PHOTOSHOP 7 at Your Fingertips

PHOTOSHOP® 7 at Your Fingertips

Get In, Get Out, Get Exactly What You Need™

JASON CRANFORD TEAGUE

San Francisco • London

Associate Publisher: Dan Brodnitz

Acquisitions Editor: Bonnie Bills

Developmental Editor: Pete Gaughan

Editor: Pat Coleman

Production Editor: Kylie Johnston

Technical Editors: Kyle McCabe, Stephen Marsh

Interior Designer and Compositor: Franz Baumhackl

Proofreaders: Emily Hsuan, Dave Nash, Laurie O'Connell, Nancy Riddiough

Indexer: Ted Laux

Cover Designer: Daniel Ziegler

Cover Illustrator/Photographer: Daniel Ziegler

Library of Congress Card Number: 2002109625

ISBN: 0-7821-4092-0

The artwork throughout the pages of this book was used with the permission of the following:

Teodoru Badiu; `teodoru.badiu@chello.at`; `www.apocryph.net`.

Sarah Beniston; `smbeniston@mac.com`; `http://smbeniston.4t.com`.

Shelley Eichholz; `shelley@fadetonoir.com`; `www.fadetonoir.com`.

Neil Evans; `nelson_evergreen@hotmail.com`; `www.nelson-evergreen.com`.

Tim Greenzweig, Greenzweig Design and Illustration; `tim@greenzweig.com`; `www.greenzweig.com`.

Kyle McCabe; `beastie@ibiblio.org`.

Maggie Taylor; `www.maggietaylor.com`.

Jim Yi; `jimmysyi@aol.com`.

Manufactured in the United States of America

10 9 8 7 6 5 4 3 2 1

Dear Reader,

Thank you for choosing *Photoshop 7 at Your Fingertips: Get In, Get Out, Get Exactly What You Need*. This book is part of a new wave of Sybex graphics books, all written by outstanding authors—artists and professional teachers who really know their stuff, and have a clear vision of the audience they're writing for.

At Sybex, we're committed to producing a full line of quality digital imaging books. With each title, we're working hard to set a new standard for the industry. From the paper we print on, to the designers we work with, to the visual examples our authors provide, our goal is to bring you the best graphics and digital photography books available.

I hope you see all that reflected in these pages. I'm very interested in hearing your feedback on how we're doing. To let us know what you think about this or any other Sybex book, please visit us at `www.sybex.com`. Once there, go to the product page, click on Submit a Review, and fill out the questionnaire. Your input is greatly appreciated.

Best regards,

Daniel A. Brodnitz
Associate Publisher
Sybex Inc.

For Johnny,
who sparked my love
of the arts at an early age.

Acknowledgments

First, I want to thank my family for their unwavering support. Thanks to my wife, Tara, who has put up with my mad tantrums and my dashing around taking photographs at odd times. Thanks to my daughter, Jocelyn, and son, Dashiel, for lifting my spirits and inspiring me with their smiles. Thanks to my parents and parents-in-law for helping take care of my family during the thick of writing this book.

A special thank you to Neil Salkind, at Studio B, for representing me and my better interests.

I am extremely thankful to the good folks at Sybex. Thanks to Dan Brodnitz, who listened to me with great patience. Thanks to Bonnie Bills, who nurtured this project from infancy. Thanks to Pete Gaughan and Kylie Johnston, who edited out my mistakes and helped direct me toward a better book, and to Kelly Winquist, who pitched in.

Thanks to Pat Coleman for dotting the *i*'s and crossing the *t*'s (not to mention providing some great input on typography). Thanks to Dave Nash, Nancy Riddiough, and Amey Garber for proofreading (which is a full-time job with me). Thanks to Franz Baumhackl and Amy Changar for taking my design concept for this book's layout and making it work.

Thanks to the many talented artists who contributed their work to the book: Jim Yi, Maggie Taylor, Neil Evans, Sarah Beniston, Shelley Eichholz, Teodoru Badiu, and Tim Greenzweig.

Great thanks go out to Kyle McCabe, who not only looked over all this book for technical accuracy but also contributed his knowledge of digital video for Chapter 29, and to David Huss, who pitched in to write chapters 19, 20, 21, 26, and 27.

I also want to thank Adobe for making such great software to write about. Specifically, I want to thank Anjali Ariathurai and Dawn Osbourne of Adobe who helped me get beta copies and answered my questions.

I am always thankful to Ms. Rhodes, Judy, Sue, Boyd, Dr. G, and the Teachers of America.

Finally, I'd like to thank the people whose art, film, music, theater, and writings inspire me daily: The The, Gustav Klimt, Fyodor Dostoyevsky, Woody Guthrie, Tim Burton, Charles Dodgson (Lewis Carroll), Neil Gaiman, Orson Scott Card, Miles Davis, Cindy Sherman, Nine Inch Nails, ZBS Studios (for the *Ruby* series), Bad Religion, H.P. Lovecraft, Arthur Miller, Elvis Costello, Graham Greene, The Sisters of Mercy, Frank Miller, The Hollies, Dashiell Hammett, New Model Army, J.R.R. Tolkien, The Smiths, Marcel Duchamp, New Order, William Gibson, James, John William Waterhouse, Blur, Phillip K. Dick, Siouxsie & the Banshees, Carl Sagan, and, of course, Douglas Adams.

About the Authors

Jason Cranford Teague works as a designer, an instructor, and a writer, specializing in multimedia and interface design. He has been using Photoshop for more than 10 years, starting in the print world and migrating to online use. Jason has written on a variety of topics for the Apple Developers Center, Adobe, C|Net, Tripod, and *The Independent* and has written several best-selling computer design books, including *Final Cut Pro 3 and the Art of Filmmaking*, *DHTML and CSS for the World Wide Web*, and *Dreamweaver MX Magic*. Jason has taught classes and seminars in the United States, Canada, and the United Kingdom, and he is currently the Creative Director for Bright Eye Media (`www.brighteyemedia.com`).

Kyle McCabe is a shooter, a producer, and an editor. He has worked on a variety of productions for Animal Planet, Bravo, HBO, the Independent Film Channel, Metro Channel, and Sky Television. On the side, Kyle takes to the streets of New York with his Soviet-era Lomo still camera.

Dave Huss has authored or co-authored 14 books on digital photo-editing. A contributing editor for *Photoshop User* magazine and the new Nikon digital photography magazine, *Capture,* Dave has been a photographer for more than 25 years, and his photo montages have won several international competitions. In addition to his appearances at conferences (including Photoshop World) and classes, he has been seen on TechTV and CNN.

Contents

Introduction

More than a decade ago, Photoshop revolutionized the way images are edited using the computer. There were image-editing programs around before Photoshop, and many more programs have come after it, but Photoshop reigns supreme as the workhorse image-editing tool of choice for photographers, designers, and artists around the world. The reason for Photoshop's success is easily explained: versatility. Despite its name, Photoshop does much more than simply allow you to edit photographs. Over the years, Adobe has added functionality and tools to Photoshop for print, art, web, and even video design.

Now, with the release of Photoshop 7, the tool set is yet further refined and expanded to meet the needs of today's designers.

Who Is This Book For?

If you are reading this, most likely you are standing in a bookstore or a library, surrounded by dozens of other books about Photoshop, trying to select the one that will best suit your needs. If you are looking for a complete resource for Photoshop, one that will help you learn new skills and improve existing ones, you have picked up the right book.

When you're faced with a particular job, would you like to be able to find out quickly how to accomplish just that task? Would you like to know the shortcuts and secrets that help you work faster and better in Photoshop? If you are a photographer, a graphic artist, a print designer, or a web designer looking for a complete resource for Photoshop, you need this book.

The concept behind writing *Photoshop 7 at Your Fingertips* was to give Photoshop users a well-organized, comprehensive, and visual resource. Regardless of your skill level, this book provides immediate access to the program.

Beginning If you are new to Photoshop, use this book to get acquainted with the Photoshop interface and get step-by-step instruction in fundamental tasks so you can get right to work on your images.

Intermediate Once you master the basic Photoshop skills, you can use this book to discover shortcuts and more efficient ways of doing routine tasks. You can use it as a springboard to specialize your skills for particular uses such as print, web, photography, and video.

Advanced Photoshop has undergone a lot of changes in the last several years, and staying ahead of the curve is never easy. This book is a comprehensive reference manual, with thorough cross-referencing to help you find the detailed information you need to stay up-to-date.

How This Book Is Organized: A Task-Based Reference

When you're working in Photoshop, you're trying to *do* something. That's why *Photoshop 7 at Your Fingertips* is organized around the many tasks you perform and breaks these down to explain the various ways to perform them.

Photoshop is a complex piece of software. It has dozens of commands, hundreds of features, and thousands of options. Yet most experienced Photoshop users tend to stick with what they know. That is, once they learn how to do a particular task in Photoshop, they rarely think to try it a different way. This is unfortunate, because they often overlook not only easier ways to do the same thing, but ways that might produce slightly different results for them to play with.

One of the great strengths of Photoshop is its ability to conform to your needs, providing functionality as you need it, rather than trying to force you to follow some set process. Although this flexibility gives you maximum creative freedom, it makes it meaningless to organize information around the program's interface. This book does have sections covering the options and features of each and every tool, preference setting, and dialog box. But the majority of the book is divided into the broad tasks users call upon Photoshop to accomplish, with one major section devoted to the universal tasks that all Photoshop users need to know.

The Photoshop Work Space Chapters 1–5 introduce you to the Photoshop interface and detail all the different parts you will be using. Here is general information about menus, tools, palettes, and preferences, with references to where in the book you can find more information for using them.

Universal Photoshop Tasks Chapters 6–18 provide the skills that every Photoshop user needs to master, regardless of how they use the program.

Print Tasks Chapters 19–21 deal with specific skills for those using Photoshop to create high-end printed pieces.

Web Tasks Chapters 22–25 deal not only with using Photoshop for creating web output but also include extensive information about ImageReady, the standalone application that can be used with Photoshop to provide further web design capabilities.

Photography and Video Tasks Chapters 26–29 deal with the specific issues involved in producing high-quality photographic and video images.

A Book for All Users

Although this book includes information about all of the most recent Photoshop features in version 7, these new features are specified as new so that those of you with older versions should be able to follow along with no difficulty. In addition, you can use this book with any of the most popular operating systems on which Photoshop 7 is available:

Windows Photoshop 7 runs on all versions of Windows, starting with Windows 98, and works the same in most versions, although the appearance of certain interface objects (such as the title bar) varies from version to version.

Mac OS X Photoshop 7 is the first version to run natively in Apple's next-generation operating system starting with version 10.1. If you are using version 10.1, however, it's recommended that you upgrade to version 10.2, which offers a significant speed boost.

Mac OS 9 Photoshop 7 is designed to still work with the older Macintosh operating system as long as you upgrade it to version 9.

We've illustrated the book with screens from both Windows and Mac operating systems. When there's a significant difference in the options or function between Windows and Macintosh, you'll see both interfaces represented.

Photoshop 7 at Your Fingertips also supplies keyboard shortcuts using both operating systems' conventions. In the margins, you'll see both the Macintosh and the Windows versions, on separate lines in that order. In text, we've run them together a bit, but still provide you with both: Command+Option/Ctrl+Alt means the Command and Option keys on a Mac, the Ctrl and Alt keys in Windows.

Using This Book

Each section in this book is organized around the idea of letting you quickly scan the information to find if a page has what you need or sending you to another section in the book to look there. Rather than burying cross-references and keyboard shortcuts in the text, we placed these in their own column, along with general tips and warnings relevant to the topic at hand.

In addition, this book makes extensive use of lettered "callout" labels on the figures to help you identify the various parts of the Photoshop interface and how they work. These are generally integrated with step-by-step instructions or bulleted lists, which refer to particular dialogs or palettes, with the callouts explaining how to set the various options.

Numbered section head Each new section in a chapter starts at the top of a page and is numbered for quick reference.

Quick cross-references Each topic points you to other sections that relate to the subject or offer alternative or more detailed information.

Keyboard shortcuts We provide the keyboard commands relevant to the section's subject.

Tips Additional notes and warnings are included about the task or tool presented in the section.

Callouts Hundreds of images in the book provide detailed labeling to eliminate the guesswork of figuring out how the Photoshop interface works.

Sidebars You'll find additional information that can be applied to the tasks presented in the chapter. Among these sidebars are "Real World" features, which present interviews with Photoshop artists who provide their own unique insights and tips.

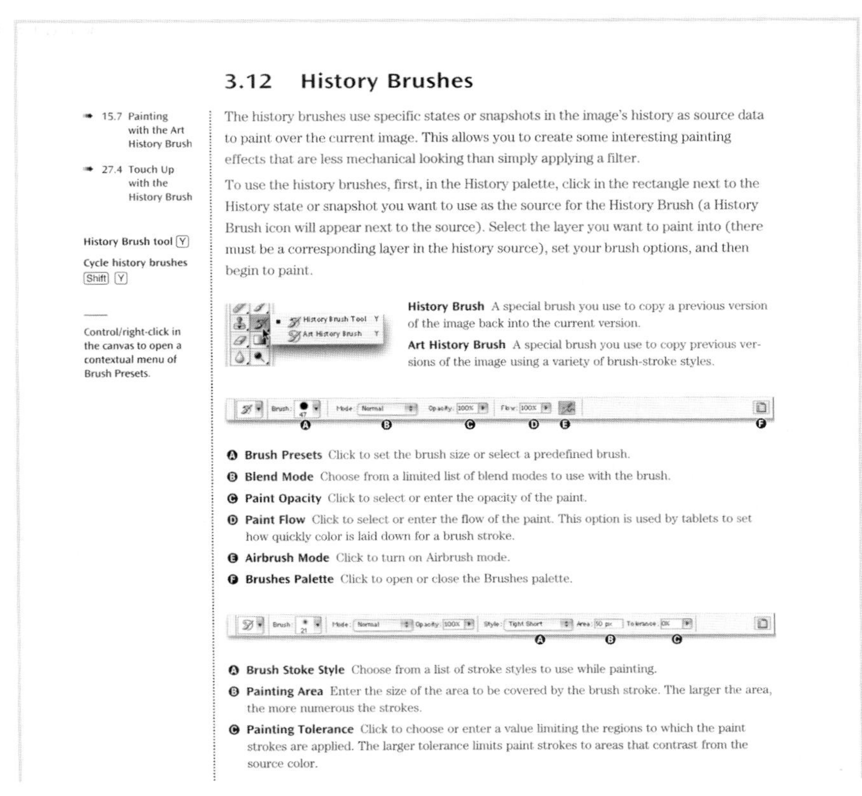

3.12 History Brushes

➠ 15.7 Painting with the Art History Brush

➠ 27.4 Touch Up with the History Brush

History Brush tool [Y]

Cycle history brushes [Shift] [Y]

Control/right-click in the canvas to open a contextual menu of Brush Presets.

The history brushes use specific states or snapshots in the image's history as source data to paint over the current image. This allows you to create some interesting painting effects that are less mechanical looking than simply applying a filter.

To use the history brushes, first, in the History palette, click in the rectangle next to the History state or snapshot you want to use as the source for the History Brush (a History Brush icon will appear next to the source). Select the layer you want to paint into (there must be a corresponding layer in the history source), set your brush options, and then begin to paint.

History Brush A special brush you use to copy a previous version of the image back into the current version.

Art History Brush A special brush you use to copy previous versions of the image using a variety of brush-stroke styles.

A Brush Presets Click to set the brush size or select a predefined brush.

B Blend Mode Choose from a limited list of blend modes to use with the brush.

C Paint Opacity Click to select or enter the opacity of the paint.

D Paint Flow Click to select or enter the flow of the paint. This option is used by tablets to set how quickly color is laid down for a brush stroke.

E Airbrush Mode Click to turn on Airbrush mode.

F Brushes Palette Click to open or close the Brushes palette.

A Brush Stoke Style Choose from a list of stroke styles to use while painting.

B Painting Area Enter the size of the area to be covered by the brush stroke. The larger the area, the more numerous the strokes.

C Painting Tolerance Click to choose or enter a value limiting the regions to which the paint strokes are applied. The larger tolerance limits paint strokes to areas that contrast from the source color.

Photoshop 7 at Your Fingertips on the Web

To see updates for this book, a list of frequently asked questions, and useful Photoshop links, check out the website set up specifically for this book at `www.webbedenvironments.com/photoshop`.

Sybex strives to keep you supplied with the latest tools and information you need for your work. Please check our website at `www.sybex.com` for additional content and updates that supplement this book. Enter the book's ISBN, 4092, in the Search box (or type "**photoshop and fingertips**"), and click Go to get to the book's update page.

Contacting the Author

Jason Cranford Teague is always happy to answer any questions that you have about Photoshop that you can't find answers for in this book. E-mail him with your questions at `photoshop@webbedenvironments.com`.

PHOTOSHOP WORKSPACE

CHAPTER 1

Interface Overview

PHOTOSHOP 7 IS AVAILABLE FOR USE in three operating systems: Windows (various versions), Mac OS 9, and the new Mac OS X (pronounced "OS Ten"). Regardless of which operating system you happen to be using, Photoshop works much the same. There may be a few operating-system–specific buttons, controls (especially with printing), and even the occasional additional menu; but understanding Photoshop in Windows is the same as understanding Photoshop on the Mac.

The first thing you notice when you open Photoshop are the controls. They are everywhere, allowing you to adjust just about anything you can possibly imagine in the images you edit. There are thousands of buttons, controls, menu options, and other objects, and each has a specific purpose. Learning all of these may seem a Herculean task, and mastering them nigh impossible. Yet all the controls in Photoshop follow a similar logic, and once you get the hang of a few controls, understanding the entire interface will quickly follow.

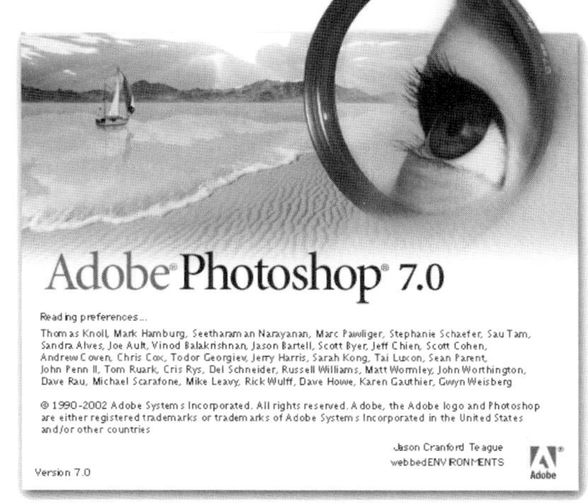

This chapter covers:

- 1.1 **The Mac interface: OS X**
- 1.2 **The Mac interface: OS 9**
- 1.3 **The Windows interface**
- 1.4 **The document window**
- 1.5 **Interface objects**

1.1 The Mac Interface: OS X

➠ 1.4 The Document Window

➠ 1.5 Interface Objects

➠ 2 Menus

➠ 3 The Toolbox

➠ 4 Palettes

Since standard Mac mice do not have a right button (as with PC mice), use Control-click whenever right mouse clicking is indicated. If your mouse does have a right mouse button, you can use either method.

Although the OS X and OS 9 versions of Photoshop 7 are almost identical, there are a few key differences, not only in the general operating-system interface, but also with the addition of new menu options only available in OS X. Throughout, this book will highlight the differences between the operating systems when necessary.

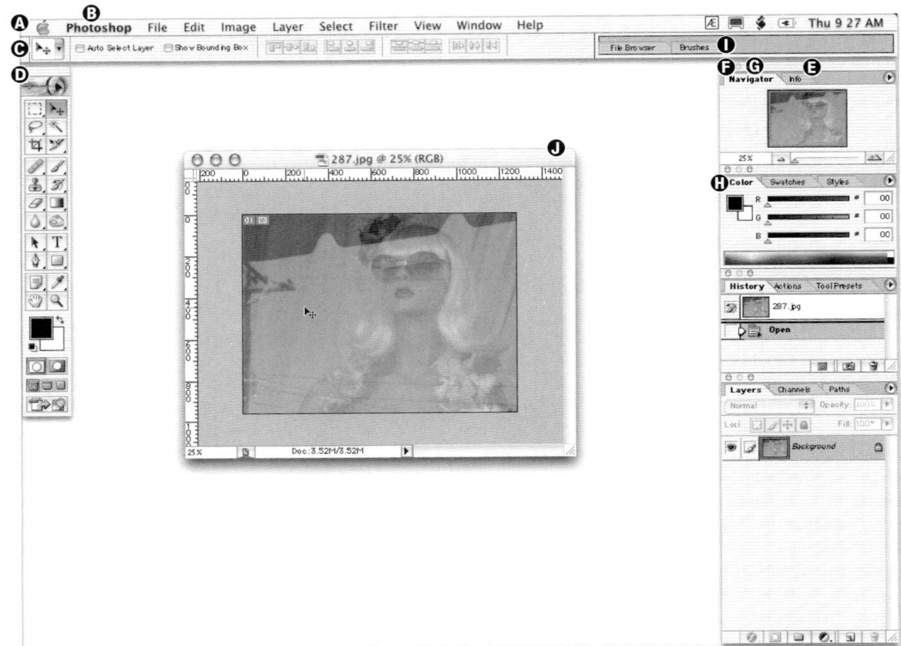

A **Menu Bar** Click any of the menu headings to view a list of menu options.

B **Application Menu (Photoshop)** This menu option is available in Mac OS X to provide access to application-specific menu options such as About Photoshop and Preferences. This menu also gives you the ability to hide Photoshop or hide other applications.

C **Tool Options Bar** This part of the interface provides options for the currently selected tool.

D **Toolbox** Click to select a particular tool to use in the canvas.

E **Palettes** Through the Window menu, you can access 17 floating palettes that contain controls and options for the various tools and the canvas. A palette is distinguished by a tab with its name.

F **Close Palette** Click to close the current window. You'll have a chance to save changes if necessary.

G **Minimize/Restore Palette** Click to minimize the window so that just its title bar is showing.

H **Palette Group** You can group palettes together and then bring an individual palette to the front of a group by clicking its tab.

I **Palette Well** This space holds palettes for quick access. Simply drag and drop a palettes tab into the area to add it to the well.

J **Document Window** The document window displays the image currently being edited (also called the image window). Multiple document windows can be open at a given time, but only one is on top and can be edited.

1.2 The Mac Interface: OS 9

Although now available for OS X, Photoshop 7 is also available to OS 9 users, and it has just as much power as it does in OS X. However, it is important to distinguish between the two versions because of the major interface changes in OS X from OS 9. These changes become especially apparent when it's time to open, save, or print a document.

➟ 1.4 The Document Window

➟ 1.5 Interface Objects

➟ 2 Menus

➟ 3 The Toolbox

➟ 4 Palettes

In Mac OS 9, use the options in the application switcher (top right corner) to hide Photoshop or hide all other applications except Photoshop.

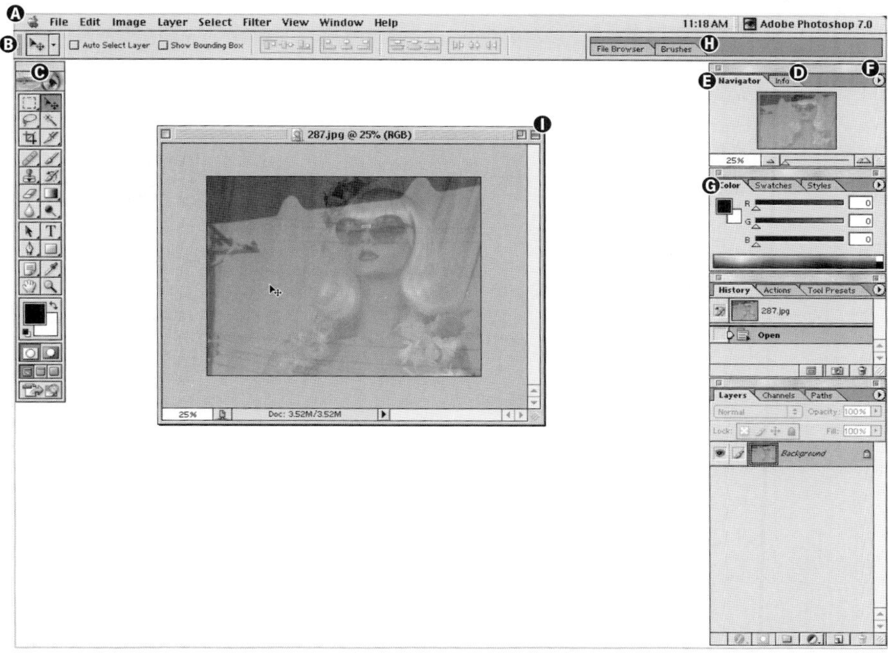

A Menu Bar Click any of the menu headings to view a list of menu options.

B Tool Options Bar This part of the interface provides options for the currently selected tool.

C Toolbox Click to select a particular tool to use in the canvas.

D Palettes Through the Window menu, you can access 17 floating palettes that contain controls and options for the various tools and the canvas. A tab with its name distinguishes a palette.

E Close Palette Click to close the current window. You'll have a chance to save changes if necessary.

F Minimize/Restore Palette Click to minimize the window so that just its title bar is showing.

G Palette Group You can group palettes together, and then you can bring an individual palette to the front of a group by clicking its tab.

H Palette Well This space holds palettes for quick access. To add a palette to the Well, simply drag and drop its tab into this area.

I Document Window The document window displays the image currently being edited (also called the image window). Multiple document windows can be open at a given time, but only one is on top and able to be edited.

1.3 The Windows Interface

- 1.4 The Document Window
- 1.5 Interface Objects
- 2 Menus
- 3 The Toolbox
- 4 Palettes

Although the appearance of the Windows interface has undergone something of a metamorphosis from Windows Me to Windows XP, the basic structure remains unchanged. The primary differences between Photoshop on the Mac and Photoshop in Windows are the placement of the menu bar, the ability to enlarge the application to fill the entire window using the application buttons in the top right corner of the screen, and the placement of the status bar at the bottom of the application window (rather than in the document window).

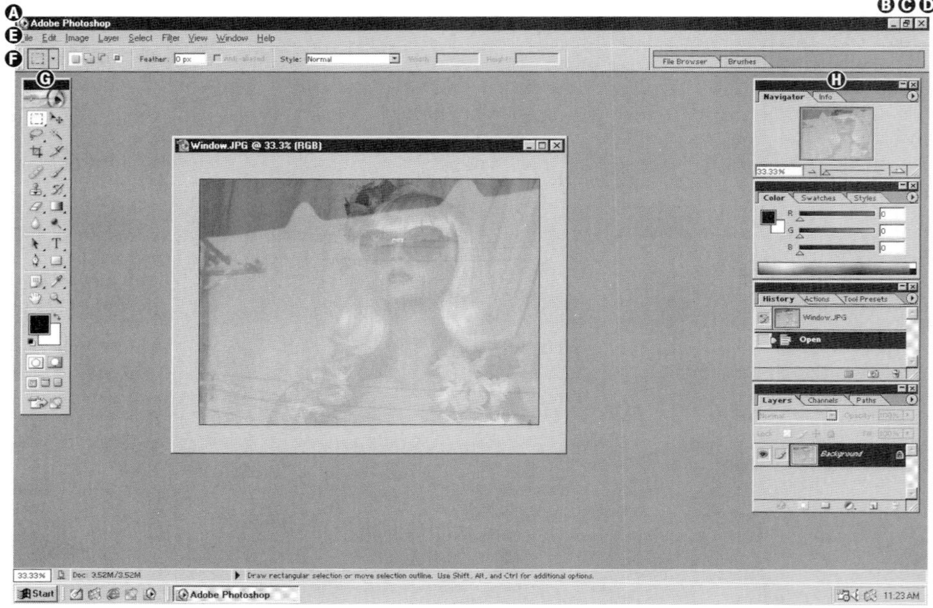

- **A** **Application Control Bar** Click to access a menu with options to restore, move, size, minimize, maximize, and close the application.
- **B** **Minimize Application** Click to minimize Photoshop into the Windows Taskbar.
- **C** **Maximize/Restore Application** Click to enlarge the application window to fill the entire screen. Click again to restore the application to window mode.
- **D** **Close Application** Click to quit Photoshop. You will be prompted to save changes if necessary.
- **E** **Menu Bar** Click a menu heading to view a list of menu options.
- **F** **Tool Options Bar** This part of the interface provides options for the currently selected tool.
- **G** **Toolbox** Click to select a particular tool to use in the canvas.
- **H** **Palettes** Through the Window menu, you can access 17 floating palettes that contain controls and options for the various tools and the canvas. A tab with the palette name distinguishes a palette.

1.3 The Windows Interface *(Continued)*

I **Minimize/Restore Palette** Click to minimize the window so that just its title bar is showing.

J **Close Palette** Click to close the current window. You'll have a chance to save changes if necessary.

K **Palette Group** You can group palettes together, and then you can bring an individual palette to the front of a group by clicking its tab.

L **Palette Well** This space holds palettes for quick access. To add a palette to the well, drag and drop its tab into this area.

M **Document Window** This window displays the image currently being edited (also called the image window). Multiple document windows can be open at a given time, but only one is on top and able to be edited.

N **Image Magnification** This space display the current magnification of the canvas. Click and enter a new magnification.

O **Workgroup Options** Click to select Save or to check out the document to and from the workgroup server.

P **Document Information** This space displays document information as chosen in the drop-down immediately to the right. Option/Alt-click to view width, height, channels, and resolution.

Q **Document Information Selection** Click to select the information displayed.

R **Action** Much like the Tool Tip, this area displays the action possible with the current tool.

1.4 The Document Window

➠ 6.1 Starting a New Image

➠ 6.5 Changing the Canvas Size

➠ 6.7 Navigating the Canvas

➠ 6.13 Saving and Closing an Image

Minimize window

⌘ M

Ctrl M

Hide everything but the document windows

Option Tab

Alt Tab

Close front document window

⌘ W

Ctrl W

You can have multiple document windows open at the same time and juggle these documents using the Window > Documents submenu. You can tile the open document windows in a variety of ways, or you can choose the document you want to work with and bring it to the front.

When you open an image or start a new image, it is placed in its own document window. The document window not only displays the image, allowing you to edit it in a variety of ways in the canvas, but also displays important information about the document and some controls for the image file.

Ⓐ Title Bar Displays the filename, the magnification, and the color mode of the document in the window. Command/Ctrl-click to view saving path.

Ⓑ Close Window Closes the current window giving you a chance to save changes if necessary.

Ⓒ Minimize Window Minimizes the window to a small icon on the Dock (OS X) or a window shade (OS 9 and Windows).

Ⓓ Resize/Restore Window Toggles the document window size between fitting to the canvas and the last size opened.

Note that in Windows, the Minimize, Resize/Restore, and Close icons occur in that order, left to right.

Ⓔ Image Mat Surrounds the area around the canvas with a gray frame to the edge of the window. Shift-click in the image mat with the paint bucket to change the color to the selected foreground color.

Ⓕ Rulers Displays the measurement of the image in selected units. Click and drag to set a guideline. Double-click to open Rulers & Units preferences.

Ⓖ Adjust Ruler Origin Click and drag to adjust the origin point for the ruler in the display area. Double-click to reset the origin to the top left corner of the image.

Ⓗ Canvas Edit the image in this work area. The canvas area in the document window depends on the dimensions, resolution, and magnification of the image. If the canvas is too large for the display area of the document window, scroll bars are added so that you can "move" the image around.

Ⓘ Mouse Pointer Use to manipulate the image on the canvas with the chosen tool. Generally the mouse pointer is an arrow, but its appearances in the canvas and in certain palettes depend on the selected tool and the settings in the Display & Cursors preferences.

Ⓙ Slice Label Displays the slice number and type.

Ⓚ Image Magnification (Mac only) Displays the current magnification of the canvas. Click and enter a new magnification.

Ⓛ Workgroup Options (Mac only) Click to check out (open) a document or check in (save) a document to a workgroup server once you are finished editing it.

Ⓜ Document Information (Mac only) Displays document information as chosen in the drop-down. Option/Alt-click to view width, height, channels, and resolution.

Ⓝ Document Information Selection (Mac only) Click to select the information displayed.

1.5 Interface Objects

Regardless of which operating system you are using to run Photoshop, several "widgets" are used in the interface. Although they look slightly different in the three operating systems, for the most part, they behave identically. To master this seemingly complex interface, you need to understand the basic nature of the various interface objects in Photoshop. When you then encounter an unfamiliar object, you'll at least understand how it behaves if not exactly what it does.

The various controls are context specific. That is, when you use them to control something (color, percentage, size), you have to look at surrounding labels to see what the control is specifically affecting. Many controls (although not all) will have a brief text label in the general vicinity of the control, or you can use Tool Tips for a more detailed explanation.

One other important, but often overlooked, fact about the Photoshop interface has to do with text labels. Many interface objects will have a text label in close proximity to identify what the object is for. Often, clicking the text label will either select the object, or, in the case of form fields, select the content of the field, allowing you to start typing to replace it.

Text Label Text labels are used to identify the data field to its right (in this case width and height). Click the text label to quickly select the text in the field.

Tool Tip

Although not technically a control, Tool Tips are available with almost all controls in the Photoshop interface. Simply place your cursor over any control or control label in the interface and wait less than a second. A small yellow box appears, displaying a brief description of the control.

If you do not see the Tool Tip, open the Photoshop General preferences (Command/Ctrl-K) and check the Show Tool Tips option. If you still do not see the Tool Tip, this object may not have one. Try a different object.

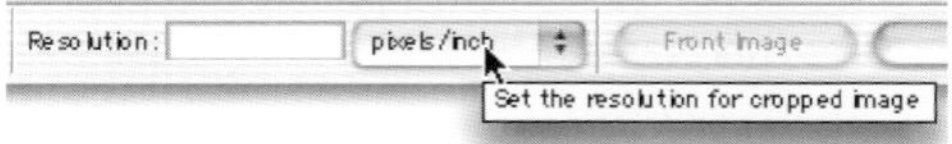

Tool Tip Place the mouse pointer over an object, and a Tool Tip describing the object will appear within a second.

➠ 2 Menus

➠ 3 The Toolbox

➠ 4 Palettes

Contextual menu

There are also two menus in each document window that will be discussed in Chapter 5.

1.5 Interface Objects *(Continued)*

If you are looking for a quicker way to get something done, check to see if a menu option in the contextual menu will save you time.

Often, selecting an option in one control changes the options available in another control.

Interface Menus

Although Photoshop comes well equipped with the menu bar across the top of the screen (Mac) or window (Windows), additional menus are available throughout the interface that fall into four basic categories: palette menus, footer menus, contextual menus, and dialog menus.

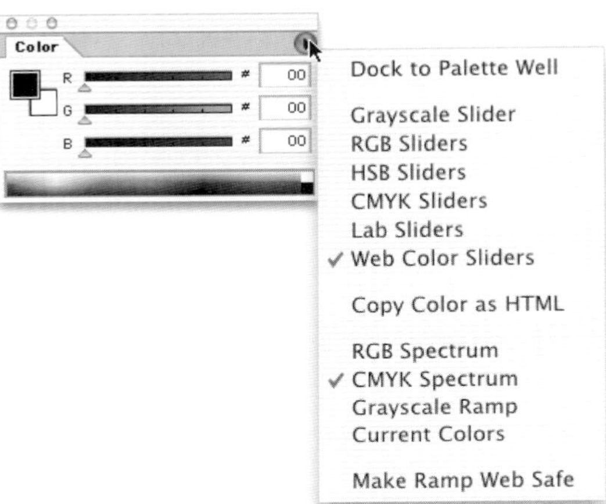

Palette Menu Click the circular arrowhead button in the top right corner of the palette or (when in the palette well) the arrowhead on the left side of the tab to open the palette menu. This menu contains palette-specific options as well as the Dock To Palette Well option. For example, the Color palette includes various options that you can use to choose how colors are set.

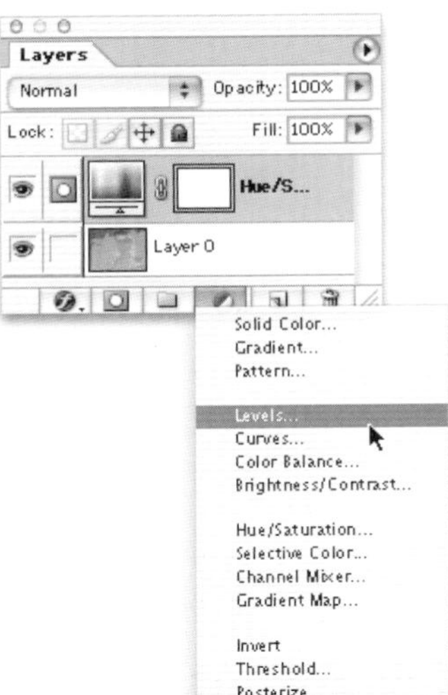

Footer Menu Click to view a list of options. The icons for footer menus come in all shapes and sizes and can be found at the bottoms of palettes in the interface. They are identified by a small arrowhead next to the icon pointing down. For example, the Layers palette includes a footer menu that you can use to quickly add adjustment layers.

1.5 Interface Objects *(Continued)*

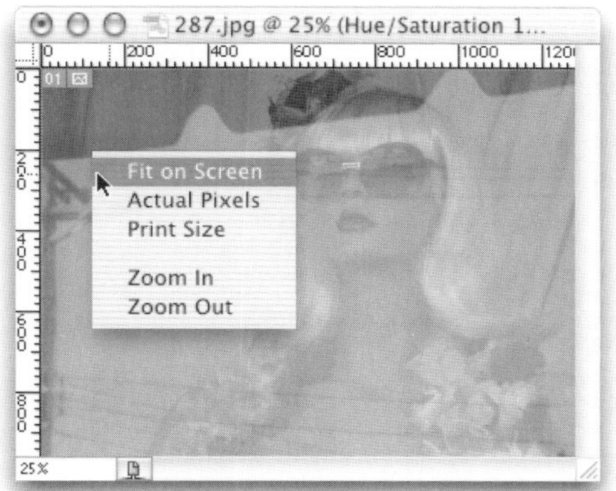

Contextual Menu Control/right-click anywhere in the document window, a palette, or a dialog window to open a contextual menu that contains options which affect the object being clicked. These options depend on what was clicked, where it was clicked, and the currently selected tool. For example, if you select the Zoom tool, clicking in the canvas displays a contextual menu that contains zooming options.

Dialog Menu Many dialog windows in Photoshop have one or more menus embedded in them. These menus generally provide window-specific options. Most of these menus are distinguished by an arrowhead in a circular button. For example, in the Preset Manager dialog, the menu provides ways to save and load gradient presets into the current list or to replace gradient presets in the current list.

Most data fields have units associated with them (such as pixels, points, or a percentage). Photoshop usually inserts the unit or percent sign if you do not include it. However, some fields have select menus next to them to specify the unit used in the data field.

Generally, sliders work in "real time," meaning that as you make a change, you see the effect of the change.

Check Boxes

You use check boxes to select or deselect a particular option. A text label always immediately follows the check box.

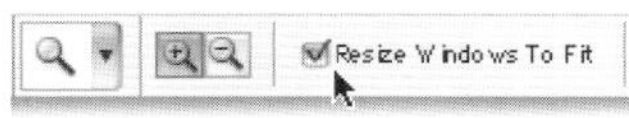

Check Box Click the check box or the text label next to the check box to toggle the option on and off. For example, you can turn Auto-Select Layer on and off for the Move tool.

Radio Button

You use radio buttons to choose between two or more mutually exclusive options. Generally, though, a select menu is used for three or more options.

Radio Button Click the radio button or its text label to select that option. All radio buttons for related options are grouped together. For example, you can choose between using Sampled and Pattern for the Healing Brush tool. If you choose Pattern, the Pattern menu is activated.

1.5 Interface Objects *(Continued)*

Select Menu

Like the Radio button, the select menu allows you to choose between two or more mutually exclusive options.

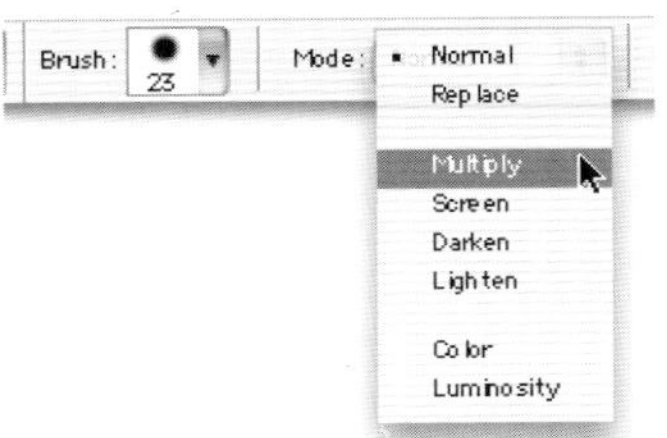

Select Menu Click the menu and then click again on the desired option or use the Up and Down arrow keys to navigate the list and press Enter to choose an option. For example, you can select the blending mode used by a paint brush.

Drop-Down Controls

Some menus are not truly menus but a set of controls used to set additional options.

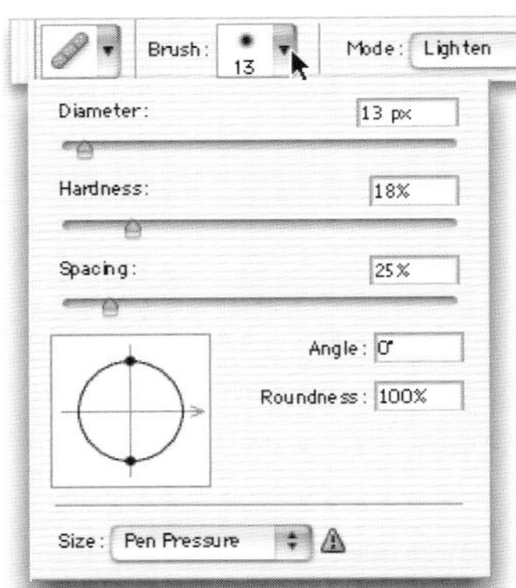

Drop-Down Click the drop-down control, make adjustments, and then click anywhere outside the control or press Enter to close it. For example, some brushes allow you to set various options to define the brush.

Data Fields

You use data fields to enter numbers in control options. Data fields can be combined with Select menus so that you can either enter a value directly or click the menu arrow (on the right side) to select an option. In addition, some data fields are accompanied by a slider control, which is helpful when a wide range of values is possible or when you need to quickly change the value for comparison purposes.

Data Field Click in the data field to insert the cursor and begin to type. You can also double-click in the field or click the field's text label to select the entire field and begin typing to erase the current value and replace it with a new value. For example, you can enter the number of pixels to feather a selection.

1.5 Interface Objects *(Continued)*

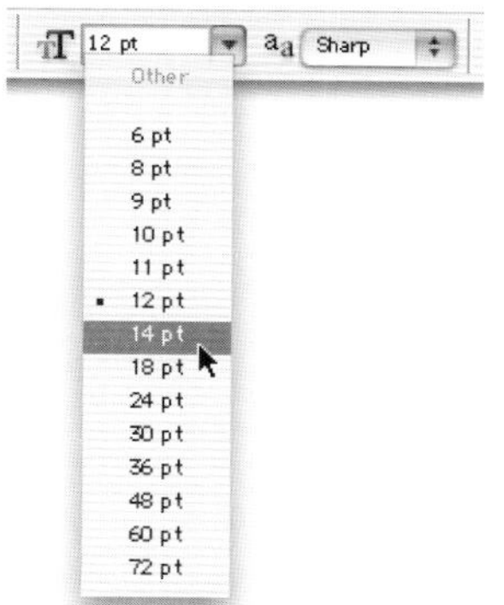

Data Field with Drop-Down Click in the data field to enter a value directly, click the drop-down arrow (on the right) to choose a value from the list. For example, you can enter the font size directly in the field or select it from a list in the drop-down. Some drop-downs allow you to adjust a slider or use the left and right arrow keys to change the value.

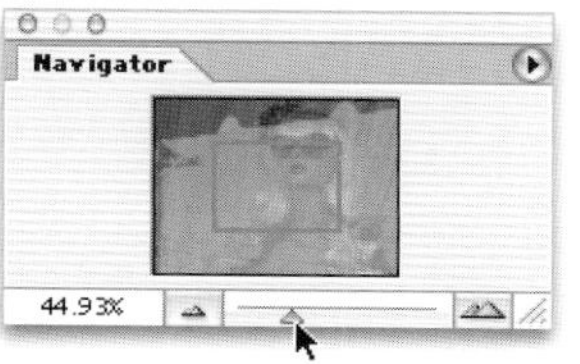

Slider Click and drag the slider to the left or right to change the value in the data field. You can also click the slider line to move the slider to that point. Sliders are sometimes next to the data field but can also be included as a drop-down. For example, the Navigator palette has a slider at the bottom of the window that controls the magnification of the image (the field is to the left).

Buttons

A wide variety of buttons are used in the Photoshop interface.

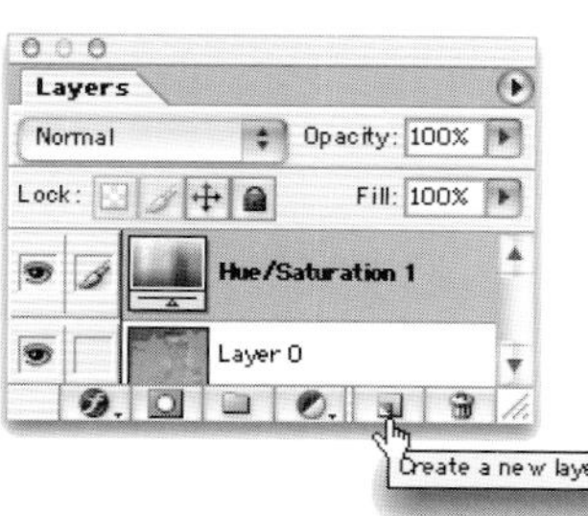

Action Button Click to perform a specific action. Click again to repeat the action. For example, every time you click the Create A New Layer button in the Layers palette, a new blank layer is added to the image.

Text Button Click to perform a specific action. Click again to repeat the action. These buttons are similar to the action buttons, but do not use an icon to represent functionality. For example, in the Zoom Tool Options bar, three text buttons allow you to magnify the image for a variety of purposes.

Select Button Click to select a single option from a group of related options, much like a radio button. However, rather than using a text label, select buttons use icons to indicate what they do. The various options are usually touching each other. For example, text allows you to select one of three justifications: left, center, or right.

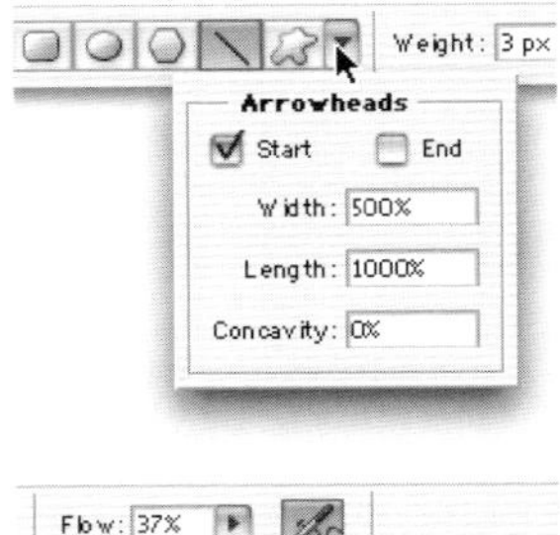

Select Button with Drop-Down Click the drop-down menu on the right side of a select button group to view additional control or a menu of options. The menu is context sensitive to the button selected in the group. For example, if you select the Line Draw tool, the drop-down provides additional options for using that tool.

Toggle Button Click to turn an option on (highlighted) or off, much like a check box. However, rather than using text labels, toggle buttons use icons to indicate what they do. For example, the Airbrush button allows you to turn Airbrush mode on or off for the selected brush.

Color Squares

You can select two general colors for use while working: Foreground and Background. However, any time you see a color square in the interface (a small rectangle or a square of color), you can double-click it to open the Color Picker. This is true virtually anywhere you see color, not only in the toolbar and Color Palette, but also in the Text Options bar and the Gradient Editor.

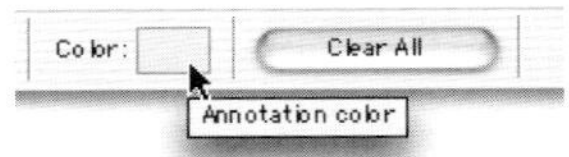

Color Swatch Double-click to open the Color Picker. For example, click the annotation color square to select the highlight color for a note.

Toggles

Several palettes, most notably the Layers palette, include one or more columns on the left side of a list of elements (layers, history states, channels) that allow you to toggle a specific option about that list element.

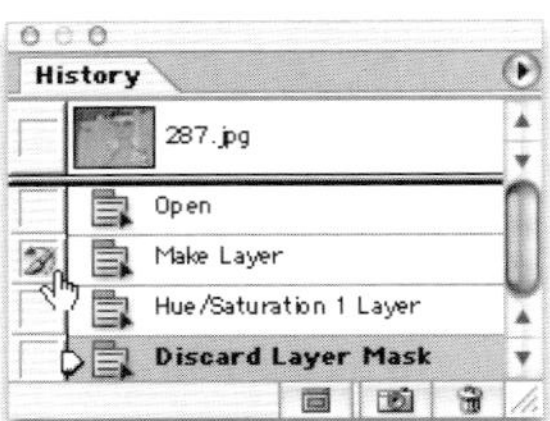

Toggle Click in the square next to the list item to toggle an option on or off for that item. Some toggles work like radio buttons, meaning that only one list item can have that option at a time. For example, you can select only one history state at a time to be used for the history brush.

CHAPTER 2

Menus

YOU USE MENUS TO PERFORM a variety of actions with the software being run. In Photoshop 7, you use menus to do everything from opening images to opening dialogs to manipulating the image content. This chapter takes a close look at each of the Photoshop 7 menus:

2.1 Menu Overview

➠ 5.3 General Preferences

Like most software, many Photoshop menu options have keyboard shortcuts that allow users to quickly activate them without using the mouse. If a shortcut is available for a menu option, it is given across from the menu option. In this book, keyboard shortcuts are listed in the margins underneath page cross-references.

You can adjust the keyboard shortcuts for Redo and printing in the General preferences.

Photoshop 7 has 9 menus (10 in Mac OS X) located at the top of the screen (Mac) or window (Windows). These menus give you access to hundreds of options that you use to create your images. On the Mac, the menu bar is always at the very top of the screen. In Windows, the menu bar is always at the top of the application window.

Photoshop menu options can be classified into six types:

Submenus A menu option with a triangle to the left contains a submenu of further options from which you must choose. *Example*: Layer > New is a submenu of options for creating a new layer.

Commands An action is performed immediately after you choose a menu option. *Example:* Edit > Cut immediately removes the selected object and places it in memory.

Dialogs These menu options end with an ellipsis (...), which indicates additional steps that are presented through one or more dialogs. *Example:* View > New Guide... asks you to specify the orientation and location of the guide you are adding to the canvas.

Show/Hide Several menu options are used to control the appearance of the Photoshop interface, allowing you to show and hide interface items as needed. When the option is set to Show, a check appears next to it in the menu. *Example:* View > Rulers shows or hides the rulers that appear around the top and left sides of the document window.

On/Off Several menu options are used to control Photoshop features, allowing you to turn certain features on or off. When a feature is on, a check appears next to the menu option. *Example:* View > Snap turns snapping on or off.

Pseudo-tools Although not in the toolbox, these menu options work much like tools in that they allow you to use the mouse cursor to change the image manually. *Example:* Edit > Free Transform allows you to rotate and resize the current layer or a selected object using the mouse.

The menu bars for Mac OS X, Mac OS 9, and Windows are all much the same. Notice, however, that the Mac OS X version includes an extra menu called Photoshop, which collects all the Photoshop-specific options into one menu (see Section 2.2 for more details).

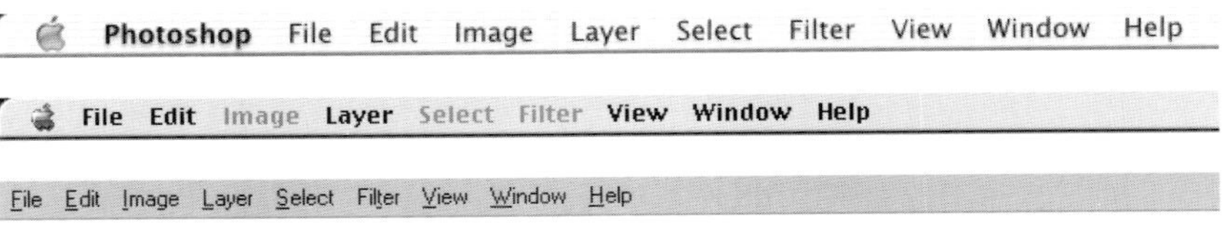

2.2 Photoshop Menu (Mac OS X Only)

Photoshop 7 is the first version of Photoshop to run natively in OS X. OS X was designed from the ground up and includes many new interface features that are completely changed from or not available in older versions of the Mac operating system. One of the most noticeable changes is the new Application menu, which appears on the left side of the screen next to the Apple menu and uses the name of the currently running application, in this case Photoshop. This menu contains options to view information about Photoshop in addition to controls for the program.

Ⓐ Displays the opening splash screen detailing information about this version of Photoshop. Click to make the splash screen go away.

Ⓑ Displays a submenu with a list of all installed plug-ins. Choosing one of the plug-ins displays its information panel. Click the panel to make it go away.

Ⓒ Opens a dialog to control program-wide color settings.

Ⓓ Displays a submenu of Photoshop preferences. Preferences allow you to control how Photoshop looks and behaves (see Chapter 5).

Ⓔ Displays submenu of system-wide actions in some applications. However, Photoshop 7 does not use this submenu.

Ⓕ Choose one of these options to hide Photoshop, hide all other running applications, or display all other running applications.

Ⓖ Quits Photoshop, allowing you to save changes to open documents first.

➠ 5 Presets and Preferences

➠ 7.3 Specifying Color Settings

➠ 16.1 Filter Basics

Color Settings dialog
Shift ⌘ K

General Preferences dialog
⌘ K

Hide Photoshop
Option ⌘ H

Quit Photoshop
⌘ Q

There is an option in the general controls to use the Mac OS X system shortcuts. Selecting this option changes a few keyboard shortcuts. For example, Hide Photoshop becomes Command-H.

In the About Photoshop screen, additional Photoshop credits will begin to scroll by if you wait a few seconds. If you can hold out, you'll see some amusing messages at the end.

Your serial number (except for the last four numbers) is displayed in the About Photoshop screen.

If you quit with unsaved changes, you will be asked to save changes. You can select to save changes, discard changes, or cancel. Canceling stops the Quit process.

2.3 File Menu

- ➠ 6.1 Starting a New Image
- ➠ 6.2 Opening an Existing Image
- ➠ 6.3 Importing Images
- ➠ 6.4 Placing a Vector Image
- ➠ 6.10 Printing Basics
- ➠ 6.11 Adding File Information and Watermarks
- ➠ 6.13 Saving and Closing an Image
- ➠ 18.5 Setting Up Workgroups
- ➠ 18.6 Checking Documents In and Out

New File dialog
⌘ N
Ctrl N

Open File dialog
⌘ O
Ctrl O

Image Browser
Shift ⌘ O
Shift Ctrl O

Close top window
⌘ W
Ctrl W

Close all windows
Option ⌘ W
Alt Ctrl W

Save changes to document
⌘ S
Ctrl S

Save As dialog
Shift ⌘ S
Shift Ctrl S

Save For Web dialog
Option Shift ⌘ S
Alt Shift Ctrl S

The File menu contains all the options for opening, acquiring, and outputting files used in Photoshop. The Windows and Mac OS 9 versions of this menu include a few different options for managing Photoshop that OS X places in the Photoshop menu.

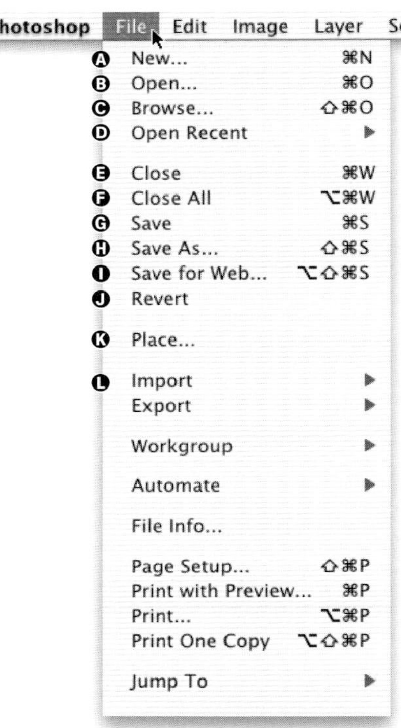

- **A** Opens a dialog you can use to start a new Photoshop file.
- **B** Opens a dialog in which you can open a Photoshop or compatible file from any available drive.
- **C** Shows the File Browser window. This is redundant to the Window > File Browser option.
- **D** Displays a submenu that lists recently opened files.
- **E** Closes the active document window, giving you a chance to save changes first.
- **F** Closes all open files giving you a chance to save changes first.
- **G** Updates the saved version of the file with any changes made since the last save.
- **H** Opens a dialog to save a file by specifying file format, name, location to be saved on the hard drive, and other options.
- **I** Opens a dialog to specify how to save an image for display on the Web.
- **J** Restores the previously saved version of the file. You cannot undo this action, and you are warned before the action is performed.
- **K** Imports an EPS or PDF image file into the current Photoshop file.
- **L** Displays a submenu that includes options to acquire images from a variety of sources (including scanners and digital cameras). The exact options listed depend on your operating system and plug-ins.

2.3 File Menu *(Continued)*

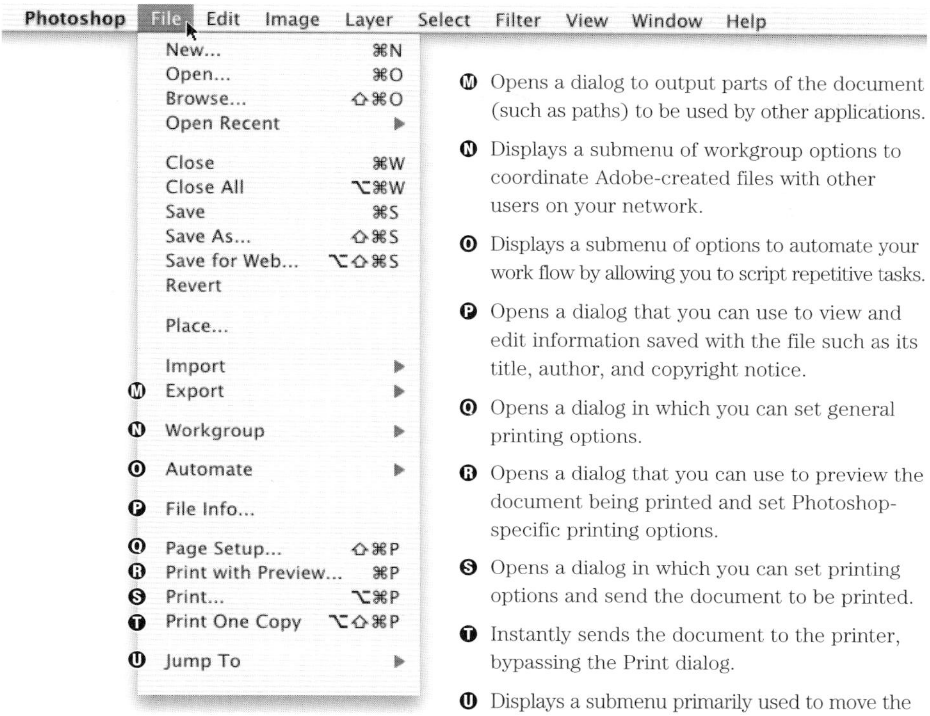

Photoshop	File	Edit	Image	Layer	Select	Filter	View	Window	Help

	Command	Shortcut
	New...	⌘N
	Open...	⌘O
	Browse...	⇧⌘O
	Open Recent	▶
	Close	⌘W
	Close All	⌥⌘W
	Save	⌘S
	Save As...	⇧⌘S
	Save for Web...	⌥⇧⌘S
	Revert	
	Place...	
	Import	▶
M	Export	▶
N	Workgroup	▶
O	Automate	▶
P	File Info...	
Q	Page Setup...	⇧⌘P
R	Print with Preview...	⌘P
S	Print...	⌥⌘P
T	Print One Copy	⌥⇧⌘P
U	Jump To	▶

M Opens a dialog to output parts of the document (such as paths) to be used by other applications.

N Displays a submenu of workgroup options to coordinate Adobe-created files with other users on your network.

O Displays a submenu of options to automate your work flow by allowing you to script repetitive tasks.

P Opens a dialog that you can use to view and edit information saved with the file such as its title, author, and copyright notice.

Q Opens a dialog in which you can set general printing options.

R Opens a dialog that you can use to preview the document being printed and set Photoshop-specific printing options.

S Opens a dialog in which you can set printing options and send the document to be printed.

T Instantly sends the document to the printer, bypassing the Print dialog.

U Displays a submenu primarily used to move the current file to ImageReady or other Adobe software.

Open As... (Windows only) Opens a dialog in which you can open a file as a specific file type, for example, to open a TIF file as a JPEG. On the Mac, this operation is handled directly in the Open dialog.

Quit/Exit (Windows and Mac OS 9 only) Closes all open documents in Photoshop (allowing you to save changes first) and quits Photoshop. This option is labeled Quit in OS 9. OS X places this option in the Photoshop menu.

Page Setup dialog
[Shift][⌘] [P]
[Shift][Ctrl][P]

Print With Preview dialog
[⌘] [P]
[Ctrl][P]

Print dialog
[Option][⌘] [P]
[Alt][Ctrl][P]

Print one copy
[Option][Shift][⌘] [P]
[Alt][Shift][Ctrl][P]

Jump image to ImageReady
[Shift][⌘] [M]
[Shift][Ctrl][M]

Quit Photoshop
[⌘] [Q]
[Ctrl][Paste]

Like most programs, Photoshop 6 used Command/Ctrl-P to open the Print dialog. Photoshop 7 opens a Print Preview dialog first before the Print dialog. You can change this behavior, though, in the General preferences.

If you close a document with unsaved changes, you will be asked to save changes. You can select to save changes, discard changes, or cancel. Canceling keeps the document from closing.

The length of the Open Recent list is set in the File Handling preferences and defaults to 10.

2.4 Edit Menu

➠ 6.9 Changing Your Mind

➠ 7.3 Specifying Color Settings

Step forward in document history
Shift ⌘ Z
Shift Ctrl Z

Step backward in document history
Option ⌘ Z
Alt Ctrl Z

Fade last filter or adjustment
Shift ⌘ F
Shift Ctrl F

Copy selection on all layers as merged layer
Shift ⌘ C
Shift Ctrl C

Paste contents of clipboard into selected layer
⌘ V
Ctrl V

Paste contents of clipboard into center of selection
Shift ⌘ V
Shift Ctrl V

Free transform selected or layers content
⌘ T
Ctrl T

Repeat previous transform
Shift ⌘ T
Shift Ctrl T

To select an entire layer to copy or cut, use *Select > All*.

You can also paste content into Photoshop that you cut or copied from another graphics or text application.

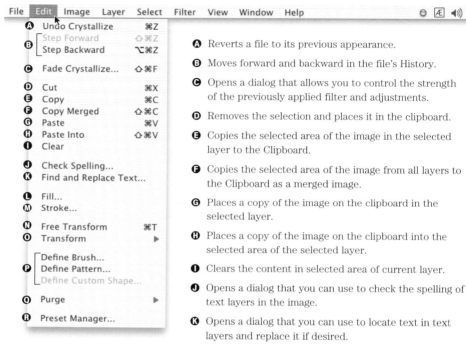

The Edit menu contains options used to work with a layer or a selection. In addition, the Edit menu contains several options for editing Photoshop tools. The Edit menu in OS X is different from the Edit menu in Mac OS 9 and Windows. The version in OS 9 and Windows has Color Settings and Preferences options, which in OS X are in the Photoshop menu.

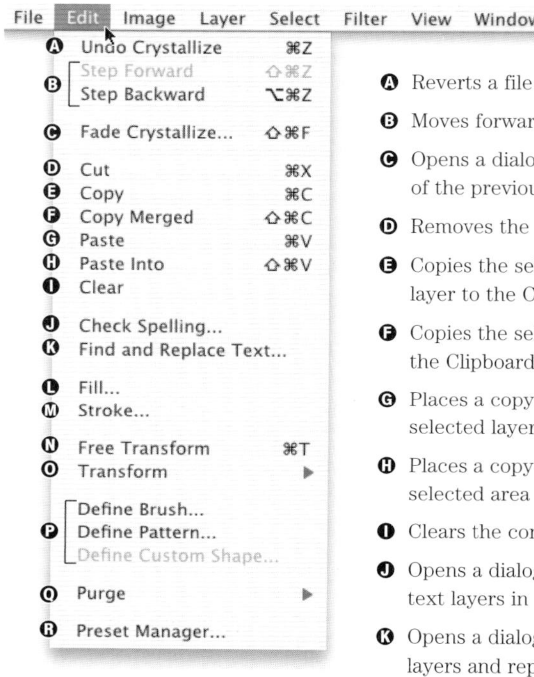

A Reverts a file to its previous appearance.

B Moves forward and backward in the file's History.

C Opens a dialog that allows you to control the strength of the previously applied filter and adjustments.

D Removes the selection and places it in the clipboard.

E Copies the selected area of the image in the selected layer to the Clipboard.

F Copies the selected area of the image from all layers to the Clipboard as a merged image.

G Places a copy of the image on the clipboard in the selected layer.

H Places a copy of the image on the clipboard into the selected area of the selected layer.

I Clears the content in selected area of current layer.

J Opens a dialog that you can use to check the spelling of text layers in the image.

K Opens a dialog that you can use to locate text in text layers and replace it if desired.

L Opens a dialog that you can use to fill a layer or selected area with a color or pattern.

M Opens a dialog that you can use to add a solid line around a selected area.

N Displays a pseudo-tool that you can use to resize, rotate, skew, distort, and add perspective to a selected area.

O Displays a submenu that lists pseudo-tools you can use to scale, rotate, skew, distort, add perspective to, and flip a selection.

P Opens dialogs that you can use to define brushes, patterns, and custom shapes.

Q Displays a submenu that has options to clear the memory used to store Undo, Clipboard, History, or all three.

R Opens a dialog that you can use to adjust Presets for Brushes, Swatches, Gradients, Styles, Patterns, Contours, Custom Shapes, and Tools.

Color Settings... (Windows and Mac OS 9) Opens a dialog that you can use to control program-wide color settings. Mac OS X places this option in the Photoshop menu.

Preferences (Windows and Mac OS 9) Displays a submenu of Photoshop preferences. You set preferences to control how Photoshop looks and behaves. Mac OS X places this option in the Photoshop menu.

2.5 Image Menu

You use the items in the Image menu to control options that will be applied to the entire canvas area, except for adjustments that are applied to the current layer or the current selection.

➠ 9 Image Layering

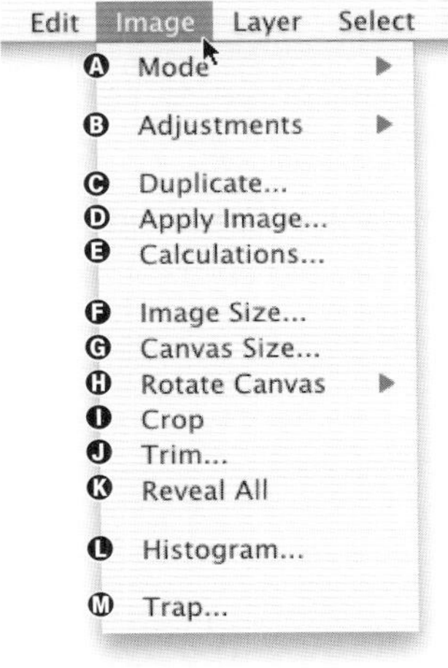

A Displays a submenu that contains options you can use to specify the image's color modes and other color table options.

B Displays a submenu that contains options you can use to change the image's properties, including color, contrast, saturation, brightness, and levels.

C Opens a dialog that you can use to create a new file, duplicating the open file as it currently appears (not its saved version). The new file is unsaved.

D Opens a dialog that you can use to blend layers and channels of an image file (including itself) into the current file if the two were duplicated from a common image.

E Opens a dialog that you can use to blend the layers and/or channels of two image files into the current image file if all three files were duplicated from a common source.

F Opens a dialog that you can use to change the width, height, and resolution of the image.

G Opens a dialog that you can use to change the width and height of the canvas. Changing the dimensions of the canvas does *not* change the size of the image, but may clip parts of the image if the sizes are smaller than the original.

H Displays a submenu that contains options to rotate the canvas (all layers). This menu also contains options to flip the canvas horizontally or vertically.

I Reduces the canvas size to the selected area.

J Opens a dialog that you can use to crop the canvas based on specific color criteria.

K Disables masks showing all the image.

L Displays a graph of the colors used in an image and other information about the image.

M Opens a dialog to add a trap width to a CMYK image used when printing the image on a four-color press.

Levels dialog
⌘ L
Ctrl L

Auto Levels
Shift ⌘ L
Shift Ctrl L

Auto Contrast
Option Shift ⌘ L
Alt Shift Ctrl L

Auto Color
Shift ⌘ B
Shift Ctrl B

Curves dialog
⌘ M
Ctrl M

Color Balance dialog
⌘ B
Ctrl B

Hue/Saturation dialog
⌘ U
Ctrl U

Desaturate Colors
Shift ⌘ U
Shift Ctrl U

Invert Image Colors
⌘ I
Ctrl I

Using the Duplicate option is the fastest way to set up an exact copy that you can then change and save independently of the original.

You can also access Auto Color Correction through the Levels and Curves dialogs, with the added advantage of being able to set options for the Auto Color Correction.

2.6 Layer Menu

New layer
Shift ⌘ N
Shift Ctrl N

Copy to create new layer
⌘ J
Ctrl J

Cut to create new layer
Shift ⌘ J
Shift Ctrl J

Group linked/ group with previous
⌘ G
Ctrl G

Ungroup
Shift ⌘ G
Shift Ctrl G

Bring layer to front
Shift ⌘]
Shift Ctrl]

Bring layer forward one level
⌘]
Ctrl]

Send layer to back
Shift ⌘ [
Shift Ctrl [

Send layer back one level
⌘ [
Ctrl [

Merge layer down
⌘ E
Ctrl E

Merge visible layers into one layer
Shift ⌘ E
Shift Ctrl E

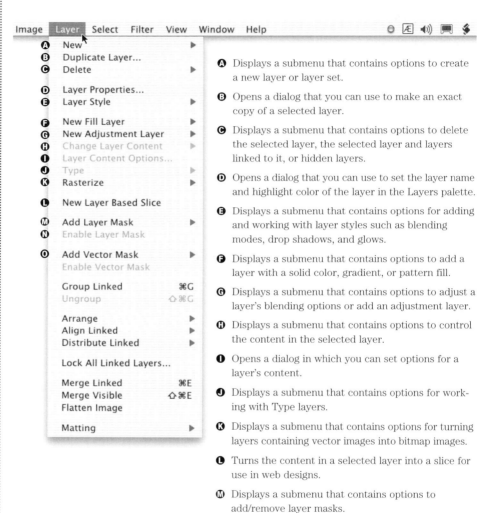

The Layer menu contains options for creating and working with individual layers in an image. The Layer menu is contextual, so which options it contains depends on the properties of the active layer: whether it is visible, linked to other layers, grouped with other layers or in a layer set.

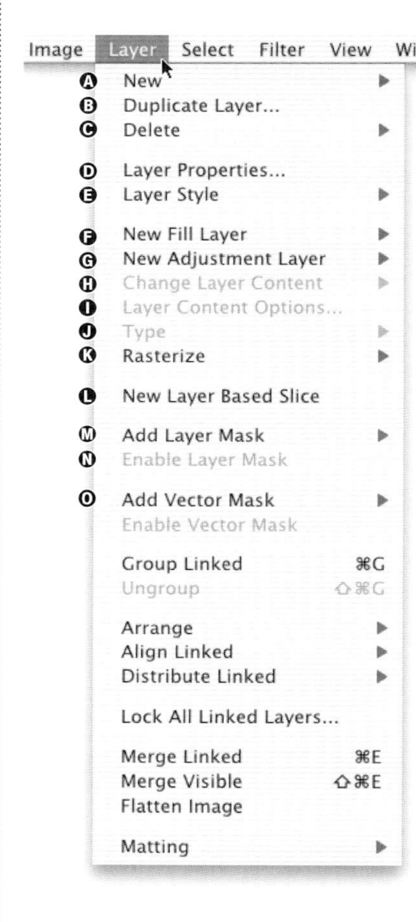

(A) Displays a submenu that contains options to create a new layer or layer set.

(B) Opens a dialog that you can use to make an exact copy of a selected layer.

(C) Displays a submenu that contains options to delete the selected layer, the selected layer and layers linked to it, or hidden layers.

(D) Opens a dialog that you can use to set the layer name and highlight color of the layer in the Layers palette.

(E) Displays a submenu that contains options for adding and working with layer styles such as blending modes, drop shadows, and glows.

(F) Displays a submenu that contains options to add a layer with a solid color, gradient, or pattern fill.

(G) Displays a submenu that contains options to adjust a layer's blending options or add an adjustment layer.

(H) Displays a submenu that contains options to control the content in the selected layer.

(I) Opens a dialog in which you can set options for a layer's content.

(J) Displays a submenu that contains options for working with Type layers.

(K) Displays a submenu that contains options for turning layers containing vector images into bitmap images.

(L) Turns the content in a selected layer into a slice for use in web designs.

(M) Displays a submenu that contains options to add/remove layer masks.

(N) Disables or enables a layer mask if it has been added to the selected layer. This will not delete the layer mask, but shows what the layer looks like without it.

(O) Submenu with options to add/remove vector masks from a layer.

2.6 Layer Menu *(Continued)*

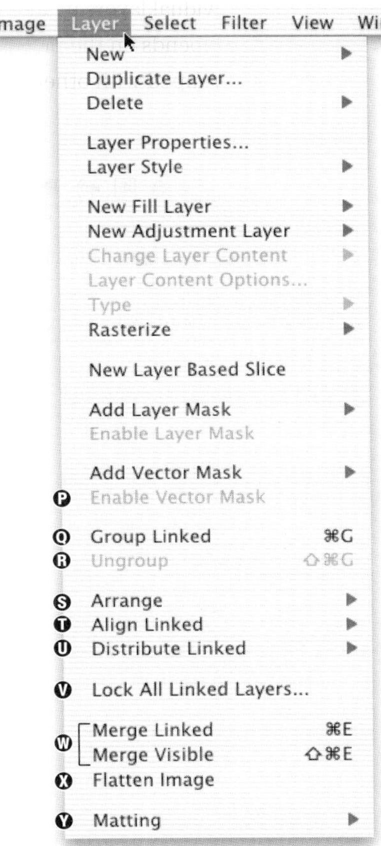

P Disables or enables a vector mask if it has been added to the selected layer. Selecting this option does not delete the vector mask, but shows what the layer looks like without it.

Q Groups the selected layer with linked layers or (if no layers are linked) with the layer beneath it.

R Ungroups layers grouped with the selected layer.

S Displays a submenu that contains options to adjust the stacking order of layers.

T Aligns the active and linked layers with the top, left, right, bottom, or center of a selection *or* the content of two or more linked layers with their top, left, right, bottom, or center.

U Distributes the content of three or more linked layers based on their top, left, right, bottom, or center.

V Locks all the layers linked to the current layer or in the selected set, preventing them from being moved.

W Merges linked layers, merges the current layer down into the layer beneath, or merges all visible layers to turn two or more layers into one layer.

X Flattens the entire image into one layer.

Y Displays a submenu that contains options for working with a layer's matte.

If you notice that Photoshop seems to perform sluggishly after you have been working in it for a while, memory might be filling up. Use Purge to clear the memory and see if that helps.

Hold down the Command/Ctrl key while selecting a layer to select only the image pixels of that layer.

When you arrange layers using the menu, you are actually moving them up or down in the Layer palette.

When layers are merged, text, styles, blending modes, and opacity changes are rasterized to create the new layer.

Align and Distribute will not work if the background layer is one of the linked layers.

2.7 Select Menu

➠ 8 Making Selections

Select All
⌘ A
Ctrl A

Deselect
⌘ D
Ctrl D

Reselect
Shift ⌘ D
Shift Ctrl D

Invert selected area
Shift ⌘ I
Shift Ctrl I

Feather selection
Option ⌘ D
Alt Ctrl D

Warning: Don't confuse inverse (reversing selected and unselected areas) with invert (reversing colors). Both have similar names and similar keyboard shortcuts, but have very different uses.

If you create a particularly complex selection, you will probably want to save it so that if you accidentally deselect it or need it again, you can quickly bring it back. Saved selections appear in the Channels palette.

You can also set a selection to be feathered before it is made using the dialog in the Options bar for the Selection tool.

You use the Select menu to work with and modify a selection in the canvas.

- **A** Selects the entire canvas area.
- **B** Removes the selection (the content of the selected area is unaffected).
- **C** Reinstates the last selection.
- **D** Swaps the selected and unselected areas.
- **E** Opens a dialog in which you can select a particular range of colors throughout an image, layer, or an existing selection.
- **F** Opens a dialog in which you can set the existing selection to gradually fade to transparent rather than using a hard edge.
- **G** Displays a submenu that contains options to change the existing selection to a border of a certain width, smooth the edges of the selection, expand the selection, or contract the selection.
- **H** Enlarges the selection to include pixels with a similar color in the selection or layer that is contiguous with the selection.
- **I** Enlarges the selection to include pixels throughout the selection or layer with a similar color.
- **J** Starts a pseudo-tool that you can use to rotate, resize, or skew (using Command/Ctrl) the selection shape, leaving the content untouched.
- **K** Opens a dialog in which you can load a saved selection shape into the current image.
- **L** Opens a dialog in which you can save the current selection shape. Saving the current selection shape does not save the content, only the shape.

2.8 Filter Menu

The Filter menu collects all the plug-in filters available, including the Extract, Liquify, and Pattern Maker dialogs. You use filters to manipulate the image in a variety of ways. Most filters work as dialogs, asking you to enter information about the changes to be made using the filter and giving you a preview of what the changes will look like. However, some filters act immediately.

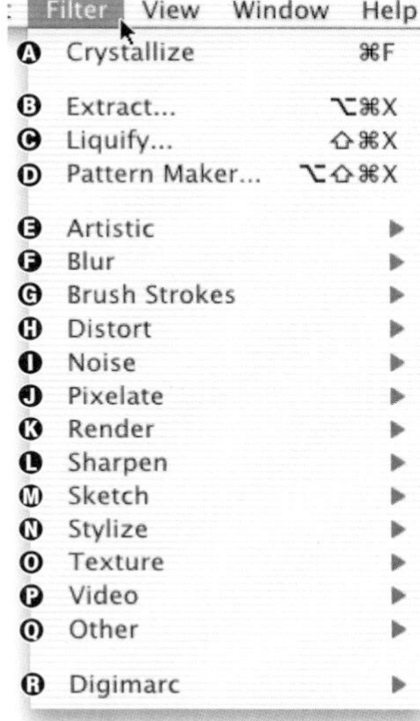

- **A** Re-performs the action of the last filter used.
- **B** Opens a dialog in which you can extract parts of the image.
- **C** Displays a submenu that contains filters used to create sophisticated smudges in the image.
- **D** Displays a submenu that contains filters used to create tiled background patterns for the image.
- **E** Displays a submenu that contains filters that simulate a variety of drawing, printing, and painting effects.
- **F** Displays a submenu that contain filters that blur a layer or selection in a variety of ways.
- **G** Displays a submenu that contains filters that simulate a variety of paintbrush stroke effects.
- **H** Displays a submenu that contains filters that manipulate the image in a variety of patterns.
- **I** Displays a submenu that contains filters used to add grainy noise, scratches, and dust effects.
- **J** Displays a submenu that contains filters used to add faceted effects.
- **K** Displays a submenu that contains filters used to create special lighting and texture effects.
- **L** Displays a submenu that contains filters used to increase the apparent sharpness of a selection or a layer.
- **M** Displays a submenu that contains filters used to add a variety of effects that simulate sketching.
- **N** Displays a submenu that contains filters used to add different stylized effects to a selection or a layer.
- **O** Displays a submenu that contains filters used to simulate a variety of textured effects.
- **P** Displays a submenu that contains filters for cleaning up images acquired from or being output to a video source.
- **Q** Displays a submenu that contains options that do not fit into other categories.
- **R** Displays a submenu that contains third-party Digimarc filters used to add and read watermarks to an image.

➠ 14.12 Using the Pattern Maker

➠ 16 Painting with Filters

Last filter
⌘ F
Ctrl F

Extract dialog
Option ⌘ X
Alt Ctrl X

Liquify dialog
Shift ⌘ X
Shift Ctrl X

Pattern Maker dialog
Option Shift ⌘ X
Alt Shift Ctrl X

As with all menu options, a filter that uses a dialog will have an ellipsis (...).

To quickly increase the effect of a filter, use the Last Filter option.

To lessen the effect of a filter, choose Edit > Fade immediately after applying the filter.

In Photoshop 6, Liquify was in the Image menu.

Photoshop allows third-parties to create filters for use in Photoshop. These filters will appear in separate menus beneath the built-in filters.

2.9 View Menu

➠ 6.7 Navigating the Canvas

➠ 6.8 Using Rulers, Guides, Grids, and Snap

➠ 14.1 Color, Gradient, and Pattern Basics

Show image in proof colors
⌘ Y
Ctrl Y

Show gamut warning
Shift ⌘ Y
Shift Ctrl Y

Zoom in
⌘ +
Ctrl +

Zoom out
⌘ −
Ctrl −

Fit image on screen
⌘ 0
Ctrl 0

Show image at 100%
Option ⌘ 0
Option Ctrl 0

Show/hide interface elements
⌘ H
Ctrl H

Show/hide target path
Shift ⌘ H
Shift Ctrl H

Show/hide grid
⌘ "
Ctrl "

Show/hide guides
⌘ ;
Ctrl ;

Show/hide rulers
⌘ R
Ctrl R

Snapping on/off
Shift ⌘ ;
Shift Ctrl ;

The View menu provides control over which windows and palettes are displayed in the Photoshop interface.

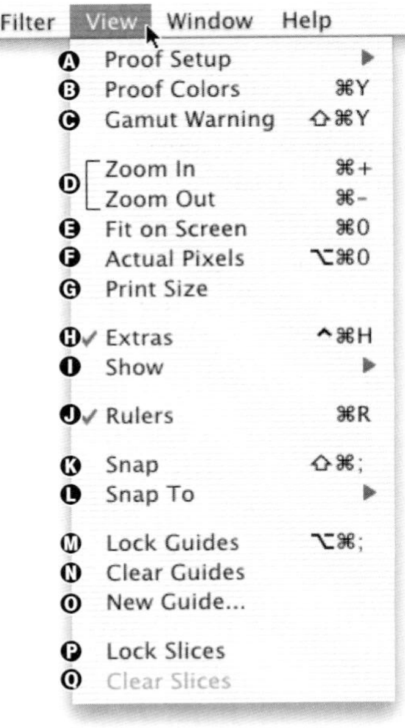

- **A** Displays a submenu that contains options for simulating how the image will look under different proof color conditions.
- **B** Turns proof colors on/off. Displays the image as it will look (or as close as possible) when printed, using the options set in the Proof Setup submenu.
- **C** Turns color out of gamut highlighting on/off. When on, colors that will not print or display properly based on the Proof Setup submenu are highlighted.
- **D** Sets the current magnification of the image in the canvas.
- **E** Changes magnification so that the image fills the screen either horizontally or vertically.
- **F** Shows the image at 100% magnification.
- **G** Shows the image in the size at which it will print.
- **H** Shows/hides interface elements as defined in the Show submenu.
- **I** Displays a submenu that you can use to select which elements will be hidden/shown using the Extras option. Select the Photoshop interface elements that you want to show, and then select the Extras option to show and hide them.
- **J** Shows/hides rulers around the edge of the document window.
- **K** Turns snapping on/off. When on, elements snap based on options selected in the Snap To submenu.
- **L** Displays a submenu of snapping options. Options are available if they are currently visible as set in the Show submenu.
- **M** Turns guide locking on/off. Prevents guides from being moved.
- **N** Removes all guides.
- **O** Opens a dialog in which you can numerically set a new guide.
- **P** Turns slice locking on/off. Prevents slices from being moved.
- **Q** Removes all slices from the canvas.

2.10 Window Menu

The Window menu has options for controlling which palettes are currently displayed on the screen. Select different palettes to show and hide them, or use the Workspace submenu to save your favorite layouts and then restore them as needed.

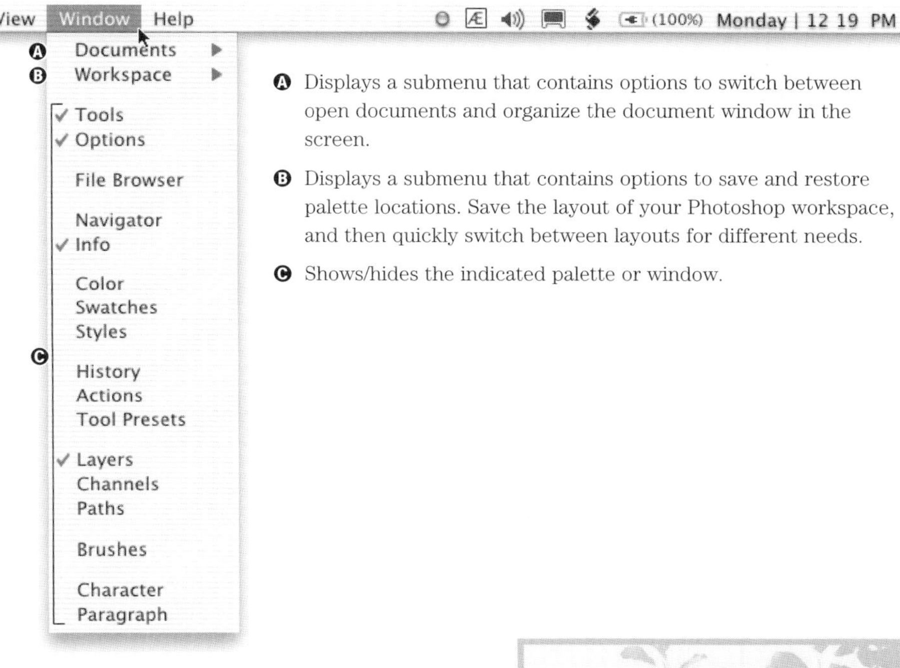

A Displays a submenu that contains options to switch between open documents and organize the document window in the screen.

B Displays a submenu that contains options to save and restore palette locations. Save the layout of your Photoshop workspace, and then quickly switch between layouts for different needs.

C Shows/hides the indicated palette or window.

➠ 1.4 The Document Window

➠ 4 Palettes

Minimize window

Ctrl ⌘ M

Alt Ctrl M

Show/hide toolbox, toolbox options, and open palettes

Tab

Show/hide open palettes

Shift Tab

Windows includes an additional option to show and hide the status bar at the bottom of the application window.

Sometimes palettes can become hidden behind other palettes. An arrow next to the menu option indicates that the palette is currently showing; if you hide it and then show it again, it should pop to the top. If you still can't see it, you might have placed it off the screen. Try hiding all other palettes and then turning on only the one you are looking for.

2.11 Help Menu

➠ 5.11 Adobe Online Preferences

➠ 6.6 Setting the Image Size

Photoshop Help
⌘ ?

You can now automatically get updates to your version of Photoshop if you have an Internet connection (see Section 5.11).

Step Backward and Step Forward are similar to the Undo option, but give you much greater control, allowing you to, in effect, undo and redo as many times as desired depending on the number of History states. You set the number of History states in the General preferences.

The Help menu not only contains an option to open the Photoshop help manual in a web browser, but it also contains several assistants (also often referred to as wizards) to help you with common but complex tasks. You will also find options to obtain additional support for Photoshop.

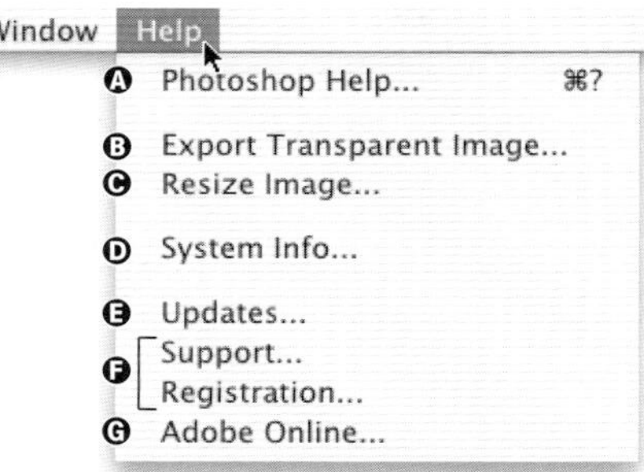

A Opens a web-based version of the Photoshop help manual. You do not need an Internet connection to open this manual.

B Opens a dialog to help with exporting an image with transparencies.

C Opens a dialog that you can use to help find the best way to resize an image with minimal quality loss.

D Displays information about the computer, operating system, version of Photoshop, and plug-ins currently in use.

E Checks for updates to this version of Photoshop. Requires an Internet connection.

F Opens a web browser to the Adobe website registration area, allowing you to register this copy of Photoshop. Requires an Internet connection.

G Opens a web browser window to the Adobe Photoshop website. Requires an Internet connection.

About Balloon Help... (Mac OS 9 only) Opens a help screen explaining balloon help.

Show/Hide Balloons (Mac OS 9 only) Toggles balloon pop-ups on and off.

About Photoshop (Windows only) Displays the opening splash screen detailing information about this version of Photoshop. Click the splash screen to make it go away. OS X places this option in the Photoshop menu. OS 9 places this option in the Apple menu.

AboutPlug-In (Windows only) Displays a submenu that lists all installed plug-ins. Selecting a plug-in displays its information panel. Click the panel to make it go away. OS X places this option in the Photoshop menu. OS 9 places this option in the Apple menu.

CHAPTER 3

The Toolbox

TO CREATE AND EDIT IMAGES, Photoshop has several dozen tools accessible through the Toolbox. To choose a tool whose icon is visible in the Toolbox, click the tool icon. Your mouse pointer will take on the appearance of the tool icon or a precision icon (depending on how your preferences are set). You can then use the tool to manipulate the image on the Canvas.

A small arrowhead in the bottom-right corner of the tool indicates that this is a tool set with other similar tools available for that box. To access the rest of the tool set, click and hold on the arrowhead and select another tool from the pop-out palette. In addition, each tool set has a single-letter keyboard shortcut that chooses the currently selected tool for that tool set. If you forget what a particular tool does or what its keyboard shortcut is, place your mouse cursor over the tool and wait a few seconds. A Tool Tip appears that labels the tool and indicates its shortcut key in parentheses. To cycle through hidden tools in a tool set, press Shift and the shortcut key, or Alt/Option-click the currently visible tool in the Toolbox.

This chapter covers:

3.1 The Toolbox

Show/hide Toolbox, tool options bar, and open palettes

Tab

Cycle through tools in a tool set

Shift **plus shortcut key**

If you do not see the Toolbox, choose Window > Tools so that a check appears next to Toolbox in the menu.

Warning: Remember, actions performed with a tool in the canvas are generally applied only to the selected layer.

The Toolbox houses icons that you can click to access all the tools used in Photoshop. To use a tool, click its icon, and then use it in the canvas. Many of the tools are part of a tool set, allowing the box to be used to house multiple tools. To select another tool from a tool set, click and hold one of the icons in the toolbox with a triangle in the bottom-right corner and then choose the desired tool. The following graphic shows the Toolbox in its default configuration with shortcut keys indicated in parentheses.

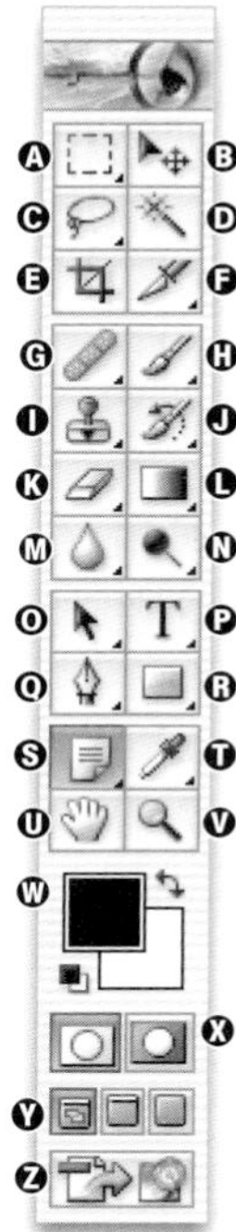

- A Marquee tools (M)
- B Move tool (V)
- C Lasso tools (L)
- D Magic Wand tool (W)
- E Crop tool (C)
- F Slice tools (K)
- G Restoration tools (J)
- H Draw and paint tools (B)
- I Stamp tools (S)
- J History Brush tools (Y)
- K Erase tools (E)
- L Fill tools (G)
- M Distortion tools (R)
- N Exposure tools (O)
- O Path tools (A)
- P Type tools (T)
- Q Pen tools (P)
- R Shape tools (U)
- S Annotation tools (N)
- T Eyedropper and Measure tools (I)
- U Hand tool (H)
- V Zoom tool (Z)
- W Background/foreground color swatches
- X Mask modes (Q)
- Y View modes (F)
- Z Jump To ImageReady

3.2 The Tool Options Bar

Most tools have attributes that specify how the tool behaves when used. You use the tool options bar to set most of these attributes (some attributes can be set in individual palettes), which is initially located at the top of the screen, but can be moved anywhere on the screen. The options in the bar depend on three criteria: the tool selected, the options selected in the bar, and the action being performed with the tool.

Show/hide Toolbox, tool options bar, and open palettes

Tab

Cycle through blending modes for the current tool or layer

Shift + or Shift −

If you do not see the tool options bar, choose Window > Options so that a check appears next to Tool Options Bar in the menu.

A Tool Preset Picker Click to choose from a list of tools with preset attributes. The icon represents the currently selected tool.

B Brush Preset Picker/Brush Picker Click to choose from a list of brushes with preset attributes (Brush Preset Picker) or to specify brush attributes (Brush Picker). This option is available for all brush types, rubber stamp, eraser, and pencil tools.

C Airbrush Mode Click to turn the brush into an airbrush tool. This option is only available for brush tools.

D Palette Toggle Click this button to show or hide this tools palette(s). The palettes displayed depend on the tool.

E Palette Well Drag and drop palettes to dock them into the Palette Well. Click a palette tab to open a palette docked in the well. Click in the canvas or click the tab again to close the palette.

Tool Preset Picker

The menu bar also has a drop-down menu that you can use to choose from a list of tools with predefined attributes. This list is initially made up of the default tools (the same as in the Toolbox), but over time you can customize the tools for specific needs and use the Tool Preset Picker to save them or load preset tools included with Photoshop.

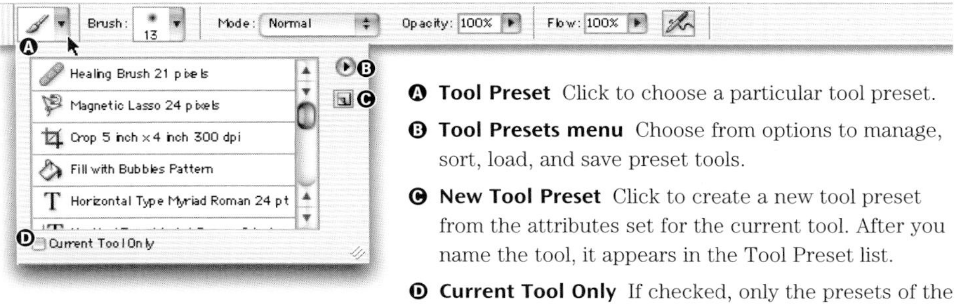

A Tool Preset Click to choose a particular tool preset.

B Tool Presets menu Choose from options to manage, sort, load, and save preset tools.

C New Tool Preset Click to create a new tool preset from the attributes set for the current tool. After you name the tool, it appears in the Tool Preset list.

D Current Tool Only If checked, only the presets of the currently selected tool are shown in the list.

Decrease brush size (with a brush tool selected)

[

Increase brush size (with a brush tool selected)

Decrease brush hardness (with a brush tool selected)

Increase brush hardness (with a brush tool selected)

Brush Preset Picker

Most brush tools include the Brush Preset Picker, which allows you to change the size of the brush being used or select a brush with predefined attributes. You can further customize brush attributes in the Brushes palette. Photoshop also comes with several lists of brush types that can be loaded.

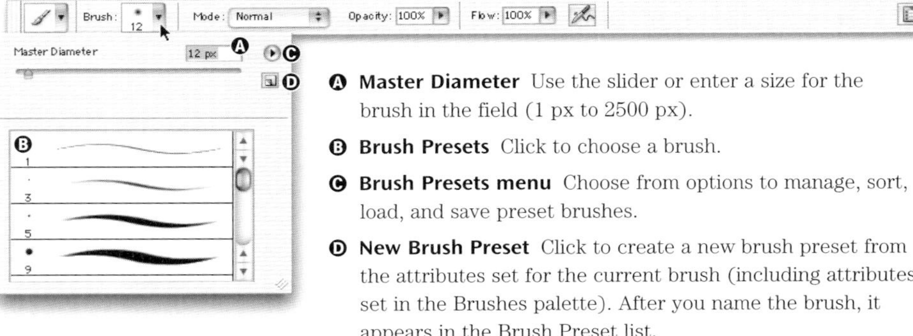

A Master Diameter Use the slider or enter a size for the brush in the field (1 px to 2500 px).

B Brush Presets Click to choose a brush.

C Brush Presets menu Choose from options to manage, sort, load, and save preset brushes.

D New Brush Preset Click to create a new brush preset from the attributes set for the current brush (including attributes set in the Brushes palette). After you name the brush, it appears in the Brush Preset list.

Brush Picker

Some brushes allow you to directly edit the brush (rather than choosing a preset) using the Brush Picker. Although the option looks the same as the Brush Preset Picker in the tool options bar, when you choose it, the Brush Picker includes not only controls for size, but also information on angle, roundness, and how the brush works with a stylus and tablet.

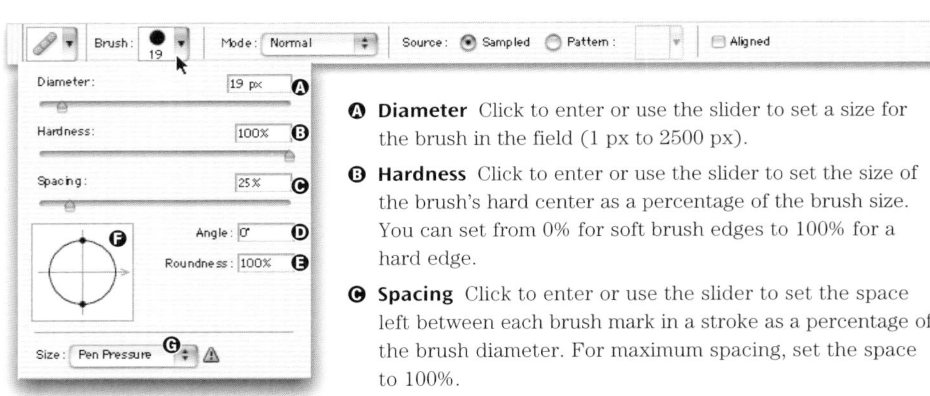

A Diameter Click to enter or use the slider to set a size for the brush in the field (1 px to 2500 px).

B Hardness Click to enter or use the slider to set the size of the brush's hard center as a percentage of the brush size. You can set from 0% for soft brush edges to 100% for a hard edge.

C Spacing Click to enter or use the slider to set the space left between each brush mark in a stroke as a percentage of the brush diameter. For maximum spacing, set the space to 100%.

D Angle Enter to set the slant of the brush.

E Roundness Enter a percentage to define elliptical shape. A circle is 100%, and a line is 0%.

F Angle & Roundness The visual shows the shape and slant of the brush. Click to make changes visually.

G Size Based On Stylus Choose an option for how to control the size of the Paintbrush using a stylus and tablet.

3.2 The Tool Options Bar *(Continued)*

Airbrush Mode

If you are familiar with previous versions of Photoshop, you will be surprised to hear that Photoshop 7 does not have an Airbrush tool. Don't panic! It makes a lot of sense. Instead of a single Airbrush tool, most brush tools now include an Airbrush option allowing you to use that tool as if it were an Airbrush tool. For example, you can use the common Brush tool in its traditional way, or, with the click of a button, you can turn it into an Airbrush tool, allowing softer edges when painting by applying gradual tones to the brush, simulating traditional airbrush techniques. The Airbrush mode is also available to the stamp tools, the eraser tools, the history brushes, and the exposure tools, which greatly enhances their capabilities.

The Airbrush Mode button

Palette Toggle Button

Some tools have a palette toggle button next to the Palette Well on the left. Clicking this button shows or hides palettes that contain the additional attributes relevant to the tool being used.

The Palette Toggle button

Palette Well

In addition to the options, the tool options bar contains the Palette Well, which is used to dock palettes that are regularly used but do not always need to be displayed. To dock a palette, simply drag its tab into the well, or select Dock To Palette Well in the palette's menu.

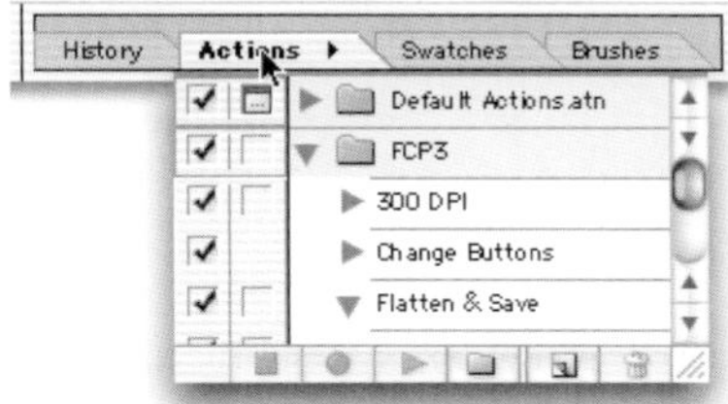

Click one of the tabs to display a drop-down version of the palette.

If you are unsure what a particular option is in the tool options bar, place the mouse cursor over the option. Within a few seconds a Tool Tip appears with a brief description. If nothing happens, turn Tool Tips on in your preferences (Command/Ctrl-K).

Click the text label next to a field to select the field.

3.3 Marquee Tools

➠ 8.3 Selecting Rectangular or Elliptical Areas

➠ 8.6 Refining the Selection

➠ 8.7 Changing the Selection

➠ 8.8 Transforming a Layer or Selected Content

➠ 8.10 Copying and Pasting Selected Content

➠ 8.11 Saving and Loading Selections

➠ 14.12 Using the Pattern Maker

Marquee tool [M]

Cycle Marquee tools
[Shift] [M] **(Rectangle and Elliptical Marquees only)**

Constrain a new selection to a square or a circle (if no existing selection)
[Shift] **plus select**

Add to current selection (with existing selection; press Shift again while selecting to constrain proportions)
[Shift] **plus select**

Subtract from current selection
[Option] **plus select**

After you make a selection, moving the selection, either with the Move tool or the arrow keys, causes the selection to collapse around the image on the selected layer.

You use the marquee tools to select regions. To make a simple rectangular or elliptical selection, select the appropriate marquee tool, place the cursor at one corner of the region you want to select, and then click and drag to the opposite corner of the region. As you drag, you will see a flashing outline (often referred to as marching ants) appear around the selected region.

For Single Row and Single Column selections, choose the tool and then click in the row or column you want to select. The selection will be 1 pixel wide or high and stretch the length or width of the entire image.

Rectangular Marquee Selects a rectangular region in a layer of the image.

Elliptical Marquee Selects a circular or elliptical region in a layer of the image.

Single Row Marquee Selects a single row of pixels in a layer in the image.

Single Column Marquee Selects a single column of pixels in an image.

Ⓐ **Selection Type** Choose how the new selection should be treated in relation to the current selection: Deselect the current selection and start new selection, add to the current selection, subtract from the current selection, or intersect with the current selection.

Ⓑ **Feather** Enter the amount of fade from the edges of the selection. You must enter this amount *before* making the selection order to affect the selection.

Ⓒ **Anti-Aliased** If checked, anti-aliasing gives the edges of the selection a smoother appearance with the elliptical marquee.

Ⓓ **Style** Choose whether the selection is Normal (unconstrained), Fixed Aspect Ratio (forces selection into a square or circle), or Fixed Size (forces selection to be a height and width entered in the fields to the right).

Ⓔ **Width** Set the width of a selection if using the Fixed Size style.

Ⓕ **Height** Set the height of a selection if using the Fixed Size style.

3.4 Move Tool

Once a selection is made, you can move it about in the image using the Move tool. If there is no selection, you can use the Move tool to move the contents of the currently selected layer.

To move an object, select the layer and then select the region you want to move (if desired). Then choose the Move tool, place the cursor within the canvas, and click and drag the selection or layer to the new location.

➠ 8.9 Moving Selected Content

➠ 9.11 Aligning and Distributing Layers

➠ 12.9 Editing Paths and Path Components

Move tool [V]

With the Move tool, Control-click or right-click any part of the image to select from a contextual menu of layers under the cursor.

Remember, you always move the selection in the selected layer. Always check your layer before making a move to make sure you have the right one.

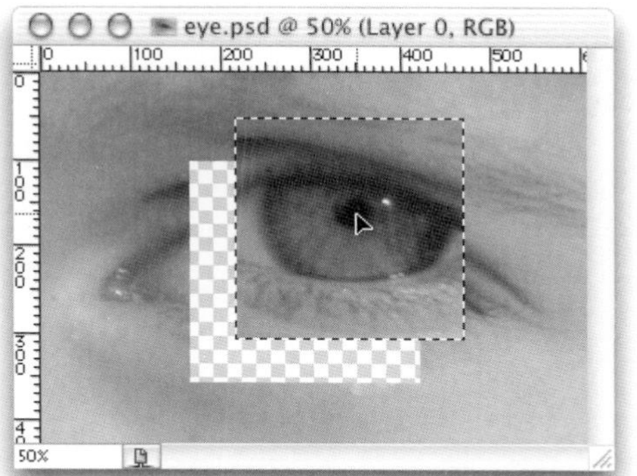

Moving a selection Use the Move tool to change the position of a selected layer or image selection.

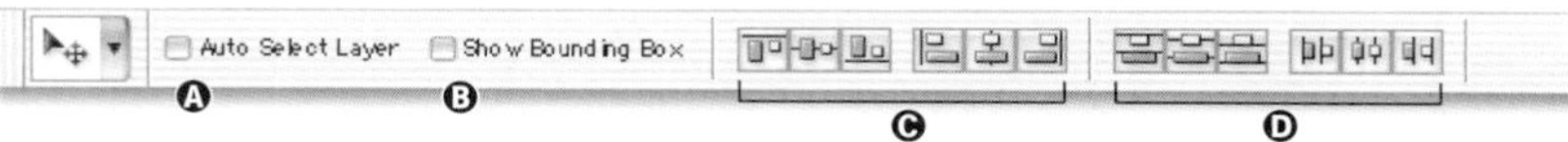

A Auto Select Layer If checked, click an object in a layer to select that layer.

B Show Bounding Box If checked, the rectangular edges of a selected region are shown. If the selection is not rectangular, the bounding box represents a rectangular region of the selection's extreme horizontal and vertical limits. You can use the bounding box to transform the selection (resize, skew, and rotate).

C Align Objects You can align two or more linked layers with their top edges, middle edges, bottom edges, left edges, center edges, or right edges.

D Distributed Objects Three or more linked layers can have their content distributed between their top edges, middle edges, bottom edges, left edges, center edges, or right edges.

3.5 Lasso Tools

→ 8.4 Creating a Free-form Selection

→ 8.6 Refining the Selection

→ 8.7 Changing the Selection

→ 8.8 Transforming a Layer or Selected Content

→ 8.10 Copying and Pasting Selected Content

→ 8.11 Saving and Loading Selections

Lasso tool [L]

Cycle Lasso tools [Shift][L]

Force selection path into 0°, 45°, or 90° angles [Shift] plus polygon select

Add to current selection [Shift] plus select

Subtract from current selection [Option] plus select

The Lasso tools allow you to make freeform selection of any shape in the canvas. You can draw the selection by hand or use either the polygonal or magnetic lasso to help you make a more precise selection.

Lasso Selects regions in the image using free-form straight edges to create a selection with as many sides as desired.

Polygonal Lasso Selects regions in the image using free-form straight edges.

Magnetic Lasso Selects regions in free form but forces the selection to stick to high-contrast boundaries in the image.

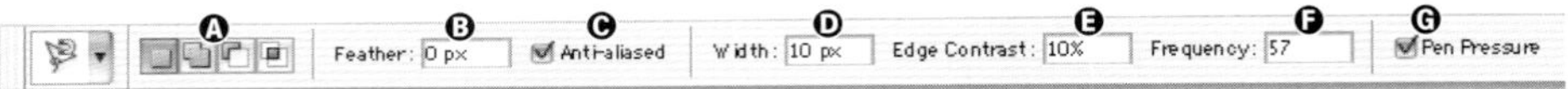

Ⓐ **Selection Type** Choose how the new selection should be treated in relation to the current selection: deselect current selection and start new selection, add to the current selection, subtract from the current selection, or intersect with the current selection.

Ⓑ **Feather** Fades the edges of the selection by the specified amount. You must enter this amount *before* making the selection in order to affect the selection.

Ⓒ **Anti-Aliased** When this option is checked, anti-aliasing gives the edges of the selection a smoother appearance.

Ⓓ **Width** (Magnetic Lasso only) Enter the width in pixels (1 to 256) to be considered around the cursor when making selection.

Ⓔ **EdgeContrast** (Magnetic Lasso only) Enter the contrast (as a percentage) to be considered between pixels for determining the selection.

Ⓕ **Frequency** (Magnetic Lasso only) Enter a number (0 to 100) to set how often anchor points are added to the selection path.

Ⓖ **Pen Pressure** (Magnetic Lasso only) If checked, a tablet's pen pressure is used to change the width.

3.6 Magic Wand Tool

The Magic Wand is a selection tool that selects only particular colors in the canvas. You can set it to select only one exact color on one layer in one area of the image, or you can set the tolerance, layers, and contiguous options to select a range of colors throughout the image.

To make a Magic Wand selection, choose the tool, set your options, and then click on (or as close as possible to) a pixel with the color you want to select. Depending on your options, you will see parts of the image selected.

➠ 8.5 Selecting Colors

➠ 8.6 Refining the Selection

➠ 8.7 Changing the Selection

➠ 8.8 Transforming a Layer or Selected Content

➠ 8.10 Copying and Pasting Selected Content

➠ 8.11 Saving and Loading Selections

➠ 13.8 Using Replace Color

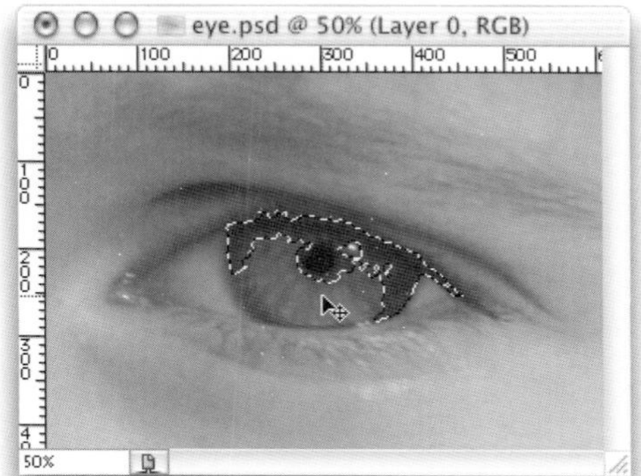

Selecting colors The Magic Wand uses the color of the pixel clicked to select all pixels with that color or similar colors based on the tolerance set. In this example, a tolerance of 50 was used to select part of the eye by clicking the iris.

Magic Wand tool [W]

Add to current selection
[Shift] plus select

Subtract from current selection
[Option] plus select

A Selection Type Choose how the new selection should be treated in relation to the current selection: deselect current selection and start new selection, add to the current selection, subtract from the current selection, or intersect with the current selection.

B Tolerance Enter a value in the range 0 to 255 (32 is the default) to specify the deviation a color can have to be included in the Magic Wand selection.

C Anti-Aliased When this option is checked, anti-aliasing gives the edges of the selection a smoother appearance.

D Contiguous If checked, only pixels touching the selected pixel and within the set tolerance and pixels touching those (and so forth) are included in the selection. Otherwise, the Magic Wand selects all pixels in the image within the tolerance level.

E Use All Layers If checked, the Magic Wand selects pixels on all layers in the image. Otherwise, the Magic Wand only works within the selected layer.

3.7 Crop Tool

➠ 6.5 Changing the Canvas Size

➠ 6.6 Setting the Image Size

If you are unsure what a particular option is in the Toolbox or what its shortcut is, place the mouse cursor over the option. Within a few seconds, a Tool Tip appears with a brief description. If nothing happens, turn Tool Tips on in the General preferences (see Section 5.3).

You can change the size of the canvas using the Crop tool to select a region to preserve and then crop to get rid of the remainder.

To crop an image, select the Crop tool, set your attributes, select the region of the canvas to preserve, and press Return/Enter.

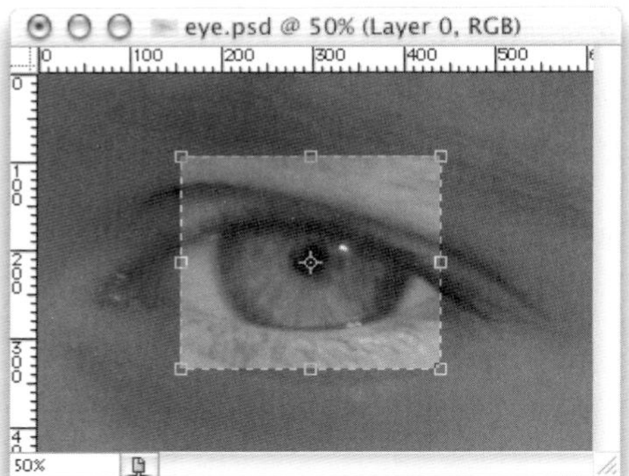

Cropping the image The selected area is preserved, but the area outside of that (shaded) is cropped out of the image when you press return or double-click.

Before a crop selection is made, you select options to specify the final size and resolution at which that the cropped region will be resized.

Ⓐ **Width, Height, Resolution** Enter the final dimensions and resolution to which the cropped image should be resized. This is optional. Leave these text boxes blank if you do not want the cropped image resized.

Ⓑ **Resolution Units** Choose the units to be used with the resolution field.

Ⓒ **Use Front Image Dimensions And Resolution** Fills the width, height, and resolution fields with the current image's values.

Ⓓ **Clear** Click to clear all values and prevent the image from being resized while cropping.

After you select the cropping region, you can use the options bar to specify what happens to cropped parts of the image and how the cropped region appears while you are working.

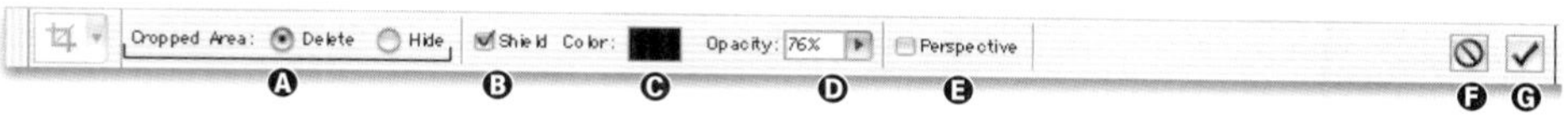

A Crop Treatment Choose Delete to permanently remove cropped regions from the image, or choose Hide to hide those regions. You can retrieve hidden parts of the image by moving the image or by resizing the image.

B Shield Region To Be Cropped If this option is checked, the region being cropped will be covered to better differentiate it from the region being preserved.

C Shield Color Click to choose the color used to cover the region being cropped.

D Shield Opacity Click to select or enter the opacity of the color used to cover the region being cropped.

E Perspective If this option is checked, the crop bounding box can be skewed.

F Cancel Click to cancel cropping.

G Commit Click to crop the image.

Crop tool [C]

Constrain proportions [Shift] plus select

Commits cropping after the selection is made [Return]

Cancel cropping after the selection is made [Esc]

REAL WORLD: KYLE MCCABE

Although Photoshop can produce some remarkable effects, some of the best effects you can create are with the camera. Kyle McCabe uses a Lomo Kompakt Automat camera, known for its unusual glass lens, which produces deep colors on photographic prints. "I never enjoyed taking photos until I discovered the Lomo camera. The Lomo philosophy is a real turn-on—which is 'don't think, just shoot.'" The Lomo is a Soviet-era camera that looks (and acts) like a poor man's spy camera.

To get the desired effects, Kyle shoots exclusively with Fuji film because he feels it provides a superior handling of reds, greens, and blues. "I generally use 200-speed films in low-level light conditions with the camera's shutter speed set to 100. In low-light conditions, the photo typically ends up with even more deeply textured saturations of color if the shot is exposed for at least one second (and sometimes three or four)."

For photo retouching in Photoshop, Kyle likes to keep things simple. "I employ only two layers for my photo editing: my source image as background, and a new layer representing the enhanced version. This helps me to see where I have made improvements and where I still need to improve."

You can see more of Kyle's work in "Don't Think, Just Shoot," a photographic anthology available from the Lomographic Society International at `www.lomography.com/justshoot/`.

3.8 Slice Tools

➠ 25.1 Slicing Your Interface

Slice tool K

Cycle slice tools Shift K

Constrain proportions Shift **plus select**

Switch between Slice and Slice Select (reverts after releasing) ⌘

If you are a web designer, the slice tools will come in handy for carving up interfaces you designed in Photoshop. You can use the Slice tool to specify particular regions of the canvas that can then be saved separate from one another using File > Save For Web....

To create a slice, select the Slice tool, set your attributes, and then select an area of the canvas to be saved independently (often a button or a header graphic). Photoshop draws a grid around the new slice, splitting the entire image into user-specified slices and auto slices. You can add as many slices as you want to a single image.

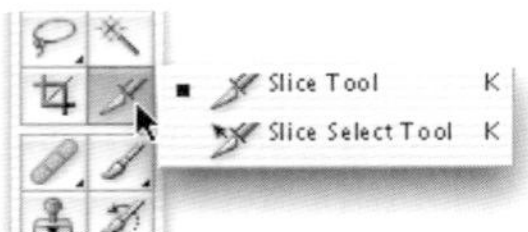

Slice A special selection tool that defines regions of the canvas (slices) to be carved up to create a web interface.

Slice Select Selects a slice to work with. Double-clicking a slice with this tool opens that slice's Options dialog.

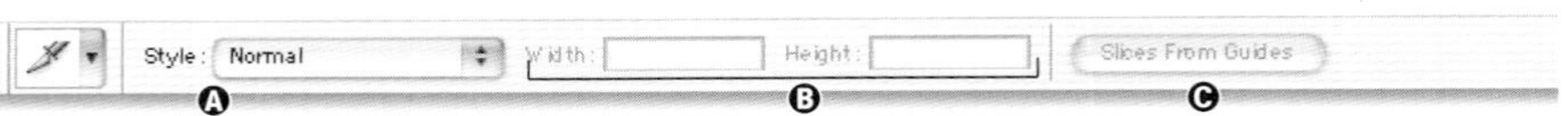

- **A Slice Selection Style** Choose Normal (unconstrained selection), Fixed Aspect Ratio (Square selection), or Fixed Size (Uses dimensions entered).
- **B Width & Height** If you select Fixed Size, enter the width and height for the slice.
- **C Slices From Guides** Click to convert the canvas guides into slices.

- **A Top** Moves the selected slice above all others.
- **B Move Up** Moves the selected slice up one level.
- **C Move Down** Moves the selected slice down one level.
- **D Bottom** Moves the selected slice below all others.
- **E Slice Options** Click to open the Slice Options dialog in which you can enter information about the selected slice.
- **F User Slice** Click to turn an auto or layer slice into a user slice.
- **G Divide Slice...** Opens a dialog that allows you to numerically divide the selected slice.
- **H Hide Auto Slices** Click to show only user slices.

3.9 Restoration Tools

Over the years, photographers have developed a dizzying array of techniques to touch up and restore photographic images using Photoshop. Now Photoshop 7 trumps many of these techniques by introducing the Heal and Patch tools, which can make getting rid of dust, scratches, or other blemishes as easy as painting them off.

The Healing Brush tool works a lot like the Rubber Stamp tool. Select the layer you want to work in and then choose the Healing Brush tool. Press Option (you will notice the cursor change) to select a region of the image with the color you want to replicate into the region being fixed. Then simply brush over the region being repaired.

The Patch tool works as a selection that allows you to copy attributes from one region of the image into another. Select the layer you want to work in, choose the Patch tool, and then select the region you want to repair. Drag the selection to an area with the coloring you want to add to the selection and release. The selected region will be reworked using the new color data.

➠ 27.3 Patching the Image

Restoration tool J

Cycle restoration tools
Shift J

Switch to Eyedropper (reverts after releasing)
Option
Alt

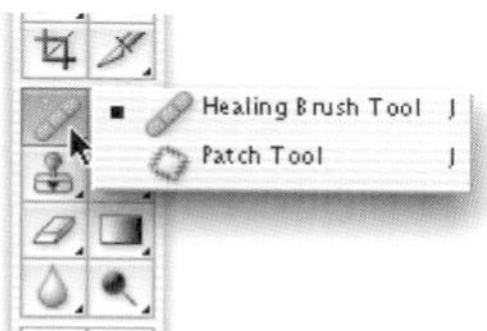

Healing Brush A special brush that you can use to copy a color from one region of the image while preserving the underlying texture, lighting, and shading of the region being brushed.

Patch A special freehand selection tool that you can use to copy one region of the image into another while preserving the underlying texture, lighting, and shading of the original region.

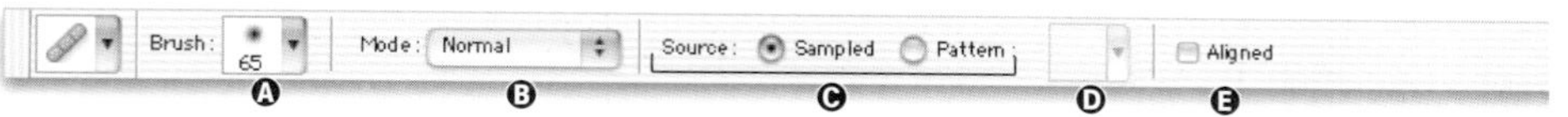

A Brush Presets Click to set a brush size or select a predefined brush.

B Blend Mode Choose from a limited list of blend modes to use with the brush.

C Source Choose the source location for healing. You can choose to either sample from the current image or use a preset pattern selected from the drop-down.

D Patterns If a pattern is selected, click to choose from a list of preset patterns.

E Aligned If this option is checked, every time the Healing Brush tool is applied to an image, the brush will remain relative to the sampling point. If this option is unchecked, every time the Healing Brush tool is stopped and then started again, it begins from the initial sampling point.

A Patch Region Choose whether the selected region is to be patched by the region moved to (source) or whether the region moved to is patched by the selection region (destination).

B Apply Pattern To Patch Click to apply the selected pattern to the patch selection.

C Pattern Choose a pattern to apply to the patch.

3.10 Drawing Tools

➠ 15.1 Brush Basics

➠ 15.5 Painting with the Brush or Pencil

Paint tool B

Cycle paint tools Shift B

Switch to Eyedropper (reverts after releasing) Option

As noted earlier in this chapter, Photoshop 7 has dropped the Airbrush tool in favor of adding an Airbrush mode to the brush tools.

Press Shift while drawing to force a straight line.

Warning: Releasing to stop a stroke is an action in the History palette. Consequently, choosing Edit > Undo removes only the last stroke you made.

Control/right-click in the canvas to open a contextual menu of the Brush Preset Picker (see Section 3.2) to choose from.

Photoshop has two primary drawing tools: the Brush and the Pencil. The difference is simply that the edges of the Brush tool are anti-aliased, and the edges of the Pencil tool are not. Other than that, they work much the same.

To use one of the paint tools, select the layer you want to paint on, choose the appropriate brush, set the brush size and other attributes, and then click and drag in the canvas. As you move, a line appears after the cursor, which is referred to as a stroke. Release to stop painting.

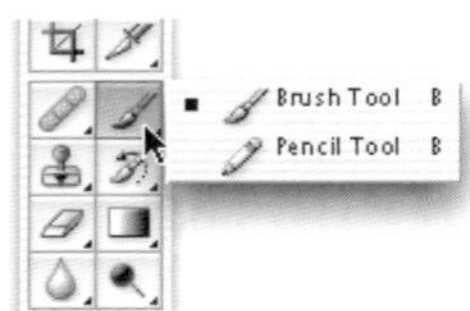

Brush Produces soft-edged, paintlike strokes.

Pencil Produces hard-edged strokes.

Ⓐ **Brush Presets** Click to set the brush size or select a predefined brush.

Ⓑ **Blend Mode** Choose from a limited list of blend modes to use with the brush.

Ⓒ **Paint Opacity** Click to select or enter the opacity of the paint.

Ⓓ **Paint Flow** Click to select or enter the flow of the paint. This option is primarily used by tablets to set how quickly color is laid down for a brush stroke.

Ⓔ **Airbrush Mode** Click to turn on Airbrush mode.

Ⓕ **Brushes Palette** Click to open or close the Brushes palette.

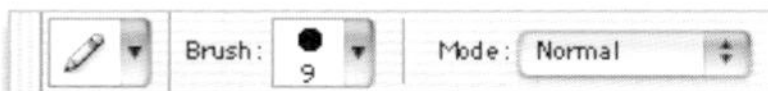

Auto Erase Click if you want the selected background color to draw over the selected foreground color.

3.11 Stamp Tools

The stamp tools are brushlike tools that you use to copy parts of the image or preset patterns into the image.

To use the Clone Stamp tool, select the layer you want to clone in, set your attributes, and Option/Alt-click in the region you want to clone from in the canvas. This is the sample point. Then move the cursor to the region you want to clone to and start painting.

To use the Pattern Stamp tool, select the layer you want to paint in, select the Pattern Stamp tool, select a pattern in the tool options bar, and set your other attributes. Then, simply click and drag to paint the selected pattern into the canvas.

➠ 15.6 Painting with Patterns

Stamp tool [S]

Cycle stamp tools [Shift] [S]

Switch to Eyedropper (reverts after releasing) [Option]

Control/right-click in the canvas to open a contextual menu of the Brush Presets.

Clone Stamp A special brush you can use to paint one region of the image over another.

Pattern Stamp A special brush you can use to paint preset patterns into the image.

Ⓐ **Brush Presets** Click to set the brush size or select a predefined brush.

Ⓑ **Blend Mode** Choose from a limited list of blend modes to use with the brush.

Ⓒ **Paint Opacity** Click to select or enter the opacity of the paint.

Ⓓ **Paint Flow** Click to select or enter the flow of the paint. This option is used by tablets to set how quickly color is laid down for a brush stroke.

Ⓔ **Airbrush Mode** Click to turn on Airbrush mode.

Ⓕ **Sample Point Alignment** If this option is checked, every time the clone brush is applied to an image, the brush remains relative to the sampling point. If this option is unchecked, every time the clone brush is stopped and then started again, it begins from the initial sampling point.

Ⓖ **Sample From All Active Layers** If checked, samples images for cloning from all layers, not just the selected layer.

Ⓗ **Brushes Palette** Click to open or close the Brushes palette.

Ⓐ **Patterns** Click to choose from a list of preset patterns to use when stamping.

Ⓑ **Impressionist Style** Check if you want the pattern to mimic the look of an Impressionist painting.

3.12 History Brushes

➠ 15.7 Painting with the Art History Brush

➠ 27.4 Touch Up with the History Brush

History Brush tool Y

Cycle history brushes Shift Y

Control/right-click in the canvas to open a contextual menu of Brush Presets.

The history brushes use specific states or snapshots in the image's history as source data to paint over the current image. This allows you to create some interesting painting effects that are less mechanical looking than simply applying a filter.

To use the history brushes, first, in the History palette, click in the rectangle next to the History state or snapshot you want to use as the source for the History Brush (a History Brush icon will appear next to the source). Select the layer you want to paint into (there must be a corresponding layer in the history source), set your brush options, and then begin to paint.

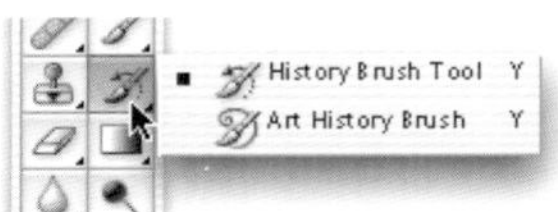

History Brush A special brush you use to copy a previous version of the image back into the current version.

Art History Brush A special brush you use to copy previous versions of the image using a variety of brush-stroke styles.

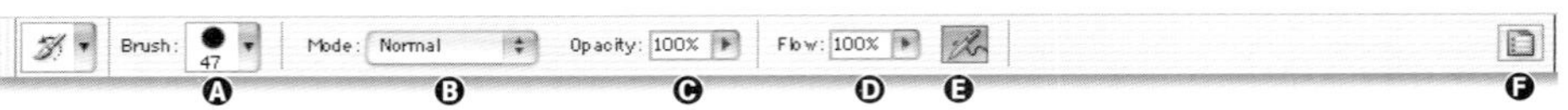

Ⓐ **Brush Presets** Click to set the brush size or select a predefined brush.

Ⓑ **Blend Mode** Choose from a limited list of blend modes to use with the brush.

Ⓒ **Paint Opacity** Click to select or enter the opacity of the paint.

Ⓓ **Paint Flow** Click to select or enter the flow of the paint. This option is used by tablets to set how quickly color is laid down for a brush stroke.

Ⓔ **Airbrush Mode** Click to turn on Airbrush mode.

Ⓕ **Brushes Palette** Click to open or close the Brushes palette.

Ⓐ **Brush Stoke Style** Choose from a list of stroke styles to use while painting.

Ⓑ **Painting Area** Enter the size of the area to be covered by the brush stroke. The larger the area, the more numerous the strokes.

Ⓒ **Painting Tolerance** Click to choose or enter a value limiting the regions to which the paint strokes are applied. The larger tolerance limits paint strokes to areas that contrast from the source color.

3.13 Eraser Tools

There is no creation without destruction, and the eraser tools are the most refined way you have of "destroying" parts of your image.

To use an eraser tool, select the layer you want to erase, choose the desired eraser tool, set the attributes for the eraser, and then click and drag over the region you want to erase.

➠ 15.9 Erasing

Eraser tool [E]

Cycle eraser tools [Shift] [E]

The Background Eraser tool ignores a layer's transparency lock.

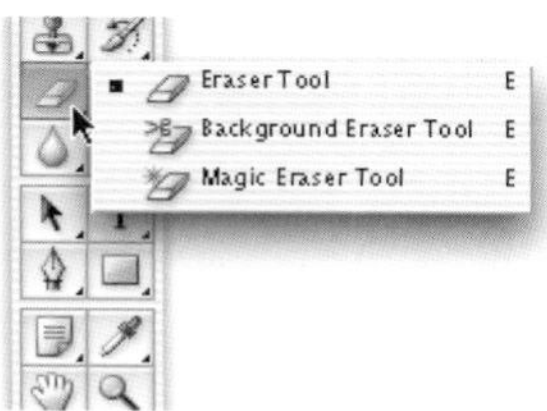

Eraser Removes pixels or makes pixels transparent on the selected layer of the canvas.

Background Eraser Removes pixels or makes pixels transparent in an image (not necessarily on the Background layer), which is useful for removing an object from a contrasting background.

Magic Eraser Removes pixels or makes pixels transparent on the selected layer for a particular color range.

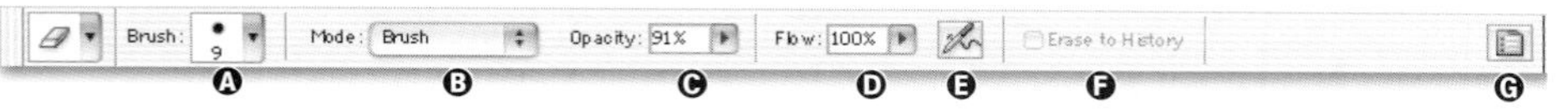

Ⓐ **Brush Presets** Click to set the brush size or select a predefined brush.

Ⓑ **Eraser Mode** Choose an eraser style: Brush, Pencil, Block (a square block).

Ⓒ **Eraser Opacity** Click to select or enter the opacity to erase.

Ⓓ **Stroke Flow** Click to select or enter the flow of the paint. This option is used by tablets to set how quickly color is laid down for a brush stroke.

Ⓔ **Airbrush Mode** Click to turn on Airbrush mode.

Ⓕ **Erase To History** Check to erase from the selected History state.

Ⓖ **Brushes Palette** Click to open or close the Brushes palette.

Ⓐ **Erase Limit Mode** Choose a limit for the color being erased: Discontinuous erases only the selected color under the brush, Contiguous erases the selected color under the brush and of any connected pixels, and Find Edges erases connected areas but preserves the sharpness and shape of edges.

Ⓑ **Tolerance** Click to set or enter a percentage for the range of similar colors to erase.

Ⓒ **Protect Foreground Color** Click to prevent the selected foreground color from being erased.

Ⓓ **Color Sampling Modes** Choose a method for selecting the color to be erased: Continuous samples colors continuously as you drag, Once erases only the first color selected, and Background Swatch erases only the currently selected background color.

3.13 Eraser Tools *(Continued)*

A Tolerance Enter a value in the range 0 to 255, which specifies the deviation a color can have to be included in the Magic Wand selection.

B Anti-Aliased When this option is checked, anti-aliasing gives the edges of the erased area a smoother appearance.

C Contiguous When checked, only pixels touching the selected pixel and within the set tolerance and pixels touching those (and so forth) are included in the selection. Otherwise, the Magic Wand selects all pixels in the image within the tolerance level.

D Sample From All Active Layers If checked, erases from all visible layers, not just the selected layer.

E Eraser Opacity Click to select or enter the opacity the eraser erases to in a single stroke.

3.14 Fill Tools

Adding dips and dabs of color is fine, but often you need to add large areas of color quickly to a canvas. Photoshop has two tools to do just that. You use the Gradient tool to add a series of colors that smoothly flow one to the next. You use the Paint Bucket tool to "pour" a solid color over all or part of the image.

To use the Gradient tool, select the layer to add a gradient to, choose the Gradient tool, and set options for the gradient. Then click where you want the gradient to begin and drag to where you want the gradient to end. The regions before and after the points are filled with the beginning and end colors of the gradient.

To use the Paint Bucket tool, select a layer to fill (you can also fill a selection in a layer), select a foreground color, and then choose the Paint Bucket tool. Set the options for the file and then click in the area you want to fill.

Gradient Fills the selection or layer with a gradiated color.

Paint Bucket Fills a selection or region in a layer with the selected foreground color.

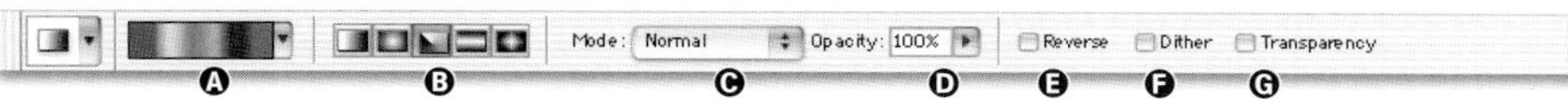

A Gradient Presets menu Click to choose a preset gradient. Double-click on gradient image to edit the gradient or create a new gradient.

B Gradient Style Choose a gradient type: Linear, Radial, Angle, Reflected, or Diamond.

C Blend Mode Choose from a blend mode for the fill to interact with the image.

D Opacity Click to select or enter the opacity for the fill.

E Reverse Direction Check to reverse the direction of the gradient colors. The effects of this show up in the Gradient Preset menu.

F Dither Gradient Check to dither the gradient colors to reduce banding.

G Transparency Mask Check to use a transparency mask with the gradient.

A Fill Type Choose to fill with the selected foreground color or with a pattern.

B Patterns If a pattern is selected in the fill type menu, click to choose from a list of preset patterns.

C Blend Mode Choose from a blend mode for the fill to interact with the image.

D Opacity Click to select or enter the opacity for the fill.

E Color Tolerance Enter a value in the range 0 to 255, which specifies the deviation a color can have from the color clicked on in order to be part of the fill.

F Anti-Aliased If this option is checked, anti-aliasing gives the edges of the fill a smoother appearance.

G Contiguous If checked, only pixels touching the selected pixel and within the set tolerance and pixels touching those (and so forth) are included in the fill.

H Fill In All Active Layers If checked, the fill affects all visible layers.

➠ 14.5 Applying Color Fills

➠ 14.8 Applying Gradient Color Fills

Fill tool [G]

Cycle fill tools
[Shift] [G]

Switch to Eyedropper (reverts after releasing)
[Option]

The farther you drag while adding a gradient, the longer and smoother the gradiated area will be.

With the Gradient tool, Control/right-click in the canvas to open a contextual menu of gradient presets.

With the Paint Bucket tool, Control/right-click in the canvas to open a contextual menu of blending modes to use for the fill.

3.15 Distortion Tools

➠ 27.6 Blurring and Sharpening with Tools

➠ 27.7 Smudging and Liquefying Images

Distortion tool [R]

Cycle distortion tools [Shift] [R]

Control/right-click in the canvas to open a contextual menu of Brush Preset Picker (see Section 3.2).

The Blur, Sharpen, and Smudge tools are brush tools that allow you to distort the image a little or a lot depending on your needs. The Blur tool does this by blurring the contrast between regions, making them look as if they are out of focus. The Sharpen tool is the Blur tool's inverse, making contrast between areas sharper. The Smudge tool gives you control as if you were running your finger over the image and smearing the colors together.

Blur A special brush that simulates a loss of focus in the image.

Sharpen A special brush that sharpens the focus of the image.

Smudge A special brush that smears the image.

All three tools share the same options except for Smudge, which adds a Finger Painting option.

Ⓐ **Brush Presets** Click to set the brush size or select a predefined brush.

Ⓑ **Blend Mode** Choose from a limited list of blend modes to use with the brush.

Ⓒ **Stroke Strength** Click to choose or enter a percentage for the strength of the stroke. The higher the percentage, the more pronounced the change.

Ⓓ **Use All Visible Layers** If this option is checked, the tool works across all visible layers, not just the selected layer.

Ⓔ **Finger Painting** If this option is checked, the Smudge tool simulates finger painting, using the selected foreground color.

Ⓕ **Brushes Palette** Click to open or close the Brushes palette.

3.16 Exposure Tools

Several tools in Photoshop are meant to mimic actual tools used during the exposure of photographic paper. Dodging is a technique that blocks light, often using a black piece of cardboard on a piece of wire, and burning is a technique that uses a hole cut in a piece of black cardboard to allow extra light into certain areas. In Photoshop, you use the Dodge tool to mimic the dodging technique, and you use the Burn tool to mimic the burning technique. You use the Sponge tool to increase color saturation and contrast.

➠ 13.6 Adjusting Brightness and Contrast

➠ 26.4 Dodging and Burning Images

Exposure tool O

Cycle exposure tools Shift O

Dodge A special brush you use to lighten the areas of the image.

Burn A special brush you use to darken areas of the image.

Sponge A special brush you use to increase the color saturation and contrast of the image.

The Dodge and Burn tools share the same options.

A Brush Presets Click to set the brush size or select a predefined brush.

B Tonal Range Choose the tonal range to burn or dodge in: Shadows, Midtones, or Highlights.

C Exposure Click to choose or enter a percentage for the exposure of the burn or dodge. The higher the percentage, the more pronounced the effect.

D Airbrush Mode Click to turn on Airbrush mode.

E Brushes Palette Click to open or close the Brushes palette.

A Brush Presets Click to set brush size or select a predefined brush.

B Saturation Choose Saturate to increase color vibrancy, or choose Desaturate to reduce color to grayscale.

C Stroke Flow Click to select or enter the flow rate for the brush. The higher the percentage, the more pronounced the effect.

D Airbrush Mode Click to turn on Airbrush mode.

E Brushes Palette Click to open or close the Brushes palette.

3.17 Path Selection Tools

➠ 12.8 Selecting Paths and Path Components

➠ 12.9 Editing Paths and Path Components

➠ 12.10 Editing Path Segments

➠ 12.11 Reshaping Curves

Path Selection tool [A]

Cycle path selection tools
[Shift] [A]

Switch between path selection tools (reverts after releasing)
[⌘]
[Ctrl]

Delete the currently selected path or path component
[Del]

Alt/Option-click with either tool inside the path and drag to duplicate the path.

You use the path tools in conjunction with the pen tools to manipulate vector paths in the image. To use them, choose a Path Selection tool and then click a path in the selected layer. The path is highlighted with direction points. Direction points appear as filled circles, selected anchor points as filled squares, and unselected anchor points as hollow squares.

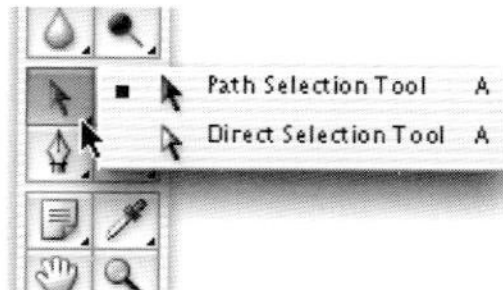

Path Selection Selects and moves paths.

Direct Selection Selects the entire path or path component and moves points or adjusts Bezier curve handles. This tool has no options.

A Show Bounding Box If checked, the rectangular edges of a path are shown. If the path is not rectangular, the bounding box represents a rectangular region of the paths' extreme horizontal and vertical limits. You can use the bounding box to transform the path (resize, skew, and rotate).

B Path Interaction Click to specify how the selected path should interact with other paths in the same layer: Add To Shape Area adds paths at overlap, Subtract From Shape Area masks overlapping paths, Intersect Shape Areas specifies that paths only show at intersections, and Exclude Overlapping Shape Areas specifies that paths only show where they do not intersect.

C Combine Paths Click to merge the paths in a layer into one path.

D Align Objects Two or more linked layers can be aligned with their top edges, middle edges, bottom edges, left edges, center edges, or right edges.

E Distributed Objects The content of three or more linked layers can be distributed between their top edges, middle edges, bottom edges, left edges, center edges, or right edges.

F Dismiss Target Path Deselects the selected path.

3.18 Type Tools

You can enter text directly into an image using any font available on the computer. Photoshop can create legible anti-aliased text for print or screen use, but often text is as an integral part of the image. It is used as a design element rather than to communicate written information. Photoshop facilitates either use of text.

To use a type tool, select the layer you want the text to appear above (type is automatically added to a new layer), select the desired type tool, set your options, and then click in the canvas where you want your text to begin (left justified), to be centered around (center), or to end (right justified).

In addition, you can create a text box for longer strings of text. Select a type tool and use it just like a selection tool to define the area of the text box. You will see a bounding box. When you enter text in the box, it will not go wider or higher than defined.

➠ 17 Typography

Type tool T

Cycle type tools Shift T

You can resize a text box using the Type tool to drag the text region's bounding box.

If there is too much text to fit in the confines of the text box, a small red plus sign appears in the bottom right corner of the box.

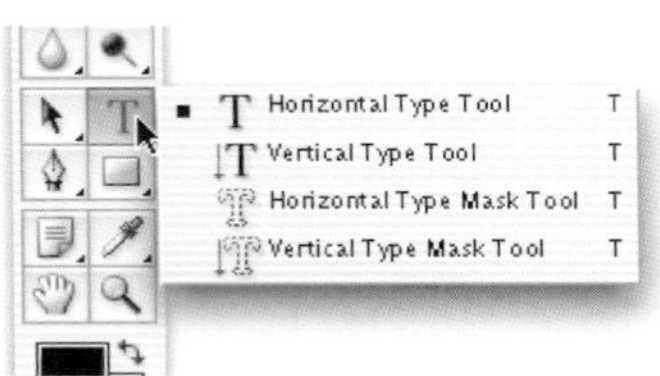

Horizontal Type Type text horizontally across the canvas.

Vertical Type Type text vertically down the canvas.

Horizontal Type Mask Type text horizontally across the canvas to create a mask.

Vertical Type Mask Type text vertically down the canvas to create a mask.

- **A Toggle Text Orientation** Click to change the text direction between horizontal and vertical.
- **B Font** Choose a font name from the list of fonts available on the computer or click to enter the font name.
- **C Font Style** Choose available styles for the selected font or click and enter the style name directly.
- **D Font Size** Choose a font size or click to enter the size directly.
- **E Anti-Aliasing** Choose an anti-aliasing method for the text: None, Crisp, Sharp, or Smooth.
- **F Text Justification** Choose a justification for the text: left, centered, or right.
- **G Font Color** Click to open the Color Picker dialog and choose a color for the text.
- **H Warped Text** Click to open the Warp Text dialog.
- **I Character & Paragraph Palettes** Click to show or hide the Character and Paragraph palettes.

3.19 Pen Tools

➠ 12.2 Setting Pen Tool Options

➠ 12.3 Setting Free-form Pen and Magnetic Pen Tool Options

➠ 12.5 Preparing to Draw Vector Paths

➠ 12.6 Preparing to Draw Shape Layers

➠ 12.7 Drawing with Pen and Shape Tools

➠ 12.11 Reshaping Curves

Pen tool [P]

Cycle pen tools (Pen and Free-form Pen only) [Shift] [P]

Delete the currently selected path or path component [Del]

Although Photoshop is primarily a bitmap-editing program, it includes several tools for adding and manipulating vector graphics. You use the pen tools to draw vector paths to create elements that can be more easily changed than bitmap elements.

To add a vector path to an image, use the Pen tool to draw anchor points, either one at a time with the Pen tool or freehand with the Freeform Pen tool. Then use the point tools to manipulate the path.

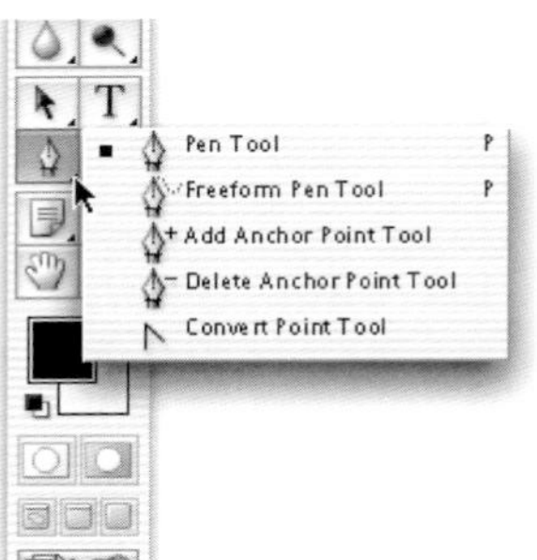

Pen Draws a vector path on a point-by-point basis.

Freeform Pen Draws a freehand vector path.

Add Anchor Point Adds a new anchor point when over an existing vector path. Otherwise, you use this tool to move and reshape exiting paths, points, and Bezier curves. This tool has no options.

Delete Anchor Point Removes an existing anchor point. Otherwise, you use this tool to reshape existing paths and Bezier curves. This tool has no options.

Convert Point Reshapes existing paths and Bezier curves. This tool has no options.

This version of the tool options bar shows the options if Shape Layer mode is selected.

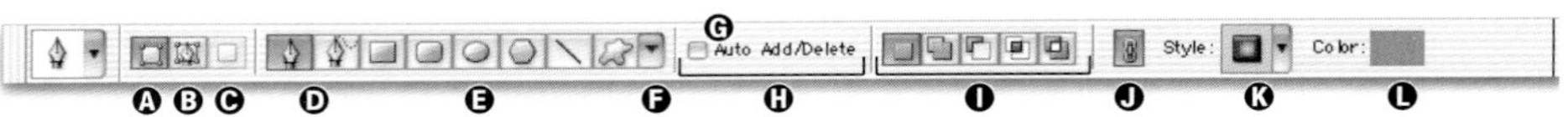

Ⓐ **Shape Layer Mode** Click to draw the vector as a layer mask. If selected, the options bar includes style and color options for the fill on the far right.

Ⓑ **Paths Mode** Click to draw a path (not filled).

Ⓒ **Fill Pixels Mode** Not available with pen tools.

Ⓓ **Pen Tools** Click to choose the Pen or Freeform Pen tool.

Ⓔ **Shape Tools** Click to choose a specific shape tool (see Section 3.20 for more details).

Ⓕ **Tool-Specific Option** This option depends on the selected tool.

Ⓖ **Auto Add/Delete** Automatically adds or deletes a point when overlapping occurs in the path. Only available to the Pen tool.

Ⓗ **Mode-Specific Options** These options depend on the mode selected.

Ⓘ **Path Interaction** Click to specify how the selected path should interact with other paths in the same layer: Create New Shape Layer starts each new path on a new layer, Add To Shape Area adds paths at overlap, Subtract From Shape Area masks overlapping paths, Intersect Shape Areas specifies that paths only show at intersections, and Exclude Overlapping Shape Areas specifies that paths only show where they do not intersect.

Ⓙ **Lock** Click to turn on or off. When on (highlighted), style changes affect the selected path. When off, style changes affect new paths only.

Ⓚ **Style Presets** Click to select a style preset.

Ⓛ **Color** Click to select a color to use if no style has been selected.

A Magnetic Check to force a freeform path to stick to high-contrast boundaries in the image. Only available to the Freeform Pen tool.

B Path Interactions Same as in Shape Layers mode but does not include Create New Shape Layer.

TOOLS AND THE MOUSE CURSOR

Every tool that you choose from the toolbox can use the tool's icon as the mouse cursor to help you identify which tool is selected. However, these icons are often clunky when you need to perform exacting manipulations of images. So Photoshop allows you to choose whether you want to use the tool icon or a more precise cursor. To set the appearance of the cursor used for tools, choose Photoshop/Edit > Preferences > Display And Cursors... (see Section 5.5). Generally, I find the Brush Size better for painting and Precision better for other tasks.

3.20 Shape Tools

➠ 12.4 Setting Shape Tool Options

➠ 12.5 Preparing to Draw Vector Paths

➠ 12.6 Preparing to Draw Shape Layers

➠ 12.7 Drawing with Pen and Shape Tools

Shape tool U

Cycle shape tools Shift U

Like the pen tools, shape tools are used to create vector paths in an image but as specific shapes (rectangles, ellipses, polygons, and so on). The shape tools share the same options as the pen tools, but add one additional mode, Pixel Fill mode, which uses a shape tool to create a bitmap rather than vector shape.

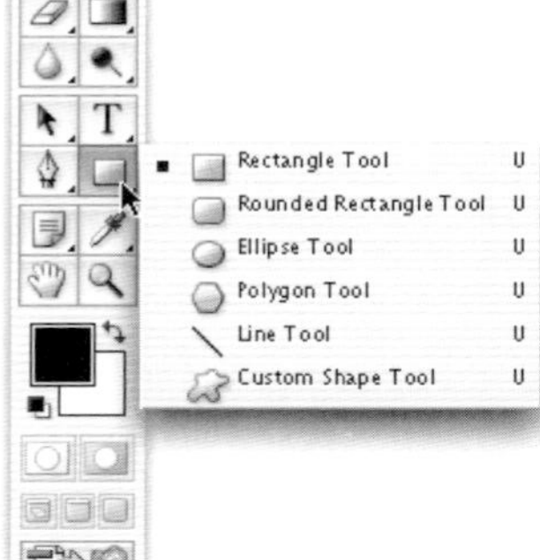

Rectangle Draws rectangular and square shapes.

Rounded Rectangle Draws rectangular shapes with rounded edges. Enter the radius of rounded edges in the tool options bar.

Ellipse Draws elliptical and circular shapes.

Polygon Draws multisided shapes. Enter the number of sides in the tool options bar.

Line Draws a straight line. Enter the line weight in the tool options bar.

Custom Shape Catch-all to draw a variety of predefined shapes. Choose the exact shape in the tool options bar.

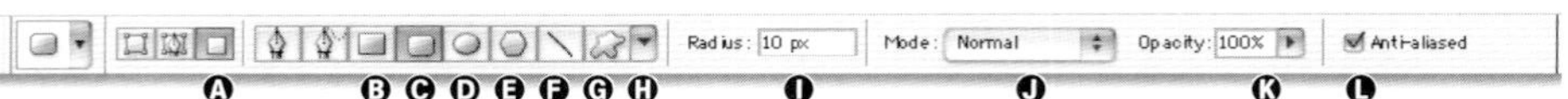

Ⓐ **Fill Pixel Mode** Uses the shape to create a bitmap image rather than a vector image.

Ⓑ **Rectangle Tool** Click to draw rectangular and square shapes.

Ⓒ **Rounded Rectangle Tool** Click to draw rectangular and square shapes with rounded rather than squared corners.

Ⓓ **Ellipse Tool** Click to draw elliptical and circular shapes.

Ⓔ **Polygon Tool** Click to draw multi-sided shapes.

Ⓕ **Line Tool** Click to draw lines.

Ⓖ **Custom Shape Tool** Click to draw customized shapes.

Ⓗ **Shape Options** Click to set additional options for the selected shape tool. Each shape tool has slightly different options.

Ⓘ **Quick Shape Options** Presents a single option for the selected shape tool (in this example, radius for the rounded rectangle corners).

Ⓙ **Blend Mode** Choose from a limited list of blend modes to use with the brush.

Ⓚ **Paint Opacity** Click to select or enter the opacity of the paint.

Ⓛ **Anti-Aliased** When this option is checked, anti-aliasing gives the edges of the selection a smoother appearance.

3.21 Annotation Tools

If you are working with others on a project, or if you simply want to remind yourself how or why you did something in an image, add a note directly to the canvas. To add a note, select the tool, click the canvas where you want the note to appear, and then enter your text.

To add an audio annotation, select the tool, click the canvas where you want an icon for the note to appear, and use the controls to record your message. Obviously, your computer must be equipped with a microphone. To play the note back, double-click the annotation icon.

Notes Adds a virtual sticky note to the document.

Audio Annotation Adds a recorded message to the document at a particular spot. Requires a computer with a microphone.

Options for both annotation tools are identical except that the Audio Annotation tool does not include font or size.

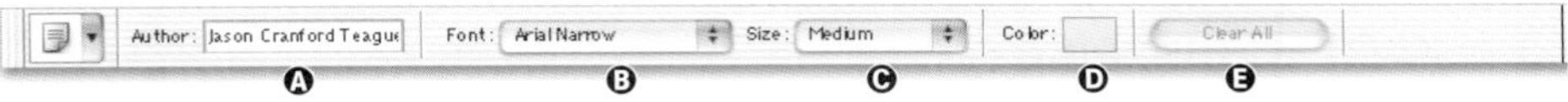

A Author Name Enter the name of the comment's author.

B Font (Notes tool only) Choose the font in which the note will appear.

C Font Size (Notes tool only) Choose a relative font size for the note: Smallest, Smaller, Medium, Larger, or Largest.

D Highlight Color Click to open the Color Picker dialog and select a highlight color for the note.

E Clear All Click to clear all notes from the current document.

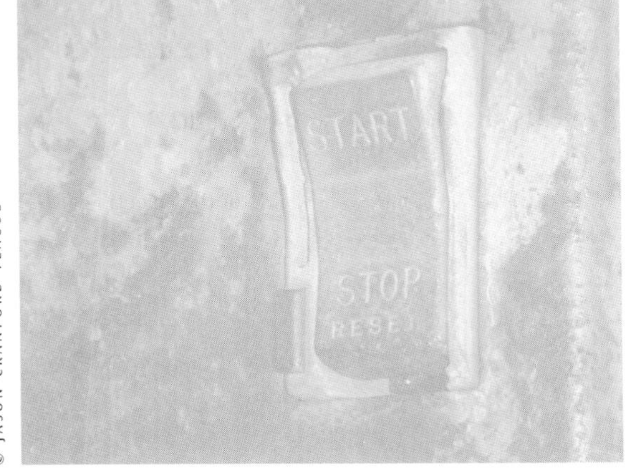

➠ 6.12 Adding Notes

Annotation tool N

Cycle annotation tools Shift N

Warning: Sound files can add considerably to the file size, so you might want to use them sparingly.

To delete a single annotation, click the Annotation icon and press Delete.

If your computer does not have a built-in microphone, you will need to plug an external microphone into the computer's "mini" input. If you have one, it will generally have a microphone icon above it.

3.22 Eyedropper and Measure Tools

➠ 14.2 Selecting Colors

Eyedropper tool [I]

Cycle eyedropper and measure tools
[Shift] [I]

Switch between Eyedropper and Color Sampler (reverts after releasing)
[Shift]

Selecting the right color is a crucial task in Photoshop. The Eyedropper tool is designed to help you select colors from anywhere on the canvas—in color swatches and even from the Color bar at the bottom of the Color palette. To compare colors, use the Color Sampler tool. This tool lets you select as many as four colors and display their color values in the Info palette.

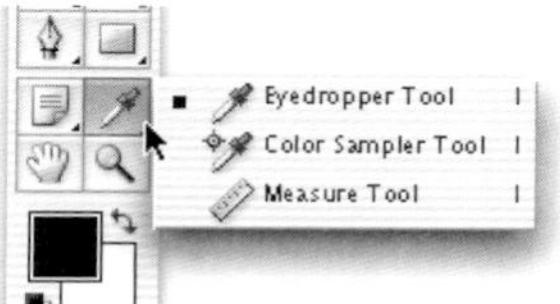

Eyedropper Selects colors from the canvas, toolbar, Swatches palette, and Color palette.

Color Sampler Select as many as four points in the canvas to display the color value for each point in the Info palette.

Measure Click and drag to measure the distance between two points in the canvas.

A Sample Size Method Choose an option to specify how the Eyedropper should select a color. Point Sample selects the color of the clicked pixel, and 3 By 3 Sample and 5 By 5 Sample both average the color of the pixels around the selection point.

B Clear Clears the selected color samples. Only available with Color Sampler tool.

A Origin Coordinates Displays the X, Y coordinates of the measurement's origin.

B Width and Height Displays the distance of the final point from the origin coordinates.

C Angle The angle of measurement.

D Distances The distances of a maximum of two measurements.

E Clear Clears the current measurement lines.

3.23 Hand Tool

Images often fill the screen and go outside the viewable area of the document window, especially if they are large or you have magnified them. Use the Hand tool to move the image within the viewing area.

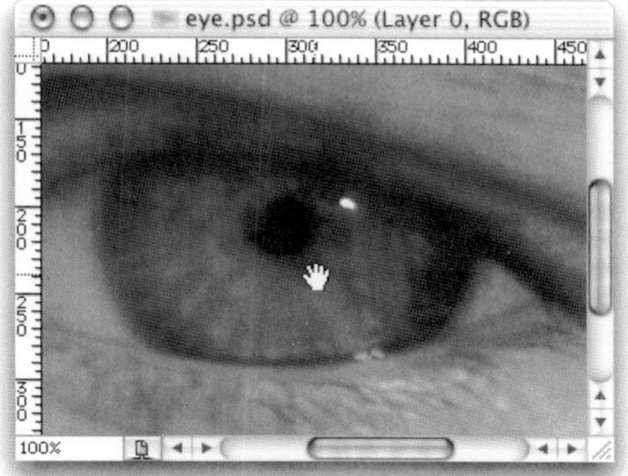

Use the Hand tool to move the canvas within the window.

Ⓐ **Actual Pixels** Click to zoom the canvas to 100%.

Ⓑ **Fit On Screen** Click to maximize the image so that it fills the screen.

Ⓒ **Print Size** Click to zoom the image to the size it will be when printed.

Hand tool H

Switch to Hand tool from any other tool (reverts after releasing)
Spacebar

Switch to Zoom In (reverts after releasing)
⌘
Ctrl

Switch to Zoom Out (reverts after releasing)
Shift

3.24 Zoom Tool

➠ 6.7 Navigating the Canvas

Zoom tool [Z]

Use the Zoom tool to magnify the image (zoom in) to get a better look at details or pull back (zoom out) to get a bird's eye view of the entire image.

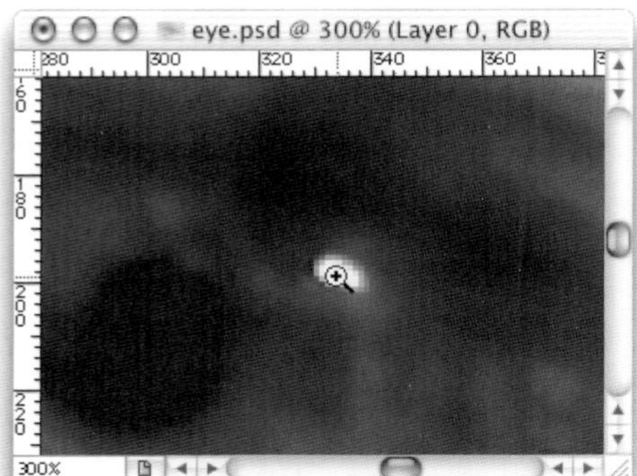

This image is zoomed to 300%.

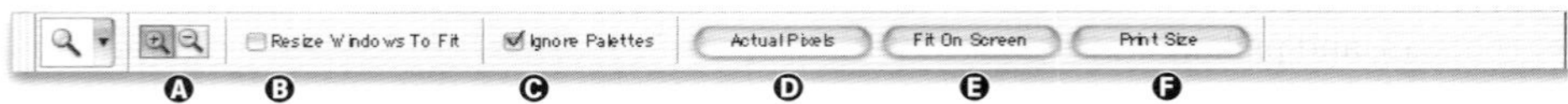

A Zoom Tools Click to select Zoom In or Zoom Out.

B Resize Windows To Fit Check to force the window to automatically resize to the size of the canvas.

C Ignore Palettes Check to allow resizing to ignore palettes on the screen. Otherwise, the window resizes to the palette edges.

D Actual Pixels Click to zoom the canvas to 100%.

E Fit On Screen Click to maximize the image to fill the screen.

F Print Size Click to zoom the image to the size it will be when printed.

3.25 Beyond the Tools

The Toolbox also contains a few other buttons that provide shortcuts to key features. You may use some of these features (such as the Foreground/Background Colors) all the time, and you may never give others a second glance (such as the Jump To ImageReady button).

Adobe Online

The Adobe Photoshop icon at the top of the menu is actually a link to the Adobe website. Click this button to open your default web browser at the Adobe Photoshop web page (www.adobe.com/products/photoshop).

Adobe Online Click to go to the Photoshop area of the Adobe website.

On this page you will find marketing information about Photoshop (which, if you already own Photoshop, won't be of much use). From here you can also download software updates and additions, find out about training and events, report problems, chat with other Photoshop users, and pick up inspiration from the Adobe Gallery.

Foreground/Background Color Swatches

Photoshop allows you to have two selected colors at any time: foreground and background. The foreground color is used by any brush, text, or other tool or option that adds pixels to the canvas. The background color is available for fills, although you can also select other colors. More important, if the image is not using a transparent background (that is, there is a Background layer), the background color fills areas whenever the canvas is resized or parts of the background are cut or deleted.

To change either color, click its color swatch to open the Color Picker. To change the foreground color, select colors in the Swatches palette, set the color in the Color palette, or use the Eyedropper tool to select a color from the image. To change the background color, use the Eyedropper tool and press Option/Alt while selecting a color from the image.

These are the same colors as shown in the Color palette.

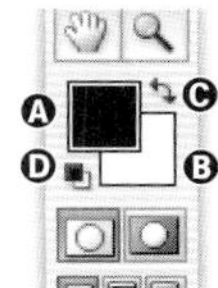

A Foreground Color Swatch Click to open the Color Picker and select a new color.

B Background Color Swatch Click to open the Color Picker and select a new color.

C Swap Click to swap the foreground and background colors.

D Reset Colors Click to reset the foreground and background colors to the default black and white.

➠ 5.11 Adobe Online Preferences

➠ 8.4 Creating a Free-form Selection

➠ 14.1 Color, Gradient, and Pattern Basics

➠ 14.2 Selecting Colors

➠ 14.3 Selecting Colors with the Color Picker

➠ 22 Working with ImageReady

Swap foreground/ background colors
X

Revert to default colors
D

Cycle mask modes
Q

Cycle view modes (Standard, Full Screen with Menu Bar, Full Screen)
P

Jump To ImageReady
Shift ⌘ M
Shift Ctrl M

3.25 Beyond the Tools *(Continued)*

Quick Mask Mode

Masks are an easy way to select parts of an image using the brush tools. The Quick Mask mode applies a mask to the entire image, which you can then edit using the standard selection and drawing tools. When you return to Standard mode, the mask is converted into a selection.

Ⓐ **Standard Mode** Click to work with the image.

Ⓑ **Quick Mask Mode** Click to edit the image mask.

View Mode

Photoshop has three distinctive view modes. You can display the image in a free-floating window that you can move around the screen, or the image can be fixed in the center of the screen with either a gray or a black background.

Ⓐ **Standard Screen Mode** Click to display the image in its own window.

Ⓑ **Full Screen Mode With Menu Bar** Click if you want the image fixed in a gray field in the center of the screen with a menu bar at the top.

Ⓒ **Full Screen Mode** Click if you want the image fixed in a black field with no menu bar available.

Jump To ImageReady

ImageReady is provided with Photoshop to add greater web-editing capabilities. You can easily move images back and forth between ImageReady and Photoshop using the Jump To ImageReady button. On the other side, ImageReady has a button to send the image back to Photoshop when you are finished in ImageReady.

Jump To ImageReady Click to open the file in ImageReady to edit for the Web.

Changes made to the image in one program are immediately imported to the other when you switch back and forth (either using the buttons or by simply using your operating system to move between programs). In addition, while one program is using the file, the document is grayed out in the other program so that there is no confusion over which version you are currently editing.

CHAPTER 4

Palettes

ALTHOUGH RECENT VERSIONS OF PHOTOSHOP have shifted attention to the tool options bar, the 17 palettes still serve as the workhorses of Photoshop, providing access to hundreds of options that control brush size to text size and everything between.

Every palette is unique and performs specific duties in the interface, yet all palettes share certain qualities. All palettes appear in a special palette window (unless docked in the Palette Well). This window is a miniature version of a regular window but has the elements commonly associated with windows.

This chapter covers:

4.1 Organizing Palettes

➠ 1.5 Interface Objects

Show/hide Toolbox, Toolbox options, and open palettes
Tab

Show/hide open palettes
Shift Tab

Hide currently open palette in the Palette Well
Esc

To avoid screen clutter, you can arrange and organize the 17 palettes in a variety of ways by docking individual palettes together, docking palette windows together, or docking pallets into a special area called the Palette Well.

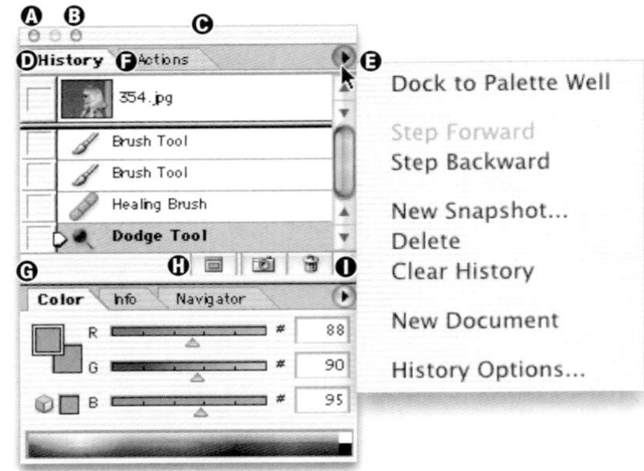

A Close Palette Window Click to close this palette window and all its palettes.

B Resize Palette Window Click to toggle between different window sizes for the currently showing palette(s) in the palette window or docked palette windows.

C Title bar Click and drag the palette window to position it on the screen. Double-click to collapse the window to just the tabs.

D Palette tab Click to display the indicated palette. Double-click to collapse the window to just the tabs. You can also use this tab to move palettes between palette windows and to the Palette Well.

E Palette menu Click to access to specific options for the palette. The menu button appears in the palette's tab when docked in the Palette Well. Each palette has different options that are usually provided in the menus at the top of the screen or application.

F Docked palettes One or more palettes grouped together into the same palette window.

G Docked palette windows One or more palette windows grouped together.

H Footer controls If available, click to use various buttons and menus depending on the palette.

I Resize Palette If available, click to change the size of the palette window.

4.1 Organizing Palettes *(Continued)*

Docking Palettes

Group two or more palettes together in the same palette window by dragging the tab of one palette into the area of another palette window (the entire palette window is highlighted by a thick black border) and release. The palettes now appear in the same palette window and move together as a single unit. To switch between palettes, simply click the tab of the palette you want to view. To ungroup a palette, click and drag its tab out of the palette window and release. The palette is now in its own palette window.

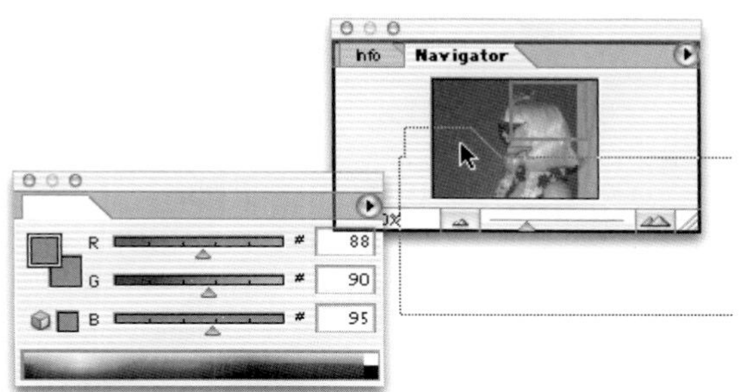

The Color palette is being docked with other palettes. Notice the thick black border around the entire palette window, indicating that the palette is being added to the window.

Docking Palette Windows

Group two or more palette windows on top of each other by dragging the tab of one palette to the top or bottom of another palette window (the area at the bottom or top of the window is highlighted) and release. The palette windows are now stacked on top of each other and not only move together but adjust their positions depending on other palette windows in the same group. You can dock and undock individual palettes as described earlier.

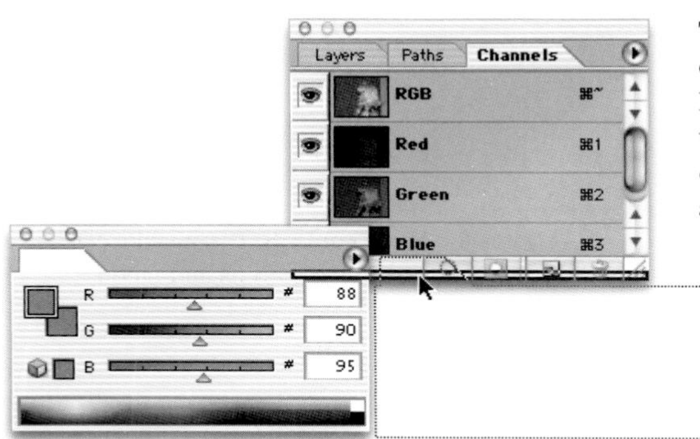

The Color palette window is being docked below another palette window. Notice the thick black border around the bottom of the palette window, indicating that the palette is being docked at the bottom.

When you move a palette window, it tends to snap around other palette windows on the screen, which makes them easier to accurately position with one another.

You can also add palettes to the Palette Well by selecting Dock To Palette Well in any palette menu.

4.1 Organizing Palettes *(Continued)*

The Palette Well is best reserved for palettes that are commonly used but not required for constant reference such as the Color and Style palette.

The more tabs you add to the Palette Well, the less space there is to display each tab. The tabs begin to overlap and become increasingly difficult to read.

Docking to the Palette Well

Add palettes to the Palette Well (located on the right side of the tool options bar) by dragging the palette's tab into the area of the Palette Well area and releasing. The tab for the palette now appears as an option in the Palette Well. To view the palette, click the tab. To close the tab, click anywhere outside its area. To remove the palette from the well, simply click and drag its tab out of the Palette Well area. The palette now appears in its own palette window.

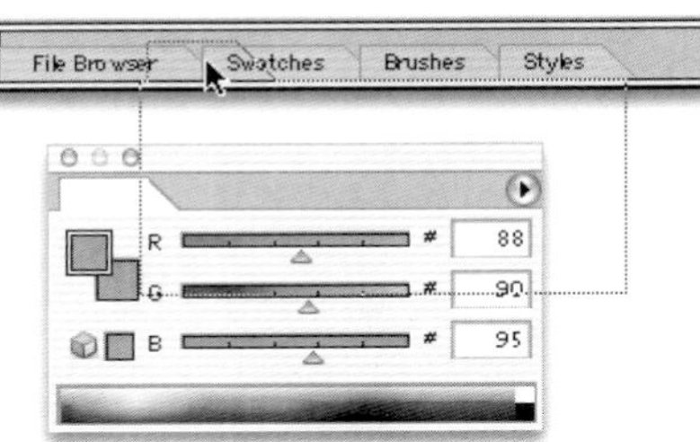

The Color palette is being added to the Palette Well. Notice the thick black border around the Palette Well, indicating that the palette is being added.

Palette Options

Many palettes have a dialog to set specific preferences for the palette. To access the palette's options, choose Palette Options… in the palette's menu.

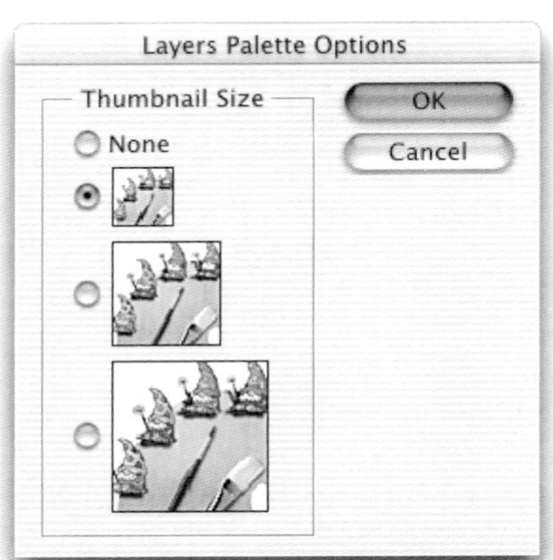

You can set the size of thumbnails displayed in the palette in the Layers Palette Options dialog.

4.2 File Browser

Photoshop 7 introduces a new feature, the File Browser, which allows you to bypass your operating system's Finder (Mac) or Explorer (Windows) to work with files, especially image files. As its name suggests, the File Browser lets you browse through your hard drive using a common interface (regardless of your operating system) to find, preview, and manipulate image files.

Although you access the File Browser through the Window menu and you can dock it to the Palette Well using its menu, the File Browser is not, in fact, a floating palette and can not be docked with other palettes. It is instead a stand-alone window with controls like other windows in your operating system.

➠ 6.2 Opening an Existing Image

Toggle between Browser and Thumbnail panes

To rename a file, select its thumbnail and double-click or press Enter to select only the image name (without selecting the image's extension), type the new name, and press Enter again. With the image name selected, you can also press Tab to move to the next filename or press Shift-Tab to move to the previous filename.

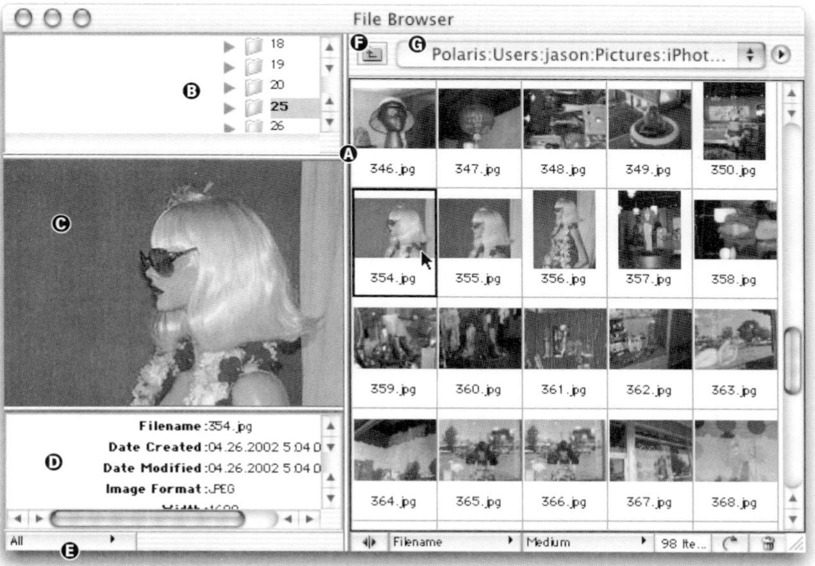

Ⓐ Frame borders Click to resize the area available for the browser: Selected Image View, Selected Information View, and Thumbnail area.

Ⓑ Browser Click a folder or a filename to select. Click a triangle/plus to open a folder. Results are displayed in the Thumbnail area.

Ⓒ Selected Image View Displays the selected image, file icon, or folder icon. Images are displayed as large as possible, depending on the area available.

Ⓓ Selected Information View Displays information about the selected image or file.

Ⓔ Information Type Select Click to choose between displaying all the information available about the image or file or only the EXIF information.

Ⓕ Up One Level Click to move up one folder level.

Ⓖ Select Level Click to view and choose previous folder levels.

Continues

Select multiple files (Shift-select) to make changes to multiple files simultaneously.

Place the mouse pointer over a thumbnail image to view a Tool Tip with the image's location, date and time created, and file format.

Since it is not a real palette, the File Browser does not have any palette options, but the palette menu contains several options for controlling the window's appearance, including the ability to flip to the expanded view showing the left column.

H Window menu Contains options for this window and selected files.

I Thumbnails Click to select. Double-click to open (including folders). Click a name to change it. Control/right-click to access a contextual menu.

J Toggle Expanded View Click to show/hide the left column.

K Sort By Click to choose the method for sorting the thumbnail list.

L View By Click to choose the size of the thumbnail as well as the information displayed with the thumbnail.

M Number Of Items In Folder Displays the number of items displayed in the Thumbnail area.

N Rotate Selected Click to rotate the thumbnail for the selected image 90° counterclockwise. The image itself is not rotated until Photoshop opens it.

O Delete Selected Click to place the selected image, file, or folder (and all its contents) in your operating system's Trash/Recycle Bin.

P Selected Image The selected image will have a thicker border around it.

4.3 Navigator Palette

The Navigator palette works as a remote control for viewing the canvas in the document window. This palette provides a thumbnail view of the entire canvas regardless of magnification, showing you the current viewable area in the canvas as a red rectangle and allowing you to quickly change the location and magnification of the viewable area.

➠ 6.7 Navigating the Canvas

The Navigator palette options let you control the color of the viewable area's border.

A magnification of 100% displays the image as it will appear on a computer screen.

Double-click the Zoom tool to return directly to 100%.

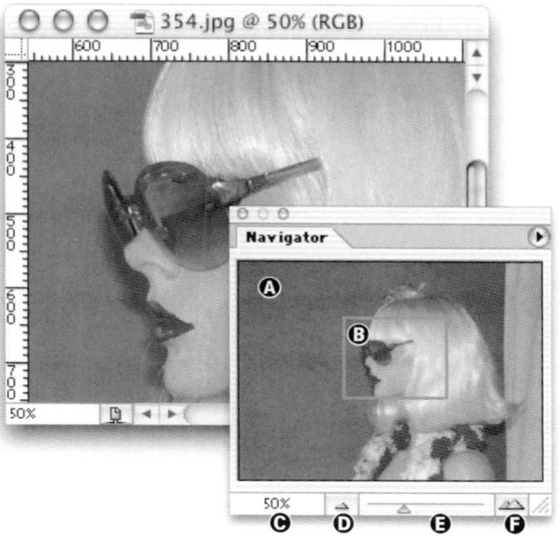

Ⓐ **Proxy Preview Area** Displays the entire image reduced to fit in the available area of palette.

Ⓑ **Viewable Area** This box shows the current area displayed in the document window's display area. Click and drag to change the area shown in the Canvas.

Ⓒ **Current Magnification** Displays the current magnification as a percentage. Click to enter a new magnification for the document directly (0.26% to 1600%).

Ⓓ **Zoom Out** Click to reduce the document's magnification.

Ⓔ **Magnification Slider** Click and drag the slider or click the slider line to change document's magnification.

Ⓕ **Zoom In** Click to increase the document's magnification.

REAL WORLD: JIM YI

Jim Yi's ideas start life as simple pen sketches, his conceptual work being done with just plain ol' ink and paper. He then scans the drawings in at 360 dpi to 600 dpi. "I usually just save files at extremely high dpi and work with the file in CMYK if it's destined for print or RGB if its meant for the Web. I generally don't give much conscious thought to the midtones, dark, and light; I don't go by histogram... mainly by eye."

But Photoshop is more than just a way to output his images. "I ran different photographs of buildings through a combo of Photoshop's filters like diffuse glow and blurs." He acknowledges that filters often get a bad rap from some Photoshop users, but feels that "filters, whether in-house or third-party, are exceptional shortcuts, and numerous unique effects can be achieved by combining filters."

You can find more of Jim's work at www.skatemafia.com.

4.4 Info Palette

➠ 8.3 Selecting Rectangular or Elliptical Areas

➠ 8.4 Creating a Free-form Selection

➠ 14.1 Color, Gradient, and Pattern Basics

➠ 14.2 Selecting Colors

Info palette options allow you to set the First Color Mode, Second Color Mode, and Ruler Units.

The Info palette displays information about the color and location of the current pixel that the cursor is over as well as the dimensions of any selections in the canvas. The palette displays as many as four color values while you are using the Color Sampler tool.

Other information that appears in the Info palette depends on which tool is active.

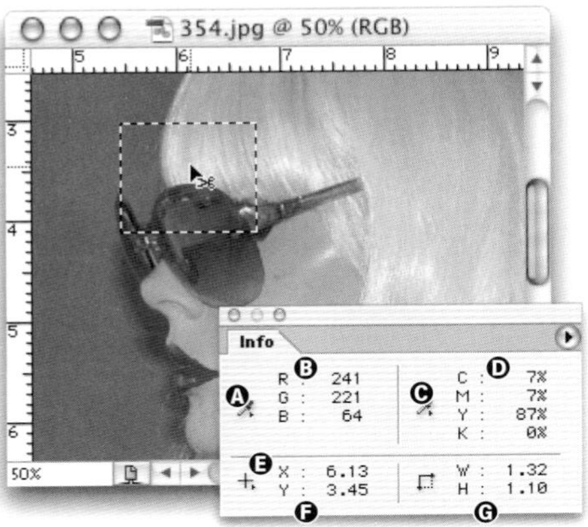

Ⓐ **First Color Mode** Click to select the color value displayed: Actual, Proof, Grayscale, RGB, Web, HSB, CMYK, Lab, Total Ink, Opacity.

Ⓑ **First Color Readout** Displays the color values (as selected) for the pixel the cursor is currently over in the image.

Ⓒ **Second Color Mode** Click to select the color value displayed: Actual, Proof, Grayscale, RGB, Web, HSB, CMYK, Lab, Total Ink, Opacity.

Ⓓ **Second Color Readout** Displays the color values (as selected) for the pixel the cursor is currently over in the image.

Ⓔ **Ruler Units** Click to select the units used (pixels, inches, centimeters, millimeters, points, picas, percentages) for the cursor position and selection size.

Ⓕ **Cursor Position** Displays the X, Y coordinates of the pixels the cursor is currently over in the selected units.

Ⓖ **Selection Size** Displays the width and height of the currently selected area in the document.

4.5 Color Palette

Although the Color Picker gives finer control over the exact foreground and background colors being used, the Color palette provides instant access to color-mixing controls, allowing you to make quick changes to colors.

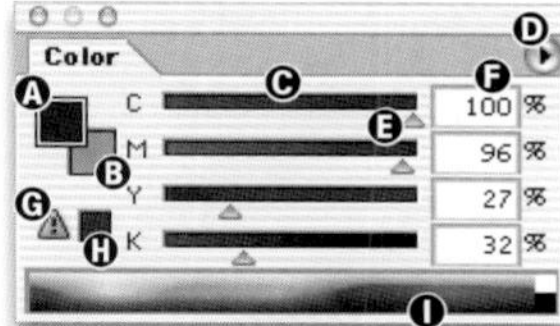

Ⓐ Foreground Color Displays the current foreground color (same as in the Toolbox). Click to select a color to make changes with the palette. Double-click to open the Color Picker.

Ⓑ Background Color Displays the current background color (same as in the Toolbox). Click to select a color to make changes with the palette. Double-click to open the Color Picker.

Ⓒ Slider Bar Displays the colors currently available to that slider. The color in the slider bar changes dynamically based on the values of the other sliders.

Ⓓ Color Mode Choose the color mode being used from the palette menu: Grayscale, RGB, HSB, CMYK, Lab, and Web.

Ⓔ Color Sliders Click and drag to change the color value.

Ⓕ Color Values Displays the color value. Click to enter the value. The possible value depends on the color mode selected.

Ⓖ Color Warning A caution symbol ⚠ appears if the color is out of range for CMYK printing. A cube appears if you are working in Web mode and the color is not browser-safe.

Ⓗ Safe Color Click to change a color to a safe color if the selected color is out of range or not a browser-safe color.

Ⓘ Color Ramp Displays a spectrum of colors from which to choose. Click to select a color.

➠ 3.22 Eyedropper and Measure Tools

➠ 14.1 Color, Gradient, and Pattern Basics

➠ 14.2 Selecting Colors

➠ 14.4 Organizing Color Swatch Presets

You use the Color palette menu to set the Color mode for the sliders (even if it is different from the document's Color mode). Select the Color mode that is being displayed in the color ramp from the palette menu (RGB, CMYK, Grayscale, Current). You can also choose to make the palette Web-safe from the palette menu or to copy the color as Web-safe.

Click and drag with the Eyedropper tool in the canvas area to display the selected colors in real time in the Color palette.

4.6 Swatches Palette

➠ 3.22 Eyedropper and Measure Tools

➠ 14.1 Color, Gradient, and Pattern Basics

➠ 14.2 Selecting Colors

➠ 14.4 Organizing Color Swatch Presets

You use the Swatches palette menu to select the size the swatches are displayed at as well as load or save various swatch color palette configurations.

The Swatches palette is a good candidate to place into the Palette Well.

The Swatches palette stores color chips (swatches) for easy access. You can add and save swatches, or you can choose pre-generated swatches for your specific needs from the extensive list in the palette's menu.

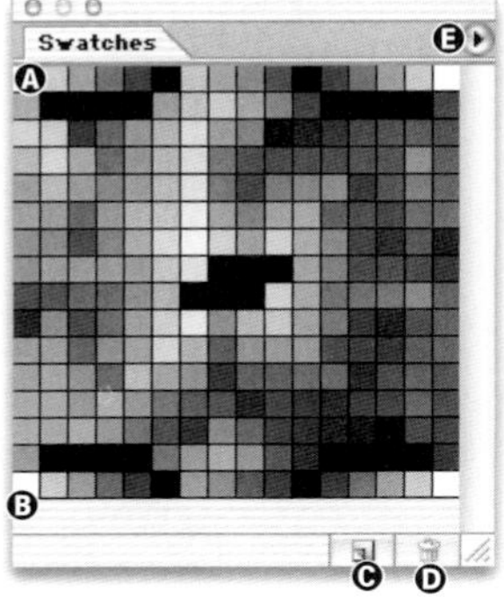

A Color swatch Click a color to select it. Option-click to remove a color from the palette. Hold the mouse over a color to view color information in a Tool Tip.

B Empty swatch Click anywhere in this area to add the current foreground color to the palette as a new swatch.

C New Swatch Click to add the current foreground color to the palette.

D Delete Swatch Click and drag a swatch to this button to delete the swatch.

E Color Swatches Presets Select the colors displayed from the extensive list of color swatch palettes to load into the palette.

© NEIL EVANS

4.7 Styles Palette

The Styles palette stores collections of effects and blending options as style presets to be applied to a selected layer.

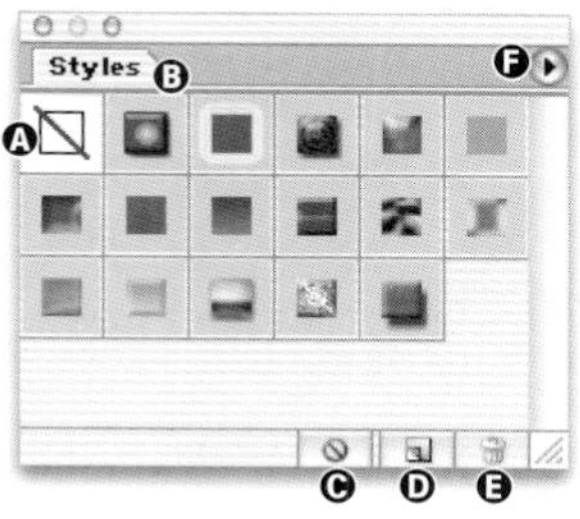

Ⓐ **Default Style** Click to apply the default style that removes other styles (the same as Clear Style).

Ⓑ **Style Preset** Click to apply this style to the selected layer.

Ⓒ **Clear Style** Click to clear all effects and blending options from the selected layer.

Ⓓ **New Style** Click to add the effects and/or blending options of the current layer as a new style to the palette.

Ⓔ **Delete Style** Click and drag a style to this button to delete the style.

Ⓕ **Style Presets** Choose from an extensive list of preset styles to load into the palette.

➠ 5.1 Preset Manager Overview

➠ 10.3 Creating and Applying Style Presets

➠ 10.4 Managing Style Presets

Use the Styles palette menu to select the size the styles are displayed at as well as load or save various style groups in the palette.

Just as with color swatches, you can click in the empty area of the Styles palette to add the styles of the currently selected layer as a style preset.

4.8 History Palette

➠ 6.9 Changing Your Mind

➠ 15.7 Painting with the Art History Brush

Undo/redo last action
⌘ Z
Ctrl Z

Step forward
Shift ⌘ Z
Shift Ctrl Z

Step backward
Option ⌘ Z
Alt Ctrl Z

The History palette menu lets you step forward or backward in the history, create a new snapshot, delete the selected History state, or clear the entire history.

The History palette options let you specify whether a first snapshot is created as soon as the image is started or opened, whether a snapshot is created whenever the image is saved, whether you are using linear or nonlinear history, and whether the new snapshot dialog opens whenever a snapshot is made.

To duplicate a History state, Option/Alt-click the History state.

Specify the number of History states in the General Preferences panel The default is 20, but adding more states requires more memory and could slow your system.

The history palette records the actions (called states in the palette) you perform while editing a document, and then allows you to move backward and forward through the History state list, basically traveling backward and forward in time. In the History palette menu, you can choose between two distinct working modes that you can set in the History palette options dialog:

Linear mode If you move backward in the history and then perform a new action, all previous actions in the history are erased. This is the easiest mode to use since you don't have to keep track of actions you are no longer using in the image; however, all those actions are lost.

Non-linear mode If you move backward in the history and then perform a new action, all subsequent actions are kept in the history (but ignored) and new actions are added to the bottom of the history. This mode tends to get a bit confusing, but does allow you to preserve actions and go back and perform them again later.

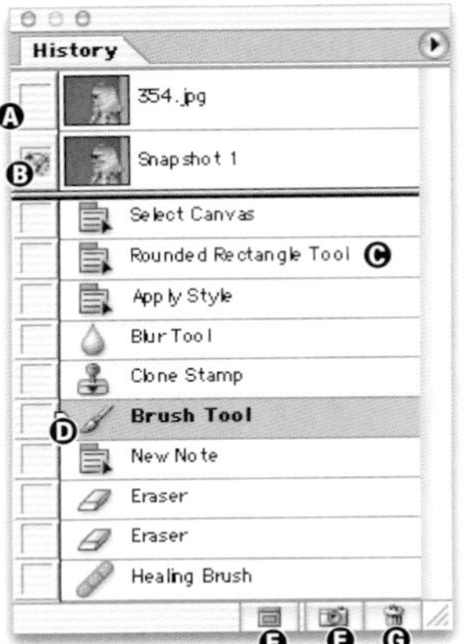

A Snap Shots Saved states for the image. Click to restore the image to its previous appearance. Click the Create Snap Shot button at the bottom of the palette to add a new snapshot based on the image's current appearance.

B History Brush Click in this column to select a state or a snapshot to be used for the history brushes.

C History state Every action performed in the canvas is recorded as a History state in this list. Click any state to revert to that point in the image.

D Current State Actions prior to this state are displayed in the canvas. Actions after this state are available, but not currently showing in the image.

E New Document Click to create a new document from the current History state.

F Create Snapshot Click to create a new snapshot from the current History state.

G Delete State Click to delete the current History state or drag a state to the button to delete it.

4.9 Actions Palette

The Actions palette stores a series of commands that you can then replay on one or a batch of images, allowing you to assign keyboard shortcuts to access these actions quickly. The Actions palette has two distinctive modes, which you can toggle between in the Actions palette menu:

Record mode Used to create or play back actions. In the Record mode, you can view all the action sets, actions, and commands.

Button mode A simplified interface that lets you click a single button to play back an action.

➠ 18.1 Playing Actions

➠ 18.2 Recording Actions

➠ 18.3 Performing Batch Actions

➠ 18.4 Creating Droplets

The Actions palette menu gives you access to all the action recording options and allows you to save and load action sets in the palette. In addition, you can select whether to use Record mode or Button mode.

Ⓐ **Toggle Action** Click to turn the action or group of actions on or off.

Ⓑ **Toggle Dialog** Click to turn the dialog for an action on or off. If on, the dialog is open. If off, the last values in the dialog are used.

Ⓒ **Action Set** A collection of actions.

Ⓓ **Action** An individual action. Click the action to select it and then click the play button to execute it.

Ⓔ **Command** An individual action.

Ⓕ **Stop Recording** If an action is being recorded, click this button to stop recording.

Ⓖ **Begin Recording** Click to start recording an action. You must have an action selected or use the menu palette to start a new action.

Ⓗ **Play Action** Click to play the currently selected action.

Ⓘ **Create New Set** Click to add a new action set folder.

Ⓙ **Create New Action** Click to start a new action.

Ⓚ **Delete Action** Click to delete the currently selected Action Set, Action, or Action Behavior or click and drag to this button to delete.

4.10 Tool Presets Palette

The Tool Presets palette menu gives you options to create and edit tool presets using the Presets Manager as well as the ability to selectively show and sort tools and load various tool presets.

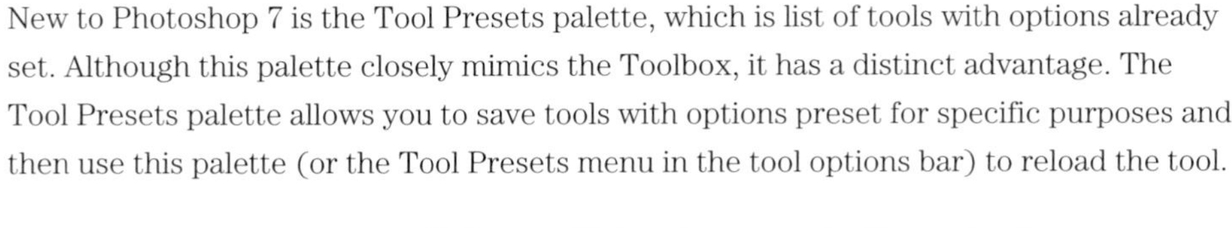

New to Photoshop 7 is the Tool Presets palette, which is list of tools with options already set. Although this palette closely mimics the Toolbox, it has a distinct advantage. The Tool Presets palette allows you to save tools with options preset for specific purposes and then use this palette (or the Tool Presets menu in the tool options bar) to reload the tool.

A Presets Click to choose a tool with preset options.

B Current Tool If checked, only versions of the currently selected tool in the Toolbox are displayed in the list.

C Create Tool Preset Click to add the current tool and options as a tool preset.

D Delete Tool Preset Click to delete the currently selected tool preset.

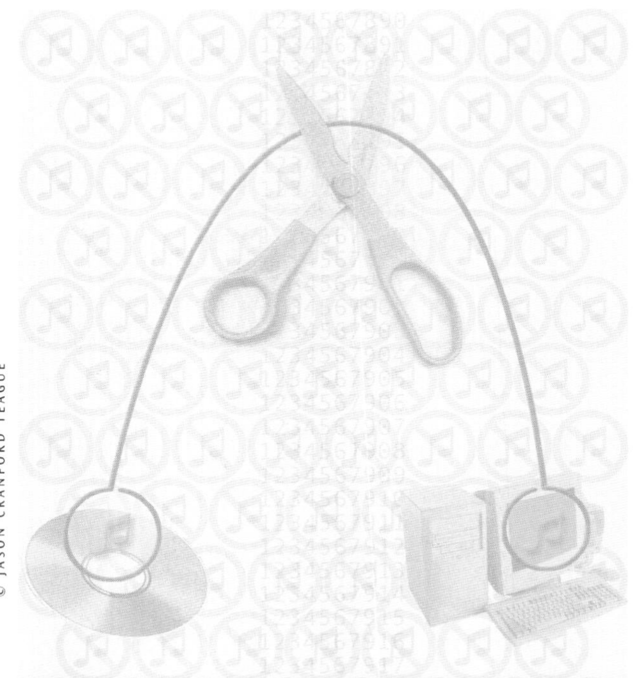

4.11 Layers Palette

You view the composited image in the document window, but the image is composed of one or more layers that you can view as thumbnails in the Layers palette. Layers allow you to independently add objects that can be edited. Each layer can have a separate blending mode, opacity, and fill opacity as well as be moved, shown/hidden, added, and deleted without affecting other layers in the image. You always edit on the *current* layer, which is highlighted and has the Paintbrush icon next to it.

There are four distinct kinds of layers:

Standard Bitmap image objects that can be edited using most tools.

Text Vector text that is edited using the text tool.

Adjustment Adds an adjustment effect to all layers beneath it.

Fill Adds a color fill to all layers beneath it.

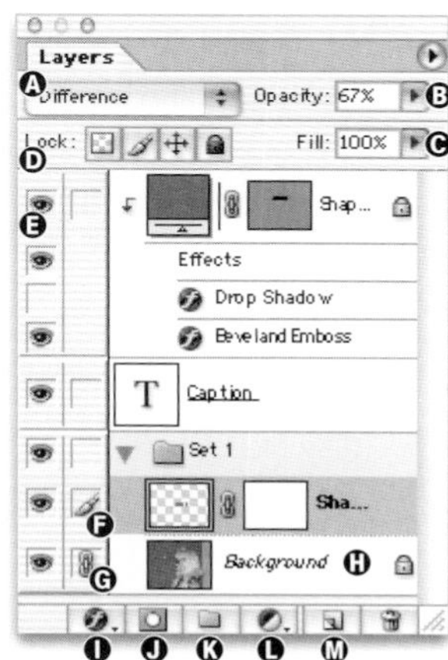

A Blending Mode Click to choose a blending mode for the layer.

B Opacity Click to enter or use the sliders to set the layer's master opacity.

C Fill Opacity Click to enter or use a slider to set the opacity of the layer without affecting the opacity of layer effects.

D Locks Click to lock transparent pixels, image pixels, layer position, or all three in a layer or layer set

E Toggle Visibility Click to show or hide a layer.

F Active Layer Click a layer name to select that layer. The Paintbrush icon is displayed to the left indicating that the layer is active and ready to be edited. Double-click the layers title to change it.

G Linked Layer Click to link or link a layer to the selected layer.

H Background Layer If included, you cannot erase or move the bottom layer.

I Add Effect Click to select a style to add as an effect to the layer.

J Add Mask Click to add a layer mask or a vector mask, depending on the layer type.

K New Layer Set Click to create a new empty layer set.

L Add Fill Or Adjustment Layer Click to select a fill or adjustment layer type to add as a new layer above the currently selected layer.

M New Layer Click to add a new layer immediately above the currently selected layer.

Continues

➠ 9 Image Layering

➠ 10 Adding Layer Styles

➠ 11 Masking Layers

New layer
Shift ⌘ Option N
Shift Ctrl Alt N

Duplicate layer
⌘ Option ↑↓←→

Ctrl Alt ↑↓←→

Merge Down/Merge Linked/Merge Group
⌘ E
Ctrl E

Merge Visible
Shift ⌘ E
Shift Ctrl E

Jump to layer above selected layer
Option [
Alt [

Jump to layer below selected layer
Option]
Alt]

Jump to bottom layer
Shift Option [
Shift Alt [

Jump to top layer
Shift Option]
Shift Alt]

4.11 Layers Palette *(Continued)*

The Layers palette menu lets you add, duplicate, delete, and merge layers as well as open the Effects dialog.

If you need to see more detail in the layer's thumbnail, use the options in the Layer palette to set the size to None, Small, Medium, or Large.

You can edit text layers only with the Type tool.

You can rasterize text layers to turn the text into a bitmap, but then you can no longer edit the text with the Type tool.

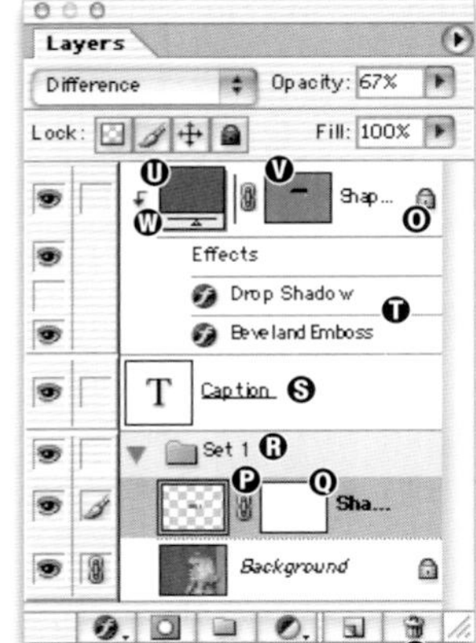

N Delete Layer Click to delete the selected layer, or drag a layer to this button to delete the layer.

O Locked Layer Indicates that the layer has one of the four lock types set.

P Linked Mask Indicates that the mask is linked to the layer.

Q Layer Mask Painting in the layer mask allows you to vary the transparency (rather than the color) of the layer.

R Layer Set A collection of layers that can all be moved, hidden/shown, and deleted as one or worked with individually. Layers in the set are indented underneath.

S Type Layer Indicates that the layer contains text.

T Effects Style applied to the layer. Double-click to change the style.

U Fill Layer Layer filled with a solid color. Click to choose a different color.

V Vector Mask Holds vector elements applied to a fill layer.

W Grouped Layer Indicates that this layer is grouped with the next to create

4.12 Channels Palette

The Channels palette displays the color or alpha channels used to create the image. The channels displayed depend on the current Color mode of the image.

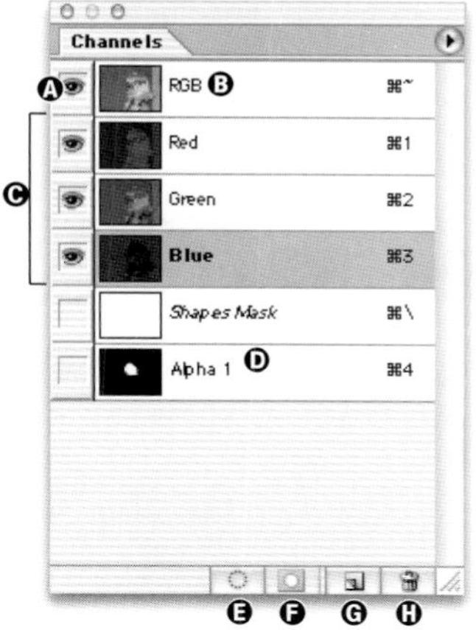

A Toggle Visibility Click to show or hide a channel.

B Combined Color Channels Controls the color channels.

C Color Channels Displays colors used to generate the image. The channels displayed depend on the Color mode of the image.

D Alpha Channel Channel used to store selection as a grayscale image which is useful for storing layer masks.

E Load Channel As Selection Click to convert the current channel into a selection.

F Save Selection As Channel Click to convert the current selection in the canvas into an alpha channel.

G Add Channel Click to create a new alpha channel.

H Delete Channel Click to delete the selected channel.

➠ 7.5 Using Color in Channels

➠ 11.2 Adding Layer Masks

➠ 11.3 Editing Layer Masks

➠ 13.2 Adjusting Tonal Range Using Levels

➠ 13.3 Adjusting Color Levels Using Curves

➠ 13.5 Adjusting Color Balance

Select composite channel

⌘ ~

Ctrl ~

Select individual color channel

⌘ 1-9

Ctrl 1-9

The Channel palette menu lets you add or delete a variety of channel types.

If you need to see more detail in the channel's thumbnail, use the options in the Channel palette to set the size to None, Small, Medium, or Large.

To add a spot color channel rather than an alpha channel, Command/Ctrl-click the Add Channel button.

REAL WORLD: SARAH BENISTON

Sarah Beniston likes to collect clippings from magazines and newspapers and then use them to create her own heavily textured illustrations. "The textures I create by scanning various objects/materials to create a rough/odd look. For example, I scan in a picture of marble to create the texture of skin. It depends on the feel of the illustration I am creating."

Commenting on her work, she notes, "I like to keep it simple both in technique and style. I don't like symmetry or anything that looks perfect. There is always an aspect of my illustrations that has an unfinished/imperfect look because I like to draw quickly, which gives my style an angle."

Her illustrations begin life in Adobe Illustrator, whether they are line or the "finished" product. "To give a 3D look, I create textures in Photoshop, which I then import into Illustrator and make a mask within a boundary."

You can find more of Sarah's work at `http://smbeniston.4t.com/`.

4.13 Paths Palette

➠ 11.6 Adding Vector Masks

➠ 11.7 Editing Vector Masks

➠ 11.8 Applying or Removing Vector Masks

➠ 12.1 Path Basics

➠ 12.12 Managing Paths

➠ 12.13 Converting between Paths and Selections

➠ 12.14 Stroking and Filling Paths

The Paths palette menu lets you start, duplicate, and delete paths as well as make the selected path a selection in the canvas, fill or stroke the path, or turn the path into a work or a clipping path.

If you need to see more detail in the channel's thumbnail, use the Channel palette options to set the size to None, Small, Medium, or Large.

The Paths palette records the vector outlines made up of curved and straight line segments using anchor points to determine curvature. You create paths using the pen tools or the shape tools and then manipulate them using the path selection tools.

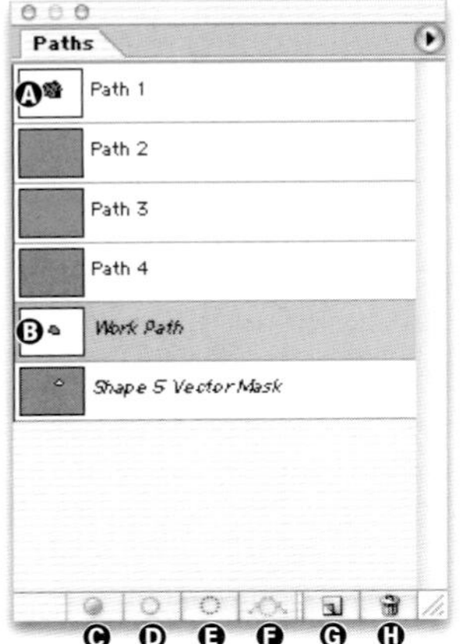

A Path Click to select the path.

B Work Path A temporary path used to define the path. Double-click it to turn it into a path.

C Fill Path Click to fill the selected path with a foreground color.

D Stroke Path Click to create a line around the path based on the current brush style.

E Turn Path Into Selection Click to load the path into the current layer as a selection.

F Turn Selection Into Work Path Click to convert the current selection into a new path.

G Add New Path Click to create a new path.

H Delete Path Click to delete the selected path.

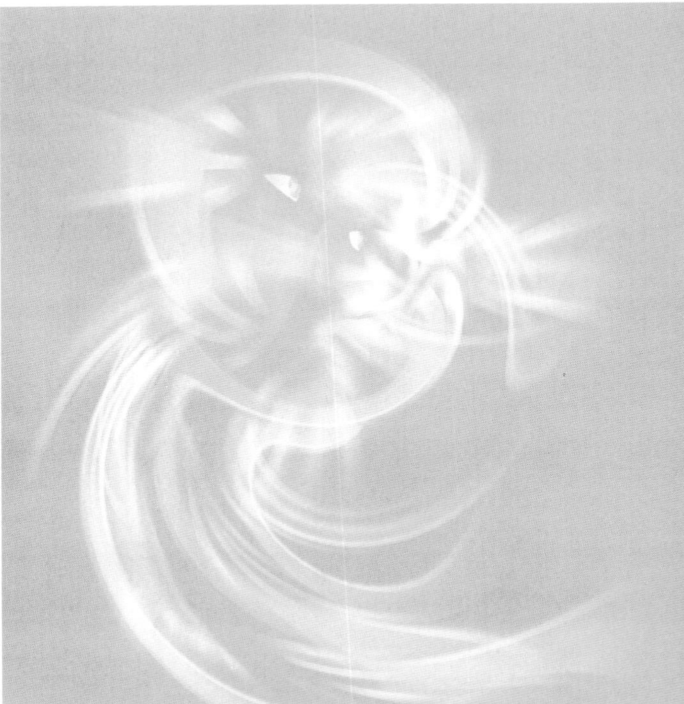

© sl eichholz 2002

4.14 Brushes Palette

The Brushes palette is not technically new to Photoshop 7. It was removed in Photoshop 6 and has returned with a vengeance. In Photoshop 7, brushes are no longer limited to options such as diameter and softness, but include a multitude of possibilities. A painting tool (brush, pencil, history brush, stamp tool, and so on…) must be selected for the options in this palette to be active.

➠ 15 Painting in Images

The Brushes palette menu lets you edit information about the selected brush, load and save collections of brushes, and set the brush preview size.

Option/Alt-click a brush preview to delete the brush.

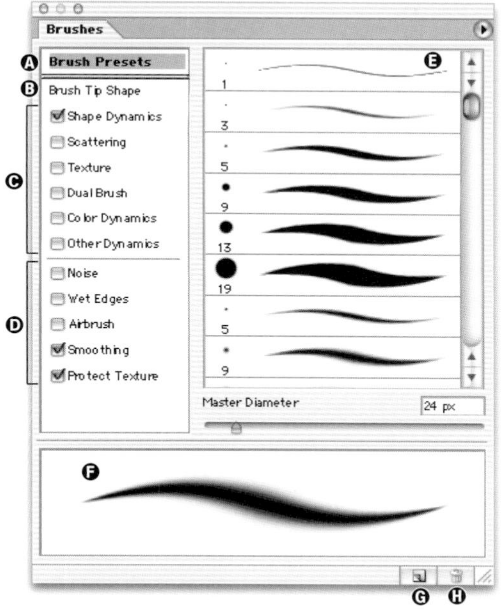

Ⓐ **Brush Presets** Click to view and choose preset brushes and master diameter in the Brush Settings area.

Ⓑ **Brush Tip Shape** Click to view and choose the brush tip in the Brush Settings area.

Ⓒ **Brush Adjustments** Check to have the brush shape adjusted based on the brush settings. Click the title to view and choose the settings for that adjustment in the Brush Settings area.

Ⓓ **Brush Options** Check to have the option used with the brush.

Ⓔ **Brush Settings** This area displays the Brush Presets, the various options for the brush tip shape, or other brush options.

Ⓕ **Brush Preview** Displays how the brush appears at flows from 0% to 100%.

Ⓖ **Create New Brush** Click to add the current brush to the Brush Presets.

Ⓗ **Delete Brush** Click to delete the selected Brush Preset or drag a Brush Preset to this button to delete it.

4.15 Character Palette

➠ 17.1 Type Basics

➠ 17.3 Formatting Characters

Cancel text changes
Esc

Commit text changes
Enter

The Character palette menu lets you select many of the style character options, including Faux Bold and Faux Italic.

Select a text layer in the Layer palette to make changes that affect all text on the entire layer.

Although the Type tool offers many of the most important options in the tool options bar when it is selected, use the Character palette for more exacting control of the shape and position of characters. Text must be selected for these options to be available.

Ⓐ **Font Family** Click to choose a font to use for selected text or text to be typed. You can also enter a font name directly in the field. Photoshop tries to match what you type to the closest font in the list.

Ⓑ **Font Style** Click to choose an available style for this font—generally regular (default), bold, italic, and bold italic although the exact styles vary from font to font. You can also enter a style name directly in the field. Photoshop tries to match what you type to the closest style in the list.

Ⓒ **Font Size** Click to choose a size for the font in points. You can also enter a numeric value directly into the field (between 0.10 points and 1296 points).

Ⓓ **Leading** Click to choose the space between lines of text in a paragraph in points. Select Auto if you want Photoshop to determine the optimum leading. You can also enter a numeric value directly into the field (between 0 points and 5000 points).

Ⓔ **Kerning** Click to choose the space between specific letter pairs in the text of a paragraph. Select Metrics to use the font's built-in kerning. You can also enter a numeric value directly into the field (between –1000 and 1000).

Ⓕ **Tracking** Click to choose the spacing between selected characters. You can also enter a numeric value directly into the field (between –1000 and 1000).

Ⓖ **Vertical Scale** Enter a percentage (between 0% and 1000%) to set the height of the letters from their standard height.

Ⓗ **Horizontal Scale** Enter a percentage (between 0% and 1000%) to set the width of the letters from their standard width.

Ⓘ **Baseline Shift** Enter a point size (between –1296 and 1296) to shift the selected letter or letters up or down from their natural position, which is especially useful to mathematical notations.

Ⓙ **Font Color** Click to choose a color for the text.

Ⓚ **Faux Styles** Click to toggle selected text between Bold and/or Italic.

Ⓛ **Caps Style** Click to toggle selected text between All Caps or Mini-Caps.

Ⓜ **Script Style** Click to toggle selected text between Superscript or Subscript.

Ⓝ **Line Style** Click to toggle selected text between Underline and/or Overline.

Ⓞ **Language** Click to select the language being used.

Ⓟ **Anti-Aliasing Method** Click to select an anti-aliasing method to be used for the text layer: None, Sharp, Crisp, Strong, and Smooth.

4.16 Paragraph Palette

You use the Paragraph palette to change the alignment and margins of a single paragraph or an entire text layer.

➠ 17.4 Formatting Paragraphs

Cancel text changes
Esc

Commit text changes
Enter

Select a text layer to make changes to the entire layer.

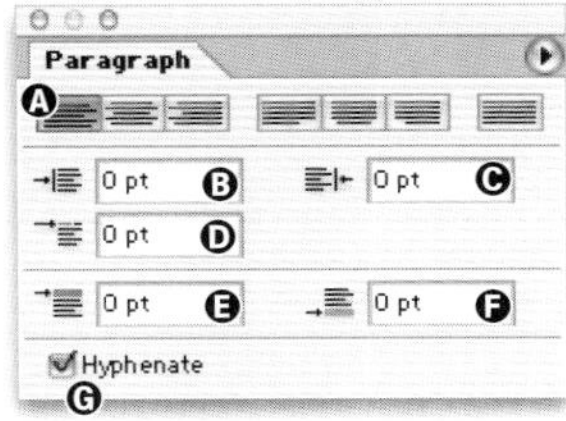

Ⓐ Align Text Click to select text alignment (left, center, or right), justified text alignment (left, center, or right), or full justified.

Ⓑ Left Indent Enter a value to set the left margin for the text layer (between 0 points and 1296 points).

Ⓒ Right Indent Enter a value to set the right margin for the text layer (between 0 points and 1296 points).

Ⓓ First-Line Indent Enter a value to set the indention of the first line for the text layer (between –1296 points and 1296 points).

Ⓔ Space Before Paragraph Enter a value to set the top margin for the text layer (between –1296 points and 1296 points).

Ⓕ Space After Paragraph Enter a value to set the bottom margin for the text layer (between –1296 points and 1296 points).

Ⓖ Hyphenate If checked, text in the layer is hyphenated rather than allowing for broken lines.

SAVING AND RESTORING THE WORKSPACE

Once you have your palettes organized and laid out the way you want them, use the workspace.

- To save the current layout, choose Window > Workspace > Save Workspace. Enter a name for the new workspace in the dialog and click OK. The configuration appears at the bottom of the Workspace submenu.
- To reset the palettes to their Photoshop default locations, choose Window > Workspace > Reset Palette Locations.
- To reset the palettes to a previously save configuration, choose Window > Workspace, and then enter the name of the desired layout configuration.
- To permanently remove a workspace layout, choose Window > Delete Workspace..., choose the workspace configuration, and then press Delete.

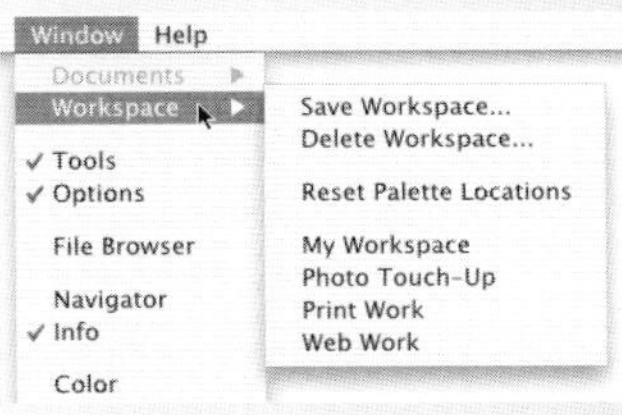

The Workspace submenu

CHAPTER 5

Presets and Preferences

PHOTOSHOP IS A POWERFUL, complex, yet elegant piece of software. Much of the complexity stems from the wide range of tasks this single application is called on to perform by its legion of users, but the elegance flows from its versatility in the face of the myriad demands. You can customize Photoshop in many, many ways to suit your individual needs.

In this chapter, you will learn the basic uses for the Preset Manager and the many preferences that you can set:

- 5.1 **Preset Manager overview**
- 5.2 **Setting Photoshop preferences**
- 5.3 **General preferences**
- 5.4 **File Handling preferences**
- 5.5 **Display & Cursor preferences**
- 5.6 **Transparency & Gamut preferences**
- 5.7 **Units & Rulers preferences**
- 5.8 **Guides, Grid & Slices preferences**
- 5.9 **Plug-Ins & Scratch Disks preferences**
- 5.10 **Memory & Image Cache preferences**
- 5.11 **Adobe Online preferences**

5.1 Preset Manager Overview

➠ 4.10 Tool Presets Palette

➠ 10.4 Managing Style Presets

➠ 14.4 Organizing Color Swatch Presets

➠ 14.7 Organizing Color Swatch Presets

➠ 14.10 Organizing Gradient Presets

➠ 15.3 Creating Brushes

Brush presets (while in Preset Manager)

⌘ 1

Ctrl 1

Swatches presets (while in Preset Manager)

⌘ 2

Ctrl 2

Gradients presets (while in Preset Manager)

⌘ 3

Ctrl 3

Styles presets (while in Preset Manager)

⌘ 4

Ctrl 4

Patterns presets (while in Preset Manager)

⌘ 5

Ctrl 5

You use the Preset Manager to specify the options that appear in the various preset drop-down menus and palettes available throughout Photoshop. Dealing with the almost infinite number of possibilities available through the program often means limiting the number of choices that you can view at any given moment so that you can see only the options relevant to your current work. To allow this, Photoshop presents you with several lists of preset common options such as brushes, color swatches, gradients, styles, patterns, contours, custom shapes, and tools. Although each of these pickers displays different items, they all have similar options, allowing the Preset Manager to deal with them similarly.

To open the Preset Manager, choose Edit > Preset Manager….

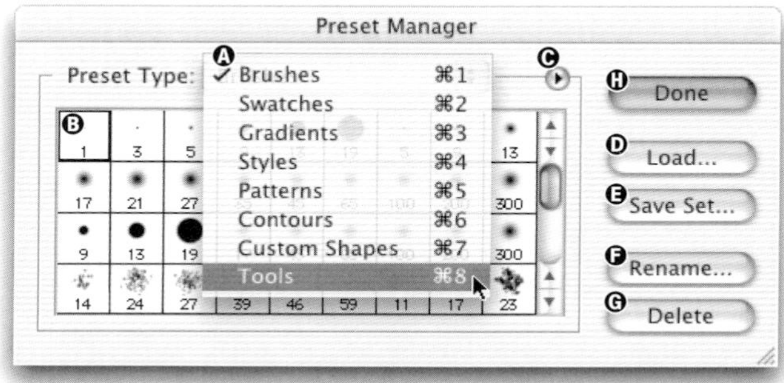

Ⓐ Preset Type Choose from a list to move instantly between preset panels.

Ⓑ Preset A single preset in the list of presets. Click to select. Double-click to rename. Control/right-click to view a contextual menu that contains options to create a new preset, delete this preset, or rename this preset. Shift-click to select multiple presets.

Ⓒ Preset Menu Choose from a list of viewing options, replace or reset the presets, and choose options to load particular preset lists instantly for this preset type.

Ⓓ Click Load…, locate a preset file for the current type, and click Load to append the selected list to the current list.

Ⓔ Select one or more presets, click Save Set…, enter a filename, making sure to preserve the preset's extension, browse to the location where you want to save the preset, and click Save.

Ⓕ Select one or more presets, click Rename…, type a new name for the preset, and click OK. If you select more than one preset, each is displayed in a separate Rename dialog.

Ⓖ Select one or more preset, then click Delete to remove the preset from the list. You cannot undo this deletion, so be careful.

Ⓗ Click Done when you are ready to return to Photoshop.

5.1 Preset Manager Overview *(Continued)*

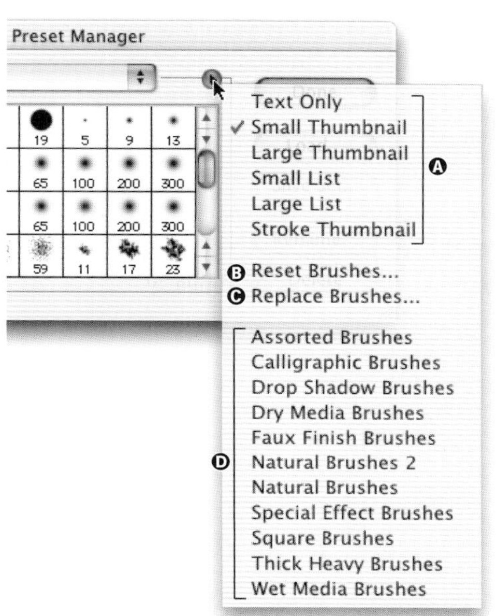

A Choose the thumbnail size of the presets.

B Choose Reset… and click Append to add the default library to the current list, or click OK to replace the current list.

C Choose Replace…, locate a preset file for the current type, and click Load to replace the current list with the selected list.

D Choose a preset library name from the bottom of the menu, and then click Append to add the library to the current list, or click OK to replace the current list.

Contours presets (while in Preset Manager)

⌘ 6

Ctrl 6

Custom Shapes presets (while in Preset Manager)

⌘ 7

Ctrl 7

Tool presets (while in Preset Manager)

⌘ 8

Ctrl 8

The options for individual Preset Managers are explained in relevant sections throughout this book.

You can share preset library files between copies of Photoshop by transferring the file.

Each preset library has its own file extension and default folder in the Adobe Photoshop 7/Presets folder.

SETTING PREFERENCES BEFORE YOU BEGIN

If you have plug-ins that are not currently in a recognized plug-ins folder, you can add their folder before Photoshop starts up, allowing you to avoid having to set the folder in the preferences and then having to restart Photoshop for the changes to take effect. Hold down Option-Command/Alt-Ctrl while starting Photoshop to set the location of additional plug-ins. After setting the folder, continue to hold down Option-Command/Alt-Ctrl set the scratch disks to be used.

5.2 Setting Photoshop Preferences

➠ 3.2 The Tool Options Bar

General Preferences dialog
⌘ K
Ctrl K

To delete preferences, hold down while starting Photoshop:
Option Shift ⌘
Alt Shift Ctrl

General preferences (while in Preferences window)
⌘ 1
Ctrl 1

File Handling preferences (while in Preferences window)
⌘ 2
Ctrl 2

Display & Cursors preferences (while in Preferences window)
⌘ 3
Ctrl 3

Transparency & Gamut preferences (while in Preferences window)
⌘ 4
Ctrl 4

Units & Rulers preferences (while in Preferences window)
⌘ 5
Ctrl 5

Guides, Grid & Slices preferences (while in Preferences window)
⌘ 6
Ctrl 6

Plug-Ins & Scratch Disks preferences (while in Preferences window)
⌘ 7
Ctrl 7

Memory & Image Cache preferences (while in Preferences window)
⌘ 8
Ctrl 8

Before you begin using Photoshop, you will want to customize options for the various features and tools. Except for Color Settings, which are handled separately, all preference settings are in the same dialog on different panels that you can choose. But you can access each separately from the Preferences submenu in either the Photoshop (OS X) or Edit (Windows and OS 9) menu. Each panel in the Preferences dialog contains a few or a few dozen options to set preferences pertaining to a specific aspect of Photoshop. These options are presented as a variety of drop-downs, input fields, color selectors, selection boxes, and check boxes to be set as you see fit.

In addition, each panel contains buttons to navigate between the other panels and to accept or cancel the changes.

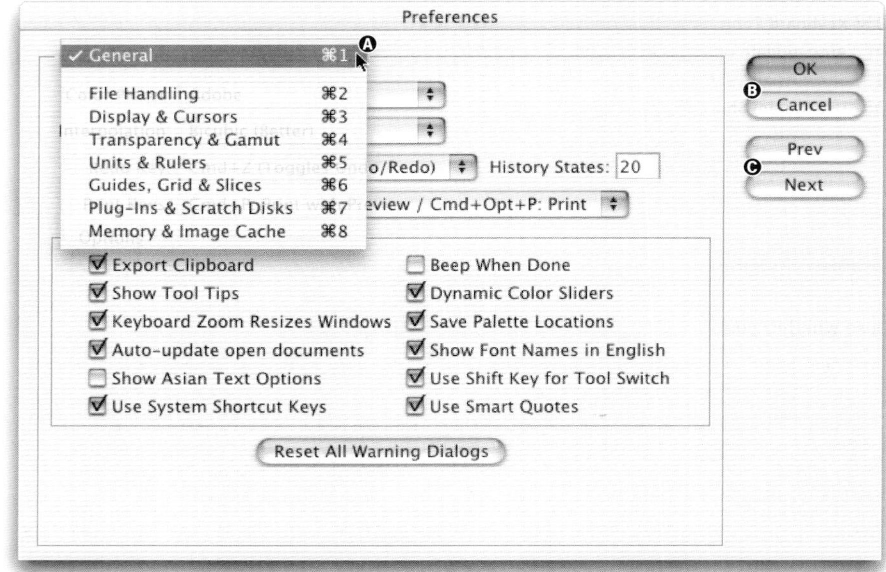

A Choose from a list to move instantly between preferences panels, or use the numeric shortcuts (Mac, press Command-1 through 8; Windows, press Ctrl-1 through 8).

B Click to accept or reject the changes. Both buttons close the Preferences dialog.

C Click to go to the previous or next Preferences panel.

5.3 General Preferences

The General preferences panel provides a catch-all screen to define several common interface options that do not readily fit into the other categories.

➠ 4.5 Color Palette

➠ 6.9 Changing Your Mind

➠ 6.10 Printing Basics

➠ 8.8 Transforming a Layer or Selected Content

➠ 8.9 Moving Selected Content

➠ 8.10 Copying and Pasting Selected Content

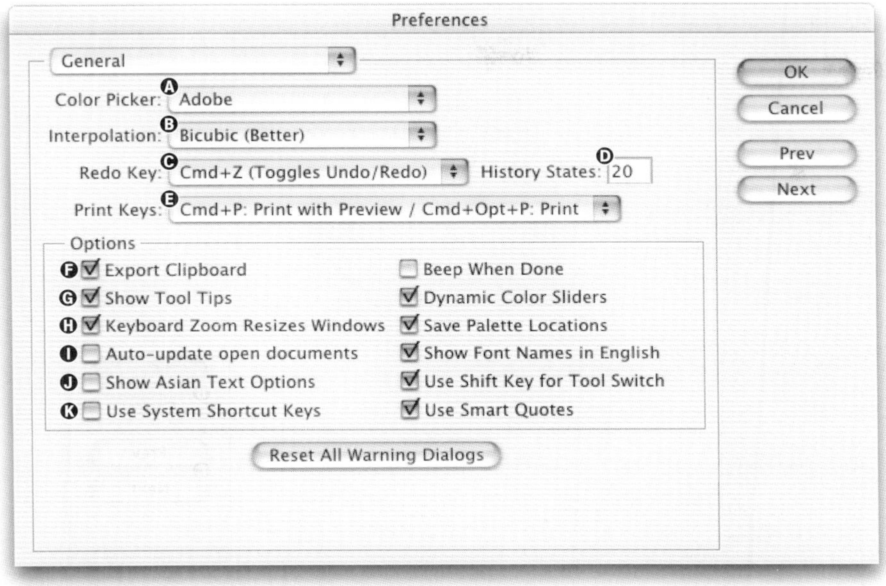

Ⓐ Choose whether you want to use Adobe's Color Picker or your system's Color Picker.

Ⓑ Choose the default means by which an image's pixels are resized (interpolated) as a result of resampling or transforming. Bicubic is slow but produces higher-quality results.

Ⓒ Choose the keystroke shortcut for the Edit > Redo menu option.

Ⓓ Enter the maximum number of History states in the History palette. After this number is exceeded, older History states are removed.

Ⓔ Choose the keystroke shortcuts for the File > Print… and File > Print With Preview… menu options.

Ⓕ Check if you want the contents of the Clipboard exported to the system Clipboard when switching between applications.

Ⓖ Check to display pop-up Tool Tips in the interface.

Ⓗ Check if you want the window to resize when you zoom using keyboard shortcuts.

Ⓘ Check if you want open documents automatically saved when you jump between Photoshop and other applications.

Ⓙ Check if you want to display Chinese, Japanese, and Korean options in the Character and Paragraph palettes.

Ⓚ (Mac OS X only) Check to override Photoshop's keyboard shortcuts with the system's keyboard shortcuts. For example, Hide Photoshop will be Command-H rather than Option-Command-H.

Continues

5.3 General Preferences *(Continued)*

General Preferences dialog

⌘ K

Ctrl K

History states require memory to store and can quickly become a memory hog.

Adobe's Color Picker is more versatile, but you might already be familiar with your operating system's Color Picker.

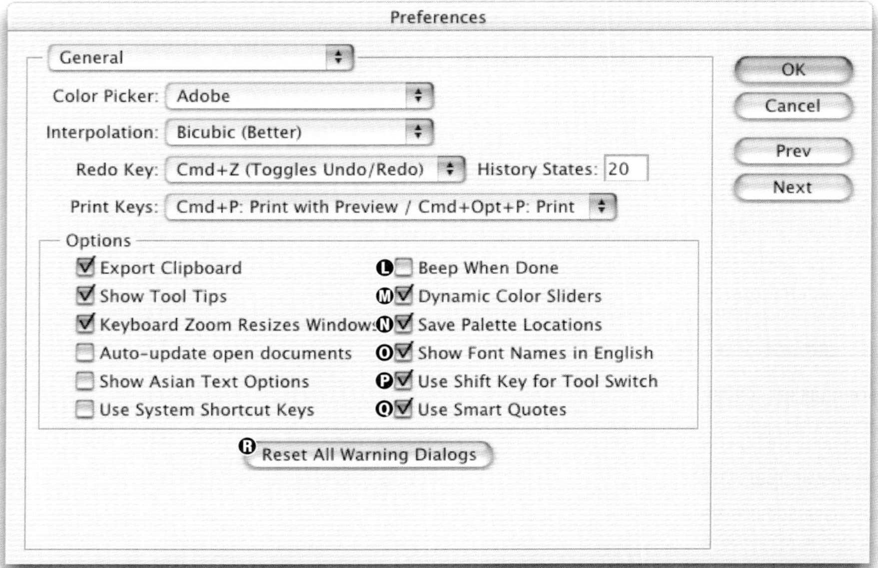

L Check if you want Photoshop to "beep" after each command that is completed.

M Check if you want color sliders to display colors in real time, changing as the slider moves.

N Check if you want the palette location saved after you quit and then restored the next time you open Photoshop.

O Check if you want to display non-Roman fonts using their Roman names. If this check box is unchecked, some font names may be illegible.

P Check if you want to require that the Shift key be pressed when you switch between tools in a group. If this check box is unchecked, pressing the tool's shortcut key switches tools in the group.

Q Check to substitute curly quotes for straight quotes while typing.

R Most warning dialogs in Photoshop include an option that prevents them from displaying a second time. Click this button to restore all warning dialogs.

5.4 File Handling Preferences

You use File Handling preferences to specify default information about how an image file should be treated when being saved using the File > Save As… menu option or when being opened as part of a workgroup.

➠ 2.3 File Menu

➠ 6.13 Saving and Closing an Image

➠ 18.6 Checking Documents In and Out

File Handling preferences (while in Preferences window)

⌘ 2

Ctrl 2

The more preview types you include, the larger the file size.

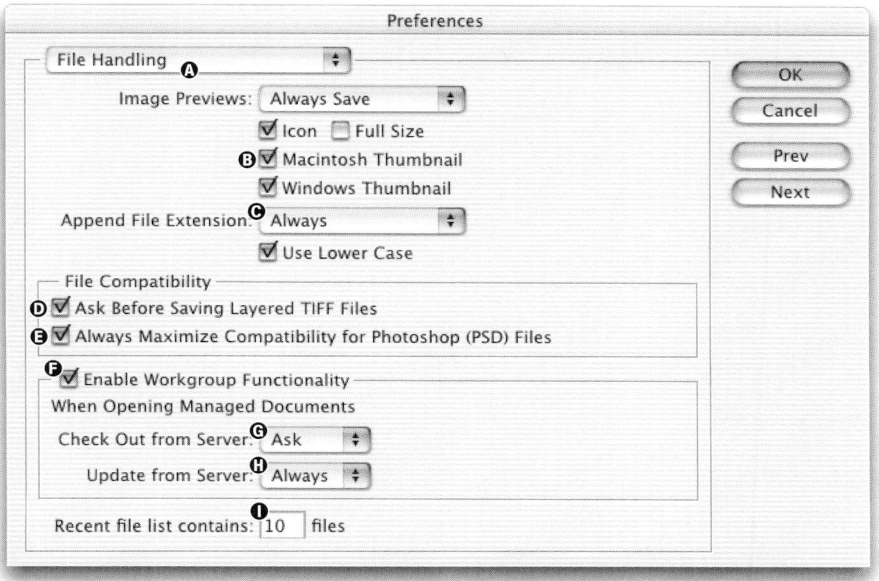

- **A** Choose when a preview should be saved.
- **B** (Mac only) Check the preview types to be included: Icon (a thumbnail image on the desktop), Full Size (low-resolution PICT used by some applications when importing non-EPS files), Macintosh Thumbnail, or Windows Thumbnail (used by the Open dialogs in those operating systems).
- **C** On Mac, choose *when* the file extension should be added to the filename, then check the box if it should be lowercase. On Windows, simply choose whether the extension should be upper- or lowercase.
- **D** Check to display the TIFF Options dialog when saving a TIFF to which layers have been added.
- **E** Check to include a flattened composite version of the image with PSD files. Doing so increases the file size but provides better compatibility with other applications and future versions of Photoshop.
- **F** Check to turn on workgroup functionality. If this option is unchecked, the Workgroup menu option is not available and will be grayed out in the File menu.
- **G** Choose whether or when to check out managed documents from the server when opened (Always, Never, or Ask When Opening).
- **H** Choose whether or when to update managed documents from the file on the server when opening (Always, Never, or Ask When Opening).
- **I** Enter the number of files to displayed in the File > Open Recent menu option.

5.5 Display & Cursors Preferences

➠ 3 The Toolbox

➠ 7.5 Using Color in Channels

➠ 8.9 Moving Selected Content

Display & Cursors preferences (while in Preferences window)

⌘ 3

Ctrl 3

Cycle cursor style: Standard to Precise Precise to Brush Size Brush Size to Precise

Caps Lock

While you are learning Photoshop, the standard icons (the literal representation of a tool, such as a paintbrush for the Brush tool) help you remember which tool you are currently working with. However, as you become more accustomed to Photoshop, you may find that these cursor icons become more of a distraction than a help. It is often difficult to tell *exactly* where the tool is affecting or over what area. The Display & Cursors preferences give you additional options for cursor display as well as monitor display.

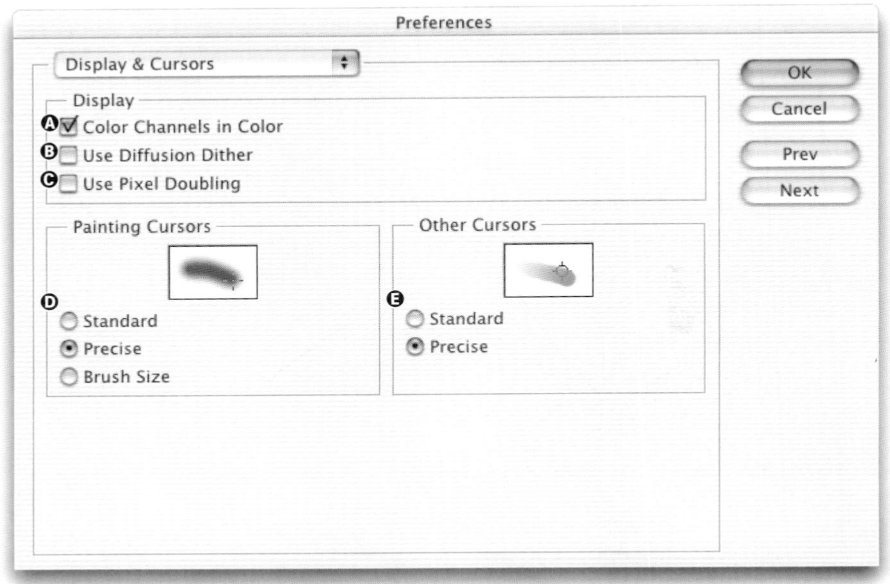

Ⓐ Check to display color channels in color rather than grayscale.

Ⓑ Check to use diffusion dithering for colors that cannot be displayed.

Ⓒ Check to reduce the resolution of objects while they are being moved, which speeds up rendering time. This will temporarily degrade the image, but the change is not permanent.

Ⓓ Choose how to display painting cursors: Standard (tool's icon), Precise (crosshair), or Brush Size (circle indicating the diameter of the brush).

Ⓔ Choose how to display other cursors: Standard (tool's icon) or Precise (crosshair).

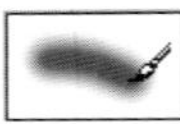

The Standard cursor uses the tool's icon.

A Precise cursor uses a crosshair with the center point marked.

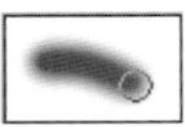

A Brush Size cursor shows a circle that is the diameter of the brush being used.

5.6 Transparency & Gamut Preferences

Transparent areas in an image—that is, areas where there are no image pixels nor a Background layer—Photoshop represents using a checkerboard grid. You can change this pattern to suit your own tastes.

Gamut settings are used when working in RGB or Lab color mode to warn you when particular colors will not print in CMYK.

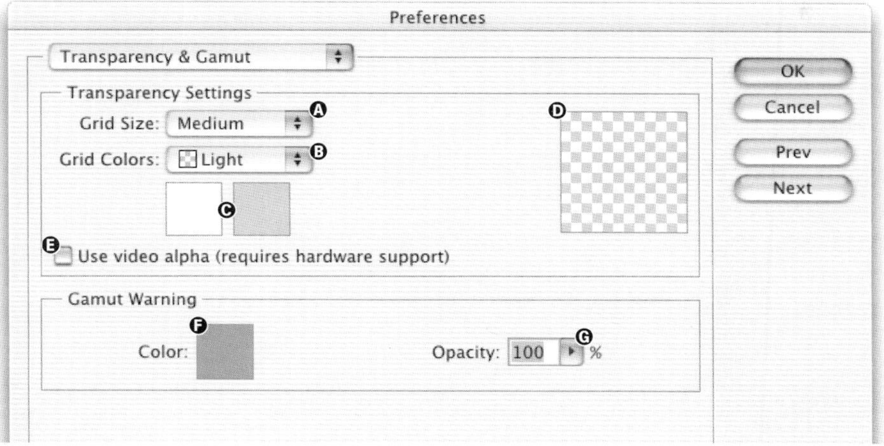

Ⓐ Choose the relative size of the transparency grid.

Ⓑ Choose a color combination for the transparency grid.

Ⓒ Displays the current color combination for the transparency grid. Click to choose other colors for the transparency grid using the color picker.

Ⓓ Displays how the transparency grid appears.

Ⓔ Check if you are using a 32-bit video card with chromakeying while editing video to enable alpha channel transparency in the video unless you are editing digital video over FireWire.

Ⓕ Click to choose the color for highlighting colors in the image that are out of the specified color mode's gamut.

Ⓖ Click to enter or select the opacity of the out-of-gamut highlight color.

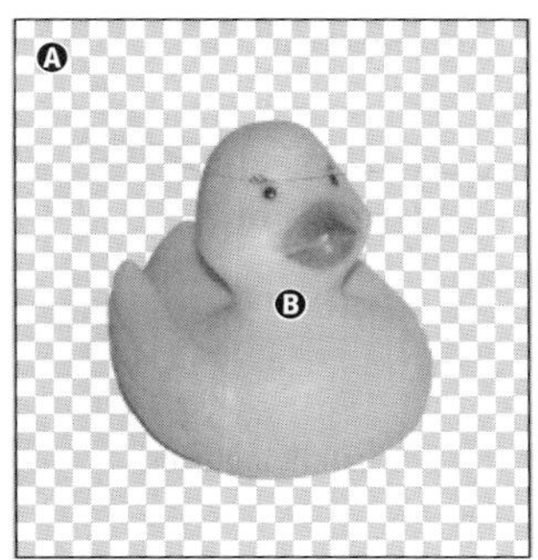

Ⓐ Transparency

Ⓑ Image pixels

➠ 6.8 Using Rulers, Guides, Grids, and Snap

➠ 9.1 Layer Basics

➠ 14.1 Color, Gradient, and Pattern Basics

➠ 14.3 Selecting Colors with the Color Picker

Transparency & Gamut preferences (while in Preferences window)

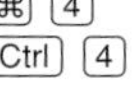

Ctrl 4

Choose View > Gamut Warning to view highlight colors that are out of the gamut range while in RGB or Lab color modes.

PHOTOSHOP WORKSPACE
UNIVERSAL PHOTOSHOP TASKS
PRINT TASKS
WEB TASKS
DIGITAL IMAGING TASKS

5.7 Units & Rulers Preferences

➠ 4.4 Info Palette

➠ 6.1 Starting a New Image

➠ 17.1 Type Basics

Units & Rulers preferences (while in Preferences window)

⌘ 5

Ctrl 5

Double-click a ruler in the document window to open the Units & Rulers preferences panel.

The units used to measure your work depend on your location (whether you use metric or imperial units) and your output medium (screen or print). You can set the default units to use in new documents (which you can easily change while you are working), as well as the resolution of new documents and a few print-specific options.

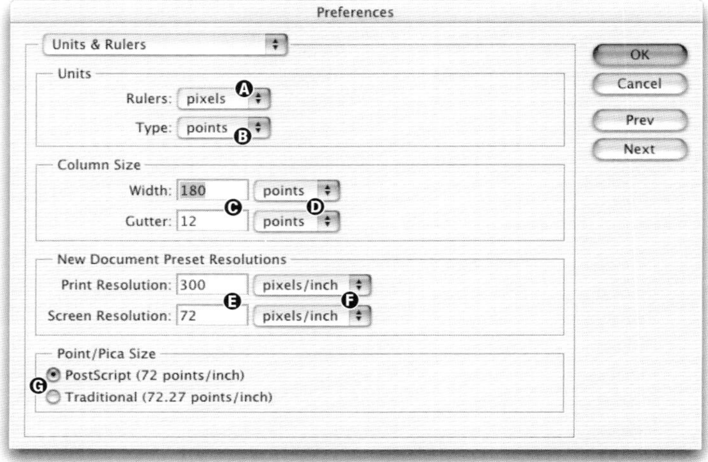

- **A** Choose the default measurement unit used in documents.
- **B** Choose the default unit used for type (generally points).
- **C** Enter the column size and the gutter size, which allows you to define the width of the document in terms of column width. These settings are useful when you import images into a page layout program with set widths for columns and gutters.
- **D** Select the units used to measure column size. This is used when exporting images to layout programs such as Quark and InDesign.
- **E** Enter the default print and screen resolutions to be used when opening new documents. You will want to use 72 for designs intended for computer or TV display and at least 300 for print.
- **F** Select the units used to measure resolution.
- **G** Select whether to use the PostScript definition or the Traditional definition to determine the number of points per inch. If you are printing to a PostScript-capable printer, you should select PostScript.

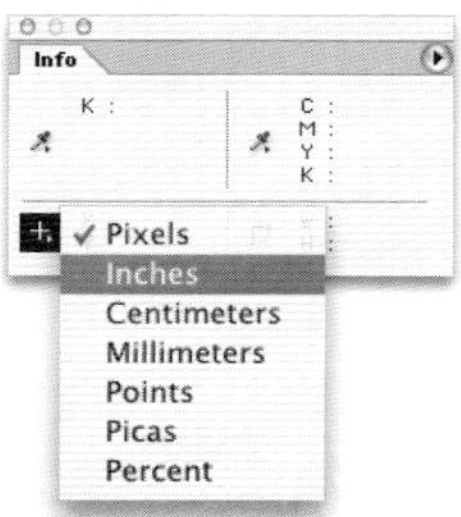

Quickly change the units being used on the Info palette.

5.8 Guides, Grid & Slices Preferences

Photoshop provides you with several guideline types to help you precisely place content in the canvas. These lines include the guides, which help you line up objects either horizontally or vertically; grid lines, which help you line up objects at regular intervals; and slice lines, which define areas to be cut in a web interface.

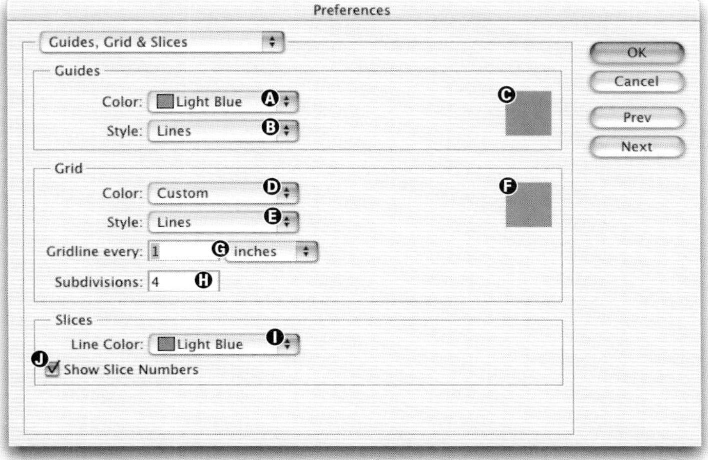

Ⓐ Choose the color used to display guide lines.

Ⓑ Choose the style for guide lines (solid lines or dashed lines).

Ⓒ Displays the color being used for the guide lines. Click to choose a different color from the Color Picker dialog.

Ⓓ Choose the color used for the foreground grid.

Ⓔ Choose the style for the foreground grid (Lines, Dashed Lines, or Dots).

Ⓕ Displays the color being used for the grid. Click to choose a different color from the Color Picker dialog.

Ⓖ Enter the distance between each grid line and select the units to be used for the grid.

Ⓗ Enter the interval for bold subdivision grid lines to appear.

Ⓘ Choose the color used to display slice lines.

Ⓙ Check to show slice numbers with slices. Slice numbers appear in the top-left corner of the slice.

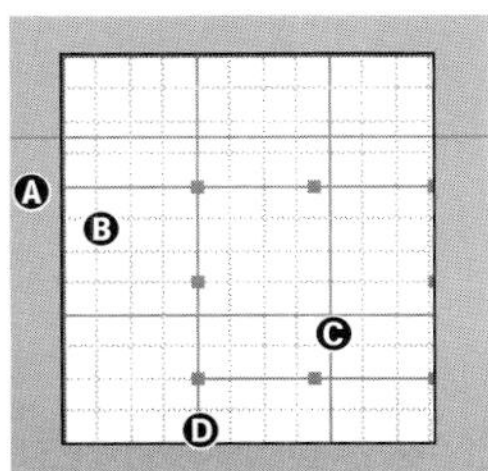

Ⓐ Guide line

Ⓑ Grid lines

Ⓒ Grid line subdivisions

Ⓓ Slice bounding box

➠ 6.8 Using Rulers, Guides, Grids, and Snap

➠ 14.3 Selecting Colors with the Color Picker

➠ 25.1 Slicing Your Interface

Guides, Grid & Slices preferences (while in Preferences window)

⌘ 6

Ctrl 6

If you set a color by clicking one of the color swatches, the color list will show it as a custom color.

5.9 Plug-Ins & Scratch Disks Preferences

➠ 7.1 Image Color Basics

➠ 16.1 Filter Basics

Plug-Ins & Scratch Disks preferences (while in Preferences window)

⌘ 7

Ctrl 7

Ideally, the first scratch disk should not be a partition on the same drive as the drive running Photoshop.

The "First" scratch disk is also commonly referred to as the "Primary" scratch disk.

Changes you make to the scratch disks do not take effect until you restart Photoshop.

Mac OS 9 plug-ins do not work in Mac OS X. If you have one, contact the plug-in maker for an update.

Photoshop automatically stores the primary plug-ins in the Photoshop application folder. But in this preferences panel you can define a second folder that contains Photoshop plug-ins in another folder on an accessible drive.

In addition, you can set as many as four hard drives to use as scratch disks to store image information while you are working in Photoshop. These can be either partitions of your primary hard drive or external hard drives.

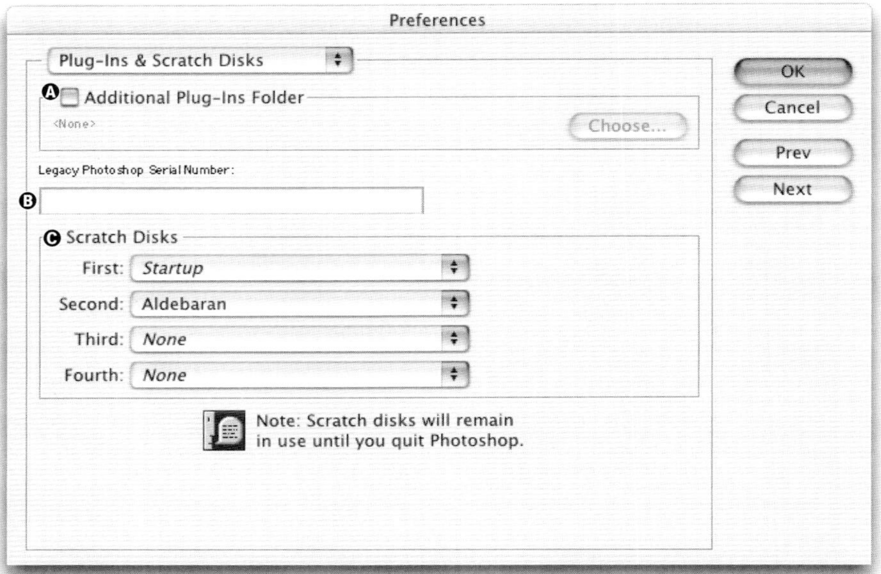

- **A** Check if you have a secondary folder of plug-ins (separate from the folder in the Adobe Photoshop 7 folder). Checking this option automatically launches a dialog to choose the secondary folder. Click the Choose... button to change the folder.
- **B** Enter older Photoshop serial numbers to associate with this copy of Photoshop to use with plug-ins that require an older Photoshop serial number.
- **C** Select the first, second, third, and fourth scratch disks used by Photoshop. All available disks are displayed in the select menus.

5.10 Memory & Image Cache Preferences

Photoshop uses lower-resolution versions of the high-resolution images being worked on to update the screen when you are working on layer or image adjustments. When you view an image at a magnification other than 100%, the displayed image is not recalculated but is based on a smaller cached version already calculated. This approach speeds redrawing, but it means that images are distorted if they are not one of the cached magnifications.

Windows and Mac OS X treat the memory used by Photoshop as a total of the memory available to the computer. The higher the percentage, the more efficiently Photoshop will run, but this efficiency may come at the expense of operation performance in other applications you are running simultaneously.

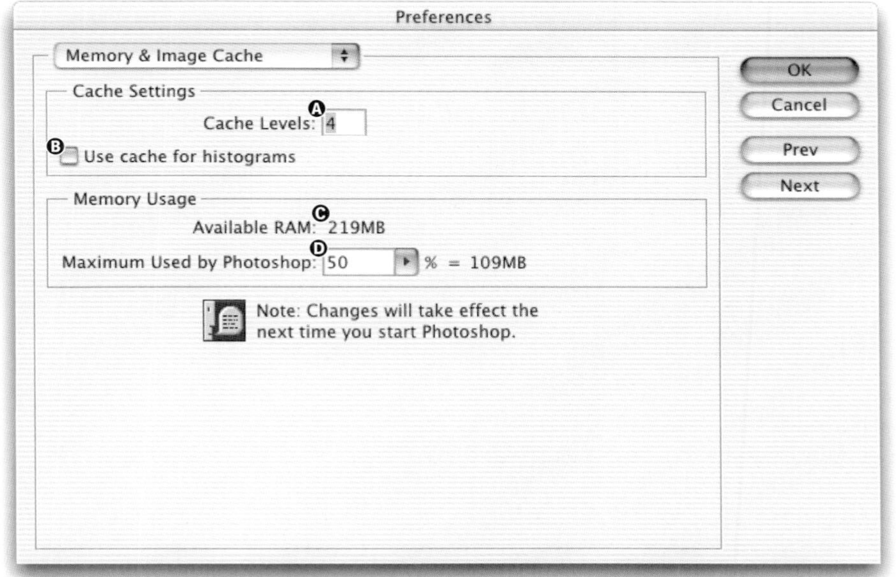

A Enter the number of levels (1 to 8) cached for image data. A higher number improves the quality of image redraw but is slower.

B Check to use sample cached data for histograms. Doing so is faster but less accurate.

C Displays the RAM currently available to Photoshop.

D (Windows and Mac OS X) Enter or select the amount of RAM devoted to Photoshop as a percentage. You will have to quit and restart Photoshop for these changes to take effect.

Memory & Image Cache preferences (while in Preferences window)

⌘ 8

Ctrl 8

The cache setting also affects the structure of the Save Image Pyramid in TIFF files.

If you do not set your memory high enough, you may spend a lot of time waiting. But if you set it too high, you may have trouble running other applications.

The memory requirements for Photoshop in Mac OS 9 are set using the information panel in the Finder.

5.11 Adobe Online Preferences

Warning: Some of the update files you will download might be quite large (1 MB or higher) and will take a while to download if you are connected to the Internet over a phone line. I would not recommend using the Adobe Online options unless you have a cable, DSL, T1, or better connection.

If you set the Adobe Online preferences to check automatically, you will notice that occasionally (depending on how often you set the option to check), as you launch Photoshop, a window will appear alerting you that updates are being checked. According to Photoshop, no personal information is collected from your computer about you when Photoshop checks for updates.

No computer is an island anymore, and in an effort to help users get updates and additions to Photoshop more quickly, Adobe provides online tools that allow you to check for and download updates as long as you have an Internet connection. You can access most of these features without the use of a web browser.

You can use the Adobe Product Updates dialog to view either updates you do not have (New) or all the updates. You can then select an update to download.

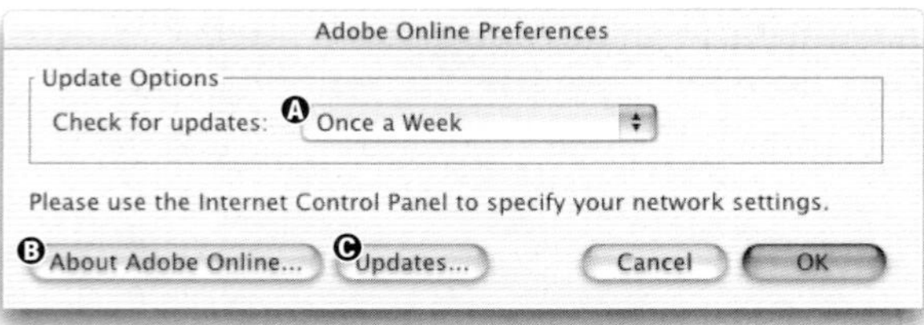

- A Select how often you want to automatically check for Photoshop updates. No personal information is sent to Adobe.
- B Click to view the Adobe Online splash screen. Click the splash screen to close it.
- C Click to run an update now.

- A Select whether to view all updates or only new updates.
- B Click a download name to select and view its description.
- C Check to add an update to the download list.
- D Click to choose where to store download updates.
- E Click to view a web page that contains additional information about the update.
- F Click to close the dialog.
- G Click to begin downloading checked updates.

UNIVERSAL PHOTOSHOP TASKS

CHAPTER 6

Starting an Image

ALL COMPUTER-GENERATED IMAGES—whether being used for print, web, or video—have a lot in common. The same processes start all of them. They are all recorded in the computer's language of 0's and 1's. In Photoshop, all images are created, edited, and manipulated in the document window using (for the most part) the same tools. In this chapter, you will learn the basics—how to create, format, and output images, regardless of their intended use.

This chapter covers:

6.1 Starting a New Image

➠ 2.3 File Menu
➠ 2.6 Image Menu
➠ 7.6 Converting between Image Modes

New File dialog
⌘ N
Ctrl N

The next time you want to create a new image, the parameters you set previously will be the defaults.

Photoshop 7 can open and save images in the following file formats. Formats marked with an asterisk (*) can only be opened; the program will not save to those file types.

Photoshop Image Formats

FORMAT	EXTENSION	USE
Photoshop	.psd	Photoshop's native format
Adobe Illustrator*	.ai	Illustrator's native format; treated as a generic PDF
BMP	.bmp	Common Windows format
CompuServe GIF	.gif	Standard web graphic format
Photoshop EPS	.eps	Common printer format
FilmStrip	.mov	QuickTime movie exported from Adobe Premiere, Final Cut Pro, or Avid
JPEG	.jpg	Standard web format for photographs
PCX	.pcx	Paintbrush native format
Photoshop PDF	.pdf	Portable Document Format used in Adobe Acrobat
Photo CD*	.pcd	Kodak's native CD file format
Photoshop 2	.psd	Older Photoshop format
PICT File	.pct	Mac graphic format
PICT Resource	.rsr	Mac system graphic format
Pixar	.pxr	3-D animation workstation format
PNG	.png	Up-and-coming web format
Raw	.raw	Mainframe graphic format
Scitex CT	.sct	Common full-color printing format
Targa	.tga	MS-DOS color format
TIFF	.tif	Standard desktop publishing format
Wireless Bitmap	.wbmp	Standard format for wireless devices such as mobile phones
Photoshop DCS 1 and 2	.eps	Common desktop publishing format
Acrobat TouchUp Image*	.pdf	Allows you to open individual images from a PDF document
Generic PDF*	.pdf	PDF file created in other applications
Generic EPS*	.eps	EPS file created in other applications
EPS PICT Preview*	.eps	PICT version of preview image associated with an EPS file
EPS TIFF Preview*	.eps	TIFF version of preview image associated with EPS file

You can start a new project in Photoshop in two ways: either create a new image file, or open an existing image file and duplicate it.

Creating a New Image File

If you are starting a new project from scratch, you'll need to set certain parameters for the image.

In Photoshop, choose File > New…. In the New dialog, specify information about the new file and click OK. The canvas for your new image file is created. You can now either begin working on your new image or save the blank image immediately.

6.1 Starting a New Image *(Continued)*

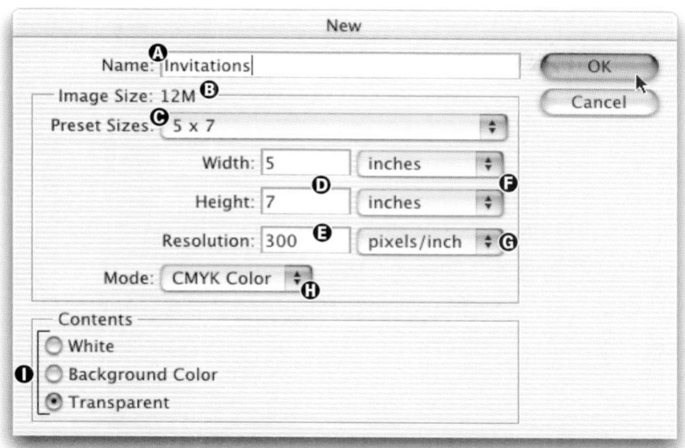

Ⓐ Enter a name for the new image. You'll use this name later when you want to save the file.

Ⓑ Displays the calculated file size for the image with the current options.

Ⓒ Choose an image size from the preset image sizes for use in different mediums: print, web, and digital video proj-ects Specifying the size saves a lot of time and guesswork, especially for web and video work. You can then customize the width, height, resolu-tion, and mode if desired.

Ⓓ Enter the dimensions of the image.

Ⓔ Enter the image resolution.

Ⓕ Choose the units used to set the width and height of the image.

Ⓖ Choose the units used to set the resolution of the image.

Ⓗ Choose a color mode: Bitmap, Grayscale, RGB Color, CMYK Color, or Lab Color.

Ⓘ Choose the color of the Background layer: white, the background color currently selected in the Toolbox, or transparent.

Duplicating an Image File

Another way to start a new project is to begin with an existing image as the framework. First, open the image you want to use as your starting point (see Section 6.2) and then do one of the following:

- Choose File > Save As… and save the file in a different location on the hard drive or with a different name in the same location.
- Choose Image > Duplicate, type a new filename for the duplicate file (if there are lay-ers in the original file, you can also merge them in the new version), and click OK. A new, unsaved version of the image is created.
- In the History palette, click New Document From Current State [icon]. A new, unsaved version of the document is created.

Duplicate Image
Duplicate: Invitations
As: Invitations copy
OK
Cancel
Duplicate Merged Layers Only

Enter a name for the new image. Check Duplicate Merged Layers Only to merge all layers when creating the duplicate. If this option is left unchecked, only the layers are used in the duplicate.

The color mode you select when starting a new image determines the output medium. Bitmap and Grayscale are fine for any output. RGB color is best for screen uses such as web and television, and CMYK color and Lab color are for use when printing.

If you are creating images for print, use a resolution of at least 244 dpi, with 300 or higher preferred.

Most of today's moni-tors display at 96 dpi, although some older Mac monitors use 72 dpi. However, both web and TV designs are cre-ated at 72 dpi.

If you are working with an image and you want to preserve the original, duplicate it immedi-ately after opening (before making changes) so that you do not accidentally save over the original.

You can also, of course, duplicate an image file using your operating system and then open the duplicate to start a new project.

6.2 Opening an Existing Image

➠ 2.3 File Menu

➠ 18.5 Setting Up Workgroups

➠ 18.6 Checking Documents In and Out

Open New File dialog
⌘ O
Ctrl O

Open As dialog (Windows only)
Ctrl O

Open File Browser
Shift ⌘ O
Shift Ctrl O

Cycle between open document windows
Ctrl Tab

Photoshop can open a variety of image file formats (see the table in Section 6.1). The Open command is the most common way of loading files into an application.

1 In Photoshop, choose File > Open… or (in Windows only) choose File > Open As… to open a file in a particular format. (On the Mac, this is handled in the same dialog as opening the file.)

2 Locate the file you want to open using your operating system's Open dialog. To display only certain file formats, select the drop-down next to Files Of Type or Show and select the file format type you want. You use the Format dialog (only available in Windows if you selected Open As…) to set the image's format when opened and defaults for the selected files format.

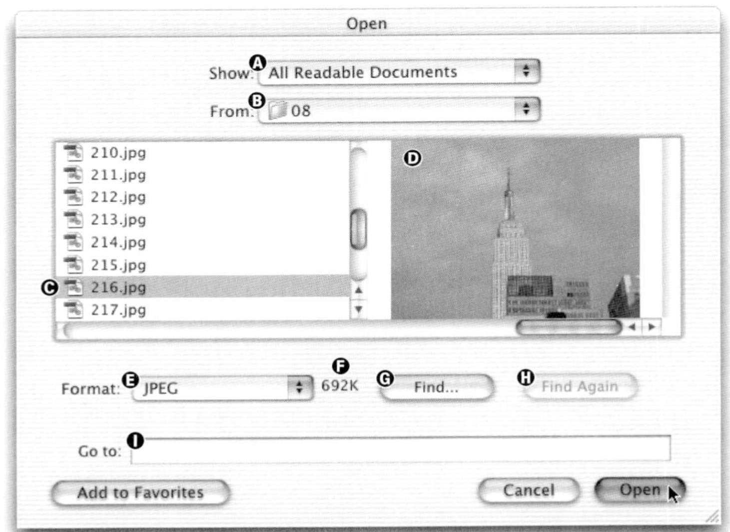

A Choose the format of the image you want to find. Select All Readable Documents or All Documents if you are not sure of the format.

B (OS X only) Choose from a list of favorite folders to jump to that location on your hard drive.

C Use the Mac OS's File Browser to locate the file you want to open. Select the file once and then click Open, or double-click a file to open it.

D Thumbnail of the selected file (if available).

E Choose the format in which to open the image.

F Displays the file size of the image if opened in the selected format.

G Click to open a Search dialog to help find files.

H Click to repeat the last search using the same parameters to find the next occurrence.

I Type the direct path of the file and click Go (which replaces the Open button).

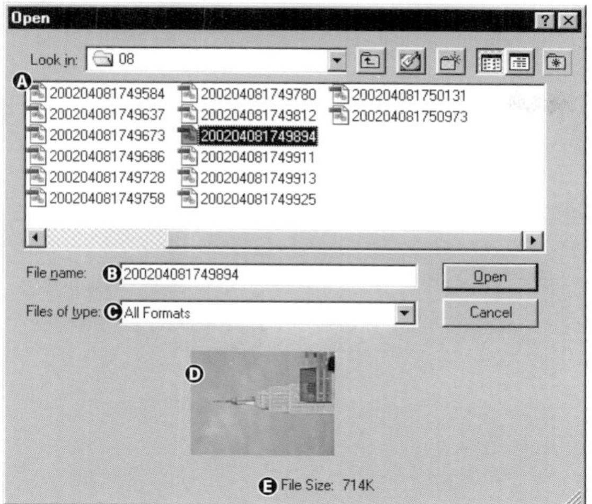

A Use the Windows File Browser to locate the file you want to open. Select the file once and then click Open, or double-click a file to open it.

B Name of the currently selected file.

C Select the image format you are looking for if you know it.

D Thumbnail of the selected file (if available).

E The selected file's size.

When opening a document, selecting All Readable Documents from the Files Of Type or Show menu displays non-Photoshop compatible files as grayed out.

Some file formats require additional information that you enter through dialogs. For example, PDF, EPS, and Adobe Illustrator files require you to enter information about rasterizing vector images.

Choose File > Open Recent to access a list of the 10 most recently opened files. Select the filename of the image you want to open. The image opens in the frontmost document window.

Using the Photoshop File Browser

New in Photoshop 7 is the File Browser, which provides a way to open and work with image files independently of the operating system.

1 Choose Window > File Browser or File > Browse… if the File Browser palette is not already open as a window or in the Palette Well. (Look for a check by its name in the Window menu.)

2 In the File Browser, navigate to the file you want to open by doing one or both of the following:

- In the Clamshell view, click the triangle (Mac) or plus sign (Windows) to expand or collapse a folder view, continuing until you find the file.
- In the Thumbnail view, double-click a folder to open it, click the Back button to move up one level, or use the Path drop-down to move back up or down several levels. Continue until you find the file you want.

6.2 Opening an Existing Image *(Continued)*

You set the length of the Open Recent list and specify whether images are saved with a thumbnail in the File Handling Preferences panel (see Section 5.4).

If you open an image that is already open in Photoshop, the image's document window is brought to the front. To open another view of the document, choose Window > Documents > New Window. Changes made in one window are duplicated in the other window.

Not all files that are compatible will be associated with Photoshop; double-clicking the file will not necessarily open it in Photoshop.

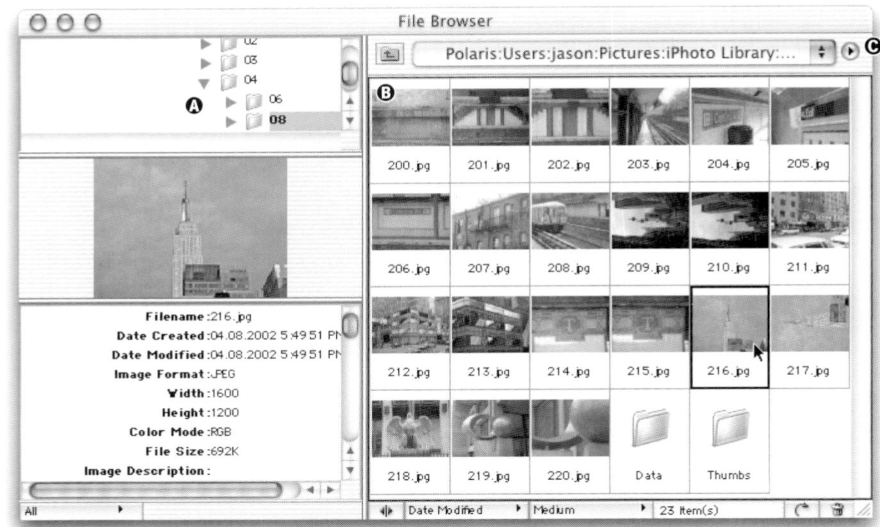

A Clamshell view

B Thumbnail view shows a small version of the hard drive, folder, or image (if one has been saved with the image)

C The File Browser drop-down menu

3 Do one of the following in the Clamshell or Thumbnail view:

- Double-click the file.
- Click the file and then choose Open from the palette's drop-down menu.

Using Your Operating System

You can also open a Photoshop-compatible image file using the Finder (Mac) or Explorer (Windows) simply by locating a Photoshop file—a PSD or other compatible image file type—and double-clicking it or dragging the file onto the Photoshop application icon or one of its aliases.

Drag a Photoshop-compatible file onto the Photoshop application icon to open the file.

6.3 Importing Images

Most images that you will use in Photoshop are either started from scratch (new) or opened from other sources. However, Photoshop does include a few other ways of acquiring images.

➠ 26.1 Scanning Basics

Using the PDF Image import is the same as opening a PDF document using the Acrobat TouchUp Image format.

Mac users can import or open a PICT file, but importing a PICT file allows you to control the size and color mode, and the image is anti-aliased.

TWAIN is a cross-platform interface used to acquire images using a scanner. You must install a TWAIN plug-in, usually provided with your scanner, before you can import an image using Photoshop and a scanner.

Windows Me and Windows XP users can import scanned documents using WIA Support.

Importing an Image

Choose File > Import and then select an import option from the submenu:

Anti-Aliased PICT (Mac) Browse and select a PICT image and then click Open. In the Anti-Aliased PICT dialog, set the size of the PICT as a constrained proportion or by unchecking that option and setting the width and height independently. Then select RGB or Grayscale mode and click OK. The PICT image opens in a new document window embedded in a white background.

PDF Image Browse and select a PDF and click Open. In the PDF Image Import dialog, select the image you want to import from the PDF and click OK or click Import All. Each image opens in a separate document window automatically named with the PDF's filename followed by a four-digit number based on the image order in the PDF.

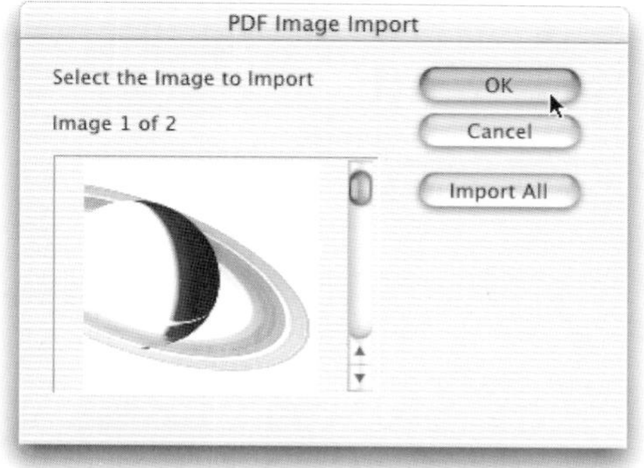

PICT Resources (Mac) Browse and select a file with PICT resources. In the PICT Resource dialog, select the PICT resource to open by using the arrows to browse the resources and then click OK. The resource opens in its own document window.

WIA Support (Windows Me or XP) Choose a destination for the imported images, check Open Acquired Images if desired, and click Start. Select the image or images from the camera and click Get Picture.

Scanning Images

Choose File > Import and then select a scanning option from the submenu, which will contain the word *TWAIN*. This option opens the scanning software provided with your scanner and then imports the image into Photoshop after completion. Follow the instructions that came with your scanner, and after completion, the image is automatically imported into a new Photoshop document.

6.4 Placing a Vector Image

➠ 8.8 Transforming a Layer or Selected Content

You can place certain vector file formats (EPS, PDF, and Adobe Illustrator) directly into an open Photoshop document. Follow these steps:

1. Open the Photoshop image into which you want to place a vector image, and choose File > Place....
2. Browse to find the vector file you want, and double-click the file or click it and click Place. The file should have the `.eps`, `.pdf`, or `.ai` extension.
3. If you are placing a PDF file with multiple pages, you will be prompted to select the page you want to place. Select the page and click OK.
4. The vector image is initially placed as a wire frame (a rectangle surrounding a low-resolution version of the image with an *X* through it). Use the mouse or the Option palette controls to transform the wire frame: move, resize, skew, or rotate the image.

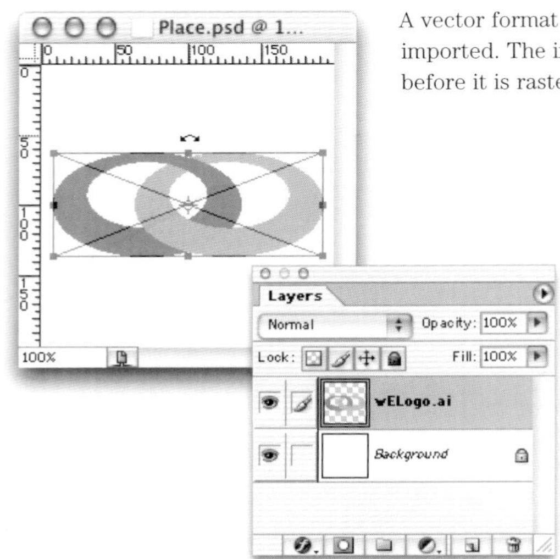

A vector format Illustrator file is being imported. The image can be transformed before it is rasterized into the image.

5. Click the Commit button ✓ or press Enter/Return. The image is rasterized and placed as a new layer on top of other layers in the image. Alternately, click the Cancel button ⃠ or press Esc to cancel the placement.

6.5 Changing the Canvas Size

The canvas is the area in which an image is displayed, and you can set the size of the canvas independently of the image size. For example, if an image is 500 pixels wide, you can size the canvas to 300 pixels, cutting off 200 pixels in the image rather than reducing the image to fit the new size.

➠ 2.4 Edit Menu

➠ 3.3 Marquee Tools

➠ 3.7 Crop Tool

➠ 8.3 Selecting Rectangular or Elliptical Areas

➠ 8.8 Transforming a Layer or Selected Content

➠ 12.1 Path Basics

Crop tool [C]

Cancel cropping action [Esc]

Commit cropping action [Enter]

Crop tool [C]

Marquee tool [M]

Setting the Canvas Size

The most accurate way to set the size of the canvas is to use the Canvas Size dialog located in the Image menu. Using this method you can enter exact measurements for the canvas size and then dictate in which quadrant the size changes should be anchored.

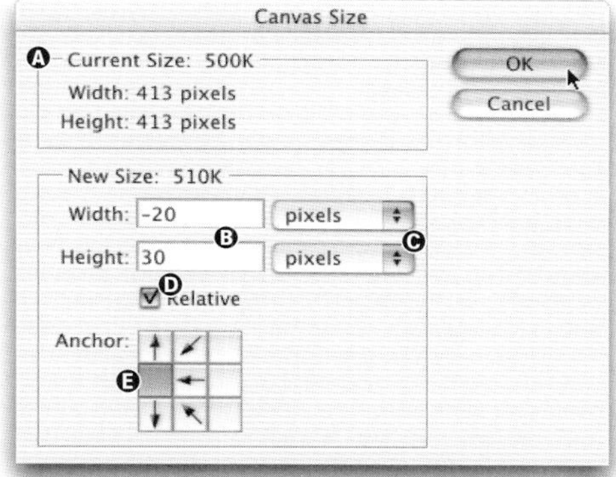

A The current dimensions and file size of the canvas.

B Enter new dimensions for the Canvas. If the Relative option is checked, use +/– units to add or subtract from the current canvas size.

C Choose units to be used for setting dimensions.

D Check if the amounts entered should be added to/subtracted from the canvas size rather than used to set the absolute size.

E Each square represents a quadrant of the canvas. Choose the quadrant around which the canvas will be enlarged or reduced. If quadrants are above and below or to the left and right of the selected quadrant, the changes to the canvas will be equally distributed between them.

Choose Image > Canvas Size…. In the Canvas Size dialog, enter the new width and height for the canvas, select an anchor point around which the size changes will be made, and click OK.

The canvas now appears at the new size. If the width and/or height of the new canvas is larger than the original, previously clipped parts of the image are revealed, or the background color set in the Toolbox fills the new area.

Cropping the Canvas

You use the Crop tool to select a rectangular area of the canvas to preserve while deleting or hiding other areas. Doing so reduces the dimensions of the canvas, as with using the Canvas Size dialog, but gives you direct visual control over what remains.

Warning: In the Canvas Size dialog, if the size for either width or height is smaller than the original size, a confirmation dialog warns that parts of the image will be clipped.

You can also crop the canvas using a Marquee tool. Choose the Marquee tool, make a selection in the canvas, and then choose Image > Crop. The canvas is now cropped to the size of the selected area. If your selection was not rectangular (for example, a circle), the dimensions of the cropped area are the extremes for the selected area.

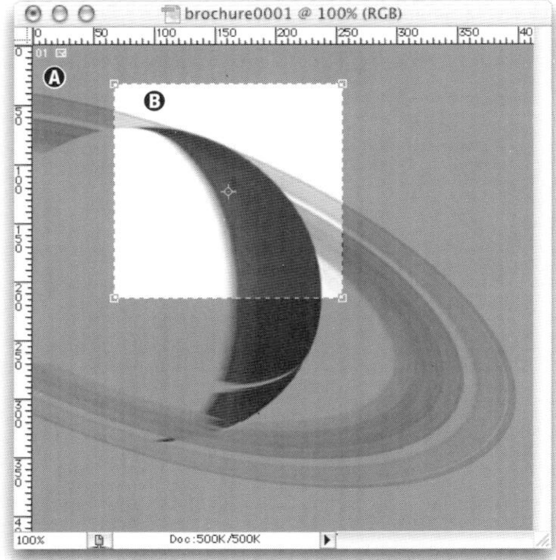

Ⓐ Area will be cropped.

Ⓑ Area will be preserved.

Follow these steps to crop the canvas:

1 Choose the Crop tool and select the area of the canvas you want to preserve. You can move and resize the crop selection.

2 Set the options bar:

- Specify whether cropped parts of the image should be hidden (allowing them to be retrieved later by resizing the canvas) or deleted after cropping.
- Checking Perspective in the options bar also allows the crop selection to be rotated and skewed as well as moved and resized.

3 Adjust the crop selection as desired, and press Enter or click the check mark icon in the options bar to crop the image.

The canvas is now cropped to the boundaries of the cropping selection.

Trimming the Canvas

Trimming allows you to quickly crop solid colors or transparent pixels from the edges of the canvas. For example, if there is a solid-colored border around the image that you want to remove, you can quickly remove it using Trim without having to resort to the crop tool.

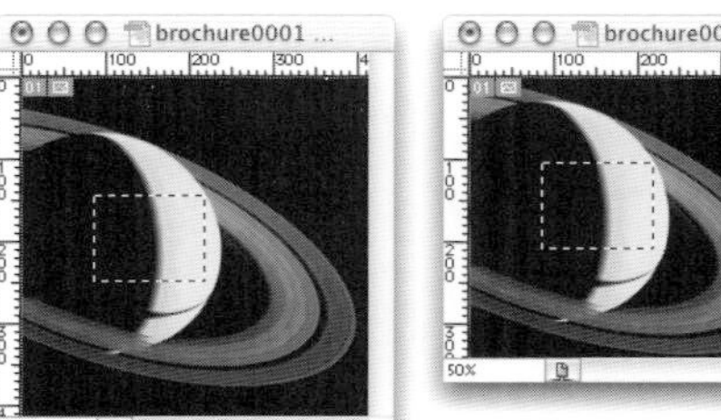

The color in the top-left corner of the selection is used to trim the border of the image.

6.5 Changing the Canvas Size *(Continued)*

Choose the Marquee tool and make a selection in the canvas. Choose Image > Trim.... Set the options in the Trim dialog and click OK. The edges of the Canvas are cropped based on the options set.

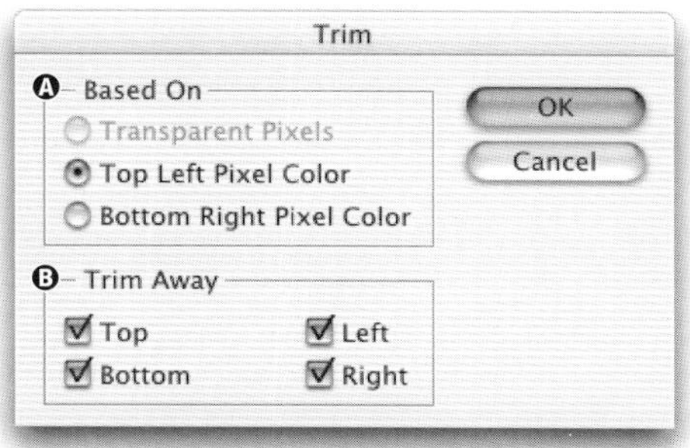

A Choose to trim transparent pixels or to use the color of the pixel in the top-left corner or bottom-right corner of the selection.

B Check the sides of the canvas to be trimmed.

Rotating the Canvas

With the document to be rotated is the top document, choose Image > Rotate Canvas and select an option from the submenu:

180°, **90° CW** (clockwise), or **90° CCW** (counterclockwise).

Arbitrary Allows you to enter a specific number of degrees in the Rotate Canvas dialog to rotate the canvas clockwise or counterclockwise. If the rotation is 180° or 360°, the canvas size remains the same. If the rotation is 90° or 270°, the width and height are swapped. For all other angles, the canvas is resized to accommodate the extreme width and height of the image.

Flip Canvas Horizontally or Vertically

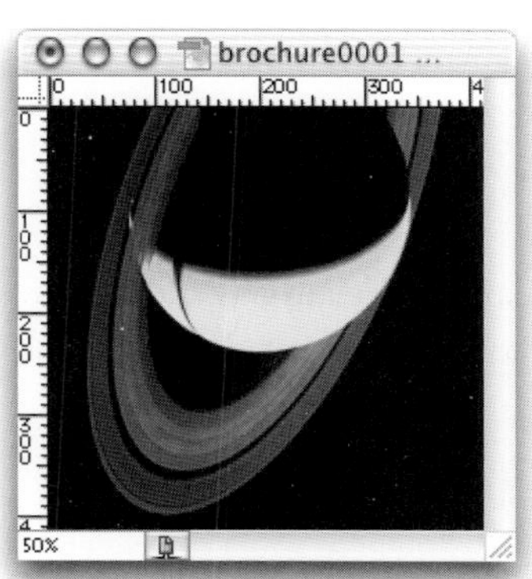

The image is rotated 90° clockwise.

You can change the canvas size directly, using the Canvas Size dialog, or by cropping the trimming or rotating the canvas.

Warning: When pasting between documents, keep in mind the documents' resolutions. Pasting into a document with a lower resolution than the original causes the pasted image to grow; pasting into an image with a higher resolution causes the pasted image to shrink (see Section 8.10).

You can also resize the image while cropping. See Section 6.6 for details.

6.6 Setting the Image Size

➡ 8.8 Transforming a Layer or Selected Content

Crop tool [C]

An image's physical size—its width and height—determine not just its dimensions, but also its file size. Larger physical images require more disk space to record. In addition, image size and image resolution are linked in such a way that an image can be enlarged or reduced without a loss of quality as long as the resolution is similarly increased or decreased. However, the image size and resolution do not have to be set in conjunction. *Interpolation* (or resampling) is the process by which pixels are added or deleted from an image to adjust the dimensions and resolution independently. Doing so causes some degradation of the image quality, but whether the viewer notices that quality loss depends on several factors, including the interpolation method used, the original quality of the image, and (of course) the degree of change.

The image resized by 15%.

Resizing an Image

You can resize the entire image (including all layers) using the Image Size dialog. Follow these steps:

1. Open the image to be resized and choose Image > Image Size... to open the Image Size dialog.
2. Enter a new width, height, and/or resolution for the image. If the image is not being resampled, all three options will change if one is changed. If resampling is on and proportions are constrained, only width and height change in unison. If resampling is on and proportions are not constrained, you can set all three options independently.
3. Click OK. The image is interpolated (if necessary), and the document window now displays the image at its new size and/or resolution. If the interpolation process takes more than a few seconds, you will see a progress bar indicating how long the process will last.

6.6 Setting the Image Size *(Continued)*

Image Size
Pixel Dimensions: 12K (was 529K)
Width: 15 percent
Height: 64 pixels
OK
Cancel
Auto...
Document Size:
Width: 0.213 inches
Height: 0.213 inches
Resolution: 300 pixels/inch
Constrain Proportions
Resample Image: Bicubic

A The image dimensions in pixels. You can enter the image dimensions here in pixels or as a percentage of the original size if resampling is checked. See H.

B Enter the image dimensions.

C Enter the image resolution.

D Choose the units for measuring the image's dimensions.

E Choose the units for measuring the image's resolution.

F Indicates that width and height are locked and cannot be set independently. See G. If resampling is off, this line extends to resolution as well as indicating that all three attributes are set together.

G Check if the dimensions and resolution need to be set independently. The lock will be removed from the Resolution field.

H Check if the width and height need to be set independently after checking Resample Image. The locks will be removed from the Width and Height fields.

I Choose the Interpolation method if you are resampling an image.

You set the default interpolation method used for resampling in the General preferences (see Section 5.3).

Choosing the right halftone screen is vital for getting the best results when printing. Always check with your print shop before specifying this setting.

Resizing While Cropping

You can also resize the image when you crop the canvas. Doing so involves using the Crop tool and then setting the image size and resolution that the newly cropped region should fit.

On the left is the image before cropping. On the right is the image after cropping, and the cropped area is resized.

To resize an image while cropping it, follow these steps:

1 Choose the Crop tool, but *do not* select a crop region yet.

2 In the options bar, enter a width, height, and resolution that the cropped area should resize to after cropping. Click the Clear button if you do not want to resize, or click Front Image to use the size of the canvas in the frontmost document window. (You can switch back and forth between documents while cropping if you want the image to be resized to the same size as another image.)

3 Select the area of the canvas you want to preserve. You can transform (move, resize, rotate, and skew the crop selection).

4 Press Enter or click the check mark icon ✓ in the options bar to crop the image.

The canvas is now cropped to the boundaries of the cropping selection but also resized to the specified dimensions and resolution. However, you may notice some distortion of the image.

Using the Resize Image Assistant

If you have difficulty producing high-quality images while manually changing the image size, the Resize Image Assistant is for you. By answering a few simple questions about the results you want from resizing, you can generally get clearer results unless you are well practiced at the art of image resizing. To use the Resize Image Assistant, follow these steps:

1. With the image you want to resize as the active document window, choose Help > Resize Image....
2. Choose whether the image is to be used for print or online and click Next.
3. Enter a new width or height for the image. Since these dimensions are linked, changing one changes the other. If you are resizing for print, select the units used. If you are resizing for the screen, click the Preview button to see what the changes will look like (displayed in a copy of the document window that is placed in the top-left corner of the screen). Click Next.
4. If you are resizing for the screen, skip to Step 6. If you are resizing for print, choose a halftone screen to use when your image is printed.
5. Use the slider to set the image quality. If you have increased the file size and then increase the "quality," you will actually be decreasing the image quality. The result of the change is displayed. Click Next.
6. Click Finish to resize your image as specified.

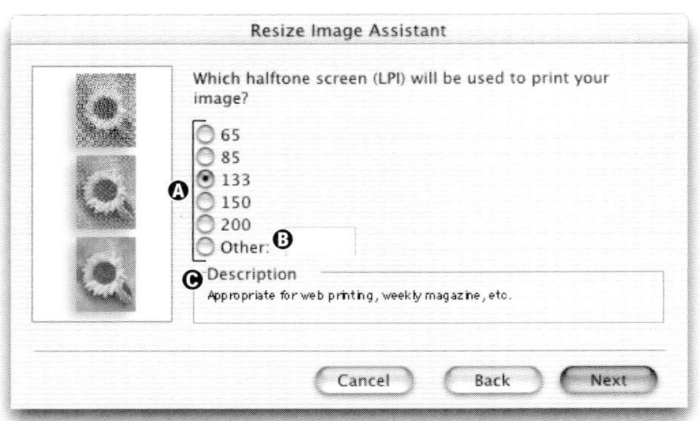

A Choose from the list of common halftone screens. Select a screen based on how your image will be printed. Most newspapers use 85, and glossy corporate reports and art books use 200, because they need sharp images.

B Choose Other and then enter a halftone screen value to the left.

C Displays information about the best use of the selected halftone screen.

6.7 Navigating the Canvas

You can enlarge or reduce images on the screen without affecting the actual image itself. Changing the apparent size of the image allows you to zoom up or down to see the entire canvas at once or to view smaller details close up.

2.9 View Menu
3.23 Hand Tool
3.24 Zoom Tool
4.3 Navigator Palette

Zooming In and Out

The Navigator palette displays a thumbnail version of the topmost document, with a rectangular box surrounding the area currently visible in the document window and the current zoom level as a percentage.

To change the zoom level, click the small mountain icon to zoom in, click the large mountain icon to zoom out, or the use the slider in between these two icons to zoom up or down. In addition, you can type a percentage directly in the Zoom Level box.

On the left is the image zoomed to 33.33%. On the right is the image zoomed to 100%.

In addition, you can use the Zoom tool to quickly zoom in and out of parts of an image. Follow these steps:

1 Select the Zoom tool.

2 Set the zoom options in the tool options bar:

- Select zoom in (+) or zoom out (–)
- Check Resize Window To Fit if you want the document window to resize every time the zoom level is changed to show the entire image (or as much of it as the screen will allow). Otherwise, the document window maintains a constant size.
- Check Ignore Palettes if you want the window to resize behind palettes. Otherwise the windows will only resize within the area of the screen not occupied by palettes.
- Click Actual Pixels to display the image at 1:1.

Switch to Hand tool from any other tool (reverts after releasing)
Spacebar

Zoom tool Z

Hand tool H

Zoom in (the window resizes to fit)
⌘ +
Ctrl +

Zoom out (the window resizes to fit)
⌘ –
Ctrl –

Zoom in (the window doesn't resize)
⌘ Option +
Ctrl Alt +

Zoom out (the window doesn't resize)
⌘ Option –
Ctrl Alt –

Fit on the screen
⌘ 0
Ctrl 0

Show actual pixels (100%)
⌘ Option 0
Ctrl Alt 0

6.7 Navigating the Canvas *(Continued)*

Double-click the Zoom tool to instantly zoom to 100%.

Double-click the Hand tool to instantly change the window size to fit the screen.

Since image resolution is independent of the monitor's resolution, an image with a resolution higher than the monitor resolution (generally 72 ppi) displays larger at 100% than its actual size when printed. How much larger depends on the image's resolution.

- Click Fit On Screen to zoom the image to fill the entire screen or the area not occupied by palettes.
- Click Print Size to display the image at the size it would appear if printed.

3 To zoom, move the Zoom tool over the canvas:

- Click a point in the image you want to use as the center of the zooming (either in or out). The image immediately changes apparent size.
- If you are zooming in, click and drag with the zoom tool in the canvas to select the rectangular area to be magnified. That area will fill the document window.
- Hold down the Alt/Option key to toggle between zooming in and out.
- Press Option/Ctrl and click in the canvas to open a pop-up menu of zoom options.

Moving the Canvas

If the size of the document window is smaller than the size of the total canvas, you will not be able to view parts of the image. You can move the image around within the viable area of the document window in several ways:

- Use the horizontal and vertical scroll bars to move the image up or down and left or right.
- Select the Hand tool and click and hold on the canvas. As you move the tool, the image moves within the viewable area of the canvas.
- In the Navigator, click and hold within the box showing the current viewable area and move it to the area of the canvas you want to view. As you move the box, the image shifts in real time, allowing you to scan through the entire image.

In the Navigator palette, grab the viewing area and move it around as desired.

6.8 Using Rulers, Guides, Grids, and Snap

Guides and grids allow you to precisely position your content in the canvas by providing lines that float over the image to show either ruler divisions (grid) or custom positions (guides) on the canvas.

Snapping increases precision when placing selections, cropping images, creating slices, and drawing shapes and paths by forcing the cursor and the graphic content to a guide, grid, slice, or the edges of content on a layer.

➠ 1.4 The Document Window

➠ 2.9 View Menu

➠ 5.7 Units & Rulers Preferences

➠ 5.8 Guides, Grid & Slices Preferences

Showing and Adjusting Rulers

Rulers are used to display the size (width and height) of the document, regardless of the image's magnification.

- To show or hide the rulers, choose View > Rulers.
- To adjust the ruler's origin, click and drag the origin box (between the horizontal and vertical ruler in the top-left corner) and drag down to the position you want the origin of the ruler to appear. To reset the origin to the top-left corner of the canvas, double-click the origin box.

Show/hide rules
⌘ R
Ctrl R

Ⓐ Ruler origin
Ⓑ Horizontal ruler
Ⓒ Vertical ruler

Showing and Setting Guides

Guides appear as either horizontal or vertical lines that you can place anywhere in the canvas

- To show or hide existing guides, choose View > Show > Guides. If there are no guides in the canvas, this option is not available and will be grayed out.

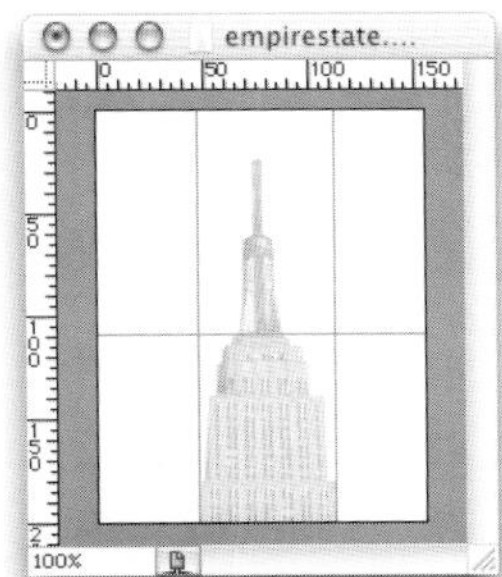

The guides are showing.

Show/hide guides
⌘ ;
Ctrl ;

Show/hide grid
⌘ "
Ctrl "

Lock/unlock guides
Option ⌘ ;
Alt Ctrl ;

Turn snapping on/off
Shift ⌘ ;
Shift Ctrl ;

Show/hide all elements selected in the Show submenu
Ctrl ⌘ H
Alt Ctrl H

An image size is the measurement of its height and width. When using units such as inches and centimeters (absolute units), the image size is the size at which it is printed. When the units are pixels or points, the image size is based on the resolution of the image.

- To quickly add a guide to the canvas, makes sure the rulers are showing, click and drag from either the horizontal or vertical ruler into the canvas and release on the desired location. As you drag, a gray line will indicate where the guide will be placed. Hold down Shift while dragging to force the guide to stop on ruler tickmarks.
- To add a guide to a precise location, choose View > New Guide, set the options for the guide in the New Guide dialog, and click OK. The guide will appear at the specified position.

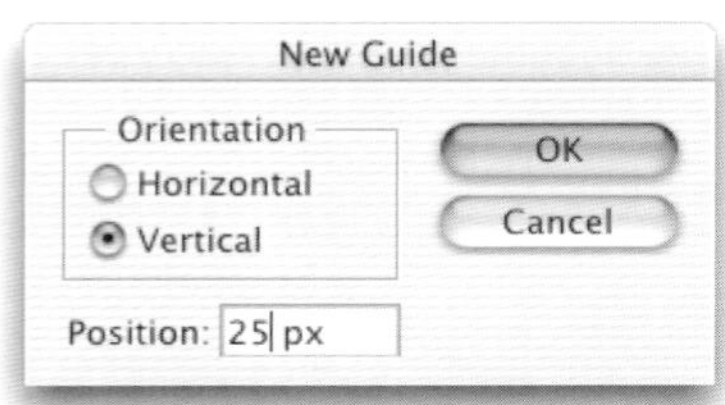

Choose whether the new guide should be Horizontal (width) or Vertical (height), and enter a value (based on the width and height of the canvas) to set the Position of the new guide.

- To lock or unlock the guides, choose View > Lock Guides. When locked, the guides can be added, but not repositioned.
- To move a guide, make sure the guides are not locked, choose the Move tool, and then click and drag on the guide. To change a guides orientation (horizontal/vertical) hold down the Option/Alt key while dragging it.
- To remove a single guide, make sure the guides are not locked and click and drag the guide out of the canvas.
- To delete all of the guides from the canvas, choose View > Clear Guides.

Showing and Setting the Grid

Like guides, the grid sets lines above the image in the canvas, but these lines are regularly spaced, based on the rulers, and cannot be moved (though you can set their spacing in the Guides, Grid & Slices preferences). To show or hide the grid, choose View > Show > Grid.

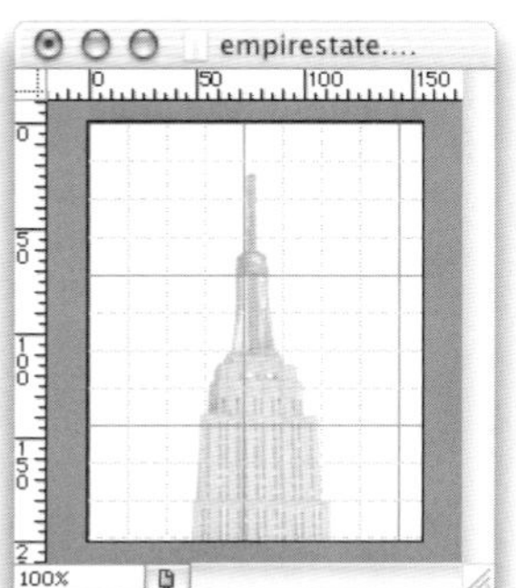

The grid is showing.

6.8 Using Rulers, Guides, Grids, and Snap *(Continued)*

Using Snap

You can set elements being drawn or painted or new guides to snap to the guides, grid, slices, or document bounds (the edges if images in a layer) if they are within 8 pixels of those elements.

- To turn snapping on or off, choose View > Snap.
- To set the elements that are snapped to, choose View > Snap To and select the element to be snapped to. You can also select All to turn on snap for all four elements or None to turn off snap for all four elements.

Double-click either of the rulers to open the Units & Rulers preferences.

You can show or hide all elements selected in the Show submenu by choosing View > Extras.

You can also show or hide all extras by choosing View > Show > All or None.

There are additional elements that you can choose to show or hide in the Show Extras options dialog. To open this dialog, choose View > Show > Show Extras Options.

INTERPOLATION METHODS

Whenever an image is resized, either by changing the canvas size or transforming the content, the image is adjusted either by adding or removing pixels. To add these pixels, Photoshop will use an interpolation method to assign color values to the new pixels based on other color values in the image. Photoshop offers three different methods for interpolation. You can set the interpolation method in the General preferences, where you can choose between the following options:

Bicubic This is a slow but precise method that generally results in better quality results.

Bilinear This method produces medium quality results.

Nearest Neighbor This method is the fastest, but generally produces lower-quality results.

6.9 Changing Your Mind

➠ 2.4 Edit Menu

➠ 4.8 History Palette

➠ 5.3 General Preferences

Undo/redo last action
⌘ Z
Ctrl Z

Step forward in image history
Shift ⌘ Z
Shift Ctrl Z

Step backward in image history
Option ⌘ Z
Alt Ctrl Z

It happens. You start to make changes to an image, more changes, and still more changes, and you realize that this is not at all what you wanted. Sometimes you only need to get rid of your last change, but sometimes you want to go back several actions or even just start over. You can change your mind in a variety of ways while working on an image in Photoshop.

Undoing/Redoing the Last Change

To instantly get rid of the last change you made in an image, choose Edit > Undo. The last change is listed beside the Undo menu option, letting you know what you will be undoing (for example, Undo Image Size).

If you change your mind and decide to keep the last change, immediately select Edit > Redo (the Redo option replaces Undo in the menu) to reinstate the change.

Navigating the History Palette

The History palette provides access to the last several actions you performed. Unlike Undo, which toggles only the last action, the History palette can be used to move back as many actions (History states) as are available. (The number of states is set in the general controls.)

To open the History palette, choose Window > History.

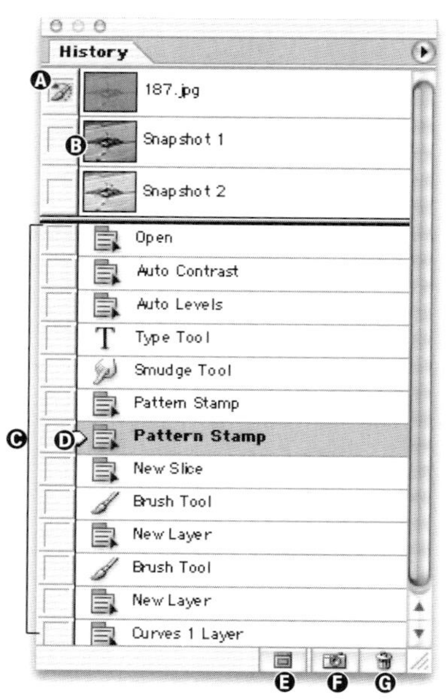

A History Brush Click in this column to use the snapshot or History state with the History Brush tool set.

B Snap shot thumbnail Click a snapshot at the top of the palette. The image reverts to the state in which the snapshot was taken, preserving all layers for that state. To take a snapshot (see F), click the Snap Shot button. The new snapshot appears at the top of the palette.

C History states Select a History state to move backward or forward in the history. Making a change erases all History states after the selected one.

D Current state Indicates that this is the state currently shown in the document window.

E New Document From Current State Click to create a duplicate document from the currently selected state, preserving all layers.

F Snap Shot Click to create new snapshot state.

G Delete State Click to delete the selected state (deletes all states forward of that state as well)

6.9 Changing Your Mind *(Continued)*

You can also use menu options to navigate the History palette:

- To move back one level in the History palette, choose Edit > Step Backward. Repeat this action as many times as desired or until there are no more previous History states.
- To move forward one level in the History palette, choose Edit > Step Forward. Repeat this action as many times as desired or until there are no more future History states.

Reverting to the Last Saved Version

If all else fails, and you want to start over from the point where you were the last time you saved the page, choose File > Revert. This action restores the version of your document currently saved.

In previous versions of Photoshop, Revert was a lot more final than it is in version 7. Reverting a document meant that all changes were lost and that there was no way to go back. In Photoshop 7, reverting a file is treated as another action in the history and can be undone easily.

Warning: Undo and the History palette do not record actions by the Zoom, Hand, and Eyedropper tools.

UNDERSTANDING RESOLUTION

The painter Georges Seurat developed the technique of Pointillism. He placed small points of paint from his palette onto the canvas close together to create the illusion of a continuous image. Both printed and computer images use the same concept, either placing dots (printing) or pixels (screen) so close together that they fool the eye into seeing a complete image. *Resolution* is the measurement of how many units (dots or pixels) are within either a linear inch or a linear centimeter of an image. Higher resolutions (more units per inch or centimeter) produce better-quality images but also mean a larger file size. In addition, printing presses measure halftone screens using lines per inch (lpi).

6.10 Printing Basics

- ➠ 19.1 Print Basics
- ➠ 19.2 Resolution and Printing
- ➠ 19.3 Previewing Color for Print
- ➠ 20 Preparing Images for Print

You can print images in Photoshop using any of a number of output devices: everything from inkjet printers to imagesetters. At its simplest, printing requires only one menu selection or keyboard shortcut, yet printing can also be an involved process that requires the setting of dozens of options to get the exact results.

This section will cover the basics of printing a document using a desktop printer. For advanced printing information, see the "Print Tasks" area of this book.

Obviously, you will need a printer to follow these instructions through completion, but even without a printer, you can view and make changes to all the dialogs.

Click and hold the status bar in the document window to display the page preview, which shows the position of the image in the current page setup.

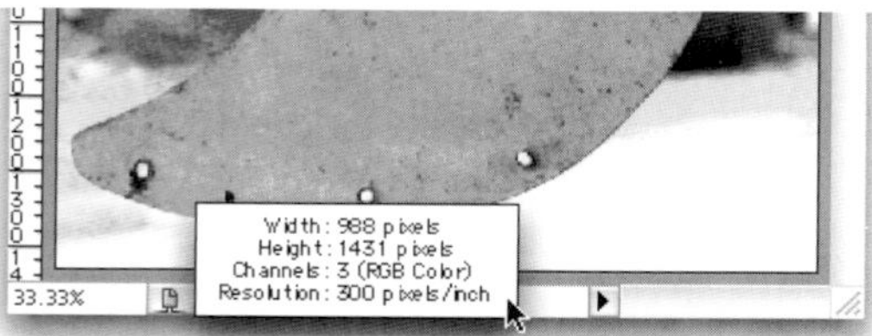

Press Alt/Option and click the status bar to view information about the image.

Setting Up the Page

Before an image is printed, Photoshop needs information about the output medium: the paper size, printer type, and page orientation and whether you want to scale the printed image. To open the Page Setup dialog, choose File **>** Page Setup…, select options, and then click OK to save the changes and close the dialog.

6.10 Printing Basics *(Continued)*

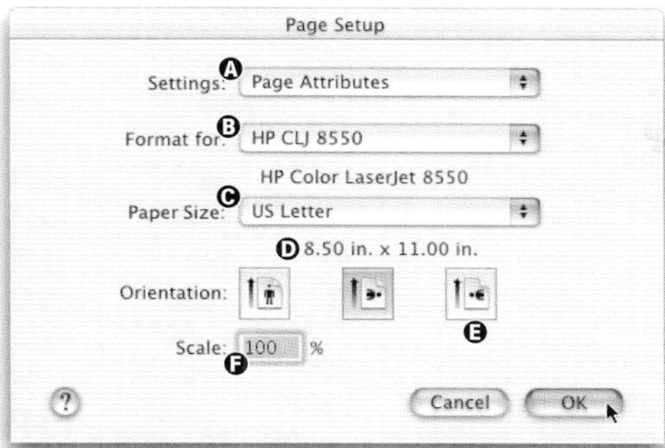

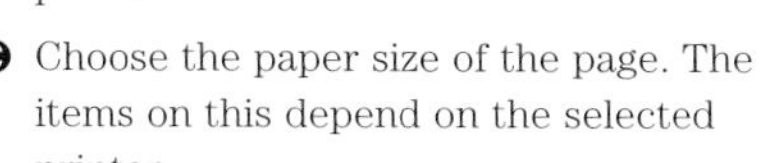

Ⓐ Choose to show and change page attribute settings (shown) or display a summary of the page attributes.

Ⓑ Choose the printer the page is being output to. Doing so displays a list of all currently configured printers, or you can select to format the page for any printer.

Ⓒ Choose the paper size of the page. The items on this depend on the selected printer.

Ⓓ The current page dimensions.

Ⓔ Choose either portrait or landscape orientation.

Ⓕ Enter a percentage to scale the image. This percentage is in addition to the percentage set in the Print Preview dialog.

Page Setup
Paper
Size: Letter 8 1/2 x 11 in
Source: Auto sheet feeder
Orientation
Portrait
Landscape
Margins (inches)
Left: 0.122" Right: 0.377"
Top: 0.361" Bottom: 0.627"
OK Cancel Printer...

Ⓐ Choose the paper size of the page.

Ⓑ Choose the paper-source tray.

Ⓒ Choose either portrait or landscape orientation.

Ⓓ Enter values for the margins of the page.

Ⓔ Click to open a dialog in which you can set the selected printer's properties.

Page Setup dialog
Shift ⌘ P
Shift Ctrl P

Print With Preview dialog
⌘ P
Ctrl P

Print dialog
Option ⌘ P
Alt Ctrl P

Print one copy
Option Shift ⌘ P
Alt Shift Ctrl P

6.10 Printing Basics *(Continued)*

Most programs (including older versions of Photoshop) use Command/Ctrl-P to open the Print dialog. Photoshop 7 defaults to using that keyboard shortcut to print but with a preview dialog screen first. You can change these keyboard shortcuts in the General preferences (see Section 5.3).

Warning: The image prints as it appears when printing is initiated. Hidden layers are not printed.

Check with your print shop to determine whether it requires positive emulsion up, negative emulsion up, positive emulsion down, or negative emulsion down before setting Emulsion Down and Negative.

Previewing the Page before Printing

The term *print preview* is a bit misleading. In the Print Preview dialog, you can do much more than preview the image. You can also adjust the position of the image on the printed page and scale the image up or down. In addition, you can set numerous advanced options for output to printing, which will be discussed in greater detail in the "Print Tasks" area of this book.

To open the Print Preview dialog, choose File > Print With Preview…. After adjusting the image size and position as desired, click OK to print the file.

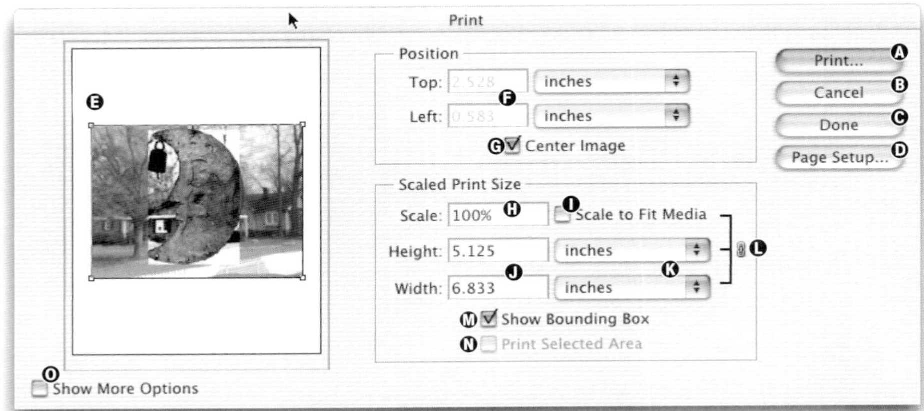

- **A** Click to open the Print dialog to print the image using these settings.
- **B** Click to return to the image without saving print settings.
- **C** Click to save print settings and return to the image.
- **D** Click to open the Page Setup… dialog to make adjustments (see the preceding section).
- **E** A thumbnail of the image with bounding box. Click and drag edges to resize.
- **F** Enter the position of the image from the top-left corner of the page.
- **G** Check to automatically center the image on the page.
- **H** Enter a value (2.5 to 15000) for the percentage to scale the image for printing. This percentage is in addition to the percentage set in the Page Properties dialog.
- **I** Check to force the image to scale to the maximum width or height allowed by the page. This is especially important for printers that make borderless prints.
- **J** Enter a value (0.014 to 416.666) for the width or height to scale the image.
- **K** Select units to measure the width and height of the image.
- **L** Indicates that these values are locked. Changing one value changes the others.
- **M** Check to turn on the bounding box in the thumbnail.
- **N** Check to print only the selected area. Select an area of the image before selecting Print Preview in order to use this option.
- **O** Click to display advanced printing options.

6.10 Printing Basics *(Continued)*

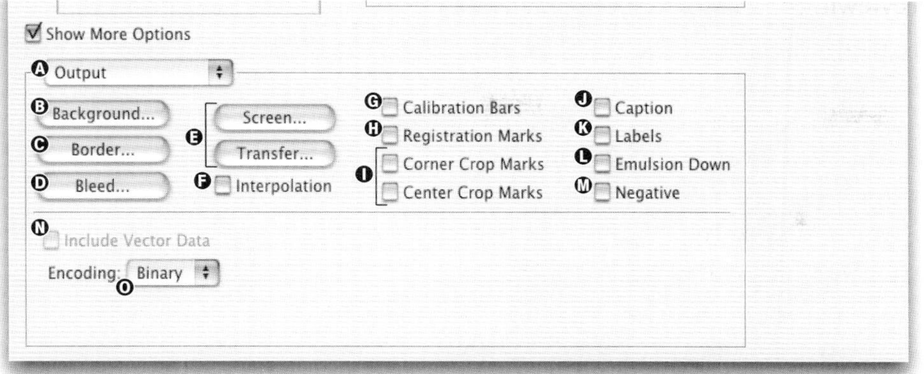

Advanced printing options:

- **A** Select Output options (shown) or Color Management options (see Section 7.3).
- **B** Click to select a background color for the page.
- **C** Click to set a black border 0 to 10 points (0 to 3.5 mm or 0 to 0.15 inches).
- **D** Click to set the amount of overlapping if the image is printing on multiple pages.
- **E** Click to set color correction options.
- **F** Check to help smooth jagged edges when printing to PostScript Level 3 or later printers.
- **G** Check to add color and/or grayscale (depending on the color mode) calibration strips outside the image area.
- **H** Check to add marks used to align color separations.
- **I** Check to add lines indicating where to trim edges for the final page. This is important when printing files that will be physically trimmed.
- **J** Check to add the caption from the File Info dialog to the outside of the image area.
- **K** Check to add the image's title and channel names to the outside of the image area.
- **L** Check to print to film or photographic paper if the photosensitive layer is facing away from you. If you are unsure which is the emulsion side, examine the developed film under a bright light. The dull side is the emulsion; the shiny side is the base.
- **M** Check to print an inverted version of the image for a photonegative. You'll want to do this if you are printing separations directly to film, although in some countries film positives are used.
- **N** Check to include the vector data in the image.
- **O** Select how the image should be encoded for printing. Binary is generally preferred.

Hold down the Alt/Option key in Print Preview to change several buttons. The Print... button becomes Print One Copy, Cancel becomes Reset, allowing you to reset the options, and Done becomes Remember, which saves the options without closing the Print Preview dialog.

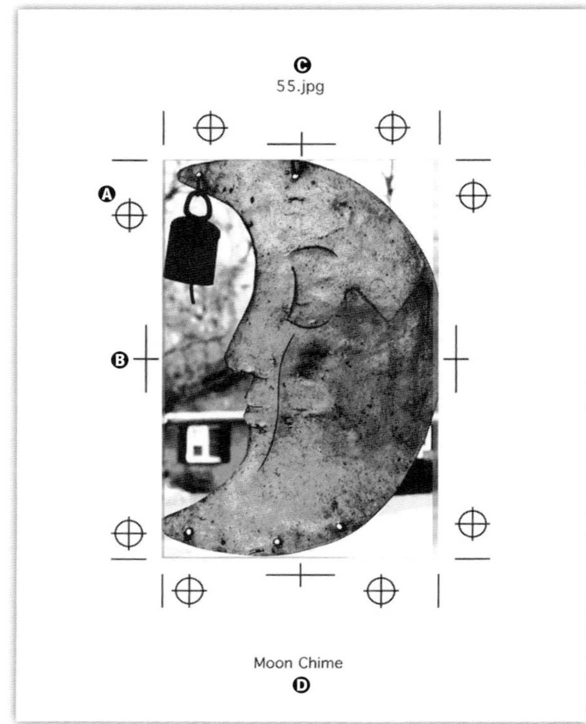

A Registration mark

B Crop mark

C Caption

D Label

Printing to a Desktop Printer

Once you set the options, you are ready to print.

- Selecting Print… in the Print Preview dialog opens the Print dialog. After adjusting the printing options, click Print.
- To print the image, choose File > Print…. After adjusting the printing options in the Print dialog, click Print.
- To quickly print a single copy of the image (bypassing the Print dialog), choose File > Print One Copy. The image is sent to the printer you choose in Page Setup.

6.10 Printing Basics *(Continued)*

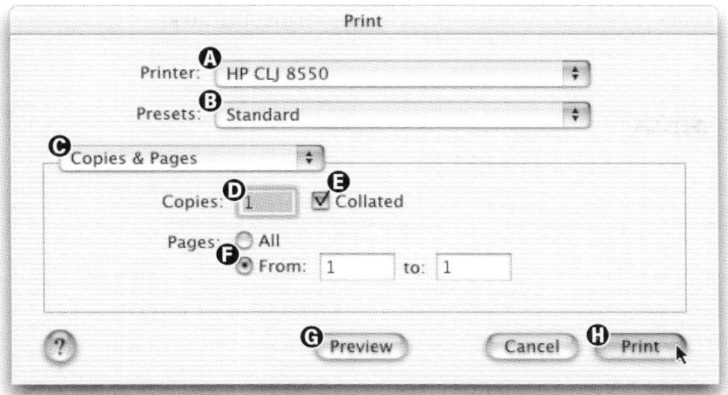

Ⓐ Choose the printer for output. If you do not see the printer you want in the list, choose Edit Printer List… to add a new printer.

Ⓑ Choose either standard options or a custom setting (saved using the Save Custom Settings dialog).

Ⓒ Choose Copies & Pages panel (shown) or Layout Options panel, or select one of the printer-specific Options panels. (Every printer has different options.) You can also choose Summary to display a list of current printing settings or choose Save Custom Settings to custom preset the current settings.

Ⓓ Enter the number of copies to be printed.

Ⓔ Check if you want each copy printed separately. Collating copies in this manner generally takes slightly longer.

Ⓕ Choose whether you want to print all the pages needed to output the image (All) or a specific range (From). If you select From, enter the page numbers for the range in the From and To fields) If you select From, enter the page range you want to printed.

Ⓖ Click to preview the image in Adobe Acrobat (if available). This is *not* the same as Print Preview.

Ⓗ Click to send the image to the printer.

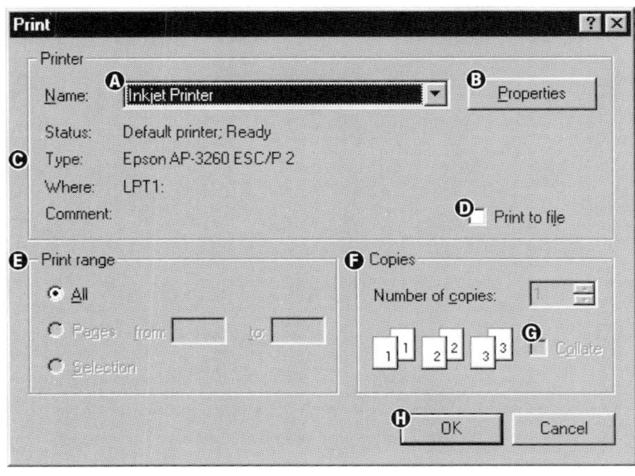

Ⓐ Choose the printer for output.

Ⓑ Click to open the Printer Properties dialog.

Ⓒ Displays the current printer information.

Ⓓ Click to output to a file rather than to a printer.

Ⓔ Choose whether you want to print all the pages needed to output the image (All), a specific range (Pages), or the selected area or the image. If you select Pages, enter the page numbers for the range in the From and To fields.

Ⓕ Enter the number of copies to be printed.

Ⓖ Check if you want each copy printed separately. Collating copies in this manner generally takes slightly longer.

Ⓗ Click to send the image to the printer.

6.11 Adding File Information and Watermarks

➠ 2.3 File Menu
➠ 2.8 Filter Menu
➠ 6.13 Saving and Closing an Image

The Internet makes the transfer of images easy and convenient. It also makes copying images without the creator's permission easy and convenient. To add copyright and other information about who generated the image and how it was generated to an image file, Photoshop provides two very different tools: File Info and Watermark.

Setting File Info

Photoshop allows you to add *metadata* information about the file—including author, copyright, descriptive keywords, and date created—using the information standard developed by the Newspaper Association of America (NAA) and the International Press Telecommunications Council (IPTC) to identify transmitted text and images.

To add metadata to an image, choose File > File Info. Enter information in the panels, and then click OK. You must save the image before the data is recorded in the image.

You can record the metadata in the following panels:

General Enter information about the document as well as its copyright state, copyright message, and a URL for the owner.

Keywords Enter a keyword that describes the image and then click Add to add it the list. Keywords help when searching for images that display a particular idea or subject.

Categories Enter a three-letter Associated Press code. You can also add a supplemental category. This is primarily used by news operations. To replace a category, select the category, type its replacement, and click Replace. To delete a category, select the category and click Delete.

Origin Enter information about the history of the image, including its creation date, credits, an Associated Press transmission reference, and editorial urgency.

EXIF If the image was created by a digital camera, this panel displays imported information such as creation date and time, resolution, f/stop, compression, and exposure time. The information in this area depends on the EXIF (a standard information format used by most modern digital cameras) information recorded by your digital camera and is not editable.

In addition to entering the information directly, file information can be saved as an XMP (Extensible Metadata Platform) file, with the .xmp extension, and then loaded into other Photoshop files. This is especially helpful if you have a series of files with similar information that you want to be able to quickly attach to them without having to retype it into the panels of each file.

6.11 Adding File Information and Watermarks

(Continued)

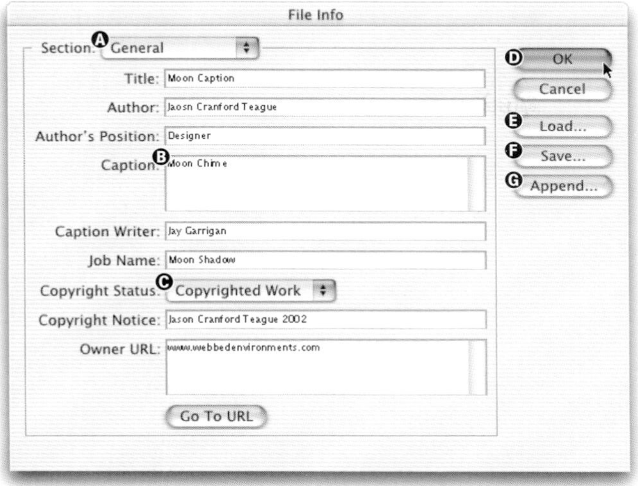

A Choose an information panel: General (shown), Keywords, Categories, Origin, EXIF.

B Type a caption for use when printing the document.

C Choose whether the image is Copyrighted, Public Domain, or Unmarked.

D Click to save the metadata and close the File Info dialog.

E Click to load a saved `.xmp` file for this document.

F Click to save the current data as an independent `.xmp` file.

G Click to add a saved `.xmp` file to fill blank fields in the information except caption and keywords, which will be appended at the end of the current list.

Watermarking is not an Adobe feature, but is contributed by the Digimarc Corporation, and your watermark information is stored on the Digimarc website. To get a unique creator ID to use a watermark, you must first register with Digimarc and then use the watermark filter. Digimarc offers a number of plans with annual fees ranging from $100 to $800, depending on the number of images covered and the length of time. A free option covers a maximum of 99 images for 1 year.

Copyright information entered for the watermark will be used by File Info.

Adding a Watermark

In addition to the file information, you can add a faint or strong watermark to your image that includes copyright information, image attributes, and intended output medium. You can't read the watermark with the naked eye, but it is embedded in the image itself and will slightly distort the image depending on the strength you choose for the watermark. Even if the image is cropped or manipulated, if the data is scrubbed from the data file, or if the image is composited with other images, the watermark information is preserved.

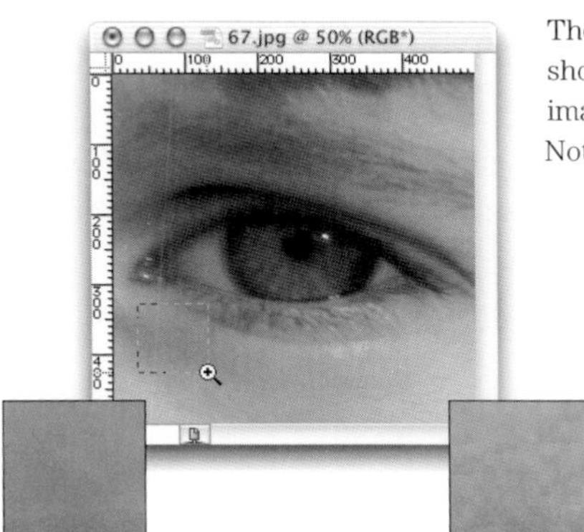

The original image is in the middle. The image on the left shows the unwatermarked version of the image, and the image on the right shows the same area with a watermark. Notice the additional noise.

6.11 Adding File Information and Watermarks

(Continued)

Windows users can include file information only in Photoshop, TIFF, JPEG, EPS, and PDF formats. Mac users can add file information to files in any format.

The metadata is embedded in the image file using XMP (Extensible Metadata Platform). XMP is an XML (Extensible Markup Language) format used for standardizing the transfer of files between workgroup members using Adobe products.

If Copyrighted Work is chosen in the File Info dialog, a copyright symbol (©) is added to the document title bar.

To add a watermark to an image, choose Filter > Digimarc > Embed Watermark…. If you haven't done so before, click Personalize and enter your Digimarc PIN and ID numbers. Then enter the watermark attributes and click OK.

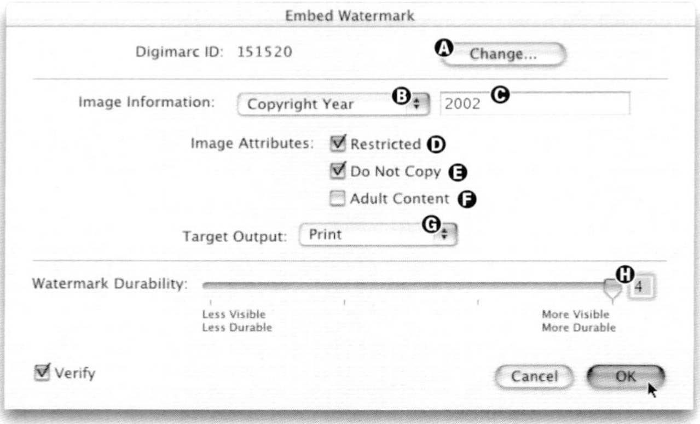

Ⓐ Click to enter your Digimarc PIN and ID. Also includes a link to the Digimarc website to set up an account (requires an Internet connection).

Ⓑ Choose to enter information regarding the copyright year, transaction ID, or image ID.

Ⓒ Enter image information.

Ⓓ Check if the use of this image is restricted.

Ⓔ Check if this image should not be copied.

Ⓕ Check if this image contains adult content.

Ⓖ Choose the medium the image is intended for: Monitor, Web, or Print.

Ⓗ Select how visible vs. how durable the watermark should appear.

Ⓘ Check to automatically view the watermark strength meter.

Once the watermark filter is applied, anyone with the proper software can read the image's watermark. In Photoshop, choose Filter > Digimarc > Read Watermark.

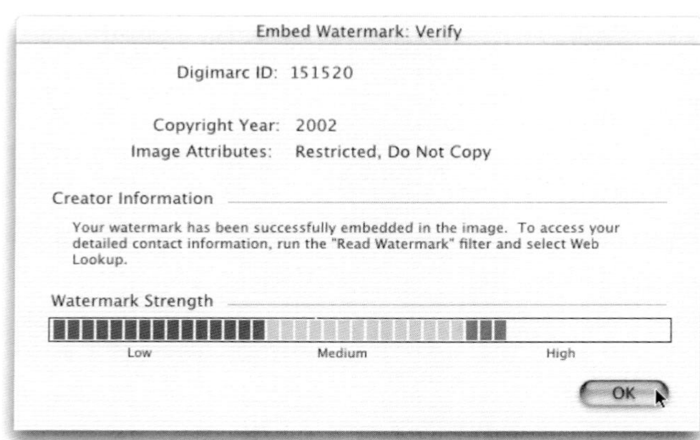

The stronger the watermark, the more difficult it is to erase it. Click OK to view the creator's information on the Digimarc website (requires an Internet connection).

6.12 Adding Notes

Often while working on an image, especially one you might be sharing with others who will be working on it, you need to add notes to the canvas itself. Notes do not affect the final output of the image.

➠ 3.21 Annotation Tools

Notes/Audio Annotation tool N

Cycle note tools
Shift N

To show or hide note icons for the image, choose View > Show > Annotations.

Warning: Sound files can add considerably to the file size, so you might want to use them sparingly.

To remove all annotations from an image, click the Clear All button in the tool options bar.

To delete a single annotation, click the Annotation icon and then click Delete.

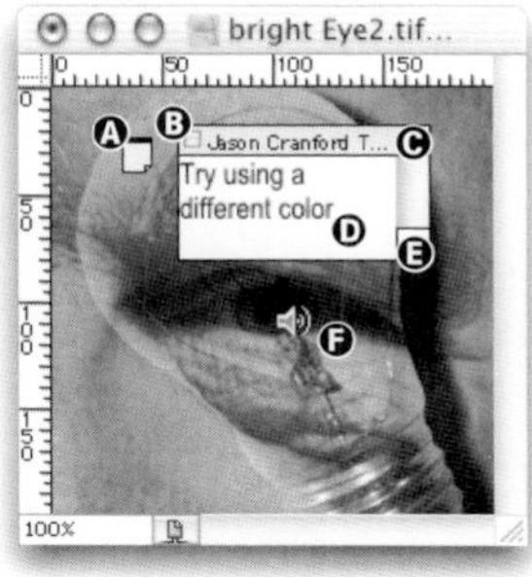

Ⓐ Click and drag the Note icon to select and move to a new location on the canvas. Double-click to show/hide the associated note. (The note might be anywhere on the canvas.) Place the mouse pointer over the note and wait for a Tool Tip displaying the note author's name.

Ⓑ Click to hide the note.

Ⓒ Displays the note's author. Click and drag to move the note.

Ⓓ Enter note comments.

Ⓔ Click and drag to resize the note.

Ⓕ Click and drag the Audio Annotation icon to move it to a new location on the canvas. Double-click to play the audio note. (Be sure your volume is sufficient.) Place the mouse pointer over the note and wait for a Tool Tip displaying the note author's name.

Text Notes

Text notes work a lot like the sticky notes available with most operating systems. The idea is that you can type a text note that has a related icon, generally placed in a specific location on the canvas that the written note is referencing. There are two parts to a note: the Note icon (a button representing the note) and the note itself that can be moved independently of the icon. To add a text note, do the following:

1 Choose the Notes tool and set the options for the note's author, font appearance, and background color.

2 Click the canvas in the location where you want the note to appear. The Note icon will appear there, and a space appears underneath where you can type the note.

3 Enter your note comments. You can then hide the note and continue working or add other notes.

Audio Notes

Audio annotations allow you to record your voice to create a note. Of course, you need a microphone hooked up to your computer and you need the proper audio software installed for your operating system. To add an audio note, do the following:

1 Choose the Audio Annotation tool and set the note's author and icon color.

2 Click the canvas in the location where you want the note's icon.

3 In the Audio Annotations dialog, click Start… to begin recording your message. Speak clearly and evenly into the microphone. Click Stop when you are finished recording.

To play back the note, double-click the Audio Annotation icon.

6.13 Saving an Image

Save the document (update saved file)
⌘ S
Ctrl S

Save As dialog
Shift ⌘ S
Shift Ctrl S

Close the current window
⌘ W
Ctrl W

Close all open windows
Option ⌘ W
Alt Ctrl W

Warning: Although you can work on a file without saving it, you will lose the image and all your work if you accidentally close the file (and this does happen) or if Photoshop or your operating system crashes. It is recommended that you save the file immediately upon creating it and then regularly save changes. Photoshop does not have an autosave feature.

Once you save the document, you can choose Save As... at any time to resave the document in a different location or with a different name or to overwrite the current version by using the same name and location.

The "Web Tasks" area of this book discusses the Save For Web... option. Save For Web, however, does not save the document, but instead saves a copy of the document or parts of the document.

At some time after starting an image (either immediately after creating a new image or after making significant changes to the image), you will need to save the image to a hard drive or other storage medium.

To save an image for the first time, choose File > Save As.... Enter information in the Save As dialog and click Save. If you click Cancel at this point, the image will not be saved.

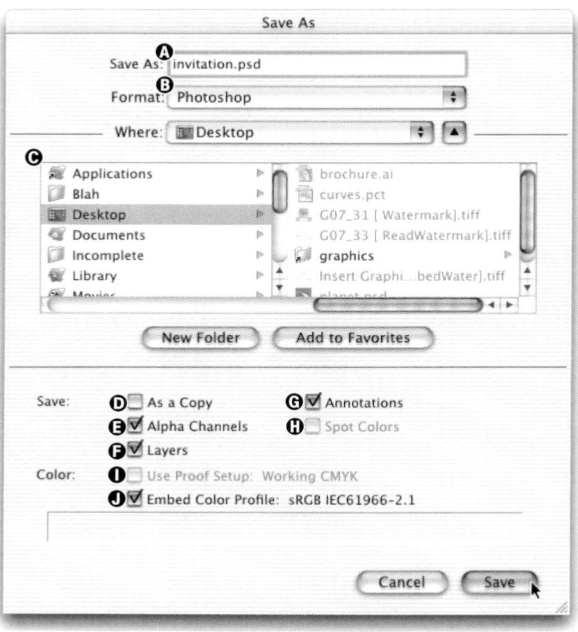

Ⓐ Enter a filename. Depending on your preferences, Photoshop automatically adds the correct extension for the file format.

Ⓑ Choose a file format in which to save the image.

Ⓒ Use your OS's file finder to browse to the location where you want the file saved.

Ⓓ Check to save this file as a copy. This option adds the word *copy* to the end of the current filename.

Ⓔ Check to preserve alpha channels in the saved document. This option is not available for all formats or if the document does not contain alpha channels.

Ⓕ Check to preserve layers in the document. This option is not available for all formats or if the document does not contain layers. Only documents saved in Photoshop, Advanced TIFF, and Photoshop PDF formats can contain layers.

Ⓖ Check to preserve annotations added to the document. This option is not available for all formats or if the document does not contain annotations.

Ⓗ Check to preserve spot colors. This option is not available for all formats or if the document does not contain spot colors.

Ⓘ Check to add a particular proof setup for printing. This option is available only in CMYK mode.

Ⓙ Check to embed the document's color profile, ensuring that the color is consistent for the document even if opened on a computer that does not have that profile. This option is not available for all formats.

Choose File > Save to add the changes made to the image since the last save to the saved file.

If you are finished with an image, you can close its window to clean up your desktop by choosing File > Close to close the topmost document. To close all open documents, choose File > Close All. You will be prompted to save any documents with unsaved changes.

CHAPTER 7

Managing Color and Image Mode

THERE IS A LOT MORE TO COLOR in Photoshop than just picking a color. By its very nature, color is difficult to pin down since it is a matter of perception—both human and digital. Just as one person will see colors differently than another person, different computers and output devices "see" colors differently.

Although a color's numeric values stay consistent regardless of the output device, how those values are output depends on a variety of factors. These differences are especially noticeable when you compare a printed image with its screen appearance, but are even visible when you move images between computers with different monitors. Using Photoshop's color management tools, you can specify certain color profiles that are embedded in the image's document file and then used by imaging software to more accurately and consistently represent the color regardless of the output device.

Photoshop can ensure that "what you see is what you get" when working on an image by managing how colors are treated and by choosing an image mode that is specific to the device with which you will be outputting your image. This chapter covers:

7.1 Image Color Basics

➠ 5.5 Display & Cursor Preferences

➠ 13.2 Adjusting Tonal Range Using Levels

➠ 13.3 Adjusting Color Levels Using Curves

➠ 15 Painting in Images

Pixels

All images on the computer screen are made of thousands of square dots called *pixels,* which are arranged in a grid to create the illusion of a single image. Each pixel is a particular color or shade, but the dots are so small and close together that the human eye blends the colors, much like the chips in a tile mosaic. An image created using this mosaic-style grid is referred to, in computer jargon, as a bitmap. Thus, Photoshop is often referred to as a bitmap-editing program. That is, it is used to edit images created using tiled pixels with painting tools that are used to recolor pixels in the image. Other programs, such as Adobe Illustrator, are referred to as vector-editing programs because images are defined mathematically using vector paths rather than as a grid of pixels.

Although Photoshop is primarily known for its bitmap-editing capabilities, it includes some sophisticated vector-editing tools as well (see Chapter 12).

Pixel is short for *picture element.*

If you magnify the image on the screen, you can see the individual pixels used to create the image.

Histograms

A *histogram* is a graph showing the number of pixels used in the image for a given color or intensity level. The histogram is used with color correction in the Levels adjustment, but you can also display a histogram of the image to check the distribution of colors throughout an image and to see if there is good tonal distribution.

To open the histogram directly, choose Image > Histogram. You can also make a selection if you want to view the histogram for a specific area of the image, or you can hold down Option/Alt while choosing the Histogram menu option to include information from spot color and alpha channels.

7.1 Image Color Basics *(Continued)*

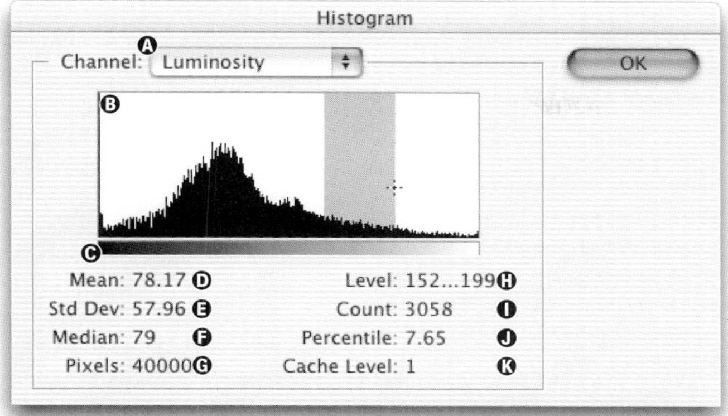

Ⓐ Choose the channel in which to view a histogram.

Ⓑ **Histogram** Displays the number of pixels, or count (see I), for a given intensity level (see H), ranging from 0 on the left to 255 on the right. As you move your mouse over areas of the histogram, values for that position's intensity level are displayed below. Click and select to display values for multiple intensity levels.

Ⓒ **Color bar** Displays the color for the intensity level in the histogram.

Ⓓ Displays the average intensity value in the selected channel.

Ⓔ Displays how widely the intensity value varies in the selected channel.

Ⓕ Displays the middle value in the range of intensity values.

Ⓖ Displays the total number of pixels in the selected area or in the image.

Ⓗ Displays the intensity level at the mouse cursor's position or selection in the histogram.

Ⓘ Displays the number of pixels for the intensity level at the mouse cursor's position or selection in the histogram.

Ⓙ Displays the total number of pixels at or below the current intensity level at the mouse cursor's position in the histogram as a percentage of the total pixels (see G).

Ⓚ Displays the setting for the image cache.

The histogram does not allow you to make any changes directly to the image. However, you can use the Levels adjustment dialog (see Section 13.2) to make tonal changes using a version of the histogram.

When you are working with a large image, Pixel Doubling (see Section 5.5) allows you to work in a lower resolution (low-rez) mode when moving and editing pixels which can significantly speed up your editing process without affecting the quality of the image.

Viewing the histogram of an adjustment layer reflects the data for all layers beneath it.

7.2 Understanding Image Modes

➠ 6.1 Starting a New Image

➠ 7.6 Converting between Image Modes

Don't confuse the general term *bitmap* with the specific image mode Bitmap. The image mode allows only black pixels and white pixels; the general term refers to any image created using tiled pixels.

All bitmap images use an image mode to define the method used to store the color or shade of their pixels. This mode determines not only how the colors are recorded, but also what colors are available for use in the image—this range of colors is called the *color gamut*—and how those colors are created when output. Therefore, picking the right color mode for the image is vitally important. You can convert between different color modes while you are working, but doing so is generally discouraged because of inevitable color shifts. This is not to say that you will never want to convert between modes, simply that you need to be cautious and always keep an original version of the image in its original color mode in case you need to go back to it.

When working with an image, you want to consider where the image is to be used and then pick the appropriate color mode. In addition, different features in Photoshop are available in different image modes. For example, many filters will not work in CMYK mode, and if you must use them, you will need to convert to RGB mode, apply the filter, and then convert back to CMYK mode. In Photoshop, you can choose from eight color modes:

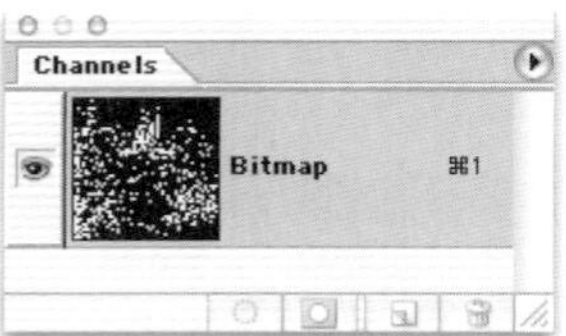

Bitmap mode: All pixels are recorded as either black or white (no shades of gray). You must convert the image to Grayscale mode and flatten all layers before converting to Bitmap mode. Filters, layers, and adjust commands are unavailable in Bitmap mode, but you can invert the image. Bitmap mode is recommended for output to older PDA or mobile phone devices.

Left: An image in Grayscale mode; right, the same image in Bitmap mode.

Grayscale mode: Pixels are recorded in black, white, or as many as 254 shades of gray, which is ideal for current PDAs. When you convert from color to grayscale, color values are removed from the pixel, leaving only luminosity to define the grayscale level. Once removed, color values cannot be restored.

7.2 Understanding Image Modes *(Continued)*

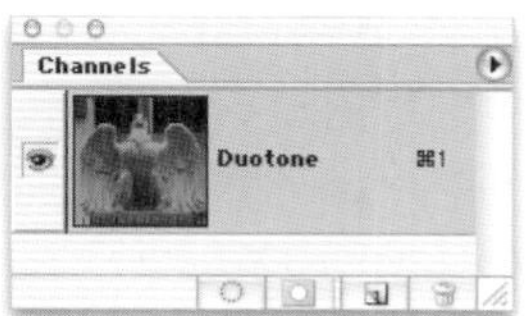

Duotone mode: Uses two (Duotone), three (Tritone), or four (Quadtone) spot colors in combination. You must convert the image to Grayscale mode before converting to Duotone mode. This mode is recommended for printing colorized grayscale images using spot color rather than process color.

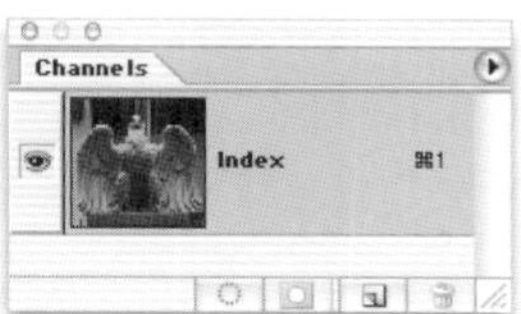

Indexed Color mode: All pixels are forced (indexed) to the closest color value in a table of as many as 256 possible color values or shades (8-bit) as set in the image color table. You must flatten layers before converting to this mode. Traditionally, this mode was recommended if you were outputting web graphics to GIF or PNG format. However, you might never need to use Indexed Color mode, since images are automatically indexed when output for the Web.

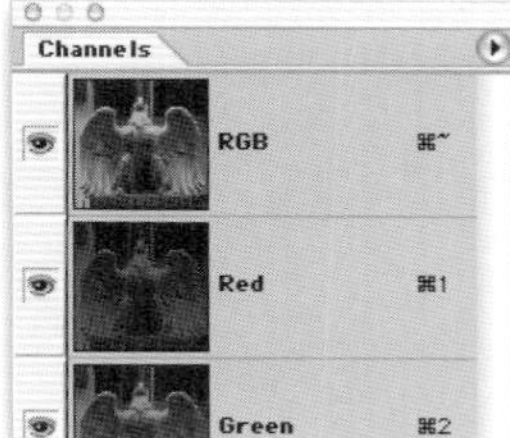

RGB mode: Pixels are recorded as a combination of Red, Green, and Blue color values. RGB mode is the most common color mode, and all Photoshop commands and tools are available in this mode. RGB mode is recommended if you are outputting to the computer or television screen or to an RGB printing device.

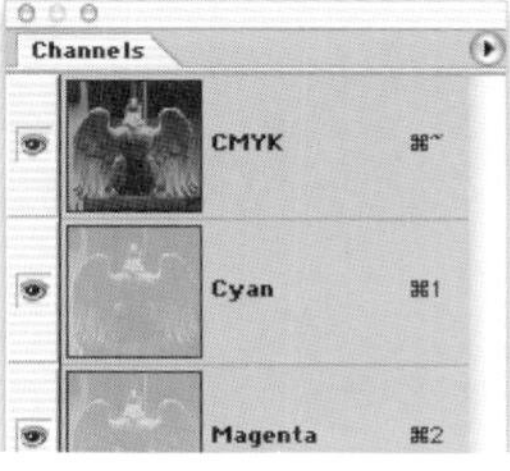

CMYK mode: Pixels are recorded as a combination of Cyan, Magenta, Yellow, and Black (K) color values. CMYK mode is recommended only if you are out putting to a color printer or creating color separations.

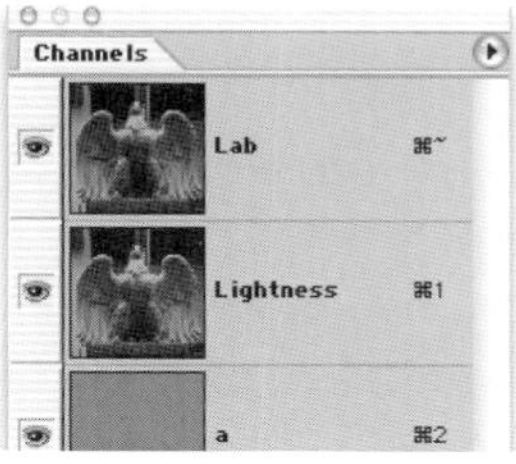

Lab mode: Pixels are recorded by their Lightness value and color values on a green–red (the "a" axis) and blue–yellow (the "b" axis) scale. This mode was developed to overcome differences and provide consistency among printers, monitors, and other output devices. Lab mode is recommended when transferring files between computers running different operating systems.

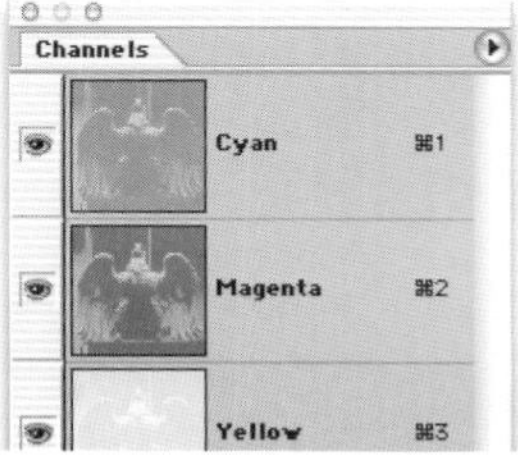

Multichannel mode: Pixels are recorded using multiple 256-level grayscale channels but without a combined channel. When you convert from other color modes, channels are converted into CMY spot colors. This mode is recommended only for special printing needs.

If you delete a channel from an image using RGB, CMYK, or Lab mode, the image mode is automatically converted to Multichannel mode.

Save images using Multichannel mode in Photoshop DCS 2.0 format.

Although image modes are used to *record* colors in an image, color models are used to *create* colors in an image. See Chapter 14 for more details on color models.

7.3 Specifying Color Settings

➠ 6.1 Starting a New Image

➠ 6.2 Opening an Existing Image

Photoshop lets you specify which color profiles (referred to as working space profiles) should be used in a document for a particular image mode in the Color Settings dialog. You use this dialog to set and save the general color management options to be used for new documents and documents being opened in the current copy of Photoshop.

Color Settings dialog
Shift ⌘ K
Ctrl Alt K

To open the Color Settings dialog, choose Photoshop > Color Settings... (Mac OS X) or Edit > Color Settings... (Mac OS 9 and Windows).

If you are new to Photoshop and computer-generated color, use the predefined color settings, and leave the advanced options at their defaults.

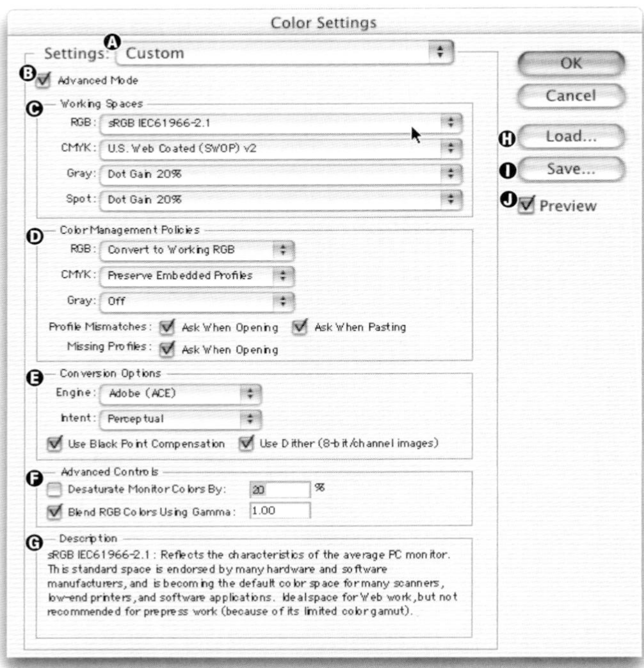

- **A** Predefined color management settings.
- **B** Check to display the Conversion Options and Advanced Controls sections of this dialog.
- **C** Choose working space profiles for RGB mode, CMYK mode, Grayscale mode, or spot color.
- **D** Choose how working space profiles in specific color modes (RGB, CMYK, or Grayscale) should be treated when an image is opened.
- **E** (Advanced mode) Set options for how the colors should be converted between different color spaces.
- **F** (Advanced mode) Set options for how the monitor renders colors.
- **G** Place the mouse cursor over any element in the web interface to view a description, which includes detailed explanations of the options in each drop-down.
- **H** Click to load a color setting file that has the `.csf` extension.
- **I** Click to save the current color settings as a file that has the `.csf` extension.
- **J** Check to show changes to the color settings in the current image.

7.3 Specifying Color Settings *(Continued)*

Choosing a Predefined Color Management Setting

The easiest way to deal with color settings is to use the predefined settings that Photoshop provides, which automatically set options for the Working Spaces, Color Management Policies, and Advanced Options. In the Settings drop-down in the Color Settings dialog, choose one of these options:

Color Management Off No color management is used. This setting is recommended for images being output to the screen or video only.

ColorSync Workflow (Mac only) Uses the Mac's ColorSync color management system; recommended if you will not be transferring the image to a Windows machine and if you are familiar with ColorSync technology.

Emulate Photoshop 4 Uses the color-handling behavior of Photoshop 4; recommended if you are transferring the image to machines that use older versions of Photoshop.

European, Japan, or U.S. Prepress Defaults Recommended if you are printing to a press in one of these areas.

Photoshop 5 Default Spaces Uses the default working spaces from Photoshop 5; recommended if you are transferring the image to machines that use that version.

Web Graphic Defaults Sets optimal color settings for creation of web graphics.

Choosing Workspace Settings

When you create a new document, a color profile is automatically associated with it depending on its color mode. In addition, you can set all new documents to be converted to the selected profile when opening. You set the default working space profile for a color mode in the Color Settings dialog. You can set the color workspace (how colors are treated in the document of a certain mode) for the following image modes:

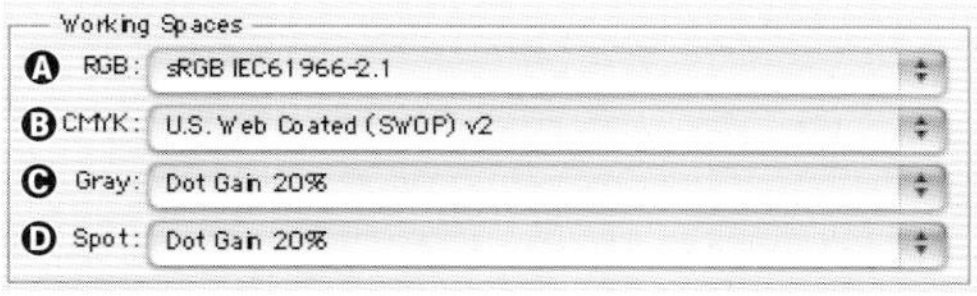

A Choose from an extensive list of RGB profiles to embed in images. The one you choose will depend on your working needs, but generally Adobe RGB (1998) is best for print work, sRGB IEC61966-2.1 is preferred for web images.

B Choose from an extensive list of CMYK profiles. Talk to your print service provider for the setting that works best with their presses.

C Choose from a list of Dot Gain percentages or gamma levels to use with grayscale images.

D Choose from a list of Dot Gain percentages to use with spot colors.

➠ 13.10 Mixing Channels
➠ 14.1 Color, Gradient, and Pattern Basics
➠ 14.2 Selecting Colors
➠ 29.1 Calibrating Color for TV Resolution

If you are working with a prepress provider, always check with them to ensure that the working space profiles you select are compatible with their workflow.

Color settings are especially useful if your image will be used in a variety of output mediums to ensure that colors are consistent when converting between different image modes.

A "working space" is a color profile used for newly created or untagged documents for the associated color mode. For example, if you start a new document using the RGB mode, and you have set the RGB Working Space to sRGB IEC61966-2.1, then this working space will be embedded in the new document.

7.3 Specifying Color Settings *(Continued)*

The location of the Color Settings preferences will vary depending on the operating system. To find the file, use your operating system Find feature to search for "Color Settings." It should be in a folder labeled Adobe "Photoshop 7.0 Settings."

If you are regularly sharing your files with other Photoshop users, you may want to save and share your Color Settings so that you are all working with the same options.

Choosing Color Management Policies

You use color management policies to specify how images being opened in RGB, CMYK, or Grayscale mode should be treated in relation to the default working space profiles you have set. Three policy options are available for each color mode:

Off No working space profiles are embedded in new documents. Working space profiles are turned off for documents being opened unless the embedded profile matches the default working space profile.

Preserve Embedded Profiles The embedded working space profile in the image being opened overrides the default working space profile.

Convert To Working Space The embedded working space profile in the image being opened is replaced by the default working space profile.

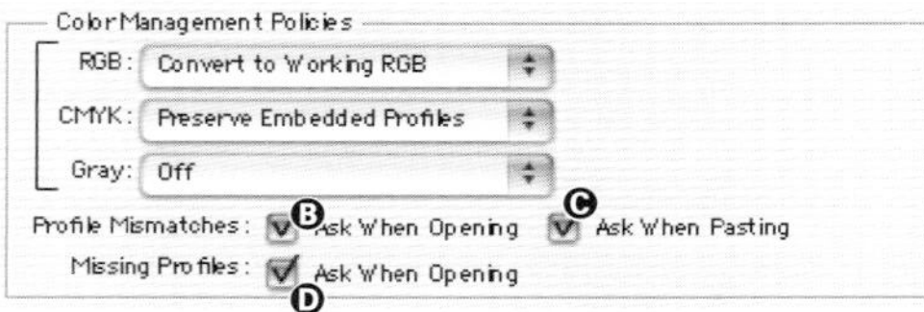

A Choose one of the three policy options for each color mode.

B Check to be alerted when the working space profile embedded in an image being opened is different from the profile specified in the working space. This option is recommended.

C Check to be alerted when the working space profile embedded in an image being pasted is different from the profile of the image into which it is being pasted. This option is recommended.

D Check to be alerted when the image opened does not contain a working space profile. This option is recommended. The alert also requires that the color management policy for the corresponding color mode is not set to Off.

WHAT IS GAMMA?

Gamma is a measurement scale used with video monitors that compares contrast and saturation. Gamma values range from 1.0 (low contrast and saturation) to 2.5 (high contrast and saturation), with Macintosh monitors generally set to a value of 1.8 and Windows monitors to 2.2. Many computers have software that allows you to adjust the gamma value used by the monitor as part of monitor calibration. Generally, if you are creating print graphics, a gamma of 1.8 is best. However, since most web surfers use a Windows PC, web and video designers should work using the 2.2 gamma setting.

7.3 Specifying Color Settings *(Continued)*

Working with Advanced Color Settings

Checking the Advanced Mode option at the top of the Color Settings dialog opens additional option areas that allow you to control the default options for how profiles are converted and how colors are displayed on the screen.

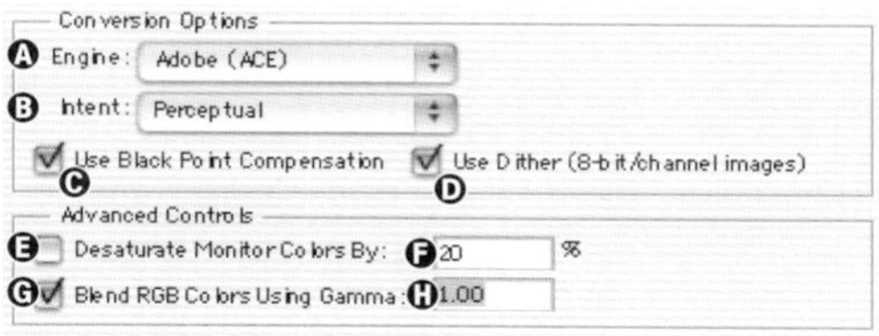

Conversion Options
A Engine: Adobe (ACE)
B Intent: Perceptual
C Use Black Point Compensation D Use Dither (8-bit/channel images)
Advanced Controls
E Desaturate Monitor Colors By: F 20 %
G Blend RGB Colors Using Gamma: H 1.00

Ⓐ Choose the conversion engine you want to use. The exact list depends on your operating system. Adobe (ACE) is recommended.

Ⓑ Choose how you want the color to be changed: Perceptual (preserves colors to appear natural to the human eye), Saturation (preserves vivid colors), Absolute Colorimetric (preserves colors as directly as possible between the color gamuts), Relative Colorimetric (shifts colors based on the extreme highlight in the image). Perceptual is recommended.

Ⓒ Check to adjust for differences between the black points (the point at which colors are 100% black) between the two profiles. If unchecked, some blacks might turn gray.

Ⓓ Check to dither colors with 8-bit/channel images when converting. This will use dithering if colors available in one color profile image model are not available in the image mode to which the color is being converted.

Ⓔ Check to desaturate the colors displayed in the image to simulate a wider gamut of colors than the monitor can actually display. Because this setting does not change how the colors are output, colors on the screen will look different from the output colors.

Ⓕ Enter a percentage value (0 to 100) for the amount by which to desaturate monitor colors. The higher the value, the more the colors are desaturated.

Ⓖ Check to blend RGB colors in the monitor using a specific gamma value instead of blending using the default RGB profile.

Ⓗ Enter a gamma value (1.00 to 2.20) to be used for blending RGB colors. A value of 1.00 is considered "colorimetricly correct" and should produce the fewest artifacts between high-contrast edges in the image.

Color is created on the computer or television screen using red, green, and blue light in an *additive* process, in which combining the colors produces lighter colors. Conversely, color is created in print by using inks (most often cyan, magenta, yellow, and black) in a *subtractive* process, in which combining the inks creates darker colors. Obviously then, if you are designing for print, you cannot see the "true" colors on the screen.

7.4 Setting a Document's Color Profile

➠ 29.1 Calibrating Color for TV Resolution

If you need to change the color profile, but do not want to change the appearance of the image, you will probably want to convert rather than simply change the color profile.

Although you can set global settings for color management in the Color Settings dialog, each individual document has its own individual profile for controlling how the image should be previewed on the screen and output.

To save the embedded profile in the document file, you must use a file format that supports embedded profiles (Photoshop, PDF, EPS, TFF) and make sure that the Embed Color Profile option is checked.

In the process of working with an image, you might want to change, convert, or even remove the image's current color profile. Change the profile by replacing the image's current profile with a new one selected in the Assign Profile dialog. The colors will be reinterpreted, which can lead to a noticeable shift in colors.

To open the Assign Profile dialog, choose Image > Mode > Assign Profile..., select a profile, and click OK.

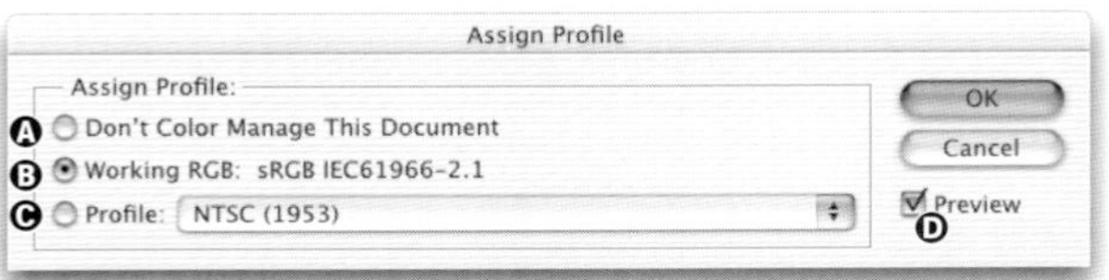

A Choose to remove all color management profiles from this document.

B Choose to use the working space defined for the image's color model (see Section 7.2).

C Choose an alternative profile from the drop-down.

D Check if you want profile changes shown in the canvas.

Converting a Profile

When you convert one profile to another, colors are recalculated in an attempt to preserve the appearance of the colors as displayed using the current color profile. Although some color shifting might occur, the shift is minimized. Choose Image > Mode > Convert To Profile..., select a profile, and specify how to perform conversion. Click OK to convert the image's profile using the selected options.

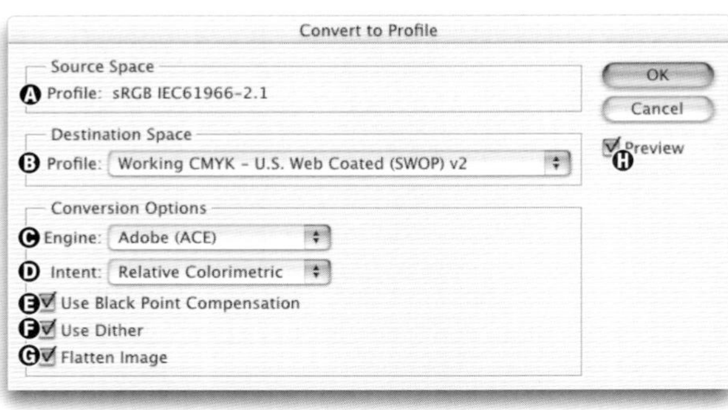

A Displays the image's current color profile.

B Choose a new color profile to translate to.

C Choose the conversion engine you want to use. The exact list depends on your operating system. Adobe (ACE) is recommended.

D Choose an option for how you want to convert the color. I generally prefer Perceptual.

E Check to adjust for differences between the black points (the points at which colors are 100% black) between the two profiles. If unchecked, some blacks might turn gray.

F Check to dither colors with 8-bit/channel images when converting. This setting uses dithering if colors available in one color profile image mode are not available in the image mode of the color being converted to.

G Check to flatten multiple layers in the image before conversion.

H Check if you want conversion changes shown in the canvas.

7.5 Using Color in Channels

All colors displayed on the computer screen are created through combining one or more semitransparent colors. The colors used in combination depend on the color mode the image is set to, but the colors are represented in the Channels palette with one channel for each color and additional channels for spot colors and alpha (transparency) channels. For example, if an image is using CMYK mode, there will be five channels: one for each color (cyan, magenta, yellow, and black) and a composite channel to show all five channels simultaneously.

➡ 4.12 Channels Palette

➡ 8.11 Saving and Loading Selections

➡ 11.2 Adding Layer Masks

Switch to Combined color channel
⌘ ~
Ctrl ~

Switch to a specific color channel
⌘ 1-4
Ctrl 1-4

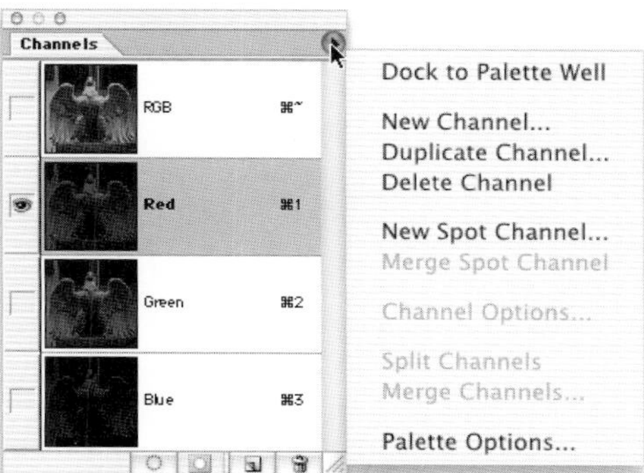

Color channels are displayed in the Channels palette, where you can edit and add channels for a variety of purposes.

- To **edit** a specific channel, select that channel in the Channels palette, and then use a painting tool to edit the pixels on just that layer. Regardless of the colors selected, you paint in shades of that channel's color.
- To **duplicate** a channel using the Duplicate dialog, select the channel in the Channels palette and then choose Duplicate Channel in the Channels palette menu. In the Duplicate dialog, enter a name for the new channel, and select where to add the channel (in the current document, in another open document, or in a new document). If you select a new document, enter a name for the new document, and then specify whether to invert the channel.
- To **quickly duplicate** a channel by dragging the channel's thumbnail to the Create New Channel button. The channel is duplicated using the channel's name with the word *copy* added after it.
- To **delete** a channel, select the channel in the Channels palette, and then click the trashcan or drag the layer to the trashcan. You can also select Delete Channel from the Channels palette menu.
- To **split** channels into separate documents, choose Split Channels from the Channels palette menu. All the channels in the current document open as new documents.

Alpha channels are used to record selections and layer masks as a grayscale image. This allow you to edit selections using any painting tool (see Chapter 15). Section 8.11 explains how to save and load alpha channels.

Spot colors use a special channel to record a single predefined color ink, such as a PANTONE ink.

Deleting one of the color channels in RGB or CMYK mode automatically converts the image to Multichannel mode.

Duplicating a color channel creates a grayscale version of the channel.

- To **merge** channels in open, single-layered, flattened grayscale documents into a single RGB, CMYK, Lab, or Multichannel document, open the documents to merge (this will also work to "unsplit" a split document). Choose Merge Channels... from the Channels palette menu on any of the open images. In the Merge Channels dialog, choose the image mode for the combined channels, choose the number of channels for the new document, and click OK. In the next dialog, assign the documents to the channels for the color mode selected, and then click OK. The new image is created using the selected options.

COLOR MODES VS. COLOR MODELS

Although many of their names are identical, it is important not to confuse color modes, which are used by the document to record and display color values, with color models (see Section 14.1), which are used to specify color values. All documents have a color mode set for them that determines the color gamut available as well as how colors are output to the monitor or printer. Color models, on the other hand, allow you to specify particular color values used to create colors on the screen. You can, for example, have a document in CMYK mode and still use the RGB color model to specify the colors. However, to avoid confusion and to make sure that the colors in the image will not fall out of the color mode's gamut, generally use the same color model to specify colors as the image's color mode.

7.6 Converting between Image Modes

All images, regardless of the color profiles embedded in them, have a specific color mode that they use to record colors. However, the image mode is not set in stone, and you can quickly move between color modes depending on your needs at any time while working. But, be careful. Although you can convert between modes easily, each mode has its own color gamut, and you will likely lose colors and degrade the image quality if you constantly convert back and forth. That said, not all commands and features in Photoshop are available in all image modes. For example, CMYK does not have access to all the filters. In that case, it is best to begin work in RGB mode, make all of your edits (making sure not to use color out of the CMYK gamut), and then convert to CMYK when you are satisfied with the image.

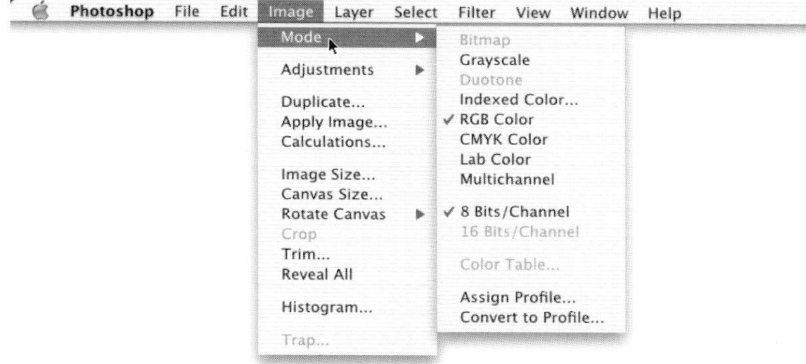

1 Choose Image > Mode and select the desired image mode. To convert to Bitmap or Duotone mode, first convert to Grayscale mode and then convert again to Bitmap or Duotone mode (see Section 7.2).

2 A dialog will appear asking whether you want to flatten or merge layers in the image.

- If you selected Multichannel, Indexed Color, or Bitmap, you must click OK to flatten the image in order to continue. If you click Cancel, the image mode is unchanged.
- If you selected Lab Color, CMYK Color, or RGB Color, you must choose whether you want to merge the layers into a single layer (Merge) or preserve the current layers (Don't Merge) in order to continue. If you click Cancel, the image mode is unchanged.
- If you selected Grayscale, and there is only one layer, you must click OK to discard the image's color information in order to continue. If there are two or more layers, you must choose whether to merge the layers into a single layer (Merge) or preserve the current layers (Don't Merge) in order to continue. If you click Cancel, the image mode is unchanged.

3 If you selected Multichannel, Lab Color, CMYK Color, or RGB Color, the image mode is changed without further interaction. The next four sections explain how to proceed using Bitmap, Grayscale, Duotone, and Indexed Color.

➟ 5.6 Transparency & Gamut Preferences

➟ 6.1 Starting a New Image

➟ 14.1 Color, Gradient, and Pattern Basics

Color modes not only determine the number of colors available to the image (gamut) but also the number of color channels available in the Channels palette and the file size.

Remember, color modes determine how color is recorded in the image while color models determine how you define color for the image.

The Gamut for RGB and CMYK modes will also depend on their Color Settings (see Section 7.3).

CMYK gamuts are smaller than other color gamuts since they consist only of colors that can be printed using process-color inks. You can highlight colors that are out of gamut in the image by choosing View > Gamut Warning. You can set the color of the Highlight color in the Tranparency & Gamut preferences (see Section 5.6).

Whenever you start a new document, one of the options you must set is the initial image mode.

7.7 Converting to Bitmap Mode

➠ 14.10 Organizing Pattern Presets

Bitmap images are not extremely common anymore except in mobile phones and certain PDAs that do not support grayscale or color. The WBMP (short for "wireless bitmap") format is a bitmap format.

Bitmap mode can be accessed only by images currently in Grayscale mode. Follow the instructions in Section 7.6 to convert the image to Grayscale, repeat those steps to convert to Bitmap, and continue with the following steps:

1 If there are multiple channels in the image, you will be asked to discard the non-grayscale channels.

2 Set the options in the Bitmap dialog and click OK.

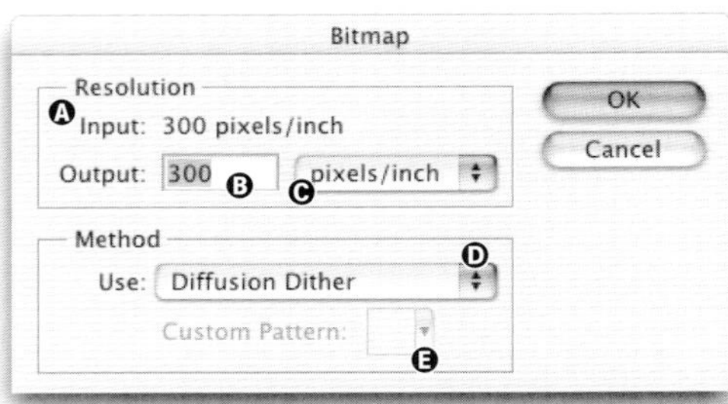

Ⓐ Displays the current resolution of the image.

Ⓑ Enter a value (1.000 to 30000.000) for the resolution of the final bitmap image.

Ⓒ Choose the units used for the output resolution.

Ⓓ Choose a method for creating the bitmap. If you select Halftone Screen…, you can set the halftone options when you click OK.

Ⓔ If you selected Custom Pattern, choose the pattern from the Pattern Presets drop-down.

3 If you set the method to Halftone Screen… in step 5, set the halftone screen options and click OK.

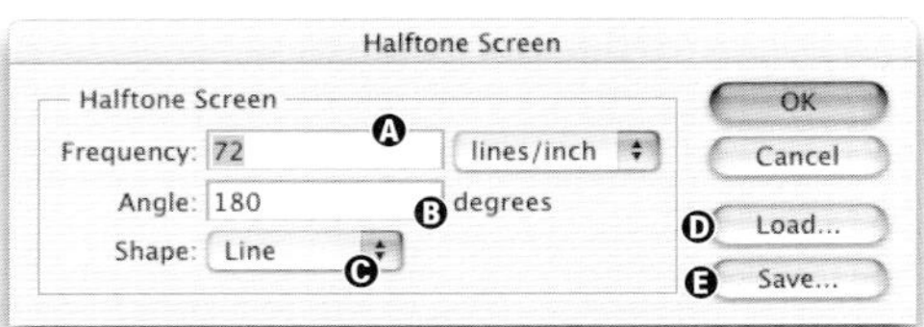

Ⓐ Enter a value (1.000 to 999.999) for the line frequency (the printing equivalent of resolution) for the bitmap. The pull-down menu to the right allows you to choose lines per inch or lines per centimeter.

Ⓑ Enter a value (–180.0000 to 180.0000) for the halftone angle.

Ⓒ Choose a shape for the halftone screen to be used in the bitmap.

Ⓓ Click to load Halftone Screen options that have the `.ahs` extension.

Ⓔ Click to save the current Halftone Screen options using the `.ahs` extension.

The image now appears in Bitmap mode.

7.8 Converting to Duotone Mode

Duotone mode can be accessed only by images currently in Grayscale mode. Follow the instructions in Section 7.6 to convert the image to Grayscale, repeat the steps to convert to Duotone, and then follow these steps:

1 In the Duotone Options dialog, choose the tone type you want to use. The number of inks available depend on the tone type selected.

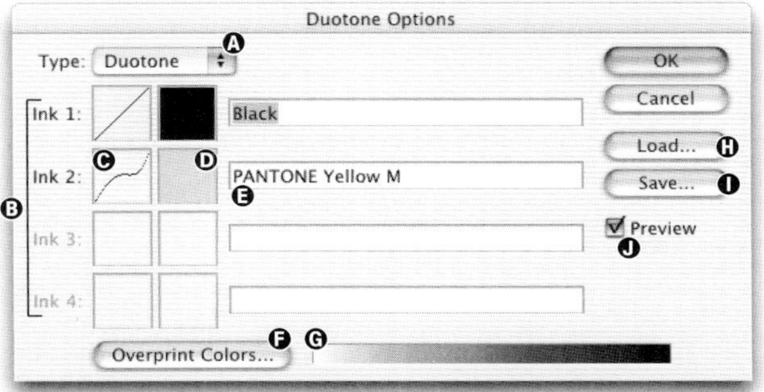

Ⓐ Choose a tone type: Monotone (one color), Duotone (two colors), Tritone (three colors), or Quadtone (four colors).

Ⓑ **Inks** Depending on the tone type selected, one to four inks are available to edit.

Ⓒ **Ink Curve** Displays a thumbnail representation of the application of the ink color at different levels. Click the thumbnail to open the Duotone Curve Editor.

Ⓓ **Ink Color** Displays the color of the ink used in this tone. Click to open the Custom Color Picker and choose a spot color.

Ⓔ **Ink Name** Displays the name of the ink. Enter a name for the color if you want to use a name that is different from the Photoshop-assigned name.

Ⓕ Click to open the Overprint Editor.

Ⓖ Displays a preview of the tonal range using the selected ink colors.

Ⓗ Click to load a file of previously saved Duotone options that have the `.ado` extension.

Ⓘ Click to save the current options as a Duotone options file that has the `.ado` extension.

Ⓙ Check if you want changes made in the Duotone Options dialog previewed in the canvas.

2 Click an ink color to use the Custom Color Picker to choose the spot color you want to use for each ink.

3 Click the ink curve to adjust the amount of ink being used at different levels (shadow to highlight) for each ink. The curve maps the grayscale value in the original image to a specific ink percentage. If you have Preview checked in the Duotone Options dialog, curve changes are reflected in the canvas. Click OK to return to the Duotone Options dialog when you are satisfied with the curve.

➠ 14.3 Selecting Colors with the Color Picker

To avoid murky colors in your Duotones, place the darkest colors at the top of the Duotone list and the lightest at the bottom. This ensures the best saturation of all colors.

If you want a Duotone to affect only part of an image, convert from Duotone to Multichannel mode (converting the Duotone colors to spot colors). You can then erase colors in the spot channels that you want printed in grayscale.

Photoshop provides several common sample duotone, tritone, and quadtone curves to get you started.

Warning: You will not be able to revert to the original duotone state (except through the History palette) if you make changes to the image in Multichannel mode. Make all adjustments in the Dutone Curves before converting to Multichannel mode for output.

Choose Duotone mode again while in Duotone mode to reopen the Duotone Options dialog.

To output duotone images for other applications, save them in EPS or PDF format, unless the image contains spot-colors in channels, in which case you should save it as DCS 2.0. Make sure to name the custom colors so that they will be recognized in the other applications.

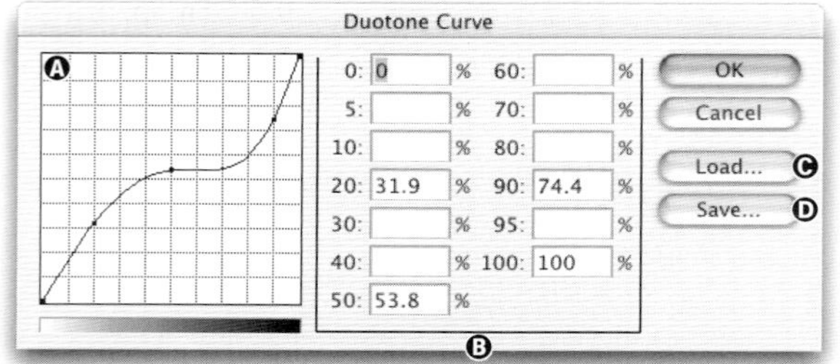

A **Ink Curve** Displays the amount of ink (vertical) for a particular level in increments of 10. Click any of the vertical lines in the graph to adjust the amount of ink being used at that level. The value is reflected in the level values input fields to the right (see B).

B **Level Values** Displays the value as a percentage for the amount of ink being used at that level. Enter a value (0.0 to 100.00) to change the value directly. The changes are reflected in the ink curve (see A).

C Click to load a file of previously saved Duotone Curve options that have the `.atf` extension.

D Click to save the current options as a Duotone Curve options file that has the `.atf` extension.

4 To view or adjust how overprinted colors display on the screen, click the Overprint Colors… button. Colors are "overprinted" when two or more unscreened inks are printed on top of each other, resulting in new color. Since several variables can affect the resulting color (paper color, order the inks are printed, slight variations in ink colors, and so on), you might need to adjust how the overprinted colors are displayed on the screen to better match how they look when printed, usually based on a preview sample from your printer. This setting does not affect the way overprinted colors are printed. Click OK when you are finished adjusting overprint colors to return to the Duotone Options dialog.

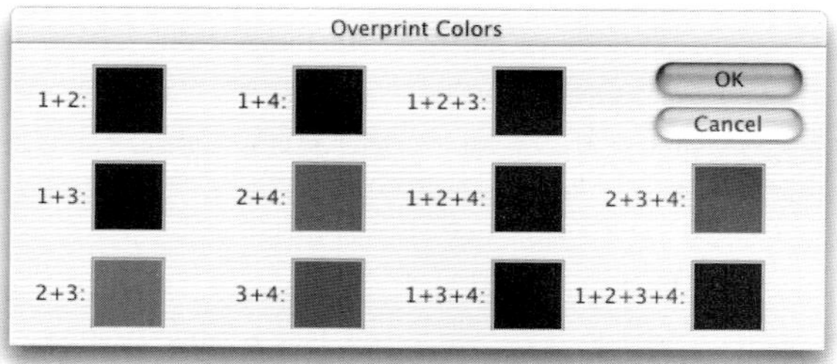

Each square represents how the two or three inks indicated next to it will appear when mixed on the screen (but *not* when printed). Click any square to open the Color Picker and adjust the color manually. Doing so is not generally recommended unless you have calibrated your monitor.

5 Click OK when you are satisfied with the Duotone. The image will now use Duotone mode.

7.9 Converting to Indexed Color Mode

Duotone mode can be accessed only by images currently in RGB, Duotone, Bitmap, or Grayscale mode. Follow the instructions in Section 7.6 to convert the image to Grayscale, Duotone, Bitmap, or RGB mode, and then repeat to convert to Indexed Color.

- If you are converting from Grayscale, Duotone, or Bitmap modes, the indexing process is automatic, and no further action is required.
- If you are converting from RGB mode, you will need to specify how the colors should be indexed in the Indexed Color dialog.

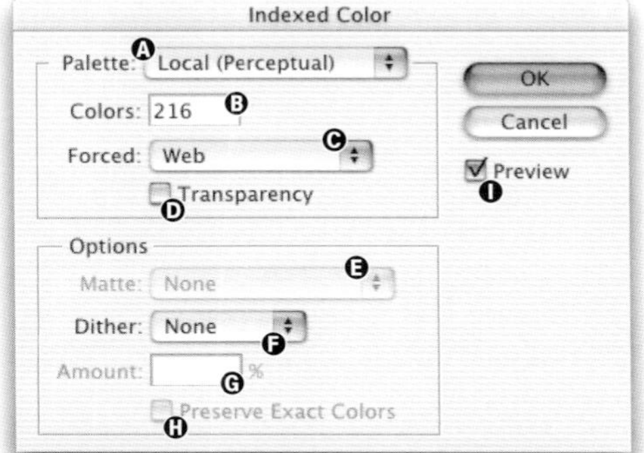

Ⓐ Choose a color palette to index to: System (Mac or Windows), Web, Uniform, Local (Perceptual, Selective, or Adaptive), Master (Perceptual, Selective, or Adaptive), Custom (allows you to edit the color table), or Previous (to use the last color palette). If there are 256 or fewer colors in the image, you can also select Exact to use all the colors in the image. Generally, Perceptual will provide the best image quality.

Ⓑ Displays the number of colors being used in the palette. For Uniform, Local, or Master palettes, enter a value (3 to 256) to set the number of colors in the palette. Fewer colors decrease file size at the expense of image quality.

Ⓒ For Exact, Local, and Master palettes, choose which colors should be forced. That is, if a color is close to a particular color value (Black And White, Primaries, or Web Safe Colors), the color is forced into that value. To edit the forced color table, select Custom….

Ⓓ Check to use 100% transparent areas of the image as a transparent color. If this option is unchecked, transparent areas in the image are filled with the matte color.

Ⓔ Choose a matte color to be used as the background of the image.

Ⓕ Choose whether you want colors dithered and the dithering type to be used.

Ⓖ If dithering is being used, enter a percentage (1 to 100) for the amount of dithering allowed in the image.

Ⓗ If diffusion dithering is being used, check to preserve the original colors for the dither.

Ⓘ Check to show a preview of the indexed image in the canvas.

➠ 25.5 Saving Your Website

Traditionally, web designers converted images to Indexed Color mode before saving them as GIFs. However, Photoshop's Save For Web dialog lets you save a copy of the image as a GIF without first converting the original image to Indexed Color.

Although you can convert an image in Indexed Color mode back to RGB or other color modes, any color lost to indexing cannot be restored.

7.10 Changing the Indexed Color Table

➠ 14.3 Selecting Colors with the Color Picker

Although you can use painting tools to edit in Indexed Color mode, you can only use colors in the indexed color palette and cannot add other colors without editing the color table.

Once a color is converted to Indexed Color mode, a color table is generated that contains all the colors in the image. You can view and edit this color table by choosing Image > Mode > Color Table….

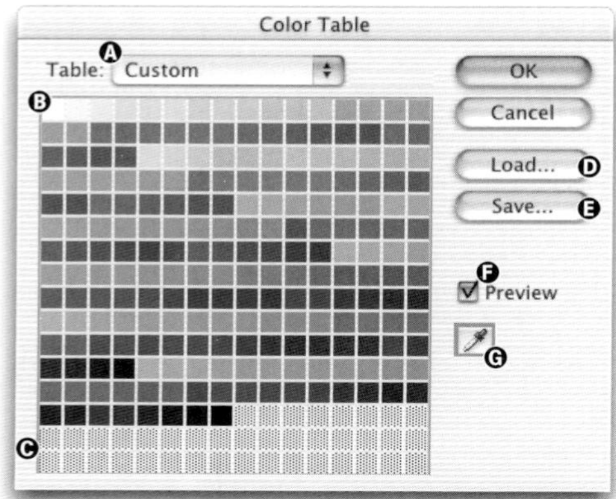

Ⓐ Select a color table to apply to the image. Custom is the color table generated when converting to Indexed Color mode. Changing the color table might produce some bizarre results.

Ⓑ **Color squares** Each square represents a color in the image. Click a square to open the Photoshop Color Picker and adjust that color's value. Command/Ctrl-click to delete the color from the table.

Ⓒ **Blank squares** Represent an unused color square in the possible 256 values in the color table. Click to open the Photoshop Color Picker and add a color in that position.

Ⓓ Click to load a color table saved with the `.act` extension.

Ⓔ Click to save the current color table as a file that has the `.act` extension.

Ⓕ Click to preview color table changes in the canvas.

Ⓖ Click and then select a color square or a color in the canvas to use as the transparent color when saving as a GIF.

CHAPTER 8

Making Selections

YOU MAKE A SELECTION in a document (whether it is a text document in Word or an image in Photoshop) to single out content to edit, copy, or move while protecting the rest of the document from changes. In Photoshop, you can select either an entire layer to edit or specific content (opaque pixels) within a layer. If you select specific content, that content is highlighted and surrounded by a marquee—a flashing dashed border often referred to as "marching ants."

This chapter looks at the various ways you can select, move, and copy content in Photoshop:

8.1 Selection Basics

➠ 2.4 Edit Menu

➠ 2.7 Select Menu

➠ 3.3 Marquee Tools

➠ 3.4 Move Tool

Lasso Tool L

Cycle Lasso Tools Shift L

Marquee Tool M

Cycle Marquee Tools Shift M

Magic Wand Tool M

Move tool V

Copy selected content to Clipboard ⌘ C / Ctrl C

Cut selected content to Clipboard ⌘ X / Ctrl X

Paste content from Clipboard ⌘ V / Ctrl V

Remember, you can keep modifying a selection at any time.

Selections can be virtually any shape within the 2-D confines of the canvas and do not have to be contiguous; that is, you can select different areas of the image that are not connected. You select content with a variety of tools—Marquees, Lassos, Magic Wands—as well as by using the Color Range and Extract dialogs. You can combine these methods to select only the areas you want to work with.

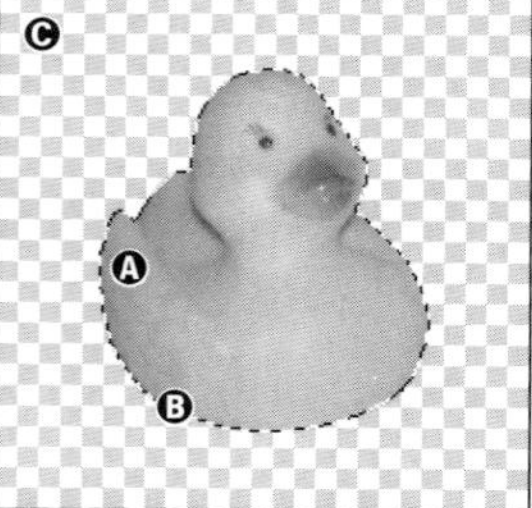

A Content Opaque pixels that you can select and edit.

B Selection border Defines the edges of the selected area(s).

C Transparent area Cannot be selected by itself although you can select a transparent area that has opaque pixels in it.

After you make a selection, you have three basic options:

Move Use the Move tool to relocate the content within the current document or to another document.

Copy/cut and paste Use the Clipboard to relocate content within the current document or to another document.

Edit Change the content.

This chapter deals with making a selection and then moving or copying that selection. Most of the rest of the book deals with editing a selection.

ANTI-ALIASING

Several selection and other tools have the option of anti-aliasing pixels. Using anti-aliasing allows Photoshop to soften the edges of images and text, making the edge pixels semitransparent so that they blend more fluidly into the background color rather than producing a hard edge.

8.2 Selecting a Layer or Its Contents

Most actions performed in Photoshop are applied to a specific layer. Therefore, before making any changes to the image, you need to make sure that the layer you want to make the changes on is selected. A selection affects the pixels in the currently selected (active) layer.

- 1.4 The Document Window
- 2.6 Layer Menu
- 2.7 Select Menu
- 4.11 Layers Palette
- 9 Image Layering

Selecting a Layer

You can select a layer in the following ways:

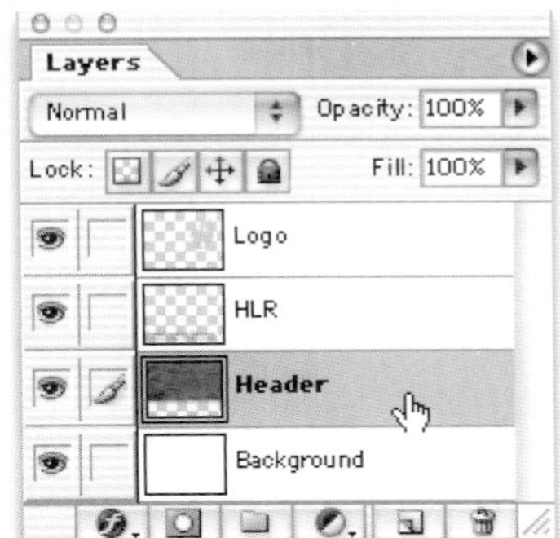

In the Layers palette, click the layer's thumbnail or title. The layer is highlighted with a brush icon in the left column to indicate it is active. Here, the layer "Header" has been selected.

Or, select the Move tool . Control/right-click in the canvas on content in the layer you want to select. A contextual menu appears listing all the layers with content currently under the mouse cursor. Select the layer from the list.

If you do not select any specific content in the layer using the techniques shown in the rest of the chapter, changes are applied to the entire layer.

Selecting a Layer's Content

To select only the opaque pixels of the layer and exclude all transparent pixels, do one of the following:

- Select a layer as described earlier, choose Select > All (a marquee appears around the entire canvas), and then move the layer using either the mouse or arrow keys.
- Command/Ctrl-click the layer in the Layers palette.
- Control/right-click a layer thumbnail in the Layers palette and choose Layer Transparency from the contextual menu.

Select All
⌘ A
Ctrl A

A few tools, such as Smudge, include an option that allows you to work with multiple layers simultaneously.

If there are no opaque pixels in a selected area (that is, the area is empty), you will not be able to move, copy, cut, or transform the selected area.

In this chapter, all the methods for making and working with selections have a common goal: surrounding the area that you want to edit, copy, or move in the fill image. With some selections, close is close enough, but for others, you need to capture the exact pixels as precisely as possible.

8.3 Selecting Rectangular or Elliptical Areas

➡ 2.4 Edit Menu
➡ 2.7 Select Menu
➡ 3.3 Marquee Tools
➡ 3.4 Move Tool
➡ 4.4 Info Palette

Marquee tool [M]

Cycle marquee tools [Shift] [M]

If there is no existing selection, constrain proportions (square or circle); if there is an existing selection, add to the current selection (press Shift again while selecting to constrain proportions). [Shift] **plus select**

Subtract from the current selection [Option] **plus select** [Alt] **plus select**

Hold down while making a selection to move the marquee [Spacebar]

Cancel a selection in progress (previous selections are preserved) [Esc]

If you move a selection, either using the Move tool or the arrow keys, the selection collapses around the content within the selection for the current layer.

As you make your selection, the width, height, and origin point of the selection are displayed in the Info palette.

A common way to begin a selection is to use the marquee tools, which allow you to select a regular rectangular or elliptical region of the canvas. Making such a selection is often a helpful way to begin a more complex selection or to define the area to begin an edit. For example, if you are creating a rectangular button, select a rectangular area to define the size of the button and then begin to edit the selection.

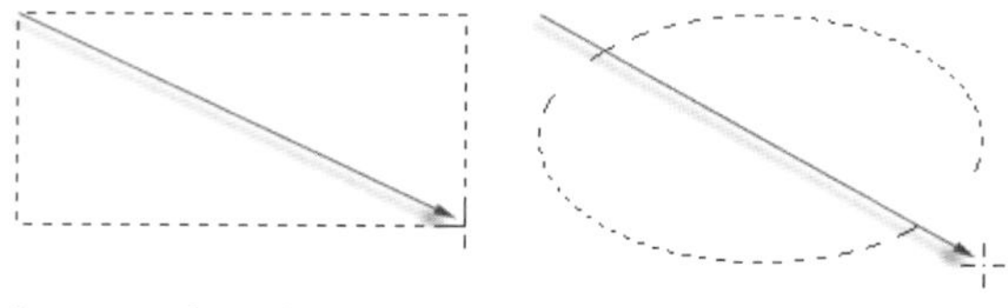

A rectangular selection — An elliptical selection

To use the marquee tools, follow these steps:

1 Select a layer as described in Section 8.2.

2 Choose a marquee tool from the toolbox:

- Rectangular Marquee
- Elliptical Marquee
- Single Row Marquee
- Single Column Marquee

3 Set the options in the tool options bar for this selection:

- Choose how the new selection should be treated in relation to the current selection: deselect the current selection and start a new selection, add to the current selection, subtract from the current selection, or intersect with the current selection.
- If you are using the Rectangular Marquee or Elliptical Marquee tools, enter the amount of feathering for the new selection (0 is no feathering), specify whether you want the selection anti-aliased so that edges are softer, and choose a style for the selection (Normal, Fixed Aspect Ratio, or Fixed Size).
- If you selected Fixed Aspect Ratio or Fixed Size, enter an aspect ratio or width and height.

4 Depending on the marquee tool and options selected, do one of the following in the canvas:

Rectangular or Elliptical Marquee Click and drag diagonally across the area you want to select. The marquee border surrounds the selected area.

Single Row or Single Column Marquee Click and drag to select a row or column.

If you selected Fixed Size, click in the top-left corner of where you want the selection and drag until the selection is positioned exactly where you want it.

5 You can now refine the selection further or edit the selection.

8.4 Creating a Free-Form Selection

To capture irregular shapes, you can use three free-form lasso tools, or you can use a Quick Mask to "paint" the area to be selected.

Using the Lasso and Polygonal Lasso Tools

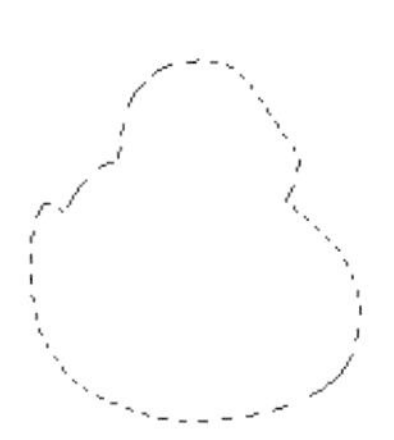

A curved selection made with the Lasso tool

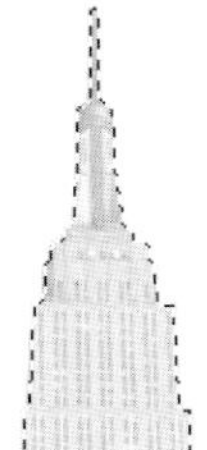

The straight edges of the Empire State Building captured with the Polygonal Lasso tool

You can use the Lasso and Polygonal Lasso tools to freehand trace the outline of the area you want to select. Follow these steps:

1 Select a layer as described in Section 8.2.

2 Choose the Lasso or Polygonal Lasso tool.

3 Set the options in the tool options bar for this selection:

- Choose how the new selection should be treated in relation to the current selection: deselect the current selection and start a new selection, add to the current selection, subtract from the current selection, or intersect with the current selection.
- Enter the amount of feathering for the new selection (0 is no feathering).
- Specify whether you want the selection anti-aliased so that edges are softer.

4 Depending on the Lasso tool selected, do one of the following:

Lasso Click and drag around the area you want to select. When you release the mouse button, the selection is automatically closed by a straight line between the starting and stopping points.

Polygonal Lasso Click at points around the area you want to select to create straight sides. To close the selection, click back on the first point (the Polygonal Lasso icon appears with a circle next to it when you are over the point). You can also Command/Ctrl-click or double-click to close the selection with a straight line between the starting and stopping points.

5 You can now refine the selection further or edit the selection as explained in the rest of the chapter.

➠ 2.7 Select Menu

➠ 3.5 Lasso Tools

➠ 7.5 Using Color in Channels

➠ 11 Masking Layers

➠ 12.7 Drawing with Pen and Shape Tools

Lasso tool [L]

Cycle lasso tools
[Shift] [L]

Add to the current selection
[Shift] **plus select**

Subtract from the current selection
[Option] **plus select**
[Alt] **plus select**

Cancel a selection in progress (previous selections are preserved)
[Esc]

8.4 Creating a Free-Form Selection *(Continued)*

Erase the last anchor point of Polygonal or Magnetic Lasso tools

Del

Switch from Magnetic Lasso to Lasso (reverts after release)

Option

Alt

Switch from Magnetic Lasso to Polygonal Lasso (reverts after first click after release)

Option click

Alt click

Increase the Magnetic Lasso width by 1 pixel

]

Decrease the Magnetic Lasso width by 1 pixel

Toggle Standard and Quick Mask mode

Q

Using the Magnetic Lasso Tool

The Magnetic Lasso tool goes one step further than other lasso tools by automatically following the edge of the object you are trying to select that is embedded in the image. Photoshop does this by looking at the contrast between pixels to determine where the boundary is. The results are not always perfect, and you will need to adjust the options for some objects, but this technique can save a lot of time. Follow these steps:

1 Select a layer as described in Section 8.2.

2 Choose the Magnetic Lasso tool .

3 Set the options in the tool options bar for this selection:

- Choose how the new selection should be treated in relation to the current selection: deselect the current selection and start a new selection, add to the current selection, subtract from the current selection, or intersect with the current selection.
- Enter the amount of feathering for the new selection (0 is no feathering).
- Specify whether you want the selection anti-aliased so that edges are softer.
- Enter the width from the mouse pointer to be considered as part of the path. If the image is high contrast, use a wide line to ensure a solid edge. If there are a lot of small shapes, use a width larger than 10 pixels.
- Enter the percentage of contrast between edges in the image to be considered for the path. Use a high percentage for high-contrast images to ensure a tighter fit.
- Under Frequency, enter a number (1 to 100) for how often anchor points are automatically added along the path. The more points, the tighter the fit, but the more jagged the selection may appear.
- If you are using the Magnetic Lasso tool and a tablet, specify whether you want to allow pen pressure to set the width.

4 Click to set the first anchor point in the selection. Drag around the edge of the object you are attempting to select. A selection path (a solid line) snaps to the edge of the object as you drag. The settings for Width, Edge Contrast, and Frequency determine the fit of the selection.

If you notice that the selection is moving away from the object's edge, move back to the point where it started to deviate (unlike the other free-form selection tools, you can move back along your path), click to manually add an anchor point, and then continue your selection.

5 To close the magnetic selection, do one of the following:

- Click back on the first point (the Magnetic Lasso icon appears with a circle next to it when you are over the point).

- Command/Ctrl-click, press Return/Enter, or double-click to close the selection with a magnetic path line directly between the starting and stopping points calculated by Photoshop.
- Option/Alt-double-click to close the selection with a straight line between the starting and stopping points.

The magnetic selection surrounds the eagle statue.

6 You can now refine the selection further or edit the selection.

Using Quick Mask to Make a Selection

Using Quick Mask to create a selection is conceptually the opposite from other selection methods. Rather than tracing the border of the selection, you use painting tools to select the interior of the selection. The Quick Mask channel works as an onionskin layer that you can manipulate independently of the image itself, allowing you to use tools to "draw" your selection as an alpha channel. Using this technique, you can create some great rough selections that would be nigh impossible with other selection tools. Follow these steps:

1 Choose the Quick Mask Mode option on the toolbar. A new Quick Mask channel appears, and your foreground and background colors are transferred to black and white.

2 Choose any painting tool to draw on and manipulate the Quick Mask channel. You will see a semitransparent red mark to show where you are painting.

The mask is being painted over the image.

3 After you paint your mask, select the Standard Mode button in the toolbar to turn the mask into a selection. Click back to Quick Mask mode to turn the current selection back into a mask and continue editing.

You can still make selections in Quick Mask mode to limit the area in which you are making your Quick Mask.

Another way to make a free-form selection is to use the Pen tool to create a path and then turn the path into a selection.

When making precise selections, it is helpful to zoom in to the image as much as possible to see greater detail.

To help make Magnetic Lasso selections, increase the difference between edges in the image by adding a Brightness/Contrast fill layer and increasing contrast.

8.5 Selecting Colors

➠ 2.7 Select Menu

➠ 3.6 Magic Wand Tool

➠ 13.8 Using Replace Color

Magic wand [W]

You can select a particular color or color range in the image. If your image contains large areas of flat color, this task is easy. If there are a lot of tonal changes in the area you want to select, you might have to play with your settings to get the desired selection.

Using the Magic Wand Tool

You can use the Magic Wand tool to click a single pixel in your image to select that color and similar colors immediately surrounding it or throughout the image. Follow these steps:

1. Select a layer as described in Section 8.2.
2. Choose the Magic Wand tool.
3. Set the options in the tool options bar for this selection:
   - Choose how the new selection should be treated in relation to the current selection: deselect the current selection and start a new selection, add to the current selection, subtract from the current selection, or intersect with the current selection.
   - Enter the color Tolerance (0 to 255) for the selection. This number specifies how similar a color has to be to the color clicked to be included in the selection. The higher the number, the more tolerant the selection.
   - If checked, anti-aliasing is used to give the edges of the selection a smoother appearance.
   - If Contiguous is checked, only pixels touching the selected pixel and within the set tolerance are included in the selection. Otherwise, the Magic Wand tool selects all pixels in the image within the tolerance level.
   - If Use All Layers is checked, the Magic Wand selects pixels on all layers in the image. Otherwise, the Magic Wand tool works only within the selected layer.
4. In the canvas, click a pixel of the color you want to select. You can now refine the selection further or edit the selection.

A Magic Wand selection with a Tolerance of 25 and Contiguous checked. The selection is stopped by the black line.

A Magic Wand selection with a Tolerance of 150 and Contiguous unchecked. More pixels are selected, and the selection is not stopped by the black line.

8.5 Selecting Colors *(Continued)*

Using the Color Range Dialog

You can use the Color Range dialog to select specific colors throughout all layers of an image or to select colors with a specific luminosity or hue range. Follow these steps:

1 Make sure all layers to be considered for the color selection are currently visible. If you want, you can also limit the area being considered by making a selection.

2 Choose Select > Color Range to open the Color Range dialog.

3 Set the options in the dialog:

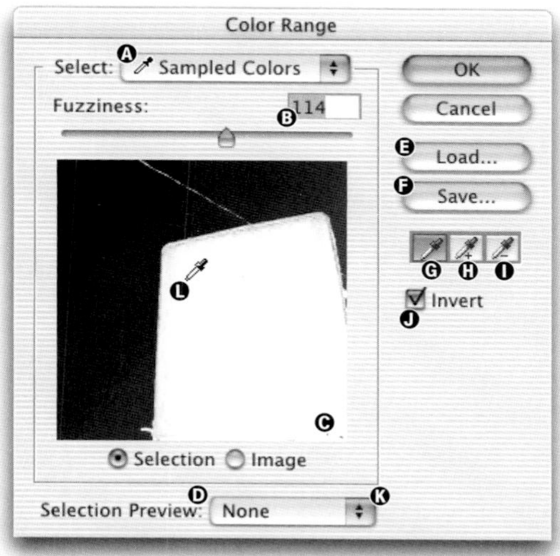

A Choose to select colors directly from the image or to select a particular color, luminosity, or out-of-gamut colors.

B Click to enter or use the slider to set the level of fuzziness (0 to 200), which is much like color tolerance.

C **Preview** Shows the image, the selected area (white indicates a selected area), or a reduced version of the original image.

D Choose a preview method for the canvas, showing the selection either as grayscale (shown) or the full image.

E Click to load previously saved settings.

F Click to save the current settings.

G **Eyedropper tool** Click to select a new color. This action deselects other colors currently selected.

H **+ Eyedropper tool** Click to select a color to add to the current range.

I **– Eyedropper tool** Click to select a color to remove from the current range.

J If checked, the selection is inverted.

K Choose a method for previewing the selection in the canvas : None, Grayscale, Black Matte, White Matte, Quick Mask.

L Use the Eyedropper tool to select colors in the preview area, in the document windows, or from any color swatch in the interface.

4 Choose the Eyedropper tool and then click a color in the selection preview or in the canvas itself (if visible behind the dialog). That color is selected. Use the + Eyedropper tool to add additional colors, or use the – Eyedropper tool to subtract selected colors. You can adjust the Fuzziness setting to include or exclude more colors.

5 When you are satisfied with the selection, click OK. You can now refine the selection further or edit the selection.

Although selecting a color range is a good way to re-color a certain color, special color correction tools are available for that as well (see Section 13.8).

When selecting specific colors for editing, be careful not to create sharp changes in the color that will look strange when printed.

8.6 Refining the Selection

➠ 2.7 Select Menu

➠ 3.3 Marquee Tools

➠ 3.5 Lasso Tools

➠ 3.6 Magic Wand Tool

Lasso tool L

Cycle lasso tools Shift L

Marquee tools Shift M

Magic wand tool W

After making an initial selection, you can add to or subtract from the selection in a variety of ways.

Ⓐ New Selection

Ⓑ Add To Selection

Ⓒ Subtract From Selection

Ⓓ Intersect Selections

Using Selection Tools to Add to or Subtract from a Selection

You can use all the selection tools (Marquee, Lasso, and Magic Wand) to add to or subtract from an existing selection. Depending on the tool you are using, the cursor icon will have a plus (+) next to it when adding or a minus (–) when subtracting.

You can add or subtract using the selection tools in two ways:

- Choose a selection tool, and then click the Add To Selection or Subtract From Selection button in the tool options bar. Set other options for the selection tool as desired, and then follow the instructions for selecting with that tool. The new selection is added to or subtracted from the original selection.
- Choose a selection tool, set options in the tool options bar, and then hold down the Option/Alt (subtract) or the Shift (add) key while following the instructions for selecting with the current tool. The new selection is added to or subtracted from the original selection.

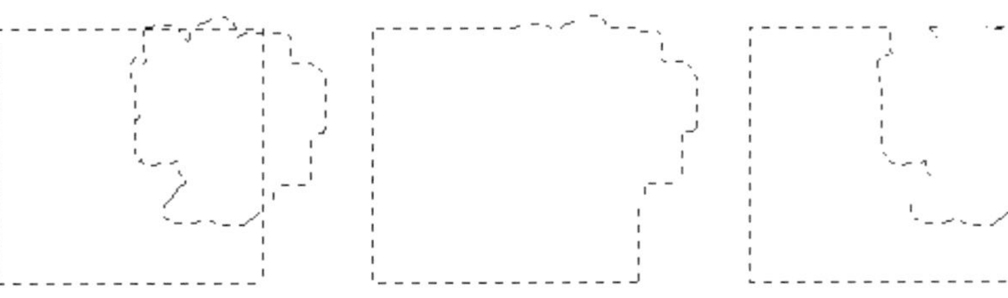

The original selection (square) and the new selection.

The new selection has been added to the original selection.

The new selection has been deleted from the original selection.

8.6 Refining the Selection *(Continued)*

Using Selection Tools to Intersect a Selection

Use selection tools to select the common area between an existing selection and a new selection. When you are creating an intersection, the cursor icon will have an *X* next to it. Follow these steps:

1. Choose a selection tool, click the Intersect button, and set the other options in the tool options bar.
2. Follow the instructions for the tools being used to make a second selection. Make sure that the new selection overlaps the existing selection; if it does not, no pixels will be selected.

The new selection has intersected the original selection.

Softening the Selection's Edges

Feathering is the process of softening the edges of a selection, making a gradual fading transition from the boundary of the selection inward. You can set feathering as an option in the tool options bar before making most selections (except with the Magic Wand), but you can also set feathering after making a selection. Follow these steps:

1. Choose Select > Feather….
2. Enter the number of pixels you want to be feathered from the edge of the selection marquee in the Feather Selection dialog. The number you choose depends not only on the amount of fade you want, but also on the size of the actual selection and the resolution of the image. A higher resolution image requires greater feathering in order to produce the same amount of fade as a lower resolution image.
3. Click OK. The selection is now feathered at the edges.

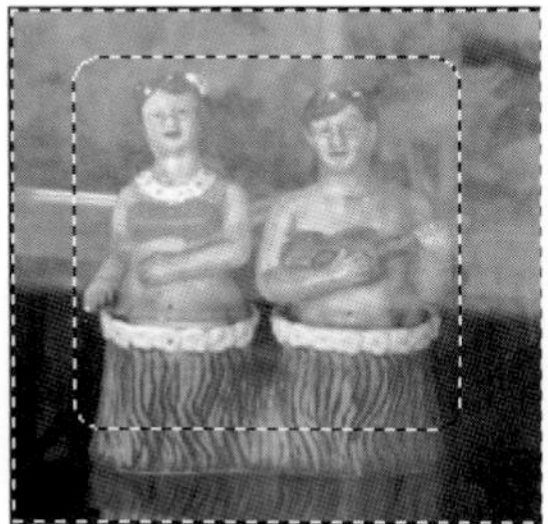

The content around the center of the image has been selected and feathered.

You can really see the effects of the feathering when the selection is deleted.

Add to the current selection

Shift plus select

Subtract from the current selection

Option plus select

Alt plus select

Cancel a selection in progress (previous selections are preserved)

Esc

Warning: Don't confuse moving the selection marquee with moving the selected content. You can move the marquee using any selection tool, and doing so does not affect the image. You can move the selected content only using the Move tool.

8.6 Refining the Selection *(Continued)*

To capture an exact area, you must use a variety of methods to make your selection and then further refine and modify the selection. You can continually modify selections at any time while working with them.

Selection marquees that have been feathered have rounded edges at the corners.

Modifying a Selection

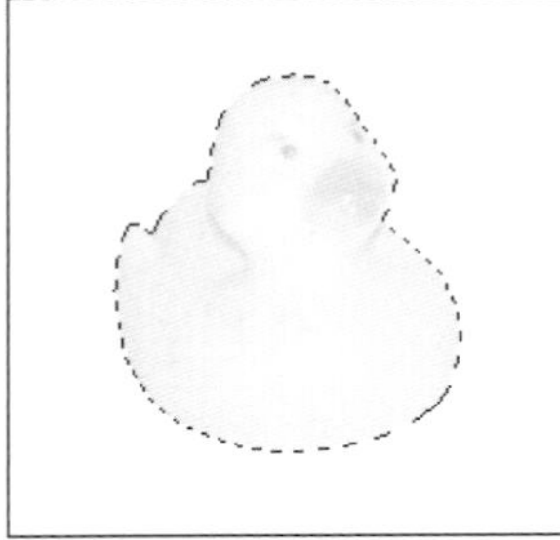

The original selection to be modified

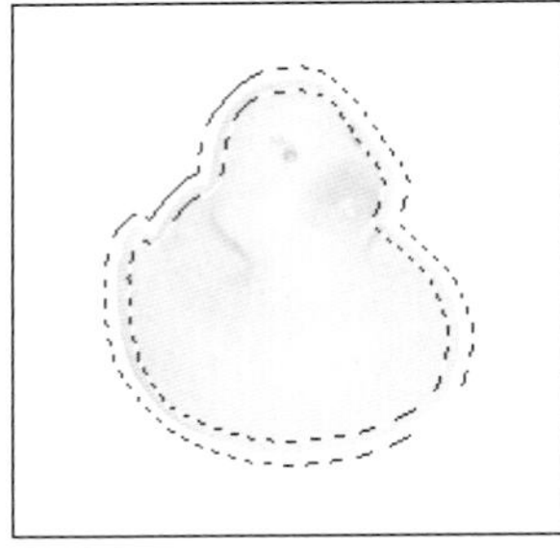

A 10-pixel border selected

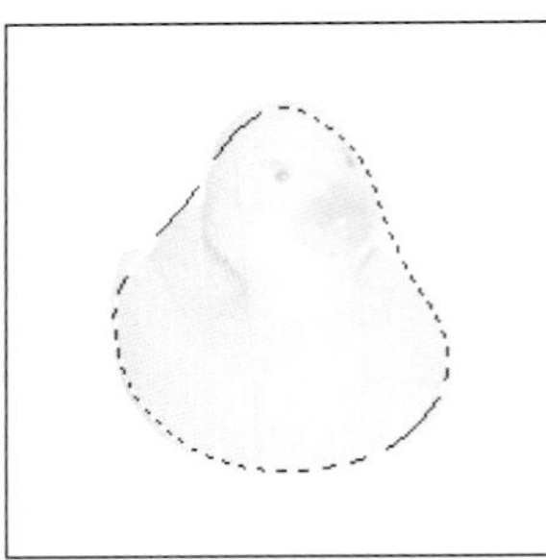

Smoothed to 20 pixels

Four modify options allow you to change the size of the selection numerically.

- To **select** a border around a selection, choose Select > Modify > Border…, enter the size of the border, and click OK. The selection is changed to a border of the set thickness around the position of the original border.
- To **smooth** a rough selection, choose Select > Modify > Smooth…, enter the amount of smoothing you want (higher numbers create smoother selections), and click OK. The selection will flatten sharp picks and dips within a jagged selection by the amount you indicated. Smooth is most effective in RGB mode.
- To **enlarge** the size of the selection, choose Select > Modify > Expand…, enter the number of pixels to enlarge the selection, and click OK. The selection expands by that amount.
- To **reduce** the size of the selection, choose Select > Modify > Contract…, enter the number of pixels by which to reduce the selection, and click OK. The selection contracts by that amount.

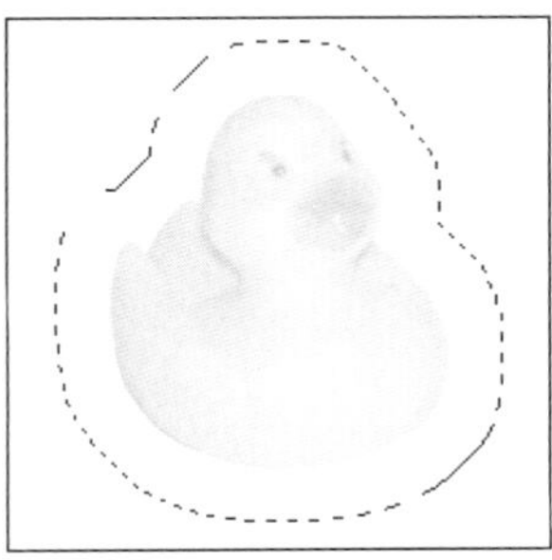

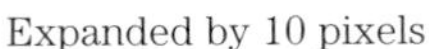

Expanded by 10 pixels

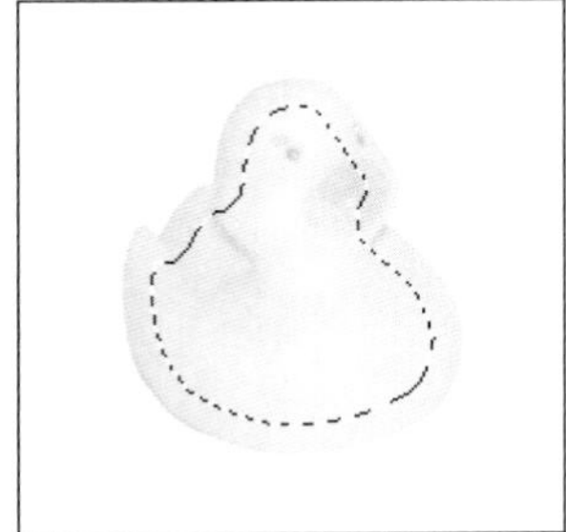

Contracted by 10 pixels

8.6 Refining the Selection *(Continued)*

Enlarging a Selection Based on Color

To enlarge a selection based on color, follow these steps:

1. Choose the Magic Wand tool, and set the color tolerance (0 to 255) in the tool options bar.
2. Choose one of the options:
   - To add *contiguous* pixels to the selection based on the current Tolerance, choose Select > Grow. The selection expands to include colors immediately around the image based on the selected area and within the set tolerance.
   - To add *noncontiguous* pixels to the selection based on the current Tolerance, choose Select > Similar. The selection expands to include colors throughout the image based on the selected area and within the set tolerance.

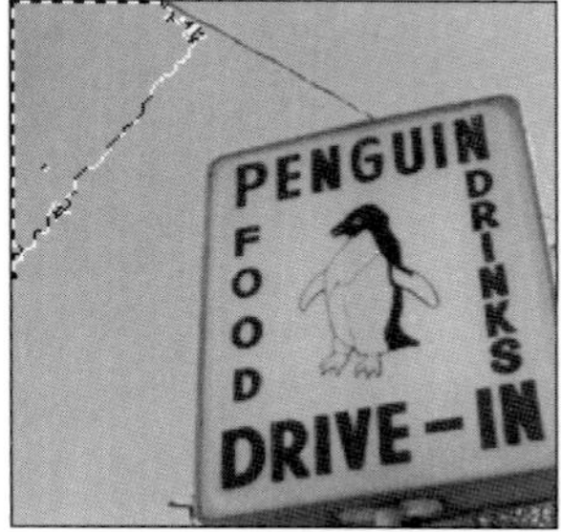

The original selection to be modified

Grow: The selection grows to include similar pixels in the same area.

Similar: The selection includes similar pixels throughout the image.

ALPHA CHANNELS AND SELECTIONS

When you save a selection, it is turned into an alpha channel and stored in the Channels palette. This feature gives you a lot of power to control and manipulate the selection, which is discussed in further detail in Chapter 11.

8.7 Changing the Selection

➠ 2.7 Select Menu
➠ 3.3 Marquee Tools
➠ 3.4 Move Tools
➠ 3.5 Lasso Tools
➠ 3.6 Magic Wand Tool
➠ 8.8 Transforming a Layer or Selected Content

After you make a selection, you can move and distort independently of the content underneath.

Moving the Selection Marquee

You can move the selection marquee independently of the actual image content, which allows you to make a selection in one layer or area and then transfer the selection to another layer or area without affecting the content.

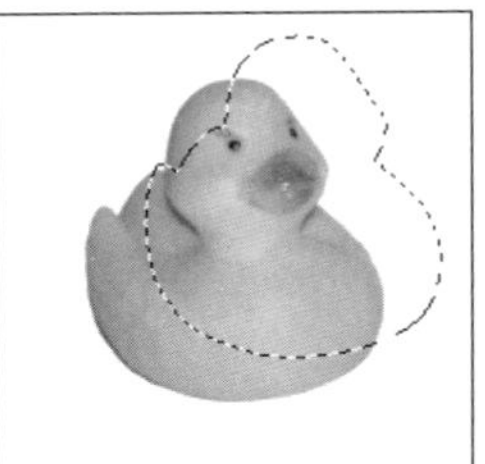

The selection is moved, but the content remains in the same place.

- To move the selection marquee **within a layer**, choose any selection tool and select the New Selection button in the tool options bar. Now either click and drag anywhere within the selection or use the arrow keys to move the selection.
- To move the selection marquee **to another layer**, simply select the target layer using one of the methods discussed in Section 8.2.
- To move the selection marquee **between open Photoshop documents**, choose any selection tool and select the New Selection button in the tool options bar. Now click anywhere within the selection and drag it from the original document into the target document's canvas. The selection is placed into the currently selected layer of the target document. The selection marquee is still available in the original document as well.

Transforming the Selection Marquee

You can transform a selection marquee: you can scale it, skew it, distort it, and add perspective to it. You transform a selection marquee on a bounding box, in much the same way that you transform content, but only the selection marquee is affected, not the selected content.

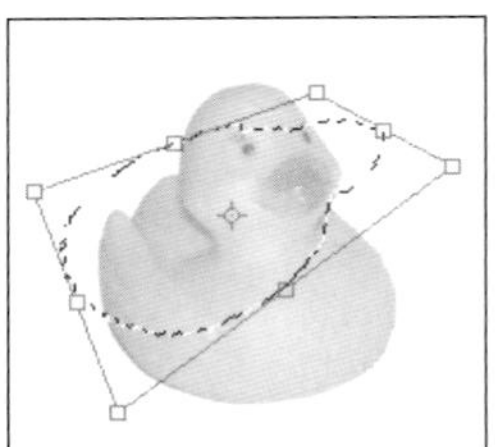

The marquee transformed with the reference point moved to the right. Notice that the content underneath remains unaffected.

8.7 Changing the Selection *(Continued)*

To transform the selection marquee, follow these steps:

1 Choose Select > Transform Selection to display a rectangular bounding box around the entire selection.

2 Make one or more of the following transformations to the marquee:

- To **move** the entire selection marquee, click and drag within the bounding box except at the exact center.

- To adjust the **reference point** (which sets the center for transformations), click and drag it to the desired location.

- To **scale** the selection marquee, click and drag an edge of the bounding box. Click corner points to resize both horizontally and vertically at the same time.

- To **symmetrically scale** the selection marquee around the reference point, Option/Alt-click and drag an edge or a corner point of the bounding box.

- To **rotate** the selection marquee around the reference point, click and drag just outside the bounding box.

- To **skew** the selection marquee, Shift-Command-click/Shift-Ctrl-click and drag an edge of the bounding box.

- To **distort** the selection marquee, Command/Ctrl-click and drag edges or corner points of the bounding box.

- To **symmetrically distort** the selection marquee around the reference point, Option-Command-click/Alt-Ctrl-click and drag edges or corner points of the bounding box.

- To add **perspective** to the selection marquee, Control/right-click and select Perspective from the contextual menu. Click and drag on an edge or a corner point to change the selection's perspective.

3 Click the Commit button ✓ in the tool options bar or press Enter to accept the transformations. Click the Cancel button ⃠ or press Esc to cancel transformations and leave the selection unchanged.

Move tool V

Invert selection
Shift ⌘ I
Shift Ctrl I

Deselect
⌘ D
Ctrl D

Reselect last selection
Shift ⌘ D
Shift Ctrl D

Warning: Don't confuse inverting the selection (the Inverse command) with inverting colors. The two processes have similar names and keyboard shortcuts, but produce very different results.

Switching Selected and Unselected Areas

Often it is easier to select the area that you do *not* want selected than the area you want selected. For example, it is easier to select a flat colored background that surrounds a complexly shaped object rather than trying to select the object itself. In these cases, you then need to invert the selection to select the desired area. First make a selection, and then choose Select > Inverse. You can then refine the selection further or edit the selection.

The selection has been inverted. Notice that the selection marquee follows the edges of the canvas.

Deselecting and Reselecting a Selection

When you are finished with a selection, you can either save it or, more likely, deselect the area to begin working on something else.

- To **deselect** a selection, choose Select > Deselect or click anywhere on the canvas outside the selected area.
- To **reselect** the last selection, choose Select > Reselect. If the last action was to deselect a selection, you can also choose Edit > Undo.
- Actions with the selections are recorded in the History palette, so you can choose Edit > Step Backward and Edit > Step Forward.

8.8 Transforming a Layer or Selected Content

After you make a selection, you can manipulate its content within. One way to do this is to transform the content by scaling, skewing, distorting, or adding perspective to the selection.

To make a transformation, you can use menu commands or use the transformation pseudotools that are accessed through menu options rather than through the Toolbox.

You perform pseudotool transformations on a rectangular bounding box that appears around the selection.

➟ 2.7 Select Menu

➟ 3.4 Move Tools

Move tool V

Free transform
⌘ T
Ctrl T

Transform again
Shift ⌘ T
Shift Ctrl T

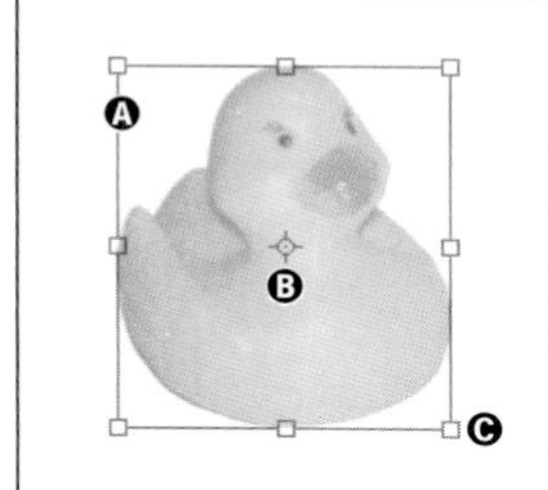

Ⓐ Bounding box edge
Ⓑ Reference point
Ⓒ Corner point

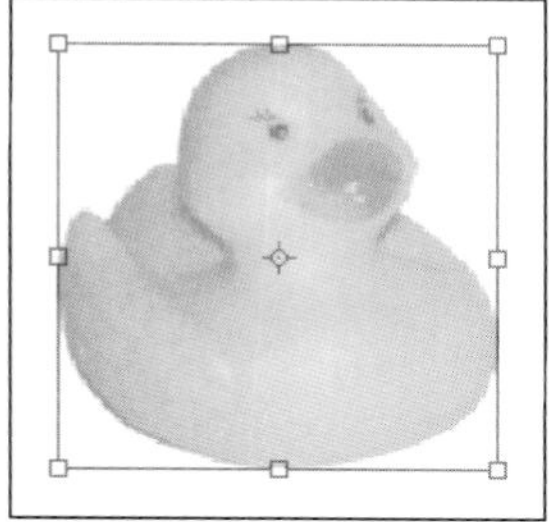

Scale transformation

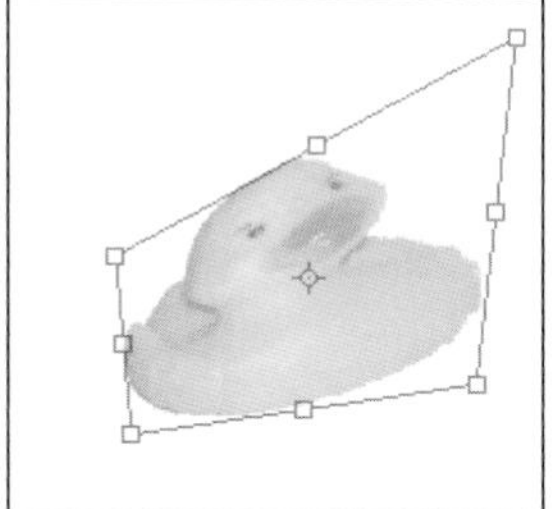

Skew transformation

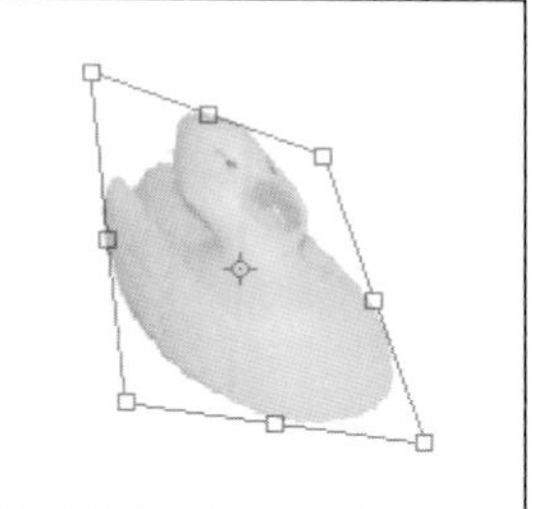

Distort transformation

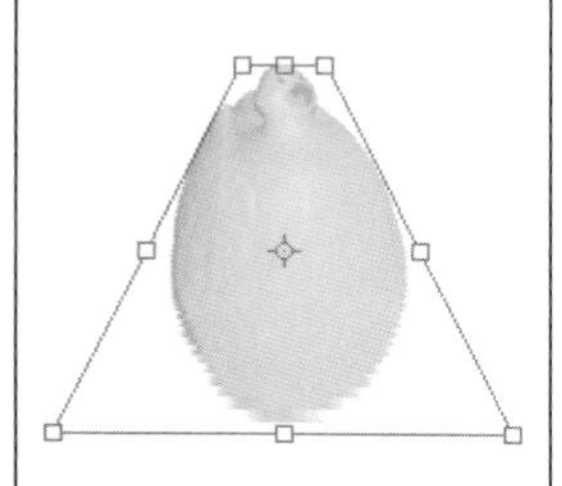

Perspective transformation

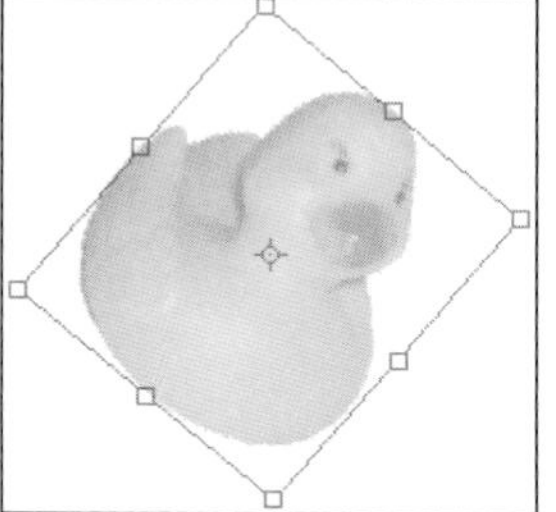

Rotate transformation

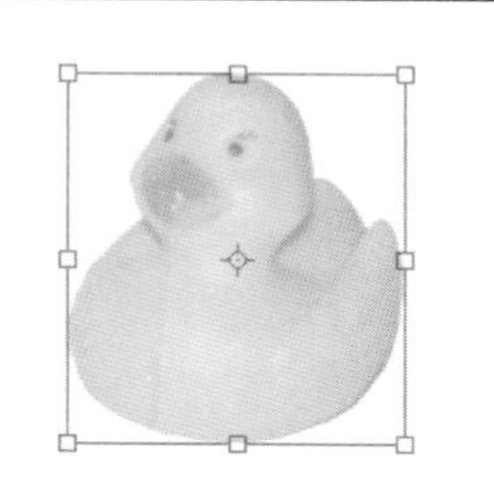

Flip transformation

8.8 Transforming a Layer or Selected Content

(Continued)

Commit transformation

Return

Enter

Cancel transformation

Esc

The Enter key is primarily used in Windows or the Mac to commit a change after it has been made. The Return key also does the same thing on the Mac.

Using the Free Transform Pseudotool

The most common way to make transformations is to use the Free Transform pseudotool, which allows you to make any of the transformations. Which transformation you make depends on where you click or which keyboard or menu modifiers you choose. To use the Free Transform pseudotool, follow these steps:

1. Select a layer to transform. You can also select specific content on the layer. If no content is selected on the layer, the transformation is applied to the entire layer.
2. Choose Select > Transform Selection to display a rectangular bounding box around the entire selection.
3. Make one or more of the following transformations:
   - To **move** the entire selection, click and drag within the bounding box.
   - To adjust the **reference point** (which sets the center for transformations), click and drag it to the desired location.
   - To **scale** the selection, click and drag an edge of the bounding box. Click on corner points to resize both horizontally and vertically at the same time.
   - To **symmetrically scale** the selection around the reference point, Option/Alt-click and drag an edge or a corner point of the bounding box.
   - To **rotate** the selection around the reference point, click and drag just outside (but not touching) the bounding box.
   - To **skew** the selection, Shift-Command-click/Shift-Ctrl-click and drag an edge of the bounding box up or down.
   - To **symmetrically skew** the selection, Option-Command-click/Alt-Ctrl-click and drag an edge of the bounding box up or down.
   - To **distort** the selection, Command/Ctrl-click and drag edges or corner points of the bounding box.
   - To **symmetrically distort** the selection around the reference point, Option-Command-click/Alt-Ctrl-click and drag edges or corner points of the bounding box.
   - To add **perspective** to the selection, Control/right-click and select Perspective from the contextual menu. Click and drag on an edge or a corner point to change the selection's perspective.
4. Click the Commit button ✓ in the tool options bar or press Enter to accept the transformations. Click the Cancel button ⃠ or press Esc to cancel transformations and leave the selection unchanged.

8.8 Transforming a Layer or Selected Content

(Continued)

Using Commands and Pseudotools

You can also access each transformation pseudotool independently. This allows you to focus on making one kind of transformation without worrying about whether you have your mouse in the right position or the right keyboard modifier pressed.

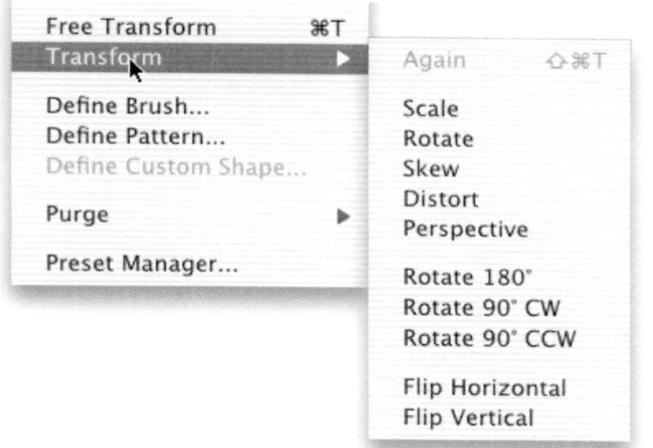

The Transform submenu

Do not confuse transforming the selection marquee and transforming the selected content.

Transformed content is interpolated using the method currently set in your preferences.

To transform using commands and pseudotools, follow these steps:

1 Select a layer to transform. You can also select specific content on the layer. If no content is selected on the layer, the transformation is applied to the entire layer.

2 Choose Edit > Transform and then one of the options in the submenu. You can select different pseudotools to work with while making transformations, using either the Edit > Transform menu or the contextual menu.

Again Choose to repeat the previous transformation performed.

Scale Choose to use the Scale pseudotool. Click and drag an edge of the bounding box to resize. Click on corner points of the bounding box to resize both horizontally and vertically at the same time. Press Option/Alt to scale symmetrically.

Rotate Choose to use the Rotate pseudotool. Click and drag just outside the edges of the bounding box to freely rotate the selection.

Skew Choose to use the Skew pseudotool. Drag an edge of the bounding box up or down to skew. Press Option/Alt to skew symmetrically.

Distort Choose to use the Distort pseudotool. Drag edges or corner points of the bounding box. Press Option/Alt to distort symmetrically.

Perspective Choose to use the Perspective pseudotool. Click and drag on an edge or a corner point to change the perspective.

Rotate 180°, 90° CW, or 90° CCW Choose to turn the entire selected region.

Flip Horizontal or Vertical Choose to reverse the area in the indicated direction.

8.8 Transforming a Layer or Selected Content

(Continued)

3 Click the Commit button ✓ in the tool options bar or press Enter to accept the transformations. Click the Cancel button ⊘ or press Esc to cancel transformations and leave the selection unchanged.

Using the Transform Tool Options Bar

Even though they are not a real tools (at least they are not in the Toolbox), all transform pseudotools have options in the tool options bar that allow you to make transformations numerically. Follow these steps:

1 Select a layer to transform. You can also select specific content on the layer. If no content is selected on the layer, the transformation is applied to the entire layer.

2 Select a Transform pseudotool from the Edit > Transform submenu, or choose Edit > Free Transform.

3 Set the options in the tool options bar.

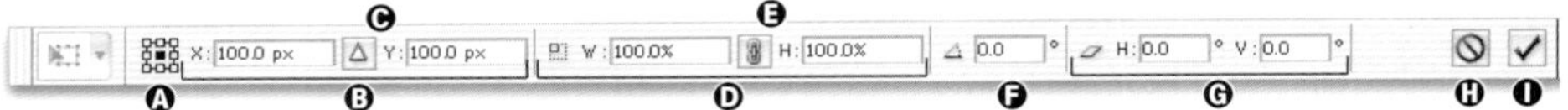

A Reference Point Location Click one of the open squares to set the relative position of the reference point in relation to the bounding box.

B Reference Point Horizontal And Vertical Position Enter an exact position for the reference point in the canvas.

C Use Relative Position For Reference Point Click if you want the units for horizontal and vertical to show the position of the reference point location relative to its initial location.

D Set Horizontal And Vertical Scale Enter the width and height (as percentages) for the bounding box.

E Link Scales Click if you want the horizontal and vertical values to remain relative to each other.

F Set Rotation Enter a value (–180 to 180) in degrees to specify the angle of the selection.

G Set Horizontal And Vertical Skew Enter values (–180 to 180) in degrees to specify the amount of twist to be applied to the selection.

H Cancel Transformation Click to reject transformation changes.

I Commit Transformation Click to accept transformation changes.

8.9 Moving Selected Content

Possibly the most common thing you will do with selected content is to move it around in the canvas window. Although this task is seemingly straightforward (select the content and then use the Move tool), several powerful options go unnoticed by many Photoshop users.

➠ 2.7 Select Menu

➠ 3.4 Move Tools

➠ 8.8 Transforming a Layer or Selected Content

Move tool [V]

Duplicate content while dragging a selection [Option] [Alt]

Switch to the Move tool from most other tools (reverts to original tool when released) [⌘] [Ctrl]

Dragging and Dropping Content

Once an area has been selected, you can use the mouse cursor to drag the selected content anywhere on the document's canvas (or even to a different document) and drop it in a new location.

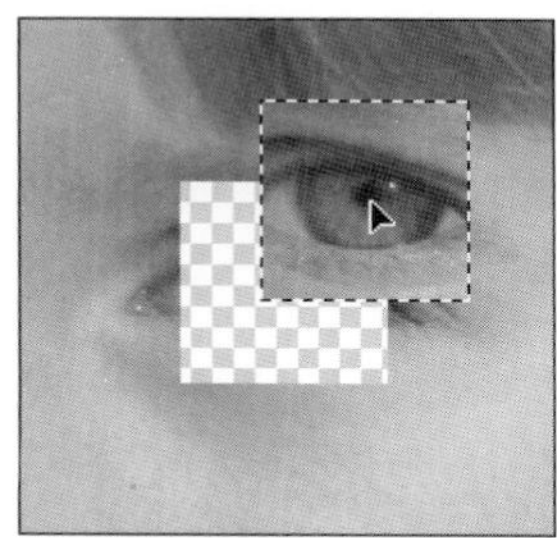

The content is being moved across the screen.

To drag and drop content, follow these steps:

1 Select a layer to transform. You can also select specific content on the layer. If no content is selected on the layer, the entire layer is moved.

2 Choose the Move tool

3 Do one of the following:

- To move the selected content **within the same document**, simply click within the selection and drag the content to the desired position. You can continue to move the selected content without dropping it until you deselect it or select another layer. The content being moved either leaves behind a hole filled with the currently selected background color (if the content was on the Background layer) or leaves a hole displaying the underlying content transparency.
- To move the content **to another open Photoshop document**, click within the selection and drag it to the canvas of the target document. The content is placed in a new layer immediately above the previously selected layer. This will not remove the content from the originating document.
- To move the content **to another application**, first make sure that the application will accept graphic input. If it does, open a document in that application, switch to Photoshop, click within the selection, and drag it to the document window of the target application.

8.9 Moving Selected Content *(Continued)*

After moving selected content, subtracting from the selection area not only removes those parts of the selection marquee, but it also removes the content

If you are moving selected content between different documents or from another application into Photoshop, remember to take into consideration the resolution of both the source and the destination.

Dragging and Dropping from Another Application

Photoshop can also receive input from other applications. To drag and drop from another application, do one of the following:

- To move a **bitmap image**, click the image in the application and drag it into the canvas of an open Photoshop document. The content is placed in a new layer immediately above the previously selected layer.
- To move a **vector image from Illustrator**, select the vector image(s) and drag them into an open Photoshop document window. The unrasterized vector image appears on a new layer with a bounding box to which you can apply transformations, or you can specify options in the tool options bar. Click the checkmark ✓ or press Enter to render the vector image at the image's resolution.
- To move **text**, select the text and click and drag it to an open Photoshop document window. The text is rasterized at the image's resolution. To move as text, you need to copy and paste it into a text layer (see Section 17.2).

Drag-Copying a Selection

If you are duplicating an object within the same document, you can simply copy it while dragging to its target location to save time. Follow these steps:

1. Select the layer with the content to be duplicated. Then, if desired, select specific content on that layer.
2. Choose the Move tool and then, in the canvas, Option/Alt-click and drag. One of two things will happen:
   - If you selected a layer, the content of the layer is duplicated into a new layer.
   - If you selected content within a layer, the content is duplicated as a selection on the same layer.
3. When you release the Move tool, the duplicated content is set. The original content remains in its initial position.

Press Option/Alt and drag the image…

…to duplicate it while moving.

8.10 Copying and Pasting Selected Content

Photoshop allows you to copy (or cut) and paste all or part of a layer in an image to a new layer in the same image or to a new layer in another image. The process for copying is the same; the difference comes when you paste.

- 2.4 Edit Menu
- 2.7 Select Menu
- 11.2 Adding Layer Masks
- 11.3 Editing Layer Masks
- 11.4 Hiding, Applying, or Removing Layer Masks
- 11.5 Turning Layer Masks into Selections

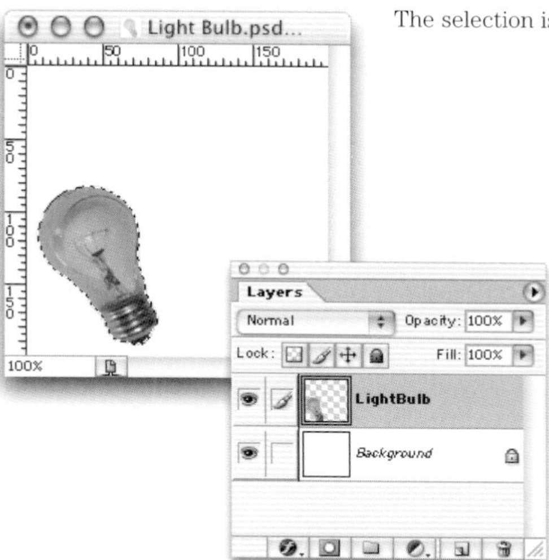

The selection is copied from the image.

When you paste an image, it is placed on a new layer immediately above the previous layer, centered in the layer.

8.10 Copying and Pasting Selected Content *(Continued)*

Copy the selection to the Clipboard

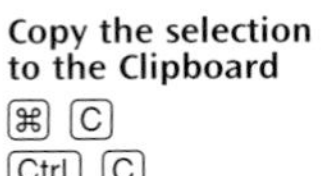

Copy the flattened selection (all layers)

Shift ⌘ C

Shift Ctrl C

Cut the selection to the Clipboard

⌘ X

Ctrl X

Paste from the Clipboard centered in the selection or layer

⌘ V

Ctrl V

Paste from the Clipboard using the selection as a mask

Shift ⌘ V

Shift Ctrl V

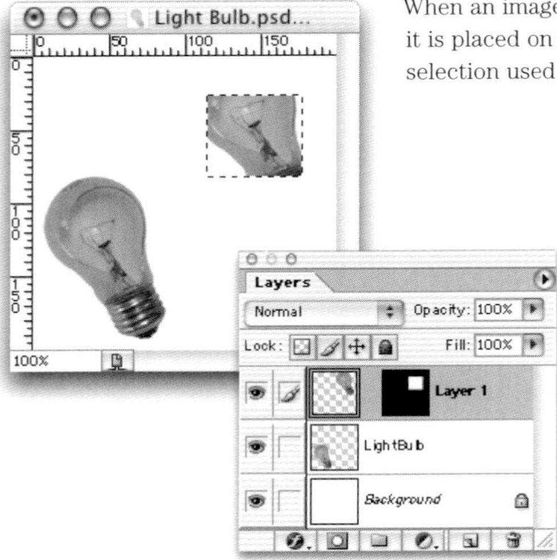

When an image is pasted into a selection, it is placed on a new layer with the selection used as a layer mask.

Copying or Cutting the Selection to the Clipboard

The Clipboard is a virtual area where you can temporarily store content. Content is moved to the Clipboard whenever you copy or paste a layer or a selected part of a layer, but only one selection at a time, and every time you copy or paste, the previous selection is replaced in the Clipboard. However, you can paste this selection from the Clipboard as many times as desired.

To move selected content to the Clipboard, use one of the following options.

- Choose Edit > Copy to move the selected content to the Clipboard but leave the original intact.
- Choose Edit > Cut to move the selected content to the Clipboard and delete the original.
- Choose Edit > Copy Merged to move the selected content on all layers to the Clipboard.

Pasting within the Same Document

To paste the content of the Clipboard into the same document, do one of the following:

- Choose Edit > Paste. The content in the Clipboard is placed into the same area as the selection but in a new layer inserted immediately above the previously selected layer.
- Deselect the selected area and choose Edit > Paste. The content in the Clipboard is placed into the middle of a new layer inserted immediately above the previously selected layer.

8.10 Copying and Pasting Selected Content *(Continued)*

- Deselect the selected area, make a new selection, and choose Edit > Paste. The content in the Clipboard is placed in a new layer (immediately above the previously selected layer) centered over the selection area.
- Deselect the selected area, make a new selection, and choose Edit > Paste Into. The content in the Clipboard is placed in a new layer (immediately above the previously selected layer) centered in the selection with the selection used as a mask effectively cropping the image.

Pasting to Another Document

To paste the content of the Clipboard into a different document, open the document and then do one of the following:

- Choose Edit > Paste. The image in memory is placed into the middle of a new layer inserted immediately above the selected layer or Background layer.
- Make a selection and choose Edit > Paste. The image is placed in a new layer (immediately above the previously selected layer) centered over the selection area.
- Make a selection and choose Edit > Paste Into. The image is placed in a new layer (immediately above the previously selected layer) centered in and cropped by the selection.

Pasting from Another Application

You are not limited to copying and pasting just within Photoshop. You can also copy images (bitmap and vector) or text in other applications and then paste them into a Photoshop document. Follow these steps:

1. Open an image file in a bitmap or text-editing application, select all or part of the image or text, and choose Edit > Copy or Edit > Cut.
2. Open the destination image file in Photoshop, and then do one of the following:
   - Choose Edit > Paste. The image in memory is placed into the middle of a new layer inserted immediately above the selected layer or Background layer.
   - Make a selection and choose Edit > Paste. The image is placed in a new layer (immediately above the previously selected layer) centered over the selection area.
   - Make a selection and choose Edit > Paste Into. The image is placed in a new layer (immediately above the previously selected layer) centered in the selection with the selection used as a mask effectively cropping the image.
   - If you are pasting text, create a text layer and then choose Edit > Paste. The text is placed in the layer as text that can be edited.

To paste content between Photoshop and another application, make sure that the Export Clipboard option is checked in the general preferences.

When you start a New document, the size and resolution automatically default to the size and resolution of the current selection in the Clipboard.

Computers sink or swim based on many factors, but chief among them is the computer's memory. If you fill up your machine's memory by copying or cutting large images, it will begin to behave sluggishly. To clear the undo, history, or Clipboard, choose Edit > Purge and then select the memory location to clear. But be careful—once purged, the information is gone from memory.

Pasting a Vector Image from Another Application

When you paste a vector image, it is initially placed as a wire frame (a rectangle surrounding a low-resolution version of the image with an *X* through it). Follow the steps in the preceding section, and then follow these steps:

1. Open an image file in a bitmap or text-editing application, select all or part of the image or text, and choose Edit > Copy or Edit > Cut.
2. Open the destination image file in Photoshop, and then do one of the following:
   - Choose Edit > Paste. The vector image in memory is placed into the middle of a new layer inserted immediately above the selected layer or Background layer.
   - Make a selection and choose Edit > Paste. The image is placed in a new layer (immediately above the previously selected layer) centered over the selection area.
   - Make a selection and choose Edit > Paste Into. The image is placed in a new layer (immediately above the previously selected layer) centered in the selection with the selection used as a mask effectively cropping the image.
3. Select whether you want the vector image placed as Pixels (bitmap), Path (vector), or Shape layer and click OK.
4. Use the mouse or the Option palette controls to transform the wire frame: move, resize, skew, or rotate the image (see Section 8.8).

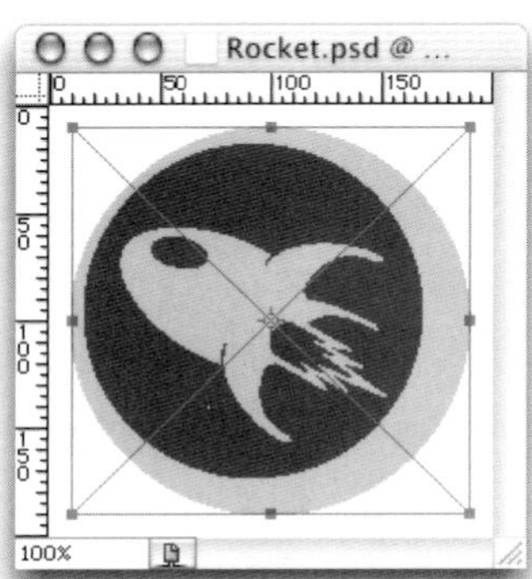

Transform the pasted vector image as desired.

5. Click the checkmark or press Enter to commit the image. The image is rasterized and placed as a new layer on top of other layers in the image. Alternately, click the Cancel button or press Esc to cancel the placement.

8.11 Saving and Loading Selections

Most of the selections you make will be of the temporary variety. That is, you make them to quickly move or edit the content and then just as quickly deselect them. However, you can also make selections that you will want to preserve even after they have been deselected. For example, you might need to make a selection in one image and then apply it to several other images. To do this, you can save selections as channels that can then be quickly turned back into selections.

➠ 2.7 Select Menu

➠ 7.5 Using Color in Channels

Save a selection as an alpha channel, bypassing the Save Selection dialog, by clicking the Save Selection As Channel button.

Saving a Selection

1 Make a selection.

2 Choose Select > Save Selection....

3 Set options in the Save Selection dialog.

Save Selection

Destination
Document: Ⓐ empire state.psd
Channel: Ⓑ Empire
Name: Ⓒ

Ⓓ Operation
Replace Channel
Add to Channel
Subtract from Channel
Intersect with Channel

OK
Cancel

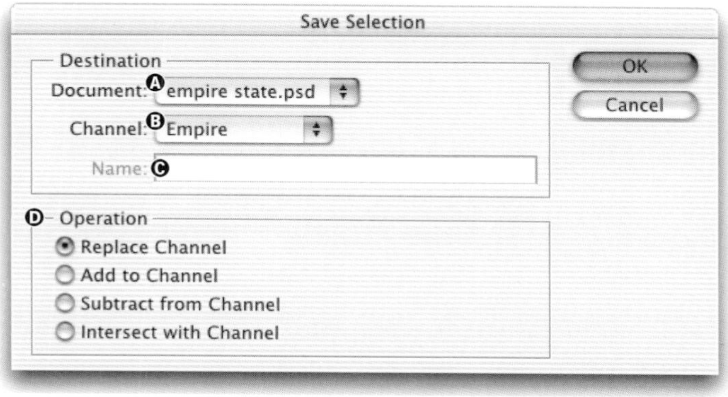

Ⓐ Specify whether you want the selection saved in the current document, an open document duplicated from this document, or a new document.

Ⓑ Select an existing channel to save the selection in, or choose to save the selection in a new channel. If you are creating a new document, New will be the only choice for channel.

Ⓒ If you are creating a new channel for the selection, enter its name.

Ⓓ If you are adding the selection to an existing channel, choose the operation for how the new selection should be placed in the channel.

4 Click OK.

- If you choose to start a new document, an untitled document is opened with the new channel.

- If you choose to add the selection to another channel, the selection is now a part of that channel.

- If you choose to start a new channel for the selection, the channel is added to the document in the Channels palette.

8.11 Saving and Loading Selections *(Continued)*

Loading a Selection

1 Select a layer into which to load the selection. You can also make an initial selection.

2 Set options in the Load Selection dialog.

3 Click OK. The new selection is on the canvas.

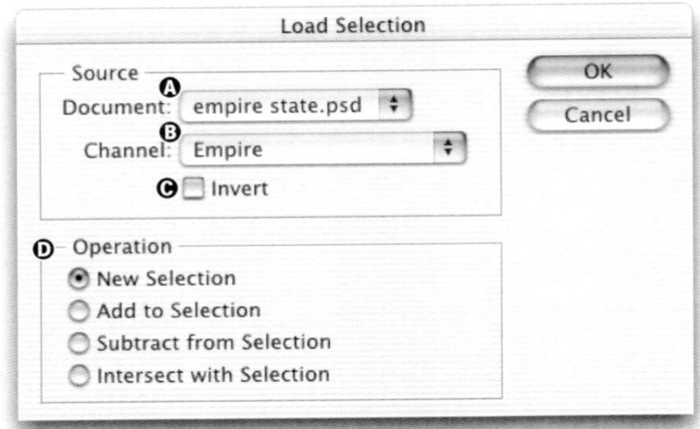

Ⓐ Choose the open document you want with the desired selection channel.

Ⓑ Choose the channel from which to load the selection.

Ⓒ Check to invert the selected area.

Ⓓ If you have an existing selection already on the canvas, choose the operation for how the new selection should be treated in relation.

Loading a Selection from the Channels Palette

You can also reload selections directly from the Channels palette.

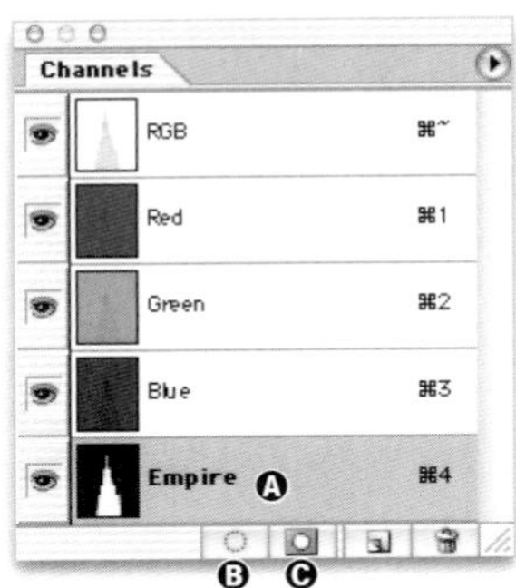

Ⓐ Selected the alpha channel that contains the selection.

Ⓑ Load the channels as selections.

Ⓒ Save the selection as a channel.

1 In the Channels palette, click the alpha channel that contains the saved selection. The canvas will show the black and white of the alpha channel. White is the selected area.

2 Click the Load Channel As Selection button [icon]. The selection will be displayed in the canvas. Select the Combined channel to view the image again.

Color Section

Fills and Adjustments

You use fills to add a solid color, a gradient, or a pattern to a layer, either directly or as part of a Fill layer. You use adjustments to control the colors and tones in an image and to correct imperfections or create interesting effects. The following images show some of the possibilities for each. The Fill or Adjustment layer's icon is shown in the top-left corner.

Original image

Color Fill A red fill color has been applied with 50% opacity.

Gradient Fill An angle gradient has been applied with 50% opacity.

Pattern Fill A pattern has been applied, scaled to 13% and with 50% opacity.

Levels Input levels have been adjusted to heighten contrast.

Color Balance More red and yellow have been added to the midtones to turn the gray areas beige.

Continues

Fills and Adjustments *(Continued)*

Curves The curve has been S-curved to solarize the image.

Brightness/Contrast The brightness and contrast have been increased to create sharp areas of black and white while preserving midtone grays.

Hue/Saturation The saturation has been drastically increased and the hue offset to create an acid effect.

Selective Color CMYK colors have been adjusted in the neutral range to colorize the image.

Channel Mixer Color channels have been mixed in the monochrome to evenly adjust the contrast.

Gradient The image's color table has been replaced by a gradient color table.

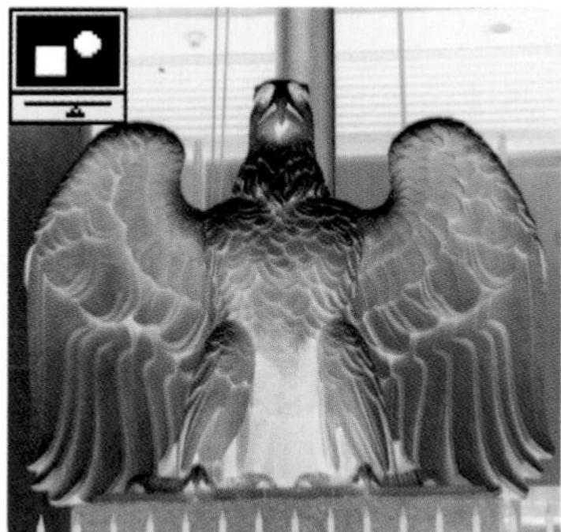

Invert The image's brightness values have been reversed.

Threshold A threshold level of 137 has been set.

Posterize A posterization level of 6 has been set.

Blending Modes

Throughout Photoshop, you use blending modes to specify how colors should be combined between layers, effects, or certain editing and painting tools. The color of each pixel in a layer is combined independently of other colors on the layer. You can specify blending modes in three primary places:

- With a **layer**, you set the blending mode in the Layers palette (see Section 4.11) or in the Blending Options of the Layer Style dialog (see Section 10.2), to specify how the colors of the active layer are combined with layers beneath it.
- With some **effects**, you set the blending mode in the Layer Style dialog for the specific effect, to specify how the colors of the effect are combined with the associated layer and layers beneath that one.
- With certain **editing or painting tools**, you set the blending mode in the tool options bar, to specify how colors applied by the tool are combined with the active layer. However, most tools use only a subset of the blending modes listed here. For example, the Healing Brush has only eight modes.

When combining colors, you must consider three color types:

Blend color Either the color of the pixel on the layer or effect with the mode being set or the color used to edit or paint the image.

Base color The color of the pixel in the underlying layer or layers being affected by the blend color.

Result color The color created by combining the blend and base colors using the specified blending mode.

The order of the blending modes shown here reflects their order in blending mode menus.

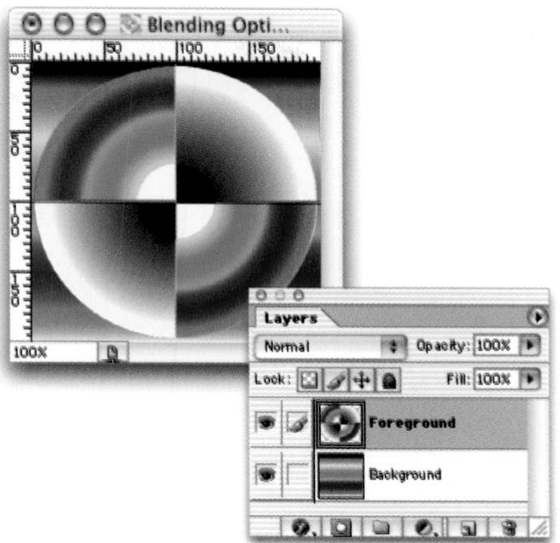

Normal The original unaltered image with two layers. The Foreground layer (currently in Normal blending mode) is the circle with color and grayscale gradients. The Background layer is a linear color gradient. Normal is called Threshold when you are working in Bitmap or Indexed Color mode.

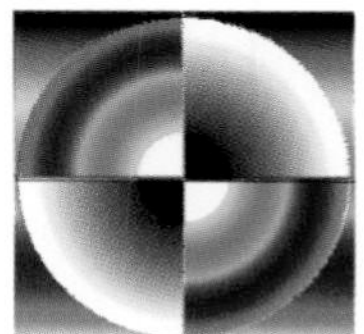

Dissolve Creates a random grainy effect based on the blend colors' opacity or the brush pressure.

Behind (Not available as a layer mode) Used to edit or paint in the transparent areas of the layer. This mode works only if the transparent lock is off.

Clear (Not available as a layer mode) Used to edit or paint only the transparency of pixels. Set the target transparency in the tool options bar. This mode works only if the transparent lock is off.

Continues

Blending Modes *(Continued)*

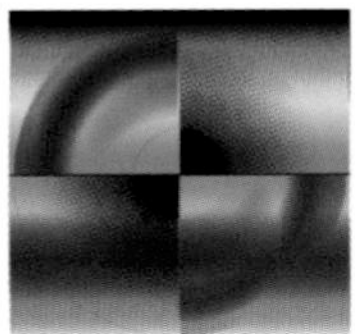

Darken If the blend color is darker than the base color, the blend color is used as the result color; otherwise, the base color is preserved.

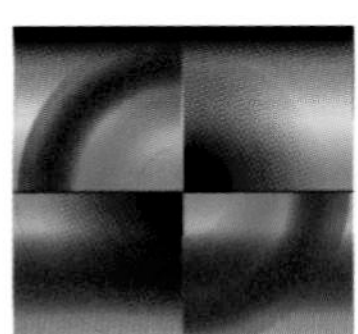

Multiply Multiplies the color value of the blend color by the base color, producing a darker color.

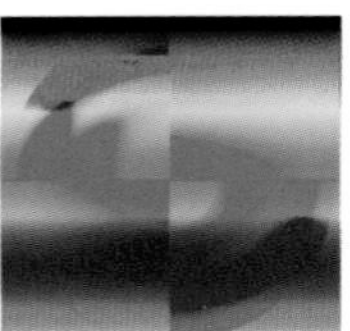

Color Burn The base color is darkened by increasing its contrast based on the blend color contrast. Blending with white produces no change.

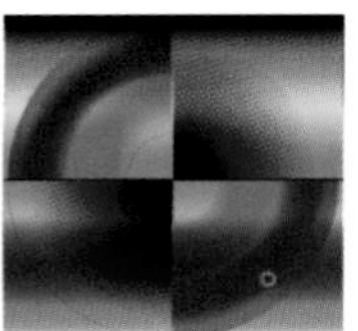

Linear Burn The base color is darkened by decreasing its brightness based on the blend color brightness. Blending white produces no change.

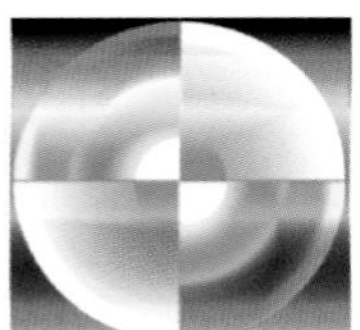

Lighten If the blend color is lighter than the base color, the blend color is used; otherwise, the base color is preserved.

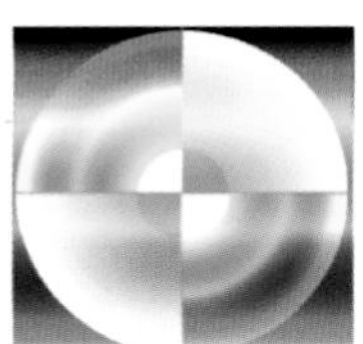

Screen Multiplies the inverse color value of the blend and base colors, producing a lighter result color.

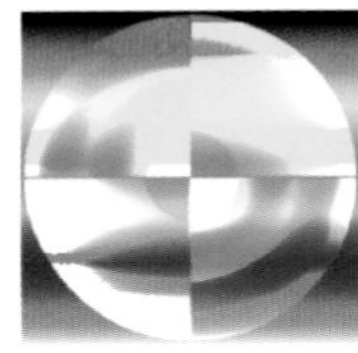

Color Dodge The base color is lightened by decreasing its contrast based on the blend color contrast. Blending with black produces no change.

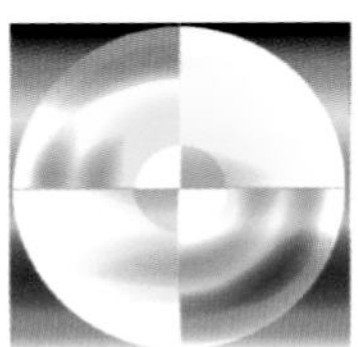

Linear Dodge The base color is lightened by increasing its brightness based on the blend color brightness. Blending with black produces no change.

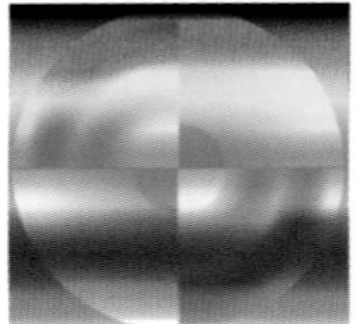

Overlay Darker blend colors darken the base color, while lighter blend colors lighten base colors, but luminosity is preserved. Black and white base colors remain unchanged, so details are preserved.

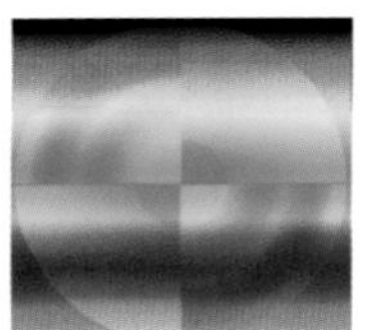

Soft Light The base color is darkened or lightened depending on the grayscale level of the blend color. If the blend color is darker than 50% gray, the base color is darkened. If the blend color is lighter than 50% gray, the base color is lightened. This produces an effect similar to shining a dim spotlight on the image.

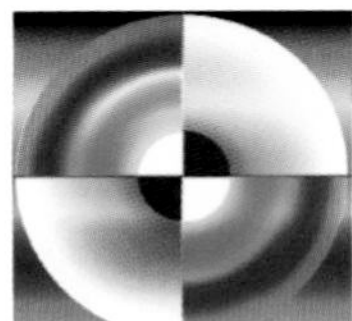

Hard Light The base color is multiplied or screened depending on the grayscale level of the blend color. If the blend color is darker than 50% gray, the base color is multiplied (darkened). If the blend color is lighter than 50% gray, the base color is screened (lightened). This produces an effect similar to shining a bright spotlight on the image.

Vivid Light The contrast of the base color is increased or decreased based on the grayscale level of the blend color. If the blend color is darker than 50% gray, the base color is darkened by increasing contrast. If the blend color is lighter than 50% gray, the base color is lightened by decreasing contrast. This produces an effect of bright sunlight.

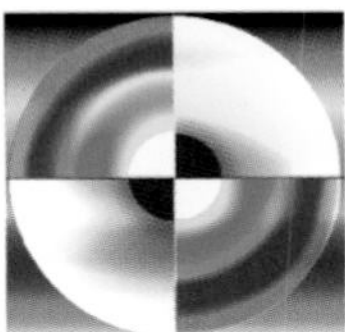

Linear Light The brightness of the base color is increased or decreased based on the grayscale level of the blend color. If the blend color is darker than 50% gray, the base color is darkened by decreasing brightness. If the blend color is lighter than 50% gray, the base color is lightened by increasing brightness. This produces an effect similar to soft light but less diffuse.

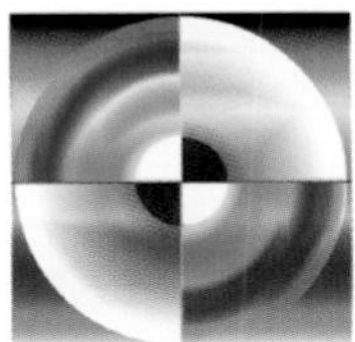

Pin Light Colors are replaced based on the grayscale level of the blend color. If the blend color is darker than 50% gray, base colors darker than the blend color are replaced by the blend color. If the blend color is lighter than 50% gray, base colors lighter than the blend color are replaced by the blend color. This produces an effect similar to shining a bright but sharp light.

Difference The blend and base color values are subtracted from each other to produce the result color. White inverts the base color, and black produces no change.

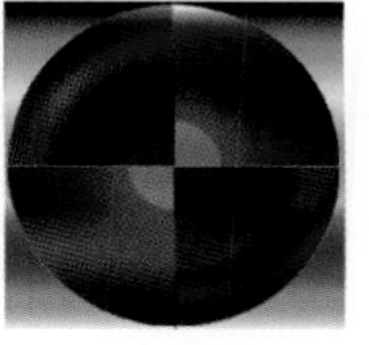

Exclusion Similar to the Difference mode, but produces result colors that are of lower contrast.

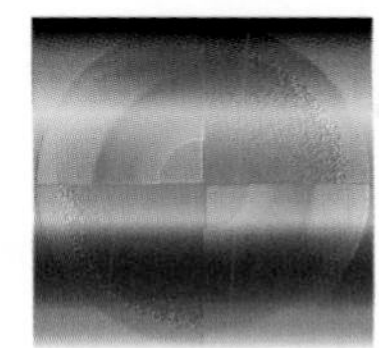

Hue Uses the luminance and saturation of the base color and the hue of the blend color to produce the result color.

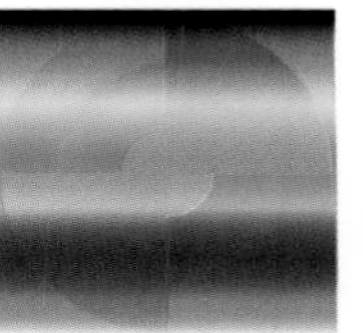

Saturation Uses the luminance and hue of the base color and the saturation of the blend color to produce the result color.

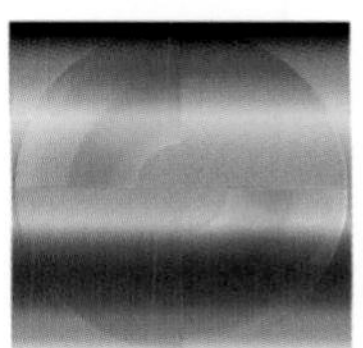

Color Uses the luminance of the base color and the hue and saturation of the blend color to produce the result color.

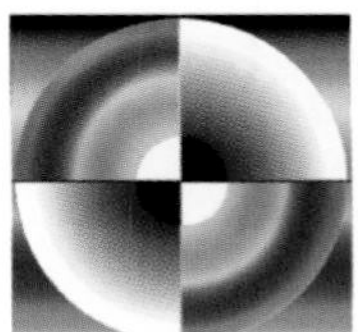

Luminosity Uses the hue and saturation of the base color and the luminance of the blend color to produce the result color.

Effects

You add effects to layers using the Layer Style dialog, discussed in Chapter 10.

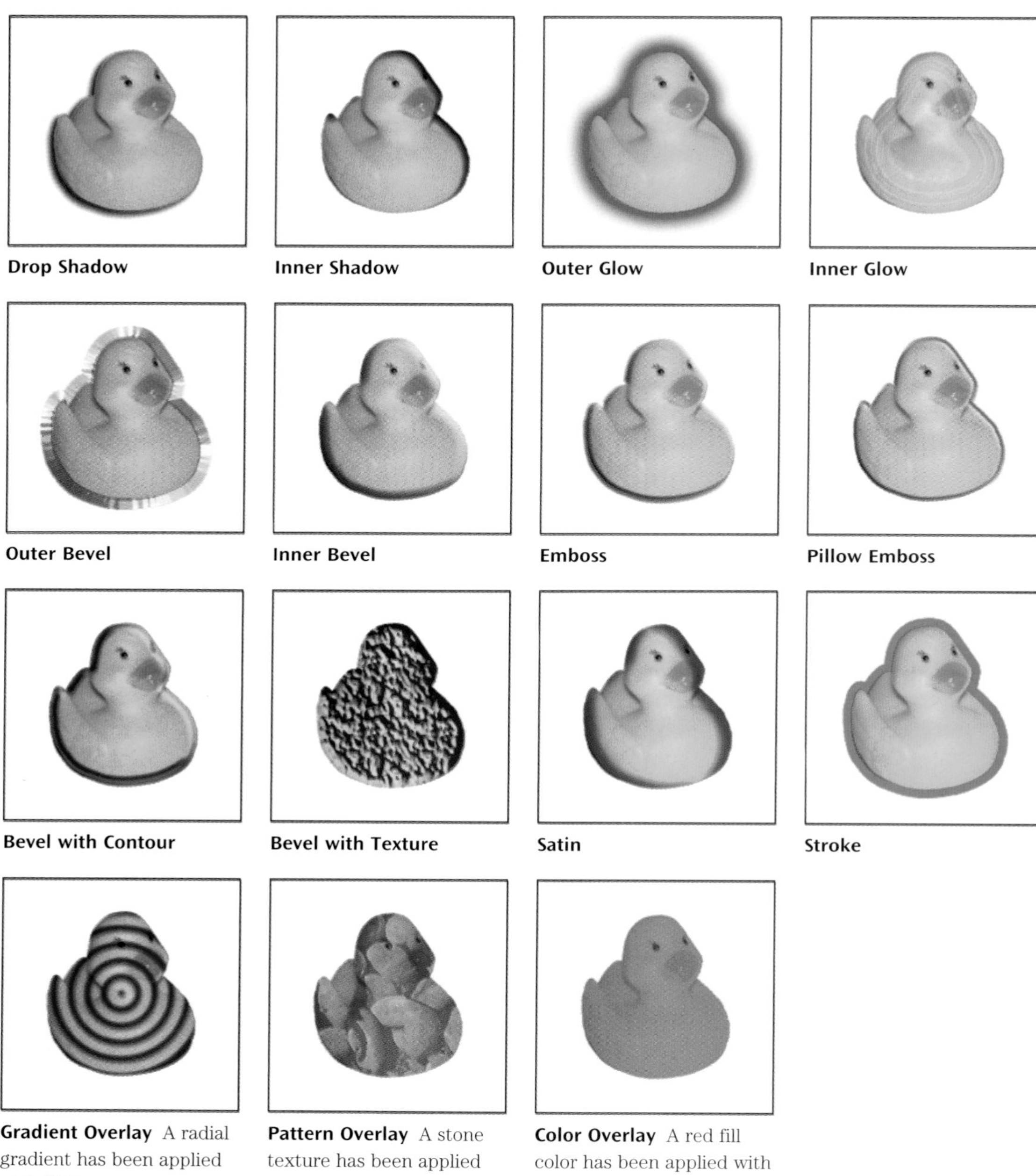

Drop Shadow

Inner Shadow

Outer Glow

Inner Glow

Outer Bevel

Inner Bevel

Emboss

Pillow Emboss

Bevel with Contour

Bevel with Texture

Satin

Stroke

Gradient Overlay A radial gradient has been applied with 70% opacity.

Pattern Overlay A stone texture has been applied with 70% opacity.

Color Overlay A red fill color has been applied with 70% opacity.

Filters

You add filters to layers using the Filter menu, discussed in Chapter 16.

Original image The foreground color is blue, and the background color is red.

Artistic > Colored Pencil (uses the background color for the pencil stroke)

Artistic > Cutout

Artistic > Dry Brush

Artistic > Film Grain

Artistic > Fresco

Artistic > Neon Glow (uses background and foreground colors)

Artistic > Paint Daubs

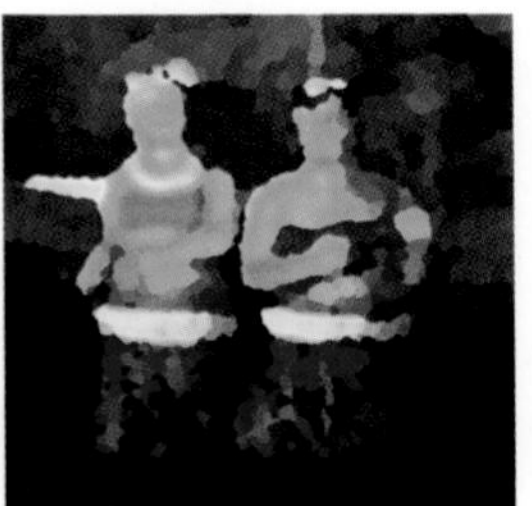

Artistic > Palette Knife

Artistic > Plastic Wrap

Artistic > Poster Edges

Artistic > Rough Pastels

Artistic > Smudge Stick

Continues

Filters *(Continued)*

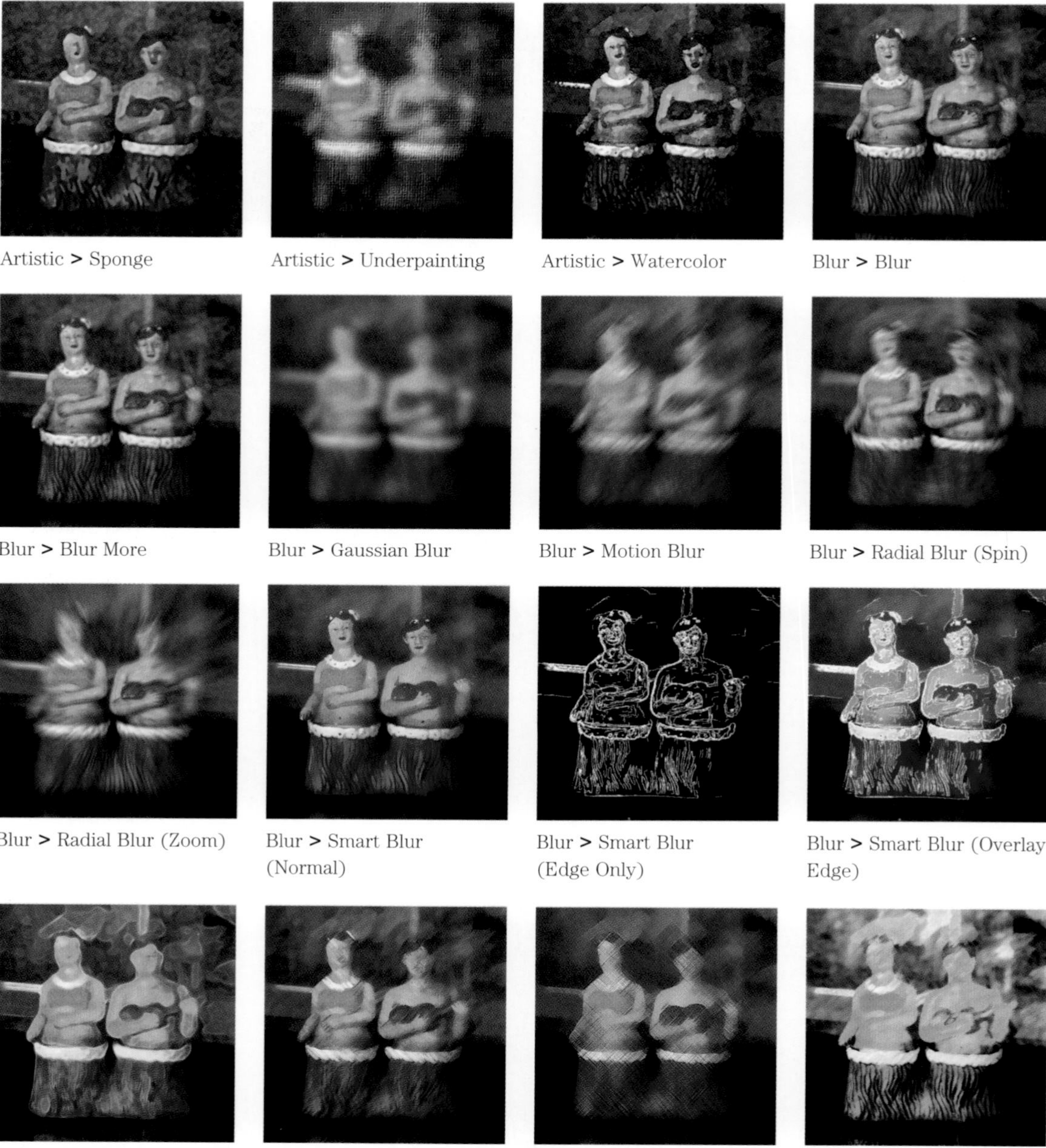

Artistic > Sponge

Artistic > Underpainting

Artistic > Watercolor

Blur > Blur

Blur > Blur More

Blur > Gaussian Blur

Blur > Motion Blur

Blur > Radial Blur (Spin)

Blur > Radial Blur (Zoom)

Blur > Smart Blur (Normal)

Blur > Smart Blur (Edge Only)

Blur > Smart Blur (Overlay Edge)

Brush Strokes > Accented Edges

Brush Strokes > Angled Strokes

Brush Strokes > Crosshatch

Brush Strokes > Dark Strokes

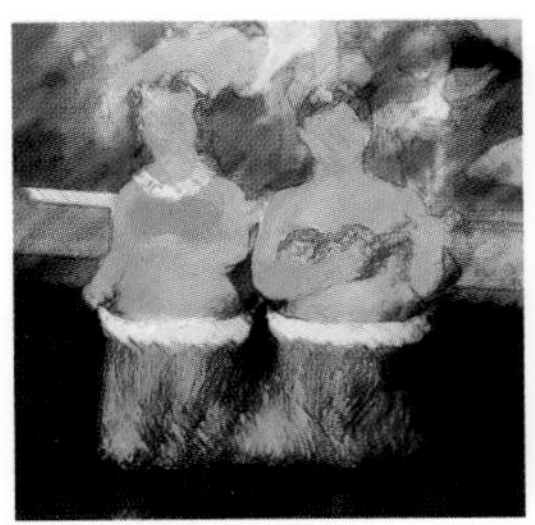
Brush Strokes > Ink Outlines

Brush Strokes > Spatter

Brush Strokes > Sprayed Strokes

Brush Strokes > Sumi-e

Distort > Diffuse Glow (uses the background color for the glow)

Distort > Displace

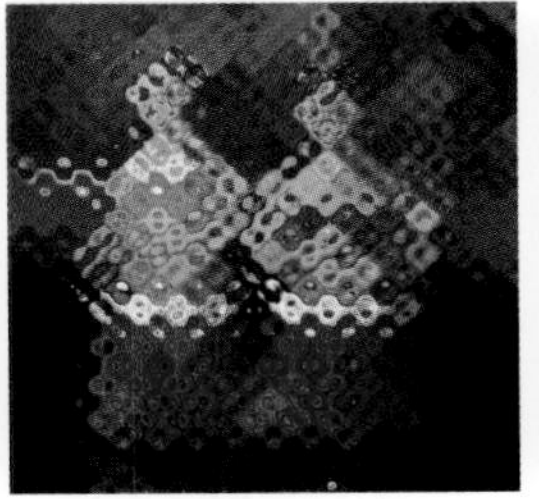
Distort > Glass

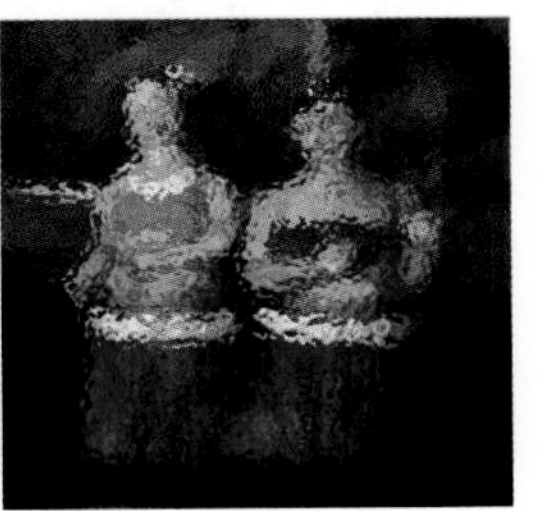
Distort > Ocean Ripple

Distort > Pinch

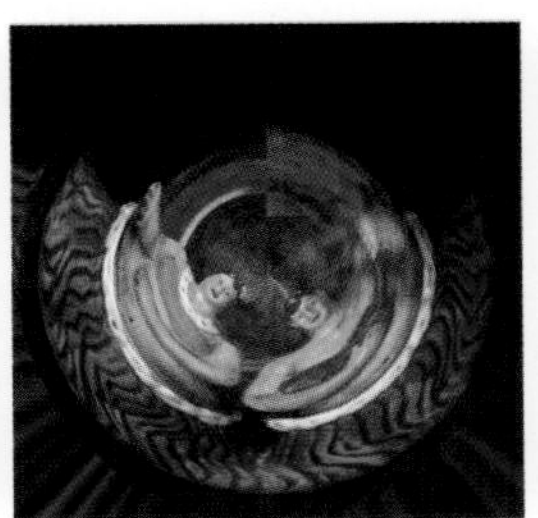
Distort > Polar Coordinates

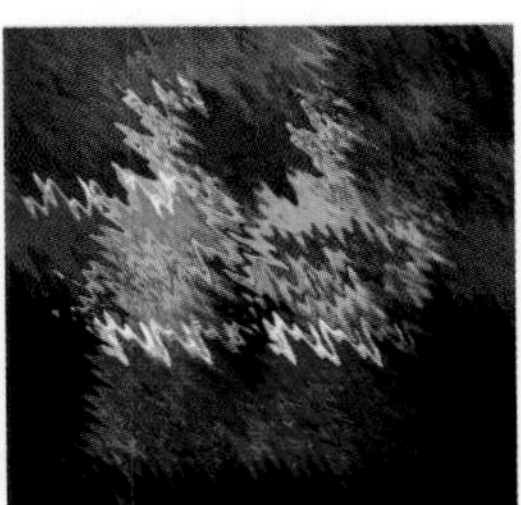
Distort > Ripple

Distort > Shear

Distort > Spherize

Distort > Twirl

Distort > Wave

Distort > ZigZag (Around Center)

Continues

Filters *(Continued)*

Distort > ZigZag (Out From Center)

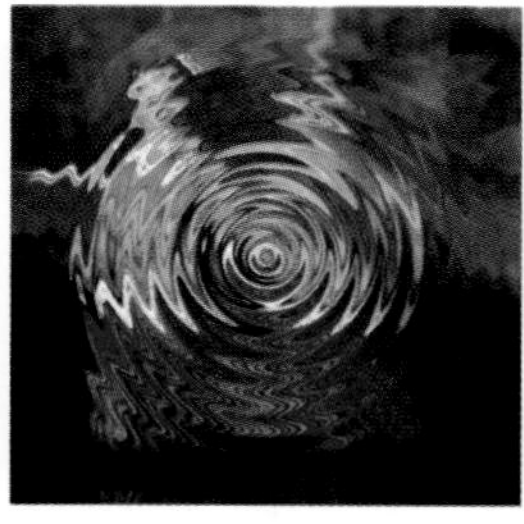
Distort > ZigZag (Pond Ripples)

Noise > Add Noise

Noise > Despeckle

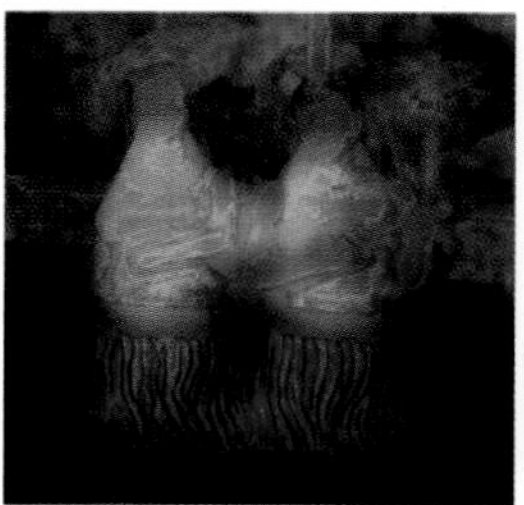
Noise > Dust & Scratches

Noise > Median

Other > Custom

Other > High Pass

Other > Maximum

Other > Minimum

Other > Offset

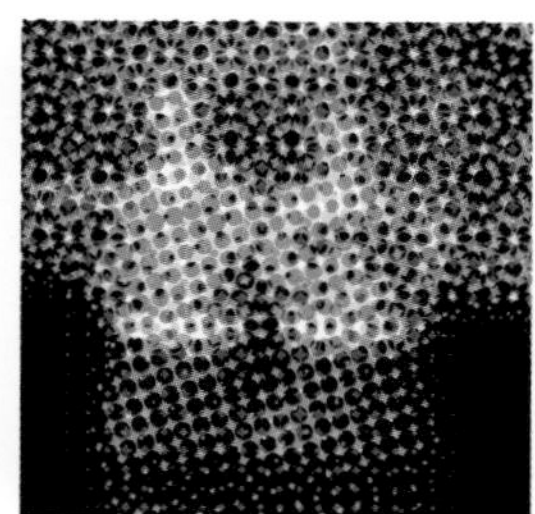
Pixelate > Color Halftone

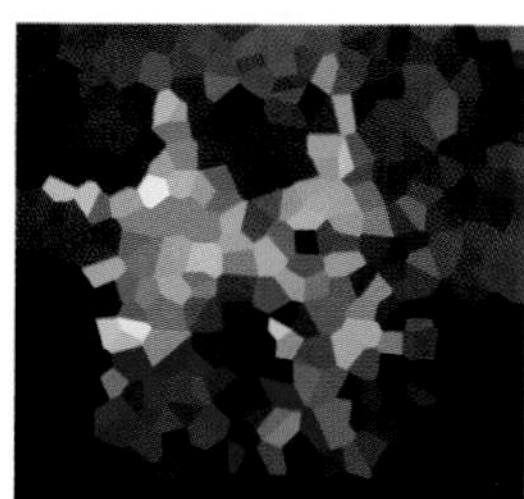
Pixelate > Crystallize

Pixelate > Facet

Pixelate > Fragment

Pixelate > Mezzotint

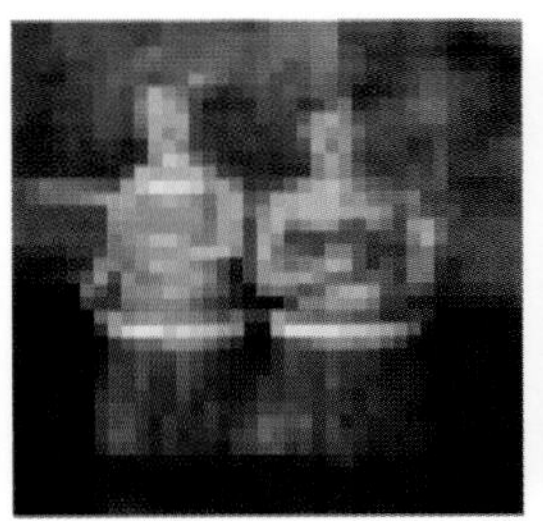
Pixelate > Mosaic

Pixelate > Pointillize (uses background color)

Render > 3D Transform

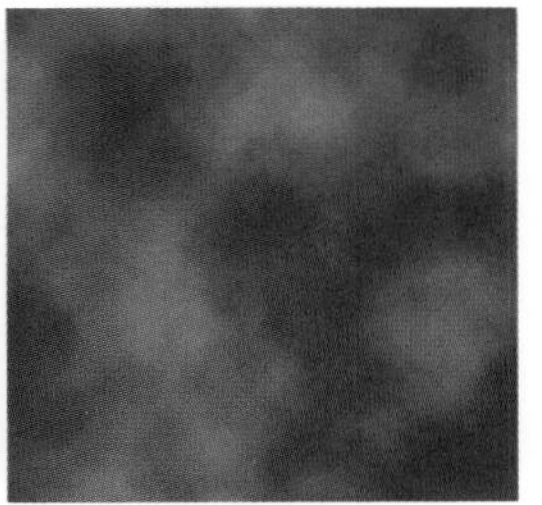
Render > Clouds (uses background and foreground colors)

Render > Difference Clouds (uses background and foreground colors)

Render > Lens Flare

Render > Lighting Effects

Sharpen > Sharpen

Sharpen > Sharpen Edges

Sharpen > Sharpen More

Sharpen > Unsharp Mask

Sketch > Bas Relief (uses background and foreground colors)

Sketch > Chalk & Charcoal (uses background and foreground colors)

Sketch > Charcoal (uses background and foreground colors)

Sketch > Chrome

Sketch > Conté Crayon (uses background and foreground colors)

Continues

Filters *(Continued)*

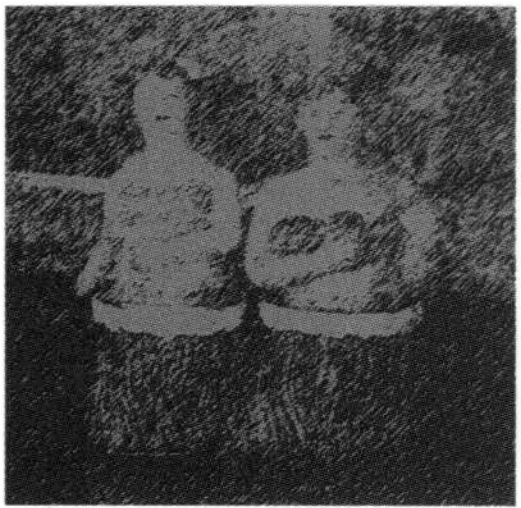
Sketch > Graphic Pen (uses background and foreground colors)

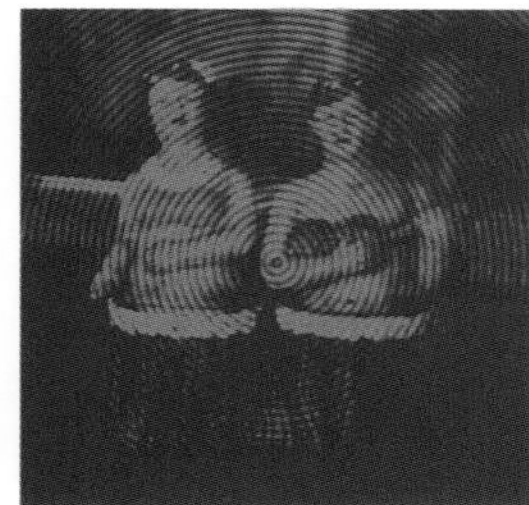
Sketch > Halftone Pattern (Circle; uses background and foreground colors)

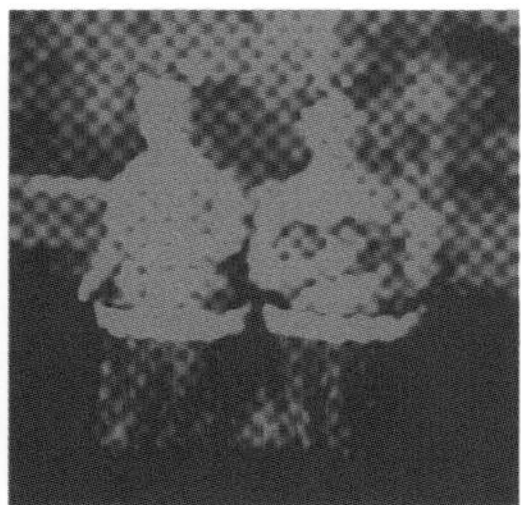
Sketch > Halftone Pattern (Dot; uses background and foreground colors)

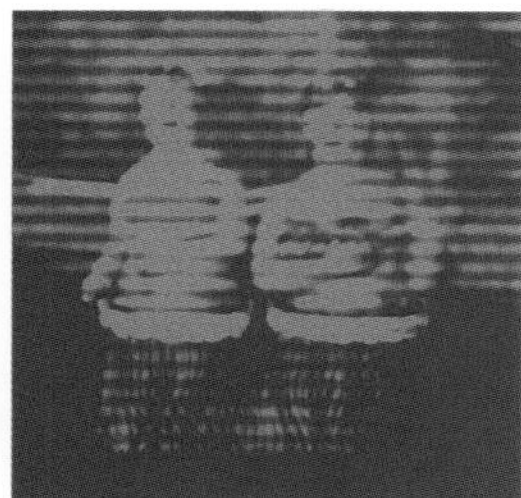
Sketch > Halftone Pattern (Line; uses background and foreground colors)

Sketch > Note Paper (uses background and foreground colors)

Sketch > Photocopy (uses background and foreground colors)

Sketch > Plaster (uses background and foreground colors)

Sketch > Reticulation (uses background and foreground colors)

Sketch > Stamp (uses background and foreground colors)

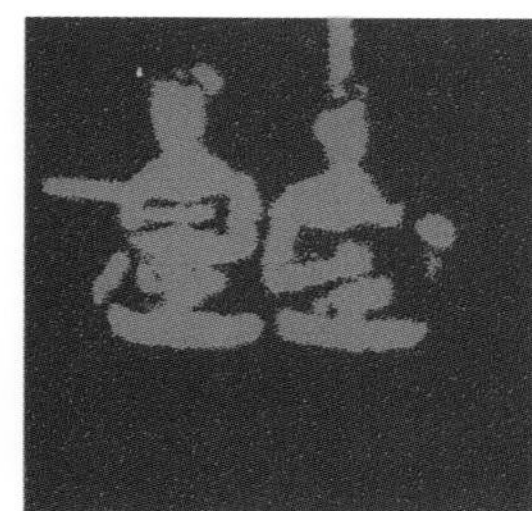
Sketch > Torn Edges (uses background and foreground colors)

Sketch > Water Paper

Stylize > Diffuse (Anisotropic)

Stylize > Emboss

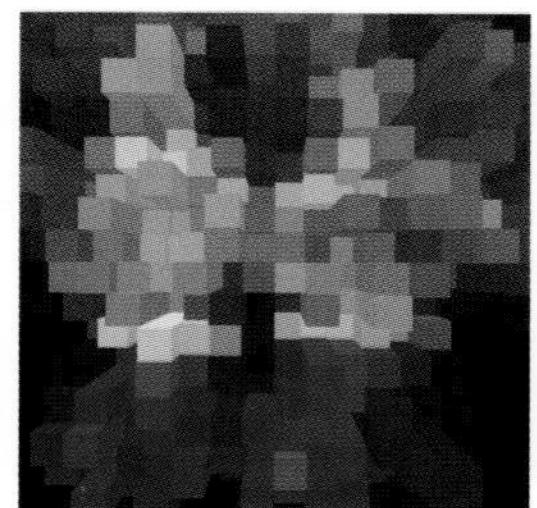
Stylize > Extrude (Cube)

Stylize > Extrude (Pyramid)

Stylize > Find Edges

Stylize > Glowing Edges

Stylize > Solarize

Stylize > Tiles (Inverse Image)

Stylize > Trace Contour

Stylize > Wind (Wind)

Stylize > Wind (Blast)

Stylize > Wind (Stagger)

Texture > Craquelure

Texture > Grain (Horizontal)

Texture > Mosaic Tiles

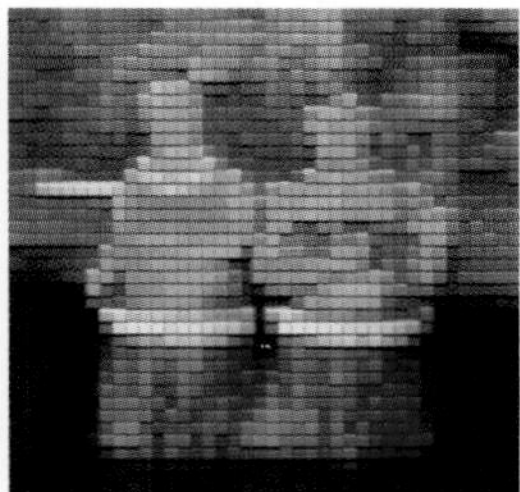
Texture > Patchwork

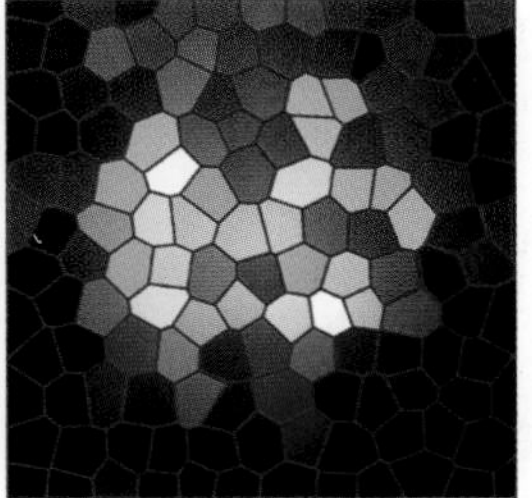
Texture > Stained Glass (uses foreground color for the border)

Texture > Texturizer

Gallery

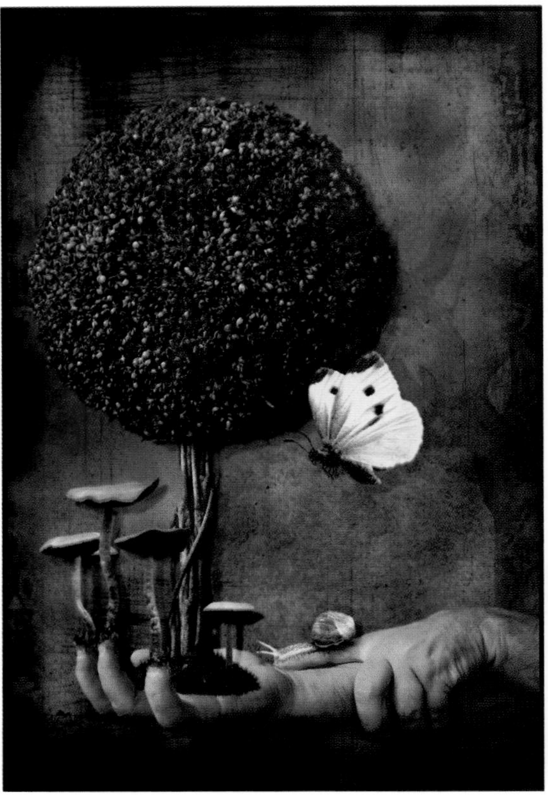

▲ **The Realm in My Hand**
© 2002 Teodoru Badiu;
`www.apocryph.net`

Theo Badiu uses masks (see Section 11.4) to blend and erase the image. He then uses the Stamp and Healing Brush tools to fill in areas before adding the background and the textures.

▲ **In the Land of the Blinds...**
© 2002 Teodoru Badiu;
`www.apocryph.net`

Badiu works with adjustment layers (see Section 9.5), blending modes (see Section 9.12), and hue and saturation controls (see Section 13.7) to bring all the elements from different photos together, creating a composition that looks as natural as possible despite its multifaceted origin.

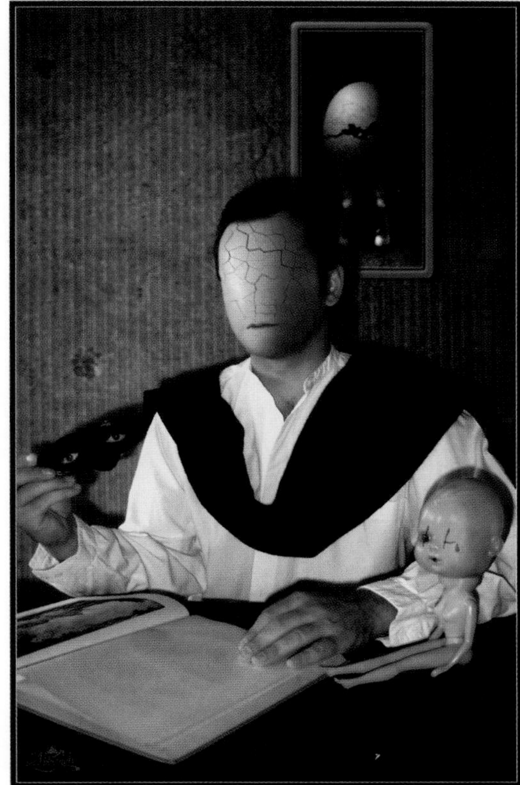

◀ **Von Eggman**
© 2002 Teodoru Badiu;
`www.apocryph.net`

To begin his images, Badiu imports all the pictures and the textures and starts to knock out the parts he need for compositing, using the Pen tool (see Section 12.2), alpha channels, Color Range (see Section 8.5), or Magnetic Lasso (see Section 8.4), depending on the complexity of the shape he needs to knock out.

▼ **Milady of the Sea**
© 2002 Teodoru Badiu;
`www.apocryph.net`

Despite the shadowy nature of his work, Badiu avoids layer effects such as drop shadows, bevels, or glows to create his effects. Instead, he works in the alpha channels (see Section 7.5), using the blur (see Section 16.3) and render filters (see Section 16.5) and with layers and selections together with blending modes and transform tools to create much deeper and more realistic shadows.

Continues

▶ © smbeniston illustrations 2002; http://smbeniston.4t.com

All of Sarah Beniston's illustrations begin life in Adobe Illustrator, but to create a 3D look, she creates textures in Adobe Photoshop, which are then imported into Illustrator (see Section 8.10).

▼ © smbeniston illustrations 2002; http://smbeniston.4t.com

Beniston creates these images by scanning various objects/materials and sizing the file depending on the output resolution required (see Section 26.1).

▲ © smbeniston illustrations 2002;
`http://smbeniston.4t.com`

Beniston occasionally uses Photoshop's drop-shadow effect (see Section 10.7) to add depth to her work.

Continues

► **the transformation**
© sl eichholz & Donald Tipton 2002;
`www.fadetonoir.com`
Special thanks to Donald Tipton (`www.donaldtipton.com`) for the use of his photography in this piece.

Shelley Eichholz thinks of her 2D work as a type of sculpture in which she uncovers the images that are already there, like a sculptor pulling objects from stone.

the transformation

◀ **Booze Demons**
© Neil Evans 2002;
www.nelson-evergreen.com

Neil Evans's works start out as black-and-white line drawings in pen and ink. He then scans these in (see Section 27.1) and works exclusively in Photoshop. He separates the black lines into their own layer using the Channels palette and places the layer at the top of the layer stack, adding layers underneath for the color (see Section 9.7).

◀ **Last One Standing**
© Neil Evans 2002;
www.nelson-evergreen.com

The entire scene for *Last One Standing* was first painted in Natural Light colors in Photoshop. It was then overlaid with a new layer, filled with dark red, and set to Multiply (see Section 9.12). Evans then created a layer mask for that layer (see Section 11.2) and used a soft-edged paintbrush to make the glitter ball lights, through which the original colors showed.

Continues

▲ **Dramatic Rehearsal**
© Greenzweig Design 2002;
www.greenzweig.com

Tim Greenzweig scans his original drawings (see Section 26.1) and assembles the composition in Photoshop using a vector program, such as FreeHand, to generate more complex black-and-white shapes that are then copied or imported into Photoshop (see Section 9.11).

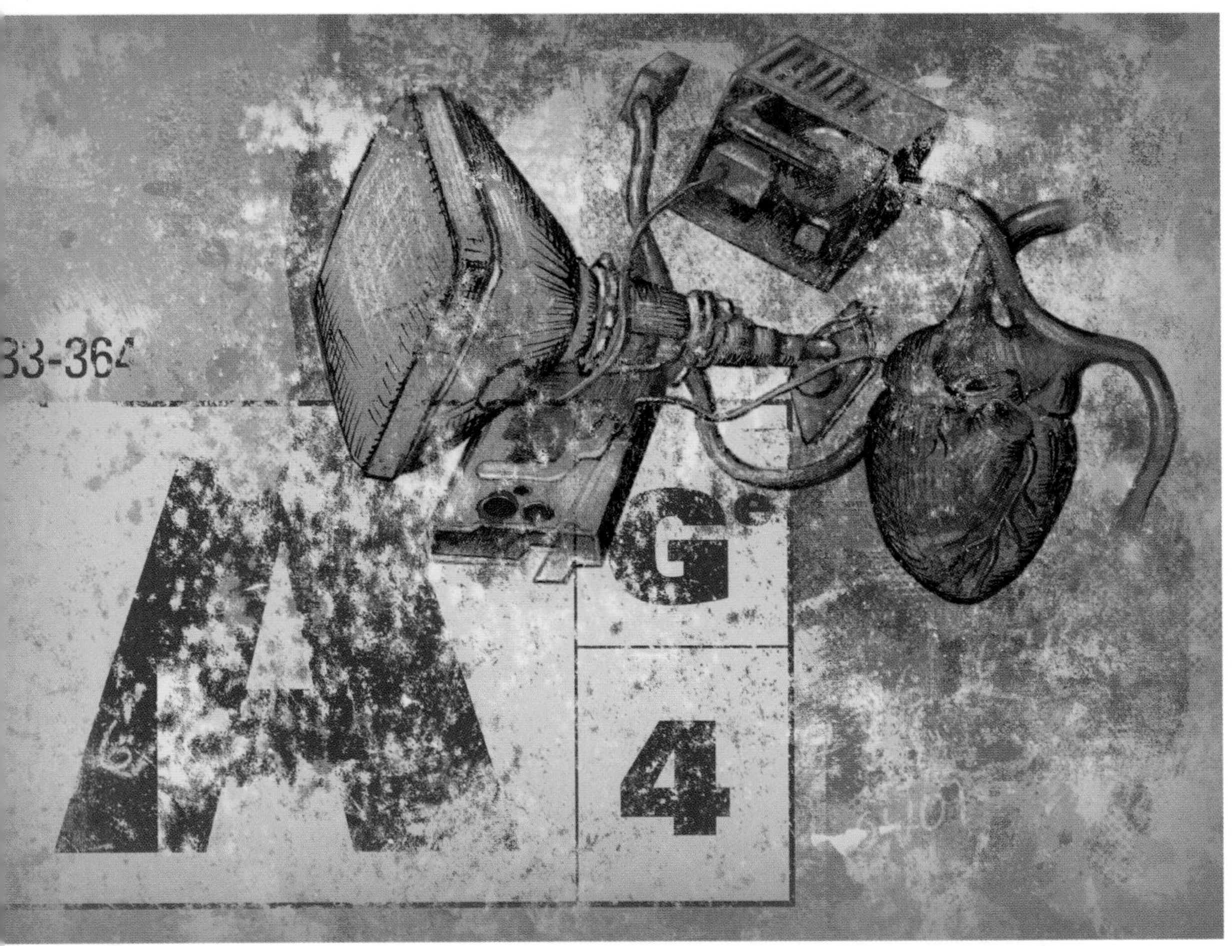

▲ **Window 364**

`www.greenzweig.com`

To get the text-erosion effect, Greenzweig scrapes some charcoal on a white piece of paper, distresses the paper (steps on it, rubs it on cement, and so on), and then scans the white sheet of paper as a grayscale image and adjusts the brightness. He then uses the Magic Wand to select the dark areas in the image (see Section 8.4) and drags that selection onto the main image. He then moves the selection around to fit the composition, selects a flattened Type layer, and deletes the selection from the type. The little bits of black that were on the original scan are deleted from the clean Type layer, creating the "eroded" look.

Continues

▶ © Kyle McCabe

Kyle McCabe shoots all his photographs using the Lomo Kompakt Automat camera. The camera is known for its unusual glass lens, which produces deep colors on photographic prints. To exploit the unusual color textures that the camera produces, McCabe uses 200-speed Fuji film with the camera's shutter speed set to 100.This technique produces shots that are doubly overexposed.

◀ © Kyle McCabe

McCabe's photos typically end up with deeply textured saturations of color. With a steady hand, he can get shots in which the framed objects have a slight blur, while still remaining intelligible.

Continues

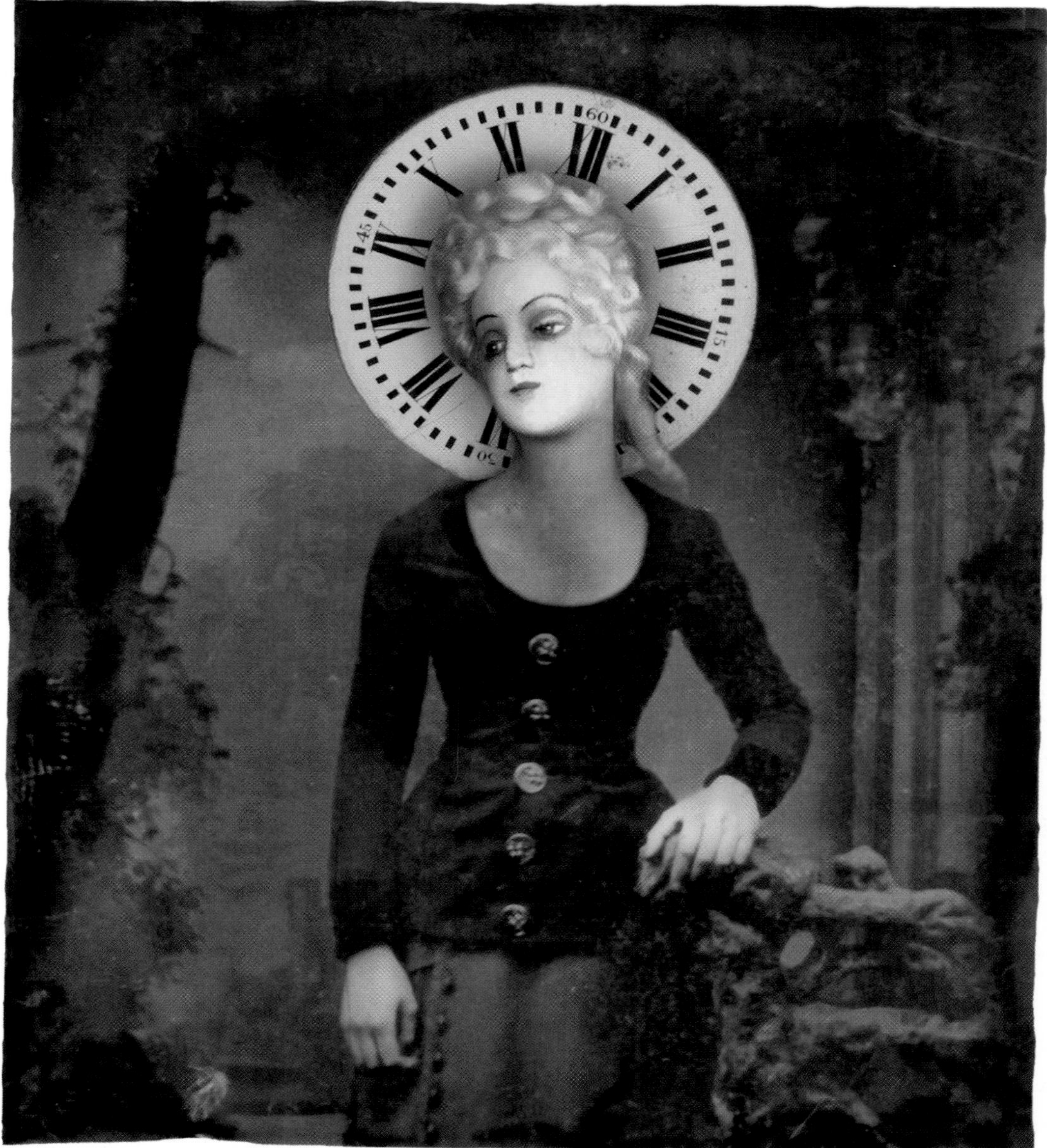

▲ **Woman with a Practical Halo**
© Maggie Taylor;
www.maggietaylor.com

Maggie Taylor collects various kinds of small objects and old tintype photographs from flea markets and eBay. She then scans the objects and photographs directly on her flatbed scanner (see Section 26.1) to produce sharply contrasting images.

◀ **Woman Holding Horse**
© Maggie Taylor;
`www.maggietaylor.com`

After scanning, Taylor begins piecing things together and tries different objects on different backgrounds, moving the layers around (see Section 9.7) until something interesting appears.

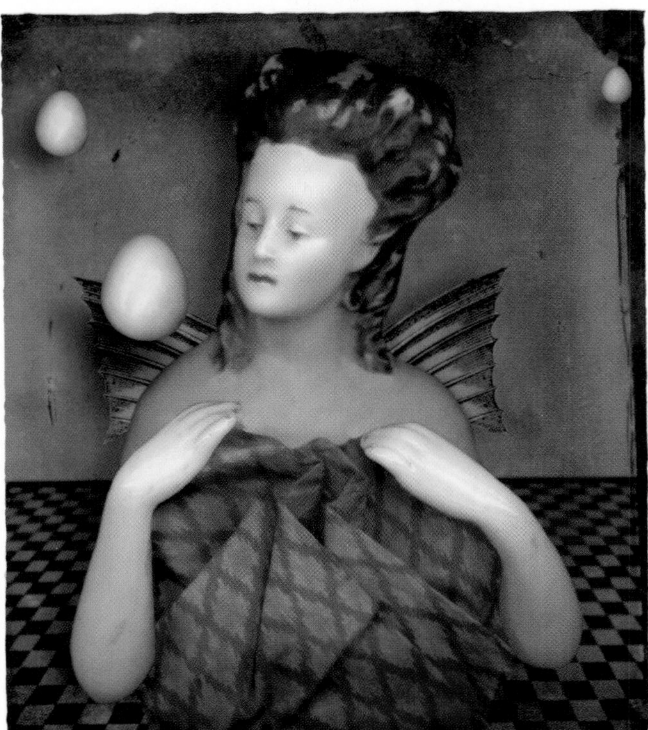

◀ **Waxing and Waning**
© Maggie Taylor;
`www.maggietaylor.com`

Although Taylor temporarily uses the drop-shadow effect (see Section 10.7), she quickly converts it to bitmap format and then directly manipulates the shadow to create a more realistic shadow (see Section 9.10).

Continues

▶ **Messenger**
© Maggie Taylor;
`www.maggietaylor.com`

Taylor uses blending modes to create some of the effects, but avoids Exclusion or Difference, relying instead on the Multiply, Overlay, and occasionally Luminosity modes (see Section 9.12).

▶ **Waders**
© Maggie Taylor;
`www.maggietaylor.com`

To create the natural-looking smoothness in her images, though, Taylor has to spend time working with the Paintbrush (see Section 15.5) and Eraser (see Section 15.9) to smooth the seam between elements on different layers.

Boris and Natasha
© Jason Cranford Teague;
`www.webbedenvironments.com`

Jason Cranford Teague likes to experiment in Photoshop, often with no final vision in mind, but trying different filters, styles, and effects until one catches his eye. Most of his images start life as photographs taken with his Coolpix 995 camera and then color corrected.

Warning Signs
© Jason Cranford Teague;
`www.webbedenvironments.com`

One of Cranford Teague's favorite techniques is to layer an image over the top of itself, make dramatic changes to the copy, and then use a layer or vector mask (see Sections 11.2 and 11.6) to partially reveal the original image.

Continues

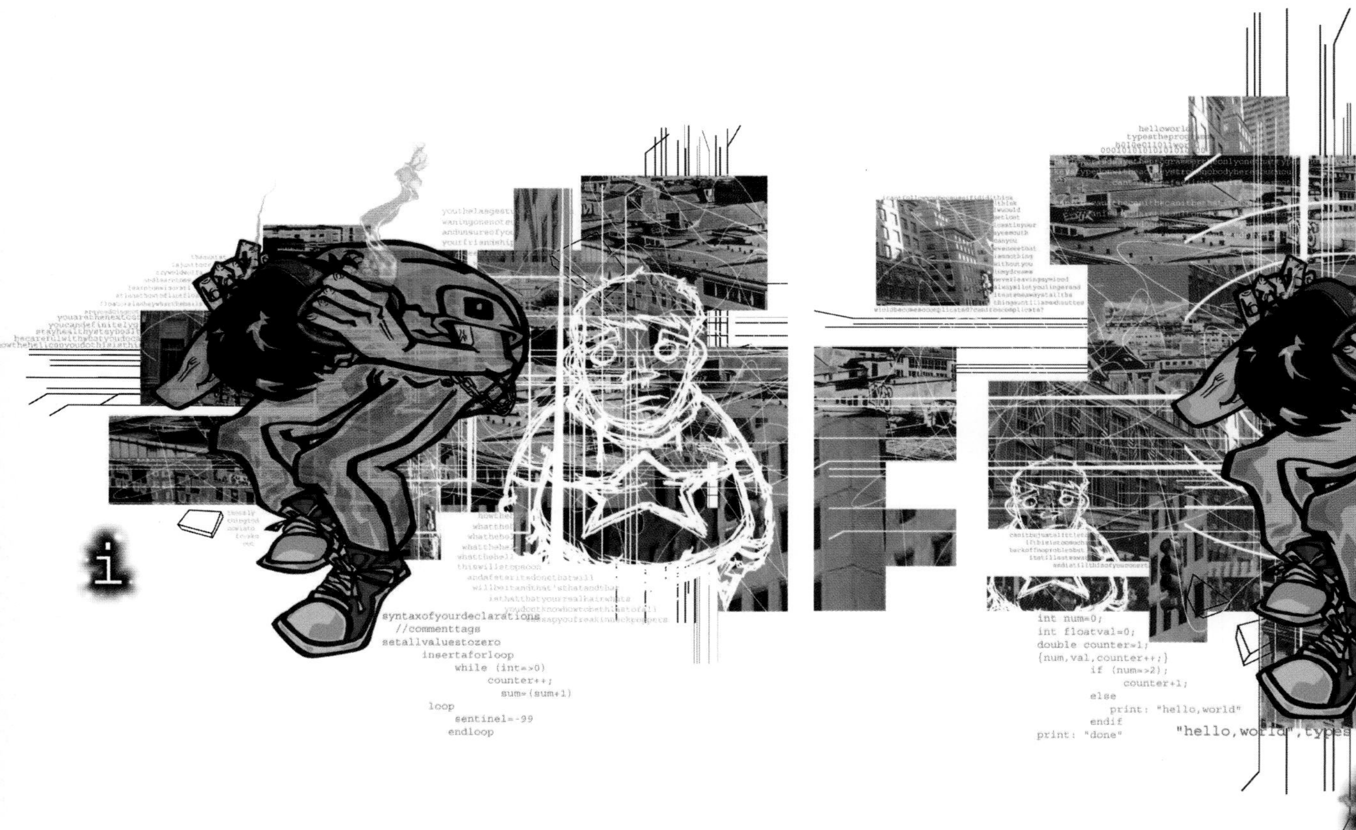

▲ **Blister**
© Jimmy Yi

Jim Yi runs different photographs of buildings through a combo of Photoshop's diffuse glow and blur filters (see Section 16.1).

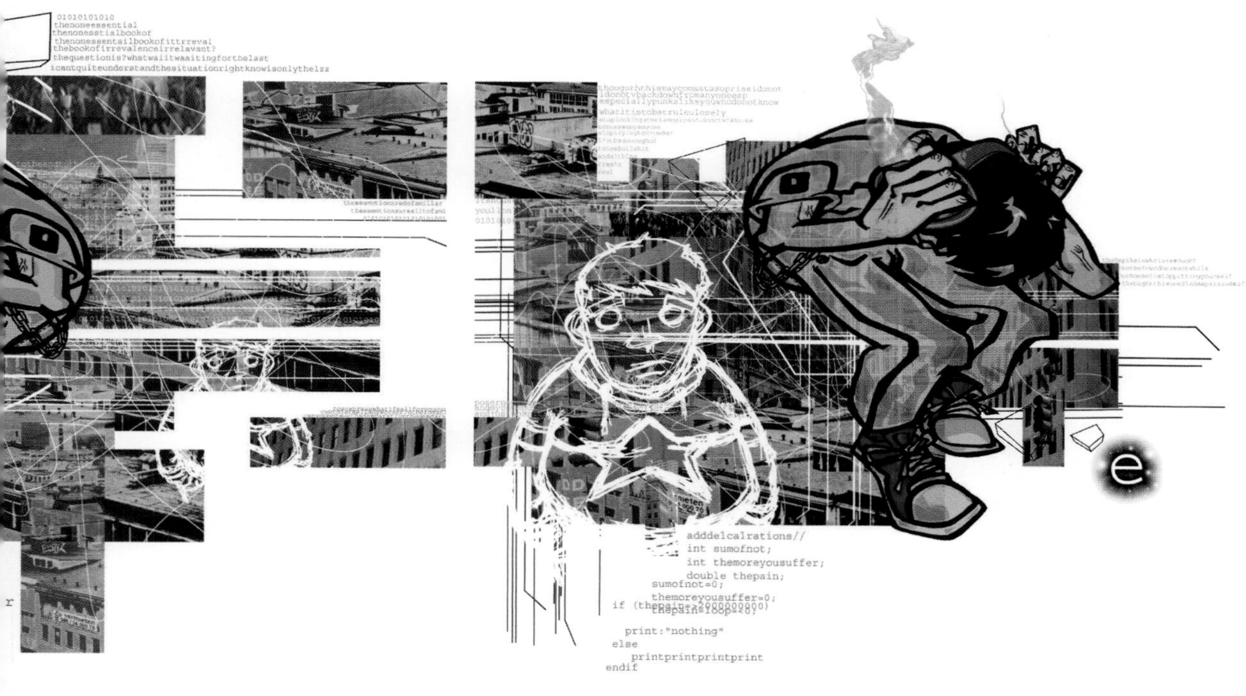
01010101010
thenoneessential
thenonesstialbookof
thenonessentailbookofittrreval
thebookofirrevalenceirrelavant?
thequestionis?whatwaiitwaaitingforthelast
icantquiteunderstandthesituationrightknowisonlythelzz
adddelcalrations//
int sumofnot;
int themoreyousuffer;
double thepain;
sumofnot=0;
themoreyousuffer=0;
if (thepain=>2000000000)
print:"nothing"
else
printprintprintprint
endif

Continues

▶ **Fame**

© Jimmy Yi

Yi's images require a lot of layers files, sometimes as many as 60 or more. He carefully organizes the image by assigning layer sets (see Section 9.6) to help keep track of each section of the image.

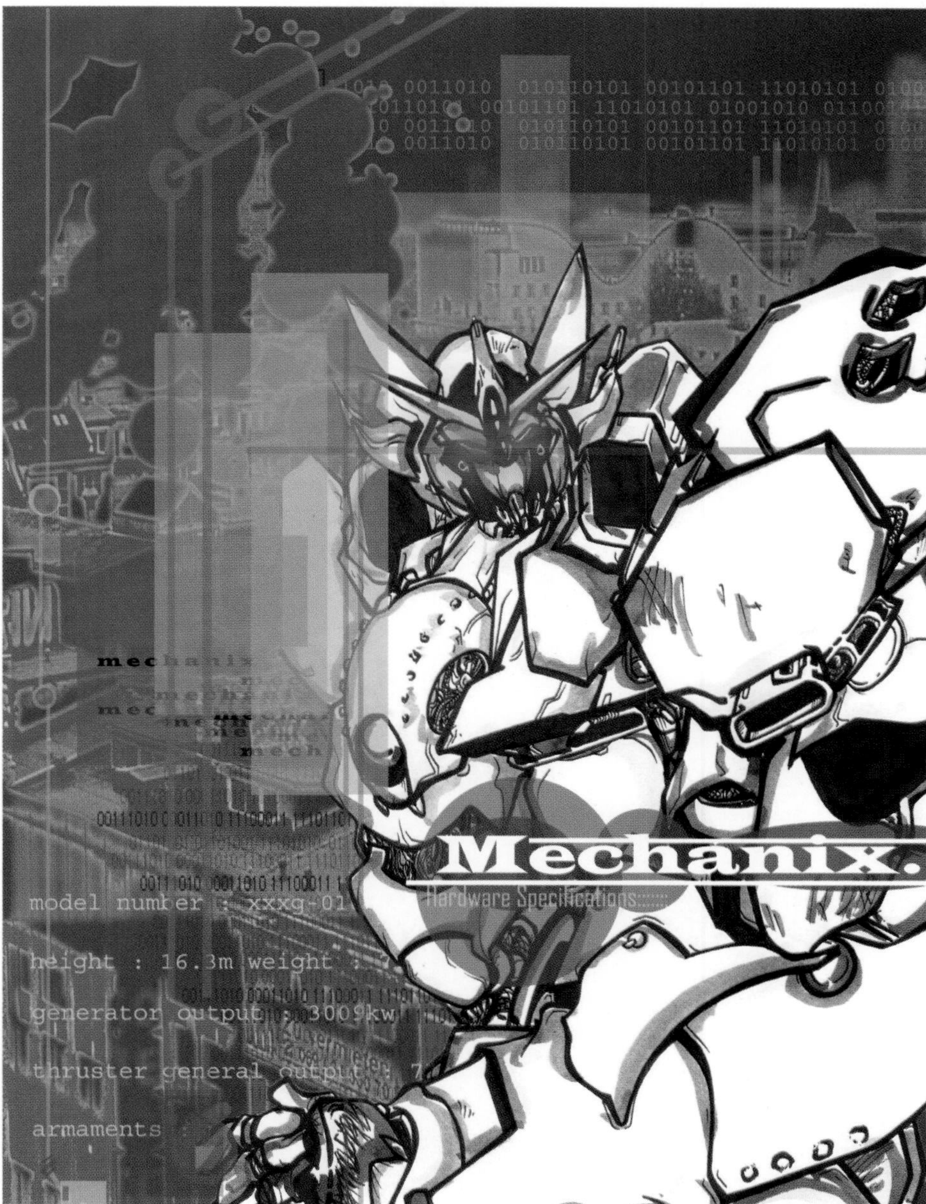

◄ **Mechanix**
© Jimmy Yi

To preserve quality, Yi saves original files at extremely high resolution. He then works on print images solely in CMYK or web images in RGB.

Continues

▶ **Punk**

© Jimmy Yi

Yi likes the Photoshop filters despite the criticism leveled at them that they are simply "push button." Filters provide Yi with effects that would be hard to achieve otherwise, especially when multiple filters are combined.

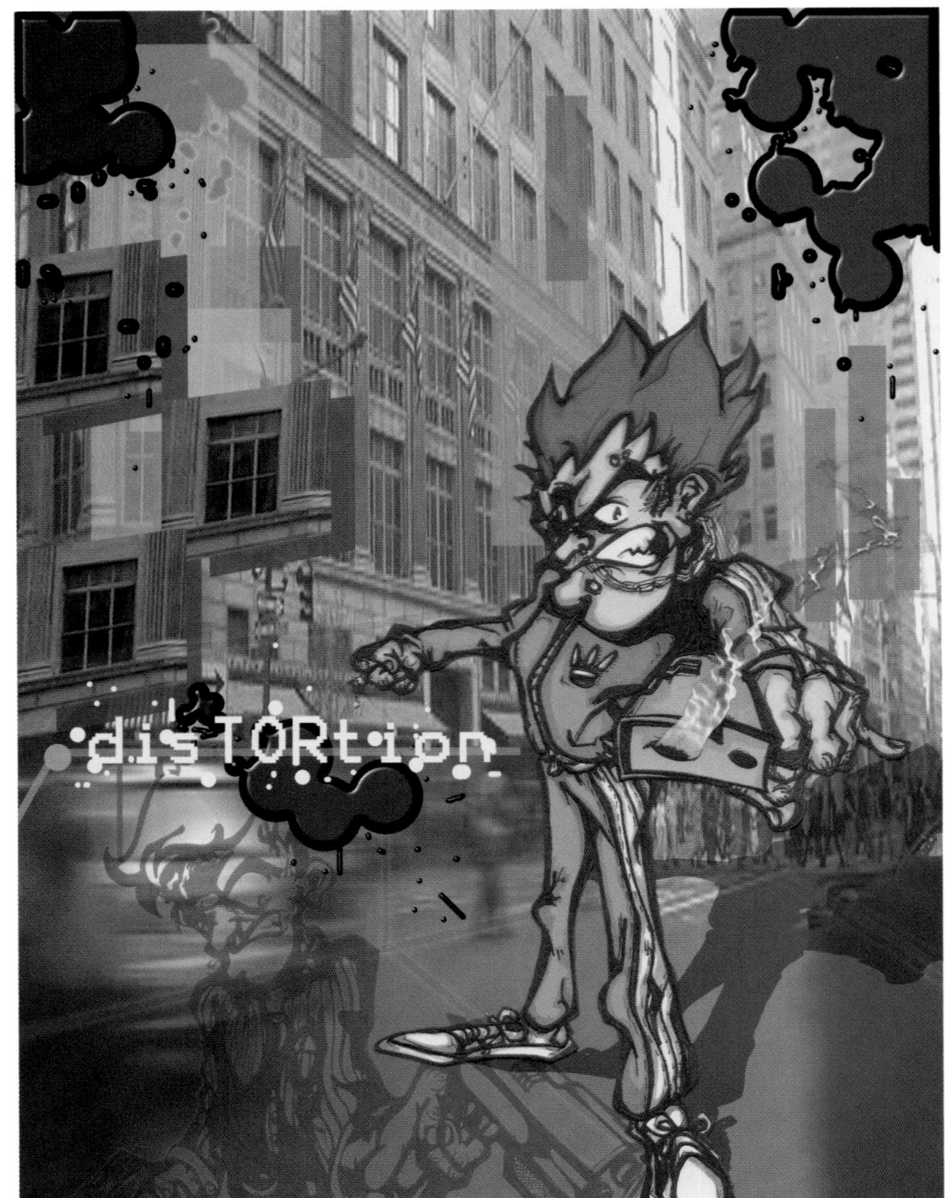

CHAPTER 9

Image Layering

ALTHOUGH YOU USE PHOTOSHOP to create two-dimensional images (even if they look 3-D, they are still output into two dimensions), you will need to move and shuffle parts of images in three dimensions. To that end, Photoshop allows you to "stack" images on top of one another. These stacked layers appear as a single composited image in the canvas, but you can control the individual layers of the image in the Layers palette.

9.1 Layer Basics

➠ 4.11 Layers Palette

In the Layers palette, each layer includes a thumbnail image that displays the content of the layer. To change the layer thumbnail size (or eliminate it entirely), choose Palette Options from the Layers palette menu. In the dialog, choose the desired thumbnail size and click OK.

Think of a layer in Photoshop as a perfectly clear piece of plastic that is placed over the canvas. You can have multiple layers in a single document, and you can add content to a single layer without changing the content above or below it. So, layers are great for building up images, allowing you greater flexibility and control. However, you can edit the content of only one layer at a time (although some tools allow you to edit across multiple layers simultaneously), and all painting, transformations, or other edits are applied to that layer or the selected region in that layer. You can adjust several variables in layers:

Blending Modes Specifies how pixels in this layer should interact with layers underneath (see Section 9.11).

Opacity Specifies the transparency of all pixels in the layer, opaque or partially transparent. Content from layers below that one show through any areas of the layer if there is no content or if the content is transparent (see Section 9.11).

Fill opacity Specifies the opacity of nongenerated pixels in the layer (see Section 9.11).

Visibility Specifies whether the layer is currently shown or hidden (see Section 9.6).

Styles Special properties generated by Photoshop, such as drop shadows (see Chapter 10).

Masks Lets you draw or paint a special mask used to remove areas of the layer without deleting the content (see Chapter 11).

Clipping groups Allows one layer to be used to clip (much like masking) the content of other layers (see Section 9.12).

Photoshop Layer Types

	LAYER TYPE	USE
	Draw layer	Paint and edit images. Thumbnail shows content of layer with transparent background.
T	Text layer	Enter and edit text. Layer name is text of layer.
	Background layer	Special draw layer that cannot be moved and does not allow transparencies. Thumbnail shows content of layer with background color.
	Adjustment layer	Filled with color, pattern, or gradient. Always includes layer mask. Thumbnail depends on fill type selected.
	Fill layer	Adjusts images on layers beneath. Always includes layer mask. Thumbnail depends on fill type selected.
Set 1	Layer set	Collects layers.
Drop Shadow	Layer effect	Adds an effect to the associated layer. Effect name listed next to icon.
	Layer mask	Paint and edit mask for layer. Thumbnail shows bitmap representation of mask.
	Vector mask	Draw and edit paths for mask. Thumbnail shows grayscale representation of paths.

9.2 The Background Layer

When creating a new image, one of the options is to use white or the current background color. If you select either of these options, a special Background layer is inserted as the bottommost layer of the image. The Background layer acts just like any other layer except for the following:

- You cannot restack the Background layer in the Layers palette.
- The Background layer will always be filled, not allowing any transparency to show through.
- You cannot change the opacity or blending mode of the Background layer.

➡ 4.11 Layers Palette

Just changing the name of a layer to *Background* does not make it a true Background layer.

If you choose Transparent when setting up a new image, no Background layer is added, and instead the transparency shows through.

You can hide the Background layer, allowing the transparency to show through.

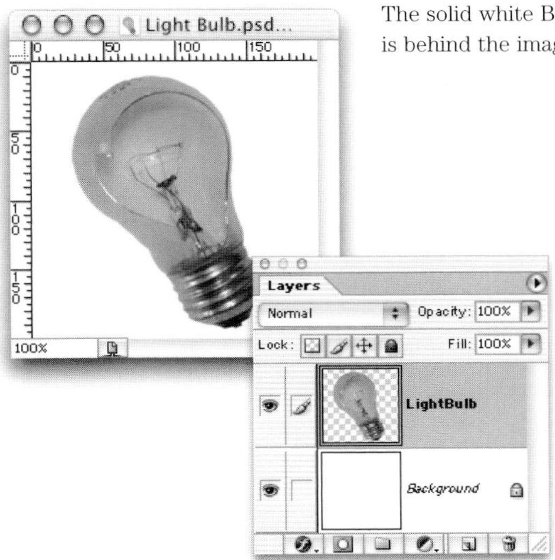

The solid white Background layer is behind the image of the light bulb.

You can convert a Background layer to a standard layer or vice versa:

- To convert a Background layer into a Draw layer, double-click the Background layer in the Layers palette or choose Layer > New > Layer From Background…, set the layer options, and click OK.
- To convert a standard layer into a Background layer, select the layer and choose Layer > New > Background From Layer.

9.3 Creating Layers

➠ 4.11 Layers Palette

➠ 8.2 Selecting a Layer or Its Contents

➠ 8.10 Copying and Pasting Selected Content

New images automatically start with a single layer (either Background or Transparent). However, with only one layer, you are limited as to what you can do to the image until you create additional layers.

The most common layer you will be using is the Draw layer, which is completely transparent until you add pixels. To add a new Draw layer to your image, select the existing layer you want the new layer to appear above in the Layers palette and then do one of the following:

- Click the Create A New Layer button in the palette to add a new empty layer above the previously selected layer.
- Choose Layer > New > Layer… or choose New Layer from the palette menu. Enter information about the new layer and click OK. The new layer is added above the previously selected layer.

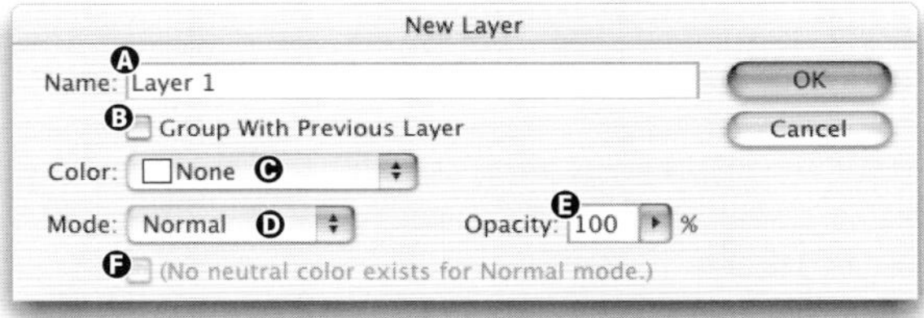

Ⓐ Enter the name for the layer.

Ⓑ Check if you want to automatically group the new layer with the selected layer.

Ⓒ Choose a color for the layer in the palette. This code does not affect the layer itself, but allows you to color-code layers depending on use.

Ⓓ Choose an initial blending mode for the layer. You can change this later in the Layers palette.

Ⓔ Enter an initial opacity for the layer. You can change this later in the Layers palette.

Ⓕ Depending on the blending mode selected, check this option to fill the new layer with a neutral color.

Duplicating Layers

Duplicating a layer makes an exact copy of the layer (including its position) into a new layer, named by default the originating layer's name plus the word *copy*. You can duplicate layers in several ways, each with slightly different outcomes:

- Click and drag a layer from the palette to the New Layer button and release. The duplicate appears above the layer from which it was duplicated.
- Select a layer and then choose Duplicate Layer… from the Layer menu, the Layers palette menu, or the layer's contextual menu. Enter information in the Duplicate Layer dialog and click OK. Depending on the options set, the duplicate layer appears above the layer from which it was duplicated.

New layer
Shift ⌘ Option N
Shift Ctrl Alt N

New layer using dialog
Shift ⌘ N
Shift Ctrl N

New layer using dialog
Option-click the New Layer icon
Alt-click the New Layer icon

New layer below selected layer/layer set
⌘-click the New Layer icon
Ctrl-click the New Layer icon

New layer from copy selection
⌘ J
Ctrl J

New layer from cut selection
Shift ⌘ J
Shift Ctrl J

New layer from copy selection with dialog
⌘ Option J
Ctrl Alt J

New layer from cut selection with dialog
Shift ⌘ Option J
Shift Ctrl Alt J

Duplicate layer
⌘ Option *any arrow key*
Ctrl Alt *any arrow key*

9.3 Creating Layers *(Continued)*

Duplicate Layer
Duplicate: Layer 2
As: Layer 2 copy (A)
OK
Cancel
Destination
Document: (B) City Scape Illo.psd
Name: (C)

A Enter a name for the duplicate layer.

B Choose whether the duplicate layer should be added to the current document or another open document or whether a new document should be started for it. If a new document is created, the document will be the same size as the original document from which the layer was duplicated.

C If you are placing the layer in a new document, enter a name for the new document.

New Layer from a Selection

When you copy or cut and paste a selection, it is automatically placed in a new layer, but you also have two—more refined—ways to create new layers using duplicated content. First, select content in a layer. Then choose either:

- Layer **>** New **>** Layer Via Copy to create a new layer from the selected region and leave the original content intact.
- Layer **>** New **>** Layer Via Cut to create a new layer from the selected region and delete the original content.

The new layer appears immediately above the previously selected layer, and the duplicated content appears directly over the top of the original content, obscuring it.

To create a layer via copy, you must select a layer. However, to create a layer via cut, you must select specific content on the layer.

Although layers give you a lot of power when creating images, they come at the cost of increased file size; so use them as needed.

After you duplicate a layer, remember that it will be over the top of, and thus obscuring, the original layer. You will need to move the duplicate content or hide the layer to see the original.

Duplicating a layer strengthens any transparencies, blending modes, or other effects.

Text layers are a special case, which are added using the Text tool and explained in Chapter 17.

9.4 Merging Layers

➠ 4.11 Layers Palette

Merge Down/Merge Linked/Merge Group
⌘ E
Ctrl E

Merge visible layers
Shift ⌘ E
Shift Ctrl E

Copy visible layers into selected layer
Shift Option ⌘ E
Shift Alt Ctrl E

Copy selected layer into layer below
Option **Merge Down (menu option)**
Alt **Merge Down (menu option)**

Copy visible layers into selected layer
Option **Merge Visible (menu option)**
Alt **Merge Visible (menu option)**

Copy linked layers into selected layer
Option **Merge Linked (menu option)**
Alt **Merge Linked (menu option)**

Because text and effects are rasterized when being merged, you can no longer edit them except as painted objects.

You can merge two or more separate layers to make one single layer, compositing the content of both, with the upper layers covering (and thus deleting) content in lower layers. The new layer reflects the opacity, blending mode, and styles of the original layers, but these characteristics are rasterized when merged. Thus, the new layer has an opacity of 100%, a normal blending mode, and no styles. You can select each of these Merge options either from the main Layer menu or from the palette menu on the Layers palette.

- To **merge a layer into the layer beneath it**, select the top layer and choose the Merge Down command in the Layer menu or the Layers palette menu. The two layers now appear as one using the bottommost layer's name.
- To **merge all currently visible layers**, select a visible layer, set the visibility of other layers to be merged to show by clicking the Show box so that the Eye icon shows, and then choose the Merge Visible command in the Layer menu or the Layers palette menu. The layers now appear as one using the topmost layer's name.
- To **merge linked layers**, select a layer, set other layers to be linked by clicking the link box so that the Link icon shows, and then choose the Merge Linked command in the Layer menu or the Layers palette menu. The layers now appear as one using the selected layer's name.
- To **merge layers in a clipping group**, select the bottom layer in the group and then choose the Merge Group command in the Layer menu or the Layers palette menu. The layers now appear as one using the bottom layer's name.
- To **merge all layers** ("flatten" the image), choose the Flatten Image command in the Layer menu or the Layers palette menu. The layers now appear as one in the Background layer. If there are hidden layers, you will be asked to confirm that these layers should be deleted.

9.5 Adding a Fill Layer or an Adjustment Layer

Fill and Adjustment layers are a special class of layer used to change the appearance of layers beneath them. Fill layers create a layer with a solid color, pattern, or gradient filling the entire layer. Adjustment layers allow you to add a single layer that adjusts images only on the layers beneath it. (Refer to the color section "Adjustments" to see how the various adjustments affect the image.)

There are 14 types of Fill and Adjustment layers, and each will be discussed individually throughout the book. However, you add each type in the same way:

1 Select the layer you want the Fill or Adjustment layer to be placed above. If a selection is an active when you add the fill or adjustment layer, it is used as a layer mask.

2 To select the Fill or Adjustment layer, choose Layer > New Fill Layer, choose Layer > New Adjustment Layer, or select it from the Layer palette's Create New Fill Or Adjustment Layer menu.

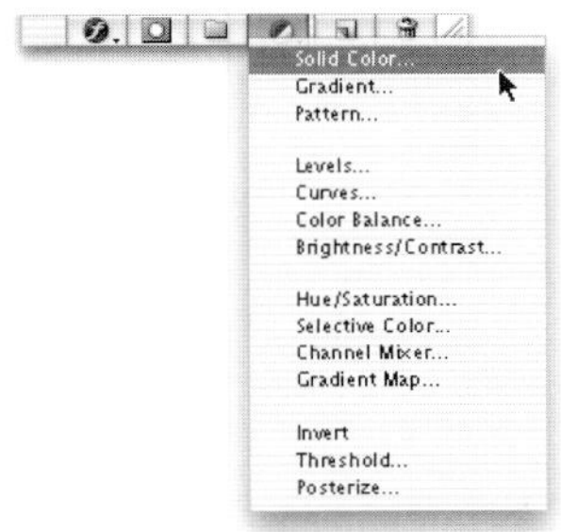

The Create New Fill Or Adjustment Layer menu; these same options are available in the Layer menu.

3 Depending on the Fill or Adjustment layer selected, you'll see a dialog in which you can specify options about the new layer. Set the options (you should see the changes affect the image in real time) and then click OK.

4 The new layer appears above the previously selected layer with a layer thumbnail and a layer mask. To change the options for the layer, double-click the layer thumbnail to reopen the dialog.

Fill and Adjustment Types

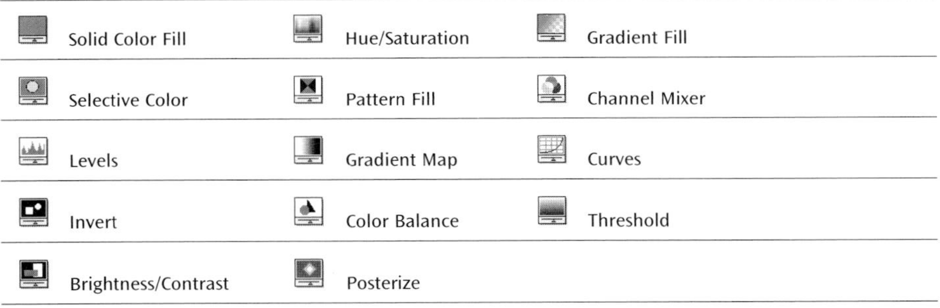

Solid Color Fill	Hue/Saturation	Gradient Fill
Selective Color	Pattern Fill	Channel Mixer
Levels	Gradient Map	Curves
Invert	Color Balance	Threshold
Brightness/Contrast	Posterize	

➠ 4.11 Layers Palette

➠ 8 Making Selections

➠ 13 Making Image Adjustments

➠ 14 Working with Colors, Gradients, and Patterns

All Adjustment and Fill layers always include a layer mask that you can use to control the shape of the layer.

A fill thumbnail displays the color, gradient, or pattern in that layer.

9.6 Creating Layer Sets

→ 4.11 Layers Palette

→ 9.8 Linking and Locking Layers and Layer Sets

Set selected layer set's blending mode to Pass Through
Shift Option P
Shift Alt P

Create new layer set below the current layer/layer set
⌘-click the New Layer Set icon
Ctrl-click the New Layer Set icon

Create a new layer set using dialog
Option-click the New Layer Set icon
Alt-click the New Layer Set icon

Layer sets are folders in which you can collect several layers. This makes it easier to show, hide, move, and make other changes to several similar layers simultaneously. When you place a layer into a set, it's indented under the set's line item in the Layers palette.

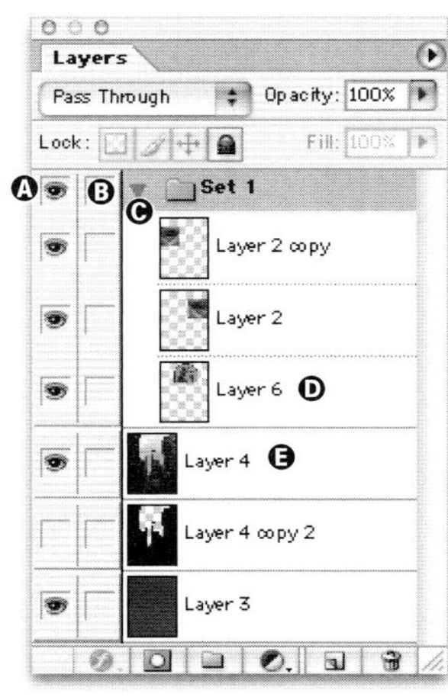

Ⓐ Click to show or hide all layers in the set.
Ⓑ Click to link all layers in the set.
Ⓒ Click to expand or contract the layer set view.
Ⓓ Layer in set.
Ⓔ Layer out of set.

Depending on how you want to initially populate the new set, do one of the following:

- To **quickly start a new empty set**, click the New Set button at the bottom of the Layers palette. The new layer set appears immediately above the previously selected layer.
- To **start an empty set**, make sure no layers are linked to the currently selected layer and choose Layer > New > Layer Set… or choose New Layer Set… from the Layers palette menu. Enter information about the new set in the dialog and click OK. The new layer set appears immediately above the previously selected layer.
- To **create a set from linked layers**, with one of the linked layers selected, choose New Layer Set From Linked… from the Layer menu or the Layers palette menu. Enter information about the new set in the dialog and click OK. The new layer set appears with the linked layers inside it immediately above the previously selected layer.

9.6 Creating Layer Sets *(Continued)*

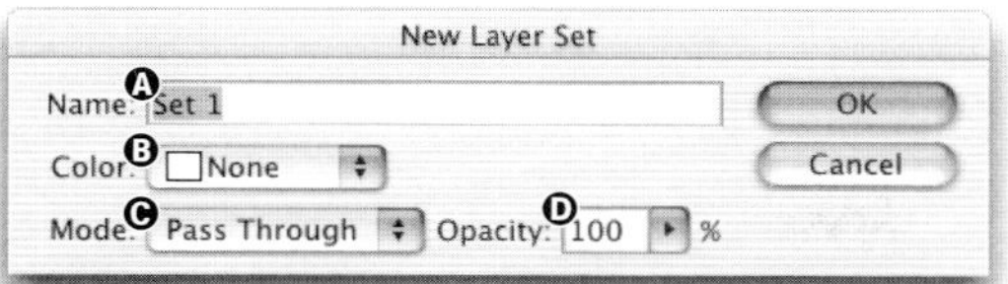

A Enter the name for the layer set.

B Choose a color for the layer set in the palette. This color does not affect the layer set itself, but allows you to color-code sets depending on use.

C Choose an initial blending mode for the layer set. This options determines how layers in the set affect layers outside the set. Modes set for individual layers affect only other layers in the same set. You can change the blending mode later in the Layers palette.

D Enter an initial opacity for the layer. You can change the opacity later in the Layers palette.

Duplicating Layer Sets

Like duplicating a layer, duplicating a layer set creates an exact copy of the layers in a set immediately above and in the same position as the originating set.

- Click and drag a layer set from the palette to the New Layer Set button and release. The duplicate set appears above the layer set from which it was duplicated.
- Select a layer set and then choose Duplicate Layer Set… from the Layer menu, the Layers palette menu, or the layer's contextual menu. Enter information in the Duplicate Layer dialog and click OK. Depending on the options set, the duplicate layer appears above the layer from which it was duplicated.

To move a layer into a set, click and drag the layer onto the layer set folder. The layer is placed at the bottom of the group.

You can also move a layer directly into a position in the group by dragging it between two layers in a group.

To move a layer out of a set, drag and drop it on the set's folder, or simply drag it out of the set to the desired position.

If you select a layer set and then add new layers, they are automatically placed in the selected layer set.

9.7 Managing Layers and Layer Sets

➠ 4.11 Layers Palette

➠ 8.2 Selecting a Layer or Its Contents

Move the selected layer backward/ forward one level

⌘ [or]

Ctrl [or]

Select the layer below/above current layer

Option [or]

Alt [or]

Move the selected layer to the back/front (or back/front of layer set)

Shift Option [or]

Shift Alt [or]

Select the back/front layer

Shift Option [or]

Shift Alt [or]

Jump to the topmost layer under the cursor

⌘ Ctrl Option -click in canvas

Alt right-click in canvas

Once you create a layer or layer set, you can manage them in a variety of ways to help you better organize them for particular uses.

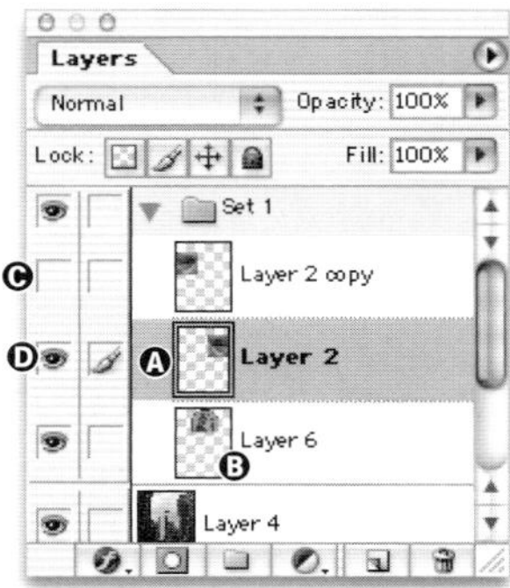

Ⓐ The currently selected (active) layer.

Ⓑ Click a layer thumbnail or name to activate it.

Ⓒ Layer hidden.

Ⓓ Layer showing.

Each layer and layer set can have a unique name and a color code associated with it. To change these properties, select the layer or layer set, click its thumbnail, and choose Layer Properties… (or Layer Set Properties…) in the Layers palette menu. In the following dialog, enter the name and color and click OK.

Activating

You can edit only the selected, active layer. The active layer or layer set is highlighted in the Layers palette. To activate a layer, do one of the following,

- Click the layer thumbnail or name in the Layers palette.
- Control/right-click content in the layer, and select the layer name from the contextual menu.
- Click the layer set folder or name. You cannot paint or edit in active layer sets (you have to select individual layers within it), but you can move active layer sets as if they were linked.

Changing Stacking Order

The order in which layers appear on top of each other dramatically affects the image itself. You can view the order of the layers in the Layers palette. The most common way to arrange layers or layer sets is to click and drag the layer or layer set in the palette up or down and release at the desired position. As you drag, a thick black bar appears between layers, indicating where the layer will be placed when dropped.

9.7 Managing Layers and Layer Sets *(Continued)*

In addition, you can select a layer or layer set and then choose one of the options from the Layer > Arrange submenu:

Bring To Front Places the layer on top.

Bring Forward Moves the layer up one level.

Send Backward Moves the layer down one level.

Send To Back Places the layer beneath all other layers except the Background layer.

Showing or Hiding

You can selectively hide or show layers, layer sets, and layer effects at any time while you are working. The Eye icon appears next to layers that are currently visible Eye icon, and clicking this icon toggles the visibility on or off for that layer or all the layers in a layer set. In addition, you can show and hide layers by doing one of the following:

- Option/Alt-click the Eye icon to hide all other layers. Option/Alt-click the icon again to show all other layers.
- Drag through the eye column to quickly change the visibility of multiple layers and layer sets.

You set a layer set's properties and visibility in much the same way that you set a layer's properties (see Section 9.4).

You can change the layer name directly in the palette by double-clicking the layer name, typing the new name, and pressing Enter.

9.8 Linking and Locking Layers and Layer Sets

➠ 4.11 Layers Palette

When layers are linked, all linked layers activate when any of the linked layers is selected (not just the originally linked layer).

You can link layers together so that you can work on them together, or you can lock them so that they cannot be edited and or moved.

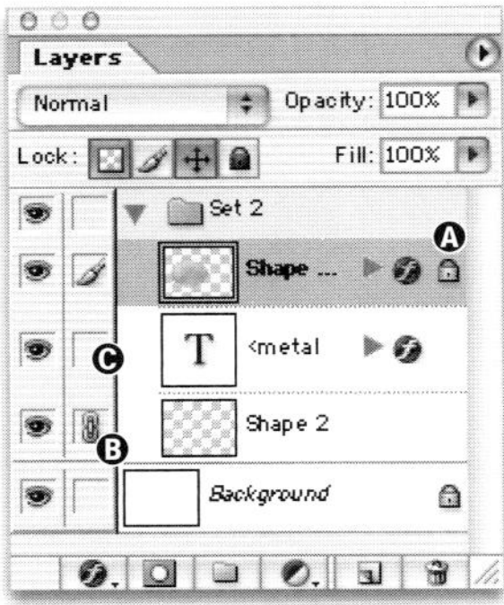

A An active layer has had its transparent pixels and positions locked.

B The layer linked to the active layer.

C The layer *not* linked to the active layer.

Linking

Linking layers lets you adjust the positions of different layers simultaneously. So, if two layers are linked, and you move one layer, the linked layer or layers move by that same amount. To link layers, follow these steps:

1. Select the first layer that will be linked to others.
2. Click in the link box next to each layer you want linked to the first layer.
3. You can now move, align, create sets, lock, merge, or delete these layers as one unit.

Locking

To prevent a layer or layer set from being moved and/or edited, you can lock it. First select the layer or layer set, and then click one of the lock icons in the Layers palette.

- Click to lock transparent pixels in the layer. You can edit only regions of the layer that currently contain content. This lock is only available to draw layers.
- Click to lock image pixels in the layer. Prevents image on the layer from being edited, but it can still be moved as a layer. This lock is only available to draw layers.
- Click to lock the layer's position.
- Click to enact all available locks for the selected layer.
- To lock the selected layer and all layers linked to it, choose Layer > Lock All Linked Layers… or choose Lock All Linked Layers… from the Layers palette menu. In the dialog, check the link types(s) you want to enact, and click OK.

9.8 Linking and Locking Layers and Layer Sets

(Continued)

- To lock a selected layer set, choose Layer > Lock All Layers in Set… or choose Lock All Layers in Set… from the Layers palette menu. In the dialog, check the link types(s) you want to enact, and click OK.

After you apply any of the locks to a layer, a lock icon appears on the far right side of the layer in the Layers palette. The specific lock icon is highlighted in the lock buttons.

Unless you always want two layers to move together, it is best to unlink layers when you are finished moving them. Otherwise, you might move both layers when you only mean to move one of them.

To unlock a layer or a layer set, select the layer or layer set and click the highlighted lock.

WHAT IS TRANSPARENCY?

Although not a literal "layer," any area of the image without content or a background image is transparent; that is, it is completely blank. However, transparency cannot be represented as simply black or white, since those colors are potential background colors. Therefore, transparent regions are represented as a checkerboard pattern of gray and white squares. You can change the appearance of the transparency grid in the Transparency & Gamut preferences.

This checkerboard appears in the absence of content (or a Background layer) in any layers and also shows through if the opacity of the pixels in a region is less than 100%.

9.9 Deleting Layers or Layer Sets

➠ 4.11 Layers Palette

If you are not sure whether you will need a layer again, you might simply want to hide the layer rather than deleting it.

You can also delete masks or effects by dragging their thumbnail or icon to the trash can.

Often you will find that you no longer need the content of an entire layer in the image, and since extra layers add to the file size even if they are not visible, it is a good idea to delete them.

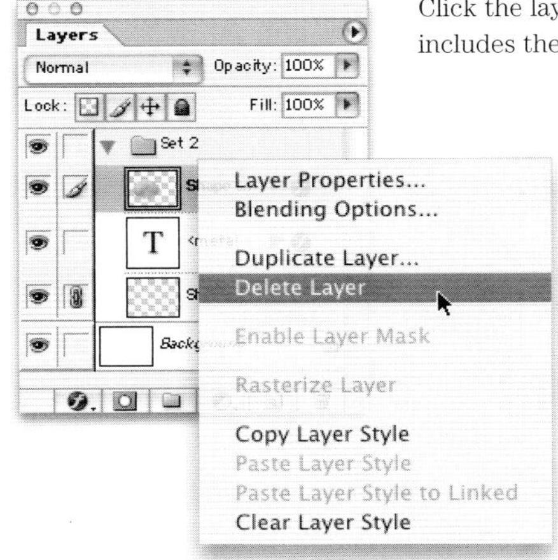

Click the layer title (not the thumbnail) to view the menu that includes the Delete Layer option.

Deleting Layers

There are about as many ways to delete a layer from your canvas as there are ways to create them, but all the deletion methods begin with the same action. First select the layer to be deleted, and then do one of the following:

- To **quickly delete** a layer, click and drag the layer to the Trash icon at the bottom of the Layers palette and release.
- To **delete the layer and all layers linked to it**, choose Layer > Delete > Linked Layers. Click Yes to confirm the deletion.
- To **delete all hidden layers** in the document, choose Layer > Delete > Hidden Layers. Click Yes to confirm the deletion. This removes all layers that do not have the Eye icon next to them in the Layers palette.
- To **delete the selected layer**, click the Trash icon at the bottom of the Layers palette and then click Yes to confirm the deletion.
- To **delete the selected layer**, Control/right-click the layer's name or click the Layers palette menu and choose Delete Layer. Click Yes to confirm the deletion.
- To **delete the selected layer**, choose Layer > Delete > Layer. Click Yes to confirm the deletion.

9.9 Deleting Layers or Layer Sets *(Continued)*

Deleting Layer Sets

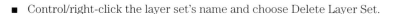

To quickly delete a layer set and all layers, in it click and drag the layer set to the trash can at the bottom of the Layers palette and release.

You can also choose whether to delete the set, but keep the layers inside it. First, access the Delete Layer Set dialog:

- Select the layer set to be deleted in the Layers palette and click the Trash icon in the Layers palette.
- Control/right-click the layer set's name and choose Delete Layer Set.
- Click the Layers palette menu and choose Delete Layer Set.

Then, in the dialog, click one of these:

- Click Set Only to remove the set, but retain the layers inside.
- Click Set And Contents to remove the set and all the layers it contains.

UNDERSTANDING FILE SIZE

The file size is how much disk space is required to store the data used to create the image on a hard drive or other storage media. How much memory an image takes is based on several factors:

Image Size The larger the dimensions of the image, the more data that has to be recorded.

Resolution The more information packed into the area of an image, the more information that has to be recorded.

Color Mode Different modes require different amounts of data to be recorded.

Layers The more layers added to an image, the more data required.

Bits/Channel The more bits used to record a single channel, the more data is required.

Metadata Any other information recorded with the image (author name, workgroups, keywords, and so on) will add slightly to the file size.

9.10 Rasterizing Vector Layers

➠ 4.11 Layers Palette

Warning: Once you rasterize a text or other vector layer, you can edit it only as a bitmap image. You can always undo the change using the History, but once the image is saved, the rasterization is fixed and cannot be undone.

Rasterizing a vector layer fixes that layer's resolution to be the image's resolution.

You cannot use filters and tools used to paint in layers in vector layers such as type, shape, and vector masks. However, you can convert vector layers into pixel-based layers by rasterizing them.

- To **rasterize a single layer**, select the layer with the vector information on it that you want to rasterize. Choose Layer > Rasterize > Layer. You can also choose to rasterize specific vector content in the layer (Type, Shape, Fill Content, or Vector Mask) or to rasterize this layer and any layers linked to it.
- To **rasterize all layers** in the document, choose Layer > Rasterize > All Layers. This will rasterize not only the vector layers, but text and vector masks as well.

EDITING ON ALL LAYERS

Most tools allow you to edit on only a single layer at a time, but a few tools allow you to use all the layers while editing for various purposes.

Magic Wand Selects colors from any visible layer rather than just from the active layer.

Clone Stamp Samples image data from all layers for cloning rather than just from the active layer.

Magic Eraser Selects the color for deletion from any visible layer but still deletes only from the active layer.

Paint Bucket The fill area is limited by all visible layers, but the fill is applied only to the active layer.

Blur, Sharpen, Smudge Copies edited areas of visible layers into the active layer. The original layers remain unaffected.

9.11 Aligning and Distributing Layers

Aligning the content of layers with the content of other layers allows you to more precisely place layers in relation to each other. Alignment and distribution work only with the active pixels in the layers.

➠ 3.4 Move Tool

➠ 4.11 Layers Palette

➠ 9.8 Linking and Locking Layers and Layer Sets

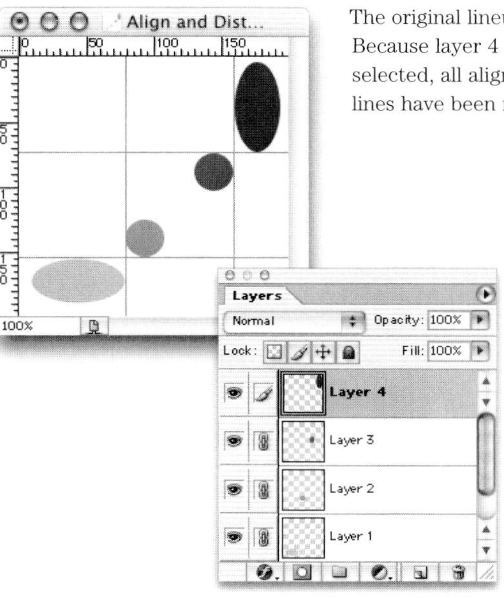

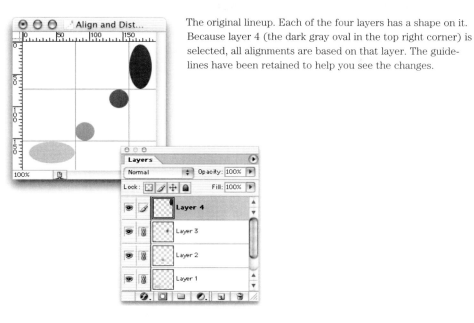

The original lineup. Each of the four layers has a shape on it. Because layer 4 (the dark gray oval in the top right corner) is selected, all alignments are based on that layer. The guidelines have been retained to help you see the changes.

Aligning Layers

To align layers, follow these steps:

1 Link two or more layers that you want to align. Select the layer to which you want the other layers to align.

2 Choose the Move tool and select the alignment buttons from the tool options bar; or with any tool, choose Layers > Align Linked and then an alignment option, or click one of the alignment buttons in the tool options bar. The entire contents of the linked layers align as defined using the selected layer as the base. So, for example, if you are aligning to the top, all layers will be aligned to the top of the selected layer.

Distributing layers may not always produce the desired results. Often you will have to manually space objects to get them to appear visually distributed the way you want them.

Remember that only the opaque pixels on the layer are aligned or distributed. If the alignment or distribution is not working as expected, you might have pixels that are not showing up for some reason (for example, they are the same color as the content behind them).

Alignment Options

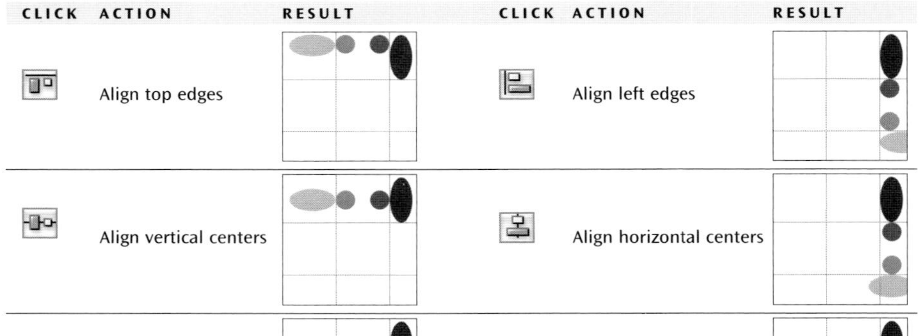

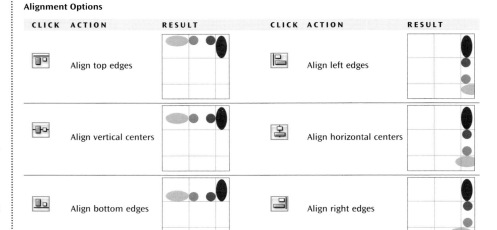

CLICK	ACTION	RESULT	CLICK	ACTION	RESULT
	Align top edges			Align left edges	
	Align vertical centers			Align horizontal centers	
	Align bottom edges			Align right edges	

Distributing Layers

To distribute layers, follow these steps:

1. Link three or more layers that you want to align. Select the layer to which you want the other layers to align.
2. Choose the Move tool and select the distribution buttons from the tool options bar, or with any tool choose Layers > Distribute Linked and then an alignment option, or click one of the distribution buttons in the tool options bar. The entire contents of the linked layers are distributed as defined using the selected layer as the base.

Distribution Options

CLICK	ACTION	RESULT	CLICK	ACTION	RESULT
	Distribute top edges			Distribute left edges	
	Distribute vertical			Distribute horizontal	
	Distribute bottom			Distribute right edges	

9.12 Blending Modes and Opacity

Layers not only allow you to build up overlapping images, but also allow you to set how those layers interact. The primary way to set how layers interact in the layer's palette is to use blending modes and opacity.

➠ 4.11 Layers Palette

➠ 10.2 Applying Effects and Styles

➠ 10.6 Applying Advanced Blending Options

➠ Color Section: Blending Modes

Setting the Blending Mode

The original layered image. A drop shadow effect has been added to Layer 2.

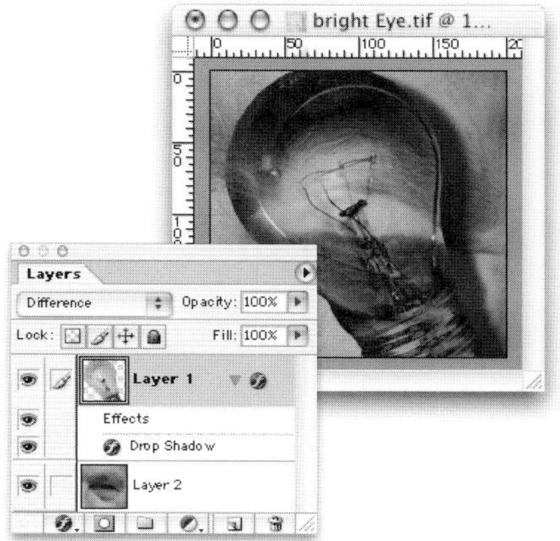

Layer 2's blending mode has been set to Difference, creating an inverted look in the area of the light bulb image.

The blending mode assigned to a layer determines how that layer affects the pixels of layers underneath it. For a description of each blending mode, see the "Blending Modes" section in the color insert.

To quickly change the blending mode, select a single layer or layer set and then choose one of the blending modes from the blending mode pop-up menu.

When you first create a layer set, its blending mode is set to Pass Through by default, which preserves the blending modes of the layers within the set . If you set a blending mode other than Pass Through for a layer set, the layers are composited (with the modes being applied only to other layers in the set) and then treated as a single layer in the image using the layer set's blending mode.

Setting the Opacity

A layer's opacity is a percentage value that defines the transparency of image pixels. If the opacity is less than 100%, the pixels are translucent, and images from layers underneath show through.

Normal blending mode
Shift Option N
Shift Alt N

Dissolve blending mode
Shift Option I
Shift Alt I

Multiply blending mode
Shift Option M
Shift Alt M

Screen blending mode
Shift Option S
Shift Alt S

Overlay blending mode
Shift Option O
Shift Alt O

Soft Light blending mode
Shift Option F
Shift Alt F

Hard Light blending mode
Shift Option H
Shift Alt H

Color Dodge blending mode
Shift Option D
Shift Alt D

Darken blending mode
Shift Option K
Shift Alt K

Lighten blending mode
Shift Option G
Shift Alt G

Difference blending mode
Shift Option E
Shift Alt E

Exclusion blending mode
Shift Option X
Shift Alt X

Hue blending mode
Shift Option U
Shift Alt U

Saturation blending mode
Shift Option T
Shift Alt T

Color blending mode
Shift Option C
Shift Alt C

Luminosity blending mode
Shift Option Y
Shift Alt Y

You can change a layer's blending mode and opacity as part of the advanced Blending Options available in the Layer Styles dialog.

You cannot change the blending mode and opacity in the Background layer or locked layers.

You cannot change blending mode and opacity selectively in a layer. Settings affect the entire layer evenly.

To change the opacity of the pixels in a layer, select the layer or layer set and then enter a new opacity, or use the Opacity slider to set the percentage. If you are using the Opacity slider, you can view the change to the layer in real time as you slide it back and forth.

If you set the opacity for a layer set, this setting is used as the base opacity for the layers in the set. Setting the opacity of a layer within the set then is not cumulative, but rather the percentage scale is compressed.

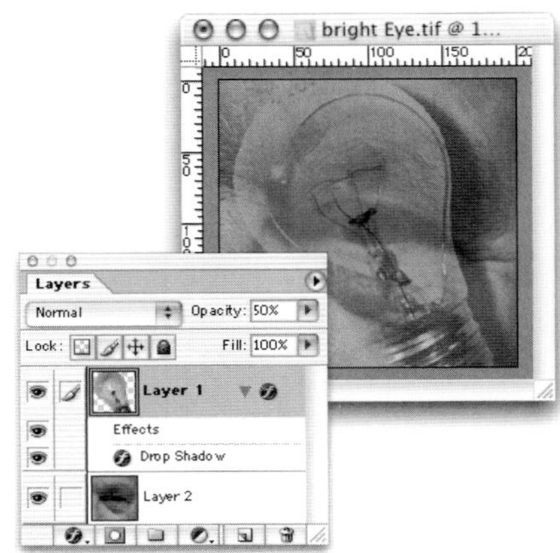

Layer 2's opacity has been set to 50%.

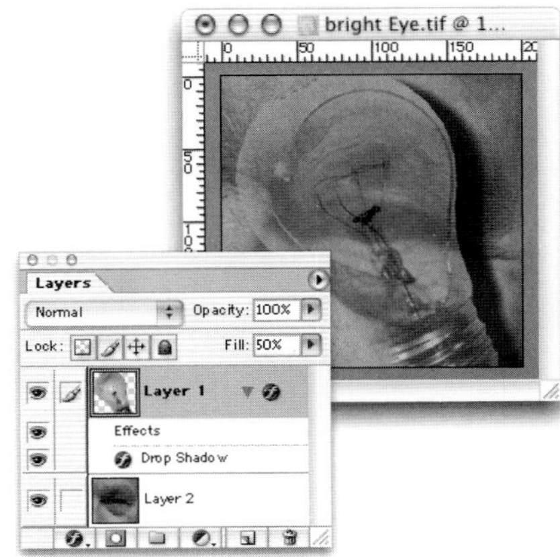

Layer 2's fill opacity has been set to 50%. Notice that the shadow remains at the original strength.

Setting the Fill Opacity

The fill opacity allows you to set the opacity of pixels that have been painted or of shapes drawn into the layer. Unlike opacity, which affects all of the content of the layer—including layer styles and blending modes applied to the layer—the fill opacity affects only pixels that you have placed on the layer using drawing, painting, or vector tools.

To change the fill opacity of the pixels in a layer, choose the layer and then enter a new fill opacity, or use the Fill Opacity slider to set the percentage. If you are using the Fill Opacity slider, you can view the change to the layer in real time as you slide it back and forth.

9.13 Clipping Groups

Clipping groups allow you to use one layer to clip (much like a layer mask) one or more layers above them. You can group as many layers as you want to a single base layer, and the layers above will only show through in active pixels of the base layer.

➠ 4.11 Layers Palette

➠ 11 Masking Layers

Don't confuse this form of grouping with the more standard use of the term *grouping* in other applications. Although you can "group" layers, creating layer sets has more in common with the function of grouping layers seen in other graphics applications such as FreeHand and Illustrator.

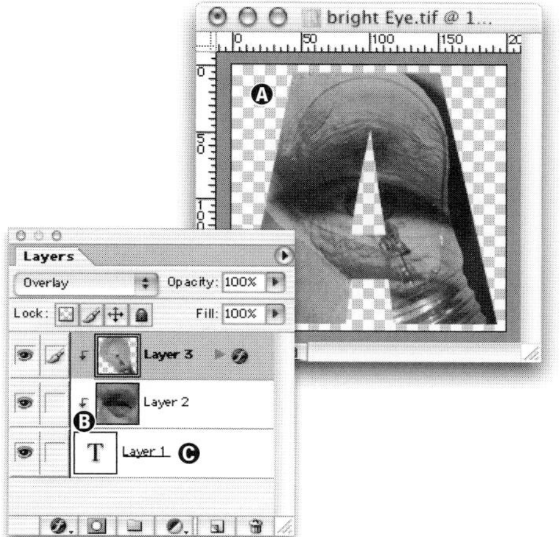

Ⓐ Layers 2 and 3 are clipped by Layer 1 underneath.

Ⓑ **Group arrow** Indicates that the layer is grouped to the layer beneath.

Ⓒ **Base layer** The bottom layer to which the above layers are grouped. The base layer is used to clip the content of the grouped layers. An underline indicates that this is the base layer.

Adding Layers to a Group

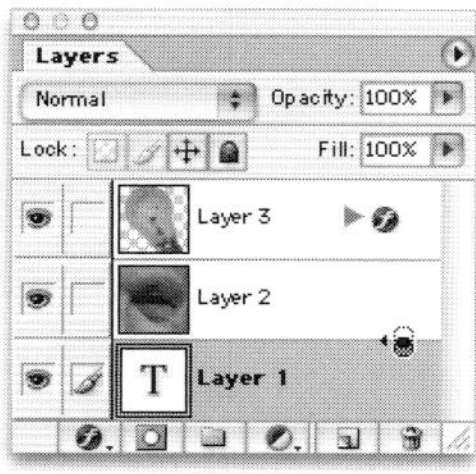

Layer 2 is being added to the text layer beneath to create a clipping group by Option/Alt-clicking the divider line between the two layers. Notice that the cursor has changed to two interlocking circles.

- To **group two adjacent layers**, press Option/Alt and place the mouse cursor on the divider between the two layers and click. You will notice, when you are right over the layer divider line, that the cursor changes to two interlocking circles. The top layer will now be clipped by the bottom (base) layer. Repeating this for any layer immediately above a grouped layer will add that layer to the group.
- To **group one layer with the layer beneath**, select the layer and choose Layer > Group With Previous.
- To **group multiple layers**, select one of the layers, link the other layers to be grouped, and choose Layer > Group Linked.

9.13 Clipping Groups *(Continued)*

Removing Layers from a Group

- To **ungroup two adjacent layers**, press Option/Alt, place the mouse cursor on the divider between the two layers, and click. You will notice, when you are right over the layer divider line, that the cursor changes to two interlocking circles. Repeat for as many layers as desired.
- To **ungroup one layer in a group**, select the layer and choose Layer **>** Ungroup.
- To **ungroup all the layers in a group**, select the base layer in the group and choose Layer **>** Ungroup.

CHAPTER 10

Adding Layer Styles

YOU USE STYLES TO APPLY special effects such as drop shadows, glows, and color overlays to a layer's content as needed to change its appearance. However, even more important, you can remove or hide these effects as easily as you apply them. In addition, you can use styles to apply a variety of blending options for layers, and you can save both the effects and blending modes for easy application to other layers.

10.1 Style Basics

2.6 Layer Menu

4.7 Styles Palette

Color Section: Blending Modes

Color Section: Effects

Effects are vector-based, which accounts for their versatility but also means that they can not be painted on until they are rasterized.

Styles are composed of two components that are applied to individual layers:

Blending options allow you to exercise exact control over how effects and other layers interact with the layer.

Effects—shadows, glows, bevels, overlays, and strokes—can be associated with a particular layer to change its appearance. When you apply an effect to a layer as a custom style, you will see an "f" icon to the right of the layer title, and you will see the name of the effect to the right. For each effect in the layer, you will also see a line item underneath the layer.

Refer to this "uneffected" version of the image throughout this chapter. You apply blending options and effects to a single layer at a time, although you can copy effects between layers and save effects as Style Presets. Style Presets are all contained in the Styles palette, which allows you to save and apply a collection of effects or blending modes.

A Style in layer Click the triangle to show or hide a list of effects applied to this layer.

B Effects Each line item represents an individual effect applied to the layer.

C All effects in the layer are currently visible. Click to show or hide all effects in the layer.

D This effect is currently visible. Click to show or hide just this effect in the layer.

10.1 Style Basics *(Continued)*

Setting Global Lighting

Several effects, such as shadows and beveling, use a simulated light source to create the effect. This lighting source is composed of two variables:

Angle Sets the position of the light source in a 360° circle around the content.

Altitude Sets the height above the content for the light source.

To keep a consistent light source for all effects, which is important for preserving realistic images, you can set a global lighting source for the image that you can then check as an option when you use lighting options in an effect. Choose Layer > Layer Style > Global Lights…, complete the dialog, and click OK.

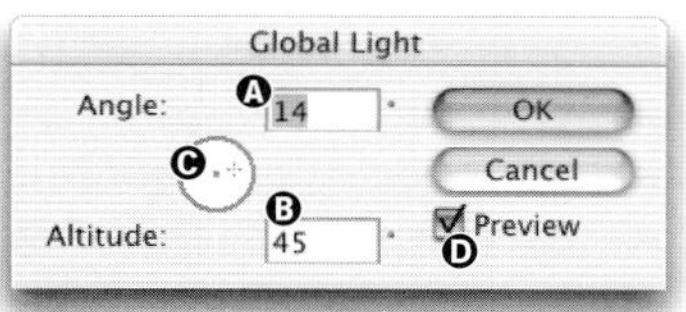

Ⓐ Enter a value (from –360 to 360) for the angle of the simulated light source.

Ⓑ Enter a value (from 0 to 90) for the altitude of the simulated light source.

Ⓒ Click around the edge to set the light angle. Click within the circle to set the altitude.

Ⓓ Check to preview the changes to styles that are using global lighting in the canvas.

Creating Contours

Several layer effects—for example, glow effects—use a contour to help shape the effect. You choose contours from a pull-down menu of contour presets that shows a thumbnail representing a side view of the contour. You can edit contours by simply double-clicking the contour thumbnail to open the Contour Editor dialog and adjusting the points of the contour.

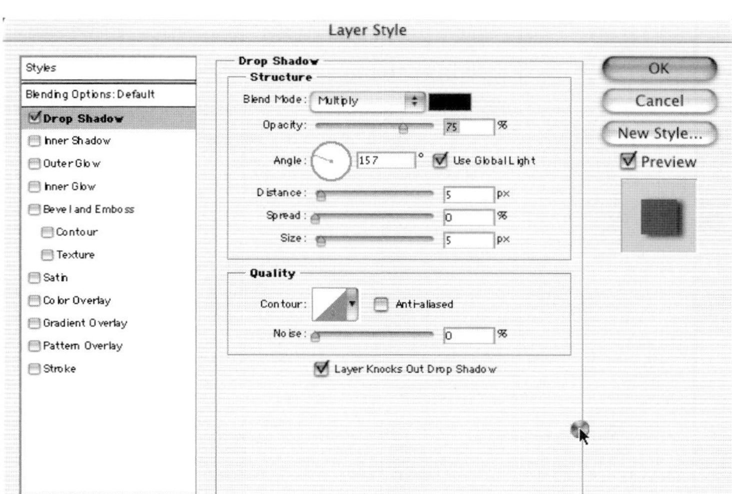

In the Layer Effects dialog, double-click the thumbnail next to the Contour drop-down menu to open the Contour Editor.

When you delete a layer, all its effects are also deleted.

It's easy to confuse styles and effects. Just remember that a group of effects is referred to as a style.

Several effects, such as shadows, only use the Global light settings angle and will ignore the altitude.

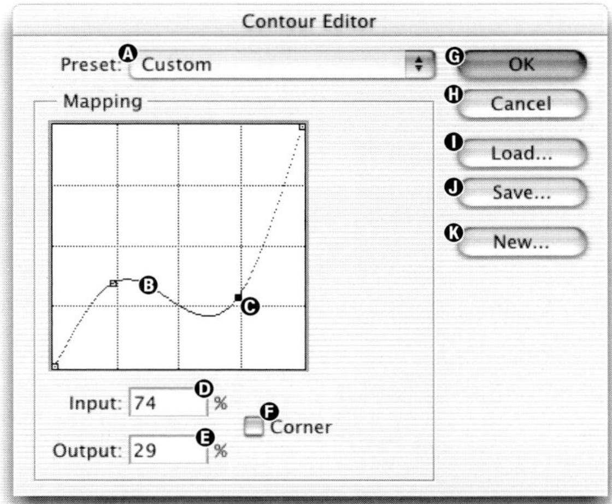

Ⓐ Choose a preset contour shape.

Ⓑ **Contour curve** Click a point on the line to select it and move it up and down or left and right to adjust the graph.

Ⓒ **Selected point** Selected points are solid black squares. You can move them directly in the graph, or enter values below.

Ⓓ Enter a value (2 to 98) to set the input level (x position) of the selected point in the graph.

Ⓔ Enter a value (0 to 100) to set the output level (y position) of the selected point in the graph.

Ⓕ Check to use the selected point as a corner, rather than as a curved, point.

Ⓖ Click to accept changes and close the Contour Editor.

Ⓗ Click to cancel changes and close the Contour Editor.

Ⓘ Click to load a saved contour.

Ⓙ Click to save the current contour.

Ⓚ Click to add the current contour to the contour presets.

10.2 Applying Effects and Styles

You can apply styles in a variety of ways, but the most direct way, and the way that offers the most versatility to setting specific effects, is through the use of the Layer Style dialog. This dialog provides controls to add any effect and provides options to control those effects. To simply add an effect to a layer, follow these steps. Further sections in this chapter then detail how to set the options for each of these effects.

1 Select the layer to which you want to apply one or more styles.

2 Open the Layer Style dialog by doing one of the following:

- Choose a specific layer style to apply from the menu at the bottom of the Layers palette [icon] or from the Layer > Layer Style submenu. The Layer Style dialog opens to that style and applies its default options to the layer.
- Double-click the layer's thumbnail or title. The Layer Style dialog opens to Blending Options with no styles applied.
- Double-click an exiting effect in the layer. The Layer Style dialog opens to the selected effect.
- Control/right-click an existing effect in the layer and choose a layer effect from the contextual menu. This list will not include Blending Options that you can select from the contextual menu opened by Control/right-clicking the layer's title.

3 Click the check box next to the effects you want to apply to the layer, and then click the title of each effect to set the options for that style. (Clicking the title also applies the style.) The options for each style are described in Sections 10.6 through 10.12.

4 Click OK when you are finished setting effects. The effects appear as a list below the layer.

➠ 2.6 Layer Menu

➠ 4.11 Layers Palette

➠ 23.3 Adding Effects with ImageReady

➠ 8.2 Selecting a Layer or Its Contents

➠ Color Section: Effects

The Contour and Texture styles are applied only if the Bevel And Emboss style is applied.

You can also apply styles to a background image, but, obviously, styles such as the drop shadow, which appear outside the content, will not appear.

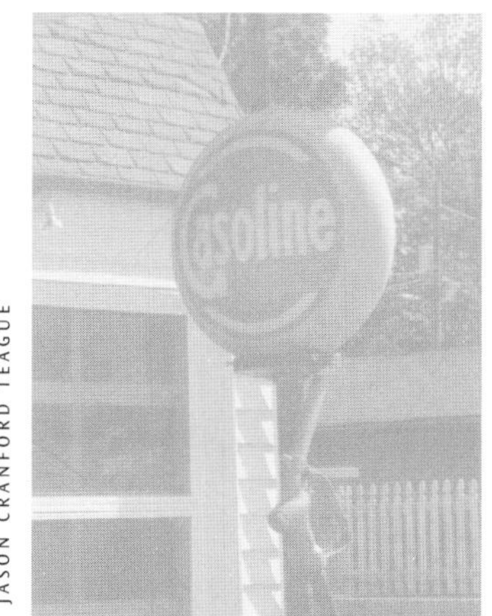

ImageReady also allows you to add effects to layers, but handles this through the Layer Effects palette rather than a dialog (see Section 23.3).

The contour and texture effects that are indented under the Bevel and Emboss effect are only applied to the area affected by the Bevel and Emboss effect and not to the entire layer.

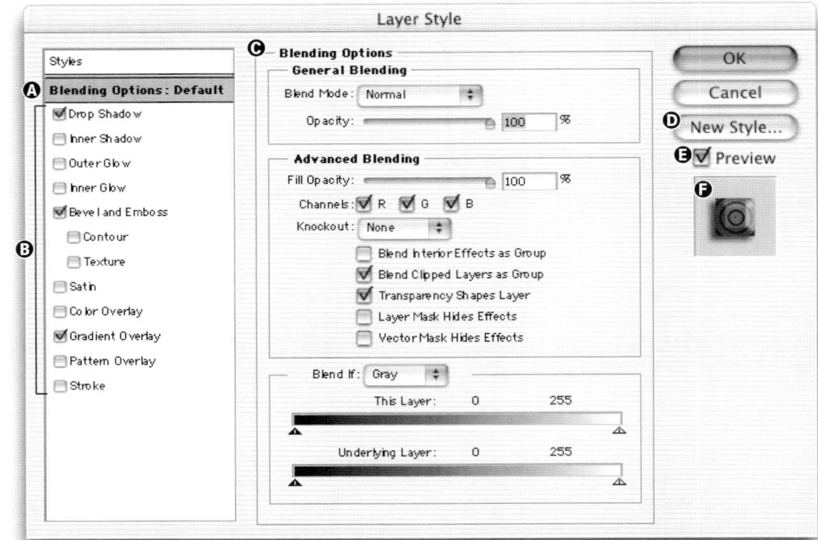

A Blending Options Select this to set specific options for how the layer should blend with other layers and how the layer's effects should blend with it and other layers.

B Effects Check the effects you want to apply to the layer. Clicking the name shows you the options for that effect.

C Effect options Select an effect in the list, and then set the options for how that effect should appear in the layer. Currently the blending options are displayed.

D Click to save the style in the Styles palette as a new Style Preset.

E Check if you want the canvas to display a preview of the applied styles.

F Preview thumbnail Displays a thumbnail representation of the combined effects associated with the current layer.

Copying and Pasting Styles

You can copy and paste the effects of one layer as a style to one or more layers. To copy a single effect from one layer to another, click the effect, drag it underneath the target layer, and drop it.

To copy all the effects from one layer to another, you can either drag the effects line underneath the layer or follow these steps:

1. Select the layer from which you want to copy styles.
2. Choose Copy Layer Style from the style's contextual menu (Control/right-click the layer or any of the styles in the layer) or from the Layer > Layer Style submenu.

10.2 Applying Effects and Styles *(Continued)*

3 The layer style is now in memory. To paste it into a layer, select the target layer and then do one of the following:

- To paste the style into the layer, choose Paste Layer Style from the style's contextual menu (Control/right-click the layer or any of the effects in the target layer) or from the Layer > Layer Style submenu.
- To paste the style to all layers linked to the selected layer, choose Paste Layer Style To Linked from the style's contextual menu (Control/right-click the layer or any of the effects in the target layer) or from the Layer > Layer Style submenu.

4 The styles display below the layer, overwriting any existing styles of the same type that were already associated with the layer.

You can save effects together as preset styles (see Section 10.3).

When copied, layer styles are placed into their own memory location independents of the one used to store content copied using Edit > Copy. The effect will stay in memory until another effect is copied.

Removing Styles

Once you apply an effect to a layer, it remains until you remove it, either individually or as part of the layer style.

- To clear a single style, open the Layer Style dialog, clear the style check box, and click OK. If you want to reinstate the style later, simply open the Layer Style dialog again, and check the style. The previous options are reapplied.
- To clear all styles in a layer, select the layer, choose Clear Layer Style from the Layer > Layer Style submenu or from the contextual menu accessed by Control/right-clicking a style in the Layers palette. Alternatively, you can click the Clear Styles button at the bottom of the Styles palette.

10.3 Creating and Applying Style Presets

➠ 2.6 Layer Menu

➠ 4.7 Styles Palette

➠ 5.1 Preset Manager Overview

➠ Color Section: Effects

You can change the size of the Style Preset thumbnail displayed in the Styles palette by selecting a size option at the top of the Styles palette menu.

Style Presets are a saved copy of a particular set of effects and/or blending options. All currently loaded Style Presets are displayed in the Styles palette.

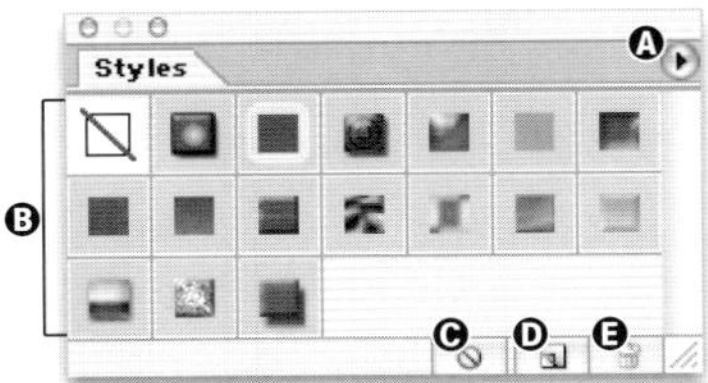

A Styles palette menu

B Style Preset thumbnails Click once to apply the style to the selected layer; double-click to rename the style.

C Clear Styles Click to remove the style from the selected layer.

D Add Style Click to add a new style to the palette based on the style in the selected layer.

E Delete Style Drag a style to this icon to delete it from the Styles palette. Deleting a style does not affect the saved version of the style group.

Creating a Style Preset

Open the Layer Style dialog and create your style as described in Section 10.1. To turn this style into a Style Preset, click the New Style… button, complete the New Style dialog, and click OK. The Layer Style dialog remains open, but the new Style Preset is inserted at the bottom of the Styles palette.

In addition, you can create Style Presets directly from styles already applied to layers. To turn a layer's styles into a Style Preset, first select the layer and then do one of the following:

- Click any blank spot in the Styles palette.
- Click the Create New Style button [icon] in the Styles palette.
- Choose New Style… from the Styles palette menu or contextual menu (Control/right-click any style).

Regardless of which method you use, complete the New Style Preset dialog, and then click OK. The new style appears at the bottom of the Styles palette.

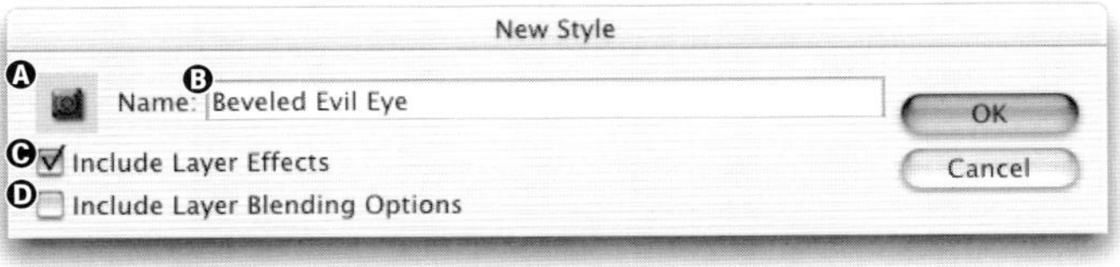

A Displays a thumbnail preview of the style.

B Enter a name for the style.

C Check to include the layer effects in the new style.

D Check to include the advanced layer blending options in the new style.

10.3 Creating and Applying Style Presets *(Continued)*

Applying a Style Preset

To apply a Style Preset to a layer, do one of the following:

- Select the layer in the Layers palette, and then click the style you want to apply in the Styles palette. The styles appear below the layer in the Layers palette, overwriting any existing styles of the same type that were already associated with the layer.
- Drag a Style Preset from the Styles palette and drop it onto the layer in the canvas to which you want to apply it. It is important to get your cursor precisely over content in the layer. The styles appear below the layer in the Layers palette, overwriting any existing styles of the same type that were already associated with the layer.

The Styles palette is a good candidate for docking in the Palette Well. You then have to quickly access it without cluttering your desktop.

ImageReady also has a Styles palette that allows you to add styles to a layer, but it also includes the ability to store rollover states as a part of the style preset.

You can keep applying style presets to the same layer to try out different looks.

STYLES AND TEXT

Although you cannot double-click the text layer icon to open the Layer Style dialog (double-clicking a text layer's icon selects the text), you can apply styles to editable text just as easily as you can apply them to any other layer type. However, effects can sometimes obscure the text if they are not applied judiciously.

10.4 Managing Style Presets

➠ 2.4 Edit Menu

➠ 4.7 Styles Palette

➠ 5.1 Present Manager Overview

Although you apply Style Presets using the Styles palette, you can manage Style Presets from the palette and from the Preset Manager. Both provide equivalent options, but the Style Preset Manager also allows you to select multiple styles to be managed simultaneously. You use this dialog to sort and manage your Style Presets and set characteristics of the palette. To open the Preset Manager, do one of the following:

- Choose Edit > Preset Manager, and then choose Styles from the Preset Type menu.
- Choose Preset Manager… from the Styles palette menu. This action opens the Preset Manager directly in the Style panel.

Ⓐ **Preset Type menu** Choose a preset type to open its panel.

Ⓑ **Style Preset menu** Choose options to change the style's thumbnail appearance, reset styles in the list, or replace styles in the list.

Ⓒ **Style Preset thumbnails** Click to select one style, double-click to change the name, or Shift-click to select multiple styles.

Ⓓ Click when finished with the Style Preset Manager.

Ⓔ Click to load preset lists.

Ⓕ Select one or more styles, and click to save them as a new Style Preset list.

Ⓖ Select one or more styles, and click to rename them.

Ⓗ Select one or more styles, and click to delete them.

Saving Style Presets

You can save a group of styles to be loaded later by doing one of the following:

- Choose Save Styles… in the Styles palette menu, enter a name for the Style Preset, making sure to preserve the .asl suffix, browse to the location on your hard drive where you want to save the Style Preset list, and click OK.
- Open the Style Preset Manager, select the styles in the list you want to save as a separate Style Preset by Shift-clicking the styles, click Save Set…, enter a name for the Style Preset, making sure to preserve the .asl suffix, browse to the location on your hard drive where you want to save the Style Preset list, and click OK.

10.4 Managing Style Presets *(Continued)*

Loading Style Presets

You can load a group of saved presets by either appending a new list to the end of the current list of presets or by replacing the current list with the new list. Both the Styles palette and the Style Preset dialog contain options to load styles, and you can perform the actions from either place. To load a group of Style Presets, do one of the following.

- To **reset** the styles in the Styles palette to the original list, choose Reset Styles… from the Styles palette menu or the Style Preset Manager menu. Click Append to add the original list to the current list, or click Replace to remove the current list and replace it with the original list.
- To **load** a style list to the current list, choose Load Styles…from the Styles palette menu or click Load… in the Style Preset Manager, browse to the location of the Style Preset list on your hard drive, and double-click it. The new list is placed below the current list.
- To **replace** the current style list with a new list, choose Replace Styles… from the Styles palette menu or the Style Preset Manager menu, browse to the location of the Style Preset list on your hard drive, and double-click it. The new list replaces the current list.
- To quickly **add** a preset list, choose a style list name from the bottom of the Styles palette menu or the Style Preset Manger menu. Click Append to add the new list to the current list, or click Replace to remove the current list and replace it with the new list.

Style Preset lists are generally saved in the Adobe Photoshop/Presets/Styles folder.

To rename a style, double-click its thumbnail in the Styles palette or click the Rename… button in the Style Preset Manager.

You can select multiple styles in the Preset Manager to save a set, rename a set, or delete a set.

10.5 Working with Effects

➠ 2.6 Layer Menu
➠ 4.11 Layers Palette
➠ 9.13 Clipping Groups

Once an effect has been applied to a layer, either as a single effect or as part of a group of effects in a style, you can work with the individual effects to show or hide them, scale them, or convert them into rasterized layers.

Hiding Effects

You can temporarily hide an effect, just like hiding a layer, so that its impact does not show up in the image.

- To hide a single effect, click the eye icon next to the effect in the Layers palette. Click again to show the effect.
- To hide all the effects in a particular layer, click the eye icon next to the Effects line for the layer in the Layers palette. All the effects for that layer are hidden. Click again to show the effects.
- To hide all the effects in a document, choose Layer > Layer Styles or Control/right-click any of the styles in the Layers palette and choose Hide All Effects. Repeat and select Show All Effects to show the effects.

Scaling Effects

You can scale the effects of a layer up or down to enlarge or shrink their appearance. To scale effects in a layer, select the layer for which you want to scale the effects, choose Layer > Layer Styles > Scale Effects…, enter the amount by which to scale the effects in the dialog, and click OK.

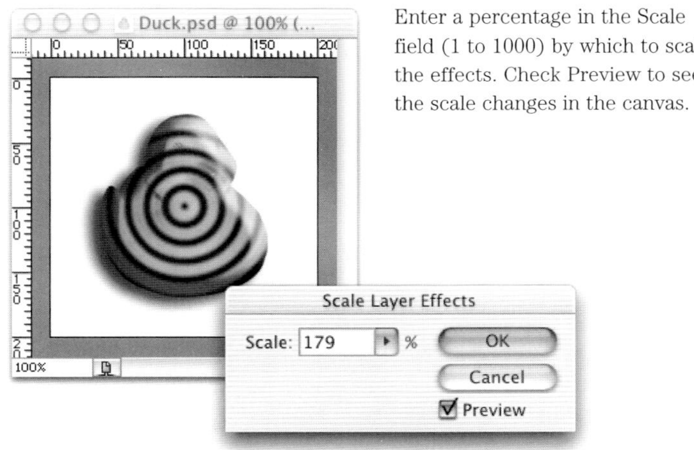

Enter a percentage in the Scale field (1 to 1000) by which to scale the effects. Check Preview to see the scale changes in the canvas.

10.5 Working with Effects *(Continued)*

Converting Effects to Layers

Styles are actually vector information that Photoshop uses to create special effects. Although you can easily change and reshape vector images, you cannot manipulate them with painting tools. To rasterize the effects into individual layers so that you can paint and edit them with other Photoshop tools, do the following.

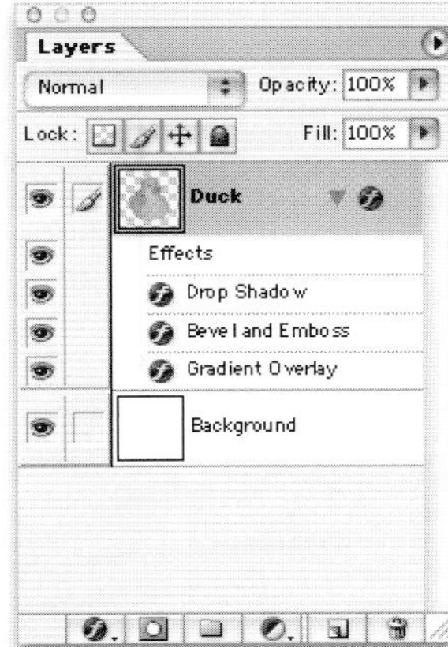

Before conversion, the effects appear below the associated layer.

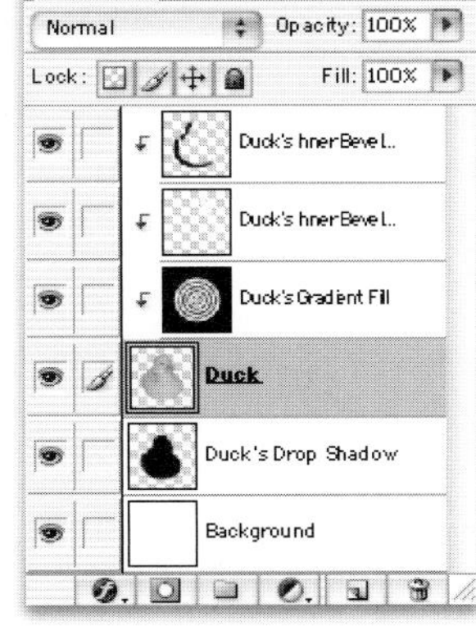

After conversion, several of the effects are layers grouped to the original layer that contained the effects, but the drop shadow is a layer beneath it.

1 Select the layer that contains the effects you want to convert to layers.
2 Choose Layer > Layer Style > Create Layers.
3 An alert may appear if some of the effects cannot be rendered as layers. If you do not want to see this alert again, check the Don't Show Again box in the bottom-left corner of the alert. Click OK to continue.

The effects now appear as layers grouped with the original layer or new layers above or below the original layer.

If you are dissatisfied with the results of rasterizing your effects, you can use Edit > Undo or the History palette to return to the state before the changes were made, thus retaining the effects.

You can reset alert messages to display in the General preferences.

10.6 Applying Advanced Blending Options

➡ Color Section: Blending Modes

The Layers palette includes options to set the blending mode, opacity, and fill opacity for an individual layer. The Layer Style dialog includes these options, but adds the ability to set the color channels used for the layer, create layer knockouts, specify how effects blend with the layer and other layers, and set blending in particular color channels.

Follow the instructions in Section 10.2 to open the Layer Style dialog, and then fill out the options for blending.

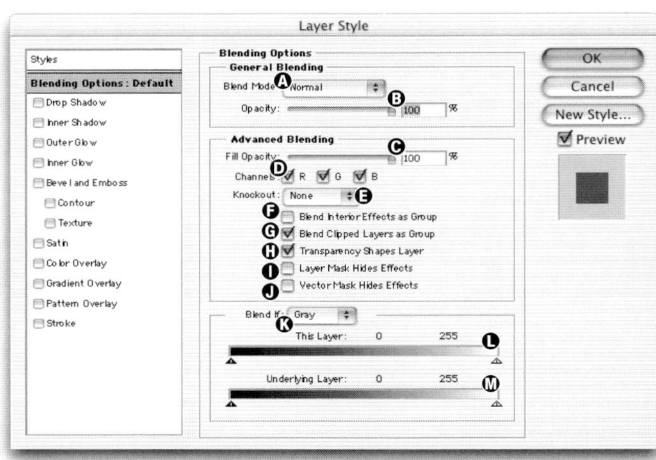

Ⓐ Click to select the blending mode for the layer. You can also change the blending mode in the Layers palette.

Ⓑ Enter a value (0 to 100) for the layer opacity. You can also change this opacity in the Layers palette.

Ⓒ Enter a value (0 to 100) for the opacity of image pixels. You can also change the fill opacity in the Layers palette.

Ⓓ Check to select the color channels being used in the layer (Red, Green, or Blue). This option affects only the selected layer.

Ⓔ Choose a Knockout style. Selecting this option makes the layer transparent, showing the content of layers beneath: None, Shallow (shows the content of the layer beneath), or Deep (punches through to the background layer or transparency).

Ⓕ Check if you want glow, satin, and interior effects blended with their associated layer before blending with the rest of the document.

Ⓖ Check to blend the clipping groups before blending with the rest of the document.

Ⓗ Check if you want the transparency of the layer to set the edges of the shape and the effects.

Ⓘ Check if you want the layer mask to hide the effects rather than reshaping them.

Ⓙ Check if you want the vector mask to hide effects rather than reshaping them.

Ⓚ Choose a color channel for which to set an individualized blending mode.

Ⓛ Set the blending range for the particular color channel in the selected layer by sliding the triangles at either end to limit the spectrum.

Ⓜ Set the blending range for the particular color channel for the layer underneath the selected layer by sliding the triangles at either end to limit the spectrum.

10.7 Applying the Shadow Effects

You use shadows to add the illusion of depth and three-dimensionality to content in the canvas. Follow the instructions in Section 10.2 to open the Layer Style dialog, and then fill out the options for the Shadow effects.

➠ Color Section: Blending Modes

➠ Color Section: Effects

With either the Drop Shadow or Inner Shadow panels open, you can drag the shadow directly on the canvas to position it. However, doing so also changes the global lighting settings.

Drop Shadow

Inner Shadow

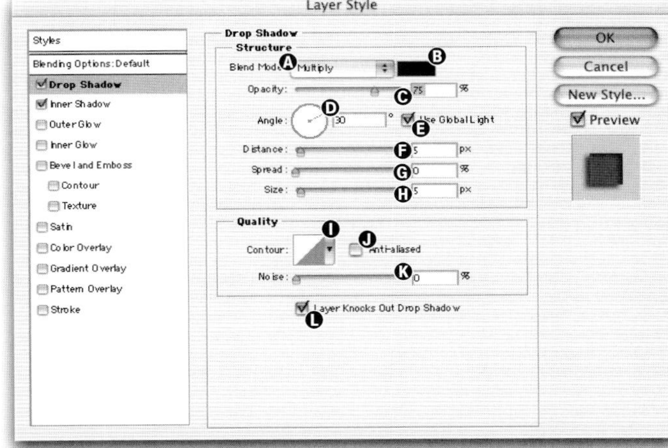

Ⓐ Click to choose the blending mode (see Section 10.1).

Ⓑ **Drop shadow color** Click to open the Color Picker and select the color for the shadow.

Ⓒ Enter a value (0 to 100) for the opacity of the drop shadow.

Ⓓ Enter a value (from –360 to 360) for the angle of the simulated light source of the shadow. You can also use the dial to change the angle.

Ⓔ Check to use global lighting with the shadow.

Ⓕ Enter a value (0 to 30000) for the distance the shadow will be offset from the source. Zero places the shadow directly beneath the source.

Ⓖ **Spread (Drop Shadow) or Choke (Inner Shadow)** Enter a value (0 to 100) for the size of the layer mask creating the shadow. For both Spread and Choke, the larger the number, the harder the edge on the drop shadow.

Ⓗ Enter a value (0 to 250), in pixels, for the size of the shadow.

Ⓘ Select a contour style for the shadow. Double-click the contour thumbnail to open the Contour Editor. The linear contour is the standard for most shadows.

Ⓙ Check to use anti-aliasing with the shadow, which can improve its smoothness.

Ⓚ Enter a value (0 to 100) for the stochastic noise to be applied to the shadow. This has the effect of dithering the shadow, making it appear less smooth.

Ⓛ (Drop Shadow only) Check to prevent the drop shadow from showing through transparent fill pixels when the fill opacity is less than 100%.

10.8 Applying the Glow Effects

- 14.3 Selecting Colors with the Color Picker
- 14.6 Creating and Editing Gradients
- 14.7 Organizing Gradient Presets
- Color Section: Blending Modes
- Color Section: Effects

A glow is a simulated lighting effect that creates the appearance of a colored light behind or inside the object. You can apply the glow outside the content of the layer (Outer Glow) or inside the content (Inner Glow) and either around the edges or emanating from the center of the layer's content. Follow the instructions in Section 10.2 to open the Layer Style dialog, and then fill out the options for the Glow effects.

Outer Glow

Inner Glow

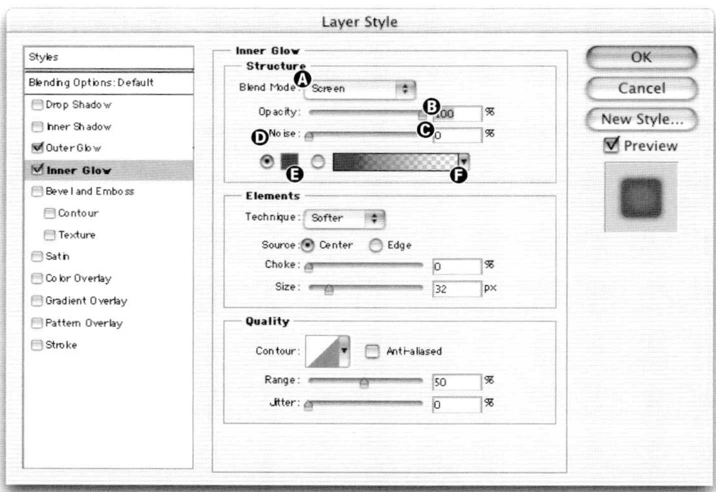

A Chose a blending mode for the glow style (see the color section "Blending Modes").

B Enter a value (0 to 100) for the opacity of the glow.

C Enter a value (0 to 100) for the stochastic noise to be applied to the glow. Selecting this option has the effect of dithering the glow, making it appear less smooth.

D Choose to use a solid color or a gradient for the glow.

E Click to open the Color Picker and select the solid color for the glow.

F Click to select a gradient preset to use for the glow. Double-click the gradient to open the Gradient Editor.

10.8 Applying the Glow Effects *(Continued)*

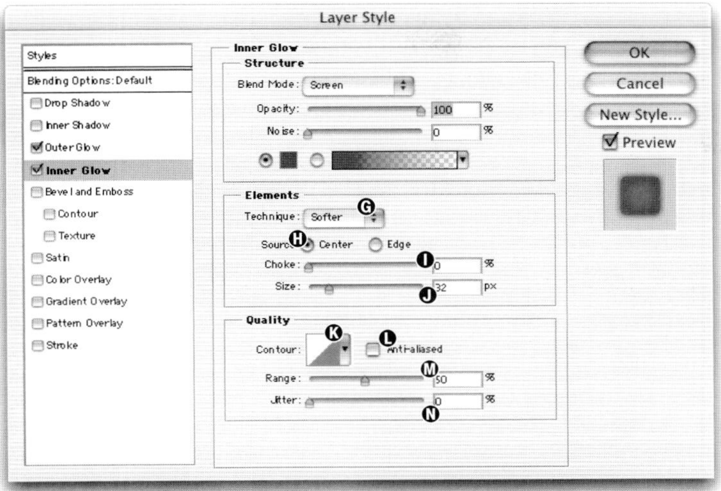

G Choose Softer if you want the color or gradient to fade to transparent gradually, or choose Precise if you want the color or gradient to fill the entire area of the glow.

H (Inner Glow only) Choose whether the glow should start at the outer edge of the source or the center.

I **Spread (Outer Glow) or Choke (Inner Glow)** Enter a value (0 to 100) for the size of the layer mask creating the shadow. For both Spread and Choke, the larger the number, the harder the edge on the drop shadow.

J Enter a value (0 to 25) for the size of the glow.

K Select a contour style for the glow. Double-click the contour thumbnail to open the Contour Editor. The linear contour is the standard for most glows.

L Check to use anti-aliasing with the glow, which can improve its smoothness.

M Enter a value (1 to 100) to control which parts of the glow are used in the contour.

N Enter a value (0 to 100) to add noise for the glow's color and transparency.

10.9 Applying the Bevel and Emboss Effects

- 14.2 Selecting Colors
- 14.3 Selecting Colors with the Color Picker
- 14.6 Creating and Editing Gradients
- 14.7 Organizing Gradient Presets
- 14.9 Creating Patterns
- 14.10 Organizing Pattern Presets
- Color Section: Effects

Beveling and embossing, like shadowing, are other ways to add a 3-D appearance to your content, but these effects create the illusion that the content is raised off the surface rather than simply floating above it. Both effects—which are mutually exclusive—work much the same, highlighting half the object while placing the other half in a shadow. Bevels create a hard edge around the content, and embossing creates a soft edge around the content. Follow the instructions in Section 10.2 to open the Layer Style dialog, and then fill out the options for the Bevel or the Emboss effect.

Left to right: Outer Bevel; Inner Bevel (Highlight Shading visible on bottom-left edge, Shadow Shading on top-right edge); Emboss; and Pillow Emboss

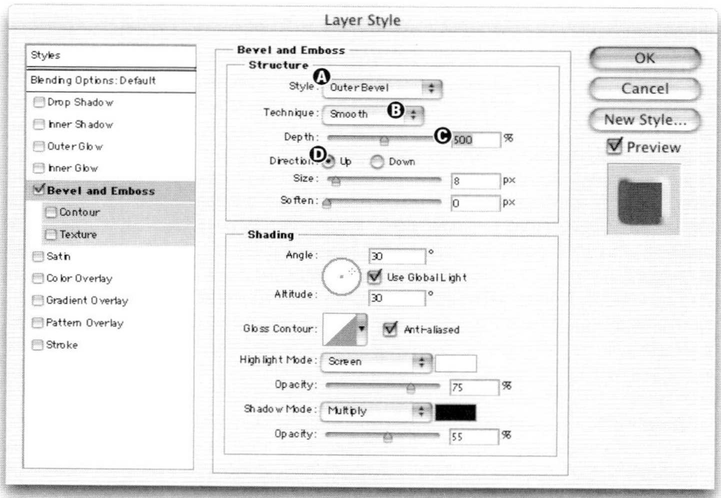

Ⓐ Choose a shading style: Outer Bevel, Inner Bevel, Emboss, Pillow Emboss, Stroke Emboss.

Ⓑ Choose an edge technique to use for the shading: Smooth, Chisel Hard, or Chisel Soft.

Ⓒ Enter a value (1 to 1000) for the depth of the shading. Selecting this option has the affect of increasing the contrast between the highlight and the shadow.

Ⓓ Choose a direction for the bevel or emboss. Selecting this option has the affect of reversing the lighting angle.

10.9 Applying the Bevel and Emboss Effects

(Continued)

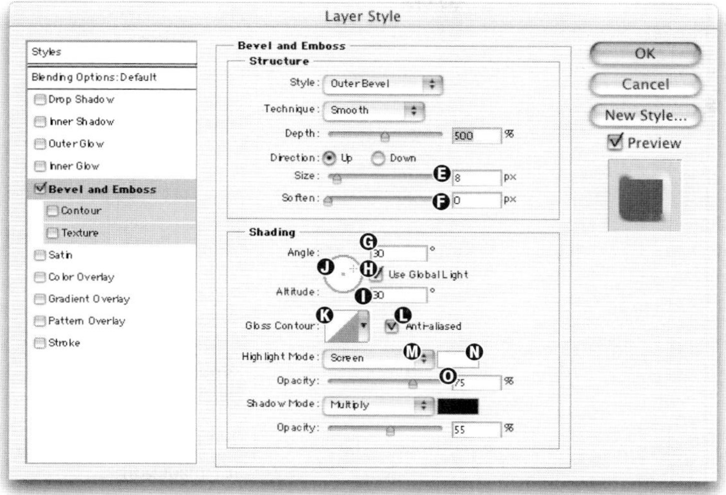

The contour and texture effects that are indented under the Bevel and Emboss effect are only applied to the area affected by the Bevel and Emboss effect and not to the entire layer.

The contour and texture effects described here are apparent only if a bevel or an emboss effect is applied to the layer.

The key to getting a good bevel is to choose the right gloss contour. Play around with different contours until you find one that works, or create your own.

- **E** Enter a value (0 to 250) for the size of the shading.
- **F** Enter a value (0 to 16) for the softness of the shading edges. The larger the number, the softer the edges.
- **G** Enter a value (–180 to 180) for the angle of the simulated lighting source used for the shading.
- **H** Check to use global lighting (see Section 10.1) for the bevel or emboss.
- **I** Enter a value (0 to 90) for the altitude of the simulated lighting source used for the shading.
- **J** Click to set the angle or altitude of the simulated lighting source (see G and I).
- **K** Select a contour style for the shading. Double-click the contour thumbnail to open the Contour Editor.
- **L** Check to use anti-aliasing with the contour shading. Using anti-aliasing can improve the smoothness of the shading.
- **M** Choose a blending mode to be used with the highlight, the shadow, the bevel, or the emboss (see "Blending Modes" in the color section).
- **N** Click to open the Color Picker and choose the highlight or shadow of the bevel or emboss.
- **O** Enter a value (0 to 100) for the opacity to be used for the highlight or shadow of the bevel or emboss.

Bevel and Emboss with Contour

This differs from the Gloss Contour setting in the Bevel And Emboss Shading options, which affects only the apparent reflection (glossiness) of the bevel and not its actual shape. Contour changes the shadows in the effect to create different shaped edges. Once you have set the Bevel or Emboss effect as described, check and click the Contour option, and then set the options.

10.9 Applying the Bevel and Emboss Effects

(Continued)

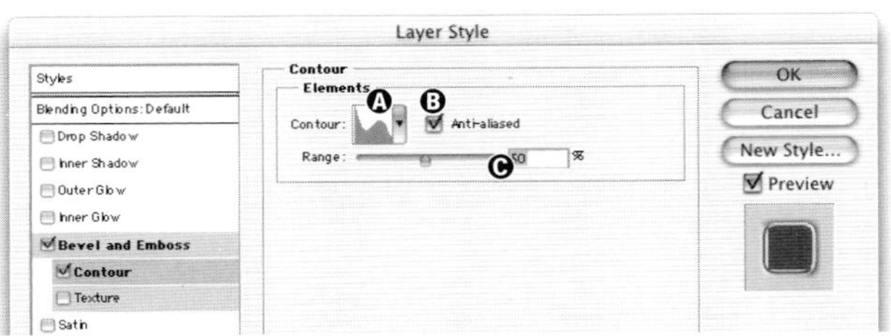

❹ Select a contour style for the shading. Double-click the thumbnail to open the Contour Editor.

❺ Check to use anti-aliasing with the contour shading. Using anti-aliasing can improve the smoothness of the contour.

❻ Enter a value (0 to 100) to control the range used in the contour. The higher the number, the sharper the edge of the contour.

Left: Contour

Right: Texture. Notice that because this is an Inner Bevel, the texture covers the entire image, much like a pattern overlay.

Bevel and Emboss with Texture

Texture allows you to apply a preset pattern to the effect's edges. Once you have set the Bevel or Emboss effect as described, check and click the Texture option, and then set the options.

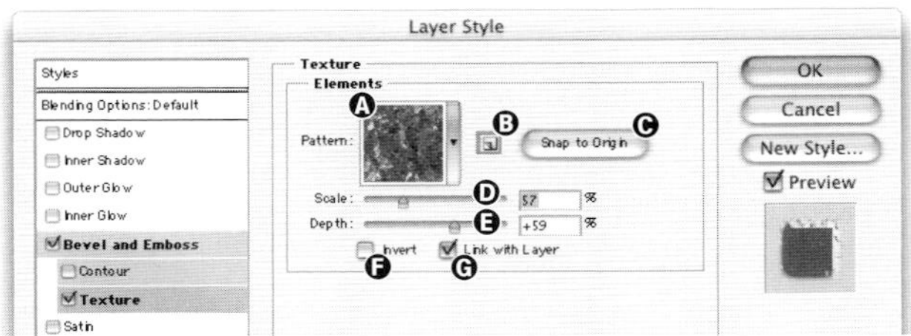

❹ Choose a texture from the list of presets to apply to the shading.

❺ Click to add the currently selected texture to the list of presets.

❻ Click if you want the texture to snap to the top-left corner of the layer or document.

❼ Enter a value (1 to 1000) to set the scale of the texture pattern.

❽ Enter a value (–1000 to 1000) to set the strength (depth) of the texture pattern. A negative number inverts the texture.

❾ Check to invert the texture pattern.

❿ Check if you want the texture linked to the layer. If this check box is cleared, the pattern will not move when you move the layer.

10.10 Applying the Satin Effect

A Satin effect creates two solid color copies of the content. When you space out these copies, you will only see the two copies where they do *not* overlap. Applying the Satin effect can create some interesting effects beyond beveling, as if the content were made from cloth. Follow the instructions in Section 10.2 to open the Layer Style dialog, select the Satin effect on the left of the dialog, and then fill out the options for the Satin effect.

➠ Color Section: Effects

➠ Color Section: Blending Modes

The satin effect works best with complex content that has multiple sides.

Satin

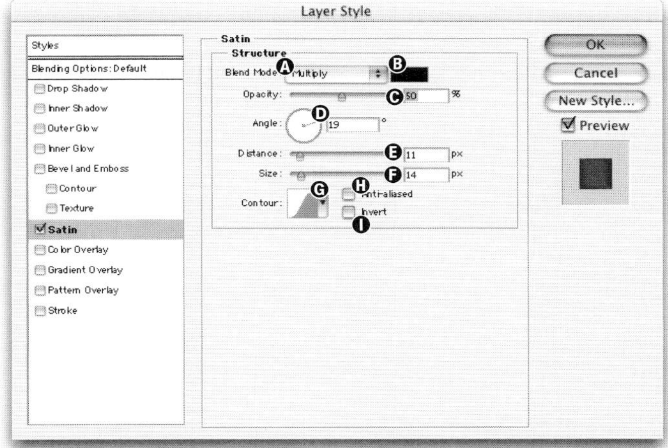

Ⓐ Click to choose the blending mode for satin shading (see "Blending Modes" in the color section).

Ⓑ **Satin color** Click to open the Color Picker and select the color for the satin shading.

Ⓒ Enter a value (0 to 100) for the opacity of the satin shading.

Ⓓ Enter a value (from –360 to 360) for the angle of the simulated light source of the satin shading. You can also use the dial to change the angle.

Ⓔ Enter a value (1 to 250) for the distance the satin shading copies will be offset from the edges of the source.

Ⓕ Enter a value (0 to 250), in pixels, for the size of the satin shading. The larger the number, the softer the edges of the shading.

Ⓖ Select a contour style for the satin effects. Double-click the contour thumbnail to open the Contour Editor.

Ⓗ Check to use anti-aliasing with the satin shading's contour, which can improve the smoothness of the contour.

Ⓘ Check to invert the satin shading.

10.11 Applying the Overlay Effects

➠ 14.3 Selecting Colors with the Color Picker
➠ 14.6 Creating and Editing Gradients
➠ 14.7 Organizing Gradient Presets
➠ 14.9 Creating Patterns
➠ 14.10 Organizing Pattern Presets

Using overlays is a quick way to add a solid color, gradient, or pattern over a layer. Using overlays is preferable in many cases to adding fill layer, since you can apply an overlay to a single layer rather than to all layers below the fill layer. Follow the instructions in Section 10.2 to open the Layer Style dialog, select one of the Overlay effects, and then fill out the options for that effect.

Color Overlay

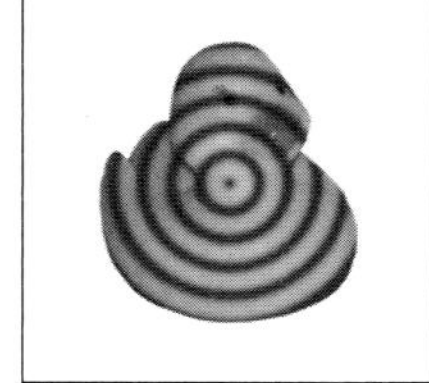

Gradient Overlay

Pattern Overlay

Color Overlay

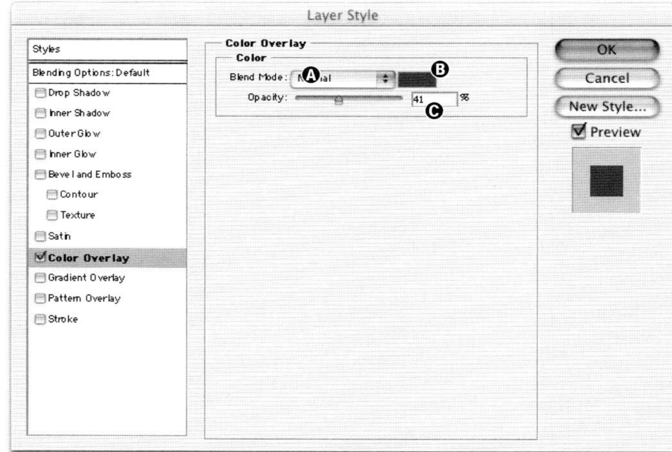

A Click to choose the blending mode for a color overlay (see Section 10.1).

B **Overlay color** Click to open the Color Picker and select the color for the overlay.

C Enter a value (0 to 100) for the opacity of the color overlay.

10.11 Applying the Overlay Effects *(Continued)*

Gradient Overlay

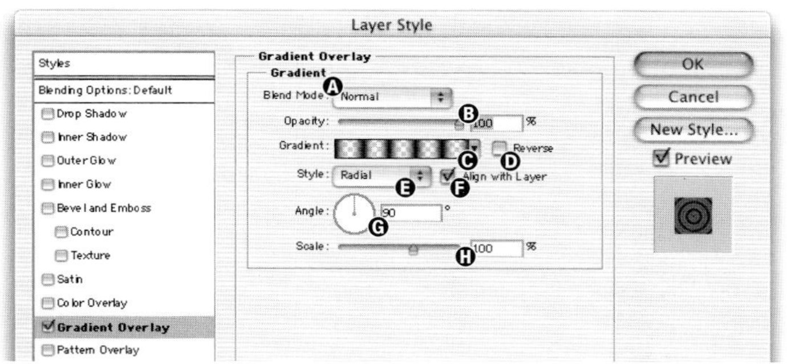

- **A** Click to choose the blending mode for color overlay (see Section 10.1).
- **B** Enter a value (0 to 100) for the opacity of the color overlay.
- **C** Click to select a Gradient Preset to use for the glow. Double-click the gradient to open the Gradient Editor.
- **D** Check to reverse the gradient direction.
- **E** Choose a gradient style: Linear, Radial, Angle, Reflected, or Diamond.
- **F** Check to center the gradient with the content of the layer. If this check box is cleared, the gradient aligns with the center of the canvas.
- **G** Enter a value (from –360 to 360) for the angle of the gradient.
- **H** Enter a value (10 to 150) for the scale of the gradient.

Pattern Overlay

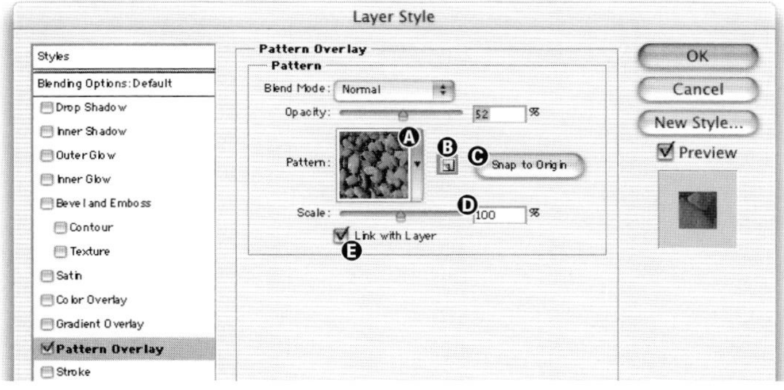

- **A** Choose a pattern from the list of presets to be used for the overlay.
- **B** Click to add the currently selected pattern to the list of presets.
- **C** Click if you want the pattern to snap to the top-left corner of the layer or document.
- **D** Enter a value (1 to 1000) for the scale of the pattern.
- **E** Check if you want the pattern linked to the layer. If this check box is cleared, the pattern will not move when you move the layer.

➠ Color Section: Blending Modes

➠ Color Section: Effects

The overlay effects are an easy way to add solid color, pattern, and gradient fills to the content of a layer that are more versatile than those shown in Chapter 14.

10.12 Applying the Stroke Effect

➠ 14.3 Selecting Colors with the Color Picker

➠ 14.6 Creating and Editing Gradients

➠ 14.7 Organizing Gradient Presets

➠ 14.9 Creating Patterns

➠ 14.10 Organizing Pattern Presets

➠ Color Section: Effects

Although you can rig the outer glow effect to do the same thing, the stroke effect adds the ability to apply a gradient or a pattern to the border.

The Stroke effect tends to round off even hard edges of shapes.

A stroke is a solid line around the contours of an object creating a border.

Stroke

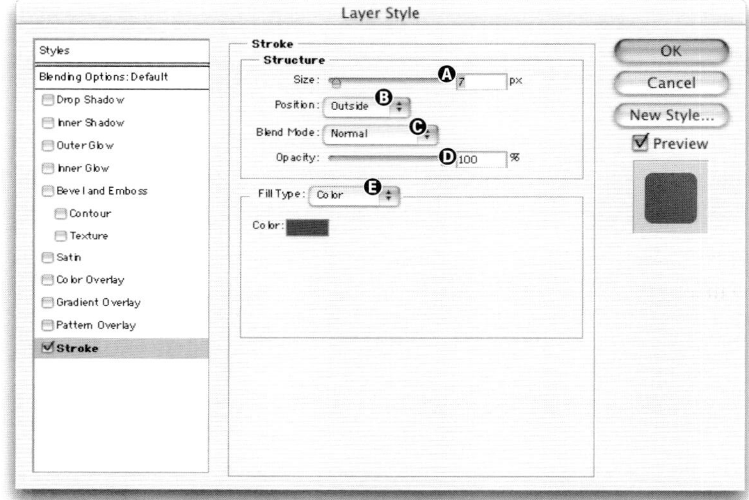

Ⓐ Enter a value (1 to 250) for the size of the stroke in pixels.

Ⓑ Choose where the stroke should be placed: outside the source, inside the source, or centered on the source's edge.

Ⓒ Click to choose the blending mode for the stroke (see Section 10.1).

Ⓓ Enter a value (0 to 100) for the opacity of the satin shading.

Ⓔ Choose a fill type to use for the stroke: Color, Gradient, or Pattern. Each fill type will have different controls identical to those in the corresponding overlay styles (described in the preceding section).

CHAPTER 11

Masking Layers

MASKS ALLOW YOU TO SELECT a part of a layer for editing and to protect the rest of the content of that layer from being changed. There are four types of masks in Photoshop. This chapter deals with the first two:

Layer mask A special sublayer placed into a layer that allows you to paint out the areas in the layer you want masked using black (masked), white (unmasked), and shades of gray (transparency).

Vector mask A special sublayer placed into a layer that allows you to add paths to mask areas in the image.

Quick Mask A mode activated in the Toolbox that allows you to paint a mask into the image that is then used as a selection. Quick Masks are discussed in Section 8.4.

Type mask A type tool that allows you to use text shapes to create a mask that is then used as a selection. Type masks are discussed in Chapter 17.

This chapter covers:

- 11.1 **Mask basics**
- 11.2 **Adding layer masks**
- 11.3 **Editing layer masks**
- 11.4 **Hiding, applying, or removing layer masks**
- 11.5 **Turning layer masks into selections**
- 11.6 **Adding vector masks**
- 11.7 **Editing vector masks**
- 11.8 **Applying or removing vector masks**

11.1 Mask Basics

➠ 2.6 Layer Menu

➠ 4.11 Layers Palette

A vector mask is always separated by a vertical line from the layer mask and/or layer thumbnail in the Layers palette.

Selected masks have an additional black box surrounding them.

All mask types allow you to create selections that can be used to protect all or part of an image from being edited. However, layer and vector masks are additionally versatile in that they provide a nondestructive way to edit the content of a layer. By "nondestructive" I mean that you can effectively erase all or part of the content of a layer without actually deleting the content. The content remains but is hidden behind the mask. Photoshop treats these masked areas as if they didn't exist for the purposes of compositing the image. However, you can edit the masks in a variety of ways to show the hidden content.

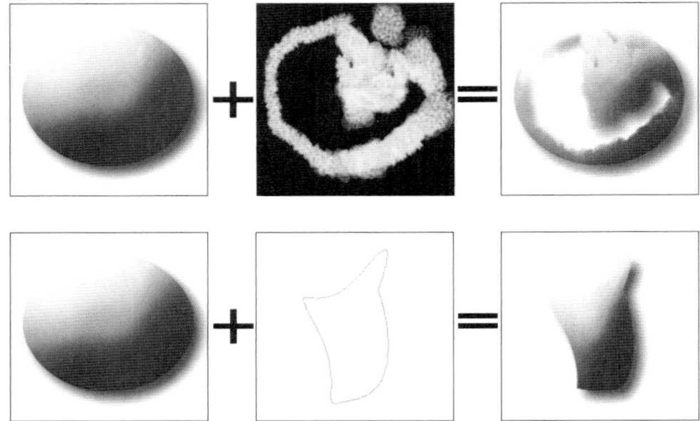

Top: A layer mask is applied to the image. Bottom: A vector mask is applied to the image.

Both layer masks and vector masks are sublayers that are attached to a master layer. They affect only the content of the associated layer, and their thumbnails always appear to the right of the layer's thumbnail.

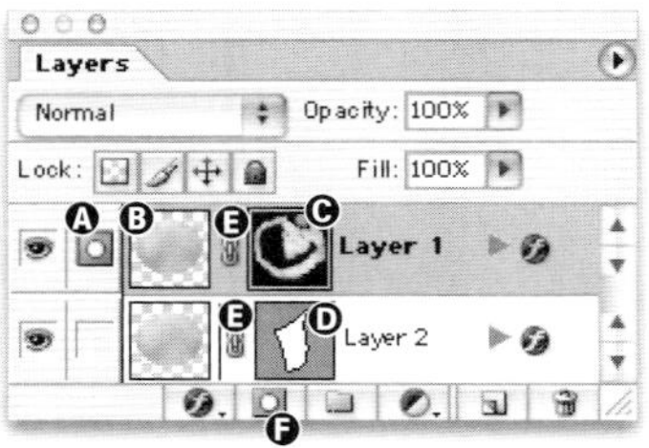

A Mask selected Indicates that the mask and not the layer is selected for editing.

B Layer thumbnail Click to select the layer and the vector mask.

C Layer mask thumbnail Click to select the mask for editing. (The layer mask is currently selected.) Double-click to open Layer Mask Options dialog.

D Vector mask thumbnail Click once to select only the layer (not the mask). Click again (not double-click) to select the vector mask. Double-click to open the Layer Style dialog.

E Mask links Click to unlink the mask from the layer's content. Click again to re-link the mask. This option allows masks and content to be moved independently.

F New Mask Click once to add a layer mask to the selected layer. Click again to add a vector mask.

11.2 Adding Layer Masks

The layer mask works as a grayscale alpha channel that can be edited or painted on in order to hide or show areas of the layer with which it is associated. Rather than erasing the image directly on the canvas, you can use a layer mask to partially or completely obscure parts of the image without actually deleting the content itself.

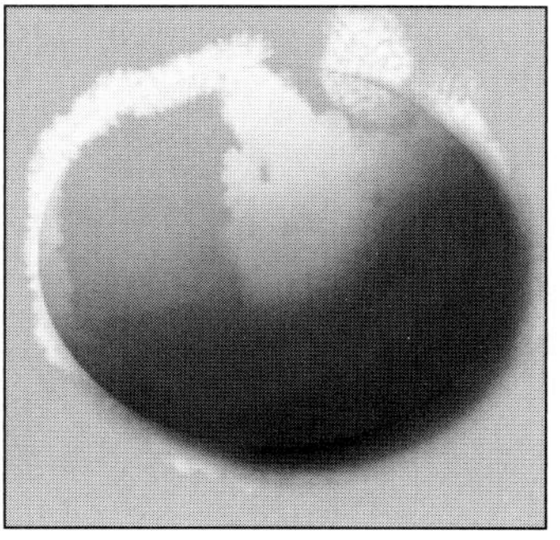

A layer mask overlay: The layer mask is superimposed over the image.

Creating a Blank Layer Mask

To start a layer mask, you can choose to add a completely empty (white) or completely filled (black) mask that you can then edit as desired. Follow these steps:

1. Select the layer to which you want to add a layer mask. The layer cannot already contain a layer mask.
2. Do one of the following:
   - To quickly add a layer mask, click the Add A Mask button [button icon] at the bottom of the Layers palette. You can also drag the layer to the Add A Mask button. Click again to add a vector mask.
   - To add an empty layer mask (regardless of current selections), choose Layer > Add Layer Mask > Reveal All. The mask will not cover any of the layer.
   - To add a filled layer mask (regardless of current selections), choose Layer > Add Layer Mask > Hide All. The mask will cover all the content in the layer.

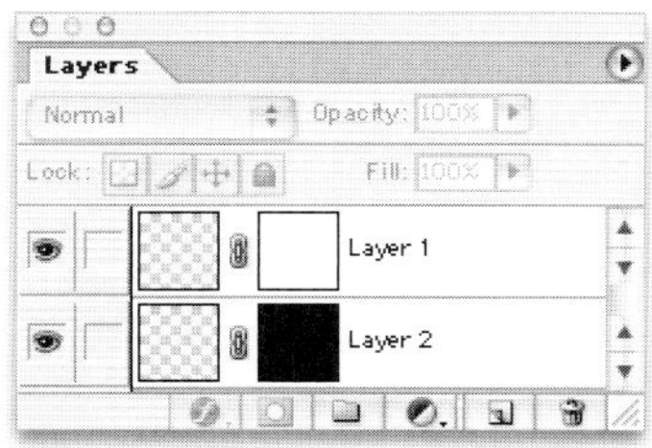

You can now use any drawing or painting tools to paint the layer and mask parts of the image on that layer. Here, Layer 1 has an empty layer mask; Layer 2 has a filled layer mask.

➠ 2.6 Layer Menu

➠ 4.11 Layers Palette

➠ 8 Making Selections

➠ 8.2 Selecting a Layer or Its Contents

Show/hide layer mask as a bitmap

Option click layer mask thumbnail

Alt click layer mask thumbnail

Show/hide layer mask overlay

Shift Option click layer mask thumbnail

Shift Alt click layer mask thumbnail

If you select a layer mask in the Layers palette, it also displays as a temporary alpha channel in the Channels palette.

11.2 Adding Layer Masks *(Continued)*

Layer masks are also accessible in the Channels palette as a temporary alpha channel, if the layer is selected. However, unlike other alpha channels, the layer mask channel can only be turned on or off for the associated layer or clipping group.

Generally you will want to set the layer mask color to contrast with the image and not be the same color as other highlight colors, such as the Gamut highlight.

Color selection defaults to grayscale when the layer mask is active.

Turning a Selection into a Layer Mask

Another way to start a layer mask is to use an existing selection as the base for the masked area. Follow these steps:

1 Select the layer to which you want to add a layer mask, and create your selection. The layer cannot already contain a layer mask.

2 Do one of the following:

- To quickly add a layer mask, click the Add A Mask button at the bottom of the Layers palette. This adds a layer mask using the selection to mask the layer.
- To hide the layer content within the selection, choose Layer > Add Layer Mask > Reveal Selection. The mask covers the selected content in the layer.
- To show only the layer content within the selection, choose Layer > Add Layer Mask > Hide Selection. The mask covers the content in the layer outside the selection.

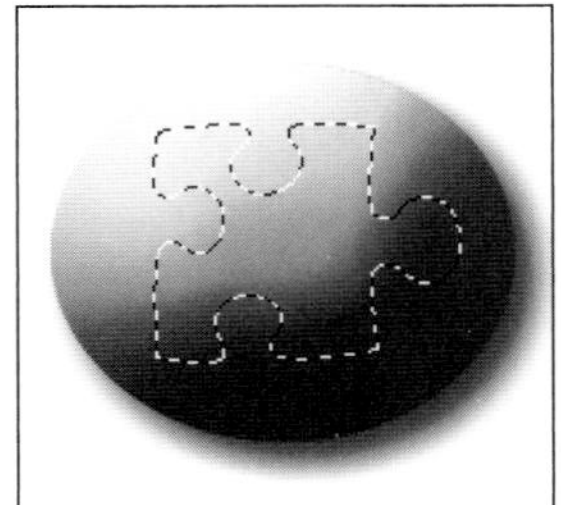

The original selection.

The selection is turned into a layer mask using Reveal Selection.

The selection is turned into a layer mask using Hide Selection.

The area of the selection now appears as the layer mask, rendering the pixels within the mask (the black areas) transparent. You can modify the mask as desired.

Turning a Layer's Content into a Layer Mask

1 Select the layer in which you want to create the layer mask. This layer cannot currently contain a layer mask.

2 Do one of the following:

- To create a mask from a layer's content in the selected layer, drag that layer's thumbnail to the Add Layer Mask button at the bottom of the Layers palette and release. You can even use the selected layer to create a mask of itself.

11.2 Adding Layer Masks *(Continued)*

- To create an inverted mask from a layer's content in the selected layer, Option/Alt drag the thumbnail of the layer mask to be copied to the Add A Mask button at the bottom of the Layers palette and release.

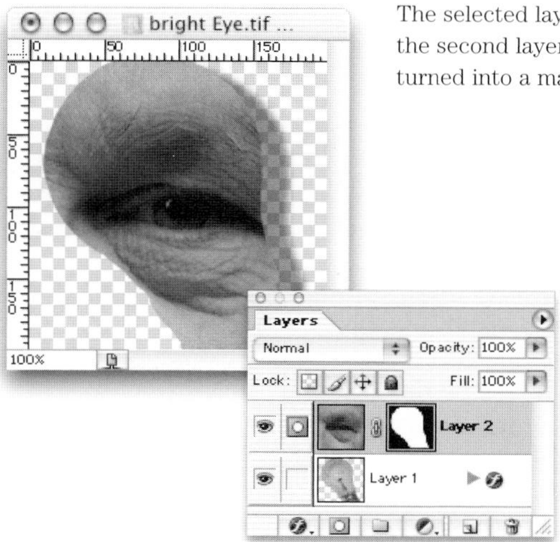

The selected layer now has a mask based on the content of the second layer, as shown here: the content in Layer 1 is turned into a mask in Layer 2.

Setting the Layer Mask Options

When a mask is viewed as an overlay by Shift-Option/Alt-clicking the layer mask's thumbnail (showing the area of the mask over the image), you can set the opacity and color in which the overlay will appear.

To set the layer mask options, open the Layer Mask Display Options dialog by double-clicking the layer mask's thumbnail or Control/right-clicking the thumbnail and choosing Layer Mask Options…. In the dialog, set the properties for the mask overlay and click OK.

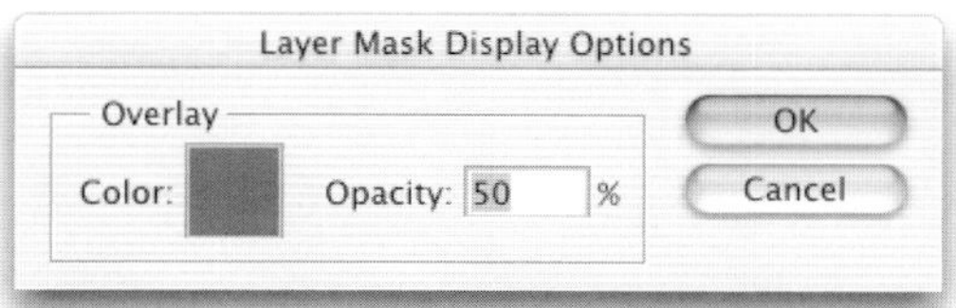

Click the swatch to choose a color for the layer mask; use the percentage field to enter the opacity for the layer mask.

11.3 Editing Layer Masks

- 2.6 Layer Menu
- 3.10 Drawing Tools
- 3.11 Stamp Tools
- 3.13 Eraser Tools
- 3.14 Fill Tools
- 3.15 Distortion Tools
- 3.16 Exposure Tools
- 4.11 Layers Palette
- 15 Painting in Images

After you add the layer mask sublayer, you can add to the mask, subtract from it, move it, or copy it.

Adding to or Subtracting from a Layer Mask

Once you add a layer mask to a layer, you can paint or draw on it as if it were a grayscale image on the canvas. You can use any tool you would normally use to edit or paint in the canvas to edit or delete the layer mask. Follow these steps:

1 Click the layer mask thumbnail in the Layers palette to make it active (indicated by a black box around the thumbnail). All edits will now be applied to the layer mask.

2 To view only the layer mask channel while editing, do one of the following:

- To view the layer mask as a grayscale mask, hiding the image underneath, Option/Alt-click the layer mask thumbnail. Repeat to return to normal viewing mode.
- To view the layer mask as a colored layer, still showing the image underneath, Shift-Option-click/Shift-Alt-click the layer mask thumbnail. You see the exact color in which the layer mask appears in the layer mask options. Darker areas represent black in the layer mask.

3 Choose any editing or painting tool. Since the layer mask works as a grayscale channel, you can paint only in black, white, or a shade of gray:

- To **add to the mask**, hiding the image on the layer, paint in black.
- To **erase from the mask**, revealing the image on the layer, paint in white.
- To **make the mask transparent**, partially revealing the image, paint in shades of gray.

After you edit the mask, click the layer thumbnail to view the results.

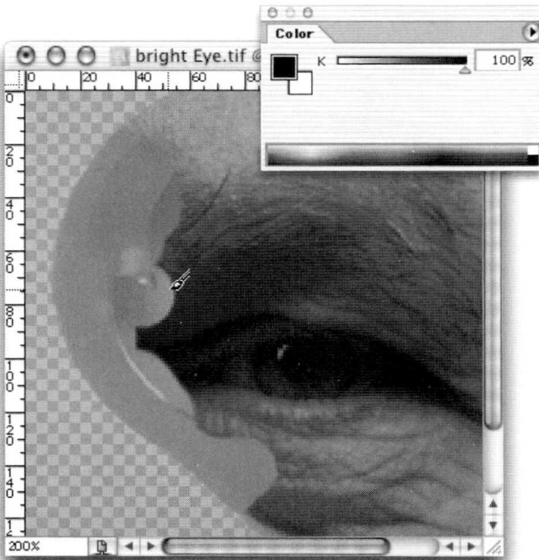

Painting in the layer mask works much like painting in the layer except you are restricted to grayscale.

11.3 Editing Layer Masks *(Continued)*

Moving a Mask within the Layer

You can link a layer mask so that it moves with the content of the layer, keeping the mask in the same relative position, or you can unlink a layer mask so that it moves independently. You can then change the content being masked.

1 Choose the Move tool .

2 To move the layer content and the layer mask independently, click the link icon between them so that it is not showing.

3 Click the layer mask thumbnail to select it, and then move the layer mask within the canvas.

Copying a Mask to Another Layer

1 Select the layer to which you want to copy the layer mask. This layer must not currently contain a layer mask.

2 Do one of the following;

- To **duplicate** the mask, drag the thumbnail of the mask to be copied to the Add A Mask button at the bottom of the Layers palette.
- To **invert the mask while duplicating**, Option/Alt drag the thumbnail of the layer mask to be copied to the Add A Mask button at the bottom of the Layers palette.

Duplicating an entire layer also duplicates that layer's masks.

To view the mask overlay in the canvas, Shift-Option-click/Shift-Alt-click the layer mask's thumbnail. This is especially useful when moving the layer mask.

To invert a layer mask, reversing the masked and unmasked regions, select the layer mask by clicking the layer mask's thumbnail and choosing Image > Adjustments > Invert.

EPS AND VECTOR MASKS

When you save an image with a vector mask as a Photoshop EPS, the vector mask will be preserved when imported into another program such as InDesign, QuarkXPress, or Illustrator. When you are saving the image as an Photoshop EPS, just make sure that Include Vector Data option is checked.

11.4 Hiding, Applying, or Removing Layer Masks

➠ 2.6 Layer Menu

➠ 4.11 Layers Palette

Enable/disable layer mask

Shift click layer mask thumbnail

You can undo the application or deletion of a layer mask.

Although masks add only a little to the overall file size, at times you will want to either apply the mask permanently to the layer or remove it altogether. First select the layer mask, then do one of the following:

- To **temporarily hide** a layer mask, choose Layer > Disable Layer Mask, or Control/right-click the layer mask thumbnail and select Disable Layer Mask, or Shift-click the layer mask thumbnail. A red *X* appears over the layer mask thumbnail, and you can see how the layer would look without the mask without deleting the mask. Repeat (selecting Enable Layer Mask instead) to show the mask.

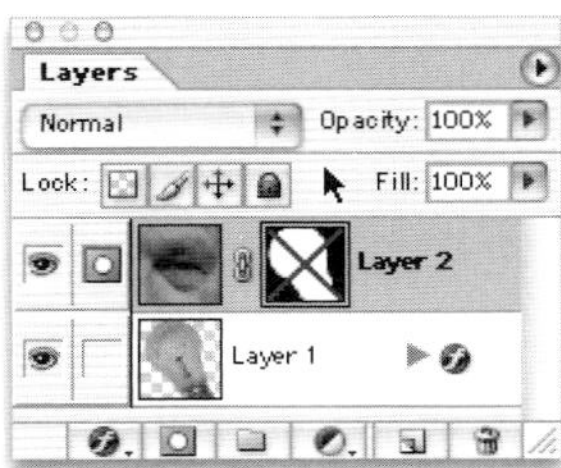

A red *X* appears next to the layer mask when it is hidden.

- To **permanently apply** the layer mask to the layer, choose Layer > Remove Layer Mask > Apply, or Control/right-click the layer mask thumbnail and select Apply Layer Mask. The layer mask is discarded, but its effects remain. This option is available only if the layer is rasterized, so it cannot be applied to type.
- To **delete** the layer mask, choose Layer > Remove Layer Mask > Discard, or Control/right-click the layer mask thumbnail and select Discard Layer Mask. The layer mask is discarded along with its effects.
- To **remove** the layer mask, click the Trash icon, or click and drag the layer mask thumbnail to the Trash icon. Click Apply to remove the layer mask while keeping the changes, click Discard to remove the layer mask and changes, or click Cancel to keep the layer mask.

USING ALPHA CHANNELS WITH LAYER MASKS

An alpha channel is a special channel used to record a selection as a grayscale. A layer mask will also appear as a temporary alpha channel in the Channels palette when the layer it is on is selected. However, the temporary alpha channel can also be saved as a permanent alpha channel and then loaded into other documents. In addition, when the layer mask is loaded, it can also be edited using painting tools.

11.5 Turning Layer Masks into Selections

Masks can quickly be turned into selections, and are, in fact a great way to create complex selections based on the layers content.

To work with the layer mask as a selection, Control/right-click the layer mask thumbnail, and choose one of the following:

- To turn the mask into a selection, choose Set Selection To Layer Mask.
- To combine the layer mask with the current selection, choose Add Layer Mask To Selection.
- To remove a selection created using the layer mask from the current selection, with a selection already active, choose Subtract Layer Mask From Selection. If none of the pixels in the selection are above 50% opacity, a dialog will appear warning you.

To overlap the current selection with a selection created using the layer mask, with a selection already active, choose Intersect Layer Mask With Selection.

➠ 2.6 Layer Menu
➠ 4.11 Layers Palette
➠ 8 Making Selections

Use layer mask as selection
[⌘]click layer mask thumbnail
[Ctrl]click layer mask thumbnail

MASKS AND EFFECTS

You will notice that the effects applied to a layer are not hidden by masks. Instead, the effects conform to the mask as if it were a transparent area in the layer. There are options in the Blending Options panel of the Layer Styles dialog (see Section 10.6) that allow you to set both vector and layer masks so that they will also mask effects in the layer.

11.6 Adding Vector Masks

➠ 2.6 Layer Menu

➠ 4.11 Layers Palette

➠ 4.13 Paths Palette

➠ 8 Making Selections

➠ 12 Drawing Paths and Shapes

Vector masks, also known as clipping paths, work much like layer mask. However, vector masks are resolution independent, meaning that they can be resized without affecting the quality of the image. To add a vector mask, follow these steps:

1 Select the layer without a vector mask to which you want to add a vector mask.

2 Do one of the following:

- To quickly add a vector mask, select a layer that already has a layer mask and click the Add A Mask button [button] at the bottom of the Layers palette.
- To add an empty vector mask , choose Layer **>** Add Vector Mask **>** Reveal All. The mask will not cover any of the layer.
- To add a filled vector mask, choose Layer **>** Add Vector Mask **>** Hide All. The mask will cover all of the content in the layer.

3 You can now edit the vector mask as desired.

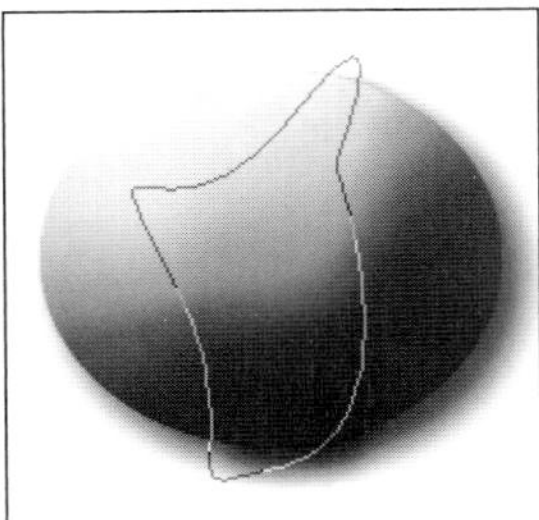

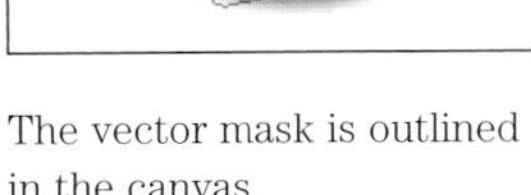

The vector mask is outlined in the canvas.

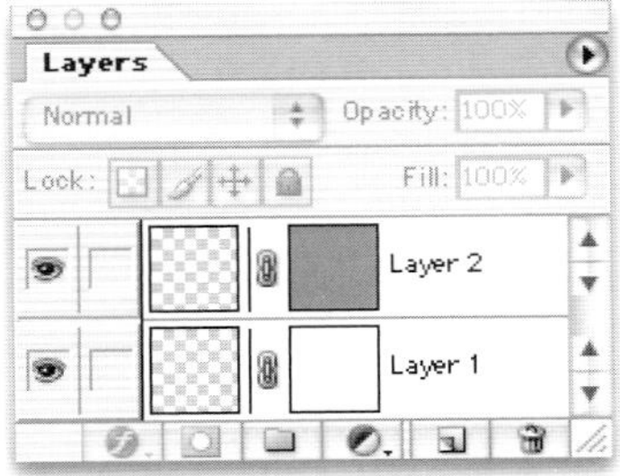

Layer 1 has an empty vector mask; Layer 2 has a filled vector mask.

Turning a Path into a Vector Mask

Any path can be turned into vector mask. (Chapter 12 covers paths in detail.)

1 Select the layer to which you want to add a vector mask, and create your path or select a path from the Paths palette.

2 Do one of the following. The area outside of the vector will be masked; you can then edit the mask as desired.

- To quickly add a vector mask to a layer that already has a layer mask, click the Add A Mask button [button] at the bottom of the Layers palette.
- To add a vector mask regardless of whether the layer has a layer mask, choose Layer **>** Add Vector Mask **>** Current Path.

11.6 Adding Vector Masks *(Continued)*

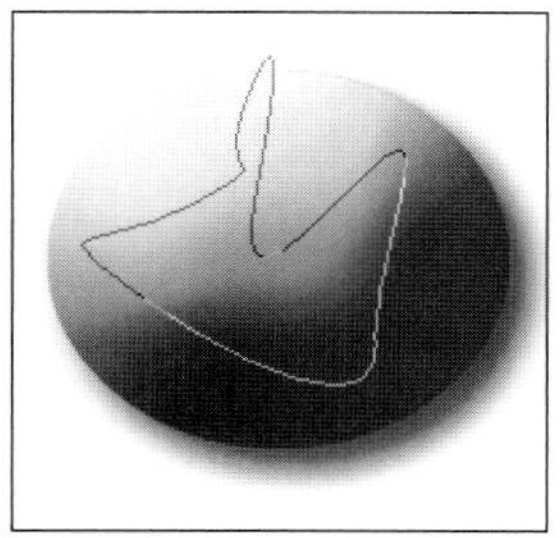

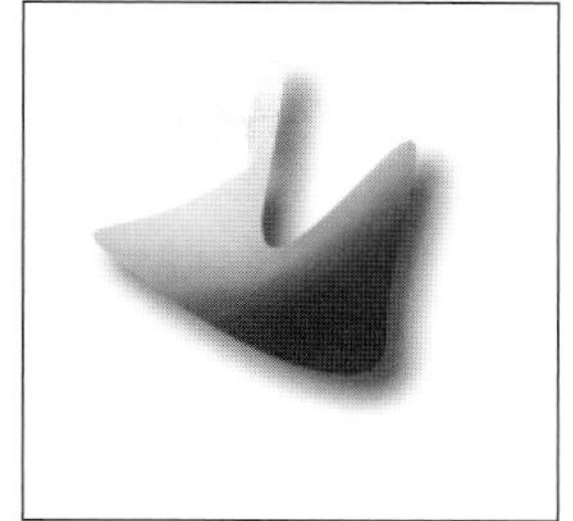

Left: The original vector path. Right: The vector path is turned into a vector mask.

Any selection in the canvas can also be turned into a path which, in turn, can then be turned into a vector mask. With the selection active in the canvas, Control/right-click the Make Work Path From Selection button.

When a vector mask is selected in the Layers palette, it will also show up as a temporary path in the Paths palette.

REAL WORLD: TIM GREENZWEIG

Tim Greenzweig's highly textual works look deceptively like they are hand drawn, and, although many of the elements start life in the physical world, many of the effects are created through manipulation in Photoshop: "Many times I am trying to create an effect in my images that resembles either spilled ink or overprinting, so I tend to blend many of my layers using the Multiply or Luminosity options in the Layers menu."

To get the eroded quality, Tim "scrapes some charcoal on a white piece of paper, steps on it, rubs it on cement, whatever... then scans the white sheet of paper as a grayscale image and adjusts the brightness and contrast to +100%." He then uses the Magic Wand (set on a low tolerance of 10 pixels for a 300 ppi image) to select the dark areas and drags that selection on to the main image. "I then move the selection around to fit the composition, select a flattened type layer, and hit the Delete key. The little bits of black that were on the original scan are deleted from the clean type layer, creating the 'eroded' look."

You can find more of Tim's work at `www.greenzweig.com/`.

11.7 Editing Vector Masks

➠ 3.17 Path Selection Tools

➠ 3.19 Pen Tools

➠ 3.20 Shape Tools

➠ 4.13 Paths Palette

➠ 12.7 Drawing with Pen and Shape Tools

➠ 12.8 Selecting Paths and Path Components

➠ 12.9 Editing Paths and Path Components

➠ 12.10 Editing Path Segments

➠ 12.11 Reshaping Curves

Pen tool P

Cycle Pen tools Shift P

Path Selection tool A

Cycle Path Selection tools Shift A

Shape tool U

Cycle Shape tools Shift U

Once a vector mask has been added to a layer, you can add additional paths to the mask, reshape existing paths in the mask, or combine different paths in the mask.

Adding Paths to a Vector Mask

A vector mask uses paths that are specifically drawn into it as the mask for the layer. These vector paths can be viewed and selected in the Paths palette whenever the layer they are on is selected in the Layers palette.

1 Do one of the following to select the vector mask:

- In the Layers palette, click the layer thumbnail (not the vector mask thumbnail) with the vector mask you want to move.
- In the canvas, click the vector mask's path.

2 Choose the Pen, Freeform Pen, or any shape tool and add paths to the vector mask. All path edits will now be applied to the vector mask.

3 After you have added the path to the mask, click the layer thumbnail to view the results. You can now edit the path as desired.

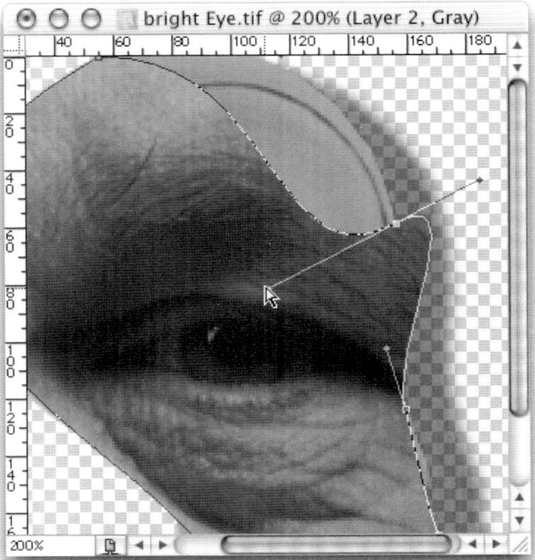

The paths in a vector mask are created using the standard vector tools.

Moving a Vector Mask within the Layer

A vector mask can be moved independent of the layer's content using the Path Component Selection tool. This differs slightly from using the move tool which can be used to either move the content and vector mask together or used to move the content independently of the vector mask by unlinking them.

11.7 Editing Vector Masks *(Continued)*

1 Choose the Path Selection tool or the Direct Selection tool.

2 Do one of the following to select the vector mask:

- In the Layers palette, click the layer thumbnail (not the vector mask thumbnail) with the vector mask you want to move.
- In the canvas, click the vector mask's path.

You can now reposition the vector mask's path in the canvas by dragging it to a new location and releasing.

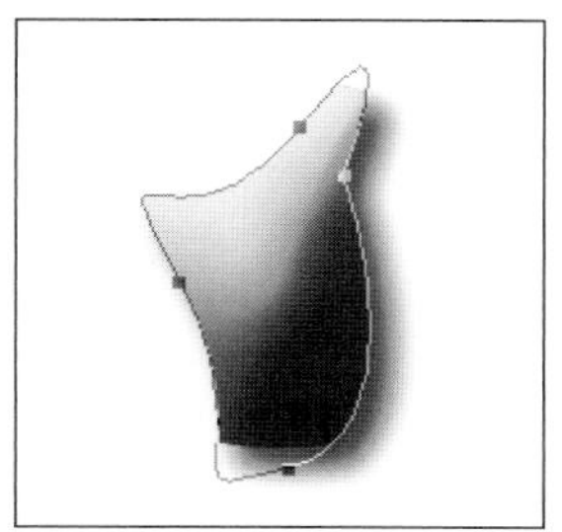

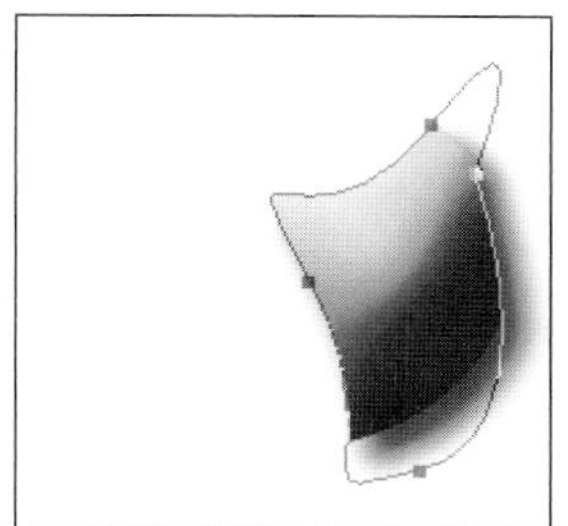

Left: The path in its original position. Right: The path is moved, masking a different part of the layer.

Copying a Vector Mask to Another Layer

You can duplicate a vector mask from one layer into another layer that does not have a vector mask.

1 Select the layer you want to copy the layer vector mask to (the target layer). This has to be a layer that does not currently contain a vector mask.

2 Do one of the following;

- To **duplicate the vector mask**, drag the thumbnail of the mask to be copied to the Add A Mask button at the bottom of the Layers palette.
- To **invert the mask while duplicating**, Option/Alt drag the thumbnail of the layer mask to be copied to the Add A Mask button at the bottom of the Layers palette.

The vector mask will now appear in the target layer.

Choose the Move tool to move the content and vector mask together or turn linking off between them and then move the content independent of the vector mask.

When you place your mouse over a vector thumbnail, after a few seconds the vector mask will be outlined in the canvas until you move off of the thumbnail. When you click to select the vector mask, the outline will be persist in the canvas.

Duplicating an entire layer also duplicates that layer's masks.

Clicking the layer's thumbnail selects the layer content and the vector mask, but not the layer mask.

Clicking the vector mask's thumbnail once selects the layer the mask is on, but not the mask itself. Once a layer is selected, click the vector mask thumbnail again to select the mask.

11.8 Applying or Removing Vector Masks

➠ 2.6 Layer Menu

➠ 4.11 Layers Palette

Once a vector mask has been rasterized, it cannot be reverted to its original vector shape, but you can convert it into a section and then convert the selection into a path and the path into vector mask. However, this will never be precisely the same vector shape.

Although masks add only a little to the overall file size, there are times you will want to either apply the mask permanently to the layer or remove it altogether.

First select the layer mask, then do one of the following:

- To **temporarily hide** a vector mask, choose Layer > Disable Vector Mask, or Control/right-click the layer mask thumbnail and select Disable Layer Mask, or Shift-click the vector mask thumbnail. A red *X* appears over the vector mask thumbnail and you see what the layer would look like without the mask without deleting the mask. Repeat (selecting Enable Vector Mask instead) to show the mask.

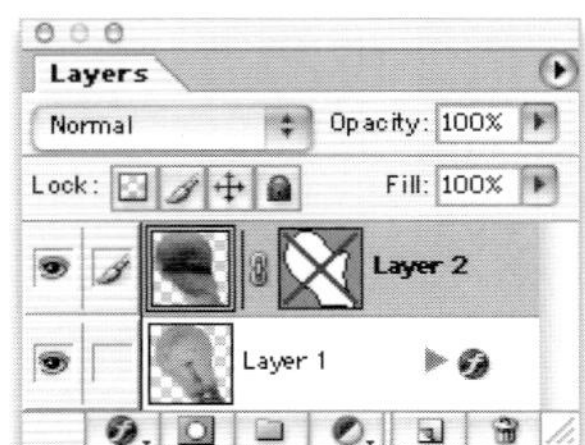

A red x will appear in the vector mask when it is disabled.

- To **apply** the vector mask to the layer, choose Layer > Rasterize > Vector Mask, or Control/right-click the layer mask thumbnail and select Rasterize Vector Mask. The vector mask is discarded, but its affects are rasterized into the layer mask.

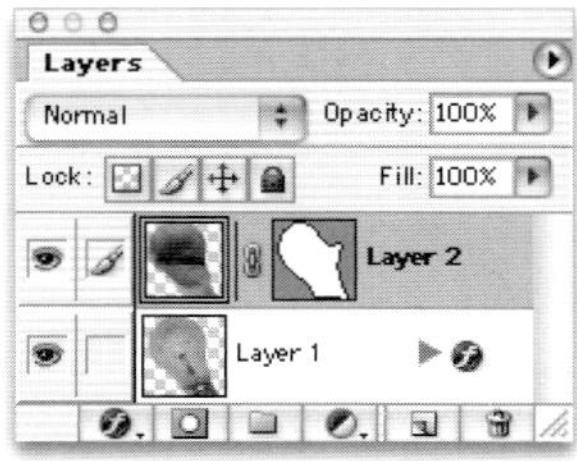

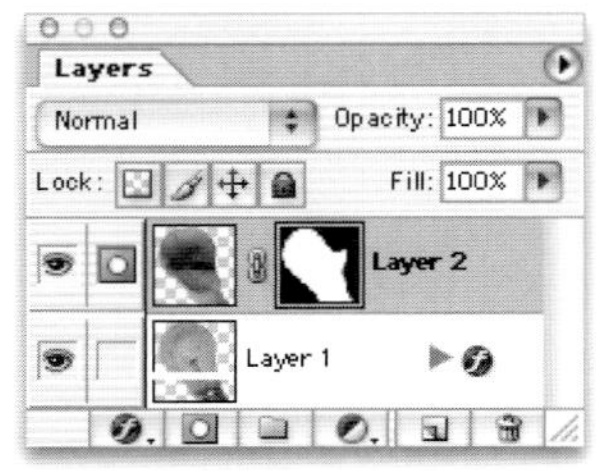

Left: The original vector mask. Right: The vector mask has been rasterized and placed in the layer mask.

- To **delete** the vector mask from the layer, choose Layer > Delete Vector Mask > Apply or Control/right-click the vector mask thumbnail and select Delete Vector Mask or click and drag the vector mask thumbnail to the trashcan icon. The vector mask is discarded along with its effects.

CHAPTER 12

Drawing Paths and Shapes

DESPITE ITS REPUTATION as a bitmap image editor, Photoshop includes an impressive array of vector-editing tools. Although it may not be on a par with Adobe Illustrator or Macromedia FreeHand, Photoshop allows you to add vector paths and shapes in a variety of ways to create images that are resolution independent. That is, by using paths in Photoshop, you can create images that can be scaled up or down in size and resolution without affecting the quality of the image. In addition, since you can apply styles to paths through the use of vector masks, paths are an especially effective way to create tactile buttons, icons, and logos that will look as good in print as on the Web.

This chapter shows you how to use the pen and shape tools to draw paths, create custom vector masks, and even draw bitmap shapes in a few seconds—all of which would have been almost impossible in older versions of Photoshop.

12.1 Path Basics

➠ 3.17 Path Selection Tools

➠ 3.19 Pen Tools

➠ 3.20 Shape Tools

➠ 4.13 Paths Palette

➠ 11.6 Adding Vector Masks

➠ 11.7 Editing Vector Masks

➠ 11.8 Applying or Removing Vector Masks

Curves in vector graphics are often referred to as Bezier curves.

You use nine tools to create vector shapes using paths:

Pen tool Allows you to draw straight-line and controlled curved-line paths.

Freeform Pen tool Allows you to draw paths of any shape.

Magnetic Pen tool Allows you to create a path base on the contrast between edges of bitmap images. Although this is not a separate tool—it is an option of the Freeform Pen tool—it is significantly different, and you can think of it as its own tool. In fact, when you are working with this tool in the canvas, it even has a cursor that is different from that of the Freeform Pen tool.

Shape tools Although you can draw most shapes using the Pen and Freeform Pen tools, Photoshop provides five ready-made shape-drawing tools (Rectangle, Rounded Rectangle, Ellipse, Polygon, and Line) as well as the Custom Shape tool, which allow you to select from libraries of pre-generated shapes and even to save your own vector custom shapes for later use.

To complicate matters, you can work with the pen tools in two different modes (Shape Layer and Path), and you can work with the shape tools in yet a third mode (Fill Pixels).

Shape Layer mode Allows you to quickly create a vector mask with a Color Fill layer.

Path mode Allows you to create vector paths independent of a layer using the Paths palette. Paths are invisible on the canvas until selected in the Paths palette.

Fill Pixels mode (shape tools only) Allows you to use the shape tools to draw rasterized (rather than vector) shapes in a layer. Once you add the shape, you cannot edit it using path tools. Using Fill Pixels is described in Section 15.8.

Anatomy of a Path

A path can contain multiple path components, which in turn are made up of two elements: anchor points and path segments.

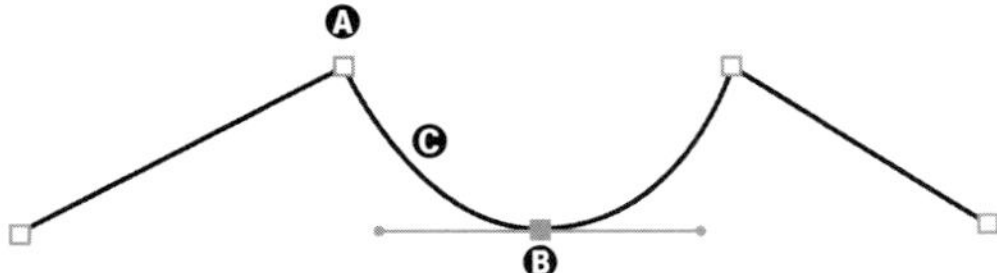

A path component (often referred to simply as a path if there is only one component) is a series of connected path segments making up a vector graphic. This image is a single path component.

A **Anchor point** Defines a corner or a curve in the path. Unselected anchor points appear as empty squares.

B **Selected anchor point** Point ready to be edited. Selected points are filled squares.

C **Path segment** The lines between anchor points that make up the path component.

Anchor Point Types

Three types of anchor points determine whether a path segment is straight or curved and how the segments intersect—as a corner, as a curve, or as both.

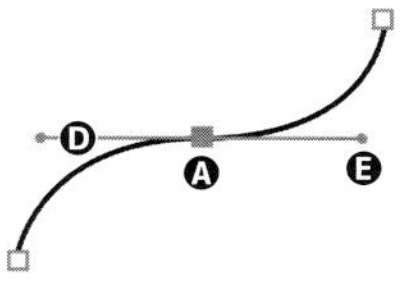

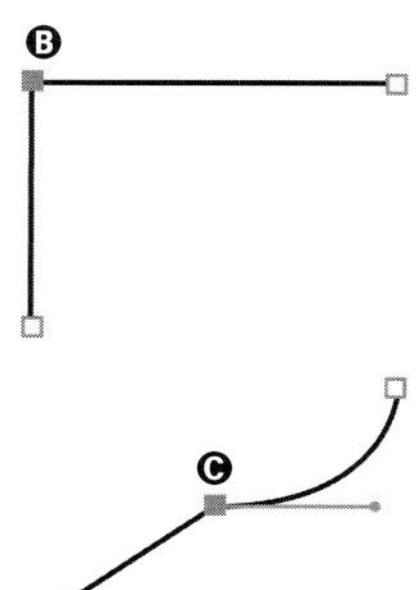

A Curve point A point where the path segments on both sides are curved and the curve on one side flows into (and affects) the curve on the other side.

B Corner point A point where the path segments on both sides are straight.

C Dual point A point where the path segment on one side does not affect the path segment on the other when reshaped. This allows you to have a straight segment on one side and a curved segment on the other or two noncontinuous curved segments.

D Direction handle Used to change the curvature of path segments connected to a curve or dual anchor point. Dragging the direction point toward the anchor point decreases the size of the curvature. Dragging the direction point around the anchor point changes the curve's angle.

E Handlebar Indicates the direction and size of the curve as set by the direction handle.

The direction handles are a common way to control Bezier curves in most vector-editing software. If you are familiar with Macromedia FreeHand or Adobe Illustrator, you'll find that the concept is much the same as in those products.

Like the Pen and Freeform Pen tools, the shape tools can be used to create paths and Shape layers. However, you can also use the shape tools to quickly draw rasterized shapes (in Fill Pixels mode) directly into a layer.

DRAWING VS. PAINTING

Computer graphics come in two basic flavors: bitmap and vector. With bitmap graphics, (not to be confused with Photoshop's "bitmap mode") images are created by placing small dots of color ("pixels") spaced closely together to fool the eye into seeing a continuous image. Vector images, on the other hand, create geometric shapes that are defined mathematically rather than mapping out each point. To distinguish between these two methods of creating images, we refer to the editing of bitmap images as painting, and we refer to the editing of vector images as drawing.

Painting is a more versatile way to create a wide variety of image types, allowing you to apply colors gradually over an area with irregular transitions. However, painted images are locked into their size and resolution, which can only be changed by sacrificing image quality.

Drawing creates more exact images that are resolution independent, allowing you to resize the image without worrying about distortion. However, drawn images have a regularity to them that makes them impractical for images such as photographs.

12.2 Setting Pen Tool Options

➠ 3.19 Pen Tools

➠ 12.5 Preparing to Draw Vector Paths

➠ 12.6 Preparing to Draw Shape Layers

Pen tool P

Cycle pen tools (Pen and Freeform Pen only)

The Pen tool is great for creating precise vector paths, especially if you require straight lines.

Regardless of the mode you are working in (Shape Layer or Path), setting the options for the Pen tool are identical, although not numerous. You can set the tool to preview the path segment as you are drawing it, and you can specify whether you want to be able to edit paths as you are working.

To begin using the Pen tool, select it in the Toolbox, and then set its options in the tool options bar. You can then follow the instructions for drawing vector paths (Section 12.5) or for drawing Shape layers (Section 12.6).

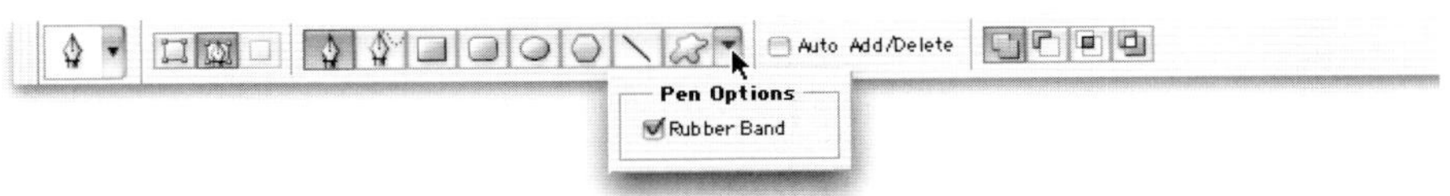

- Check Rubber Band to preview the path segment between the last anchor point and the next anchor point as you draw it. If this option is cleared, the path segment does not appear until you add the next anchor point.
- Check Auto Add/Delete if you want to be able to add new anchor points to an existing path while working. If this option is checked, clicking an existing segment adds a new anchor point to the segment, splitting it into two new segments. If this option is cleared, clicking an existing segment creates a new anchor point over the segment. This is useful if you want to be able to edit the path on the fly, but might get in the way if you need to create tight paths where anchor points are close together.

CREATING CUSTOM SHAPES

You can add paths to the Custom Shape menu by selecting the path to be added and then choosing, Edit > Define Custom Shape.... Enter a name for the new shape in the dialog, and click OK. The new shape appears in the Shapes drop-down menu with the Custom Shape tool.

12.3 Setting Freeform Pen and Magnetic Pen Tool Options

If you need to draw objects with more flowing lines, rather than straight or regularly curved lines, the Freeform Pen might provide the options you need. In addition, the Freeform Pen tool includes the Magnetic option, which allows you to closely trace the edges in an image to create a path (much like the Magnetic Lasso tool).

Both the path and shape modes use the same options as the Freeform Pen tool. Magnetic is actually an option of the Freeform Pen tool, not a stand-alone tool itself, but it acts as its own unique tool.

To begin using the Freeform Pen tool, select it in the Toolbox, and then set its options in the tool options bar. You can then follow the instructions for drawing vector paths (Section 12.5) or for drawing Shape layers (Section 12.6).

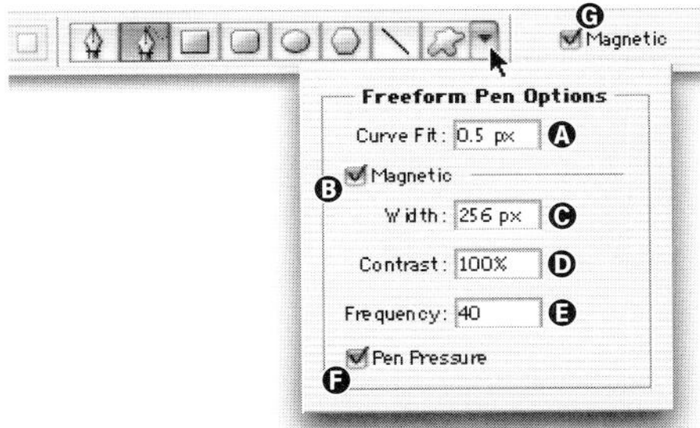

A Enter a value (0.5 to 10) to set the error tolerance for fitting curves. A higher value smoothes the path you draw; a lower value keeps the path closer to the way you draw it.

B Check to use the Magnetic Pen tool (similar to the Magnetic Lasso tool), which creates a path by following the sharp contrast contours of the image in the selected layer.

C (With Magnetic only) Enter a value (1 to 256) for the width from the mouse pointer to be considered part of the path. If the image is high contrast, use a wide line to ensure a solid edge. If there are a lot of small shapes, use a larger width.

D (With Magnetic only) Enter a value (1 to 100) for the percentage of contrast between edges in the image to be considered for the path. Use a high percentage for high-contrast images to ensure a tighter fit.

E (With Magnetic only) Enter a value (5 to 40) for how often anchor points are automatically added along the path. The more points, the tighter the fit but the more jagged the selection may look.

F (With Magnetic only) If you are using a tablet, check this if you want to allow pen pressure to set the width value.

G Check to turn the Magnetic option on. This option is redundant to the one in the tool's drop-down options panel.

➠ 3.19 Pen Tools

➠ 8.4 Creating a Free-form Selection

➠ 12.5 Preparing to Draw Vector Paths

➠ 12.6 Preparing to Draw Shape Layers

Pen tool [P]

Cycle pen tools (Pen and Freeform Pen only) [Shift] [P]

The Freeform Pen tool is great for creating vector paths of oddly shaped objects, however, it takes a steady and practiced hand to get the shapes just right.

The Magnetic Pen tool allows you to create paths based on bitmap images. In many ways this is superior to using the magnetic lasso tool, since vectors can be used for selections and much more.

12.4 Setting Shape Tool Options

➠ 3.2 The Tool Options Bar
➠ 3.17 Path Selection Tools
➠ 3.20 Shape Tools
➠ 4.13 Paths Palette
➠ 12.5 Preparing to Draw Vector Paths
➠ 12.6 Preparing to Draw Shape Layers
➠ 15.8 Painting with shapes
➠ Color Section: Blending Modes

Shape tool U

Cycle shape tools Shift U

Each shape tool has different option settings that you must consider when drawing the shape.

To begin using a shape tool, select the desired shape in the Toolbox, and then set its options in the tool options bar. You can then follow the instructions for drawing vector paths (Section 12.5) or for drawing Shape layers (Section 12.6).

Rectangle and Rounded Rectangle Tool Options

The settings for the Rectangle and Rounded Rectangle tools are almost identical, except for the ability to set the corner radius for rounded rectangles.

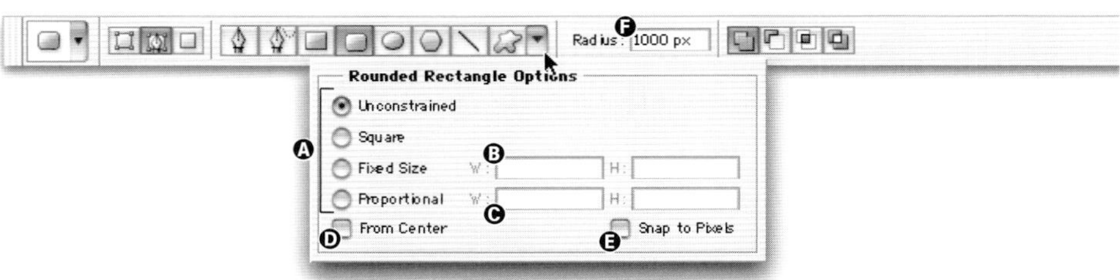

Ⓐ Choose a shape constraint: Unconstrained (freeform rectangle), Square, Fixed Size, or Proportional.

Ⓑ If you chose Fixed Size, enter a value (1 to 30000) in pixels for the width and height of the rectangle.

Ⓒ If you chose Proportional, enter a value (1 to 1000) for the width and height proportions.

Ⓓ Check to draw the shape from the center rather than from the top-left corner.

Ⓔ Check to snap the edges of the shape to the pixel's edges in the image.

Ⓕ (Rounded Rectangle only) Enter a value (0 to 1000) for the corner radius of the rounded rectangle. A value of 0 produces square corners.

Ellipse Tool Options

You use the Ellipse tool to draw circles and elliptical shapes, either in freeform or with precision by setting the exact or relative dimensions of the shape.

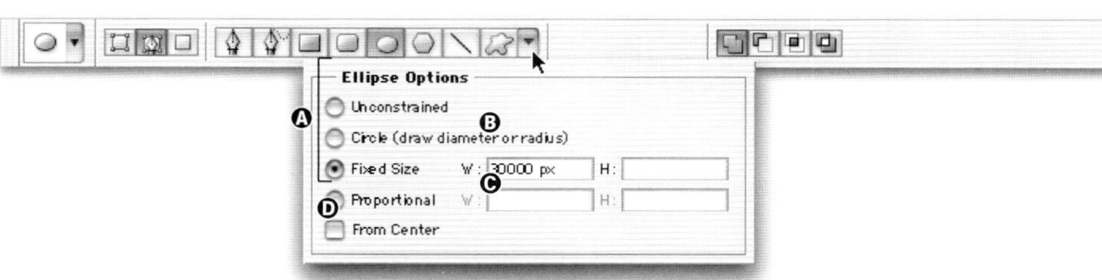

Ⓐ Choose a shape constraint: Unconstrained (freeform ellipse), Circle, Fixed Size, or Proportional.

Ⓑ If you choose Fixed Size, enter a value (1 to 30000) in pixels for the width and height of the ellipse.

Ⓒ If you choose Proportional, enter a value (1 to 1000) for the width and height proportions.

Ⓓ Check to draw the shape from the center rather than from the top-left corner.

12.4 Setting Shape Tool Options *(Continued)*

Polygon Tool Options

You use the Polygon tool to draw multisided shapes with anywhere from 3 to 100 sides. In addition, you can turn these shapes into star patterns in which the interior of the path segments indent.

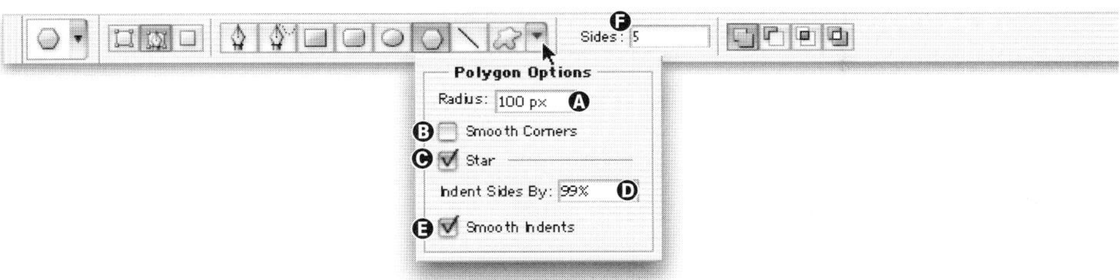

- Ⓐ Enter a value (1 to 15000) for the radius of the polygon.
- Ⓑ Check to round off the corners.
- Ⓒ Check to indent the polygon sides to create a star shape.
- Ⓓ (With Star only) Enter a value (1 to 99) to set the percentage that the sides are indented.
- Ⓔ (With Star only) Check to round off the indentions.
- Ⓕ Enter a value (3 to 100) to set the number of sides for the polygon.

Line Tool Options

Not only can you quickly draw a line, often referred to as a "rule" in printing, but you can also add arrowheads to each end of a line and adjust the arrowhead shape.

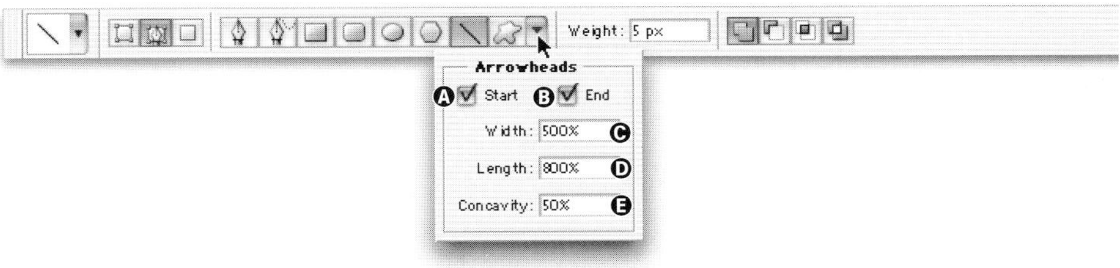

- Ⓐ Check if you want an arrowhead at the start of the line.
- Ⓑ Check if you want an arrowhead at the end of the line.
- Ⓒ Enter a value (10 to 1000) for the width of the arrowheads relative to the weight of the line.
- Ⓓ Enter a value (10 to 5000) for the length of the arrowheads relative to the weight of the line.
- Ⓔ Enter a value (from –50 to 50) for the concavity of the back of the arrowheads.

Top, Concavity 50%; bottom, Concavity –50%

Shapes can not only be added to the canvas as vector paths or shape layers as discussed in this chapter but also as painted shapes as shown in Section 15.8.

Custom shapes are managed in the Preset manager (see Section 5.1).

You can also edit the arrowheads after they have been drawn using the path and direct selection tools (see Sections 12.8 and 12.9).

Although ImageReady does not include either of the path drawing tools, it does include several of the shape tools, which can be used to add draw layers or painted shapes.

12.4 Setting Shape Tool Options *(Continued)*

Custom Shape Tool Options

The Custom Shape tool is the catchall for other freeform shape types that do not fit into the other shape categories. You can find everything from fleurs-de-lis to footprints in this category. You can also load various preset custom shape libraries and even create your own custom shapes from paths you create. The custom shape has two pull-downs. You use the first to set general options about drawing, and you use the second to select a specific shape to draw.

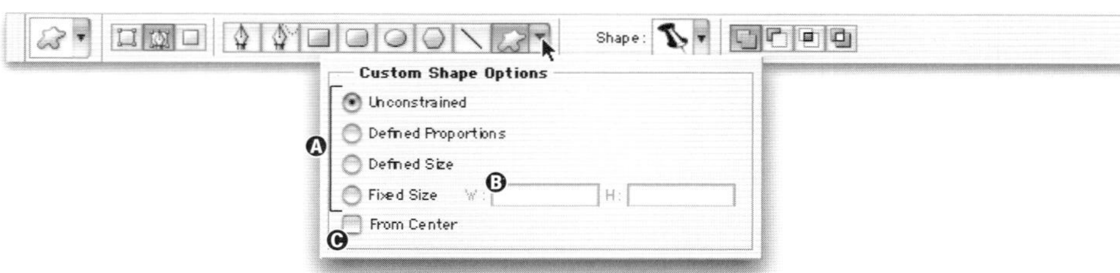

A Choose a shape constraint: Unconstrained (freeform shape), Defined Proportions (uses the proportions set when the shape was created), Defined Size (uses the size set when the shape was defined), or Fixed Size.

B If you chose Fixed Size, enter a value (1 to 30000) in pixels for the width and height of the shape.

C Check to draw the shape from the center rather than from the top-left corner.

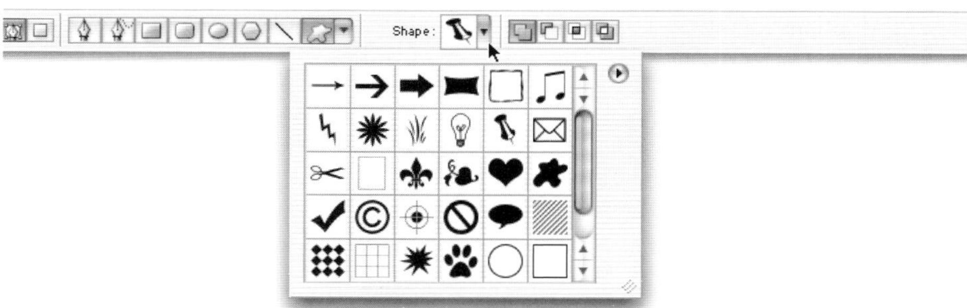

Click a preset shape thumbnail to select a shape. Click the arrow at the top right to access the preset shapes menu, where you can set the thumbnail size, load other preset shape groups, or save the current group.

12.5 Preparing to Draw Vector Paths

Vector paths are added to the Paths palette and can be used for a variety of purposes when drawing and painting in the canvas. However, they do not, by themselves, add to the image.

You use the Pen tool to create path components by plotting anchor points in the canvas that can be either straight (corner points) or curved (curved points). (You can also use the shape tools to draw vector paths, as described shortly.) To prepare to draw a vector path, follow these steps:

1. Choose the Pen tool, Freeform Pen tool, or one of the shape tools in the Toolbox; if you want to use the Magnetic Pen tool, choose the Freeform Pen tool and check Magnetic in the tool options bar. You can also select any of these tools and then switch between them in the tool options bar (see Section 3.19).
2. Click the Paths button in the tool options bar, and select a path in the Paths palette:
   - To add a path component to a new path, click the Create New Path button at the bottom of the palette.
   - To add a path component to the work path, either select the work path or, if there is no work path, deselect all paths by Shift-clicking the currently selected path. (When you start to draw, the Work path is automatically added.)
   - To add path components to an existing path, select that path.
3. Set the options for your tool in the tool options bar, and choose the overlap mode for the new path component:

Add	The new path component is added to the path.
Subtract	The new path component is subtracted from existing path components.
Intersect	Path components are created from the intersection of the new path component and existing path components.
Exclude Overlapping	Paths are created by removing the overlapping areas of the new path component and existing path components.

Now follow the instructions in Section 12.7 for the tool you selected.

➠ 3.19 Pen Tools

➠ 3.20 Shape Tools

➠ 12.2 Setting Pen Tool Options

➠ 12.3 Setting Freeform Pen and Magnetic Pen Tool Options

➠ 12.4 Setting Shape Tool Options

Pen tool P
Cycle pen tools Shift P

Shape tools U
Cycle shape tools Shift U

12.6 Preparing to Draw Shape Layers

➠ 9.5 Adding a Fill Layer or an Adjustment Layer
➠ 11.6 Adding Vector Masks
➠ 11.7 Editing Vector Masks
➠ 12.2 Setting Pen Tool Options
➠ 12.3 Setting Freeform Pen and Magnetic Pen Tool Options
➠ 12.4 Setting Shape Tool Options

Shape tool U

Cycle shape tools
Shift U

Pen tool P

Cycle pen tools
Shift P

Using Shape layers is an easy way to add a vector mask with a Fill layer to your image. This allows you to quickly add shaped designs of solid color or styles. Although this uses paths to create shapes, this tool is used to add vector shapes directly to the selected layer in the Layers palette, rather than to the Paths palette. However, the path will show up as a work path in the Paths palette when the layer is selected. When you are adding shapes to a Shape layer, you are in fact adding path components to the layer's vector mask, which is a work path for that layer.

Drawing a Shape layer with a pen tool is similar to drawing vector paths and using the shape tools to draw. To prepare to draw a Shape layer, follow these steps:

1 Choose the Pen tool, Freeform Pen tool, or one of the shape tools; to use the Magnetic Pen, choose the Freeform Pen tool and check Magnetic in the options bar.

2 Click Shape Layers in the tool options bar, and select a layer in the Layers palette:

- To create a new Shape layer, click the layer you want the Shape layer to appear above. Make sure that Create New Shape Layer is selected in the options bar.
- To add additional shapes to an existing Shape layer's vector mask, select that layer, then, in the tool options bar, choose the overlap mode for the new component:

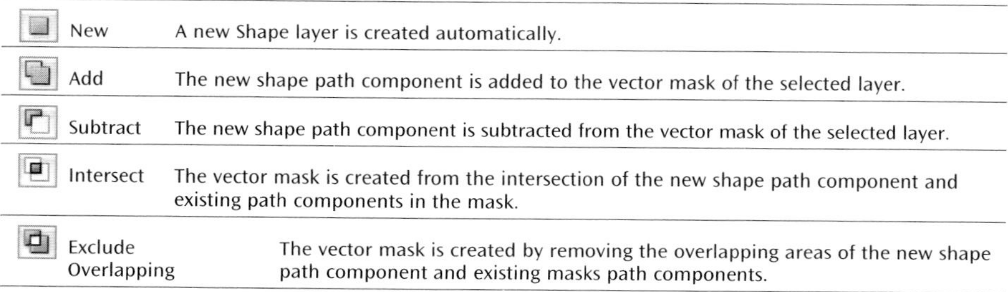

New	A new Shape layer is created automatically.
Add	The new shape path component is added to the vector mask of the selected layer.
Subtract	The new shape path component is subtracted from the vector mask of the selected layer.
Intersect	The vector mask is created from the intersection of the new shape path component and existing path components in the mask.
Exclude Overlapping	The vector mask is created by removing the overlapping areas of the new shape path component and existing masks path components.

3 Set the options for your tool in the tool options bar, then:

- If you are adding to an existing vector mask and want to apply a new style to the layer or change that layer's style or color, click the Link button so that the button is highlighted (darker). Otherwise, style and color changes made in the tool options bar are applied only to new Shape layers.
- Choose a style for the Fill layer. If you do not want to apply a style, choose Default Style (none) with the red slash.
- Click the color swatch and choose a color for the Fill layer. If a style is used, it covers the color of the Fill layer.

Now follow the instruction in Section 12.7 for the tool you selected.

12.7 Drawing with Pen and Shape Tools

Whether you are drawing a vector path or a Shape layer, the process is pretty much the same depending on the tool you are using. Follow the steps in either Section 12.5 (to prepare to draw vector paths) or 12.6 (to draw Shape layers) and then continue here.

After you draw the path, you can edit it or use it to create fills, strokes, selections, or vector masks as explained in the rest of this chapter.

➠ 3.17 Path Selection Tools

➠ 3.19 Pen Tools

➠ 4.13 Paths Palette

Using the Pen Tool

To use the Pen tool, first follow the steps in either Section 12.5 or 12.6. Next, click in the canvas to place your first anchor point, then place the next anchor point by doing one of the following:

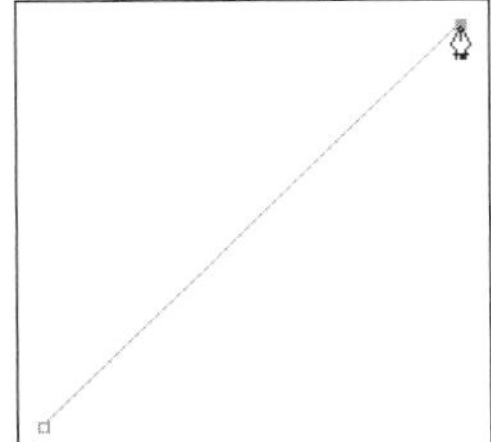

Corner point: Click to create the next anchor point. Release the mouse immediately after clicking to make it a corner anchor point. This creates a straight path segment between the current anchor point and the previous anchor point.

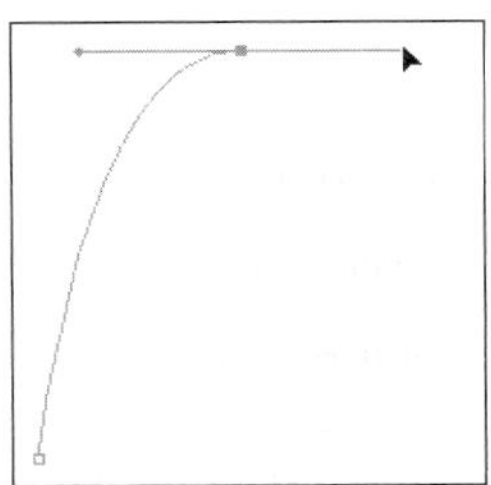

Curved point: Click and drag away from the anchor point to add a curved anchor point using Bezier curves. This creates a curved path segment between the current anchor point and the previous anchor point. Direction handles appear as you drag, allowing you to control the shape and direction of the curve as you move the handlebars. When you are satisfied with the curve, release the mouse button. You can edit the curve of the last anchor point added by clicking it and adjusting the handlebars.

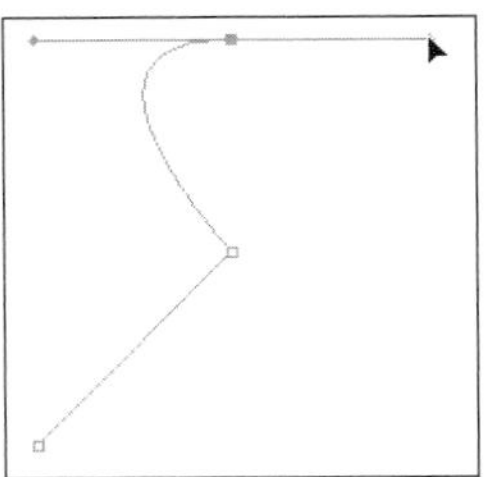

Dual point: Option/Alt-click when placing an anchor point to add a dual anchor point. The next segment you create by clicking will be curved independent of the previous segment. This allows you to have a straight-line segment on one side and a curved-line segment on the other or two curved line segments that can be independently shaped.

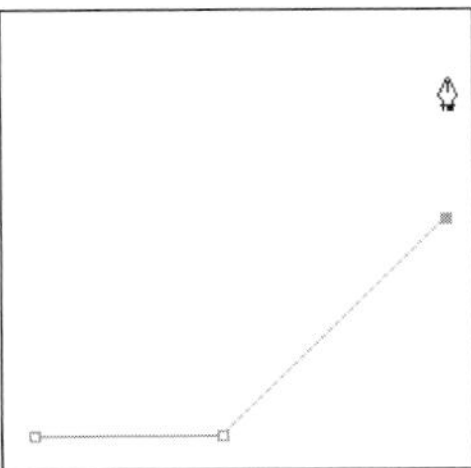

45° straight line: Shift-click to add the next anchor point at 45° increments from the previous anchor point.

Path Selection Tool [A]

Cycle Path Selection Tools [Shift] [A]

Pen Tool [P]

Cycle Pen Tools (Pen and Freeform Pen only) [Shift] [P]

Shape Tool [U]

Cycle Shape Tools [Shift] [U]

If you are using the Pen tool to draw a Shape layer, then as you add anchor points, the style or color you selected in Step 3 automatically begins to fill the area defined by the path. If you are not adding to an existing vector mask, a new Fill layer appears in the Layers palette with a vector mask.

Repeat creating anchor points as many times as necessary. When you are finished drawing your path, do one of the following:

- To leave the path open, Command/Ctrl-click the canvas or choose any tool. Any fills added to the path will assume a straight-line closure between the first and final anchor points.
- To close the path, click the first anchor point. When your mouse pointer is positioned over the first anchor point, the cursor will show the Pen tool icon with a circle next to it. You can still click and drag to make the final path segment curved.

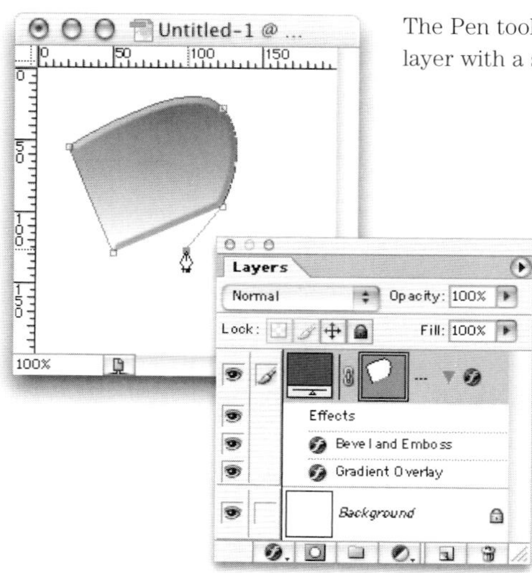

The Pen tool is creating a Shape layer with a style applied.

Using the Freeform Pen Tool

If you are using the Freeform Pen tool *without* the Magnetic option, first follow the steps in either Section 12.5 or 12.6. Then click in the canvas and draw your path without releasing the mouse button. When you are finished drawing your path, do one of the following:

- To leave the path open, release the mouse button. Any fills added to the path will assume a straight-line closure between the first and final anchor points.
- To close the path, click the first anchor point. When your mouse pointer is positioned over the first anchor point, the cursor will show the Freeform Pen tool icon with a circle next to it.

12.7 Drawing with Pen and Shape Tools *(Continued)*

- To close the path with a straight line from the current position to the first anchor point, press Command/Ctrl and release the mouse pointer.

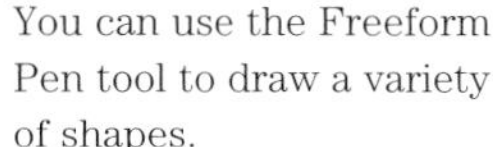

You can use the Freeform Pen tool to draw a variety of shapes.

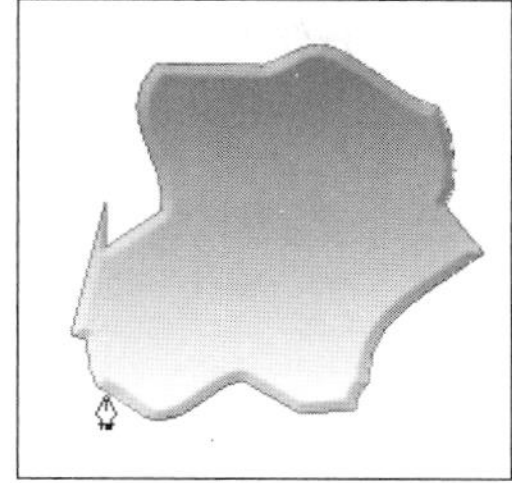

A freeform path drawn with a style applied.

Using the Magnetic Pen Tool

To use the Freeform Pen tool *with* the Magnetic option, first follow the steps in either Section 12.5 or 12.6. Then, click in the canvas to set the first anchor point in the path. Drag around the edge of the object for which you are attempting to draw a vector path.

A path (a solid line) snaps to the edge of the object as you drag. The settings for Width, Edge Contrast, and Frequency determine the fit of the path. If you notice the path moving away from the object's edge, move back to the point where it started to deviate, click to manually add an anchor point, then continue your selection.

When you are finished tracing the path, do one of the following:

- To close the path, click the original anchor point. When you place the mouse cursor over the original anchor point, the cursor will change to a Pen icon with a circle next to it.
- To close the path with a magnetic path line drawn between the starting and stopping points (as calculated by Photoshop), Command/Ctrl-click, press Return/Enter, or double-click.
- To close the selection with a straight line directly between the starting and stopping points, Option/Alt-double-click.

The Magnetic Pen tool is being used to trace the outline of the light bulb.

Switch from Pen or Freeform Pen to Direct Selection tool (reverts after releasing)

⌘
Ctrl

Switch from Pen or Freeform Pen to Convert Point tool while over an anchor point other than the first or last (reverts after releasing)

Option
Alt

Delete currently selected path or path component

Del

Move path while drawing

Spacebar

Constrain shape proportions while drawing

Shift

12.7 Drawing with Pen and Shape Tools *(Continued)*

You can move a shape while drawing by holding down the space bar and dragging.

To create an "S" curve between two anchor points, drag the handle bars in the same directions.

To create a smooth curve between two anchor points, drag the handlebars in opposite directions.

If you want to keep path segments separate, you need to add a new path using the Paths palette every time you draw a new path segment.

The more anchor points you include, the larger the file size will get.

Using a Shape Tool

To use any of the shape tools, follow the steps in either Section 12.5 or 12.6, then simply click and drag to draw the shape. Release the mouse button when the shape is the desired size.

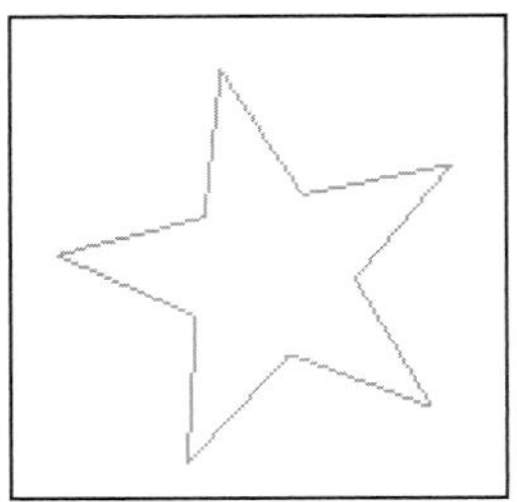

The Polygon Shape tool is being used to draw a star by indenting the sides.

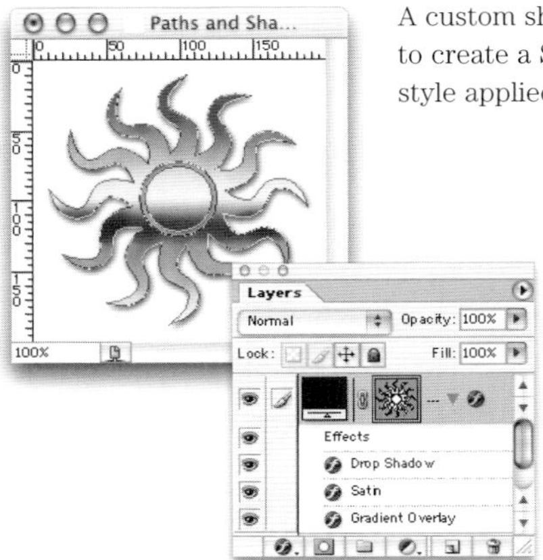

A custom shape is being used to create a Shape layer with a style applied.

12.8 Selecting Paths and Path Components

After you draw a path or Shape layer using any of the drawing tools, it appears in the Paths palette where you can select and edit it.

Switch from Path Selection to Direct Selection tool (reverts after releasing)

Ctrl

Selecting Paths

The Paths palette contains three types of paths: paths (also referred to as saved paths), the work path (of which there is only one at a time), and vector mask paths. Work paths and vector mask paths are temporary paths, and their names are always italicized.

- To **select** a path, click the path name in the Paths palette. The selected path is highlighted.
- To **deselect** a path, Shift-click the path name in the Paths palette, press Esc, or click in the empty area beneath all the paths in the Paths palette.

Once selected, paths and path components can be transformed (scaled, rotated, skewed, distorted) just like a selection except that the menu option is Transform Path instead of just Transform (see Section 8.8).

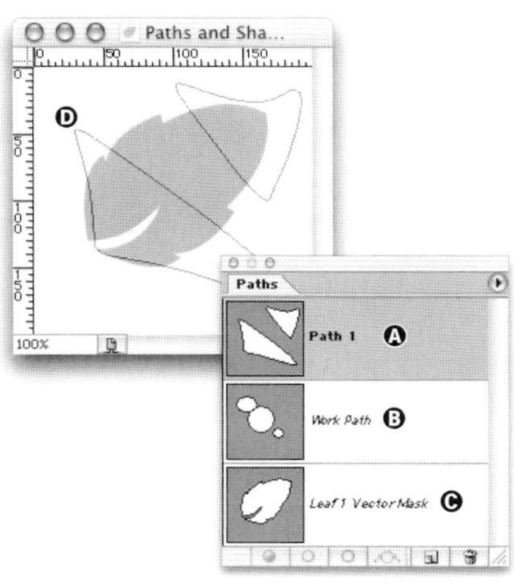

Ⓐ **Path** Click to select the path. Shift-click to deselect the path. Both shapes in this path are individual path components.

Ⓑ **Work path** Click to select the path. Shift-click to deselect the path. Double-click or drag it to the Create A New Path button at the bottom of the Paths layer to turn the path into a saved path. The work path is a temporary path used to record paths' components until they are saved.

Ⓒ **Vector mask path** Click to select the path. Shift-click to deselect the path. Double-click or drag it to the Create A New Path button to save as a path. A vector mask is a temporary path that appears only if the layer it is in is selected. The name of the layer is part of the path's name.

Ⓓ **Selected path** Selected paths are highlighted in the Paths palette and appear as an outline in the canvas.

Selecting Path Components

After you select a path in the Paths palette, you can select an individual path component within the path or a path segment within a component. To select paths, you will need to first choose the Path Selection tool, select the path in the Paths palette or the layer with the vector mask in the Layers palette, and then do the following:

- To select a path component in the canvas, click anywhere within the path component in the canvas. The anchor points for that path component will appear, letting you know it was selected. If there are multiple path components in the path, only the path component under the mouse pointer is selected.
- To select multiple path components, click and drag over one or more components. All path components within the selection marquee (even if only partially) are selected.
- To add path components to the selection, Shift-click the desired path components.

12.9 Editing Paths and Path Components

➠ 9.11 Aligning and Distributing Layers

➠ 12.10 Editing Path Segments

Switch from Path Selection to Direct Selection tool (reverts after releasing)
⌘
Ctrl

After you drawn a path or Shape layer using any of the drawing tools, it appears in the Paths palette where you can select and edit it.

Changing a Path Component's Overlap Mode

When drawing paths, you specify how the new path component interacts with the path and other components already on the path. You can change the overlap mode of an existing path component using the icons on the tool options bar.

1 Using the Path Selection tool, select one or more path components in the canvas.

2 In the tool options bar, select one of the overlap modes:

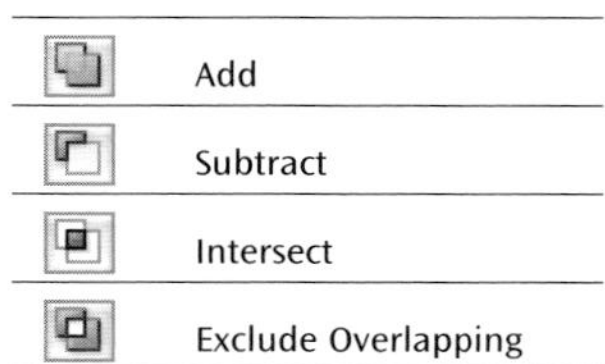

	Add
	Subtract
	Intersect
	Exclude Overlapping

Adjusting Paths and Path Components

You can move path components as a group by selecting the path they are on, or you can move them individually by selecting one or more path components. In addition, you can align path components, you can combine them into a single path component, and you can delete a single path component or an entire path.

- To move a path, select it in the Paths palette, choose the Move tool, click and drag within the canvas, moving the path to the desired location.

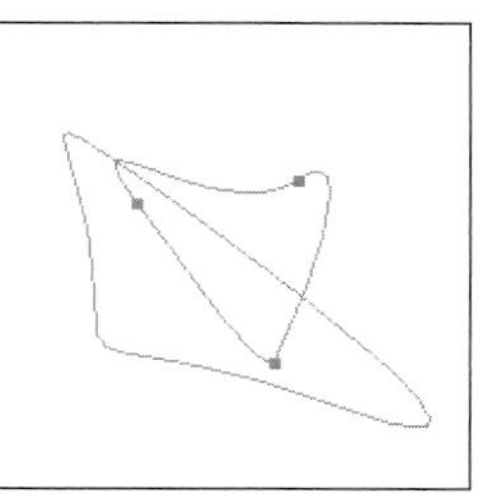

- To move path components, select one or more path components in the canvas, choose the Path Selection tool or the Move tool, and then click and drag within any of the selected path components, moving them about on the canvas to the desired location.

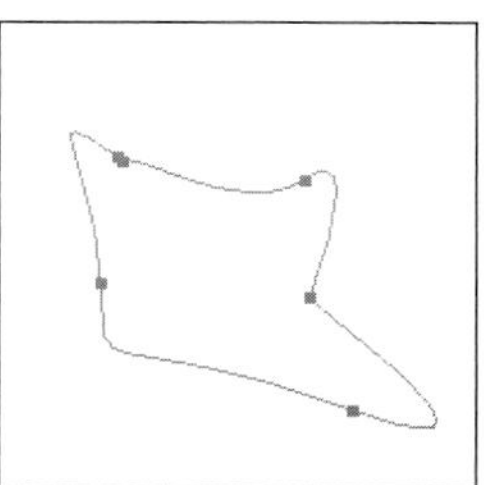

- To combine path components, select two or more path components in the canvas (they must be in the same path), and use the Path Selection tool. Click the Combine button in the tool options bar. The selected path components merge (based on their overlap mode) into a single path component.

12.9 Editing Paths and Path Components *(Continued)*

- To align and distribute path components, use the Path Selection tool, and select two or more path components to align or three or more path components to distribute. Click one of the alignment or distribution options in the tool options bar.
- To delete a path, select the path in the Paths palette and click the trash can icon, drag the path to the trash can icon, or choose Delete Path from the Paths palette menu.
- To delete a path component, select the path component and press Delete. If this is the last path component in a vector mask, you will be asked whether you want to delete the entire layer, delete only the mask and retain the layer's content, or delete only the contents of the layer and retain the vector mask.

Once selected, paths and path components can be transformed (scaled, rotated, skewed, distorted) just like a selection, except the menu option is Transform Path instead of Transform (see Section 8.8).

If you are moving a curved segment, hold down the Shift key to constrain the movements to 45° multiples.

Hold down Option/Alt and move the path component to duplicate it in the mask.

REAL WORLD: MAGGIE TAYLOR

Maggie Taylor pulls the inspiration for her work from a variety of Surrealist painters, films, folk art, and mythological figures, yet looking at her works, you can't help but notice that she takes inspiration also from the objects she finds to collage into her images. She is "a collector of various kinds of small objects and old tintype photographs. I buy them at flea markets and on eBay and scan the objects and photographs directly on my flatbed scanner."

She generally begins projects in 16-bit mode, scanning objects in high-bit depth, and then adjusts the levels and curves to bring out softer tones. She will then change the image mode to 8 bits per channel to take advantage of working with layers and use image adjustment layers from that point on to make changes to the contrast or colors.

Maggie relies on Photoshop's layers to build her work: "Sometimes with all the image adjustment layers, I might have 40 or 50 layers in a file. Many times I use blending modes; however, I try to stay away from the more bizarre ones such as Exclusion or Difference. Most often I use Multiply, Overlay, or Luminosity. I try to keep a certain sense of reality in the work—a believable pictorial space that is not as difficult to read as some layered images I have seen." You can find more of Maggie's work at `www.maggietaylor.com/`.

12.10 Editing Path Segments

➡ 3.17 Path Selection Tools

➡ 3.19 Pen Tools

➡ 4.13 Paths Palette

Switch from Path Selection to Direct Selection tool (reverts after releasing)

⌘

Ctrl

Remember that styles can be applied and changed for the Fill layer.

To change the shape of a path component, you must edit the path segments or the anchor points used to define the path segments. First, you select the anchor point or path segment to be edited, and then you can adjust or reshape the segments as desired.

Selecting Anchor Points and Path Segments

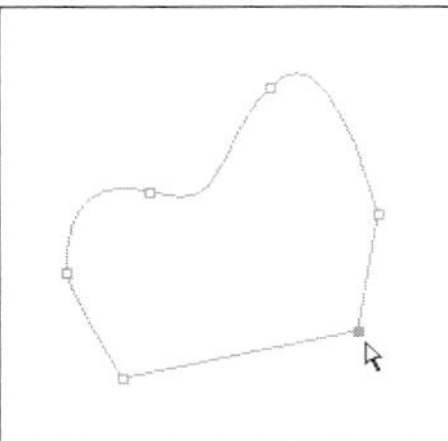

First, choose the Direct Path Selection tool, and then do one of the following:

- To select an anchor point, click it and the point's direction handles will appear. Shift-click additional anchor points to include them in the selection.
- To select a path segment, click it.
- To select multiple path segments, click outside the path component and drag over the path. All anchor points within the selection marquee are selected, even those between path components. You can also Shift-click each anchor point individually.
- To select all anchor points within a path component, Option/Alt-click within the path component. To add path components to the selection, Shift-Option-click/Shift-Alt-click within other path components in the same path.

Moving and Deleting Path Segments

First choose the Direct Path Selection tool, then do one of the following:

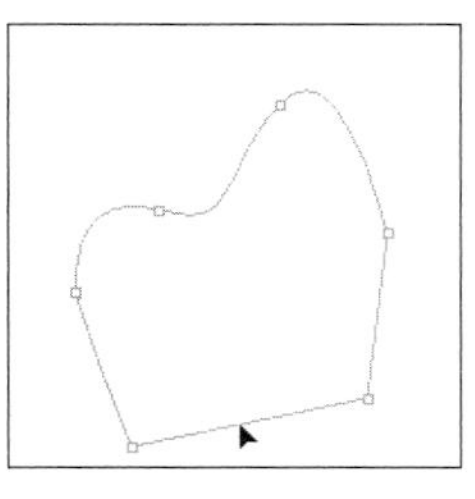

- To move a straight path segment, click and drag the path segment to the desired position. You can also select multiple path segments, even those between path components, and move them together.

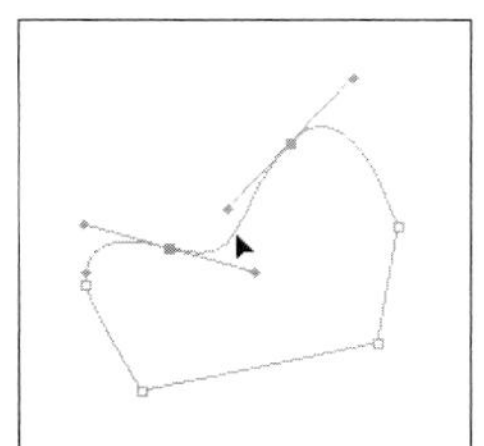

- To move a curved path segment, select the path segment by clicking the anchor points on either side, and then move the segment as desired. The curve does not change shape as it moves, but the segments on either side of it change shape to adjust.

12.10 Editing Path Segments *(Continued)*

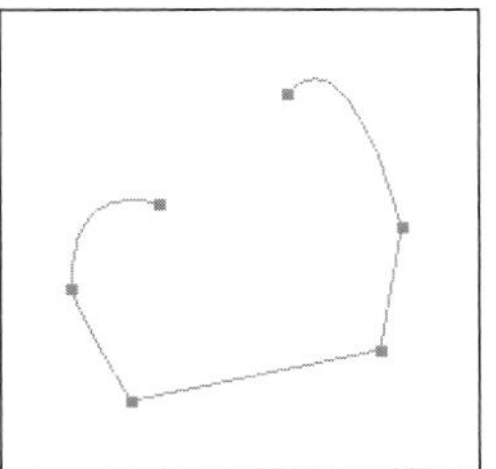

■ To delete a segment, select the path segment and press Delete/Backspace. The segment is removed, leaving a blank space between the two anchor points. Pressing Delete/Backspace again deletes the entire path component.

Adding and Deleting Anchor Points

You can add or delete anchor points from a path component to change the shape of the component or to simplify the shape.

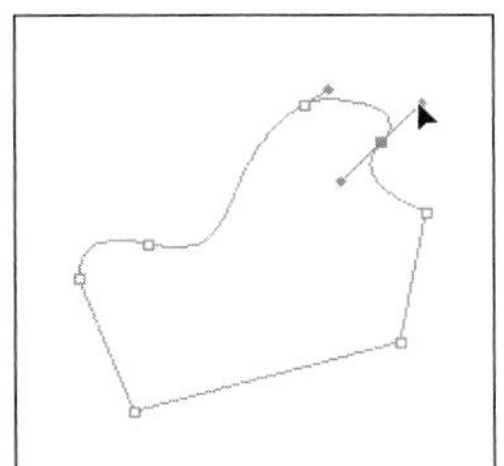

■ To add an anchor point to a path segment, choose the Add Anchor Point tool and click the position in the path segment where you want to add the new anchor point. You can click and move to immediately adjust the curvature of the path segments around the new anchor point.

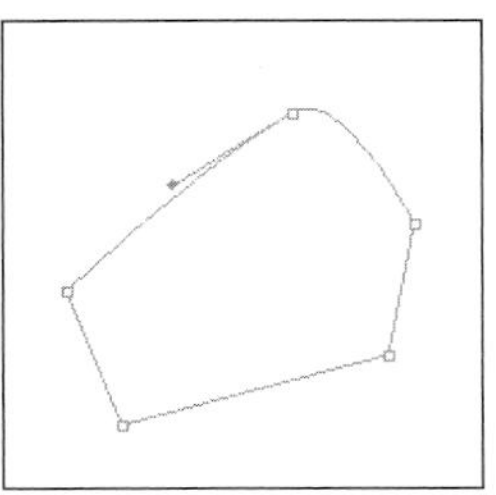

■ To delete an anchor point without erasing the line segment, choose the Delete Anchor Point tool, click the path component to select it, and then click the anchor point you want to remove. If you want to reshape the curve while removing the anchor point, click the anchor point and then drag the path.

- To convert a curve into a corner point, choose the Point tool, click the path component to select it, and click a curved anchor point. This will now be a corner anchor point.
- To convert a corner into a curved point, choose the Point tool, click the path component to select it, click a corner anchor point, and drag out to adjust the curve using the direction handle. This will now be a curved anchor point.
- To create a corner point with curves, choose the Point tool, click the path component to select it, and then click and adjust the direction points on one side of a curved anchor point. The curves on either side of the anchor point can now be adjusted independently.

If you have the Pen tool selected and have the Auto Add/Delete options checked in the tool options bar, anytime you place the pen tool over a line segment of a selected Path Component, it will automatically switch to the Add Anchor Point tool. Likewise, when you are over an anchor point, the Pen tool will switch to the Delete Anchor point tool.

Hold down Option/Alt and move the path component with the Move tool to duplicate it in the mask.

12.11 Reshaping Curves

➠ 3.17 Path Selection Tools

➠ 4.13 Paths Palette

Switch from Direct Selection to Path Selection tool (reverts after releasing)

⌘

Ctrl

The Add Anchor, Delete Anchor, and Convert Point tools will be the Direct Selection tool until they are over a path segment or anchor point.

You create curves initially by clicking and dragging while adding an anchor point with the Pen tool, by using the Freeform Pen tool to draw curved shapes, or by using part of a predefined custom shape. After you add a curve to a path, you can reshape the curve in a variety of ways to get the desired affect.

To reshape a curve, first choose the Direct Path Selection tool, then do one of the following:

- Click a curved path segment and move the cursor. As you move the cursor, the curve changes its shape, adjusting both anchor points.
- Click a curved path segment and adjust the direction handles of the anchor points on either side. This allows you to adjust the curvature of both anchor points independently.
- Click an anchor point connected to a curved path segment, and use the direction handles to reshape the curves in segments on both side of the anchor point.

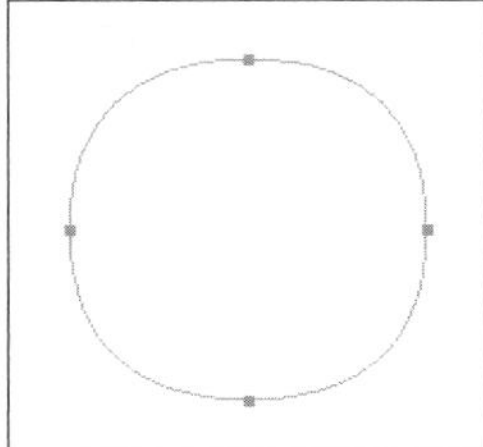

The original curve

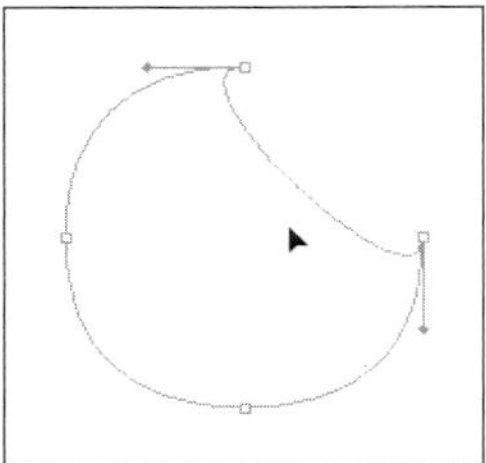

Moving the path segment directly adjusts the entire curve, but leaves curves on either side unchanged.

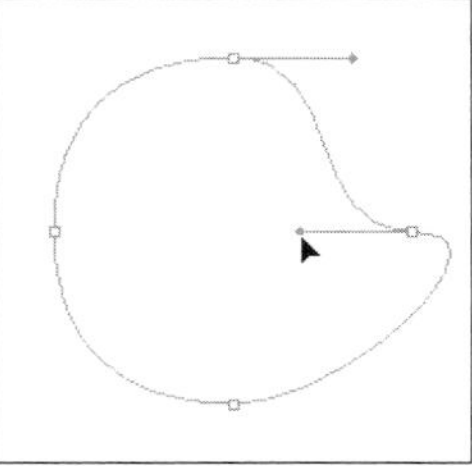

Selecting the curve and then adjusting the direction handles allow you to change the curvature at the anchor points for curves on both sides.

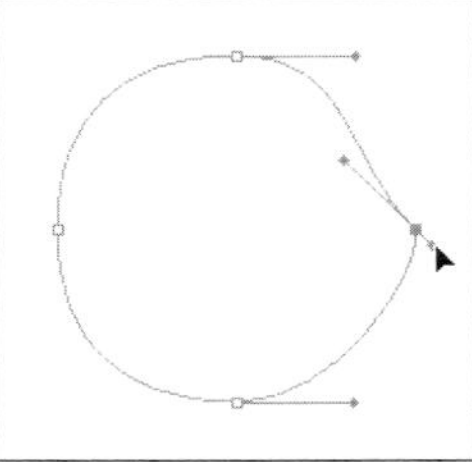

Selecting a single anchor point allows you to reshape curves on both sides of that anchor point.

12.12 Managing Paths

You manage paths using the Paths palette. You can create new blank paths, convert temporary paths into saved paths, duplicate paths and path components, and set options for the paths.

➠ 3.17 Path Selection Tools

➠ 4.13 Paths Palette

If you need to see more detail in the channel's thumbnail, use the Channel palette options to set the size to Medium or Large.

If you have a hard time seeing the paths in the Paths palette, set the thumbnail size by choosing Palette Options… in the Paths palette menu and then choosing a new size.

Creating a New Path

In the Paths palette, do one of the following:

- To create a new path in the Paths palette, click the New Path button.
- To create a new path using the New Path dialog, choose New Path from the Paths palette menu, or Option/Alt click the New Path button. Enter the name for the new path and click OK.
- To convert a vector mask path or work path into a path, double-click its name. In the dialog, enter a new name for the path. The new path appears in the palette. Changes to this path do not affect the vector mask path.

Duplicating a Path or Path Component

To duplicate a path component, choose the Path Selection tool from the Toolbox, and Option/Alt click inside the path component and drag. The original path remains, but the duplicate moves with the mouse.

To duplicate a path, drag the path to the New Path button in the Paths palette at the bottom of the Paths palette.

To duplicate a path using the Duplicate Paths dialog, select the path in the Paths palette, choose Duplicate Path… from the Paths palette menu, enter a name for the new path, and click OK.

Setting Path Options

To rename a path, double-click the path name in the Paths palette, type the new name, and press Enter.

To change the stacking order of a path, click and drag the path up or down within the Paths palette until a heavy black line appears in the location where you want the path and then release the mouse button. You cannot move vector mask paths or the work path.

12.13 Converting between Paths and Selections

➡ 3.17 Path Selection Tools

➡ 4.13 Paths Palette

➡ 8 Making Selections

Turn path into selection

⌘ click path thumbnail

Ctrl click path thumbnail

Although you can convert from selections to path and back again, even with the tolerance set low, there will always be some distortion in the process, and you will never get exactly the same selection or path when converting back and forth.

Paths and selections are easily interchangeable. Consequently, you can use the Pen tool to define an area and then quickly change it into a selection or take a selection and convert it into a vector path, turning a bitmap image into a resolution-independent vector image.

Converting a Path into a Selection

1 Select the path in the Paths palette.

2 Do one of the following:

- To convert the path directly to a selection, click the Load Path As Selection button at the bottom of the Paths palette.
- To convert the path to a selection using the Make Selection dialog, Option/Alt-click the Load Path As Selection button at the bottom of the Paths palette, or choose Make Selection in the Paths palette menu.

3 If you chose to convert using the Make Selection dialog, specify the selection options and then click OK.

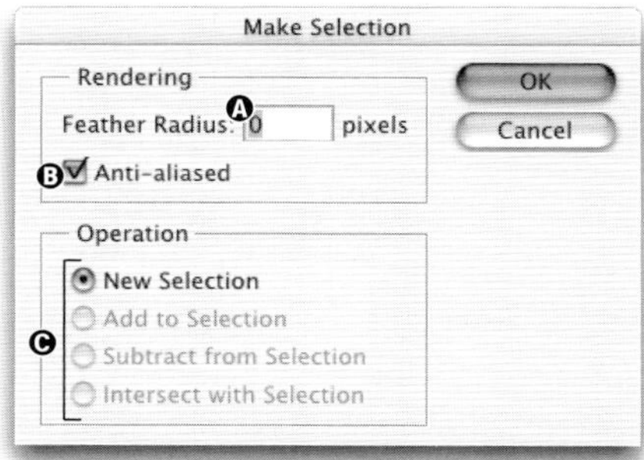

Ⓐ Enter a value (0 to 250) for the Feather Radius to set the softness of the edges of the selection.

Ⓑ Check to use anti-aliasing to smooth the edges of the selection. If checked, set Feather Radius to 0.

Ⓒ Choose how the selection should be added to existing selections in the layer. If there are no other selections in the layer, only New Selection is available.

Converting a Selection into a Path

1 Make a selection in the canvas (see Chapter 8).

2 Do one of the following:

- To convert the selection directly into a path, click the Make Work Path button at the bottom of the Paths palette.
- To convert the selection to a path using the Make Work Path dialog, Option/Alt click the Make Work Path button, or choose Make Work Path from the Paths palette menu.

4 If you chose to convert using the Make Work Path dialog, enter a value (0.5 to 10) for the tolerance used to create the path. A higher tolerance smoothes the edges of the selection when making the path.

The new work path appears at the bottom of the Paths palette, replacing the previous work path.

12.14 Stroking and Filling Paths

You can also use paths to add bitmap elements to a layer. A stroke is line that follows the path outline; a fill simply fills the area of the path with a particular color or pattern. You can perform both stroke and fill actions with the click of single palette button, or you can use a special dialog to set options.

➠ 3.17 Path Selection Tools

➠ 4.13 Paths Palette

➠ Color Section: Blending Modes

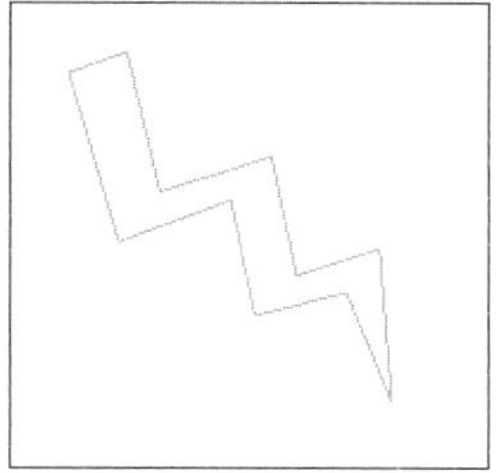

The original path

The path has been stocked with a solid black line and simulated pressure.

The path has been filled with a stone pattern.

To use a path to add a stroke or a fill to a layer, select the path or path component you want to use, select the layer you will be working in, and then do one of the following.

- To fill the path with the foreground color, click the Fill Path button at the bottom of the Paths palette.
- To stroke a path using the settings in the Stroke Path dialog and foreground color, click the Stroke Path button at the bottom of the Paths palette.
- To fill a path using the Fill Path dialog, choose Fill Path… from the Paths palette menu. Specify your options in the dialog and click OK. The filled area now appears on the selected layer.
- To stroke a path using the Stroke Path dialog, choose Stroke Path… from the Paths palette. Specify your options in the dialog and click OK. The filled area now appears on the selected layer.

The stroke and the fill are rasterized (that is, painted) rather than vector, so you edit them with painting tools.

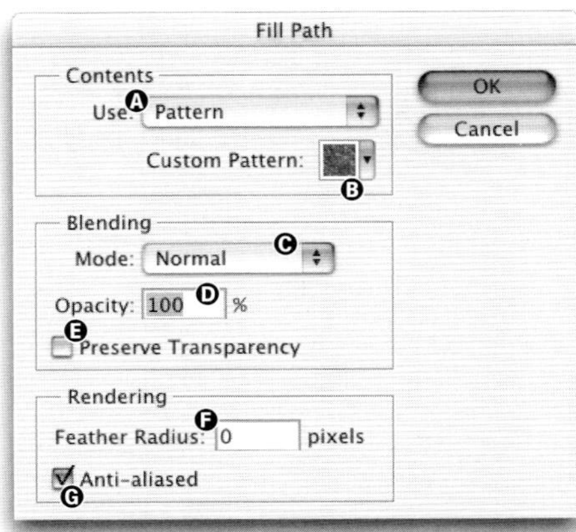

- **A** Choose the color to be used: Foreground Color, Background Color, Pattern, History (using the selected History state), Black, 50% Gray, or White.
- **B** If you selected Pattern (see A), choose the pattern to be used for the stroke.
- **C** Choose a blending mode to be used with the fill.
- **D** Enter a value (1 to 100) for the opacity of the layer.
- **E** Check to keep the current transparency of the selected layer.
- **F** Enter a value (0 to 250) for the Feather Radius to set the softness of the edges of the selection.
- **G** Check to use anti-aliasing to smooth the edges of the selection. If checked, set Feather Radius to 0.

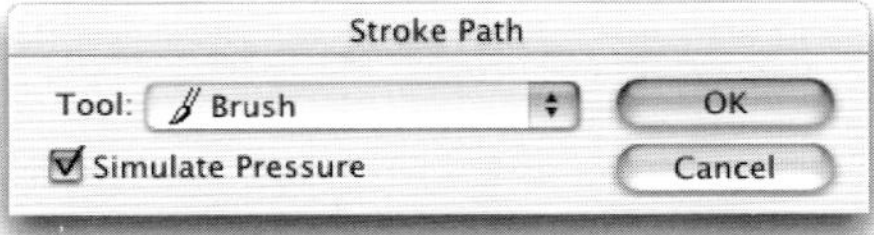

Choose a tool type from the Tool pull-down to be used when creating the stroke. The current settings for that tool are used to create the stroke with the current foreground color. Check the Simulate Pressure check box to vary the width of the stroke.

WHAT ARE BEZIER CURVES?

Vector lines that use handlebars to modify their shape are referred to as Bezier curves, named after the programmer Pierre Bézier, who developed them for use in computer-aided design (CAD) programs. For more details about the mathematics behind the design, visit `http://www.moshplant.com/direct-or/bezier/`.

CHAPTER 13

Making Image Adjustments

ADJUSTMENTS ARE USED TO CHANGE the tones and colors in an image to correct imbalances, fix blemishes, and sometime simply for affect. By editing the image using adjustments, you can minutely refine color to produce better print results, colorize an image, or create wild special effects.

To these ends, you can adjust not only "color," but brightness, contrast, hue, and saturation. You can selectively replace colors, desaturate colors, invert colors, and equalize color luminance. And that's just the beginning. It's easy to be overwhelmed with all the options. The key, therefore, is to know what you want to change, color-wise, in the image before starting and to know how to get the desired results.

This chapter covers the following topics:

13.1 Adjustment Basics

➠ 9.5 Adding a Fill Layer or an Adjustment Layer

➠ Color Section: Adjustments

All adjustments/commands are applied to the layer selected in the Layers palette. You can confine the area that the adjustment affects by selecting an area in that layer.

If you are using an Adjustment layer with a selection, the selection is turned into a layer mask limiting the area affected by the adjustment.

If the Preview option is on while you're making adjustments, but you don't notice the changes in the canvas, it could be that Photoshop is still calculating the adjustment. While Photoshop is thinking, a line blinks under the Preview check box.

Pressing Alt/Option when any Adjustment dialog is open changes the Cancel button to Reset.

You can apply adjustments to a layer in two distinct ways depending on whether you want to permanently change the contents of a single layer or create a new layer which can be used to dynamically change the layers beneath it:

Adjustment commands Applying an adjustment to a layer using a command (Image **>** Adjustments) affects only the pixels on that layer once, but the changes are permanent.

Adjustment layer Adjustment layers offer greater flexibility than using commands. You can hide and delete an Adjustment layer, removing the affects of the adjustment. In addition, you can apply layer masks to mask portions of the adjustment. However, the Adjustment layer applies the adjustment to all layers beneath it.

This chapter references three image properties: shadows, midtones, and highlights. Although these concepts are straightforward, illustrating them is important.

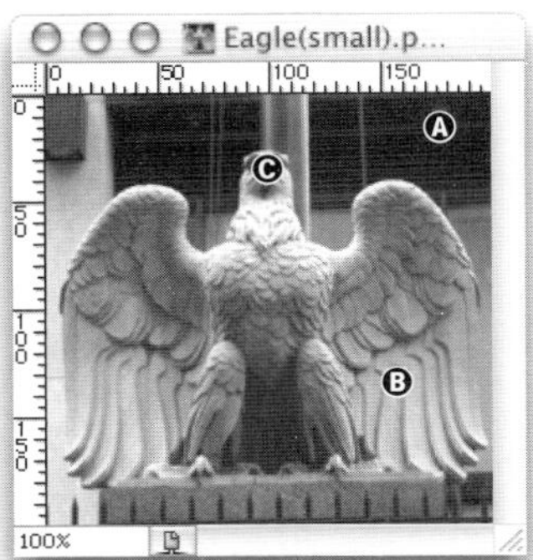

Ⓐ Shadows are the darkest regions of an image.

Ⓑ Midtones are colors in the 50% gray luminosity range.

Ⓒ Highlights are the brightest colors in the image.

BALANCING COLOR CHANNELS

Adding color to one channel means adding or subtracting color from another. For example, when you add blue to the blue channel, that means removing yellow from the yellow channel. However, this can lead to unattractive color casts (the colors change abruptly rather than blending smoothly). When you adjust an individual channel, consider making changes in other channels to offset color casts.

13.2 Adjusting Tonal Range Using Levels

The Levels dialog presents you with a Histogram of the image's pixels displaying the number of light to dark pixels. You can adjust the image's brightness and contrast by adjusting the shadows, midtones, and highlight levels to set pixels before a certain level to be black, to set pixels after a certain level to be white, and to adjust the midtones' intensity. Follow these steps:

1 Select the layer you want to apply level changes to, or select the layer you want to insert a Levels Adjustment layer above.

2 To start adjusting levels, do one of the following:

- Choose Image > Adjustments > Levels....
- Choose Levels... from the Create New Fill Or Adjustment Layer menu at the bottom of the Layers palette.

3 Set the level options in the Levels dialog.

4 Click OK to apply the changes to the layer or the Adjustment layer.

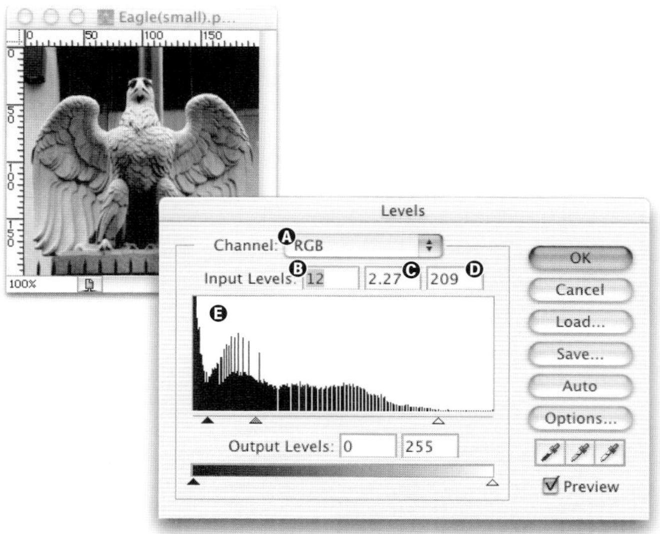

Ⓐ Choose the color channel for which you want to set the levels. The channels that appear in this drop-down depend on the current color mode. Generally, you want to edit the combined color channels.

Ⓑ **Shadow input** Enter a value (0 to 253) for the shadow input level. Increasing the value darkens the shadows in the image. The shadow input slider will adjust accordingly (see F).

Ⓒ **Midtone input** Enter a value (9.99 to 0.10) for the midtone input level. A value higher than 1 lightens the image's midtones. A value lower than 1 darkens the image's midtones. The midtone input slider adjusts accordingly (see G).

Ⓓ **Highlight input** Enter a value (2 to 255) for the highlight input level. The highlight input slider adjusts accordingly (see H).

Ⓔ **Input histogram** This graph displays the relative number of pixels for a particular luminance from dark to light. The higher the peak, the more pixels have that particular luminance in the image. More pixels to the left of the shadow slider will result in more pronounced and darker shadows. More pixels to the right of the highlights slider will result in more vibrant and brighter highlights.

- 2.5 Image Menu
- 2.6 Layer Menu
- 4.11 Layers Palette
- 7.1 Image Color Basics
- 13.4 Setting the Auto Color Correction Options
- Color Section: Adjustments

Levels dialog
⌘ L
Ctrl L

Auto Levels
Shift ⌘ L
Shift Ctrl L

(Levels dialog) Switch to combined channel
⌘ ~
Ctrl ~

(Levels dialog) Switch to a specific color channel
⌘ 1–4
Ctrl 1–4

Continues

To automatically adjust the image levels based on the options set in the Auto Color Correction Options dialog, choose Image > Adjustments > Auto Levels. The image immediately changes if any adjustments are needed. This is the same as clicking the Auto button in the Levels dialog and using Enhance Per Channel Contrast.

You can select multiple channels, but not necessarily all of them, in the Channels palette to edit only those channels.

Reversing the positions of the two output sliders inverts the image.

You can adjust the levels set by a Levels Adjustment layer by double-clicking its thumbnail icon in the Layers palette.

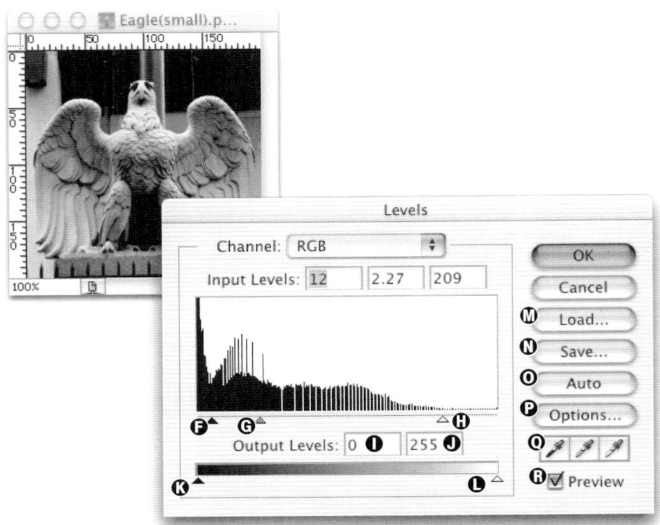

(F) **Shadow slider** Use this slider to adjust the shadow input value manually (see B). As you slide, the midtone slider adjusts the relative position of the midtones in the histogram, but not the midtone input level.

(G) **Midtone slider** Use this slider to adjust the midtone input manually. (See C).

(H) **Highlight slider** Use this slider to adjust the highlight input value manually (see D). As you slide, the midtone slider adjusts the relative position of the midtones in the histogram, but not the midtone input level.

(I) **Black output** Enter a value (0 to 255) to set the black output level. The higher the value, the lighter the image up to 255, which turns the image white (see K).

(J) **White output** Enter a value (255 to 0) to set the white output level. The lower the value, the darker the image down to 0, which turns the image black (see L).

(K) **Black slider** Use this slider to manually set the black output (see G).

(L) **White slider** Use this slider to manually set the white output (see H).

(M) Click to load saved Levels settings. Levels settings have .alv as their extension.

(N) Click to save the current level settings as a file using the .alv extension.

(O) Click to use the Auto Color Correction Options dialog to adjust the levels (same as the Auto Levels command).

(P) Click to open the Auto Color Correction Options dialog.

(Q) **Set Black, Gray, or White Point tools** Click one of these eyedropper tools and then select a pixel in the canvas, or double-click the tool's icon and select a color using the Color Picker. The selected color is used to "clip" other the colors in the image. Clipping uses the selected color as either the darkest (black point), midtone (gray point), or lightest (white point) color in the image, and adjusts all other colors in the image accordingly.

(R) Check to show a live preview of level changes on the canvas.

13.3 Adjusting Color Levels Using Curves

You can also use the Curves dialog to adjust an image's levels. Instead of a histogram, the Curves dialog uses a line graph that can be adjusted at any point along the Input/Output axis. This gives you much greater control over the image's tones and even lets you produce some surprising effects through sharp color changes. For example, by creating a double-crested curve, you can solarize the image, inverting some colors while leaving others alone. To adjust the image using Curves, follow these steps:

1 Select the layer you want to apply level changes to using curves, or select the layer you want to insert a Curves Adjustment layer above.

2 To start adjusting curves, do one of the following:

- Choose Image > Adjustments > Curves....
- Choose Curves... from the Create New Fill Or Adjustment Layer menu [icon] at the bottom of the Layers palette.

3 Set the level options in the Curves dialog.

4 Click OK to apply the changes to the layer or Adjustment layer.

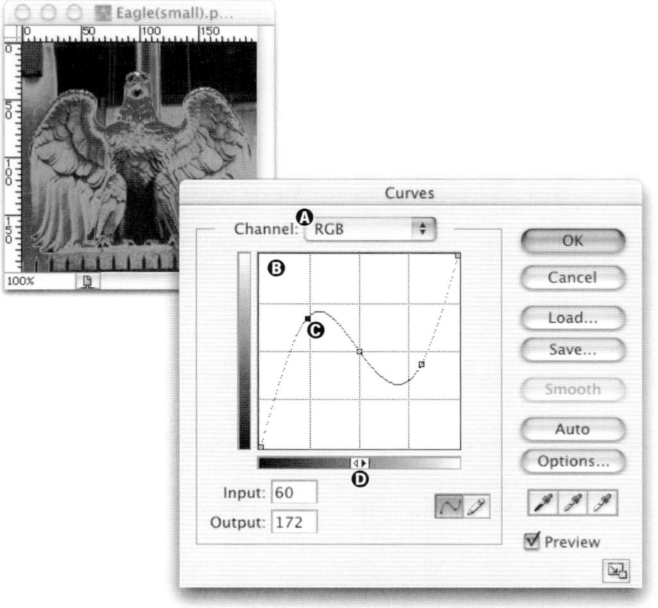

Ⓐ Choose the color channel for which you want to set the levels. The channels that appear in this drop-down depend on the current color mode. Generally, you want to edit the combined color channels.

Ⓑ **Curve graph** Plots the color input versus output. Highlight colors are in the top-right corner, and shadow colors are in the bottom-left corner. Option/Alt-click in the graph to change the grid size.

Ⓒ **Anchor point** With the Curve tool selected, click to select and then drag in the graph to manually adjust its input (see E) or output (see F) values. The selected anchor points is a solid black square. Press Delete to remove a selected anchor point.

Ⓓ **Value toggle** Click to toggle input and output values between numeric and percentage.

Continues

➠ 2.5 Image Menu

➠ 2.6 Layer Menu

➠ 4.11 Layers Palette

➠ 13.4 Setting the Auto Color Correction Options

➠ Color Section: Adjustments

Curves dialog
⌘ M
Ctrl M

(Curves dialog) Switch to combined channel
⌘ ~
Ctrl ~

(Curves dialog) Switch to color channel
⌘ 1–4
Ctrl 1–4

To automatically adjust the image levels based on the options set in the Auto Color Correction Options dialog, choose Image > Adjustments > Auto Levels. The image immediately changes if any adjustments are needed. This is the same as clicking the Auto button in the Curves dialog and using Enhance Per Channel Contrast.

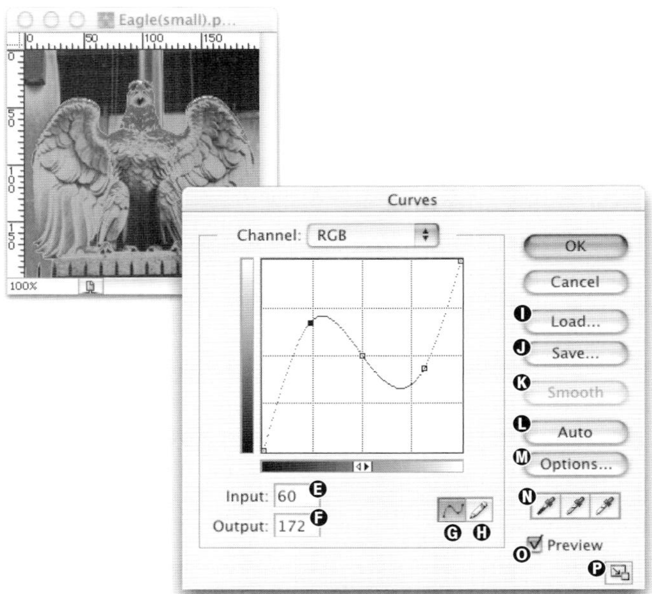

E Displays the input value of the cursor's location or selected anchor point. With an anchor point selected, enter a value for the anchor point's input value. The possible values cannot be higher or lower than the values of adjacent anchor points, but will vary from 0 to 255 (numeric) or from 1 to 100 (percent). The higher the value (the farther left in the graph), the darker the image.

F Displays the output value of the cursor's location or selected anchor point. With an anchor point selected, enter a value for the anchor point's output value. The possible values cannot be higher or lower than the values of adjacent anchor points, but will vary from 0 to 255 (numeric) or from 1 to 100 (percent). The higher the value (the farther up in the graph), the lighter the image.

G **Curve tool** Click to select and adjust anchor points in the curve graph.

H **Freeform tool** Click to draw freeform curves in the curve graph.

I Click to load saved Curves settings. Curves settings have .acv as their extension.

J Click to save the current Curves settings as a file using the .acv extension.

K With the Freeform tool selected, click to smooth the line into a continuous curve.

L Click to use the Auto Color Correction Options dialog to adjust the levels (same as the Auto Levels command).

M Click to open the Auto Color Correction Options dialog.

N **Set Black, Gray, or White Point tools** Click one of these eyedropper tools and then select a pixel in the canvas, or double-click the tool's icon and select a color using the Color Picker. The selected color is used to "clip" other the colors in the image. Clipping uses the selected color as either the darkest (black point), midtone (gray point), or lightest (white point) color in the image, and adjusts all other colors in the image accordingly.

O Check to show a live preview of curve changes on the canvas.

P Click to enlarge/reduce the size of the Curves dialog while working.

13.4 Setting the Auto Color Correction Options

You use the Auto Color Correction Options dialog, accessed through the Levels or Curves dialog, to adjust the tonal range of an image, specify clipping percentages, and assign color values for shadows, midtones, and highlights. You can apply these settings once as part of the Levels or Curves dialog, or you can save the settings as the default and apply them again using the Levels, Curves, Auto Levels, Auto Curves, or Auto Colors commands. To adjust the auto color correction options, follow these steps:

1 In the Levels dialog (see Section 13.2) or the Curves dialog (see Section 13.3), click the Options… button.

2 Set the options you want. If the Preview option is checked in the Levels or Curves dialog, the changes display in the canvas as you make them. Click OK when you are finished.

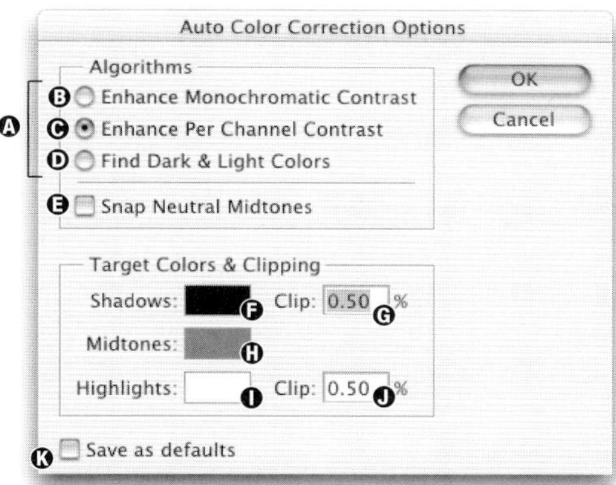

Ⓐ Choose an algorithm option to specify whether you will adjust the levels, contrast, or color of the image.

Ⓑ Click to use Auto Levels (see Section 13.6), which preserves the colors while increasing the contrast between shadows and highlights evenly across color channels.

Ⓒ Click to use Auto Levels (see Section 13.6), which changes colors by increasing the contrast between shadows and highlights on a per channel basis.

Ⓓ Click to use Auto Levels (see Section 13.6), which averages the lightest and darkest pixels in the image and uses this average to maximize contrast while minimizing the color change.

Ⓔ Check to force color values close to a neutral color value in the image to true neutral values.

Ⓕ Click to select a color for the image's shadows. This has the effect of colorizing the darkest areas of the image with this color. The default is black.

Ⓖ Enter a value (0.00 to 9.99) to specify the percentage of colors that should be ignored when determining the darkest colors. In other words, if you set 1%, the first 1% of the darkest colors in the image are ignored when identifying the darkest colors.

Ⓗ Click to select a color for the image midtones. This has the effect of colorizing the neutral areas of the image with this color. The default is 50% gray.

Ⓘ Click to select a color for the image highlights. This has the effect of colorizing the lightest areas of the image with this color. The default is white.

Ⓙ Enter a value (0.00 to 9.99) to specify the percentage of colors that should be ignored when determining the lightest colors in the image. In other words, if you set 1%, the first 1% of the lightest colors in the image are ignored when identifying the lightest colors.

Ⓚ Check to save these settings for use as the defaults when using the Auto… buttons in the Levels or Curves dialog or when using the Auto Levels, Auto Contrast, or Auto Colors commands.

➠ 2.6 Layer Menu

➠ 4.11 Layers Palette

➠ 13.2 Adjusting Tonal Range Using Levels

➠ 13.3 Adjusting Color Levels Using Curves

➠ 13.5 Adjusting Color Balance

➠ 13.6 Adjusting Brightness and Contrast

➠ Color Section: Adjustments

If you are new to color correction, it is best to stick with the default values until you become more familiar with how changing the auto options will affect your image.

Generally a range of 0.5% to 1.0% is recommended for clipping to preserve pure white or pure black areas of the image.

13.5 Adjusting Color Balance

➠ 2.5 Image Menu
➠ 2.6 Layer Menu
➠ 4.11 Layers Palette
➠ 13.4 Setting the Auto Color Correction Options
➠ Color Section: Adjustments

Color Balance dialog
⌘ B
Ctrl B

Auto Color
Shift ⌘ B
Shift Ctrl B

To automatically adjust the image colors based on the options set in the Auto Color Correction Options dialog, choose Image > Adjustments > Auto Colors. The image immediately changes if any adjustments are needed. This is the same as clicking the Auto button in the Levels or Curves dialog and using Find Dark & Light Colors.

Unless you are going for a specific color effect, you will probably only need to adjust the color balance slightly to correct color problems in the image.

Just like an old-fashioned TV set, you can directly control the color balance of an image by mixing the relative amounts of the colors being used in the image. To adjust the color balance of an image, follow these steps:

1. Select the layer to which you want to apply color changes, or select the layer you want to insert a Color Balance Adjustment layer above.
2. To start adjusting curves, do one of the following:
   - Choose Image > Adjustments > Color Balance….
   - Choose Color Balance… from the Create New Fill Or Adjustment Layer menu at the bottom of the Layers palette or in the Layer > New Adjustment Layer submenu.
3. Set the color options in the Color Balance dialog.
4. Click OK when you're done.

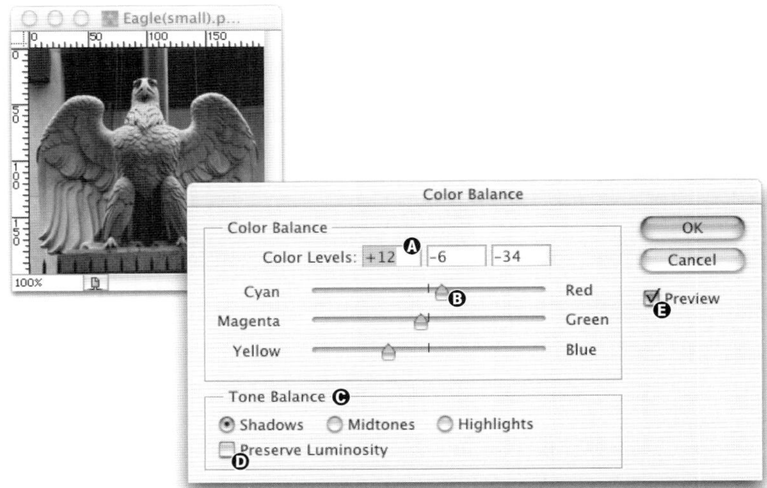

A Enter values (–100 to 100) for the Cyan/Red, Magenta/Green, and Yellow/Blue color levels. A negative value adjusts the colors in the image toward the first color in the pair. A positive value adjusts colors toward the second value in the pair (see B).

B Use the sliders to manually adjust color level values (see A).

C Choose whether you want the changes to the color levels to affect the shadows, midtones, or highlights in the image.

D Check to prevent color changes from affecting the luminosity of individual pixels. This tends to increase the contrast and preserve image details.

E Check to show a live preview of color balance changes on the canvas.

13.6 Adjusting Brightness and Contrast

To control the tonal range of the entire image, use the Brightness and Contrast controls. Follow these steps:

1 Select the layer to which you want to apply brightness and contrast changes, or select the layer you want to insert a Brightness/Contrast Adjustment layer above.

2 To start adjusting the brightness and contrast, do one of the following:

- Choose Image > Adjustments > Brightness/Contrast....
- Choose Brightness/Contrast... from the Create New Fill Or Adjustment Layer menu at the bottom of the Layers palette or in the Layer > New Adjustment Layer submenu.

3 Set the Brightness and Contrast options in the Brightness/Contrast dialog.

4 Click OK to apply the changes to the layer or the Adjustment layer.

A Enter a value (–100 to 100) to change the image's brightness. Values above 0 brighten the image, and values below 0 darken it. You can also use the slider to manually change these values.

B Enter a value (–100 to 100) to change the image's contrast. Values above 0 increase the image's contrast toward stark black and white, and values below 0 reduce the image's contrast toward a neutral gray. You can also use the slider to manually change these values.

C Check to show a live preview of brightness and contrast changes on the canvas.

➠ 2.5 Image Menu
➠ 2.6 Layer Menu
➠ 4.11 Layers Palette
➠ Color Section: Adjustments

Auto Contrast
Option Shift ⌘ L
Alt Shift Ctrl L

To automatically adjust the image contrast based on the options set in the Auto Color Correction Options dialog, choose Image > Adjustments > Auto Contrast. The image immediately changes if any adjustments are needed. This is the same as clicking the Auto button in the Levels or Curves dialog and using Enhance Monochromatic Contrast.

Adjusting brightness and contrast is not generally recommended for high-quality print output because it may result in the loss of detail in the image.

13.7 Adjusting Hue, Saturation, and Lightness

➠ 2.5 Image Menu

➠ 2.6 Layer Menu

➠ 4.11 Layers Palette

➠ Color Section: Adjustments

Hue/Saturation dialog
⌘ U
Ctrl U

Desaturate Colors
Shift ⌘ U
Shift Ctrl U

Switch to Master color range
⌘ ~
Ctrl ~

Switch to Red color range
⌘ 1
Ctrl 1

Switch to Yellow color range
⌘ 2
Ctrl 2

Switch to Green color range
⌘ 3
Ctrl 3

Switch to Cyan color range
⌘ 4
Ctrl 4

Switch to Blue color range
⌘ 5
Ctrl 5

Switch to Magenta color range
⌘ 6
Ctrl 6

You can adjust the hue (color value), saturation (amount of gray), and lightness (amount of black and white) of an image in the Hue/Saturation dialog. Using this dialog is a coarser way to correct color than using levels or curves, but you can nevertheless produce some interesting effects. For example, you can desaturate and lighten the color of an image for a faded look or increase the saturation for an over-the-top but colorful affect. To adjust the hue, saturation, and color, follow these steps:

1 Select the layer to which you want to apply hue and saturation changes, or select the layer you want to insert a Hue/Saturation Adjustment layer above.

2 To start adjusting curves, do one of the following:

- Choose Image > Adjustments > Hue/Saturation….
- Choose Hue/Saturation… from the Create New Fill Or Adjustment Layer menu at the bottom of the Layers palette or in the Layer > New Adjustment Layer submenu.

3 Set the color options in the Color Balance dialog.

4 Click OK to apply the changes to the layer or the Adjustment layer.

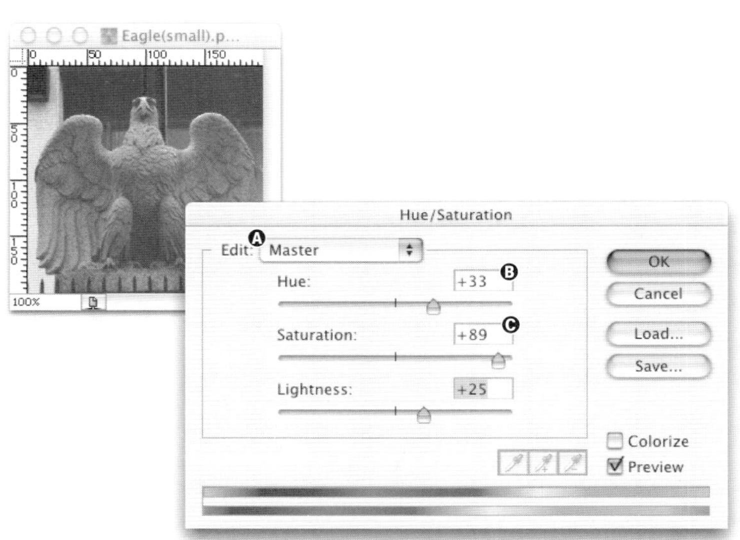

A Choose Master to adjust all colors, or choose from the list of preset color ranges to edit.

B Enter a value (–180 to 180) for the color's hue based on a standard color wheel. If you are making changes to a particular color range, hue changes are reflected in the Color Adjustment bar at the bottom of the dialog.

C Enter a value (–100 to 100) for the saturation of colors. The higher the value, the more saturated the colors appear. A value of –100 changes all colors to grayscale. If you are changing a particular color range, saturation changes are reflected in the Color Reference bar at the bottom of the dialog.

13.7 Adjusting Hue, Saturation, and Lightness

(Continued)

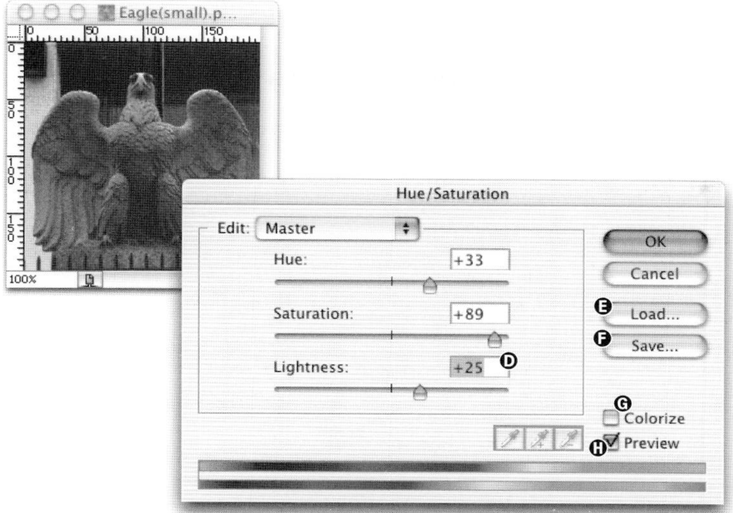

D Enter a value (–100 to 100) for the lightness of colors. The higher the value, the lighter the colors appear. A value of –100 turn the image black. If you are changing a particular color range, lightness changes are reflected in the Color Reference bar at the bottom of the dialog.

E Click to load saved hue and saturation setting files that use the .ahu extension.

F Click to save the current level settings as a file using the .ahu extension.

G Check to colorize the image using the color created by the selected hue, saturation, and lightness. This option is available only for the master color range (see A).

H Check to show a live preview of color balance changes on the canvas.

Adjusting hue, saturation, and lightness allows you to do some very deep fine-tuning with color that is less constricted than using levels or tools. This is especially true if you need to make careful adjustments to individual color channels.

To colorize an image, the image must be in RGB color mode.

Another way to desaturate the image is to turn it to black and white, and set the saturation to –100.

Adjusting in a Color Range

You can also adjust the hue, saturation, and lightness of a selected color range, without affecting other colors in the image. Follow these steps:

1. In the Hue/Saturation dialog, choose the color range and then use the range editing options to refine the exact color range to edit.
2. Enter hue, saturation, and lightness values for the color range. These changes are reflected in the Color Adjustment bar.
3. You can repeat Steps 1 and 2 as necessary to refine the color range adjustment.

13.7 Adjusting Hue, Saturation, and Lightness

(Continued)

As you can do with other actions in Photoshop, you can fade the effects of an adjustment immediately after the action. Fading dilutes and blends the effect of the adjustment. To fade the adjustment, choose Edit > Fade *Name*... (the name of the adjustment appears in the menu option), set the opacity and blending mode for the faded adjustment, and click OK. The fade command will be grayed out if the previous action cannot be faded.

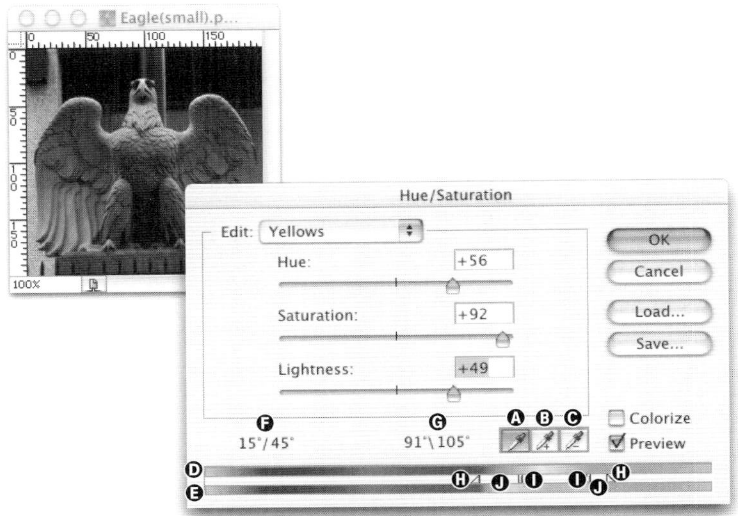

A Select Color Click and then select a color in the canvas to choose the color range to edit. Shift-click to add colors to the selection or Option/Alt-click to subtract colors. The changes are reflected in the color range extremes (see H).

B Add Color To Selection Click and then select a color in the canvas to add colors to the color range being edited. The changes are reflected in the color range extremes (see H).

C Subtract Color From Selection Click and then select a color in the canvas to remove colors from the color range being edited. The changes are reflected in the color range extremes (see H).

D Color Reference Bar Displays the natural full-color spectrum for reference with the color adjustment bar.

E Color Adjustment Bar Displays the current color spectrum for the selected color range. This spectrum depends on the hue, saturation, and lightness values.

F Left Color Value Extremes Displays the color values for the leftmost color range extreme and color fall-off point (see H and I).

G Right Color Value Extremes Displays the color values for the rightmost color range extreme and color fall-off point (see H and I).

H Color Range Extremes Click and drag to define the color extremes of the color range (see F and G).

I Color Fall-Off Points Click and drag to define the point at which the color begins to blend with surrounding colors (see F and G).

J Color Fall-Off Ranges The area between the range extreme and fall-off point defines the range of colors to blend with surrounding colors in the image. Click and drag this area to adjust the fall-off range without changing the relative positions of the range extreme and fall-off point.

13.8 Using Replace Color

The Replace Color command works a lot like the Color Range dialog for selecting colors, but you can immediately replace the selected color with a new color. To replace colors, follow these steps:

1 Select the layer in which you want to replace the colors.

2 Choose Image > Adjustments > Replace Color....

3 Set the color options in the Replace Color dialog. First, select the color or range of colors to be replaced, and then use the Hue, Saturation, and Lightness controls to define the replacement color.

4 After you make your adjustments, click OK to apply the changes to the layer or the Adjustment layer.

➠ 2.5 Image Menu

➠ 8.5 Selecting Colors

➠ Color Section: Adjustments

The Replace Color command is one of the few adjustments without a corresponding Adjustment layer.

Ⓐ Enter a value (0 to 200) for the fuzziness to use when selecting colors to change. The higher the value, the more colors similar to the selected color or colors are included in the change.

Ⓑ **Image Preview** Displays a color preview of the original image or the selected colors to be replaced. In Selection mode, white shows selected regions of the image.

Ⓒ Click to load saved replacement color setting files that use the .axt extension..

Ⓓ Click to save the current replacement color settings as a file using the .axt extension.

Ⓔ Check to show a live preview of color replacement changes on the canvas.

Continues

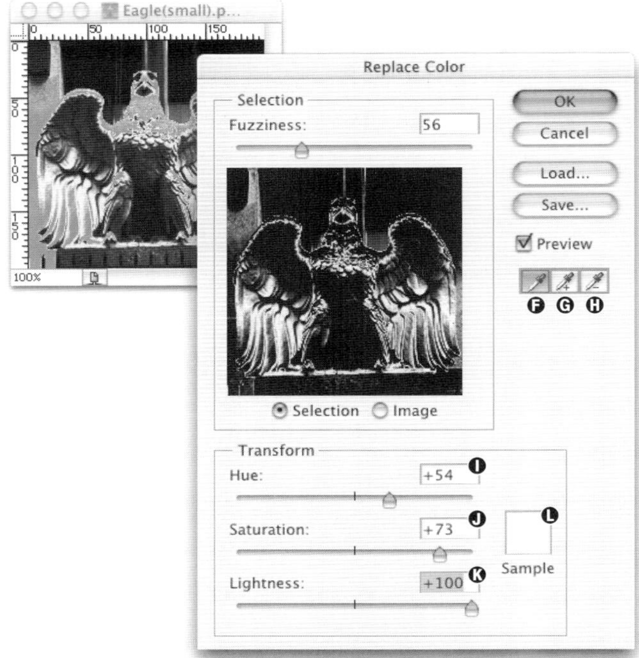

- **F** **Select Color** Click the Eyedropper tool and then select a color in the canvas or image preview (see B) to choose the color to replace. Shift-click to add colors to the selection, or Option/Alt-click to subtract colors.
- **G** **Add Color To Selection** Click and then select a color in the canvas or image preview (see B) to add colors to the color range being replaced.
- **H** **Subtract Color From Selection** Click and then select a color in the canvas or image preview (see B) to remove colors from the color range being replaced.
- **I** Enter a value (–180 to 180) for the replacement color's hue.
- **J** Enter a value (–100 to 100) for the replacement color's saturation.
- **K** Enter a value (–100 to 100) for the replacement color's lightness.
- **L** Displays a sample swatch of the replacement color.

13.9 Adjusting Selective Colors

You can use Selective Color to increase and decrease the amount of process colors (cyan, magenta, yellow, and black) needed to print the primary colors (red, green, blue, black, neutral, and white) of an image. This feature is generally only used for high-end printing jobs in which the amount of ink used to create a primary color needs to be adjusted without affecting the CMYK values in the rest of the image. To adjust colors selectively in an image, follow these steps:

➠ 2.5 Image Menu
➠ 2.6 Layer Menu
➠ 4.11 Layers Palette
➠ Color Section: Adjustments

Even if you are using RGB mode, you can still adjust the colors using CMYK colors to correct the image.

1 Select the layer to which you want to apply color changes, or select the layer above which you want to insert a Color Balance layer.

2 To start replacing selective colors, do one of the following:
- Choose Image > Adjustments > Selective Color….
- Choose Selective Color… from the Create New Fill Or Adjustment Layer menu at the bottom of the Layers palette or in the Layer > New Adjustment Layer submenu.

3 Set the color options in the Selective Color Options dialog.

4 Click OK to apply the changes to the layer or the Adjustment layer.

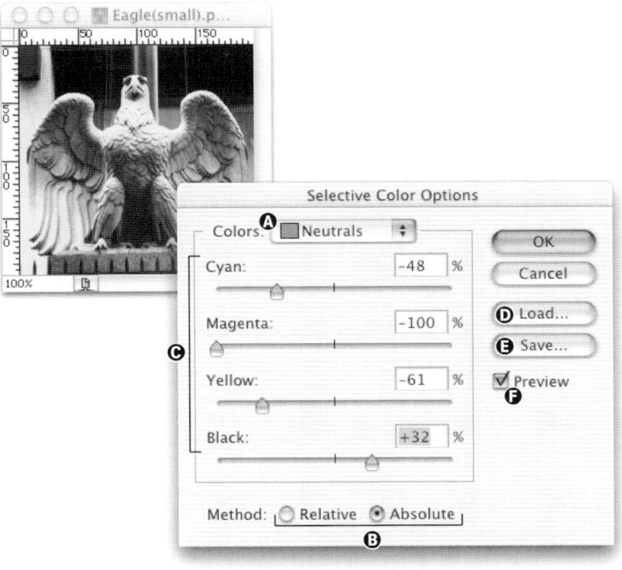

Ⓐ Select the color you want to selectively modify from the list.

Ⓑ Choose whether the values entered should be treated as a percentage relative to the current amount of cyan, magenta, yellow, or black used in the selected color or as an absolute amount of that color added to the selected color. For example, if there is currently a 10% value for cyan in the selected color, increasing it by 20% relatively changes the value to 12%. The same change made absolutely changes the value to 30%.

Ⓒ Enter values (–100 to 100) as a percentage to increase or decrease the cyan, magenta, yellow, or black mix for the selected color.

Ⓓ Click to load saved selective color setting files that use the .asv extension..

Ⓔ Click to save the current selective color settings as a file using the .asv extension.

Ⓕ Check to show a live preview of color replacement changes on the canvas.

13.10 Mixing Channels

➠ 2.5 Image Menu

➠ 2.6 Layer Menu

➠ 4.11 Layers Palette

➠ 7.5 Using Color in Channels

➠ Color Section: Adjustments

When you click the Monochrome option, you can precisely control the amount of detail and contrast when converting an image to black and white. You can then turn Monochrome off and modify each channel separately to produce a sharp, hand-tinted effect.

You use the Channel Mixer dialog to modify a single color channel using a mix of the other color channels in the image. With some practice, you can correct color more precisely this way than using the other adjustment methods, or you can create high-quality black-and-white or colorized images. To mix channels, follow these steps:

1 Select the layer to which you want to apply channel mixing, or select the layer you want to insert a Channel Mixer Adjustment layer above.

2 To start mixing channels, do one of the following:

- Choose Image > Adjustments > Channel Mixer….
- Choose Channel Mixer… from the Create New Fill Or Adjustment Layer menu at the bottom of the Layers palette or in the Layer > New Adjustment Layer submenu.

3 Set the color options in the Channel Mixer dialog.

4 Click OK to apply the changes the layer or the Adjustment layer.

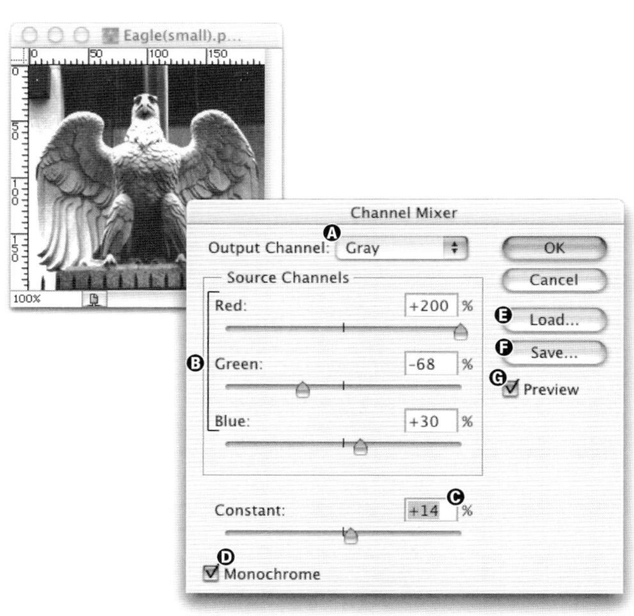

A Choose the output channel where one or more source channels will be blended. The options in the Output Channel drop-down depend on the image's color mode.

B Enter values (–200 to 200) as a percentage to increase or decrease the source channel color in the selected output channel. Negative values invert the source channel before blending it with the output channel. The Source Channels options depend on the image's color mode.

C Enter a value (–200 to 200) as a percentage to add either a black or a white channel. This results in positive values increasing the amount of the selected color in the blend and negative values increasing the amount of the blend's inverse color.

D Click to apply the settings to all output channels, creating a monochrome image.

E Click to load saved channel mixer setting files that have the .cha extension.

F Click to save the current channel mixer settings as a file using the .cha extension.

G Check to show a live preview of channel mixing changes on the canvas.

13.11 Mapping a Gradient to the Image Colors

You can completely replace an image's color table with a graduated color table. This can produce sublime tint effects or stark high-color effects depending on the gradient you select. To map a gradient to the image colors, follow these steps:

1. Select the layer to which you want to apply gradient map changes, or select the layer you want to insert a Gradient Map Adjustment layer above.
2. To start adjusting curves, do one of the following:
   - Choose Image > Adjustments > Gradient Map….
   - Choose Gradient Map… from the Create New Fill Or Adjustment Layer menu at the bottom of the Layers palette or in the Layer > New Adjustment Layer submenu.
3. Set the gradient options in the Gradient Map dialog.
4. Click OK to apply the changes to the layer or Adjustment layer.

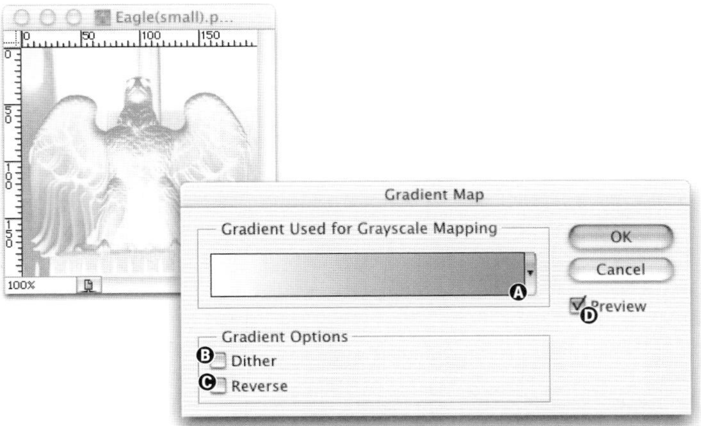

Ⓐ Select a gradient you want to use from the drop-down menu, or double-click the gradient pattern to open the Gradient Editor and create your own gradient.

Ⓑ Check to use a dithered gradient rather than a smooth gradient. This will have the effect of adding noise to the image on low-resolution monitors. If your monitor supports thousands or more colors, you will not notice any change.

Ⓒ Check to reverse the direction of the gradient.

Ⓓ Check to show a live preview of gradient changes on the canvas.

➠ 2.5 Image Menu

➠ 2.6 Layer Menu

➠ 4.11 Layers Palette

➠ 14.6 Creating and Editing Gradients

➠ 14.7 Organizing Gradient Presets

➠ Color Section: Adjustments

Although you can map a black-to-white gradient to desaturate the image, mapping a gradient is really best reserved for special effects.

13.12 Setting Posterize and Threshold Levels

- 2.5 Image Menu
- 2.6 Layer Menu
- 4.11 Layers Palette
- Color Section: Adjustments

Although it may not seem to be a helpful effect, Threshold is useful for identifying the darkest and lightest areas in our image.

Using Posterize, you can convert the image so that it uses large areas of flat color, drastically reducing the tonal values. You can specify the number of colors (levels) available to each color channel. For example, if you set the level to 3, the image is composed of nine colors, three on each channel.

Similarly, you can use Threshold to set a level above which all lighter pixels are converted to white and all darker pixels are converted to black. This produces a stark black-and-white image with no grayscales.

To posterize or add a threshold to an image, follow these steps:

1 Select the layer to which you want to apply the poster or threshold changes, or select the layer you want to insert a Posterize or Threshold Adjustment layer above.

2 Do one of the following:

- Choose Image > Adjustments > Posterize… or Threshold….
- Choose Posterize… or Threshold… from the Create New Fill Or Adjustment Layer menu [icon] at the bottom of the Layers palette.

3 Set the number of levels in the dialog.

4 Click OK to apply the changes to the layer or the Adjustment layer.

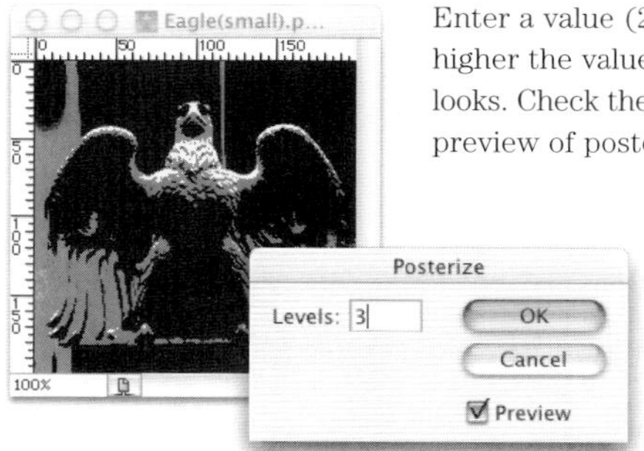

Enter a value (2 to 255) for the tonal level. The higher the value, the less posterized your image looks. Check the Preview option to show a live preview of posterized changes on the canvas.

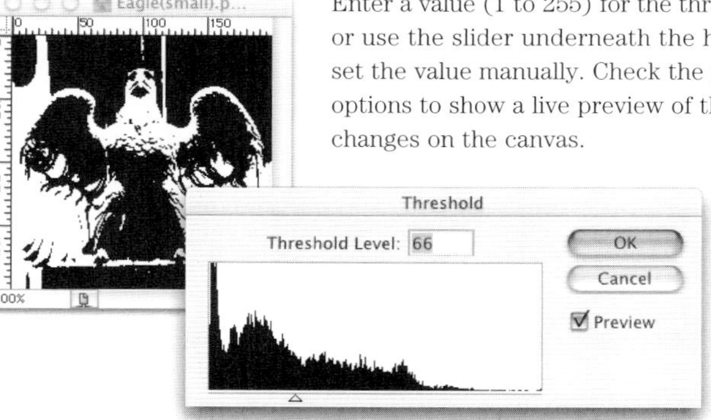

Enter a value (1 to 255) for the threshold level, or use the slider underneath the histogram to set the value manually. Check the preview options to show a live preview of threshold changes on the canvas.

13.13 Using Color Variations

You can use the Variations dialog to quickly change the color balance, contrast, and saturation in a single, highly visual interface. Rather than using precise numeric input and abstract sliders, you can view a thumbnail preview of how the change you are about to make will affect the image. This tends to work if you are more intuitive in your color correction and less worried about precision. To make color variations in the image, follow these steps:

1 Select the layer in which you want to adjust the colors using color variations.

2 Choose Image > Adjustments > Variations....

3 Set the tonal range to adjust (Shadows, Midtones, Highlights, or Saturation), set the coarseness level, and then begin adding colors or lightening or darkening the image.

4 After you make your adjustments, click OK to apply the changes to the layer or the Adjustment layer.

➠ 2.5 Image Menu

➠ Color Section: Adjustments

Variations do not work with images in Indexed Color mode.

Clicking a color preview diagonally across from the last color added will have the affect of canceling that color change. For example, if you click blue and then click yellow, the blue color addition is essentially undone.

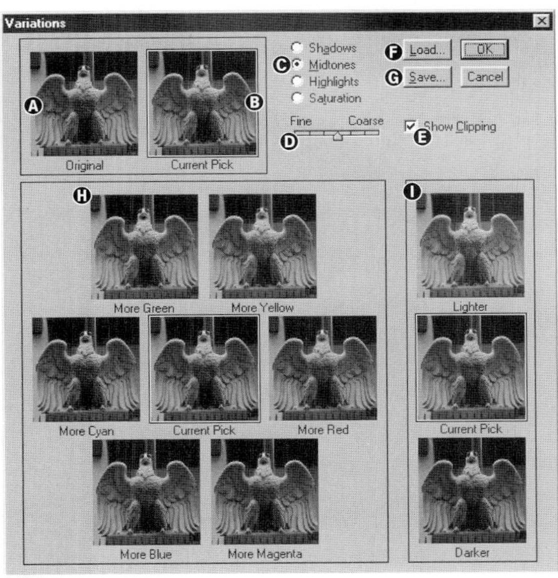

Ⓐ Displays the original image. Click to revert to this version.

Ⓑ Displays the image based on the current settings.

Ⓒ Choose whether to apply color variations to the image's shadows, midtones, highlights, or saturation.

Ⓓ Use the slider to set how much color is applied using the variations. Fine applies only a little color at a time, and Coarse applies the maximum amount of color.

Ⓔ Check to highlight areas in the preview that will be clipped by the color adjustment. Clipped areas are converted to pure black or white and may cause unwanted color shifts. Clipping does not occur when you are working with midtones.

Ⓕ Click to load saved variation settings files.

Ⓖ Click to save the current variation settings as a file.

Ⓗ Each "More" preview thumbnail displays how adding that color will affect the image. Click one of the color previews to add more of that color to the image. You can repeat this as many times as desired for as many colors as desired. Each click updates the preview thumbnails to display the current options. The amount of color added with any single click depends on the coarseness setting (see D).

Ⓘ Displays a thumbnail preview of how lightening or darkening will affect the image. Click the preview as many times as desired to lighten or darken the image. Each click updates the thumbnails to display the current options. The amount of color added with any single click depends on the coarseness setting (see D).

13.14 Other Adjustments: Brightness, Desaturation, and Inversion

➠ 2.5 Image Menu

➠ Color Section: Adjustments

Invert image colors

You can use Equalize to quickly correct scanned images that appear darker than the original.

Desaturating an image is the same as setting the saturation to –100 in the Hue/Saturation dialog.

Although an inverted image looks a lot like a film negative, you can't use the Invert command to create an exact color negative of the image because a true color negative also contains an orange mask.

Invert is often used in low-budget sci-fi television shows as a special effect for laser blasts. Watch out for Daleks.

Equalizing Image Brightness

The Equalize command evens out the distribution of brightness values in an image to create a smoother range and often has the effect of improving overall image quality. Here is our eagle demonstration image after equalization.

To equalize the brightness in the image, select the layer you want equalized (you can also select part of that layer), choose Image > Adjustments > Equalize. If you select part of the layer, specify whether you want to equalize only the selected area or the entire area based on the selection, and then click OK.

Desaturating the Image

Desaturation removes all color information from the selected layer, changing it to grayscale, without changing the image's color mode. This is the same as setting the saturation to –100 in the Hue/Saturation dialog. To desaturate the selected layer, choose Image > Adjustments > Desaturate.

Inverting the Image

The Invert command inverts the color values for each pixel. The affect looks something like a photographic negative of the image and can produce some stark images. Here is our eagle demonstration image after inversion.

- To invert the selected layer, choose Image > Adjustments > Invert.
- To add an Inversion Adjustment layer, select the layer above which you want the Adjustment layer to be added and choose Invert from the menu at the bottom of the Layers palette. All layers below this Adjustment layer are inverted.

CHAPTER 14

Working with Colors, Gradients, and Patterns

WHEN YOU'RE PAINTING, DRAWING, or editing in Photoshop, you need to select a color, even if that "color" is a shade of gray in a black-and-white image. But you can fill an area in more than one way. You can use gradients and patterns in much the same way as you use a solid color. In this chapter, you will learn how to choose and fill areas of the canvas as well as how to manage sets of colors, gradients, and patterns.

14.1 Color, Gradient, and Pattern Basics

➠ 3.25 Beyond the Tools

➠ 4.4 Info Palette

➠ 4.5 Color Palette

➠ 4.6 Swatches Palette

➠ 7.2 Understanding Image Modes

➠ 9.5 Adding a Fill Layer or an Adjustment Layer

➠ 13 Making Image Adjustments

You can enter colors in any of the five color models regardless of the color mode of the image.

The CMYK model is generally used for high-quality print work. The HSB, RGB, and Hex models are generally for web and television work, although they can be used when printing to RGB printers. Use the Lab model when you are striving for consistency between different computer platforms.

You set the colors, gradients, and patterns in Photoshop at various places throughout the interface. No matter where you set the color value, though, you have access to the same color models; you control gradients and patterns through a drop-down menu; and you can apply all three to the image using a Fill layer.

A document's color mode specifies how colors are defined. However, when you create colors in Photoshop, you use one of six color *models*. A model is based on the color mode of the same name, but you use a color model to directly input values to create a color.

HSB Enter values for hue (0 to 360), saturation (0 to 100), and brightness (0 to 100).

RGB Enter values (0 to 255) for the amount of red, green, and blue in the color.

Lab Enter values for luminance (0 to 100); "a" axis (–128 to 127), which represents the green-to-red value; and "b" axis (–128 to 127), which represents the blue-to-yellow value.

CMYK Enter values (0 to 100) as percentages of the amount of cyan, magenta, yellow, and black in the color.

Hex (web) Enter a value (#000000 to #FFFFFF) for the color.

Grayscale Enter a value (0 to 100) for the percentage of black to use.

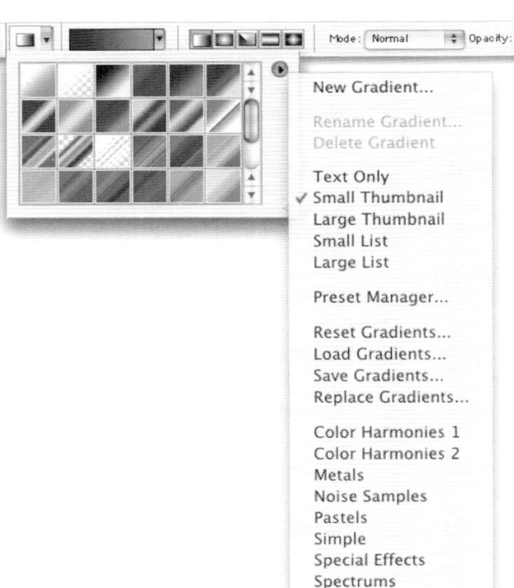

Gradient and Pattern Preset drop-downs: Both gradient and pattern presets are stored in a drop-down. The preset drop-down appears as a thumbnail of the currently selected gradient or pattern with an arrow next to it. Click the arrow to open a list of the currently loaded presets; click a thumbnail in the presets to use that gradient or pattern. In addition, this drop-down includes a menu from which you can edit, load, and save presets as well as open the Preset Manager.

Fill layers work a lot like Adjustment layers. In fact, their shortcut is in the menu at the bottom of the Layers palette. But a Fill layer is simply a layer with a solid color, pattern, or gradient. After you apply a Fill layer, you can double-click its icon to edit all its options.

14.2 Selecting Colors

Although you can set the colors for a few elements (such as text) individually, most tools and commands in Photoshop use the foreground and background colors. The selected color swatch—Foreground or Background—is surrounded by a black box in the Color palette or Toolbox. Choose the one you want to set by clicking the appropriate color square if it is *not* already selected. (Clicking a selected color square opens the Color Picker.)

➠ 3.10 Drawing Tools
➠ 3.14 Fill Tools
➠ 3.22 Eyedropper and Measure Tools
➠ 3.25 Beyond the Tools
➠ 4.4 Info Palette
➠ 4.5 Color Palette
➠ 4.6 Swatches Palette

(with Eyedropper) Switch selection of foreground or background as color (reverts after release)
Option
Alt

Using the Eyedropper Tool

You can use the Eyedropper tool to sample colors directly from any open image, color swatch, or color square. To use the Eyedropper, follow these steps:

1. Choose the Eyedropper tool from the tool options bar. You can also press Option/Alt with the Pencil, Brush, Gradient, or Paint Bucket tool or any shape tool selected to temporarily switch to the Eyedropper tool.
2. Choose the foreground or background color square in the Color palette. If the color square is already selected, do not click again (this opens the Color Picker).
3. Select a color by doing one of the following:
   - Click a pixel in the canvas of any open document; the document does not have to be in the front.
   - Click and drag over the canvas of any open document. The color of the pixel the cursor is currently over is previewed with its color value in the Color palette. Release to select the current color.
   - Click any visible color square or color swatch.

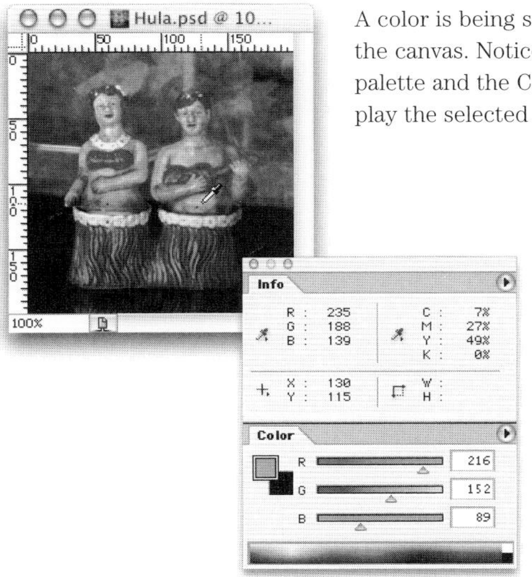

A color is being selected from the canvas. Notice that the Info palette and the Color palette display the selected color's values.

14.2 Selecting Colors *(Continued)*

As you move the cursor over an image, the color value of the pixel the cursor is currently over is displayed in the Info palette.

If you want the Eyedropper to pick a color based on an average of the selected pixels, choose 3 By 3 Average or 5 By 5 Average in the tool options bar's Select Size drop-down.

Although you can select the color model to use for the sliders in the Color palette from the palette's menu, using the same model as the color mode of the image is recommended.

You can change the colors displayed in the Color palette ramp by selecting a different color model in the palette's menu. You can choose RGB Spectrum, CMYK Spectrum, Grayscale Ramp, or Current Colors (the colors in the current image).

When in bitmap or indexed color mode, you can only choose colors currently in the image's color table.

Using the Color Palette

To choose a color from the Swatches palette, specify in the Color palette whether it will be the foreground or background color, move your cursor over the Swatches palette (the cursor will automatically switch to the Eyedropper), and then click a color swatch.

Using the Color Palette Ramp

At the bottom of the Color palette is the color spectrum ramp from which you can select colors. Specify whether it will be the foreground or background color. Move your cursor over the color ramp in the Color palette (the cursor will automatically switch to the Eyedropper) and then click a color. You can also select the black or white color squares to the far right of the spectrum.

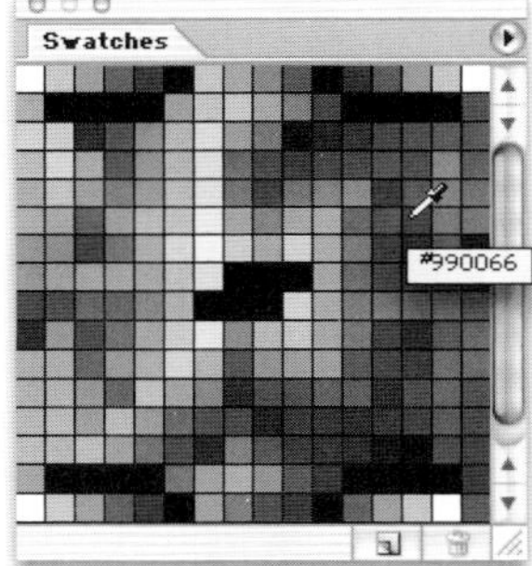

Selecting a color swatch from the Swatches palette

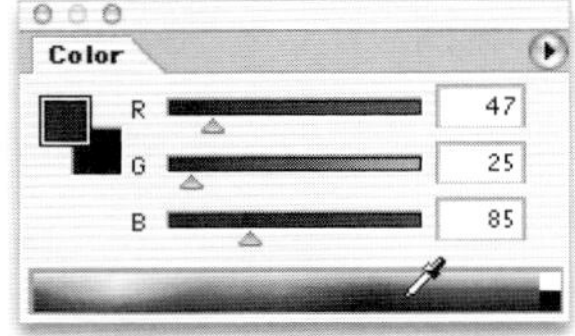

Selecting a color from the Color palette's spectrum

Adjusting Colors in the Color Palette

After you set a foreground or background color using any of the means discussed (Eyedropper, swatches, Color palette, or Color Picker), you can still adjust its color values using the Color palette. In the palette, choose whether you want to edit the foreground or background color, and set the color sliders to the desired values or enter values directly.

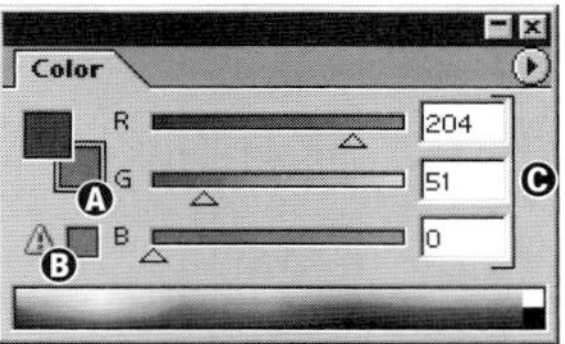

A Selected Color The background color is currently selected for editing as indicated by the black box highlighting it.

B Gamut or Web Safe Warning A triangle with an exclamation mark indicates that the selected color is out of the print gamut and cannot be printed. A cube indicates that the selected color is not browser-safe and may not display properly on all computer monitors. Click the color swatch underneath to convert the color to a similar color that is in gamut or web safe.

C Color sliders and values Displays the current color values using the selected color model. Slide the triangle underneath to change the color value, or enter the color value directly in the text field. Any changes are immediately reflected in the selected color square.

14.3 Selecting Colors with the Color Picker

Although the Color palette provides basic controls for quickly choosing and adjusting colors, you will probably find that it is difficult to use when you are searching for that perfect color. To that end, Photoshop places advanced color selection options into a separate dialog called the Color Picker. In addition, since printers need quick access to spot color catalogs, you can use the Custom Colors dialog to search through the most common spot color books.

➠ 7.5 Using Color in Channels

➠ 7.8 Converting to Duotone Mode

(in Preset Manager) Jump to swatches

⌘ 2

Ctrl 2

While you are using the Color Picker, you can also click any color square, swatch, or image to choose a color using the Color Picker.

You'll find color squares at various locations in the Photoshop interface—the two most prominent being the foreground and background squares—but they also often appear in the tool options bar and in dialogs (although color squares may be more rectangular than square). These squares generally define the color to be used by specific tools or commands, and you change them using the Color Picker. Follow these step:

1. Double-click a color square in the Photoshop interface. (Color swatches in the Swatches palette can not be changed in this way.)
2. In the Color Picker, select the color by using the color slider and field or by entering a color value directly into one of the text fields.
3. Click OK when you are finished. The color appears in the selected color square and is ready for use.

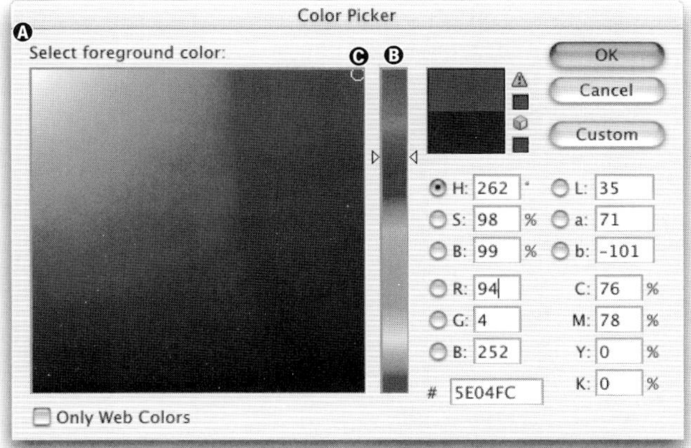

A Indicates the type of color square currently being selected. In this example, the foreground color is being selected.

B **Color slider** Displays the values available for the selected color value (see I). Move the triangles on either side up or down to change the value. For example, if you select S (for Saturation in HSB), the slider displays all the saturation levels for the current hue and brightness settings. If you select G (for Green in RGB), the slider displays all the greens.

C **Color field** Displays all the colors available based on the color currently selected in the Color slider. Click any color in this area to select it. The circle indicates the currently selected color.

Continues

You can use your operating system's color picker instead of the Photoshop Color Picker by changing the preference in the General preferences (see Section 5.3).

With the Custom Colors dialog open, start typing the name of a particular spot color in the selected catalog, and Photoshop will attempt to find it.

Spot colors are still used as process colors (except in Duotone) unless you add them to specific spot color channels.

Spot colors are especially useful when creating a Duotone.

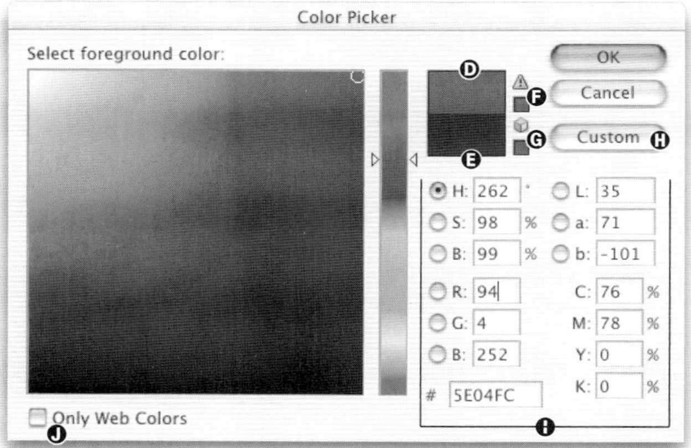

D **New Color** Displays the color selected in the Color field.

E **Current Color** Displays the color being replaced. Click to reset to this color.

F **Gamut Warning** Indicates that the selected color is out of the print and NTSC television gamut and cannot be printed or be displayed on North American televisions. Click the color swatch underneath to convert the color to a similar color that is in gamut.

G **Web Safe Warning** Indicates that the color is not web safe and might not display properly on all computer monitors. Click the color swatch underneath to convert the color to a similar color that is web safe.

H Click to open the Custom Color dialog, in which you can select Pantone and other special colors.

I **Color values** Displays the numeric values of the selected color in HSB, RGB, Lab, CMYK, and Hex (see Section 14.1 for values). You can enter the numeric values for the color directly, or you can choose a radio button next to a color value if you want the Color slider (see B) and Color field (see C) to display using that value type.

J Check to only display web-safe colors in the Color slider and Color field.

Selecting Custom Spot Colors

If you are using spot colors instead of process colors for printing, you can select from a wide range of spot color books in the Custom Color dialog. Follow these steps:

1. In the Color Picker, click the Custom button.
2. Select the spot color catalog from which you want to choose colors, select the color range in the slider, and then select the exact spot color to use.
3. Click OK when you are finished. The color now appears in the color square you selected. If you are actually using this as a spot color for printing, add an additional channel for this color.

14.3 Selecting Colors with the Color Picker *(Continued)*

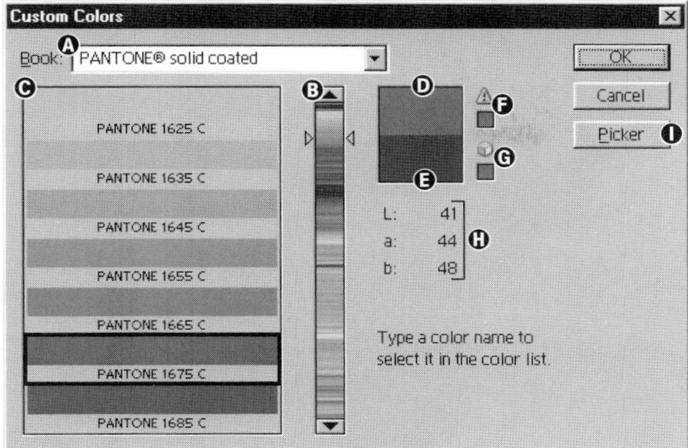

A Spot color books Select the spot color catalog you want to use. The most common of these are the Pantone color books, but check with your printer or service bureau to see what ink colors are available.

B Color Range Displays a compressed list of the colors. Click a color to select that range for it and display in the color display. You can also drag the triangles on either side up and down or use the arrows at the top and bottom to move through the list.

C Color Display Displays a list of colors based on the color range selected. Click a color to select it or use the up and down arrow keys to scroll through the list.

D New Color Displays the color currently selected in the Color field.

E Current Color Displays the color being replaced. Click to reset to this color.

F Gamut Warning Indicates that the selected color is out of the print gamut and cannot be printed. Click the color swatch underneath to convert the color to a similar color that is in gamut.

G Web Safe Warning Indicates that the color is not web safe and might not display properly on all computer monitors. Click the color swatch underneath to convert the color to a similar color that is web safe.

H Displays the Lab color values for the selected spot color.

I Click to open the Color Picker. The selected spot color is converted to a process color value.

14.4 Organizing Color Swatch Presets

➟ 4.5 Color Palette

➟ 4.6 Swatches Palette

➟ 5.1 Preset Manager Overview

(in Preset Manager) Jump to swatches
⌘ 2
Ctrl 2

Storing frequently used colors in color swatches is a handy way to have quick access to colors. For example, if you are a web designer, you might want to store all the web-safe colors. If you are working on a client project, you'll want to store your client's colors, especially if they are specific Pantone colors. You can make most changes to the Swatches palette in the Swatches palette itself or in the Swatches Preset Manager, which can be opened directly from the Swatches palette menu.

Editing Presets

The color swatch list is made up of color swatches, the small squares in the Swatches palette. Each swatch has a name, and you can easily add or delete swatches from the list.

- To **delete a color swatch**, Option/Alt-click the swatch (a the mouse cursor turns into a pair of scissors) in the Swatches palette or in the Swatches Preset Manager. You can also click and drag the swatch to the trash can button or, in the Swatches Preset Manager, click one or more colors and press Delete. The color is removed, and all other colors in the palette shift to fill its space.
- To **add the currently selected color** (foreground or background) to the Swatches palette, click anywhere in the blank area of the palette or choose New Swatch from the palette menu. Enter a name for the new swatch in the New Color Swatch Name dialog and click OK. The new color is added at the bottom of the list.
- To **change a swatch's name**, double-click the swatch in the Swatches palette, enter the new name in the Color Swatch Name dialog, and click OK. You can also select the swatch in the Swatches Preset Manager, click the Rename… button, enter a new name in the Color Swatch Name dialog, and click OK.
- To **change a swatch's position** in the list, click and drag the swatch in the Swatches Preset Manager to the desired location.

Loading Presets

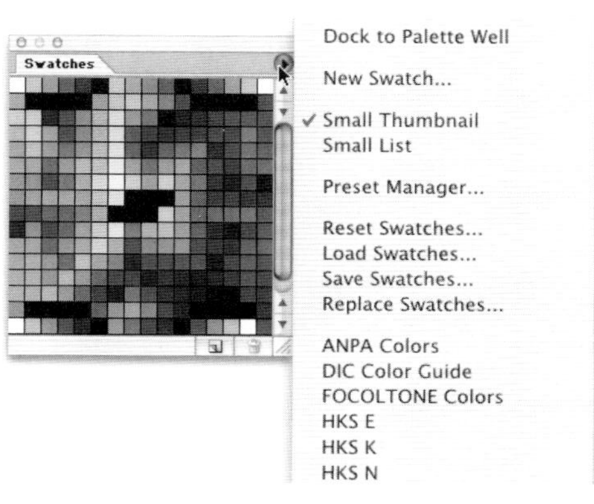

You can add to or completely replace the color swatches in the Swatches palette, selecting other saved lists.

14.4 Organizing Color Swatch Presets *(Continued)*

- To **reset the swatches** to factory fresh, choose Reset Swatches… from the Swatches palette menu or the Swatches Preset Manager menu. Choose whether you want to append the default colors to the current list (at the bottom) or to replace the current list.
- To **load a list of swatches**, choose Load… from the Swatches palette menu or click the Load… button in the Swatches Preset Manager. Browse to locate the swatch file that has the `.aco` extension, and double-click the file. The colors are appended to the bottom of the current list.
- To **quickly load a new list** of swatches, choose from the list at the bottom of the Swatches palette menu or the Swatches Preset Manager menu. Choose whether you want to append the new list to the current list (at the bottom) or to replace the current list.
- To **replace the current swatches** with a new list, choose Replace Swatches… from the Swatches palette menu or the Swatches Preset Manager menu. Browse to locate the swatch file that has the `.aco` extension, and double-click the file.

Saving color swatches is great for storing color palettes used in particular projects.

A good place to save your swatches is the Color Swatches folder in the Photoshop folder.

Hold the mouse cursor over a color in the Swatches palette to view the color name in a Tool Tip.

Although Adobe offers a wide assortment of color swatches, the Visibone 2 swatches are highly recommended for web designers.

Saving Presets

After you create and edit a personalized color swatch list, you can easily save the list for later use. To save your color swatch, do one of the following:

- Choose Save Swatches from the Swatches palette menu. Enter a name for the new swatch list, making sure to preserve the `.aco` extension, browse to the folder in which you want to save the swatch list, and click Save.
- In the Swatches Preset Manager, select the colors you want to save as a list (click the first color and then Shift-click additional colors), and then click the Save Set… button. Enter a name for the new swatch list, making sure to preserve the `.aco` extension, browse to the folder in which you want to save the swatch list, and click Save.

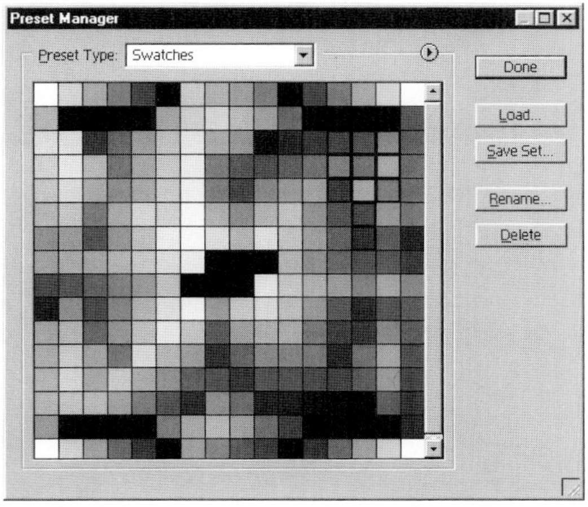

The selected colors in the Preset Manager (top right) are surrounded by a heavy black line.

14.5 Applying Color Fills

➠ 3.14 Fill Tools

➠ 9.1 Layer Basics

➠ 10.11 Applying the Overlay Effects

➠ 15 Painting in Images

Fill visible pixels in layer using foreground color
Option Shift Del
Alt Shift Bksp

Fill visible pixels in layer using background color
⌘ Shift Del
Ctrl Shift Bksp

You can also apply patterns to an entire layer using the Pattern Overlay effect.

Remember, the selection you use with a fill can be feathered to soften the edges of the fill.

You can apply color to the canvas in a variety of ways, but often you need to fill large areas or even the entire canvas with a solid color. You can do this with the Fill command, the Paint Bucket tool, or a Solid Color Fill layer.

The selection to be filled

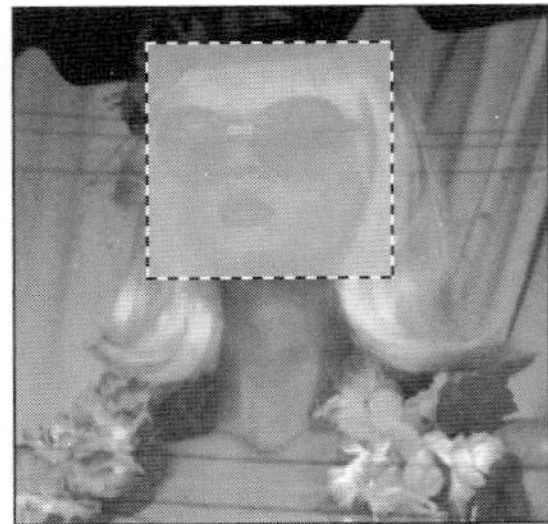

After the Fill command. The fill was performed with an Overlay blending mode and 75% opacity.

Using the Fill Command

You can use the Fill command to fill an entire layer or a selection within a layer without worrying about the content in that layer. To use the Fill command, follow these steps:

1 Pick the color you want to fill with. (The color can be in either the foreground or background square.)

2 Select the layer you want to fill. You can also make a selection to fill.

3 Choose Edit > Fill, set the options in the Fill dialog, and then click OK. The layer or selection is now filled.

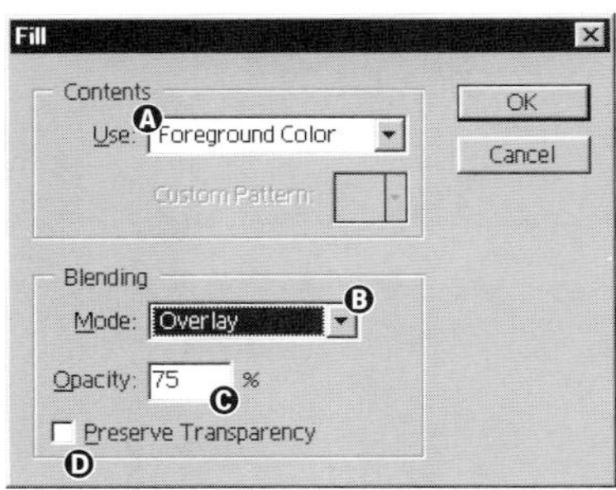

A Choose the source for the fill. You can choose the foreground color, the background color, black, 50% gray, or white.

B Choose a blending mode to use with the fill. Since you are editing a layer, you can choose Behind and Clear in addition to the standard blending modes.

C Enter a value (1 to 100) to specify the opacity of the fill as a percentage.

D Check to preserve the transparency of pixels in the layer when the fill pixels are applied. This will change the colors without affecting the opacity of pixels in the image.

14.5 Applying Color Fills *(Continued)*

Using the Paint Bucket Tool

The Paint Bucket tool will also fill the layer, but will confine the area of the fill based on the content in the selected layer. Follow these steps:

1 Pick the color you want to fill with as the foreground color.

2 Select the layer you want to fill. You can also make a selection to confine the area of the fill.

3 Select the Paint Bucket tool and set the options in the tool options bar:

- Make sure the Fill menu is set to Foreground.
- Choose a blending mode to use with the fill. Since you are editing a layer, you can choose Behind and Clear in addition to the standard blending modes.
- Set the opacity for the fill.
- Set the tolerance for the fill. The higher the number, the larger the area that is filled.
- Check whether you want the fill to be anti-aliased, contiguous (only pixels touching each other), and/or using all layers.

4 Click with the Paint Bucket on the spot where you want the fill to begin. The area of the fill is limited by the first color click, the tolerance value, any selection, whether the fill is contiguous, and whether the fill is using all layers.

After using the Paint Bucket tool to fill. The blending mode is set to Overlay, opacity is set to 50%, and tolerance is set to 100%.

Since the Fill command is only available using the Edit menu, you have to be in Standard or Full Screen Mode with Menu bar to access it.

If you fill an image in CMYK mode using the *Black* option in the Fill dialog, this will fill all channels with 100% black, which may cause problems with your printer. Instead, choose black for the foreground color, and then fill using the foreground color.

Hold down the shift key while using the fill bucket to only fill visible pixels in the selected layer.

14.5 Applying Color Fills *(Continued)*

Adding a Solid Color Fill Layer

The most versatile way to add a fill to the canvas is to use a Fill layer, which allows you to create a layer devoted to a single color that you can easily edit. Follow these steps:

1. Select the layer above which you want to insert a Solid Color Fill layer. You can also make an addition selection in that layer. The selection will be used as a layer mask in the Fill layer.
2. To insert the Solid Color Fill layer, do one of the following:
   - Choose Layer > New Fill Layer > Solid Color…. Set options in the New Layer dialog and click OK.
   - Choose Solid Color… from the Adjustments menu at the bottom of the Layers palette.
3. Choose the color to be used in the Fill layer, and click OK.

After adding a Solid Color Fill layer. The selection is used as a layer mask.

WHAT ARE WEB SAFE COLORS?

Web-safe colors are the 216 color values that display more or less consistently across both the Mac and Windows operating systems. Although web-safe colors are rapidly becoming a moot point, since most monitors can display thousands or more colors, many web designers still stick to them.

It's actually not that hard to remember all 216 safe colors, not by name of course, but either on the RGB or hexadecimal scales. Both scales use a list of three separate values. The first value tells the computer how much red to mix in the color, the second is green, and the third is blue. To be browser safe, for RGB you can use 0, 51, 102, 153, 204, or 255. For hexadecimal you can use 00, 33, 66, 99, CC, and FF, in any combination in the three slots. So 153 0 102 is the same as 990066 and produces a reddish purple.

14.6 Creating and Editing Gradients

Although Photoshop provides dozens of preset gradients, more than likely you will need to create your own with specific colors. There is no way to create a gradient from scratch. Instead, you need to select the gradient closest to the one you want to create and edit it. To edit or create a gradient, follow these steps:

1 Double-click a gradient pattern to open the Gradient Editor with this gradient loaded.

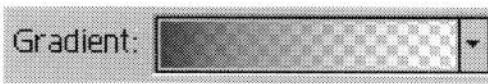

Although the size can vary, the gradient pattern is always located next to the triangle used to open the Gradient drop-down. Double-click the pattern to open the Gradient Editor.

2 Choose a Gradient Type: Solid or Noise. The options in the Gradient Editor depend on your choice. If you choose Solid, edit the gradient by adjusting opacity and color stops; if you choose Noise type, adjust the color model and other settings. Both sets of options are illustrated here.

3 Click OK when you're done. The new gradient appears in the Gradient Presets drop-down.

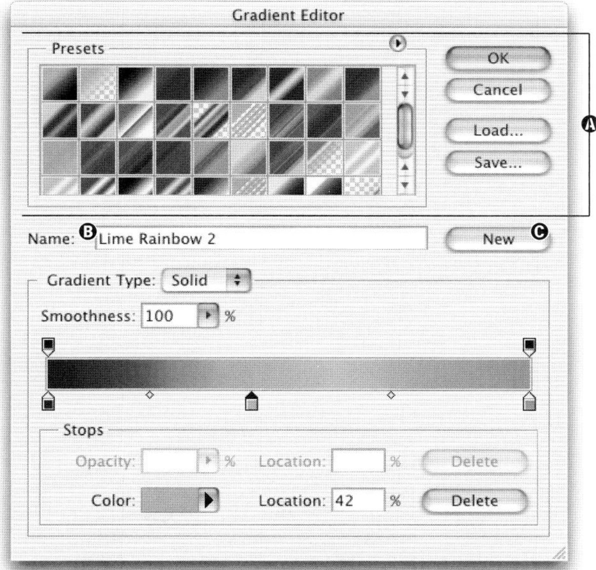

A **Presets** This area works the same as the Gradients Preset Manage (see Section 14.7). Click one of the gradient presets to load it into the editor below.

B Displays the name of the current gradient. Although you cannot change the name here, you can enter a new name to create a new gradient.

C Click to record the gradient using the name (see B) in the Presets list. This does not permanently save the gradient in the Presets list.

Continues

➠ 1.5 Interface Objects

➠ 3.14 Fill Tools

➠ 14.7 Organizing Gradient Presets

Fill Tools G

Cycle Fill Tools Shift G

Warning: This gradient is not permanently saved until you save the list of gradients in which it is stored.

14.6 Creating and Editing Gradients *(Continued)*

The gradient pattern and drop-down are accessible with the Gradient tool selected.

Gradients cannot be added to images in bitmap, indexed, or 16-bit color modes.

You can not only control the color but also the opacity of a gradient at any point, allowing you to create opacity gradients.

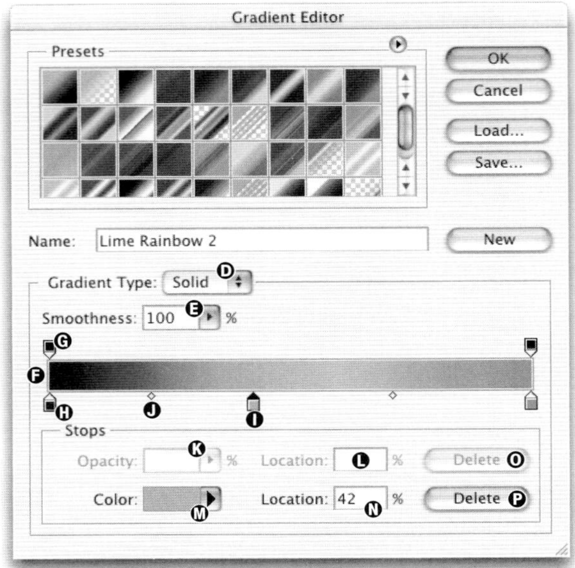

D Select either Solid or Noise for the Gradient Type. Solid is the more traditional gradient in which you set color points along the line. Noise allows you to adjust overall color values for the gradient, but randomizes the color points.

E Use the drop-down slider or enter a value (0 to 100) for the smoothness of the gradient.

F **Gradient line** Displays the current appearance of the gradient. Click anywhere immediately above the gradient line to add an opacity stop. Click anywhere immediately below the gradient line to add a color stop.

G **Opacity stop** Defines the opacity (see K) at a location (see L) in the gradient line. Click to select and change the values. Click and drag to move along the line or up to remove the stop.

H **Color stop** Defines the color (see M) at a location (see N) in the gradient line. Click to select and change the values, or click anywhere immediately above the gradient line to add an addition point.

I **Selected stop** The currently selected stop (opacity or color) has a black triangle rather than white. Click and drag to move or press Delete to remove the selected stop.

J **Midpoint** Defines the midpoint location between two colors. Click and drag to move or enter the location below.

K Enter a percentage value (0 to 100) for the selected opacity stop (see G).

L Enter a percentage value (0 to 100) for the location of the selected opacity stop (see G).

M Click to choose a color using the Color Picker for the selected color stop (see H). You can also choose one of the color options from the drop-down. In addition, you can click in the gradient line, in any open image, in any color swatch, or in any color square to select that color using the Eyedropper tool, which appears automatically.

N Enter a percentage value (0 to 100) for the location of the selected color stop (see H).

O Click to delete the selected opacity stop.

P Click to delete the selected color stop.

14.6 Creating and Editing Gradients *(Continued)*

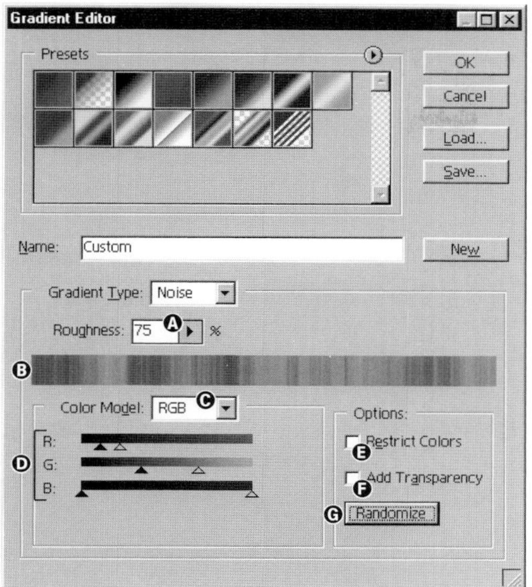

Ⓐ Use the slider or enter a percentage value (0 to 100) for the gradient roughness. The higher the value, the more distinct the noise lines.

Ⓑ **Gradient line** Displays the current appearance of the gradient.

Ⓒ Select a color model to use: RGB, HSB, or Lab.

Ⓓ **Color range** Use the three bars to define the color range for the random noise in the gradient "in" (filled triangle) and "out" (empty triangle) points. The exact bars that appear depend on the selected color model.

Ⓔ Check to prevent the colors from becoming oversaturated. This generally has the effect of washing out the gradient.

Ⓕ Check to add random opacity stops.

Ⓖ Click to randomize the gradient noise. Every time you click this button, the gradient changes according to the settings

14.7 Organizing Gradient Presets

➠ 3.14 Fill Tools

➠ 5.1 Preset Manager Overview

(Preset Manager) Jump to gradients
⌘ 3
Ctrl 3

Fill Tools G

Cycle Fill Tools
Shift G

You can add, delete, rename, and reorder gradients in the Gradient Preset list. In addition, lists of gradient presets can be saved and loaded as needed. Gradients are organized either in gradient drop-downs located throughout the interface, or in the Gradient Preset Manager.

Editing the Gradients Preset List

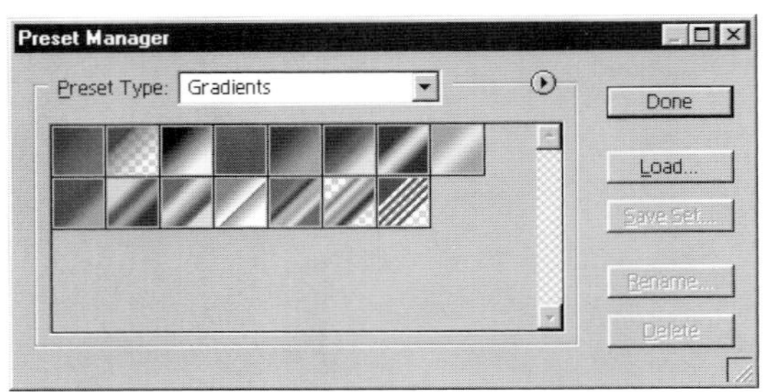

You can open the Gradients Preset Manager from the Gradient drop-down's menu. You can remove, rename, or move the gradients in the drop-down.

- To **delete a gradient preset**, Option/Alt-click the thumbnail in the Gradients drop-down, the Gradients Editor, or the Gradients Preset Manager. The gradient is removed, and all other gradients in the drop-down shift to fill its space.
- To **change a gradient's name**, click the gradient in the Gradients drop-down, select Rename Gradient… in the drop-down's menu, enter the new name, and click OK. You can also select the gradient in the Gradients Preset Manager. Click the Rename… button, enter a new name, and click OK.
- To **change a gradient's position** in the list, click and drag the gradient in the Gradients Preset Manager to the desired location.

Loading Presets

You can load lists of default gradient presets or lists that you created.

- To **reset** the gradients in the Gradients drop-down, choose Reset Gradients… from the Gradients drop-down's menu, the Gradients Editor's menu, or the Gradients Preset Manager's menu. Choose whether you want to append the default gradients to the current list (at the bottom) or to replace the current list.
- To **load** a list of gradients, choose Load… from the Gradients drop-down's menu or click the Load… button in the Gradients Preset Manager or Gradients Editor. Browse to locate the gradient file that has the `.grd` extension, and double-click the file. The gradients are appended to the bottom of the current list.

14.7 Organizing Gradient Presets *(Continued)*

- To **quickly load** a new list of gradients, choose from the list at the bottom of the Gradients drop-down's menu or the Gradients Preset Manager's menu. Choose whether you want to append the new list to the current list (at the bottom) or to replace the current list.
- To **replace** the current gradients with a new list, choose Replace Gradients… from the Gradients drop-down, the Gradients Editor, or the Gradients Preset Manager's menu. Browse to locate the gradient file that has the `.grd` extension, and double-click the file.

Saving Presets

To save a list of gradients, do one of the following:

- Choose Save Gradients from the menu in the Gradients drop-down. Enter a name for the new Gradients list, making sure to preserve the `.grd` extension, browse to the folder in which you want to save the swatch list, and click Save.
- In the Gradients Preset Manager or the Gradients Editor, select the gradient thumbnails you want to save as a list (click the first color and then Shift-click additional colors), and then click the Save… button. Enter a name for the new swatch list, making sure to preserve the `.grd` extension, browse to the folder in which you want to save the swatch list, and click Save.

If you create a gradient, as shown in Section 14.5, you have to save it as a preset or else it will be lost if you replace the gradients in the list.

It is a good idea to save all of the gradients you use in a project as a single gradients file which you can then quickly load as needed.

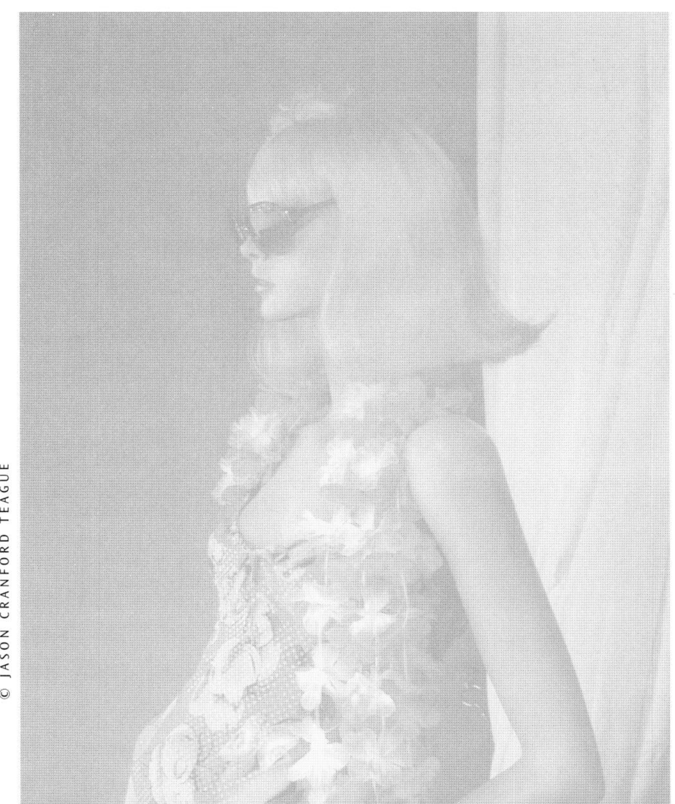

14.8 Applying Gradient Color Fills

➠ 3.14 Fill Tools

➠ 9.5 Adding a Fill Layer or an Adjustment Layer

➠ 10.8 Applying the Glow Effects

➠ 10.11 Applying the Overlay Effects

➠ 14.7 Organizing Gradient Presets

Gradients are added to the canvas either across an entire layer, within a selection, or as part of a fill layer. Whenever you apply a gradient, you can select from five gradient styles.

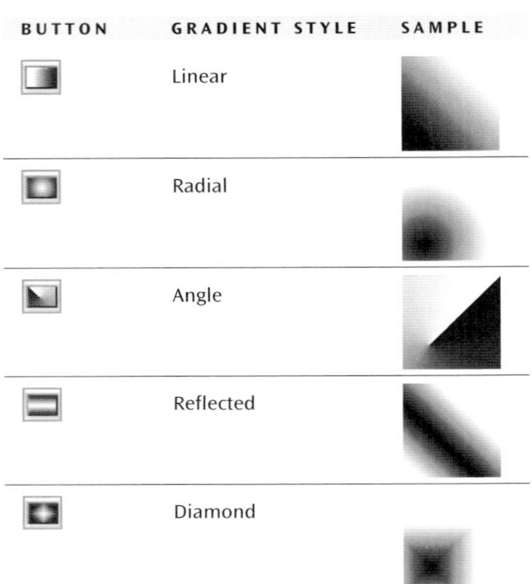

BUTTON	GRADIENT STYLE	SAMPLE
	Linear	
	Radial	
	Angle	
	Reflected	
	Diamond	

Using the Gradient Tool

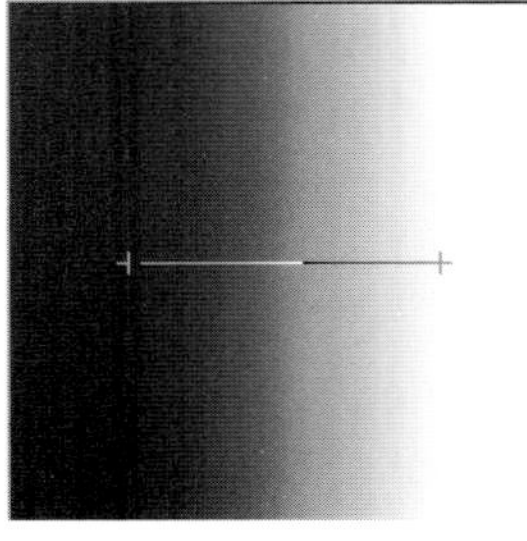

The linear gradient applied straight across the canvas

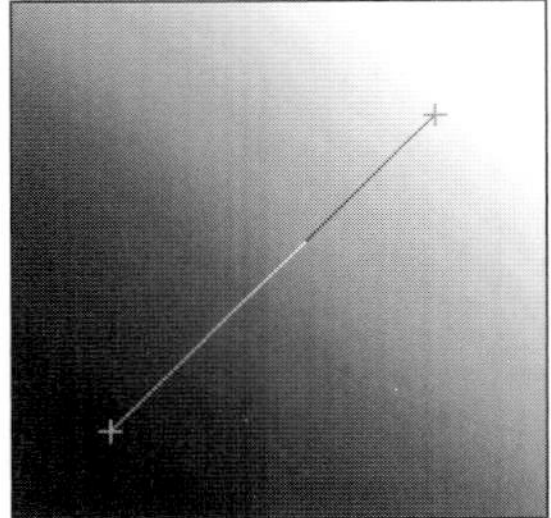

The linear gradient applied at an angle

1 Select the layer to which you want to add a gradient. You can also make a selection to confine the area of the fill. You may want to create a new layer to add the gradient to; otherwise, images on the current layer will be replaced by the gradient.

3 Select the Gradient tool and set the options in the tool options bar:

- Choose a gradient from the Gradient drop-down or double-click the gradient thumbnail to open the Gradient Editor. The first two gradients in the list are based on the currently selected foreground and background colors.

14.8 Applying Gradient Color Fills *(Continued)*

Fill Tools [G]

Cycle Fill Tools [Shift] [G]

- Choose a gradient style: Linear, Radial, Angle, Reflected, or Diamond.
- Choose a blending mode to use when applying the gradient. Since you are editing a layer, you can choose Behind and Clear in addition to the standard blending modes.
- Set the opacity for the gradient when applied.
- Check whether you want to reverse the gradient direction, dither the gradient, and use gradient transparency settings.

4 Click with the Gradient tool at the point where you want the first color to set the stop location of the first color in the gradient and then drag and release to set the stop location of the last color in the gradient. The gradient is applied based on the style selected.

Adding a Gradient Fill Layer

A Fill layer has been added. The gradient is from black to transparent using the Angle style set to a 43° angle.

1 Select the layer above which you want to insert a Solid Color Fill layer. You can also make an additional selection in that layer. The selection will be used as a layer mask in the Gradient Fill layer.

2 To insert the Solid Color Fill layer, either choose Layer > New Fill Layer > Gradient…, or choose Gradient… from the Adjustments menu at the bottom of the Layers palette.

3 In the Gradient Fill dialog, choose the gradient to use and set other options. You can also adjust the gradient's position by clicking it and the canvas and dragging.

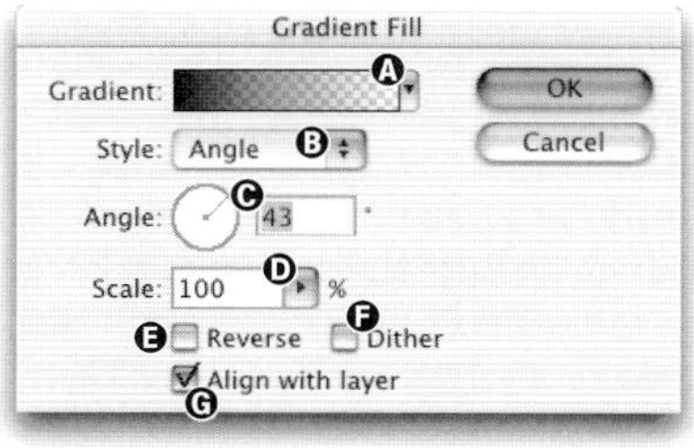

Ⓐ Select a gradient from the Gradient drop-down, or double-click the gradient thumbnail to open the Gradient Editor.

Ⓑ Select a gradient style.

Ⓒ Use the angle wheel or enter an angle value (–360 to 360) for the gradient.

Ⓓ Use the drop-down slider or enter a percentage value (10 to 150) for the gradient's scale.

Ⓔ Check to reverse the direction of the gradient.

Ⓕ Check to dither the gradient. If your monitor supports thousands or more colors, you will not notice a difference.

Ⓖ Check to align the fill with the layer rather than with the selected area.

14.9 Creating Patterns

➠ 2.4 Edit Menu

➠ 2.7 Select Menu

➠ 3.3 Marquee Tools

➠ 8.3 Selecting Rectangular or Elliptical Areas

➠ 14.12 Using the Pattern Maker

You can make more complex and abstract patterns using the Pattern Maker filter (see Section 14.12).

Warning: A pattern is not permanently saved until you save the list of presets in which it is stored. If you replace the current list before saving, the pattern will be lost.

You cannot use feathering to create a pattern.

You can import or copy a shape created in a vector image into the canvas to create more precise geometric patterns.

You create patterns using rectangular selections in the canvas. This selection is then used to define the pattern and added to the pattern presets for use. Follow these steps:

1 Using the Rectangular Marquee tool, select an area in the canvas from which you want to create a pattern. This selection will be used to create the pattern sampling from all visible layers.

2 Choose Edit > Define Pattern....

3 Enter a name for the new pattern and click OK. The new pattern appears in the Patterns Preset drop-down and the Patterns Preset Manager.

The selection in the canvas to be used to define a pattern

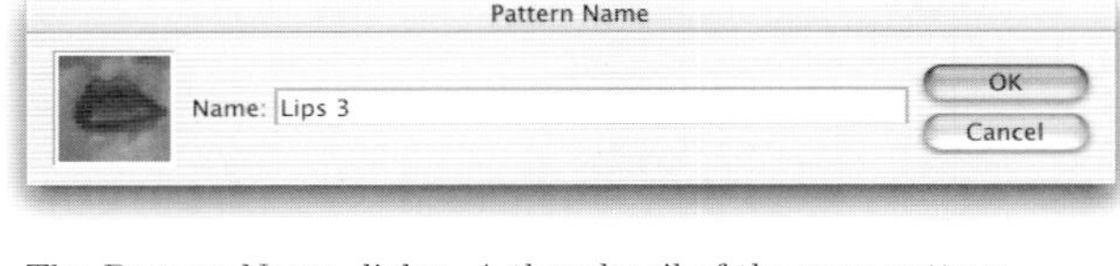

The Pattern Name dialog. A thumbnail of the new pattern appears next to the name.

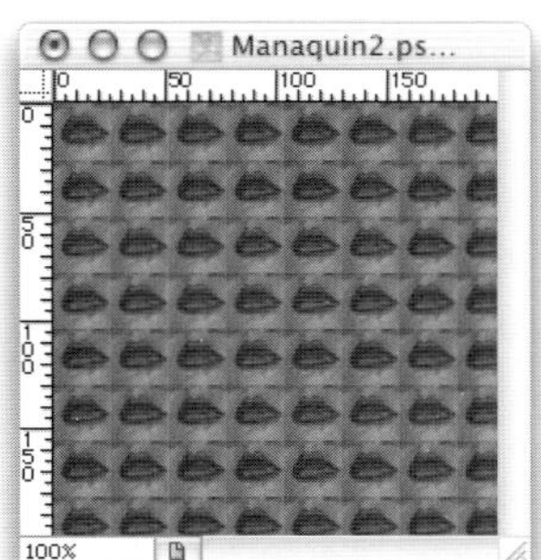

The pattern applied to the canvas using a Fill layer

14.10 Organizing Pattern Presets

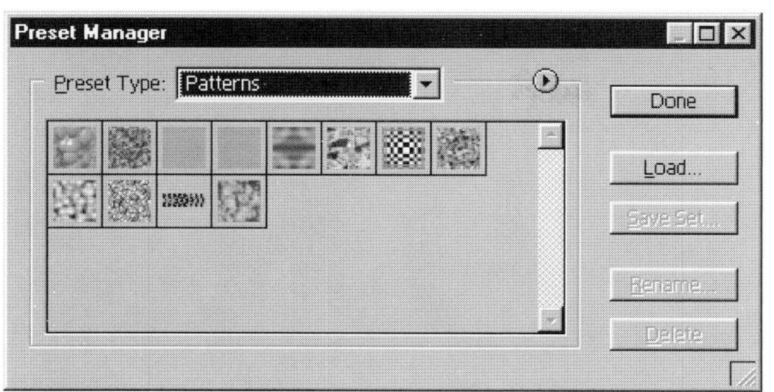

You can add patterns to and remove patterns from the presets either through a Pattern drop-down or using the Patterns Preset Manager. In addition, you can rename or save patterns as a set.

➠ 5.1 Preset Manager Overview

(Preset Manager) Jump to patterns

⌘ 5

Ctrl 5

Editing the Patterns Preset List

You can use the Pattern drop-down or Patterns Preset Manager to remove, rename, or move particular presets.

- To **delete a pattern preset**, Option/Alt-click the thumbnail in the Pattern drop-down or the Patterns Preset Manager. The pattern is removed, and all other patterns in the drop-down shift to fill its space
- To **change a pattern's name**, click the pattern in the Pattern drop-down, select Rename Pattern… in the menu, enter the new name, and click OK. You can also select a pattern in the Patterns Preset Manager, click the Rename… button, enter a new name, and click OK.
- To **change a pattern's position** in the list, click and drag the pattern in the Patterns Preset Manager to the desired location.

Loading Presets

You can change the presets listed in the Patterns drop-down by loading new lists to append to or replace the existing list. The easiest place to do this is in the Pattern Presets manager, but you can also directly edit the patterns that show up in the Pattern Presets drop-down accessible throughout the Photoshop interface.

- To **reset** the patterns in the Pattern drop-down to their defaults, choose Reset Patterns… from the Patterns palette or the Patterns Preset Manager. Choose whether you want to append the default patterns to the current list (at the bottom) or to replace the current list.
- To **load** a list of patterns, choose Load… from the Patterns palette menu or click the Load… button in the Patterns Preset Manager. Browse to locate the pattern file that has the `.pat` extension, and double-click the file. The pattern is appended to the bottom of the current list.

- To **quickly load** a new list of patterns, choose from the list at the bottom of the Patterns palette or the Patterns Preset Manager. Choose whether you want to append the new list to the current list (at the bottom) or to replace the current list.
- To **replace** the current patterns with a new list, choose Replace Patterns… from the Patterns drop-down or the Patterns Preset Manager. Browse to locate the pattern file that has the `.pat` extension, and double-click the file.

Saving Presets

To save a list of preset patterns, do one of the following:

- Choose Save Patterns from the menu in the Pattern drop-down. Enter a name for the new pattern list, making sure to preserve the `.pat` extension, browse to the folder in which you want to save the swatch list, and click OK.
- In the Patterns Preset Manager, select the pattern thumbnails you want to save as a list (click the first pattern, Shift-click additional patterns), and then click the Save Set… button. Enter a name for the new pattern list, making sure to preserve the `.pat` extension, browse to the folder in which you want to save the pattern list, and click OK.

WHEN IS A COLOR OUT OF PRINT GAMUT?

Gamut refers to the range of colors that a particular color model can display. When you select a color using one of the color models other than CMYK, it is possible to create a color that cannot be printed. Selecting a color that is out of gamut means that there is no ink combination that can be used to create the color. If the image is being used for the screen only, this is not a problem, but, obviously, if you are printing using CMYK, you will want to select a different color.

14.11 Applying Patterns

You can apply a pattern to an entire layer, to a selection in a layer, or as part of a Pattern Fill layer.

➠ 10.9 Applying the Bevel and Emboss Effects

➠ 10.11 Applying the Overlay Effects

➠ 10.12 Applying the Stroke Effect

➠ 15.6 Painting with Patterns

Using the Paint Bucket Tool

The Paint Bucket tool will also fill the layer, but will confine the area of the fill based on the content in the selected layer.

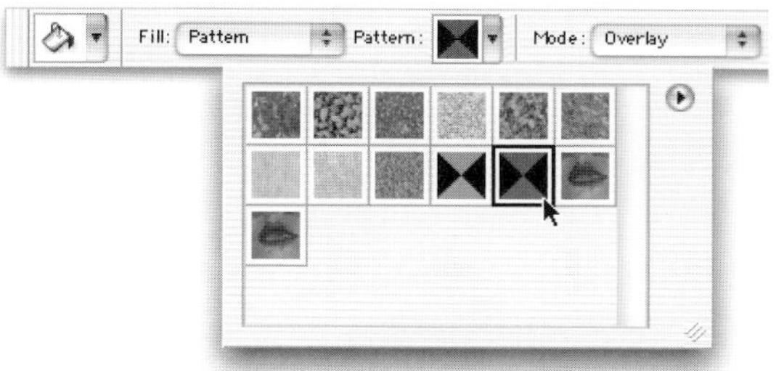

A pattern being selected from the Pattern drop-down in the tool options bar for the Paint Bucket tool

The diamond pattern applied to the image with 75% opacity

1 Pick the color you want to fill with as the foreground color.
2 Select the layer you want to fill. You can also make a selection to confine the area of the fill.
3 Select the Paint Bucket tool and set the options in the tool options bar:
   - Make sure the Fill menu is set to Pattern.
   - Choose a blending mode to use with the fill. Since you are editing a layer, you can choose Behind and Clear in addition to the standard blending modes.
   - Set the opacity for the fill.
   - Set the tolerance for the fill. The higher the number, the larger the area filled.
   - Check whether you want the fill to be anti-aliased, contiguous (only pixels touching each other), and/or using all layers.
4 Click with the Paint Bucket tool on the spot where you want the fill to begin. The area of the fill is limited by the first color click, the tolerance value, any selection, whether the fill is contiguous, and whether the fill is using all layers.

You can also apply patterns to an entire layer using the Pattern Overlay effect.

You can transform scaling patterns using the default interpolation method.

Adding a Pattern Fill Layer

Using a Pattern Fill layer is the most flexible way to apply a pattern to an image since it allows you to edit and mask the pattern without affecting the other layers in the image.

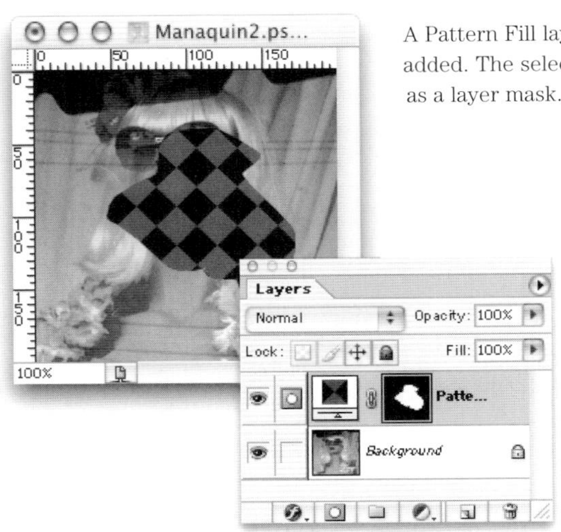

A Pattern Fill layer has been added. The selection is used as a layer mask.

1 To insert the Pattern Fill layer, either choose Layer > New Fill Layer > Pattern..., or choose Pattern ... from the Adjustments menu at the bottom of the Layers palette.
2 In the Pattern Fill dialog, choose the pattern to use and set other options. You can also adjust the pattern's position by clicking it and the canvas and dragging.
3 Click OK to place the pattern layer.

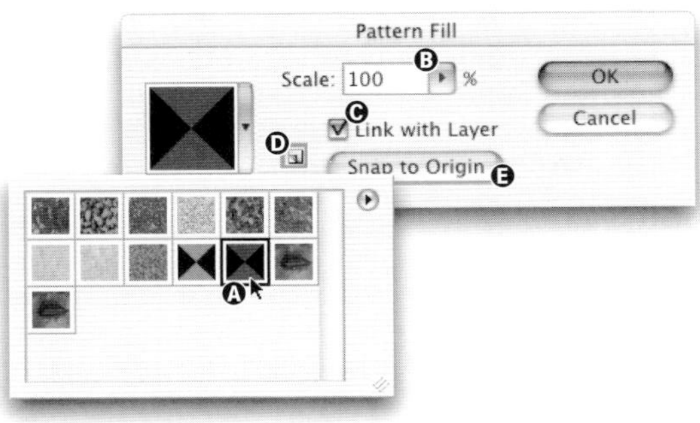

A Choose a pattern form the Pattern drop-down.

B Use the slider or enter a percentage value (1 to 1000) to scale the pattern.

C Check to link the pattern with the layer. When this option is checked, the pattern moves with the layer.

D Click to add the current pattern to the Pattern Presets list.

E Click if you want the top-left corner of the pattern to align with the origin (usually the top-left corner of the image unless it has been shifted).

14.12 Using the Pattern Maker

Simply tiled patterns are created using the Edit > Define Pattern command, but for more organic patterns, you will need to use the Pattern Maker filters. The Pattern Maker works by randomly rearranging the pixels in a selected region of the image. The tiles can be as small as 1 pixel or as large as the image from which they are being generated. This feature is especially useful for generating seamless backgrounds for web pages, but has a variety of other design uses as well.

- 3.3 Marquee Tools
- 3.23 Hand Tool
- 3.24 Zoom Tool
- 8.3 Selecting Rectangular or Elliptical Areas
- 8.10 Copying and Pasting Selected Content
- 14.9 Creating Patterns
- 14.12 Using the Pattern Maker

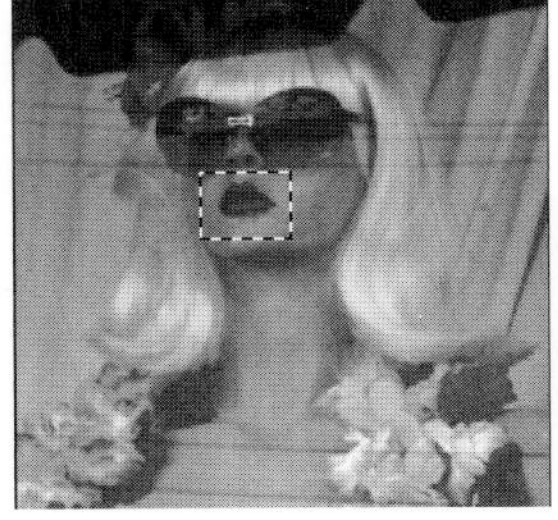

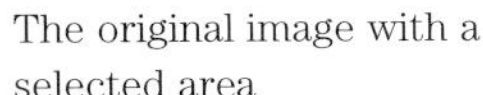

The original image with a selected area

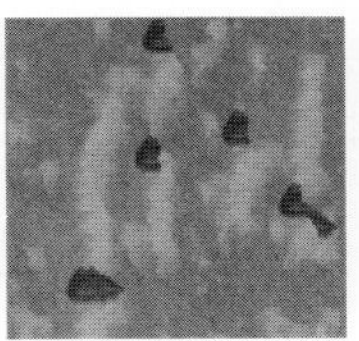

A tile created from that selection

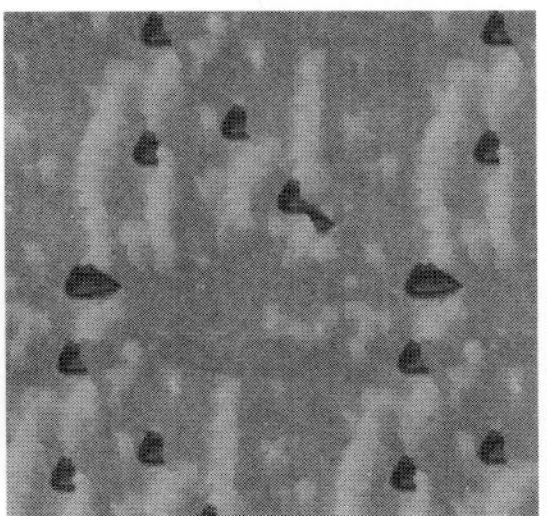

The tiled pattern

To create a pattern using the Pattern Maker, follow these steps.

1. In the original image, make a rectangular selection. You can reshape this selection in the Pattern Maker dialog.
2. Choose Filter > Pattern Maker.
3. In the Pattern Maker dialog, adjust the selection as desired, set the pattern options as desired, and then click Generate. The new tile is displayed in the tile history, and the tiled pattern is displayed in the pattern preview. To generate a different pattern, click Generate Again. All the patterns you generate are recorded in the tile history.
4. Once you have a tile you want to apply to the entire layer, display the tile in the tile history, and click OK.

14.12 Using the Pattern Maker *(Continued)*

The Pattern Maker can only be used with 8-bit images in RGB Color, CMYK Color, Lab Color, and Grayscale image modes.

If the transparency in the selected layer is locked, the pattern maker will not allow the pattern to tile into transparent pixels.

Increase the smoothness value to produce better tiling images.

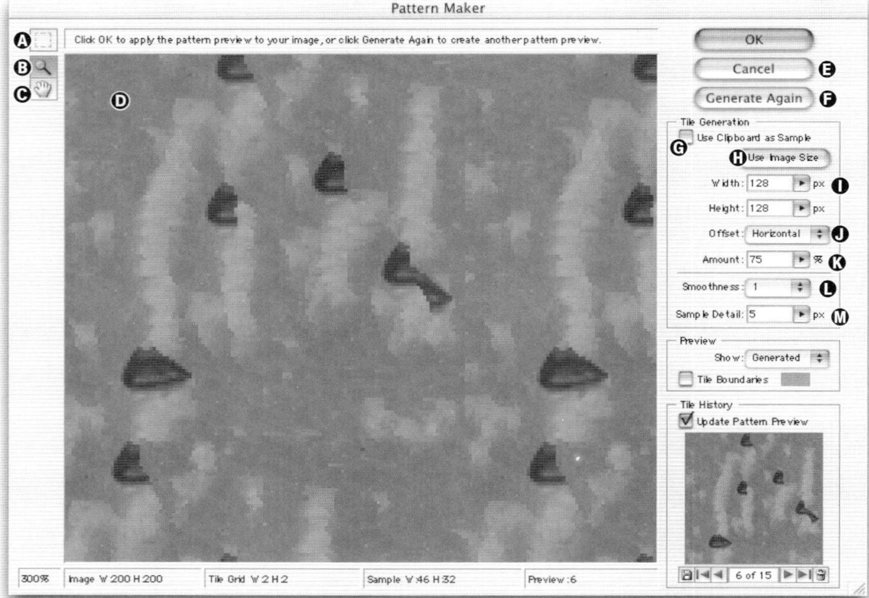

Ⓐ **Rectangular Marquee tool** Used to make a selection in the pattern preview to use as the source to generate the pattern.

Ⓑ **Zoom tool** Used to zoom into the pattern preview.

Ⓒ **Hand tool** Used to move the pattern in the pattern preview.

Ⓓ **Pattern Preview** Displays what the pattern displayed in the tile preview will look like when tiled.

Ⓔ Press Option/Alt and then click to reset the dialog to its state when you originally opened it.

Ⓕ Click to generate a new pattern based on the options set in G–M.

Ⓖ Check to use the image stored in the Clipboard to generate the pattern rather then the selection.

Ⓗ Click to set the width and height to the width and height of the image.

Ⓘ Use the slider or enter a pixel value for the width and height of the pattern. These values must be at least 1, but cannot exceed the width or height of the image.

Ⓙ Choose an offset for the pattern tiles. This can help prevent the pattern from looking too regular.

Ⓚ Use the slider or enter a percentage value (0 to 99) for the selected offset.

Ⓛ Choose a value (1 to 3) for how smooth the transition between tiles should appear.

Ⓜ Use the slider or enter a pixel value (3 to 21) to set the size of details in the pattern. Larger values take longer to generate.

14.12 Using the Pattern Maker *(Continued)*

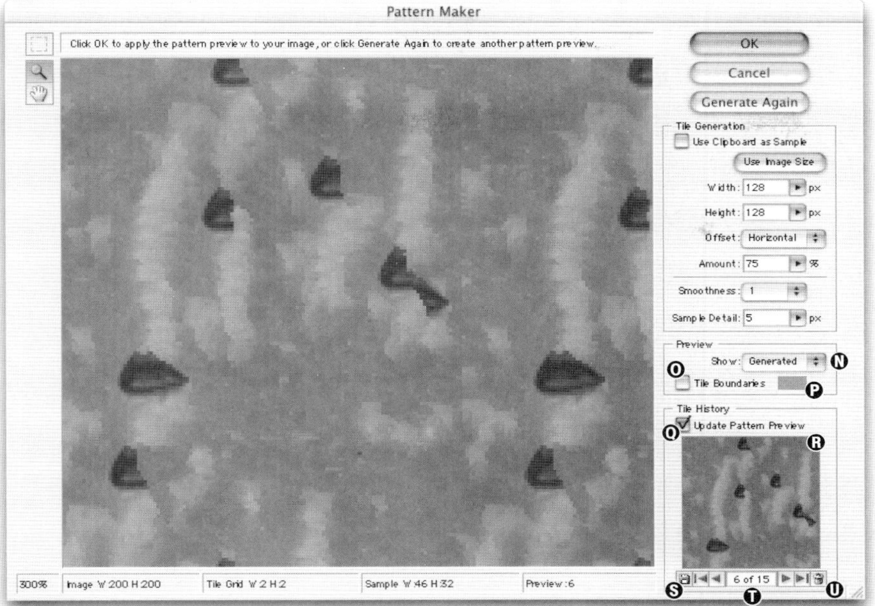

You cannot create a pattern from a nonrectangular selection. If you open the Pattern Maker dialog with a nonrectangular selection active, the Pattern Maker selects the extreme width and height of the selection as the rectangular selection.

N Choose whether the preview displays the original image or the current pattern tile sample.

O Check to show colored boundaries between tiles in the preview.

P Click to use the Color Picker to set the boundary line color.

Q Check to show the tiles in the tile history in the pattern preview.

R **Tile Preview** Every time you click the Generate Again button, the tile is added to the history and previewed here.

S Click to save the tile displayed in the tile preview as a Pattern Preset.

T Click controls to move forward or backward in the tile history. The tile is displayed in the Tile Preview.

U Click to delete the tile displayed in the Tile Preview.

CHAPTER 15

Painting in Images

PAINTING IS ONE OF PHOTOSHOP'S strong points. With Photoshop 7, Adobe completely revamped the painting tools, not only adding some new tools and combining old tools, but also completely revising how brushes are selected and created. If you are familiar with older versions of Photoshop, hold on to your hats. Choosing a brush is no longer a matter of picking from a few presets and adjusting a few options. Brushes can now be minutely detailed to produce an outstanding array of effects that are controlled, for the most part, through the new Brushes palette.

This chapter covers:

15.1 Brush Basics

➠ 3.11 Stamp Tools
➠ 3.12 History Brushes
➠ 3.13 Eraser Tools
➠ 3.15 Distortion Tools
➠ 3.16 Exposure Tools
➠ 4.14 Brushes Palette

Photoshop includes 15 individual tools that use the brush options to paint a color or a pattern onto the canvas. Most of these (except for the Healing Brush and Background Eraser) use the Brush Presets to quickly set the brush style and then allow you adjust the exact nature of the brush in the Brushes palette. This chapter refers to these tools collectively as the painting tools.

Painting Tools

	BRUSH NAME	SEE ALSO
	Healing Brush	27.2 Touch Up with the Healing Brush
	Brush	15.5 Painting with the Brush or Pencil
	Pencil	15.5 Painting with the Brush or Pencil
	Clone Stamp	27.1 Touch Up with the Clone Stamp Tool
	Pattern Stamp	15.6 Painting with Patterns
	History Brush	27.4 Touch Up with the History Brush
	Art History Brush	15.7 Painting with the Art History Brush
	Eraser	15.9 Erasing
	Background Eraser	15.9 Erasing
	Blur	27.6 Blurring and Sharpening with Tools
	Sharpen	27.6 Blurring and Sharpening with Tools
	Smudge	27.7 Smudging and Liquefying Images
	Dodge	26.4 Dodging and Burning Images
	Burn	26.4 Dodging and Burning Images
	Sponge	26.5 Using the Sponge Tool

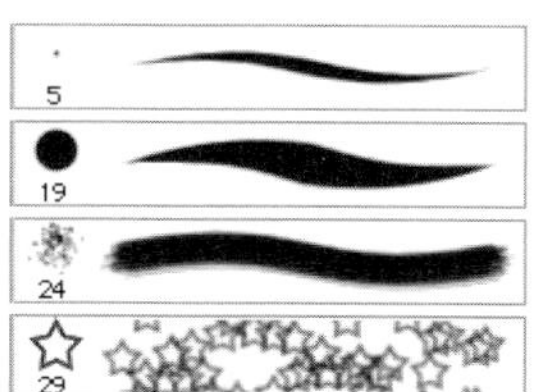

A brush tip defines the shape, size (diameter), angle, roundness, hardness, and spacing. These options define the general nature of how the brush's stroke will appear. However, Photoshop provides several other options to adjust the exact way in which the brush tip is applied to create a stroke. Brush tips are shown with their sizes underneath and a sample stroke next to them.

15.1 Brush Basics *(Continued)*

Dynamic Brush Controls

You can control several brush options dynamically while painting in the canvas. Three of these options require a pen-and-tablet device, which you must purchase separately. The dynamic control pull-down menu options are:

Fade Reduces the value of the option to a value of 0 over the entered number of steps. This creates an illusion of the brush fading over the course of a stroke.

Pen Pressure (Requires tablet) Uses the pressure you apply to a tablet to vary the value for the option between its minimum and maximum.

Pen Tilt (Requires tablet, but not available with all tablets) Uses the angle of the pen on the tablet to vary the value for the option between its minimum and maximum.

Stylus Wheel (Requires tablet) Allows you to use the pen's wheel (if it has one) to change the values of the option between its minimum and maximum.

Initial Direction (Angle Jitter only) Sets the jitter angle based on the direction in which the stroke starts.

Direction (Angle Jitter only) Sets the jitter angle value based on the current direction of the stroke.

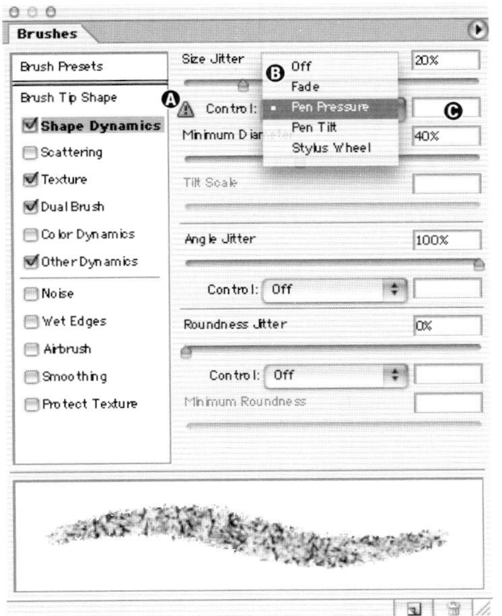

A **Alert icon** Indicates that a tablet is not connected to this computer. This icon disappears when a tablet is connected.

B Select controller options.

C **Steps** If you select Fade, enter a value (1 to 9999) for the number of fade steps.

Restoration tool [J]

Paint Brush tools [B]

Stamp tool [S]

History Brush tool [Y]

Eraser tool [E]

Distortion tool [R]

Exposure tool [O]

In Photoshop 7, the Airbrush tool is replaced with Airbrush mode, in which you can use a variety of brush types as if they were airbrushes (see Section 3.2).

Jitter refers to variations in the brush stroke to simulate the random oscillations that might occur while painting with a physical brush.

The term *paint* is used throughout this chapter either as a noun meaning any color or pattern that is applied with a brush or as a verb referring to the action of painting.

15.2 Selecting and Adjusting Brushes

➡ 3.2 The Tool Options Bar

Decrease brush size (with a brush tool selected)

Increase brush size (with a brush tool selected)

Decrease brush hardness (with a brush tool selected)

Shift [

Increase brush hardness (with a brush tool selected)

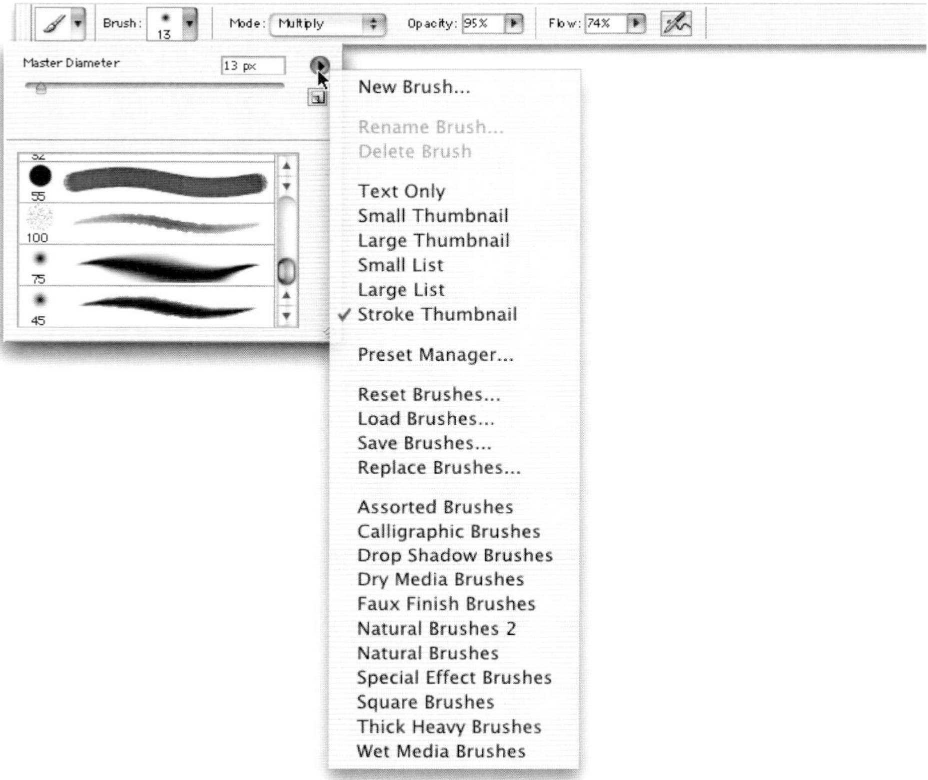

You will want to start painting by selecting a Brush Preset, either from the tool options bar or from the Brushes palette. Regardless of where you select your brush preset from, a painting tool has to be selected first. To choose a Brush Preset, follow these steps:

1. Choose a painting tool (except the Healing Brush or Background Eraser).
2. Choose a Brush Preset either in the Brush drop-down in the tool options bar or in the Brush Presets panel in the Brushes palette. Each preset has a default value for its diameter that is displayed beneath the brush thumbnail.
3. Adjust the diameter of the brush using the slider or by entering a value (1 to 2500) in the Master Diameter field.

You can now adjust the brush further in the Brushes palette or begin to paint with the selected brush in the canvas.

15.2 Selecting and Adjusting Brushes *(Continued)*

Adjusting Brush Settings

Choose one of the painting tools (except the Healing Brush or Background Eraser) and set the brush options in the Brushes palette. As you make changes to the options, a simulated stroke will appear at the bottom of the palette.

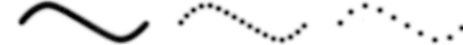

You can also select Brush Presets from the Tool Presets drop-down in the tool options bar or in the Tool Presets palette (see Section 4.10).

Brush options not available for a particular painting tool are grayed out in the Brushes palette. For example, Wet Edges is not available for the Pencil tool.

You use Brush Tip Shape to set the basic shape of the brush when it is applied to the canvas as a stroke. Left to right: spacing is set to 25%, 75%, and 150%.

Shape Dynamics Check to add options to the brush that "jitter" (randomize) the size, angle, and roundness of the brush stroke.

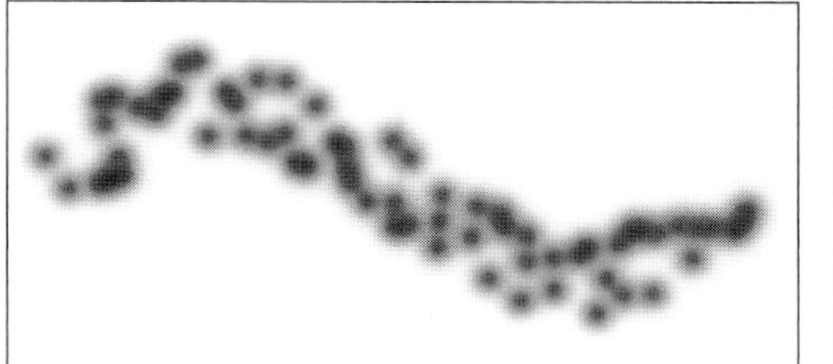

Scattering Check to add options that simulate the scattering of paint as it is applied to the canvas.

Texture Check to add options that simulate a texture for the canvas as brush strokes are being applied.

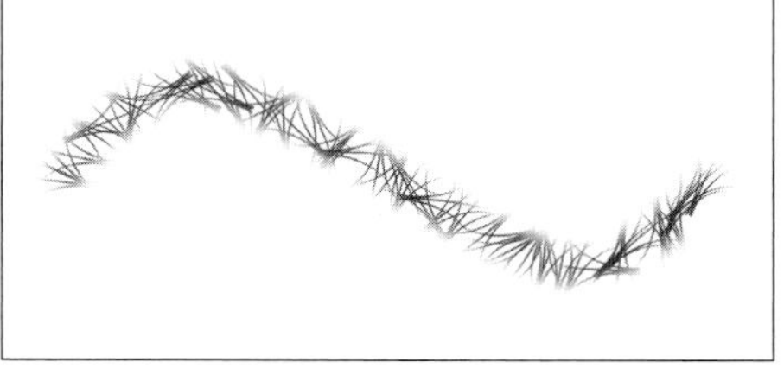

Dual Brush Check to add a second brush shape to mask the first brush, creating more organic brush strokes from their overlap.

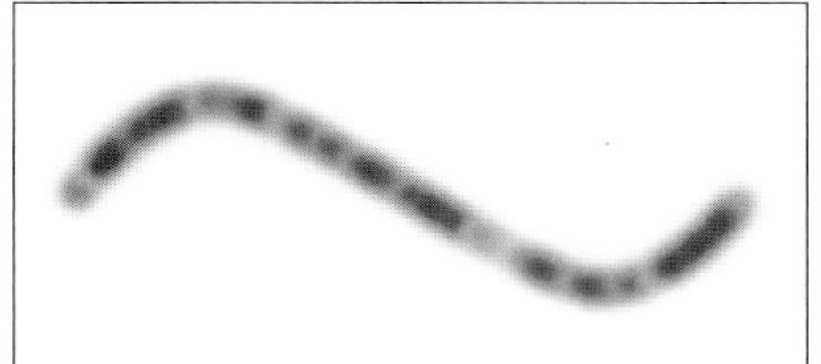

Color Dynamics Check to add options to change the color used by the brush as the stroke is applied.

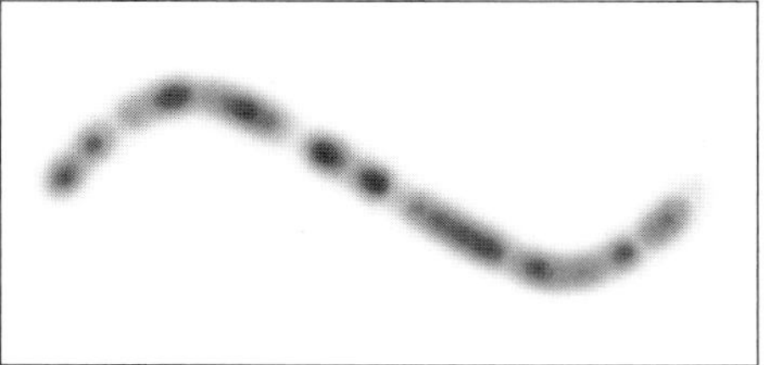

Other Dynamics/Opacity Check to vary the opacity of the stroke.

When you switch to a different painting tool, the options in the Brushes palette are set to the previous options used with this painting tool.

For instructions on using the Healing Brush, see Section 27.2.

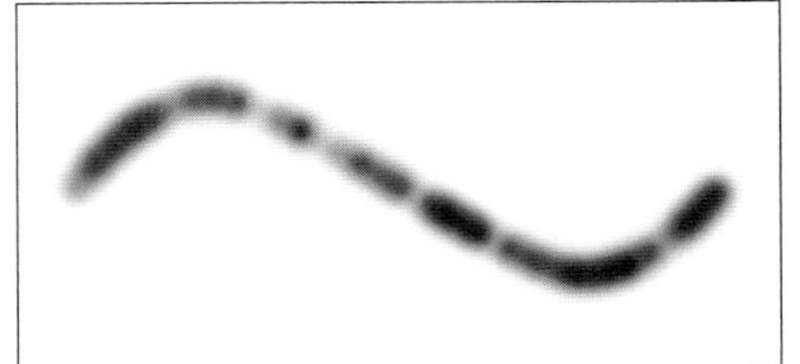

Other Dynamics/Flow Jitter Check to allow the flow value to jitter between its maximum and minimum values.

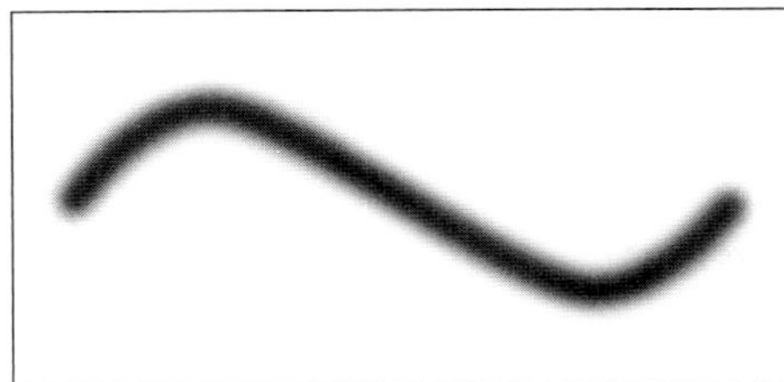

Noise Adds random static to the brush edges.

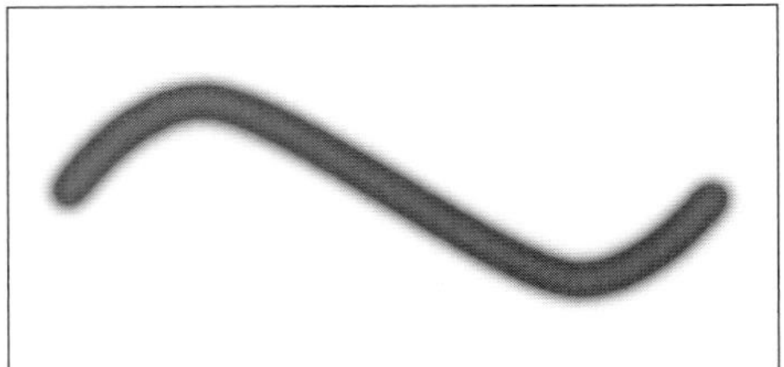

Wet Edges Simulates painting with wet paint; edges are darker than the stroke.

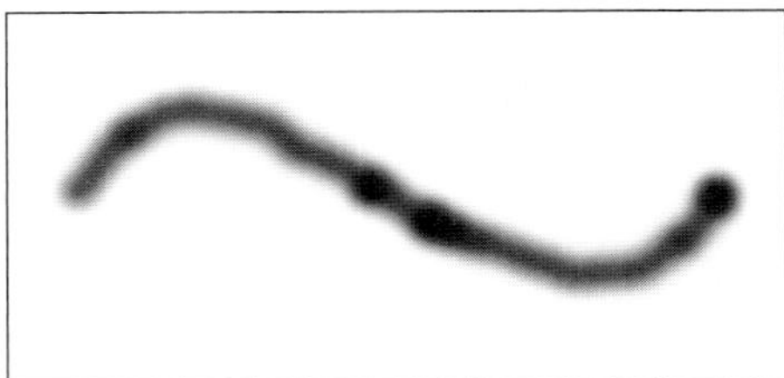

Airbrush mode A painting stroke in Airbrush mode will build up paint wherever the brush lingers in the canvas.

You can now save this brush as a new Brush Preset or begin using it in the canvas with the selected brush.

In the following table, an asterisk (*) indicates that the setting can be controlled dynamically (see Section 15.1).

Brush Settings

SETTING	VALUE RANGE	DESCRIPTION
TIP SHAPE		
Brush Presets		Select the initial brush shape from the list of presets.
Diameter	1 to 2500px	Circular width and height of the brush tip in pixels.
Angle	–180° to 180°	Simulated angle that the brush is applied.
Roundness	1 to 100%	Shape of the brush from 1 (elliptical) to 100 (circular).
Hardness	0 to 100%	Area of the brush tip with maximum application of paint.
Spacing	1 to 1000%	Interval between brush strokes.

Continues

15.2 Selecting and Adjusting Brushes *(Continued)*

Brush Settings *(Continued)*

SETTING	VALUE RANGE	DESCRIPTION
SHAPE DYNAMICS		
Size Jitter*	0 to 100%	Random variation in the diameter of the brush as you are painting.
Minimum Diameter*	1 to 100%	Smallest diameter the brush can have as a percentage of the maximum diameter.
Tilt Scale*	1 to 100%	Scale factor applied to the brush when the Size Jitter control is set to Pen Tilt.
Angle Jitter*	0 to 100%	Random variation in the angle of the brush as you are painting.
Roundness Jitter*	0 to 100%	Random variation in the roundness of the brush as you are painting.
Minimum Roundness*	1 to 100	Smallest roundness the brush can have as a percentage of the maximum roundness.
SCATTERING		
Scatter*	0 to 1000%	Simulated scattering of daubs of paint while painting.
Both Axes		Check to use symmetrical scattering.
Count*	1 to 16	Number of paint daubs used in the scatter.
Count Jitter*	0 to 100%	Random variation in the count as you are painting.
TEXTURE		
Pattern		Pattern to be used as a texture (see Section 14.10).
Scale	1 to 1000%	Size of the pattern used to create the texture. If you use a value other than 100%, Photoshop resizes the pattern using the default interpolation method (see Section 5.1).
Texture Each Tip		Check to add texture to each tip in the brush rather than a single stroke.
Blending Mode		Mode used between the brush and the texture (see Section 9.12).
Depth	0 to 100%	Simulated depth of the texture. Higher values create more contrast between "high" and "low" areas of the texture.
Minimum Depth	0 to 100%	Restrains the variation between lowest and highest values.
Depth Jitter	0 to 100%	Random variation in the depth as you are painting.
DUAL BRUSH		
Blending Mode		Select the blending mode used between the two brushes (see Section 9.12).
Brush Presets		Select the second brush shape.
Diameter	1 to 2500px	Circular width and height of the second brush stroke in pixels.
Use Sample Size		Click to reset the brush diameter to its default.
Spacing	1 to 1000%	Interval between brush strokes for the second brush.

Continues

Brush Settings *(Continued)*

SETTING	VALUE RANGE	DESCRIPTION
DUAL BRUSH		
Scatter	0 to 1000%	Simulated scattering of daubs of paint for the second brush while painting.
Both Axes		Check to use symmetrical scattering for the second brush.
Count	1 to 16	Number of paint daubs used in the scatter for the second brush.
COLOR DYNAMICS		
Foreground/Background Jitter*	0 to 100%	Random fluctuation between the foreground and background color (including colors in between) while painting. Values above 50 favor the background color.
Hue Jitter	0 to 100%	Random variation in paint color hue while painting.
Saturation Jitter	0 to 100%	Random variation in paint color saturation while painting.
Brightness Jitter	0 to 100%	Random variation in paint color brightness while painting.
Purity	–100 to 100%	Shift in the color toward or away from the neutral value (0%).
OTHER DYNAMICS		
Opacity Jitter*	0 to 100%	Random variation in paint opacity (set in the tool options bar) while painting.
Flow Jitter*	0 to 100%	Random variation in paint flow (set in the tool options bar) while painting.
OTHER OPTIONS		
Noise		Applies random noise to the brush stroke.
Wet Edges		Simulates a wet brush while painting with opaque edges and a transparent center.
Airbrush		Check to use Airbrush mode with this brush (see Section 15.1).
Smoothing		Check to have strokes smoothed from the actual mouse path used. This may slow painting.
Protect Texture		Check to apply the same texture for all brushes used while editing the image. This allows you to keep a consistent simulated texture for the canvas.

15.3 Creating and Saving Brushes

You can create a new brush either by creating your own brush tip or by simply adjusting the options for an existing brush tip and then saving the changes as a new brush.

The brush tip defines the overall shape of the brush. Often the brush is circular or elliptical, but brushes can actually be any shape you want. To create a new brush with a customized brush tip, follow these steps:

1 Choose the Rectangular Marquee tool and set Feathering to 0.

2 Select the part of the image you want to turn into a brush. The selection can be a maximum of 2500px by 2500px.

3 Adjust the brush options in the Brushes palette (see Section 15.1). These will be used as the default settings for your new brush.

4 Choose Edit > Define Brush. This will sample from all visible layers in the selection to create a grayscale image that is then used as a brush tip. White areas will be empty and darker areas will be filled when used as a brush.

5 Enter a name for the new brush in the New Brush dialog and click OK.

The new brush will appear in the Brush Presets list, ready to be adjusted or used for painting in the canvas.

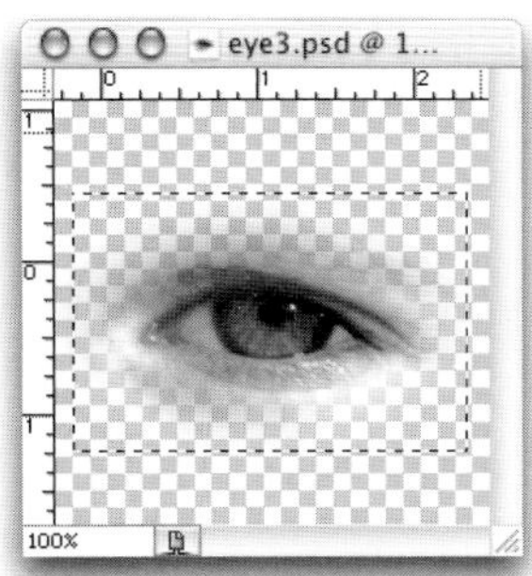

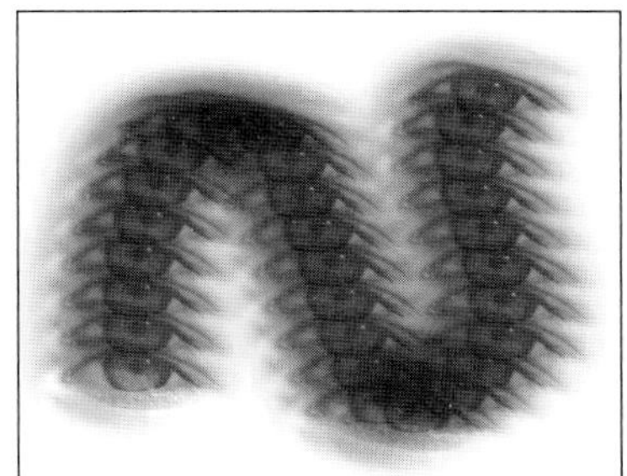

The selected area of the image can be turned into a brush.

Saving Brushes

Changing a brush's options does not change the original Brush Preset's options permanently; the next time you select that Brush Preset, it returns to the default options set for it. To save the current options as a new brush, choose New Brush… from the Brushes palette menu or the Brushes drop-down, or click the New Brush button at the bottom of the Brushes palette or in the Brushes drop-down. Enter a name for the new brush in the New Brush dialog, and click OK. The new brush appears in the Brush Presets list.

➠ 3.2 The Tool Options Bar
➠ 3.10 Drawing Tools
➠ 3.11 Stamp Tools
➠ 3.12 History Brushes
➠ 3.13 Eraser Tools
➠ 3.14 Fill Tools
➠ 3.15 Distortion Tools
➠ 3.16 Exposure Tools
➠ 4.14 Brushes Palette

If you create a new brush, the brush has not been permanently saved until you save it as part of a Brush Presets list (see Section 15.4).

15.4 Organizing Brush Presets

➠ 3.2 The Tool Options Bar

➠ 4.14 Brushes Palette

➠ 5.1 Preset Manager Overview

Jump to brushes (in Preset Manager)
⌘ 1
Ctrl 1

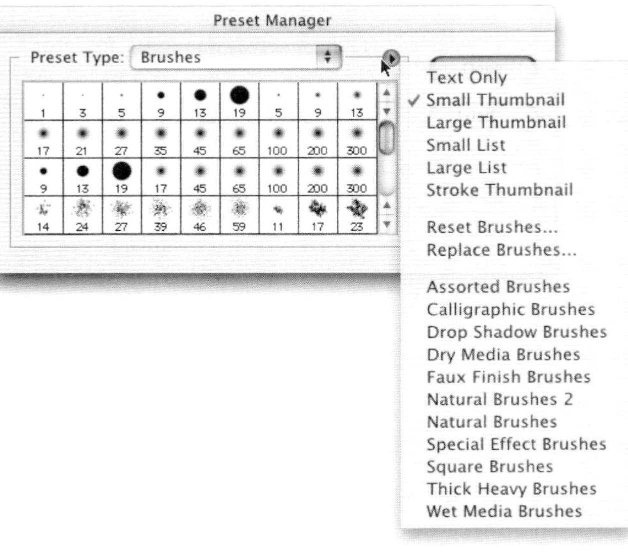

Both the Brush drop-down in the tool options bar and the Brushes palette have a list of Brush Presets. In addition, as with all presets, you can organize Brush Presets in the Preset Manager (Edit > Preset Manager…). To organize Brush Presets in the Brushes palette, the Brush Presets panel must be displayed.

Editing Presets

Photoshop comes with dozens of Brush Presets, but it is unlikely that you will use all of them. To spend less time scrolling through long lists of brushes, edit the list.

- To **delete a Brush Preset**, Option/Alt-click the brush (the mouse cursor turns into a pair of scissors) in the Brushes palette, Brushes drop-down, or Brushes Preset Manager. In the Brushes palette, you can also drag the brush to the trashcan [trashcan icon] or select a brush, click the trashcan icon, and click OK to confirm deletion.
- To **delete multiple Brush Presets** at the same time in the Brushes Preset Manager, Shift-click one or more brushes and click Delete. The brushes are removed, and all other brushes in the palette shift to fill its space.
- To **change a brush's name**, double-click the brush in the Brushes palette or Brushes Preset Manager, enter the new name in the Brush Name dialog, and click OK. You can also select the brush in the Brushes Preset Manager and click Rename… to open the dialog.
- To **change a brush's position** in the list, click and drag the brush in the Brushes Preset Manager to the desired location.

15.4 Organizing Brush Presets *(Continued)*

Saving Presets

After you create and edit a personalized brush list, you can easily save the list for later use. To save your list of Brush Presets, do one of the following:

- Choose Save Brushes… from the Brushes palette menu or Brushes drop-down.
- In the Brushes Preset Manager, select the brushes you want to save as a list (click the first brush and then Shift-click additional brushes), and then click the Save Set… button.

Enter a name for the new brush list, making sure to preserve the `.abr` extension, browse to the folder in which you want to save the brush list, and click Save.

It is a good idea to save lists of customized brushes you are using on a project so that you can quickly load them again when you need them.

The Photoshop folder contains a Brushes folder, which is a good place to save your brush lists.

Hold the mouse cursor over a brush in the Brushes palette or Brush drop-down to view the brush name in a Tool Tip.

Loading Presets

You can load additional brushes into the Brush Presets list. Photoshop comes with several lists, but you can also load your own saved lists or even trade brushes with other Photoshop users. To load a Brush Presets list, use one of the following commands or options from the Brushes palette menu, Brushes drop-down, or Brushes Preset Manager menu:

- To **reset the brushes** to factory fresh, choose Reset Brushes….
- To **load a list of brushes**, choose Load… or click the Load… button.
- To **quickly load a new list** of brushes, choose it.
- To **replace the current brushes** with a new list, choose Replace Brushes….

When loading or replacing, browse to locate a brush file that has the `.abr` extension, and double-click the file. When resetting or doing a quick load, you can choose whether you want to append the default brushes to the current list (at the bottom) or to replace the current list.

PAINTING BEHIND CONTENT

One of the blending modes that is available with painting tools (but not with individual layers) is the Paint Behind mode. In this mode, you can paint in the transparent areas of the layer, but mask solid pixels and blend semitransparent pixels. The upshot is that it will look as if you are painting behind the content already on the layer.

15.5 Painting with the Brush or Pencil

➠ 3.10 Drawing Tools

➠ 14.2 Selecting Colors

➠ Color Section: Blending Modes

Paint a straight line
Shift *click*

Switch from brush to Eyedropper tool (reverts after release)
Option
Alt

Cycle blending modes in tool options bar (with painting tool)
Shift + *or* Shift −

Cycle Brush Presets (with painting tool)
[or]

Choose Opacity (example 7 = 70%)
0 *to* 9

If you are using Airbrush mode, the longer you keep the brush in an area, the more paint builds up.

In the Clear blending mode, you can remove rather than add paint to the canvas (much like an eraser), leaving behind transparent pixels. Brushes in Clear mode do not work on the Background layer.

The most common way to apply colors to the canvas is using the basic Brush tool or the Pencil tool. Really, there is little difference between the two, except that the Brush produces soft anti-aliased edges while the pencil produces hard jagged edges. This means that a few of the edge-based brush options (Airbrush, Wet Edges, and Flow Jitter) are not available to the Pencil. To paint using the Brush or Pencil, follow these steps:

A brush stroke and a pencil stroke. The brush stroke shows jagged edges while the brush stroke is anti-aliased.

1 Select the layer in which you want to paint. Additionally, you can limit the area in the canvas to be painted by making a selection (see Chapter 8).

2 Choose the Brush tool or Pencil tool from the Toolbox.

3 Set your brush options:

- Select a foreground color. You will paint with this color.
- Choose a brush type and set the brush master diameter from the Brushes pull-down or Brush Presets panel in the Brushes palette.
- In the tool options bar, choose a blending mode and set the opacity and flow rate for the color being applied to the canvas.
- If you want to use the Brush tool as an Airbrush, choose that option in either the tool options bar or in the Brushes palette.
- Adjust the brush settings in the Brushes palette (see Section 15.2).

4 Place the mouse cursor in the canvas where you want to begin your stroke and click and drag to paint a stroke. Repeat this step as many times as desired.

15.6 Painting with Patterns

Although it is one of the stamp tools, the Pattern Stamp really works as a paintbrush for applying patterns (instead of colors). To paint using the Pattern Stamp, follow these steps:

➠ 3.11 Stamp Tools

➠ 14.9 Creating Patterns

➠ 14.10 Organizing Pattern Presets

➠ Color Section: Blending Modes

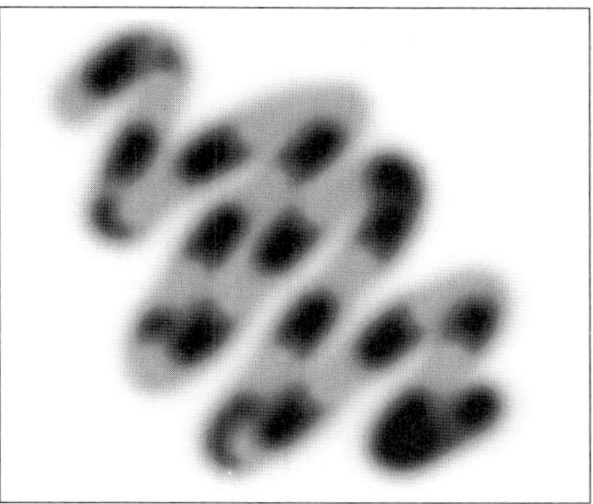

Painting with a pattern: left, with Impressionistic unchecked, and right, with Impressionistic checked.

1 Select the layer in which you want to paint. Additionally, you can limit the area in the canvas to be painted by making a selection.

2 Choose the Pattern Stamp tool from the Toolbox.

3 Set your brush options:

- Select a pattern to paint with in the tool options bar. In addition, specify whether you want the pattern aligned with the top-right corner of the canvas and whether you want to paint in Impressionistic (blurred) mode.
- Choose a brush type and set the brush's diameter from the Brushes pull-down or Brush Presets panel in the Brushes palette.
- In the tool options bar, choose a blending mode and set the opacity and flow rate for the color being applied to the canvas.
- If you want to use the brush as an Airbrush, choose that option in either the tool options bar or the Brushes palette.
- Adjust the brush settings in the Brushes palette.

4 Place the mouse cursor in the canvas where you want to begin your stroke and click and drag to paint a stroke. Repeat this step as many times as desired.

Stamp tool [S]

Cycle Stamp tools
[Shift] [S]

Paint a straight line
[Shift] *click*

Cycle blending modes in tool options bar (with painting tool)
[Shift] [+] *or* [Shift] [−]

Cycle Brush Presets (with painting tool)
[[] *or* []]

Choose Opacity (example 7 = 70%)
[0] *to* [9]

If you are using Airbrush mode, the longer you keep the brush in an area, the more paint builds up.

15.7 Painting with the Art History Brush

➠ 3.12 History Brushes

➠ 4.8 History Palette

➠ 6.9 Changing Your Mind

➠ 14.2 Selecting Colors

History Brush tool [Y]

Cycle History Brush tools
[Shift] [Y]

Paint a straight line
[Shift] *click*

Cycle blending modes in tool options bar (with painting tool)
[Shift] [+] *or* [Shift] [−]

Cycle Brush Presets (with painting tool)
[or]

Choose Opacity (example 7 = 70%)
[0] *to* [9]

To help guide you while painting, make a copy of the layer you are painting in and set its opacity to a low value (such as 25%). Then, fill the original layer with a color and begin painting.

If you are using Airbrush mode, the longer you keep the brush in an area, the more paint builds up.

You use the Art History Brush tool to paint Impressionistic, highly stylized works in the canvas based on previous History states or snapshots. Using the Art History Brush takes some practice to break away from simple swirling shapes, but by combining a variety of paint styles, tolerance options, blending modes, and opacities, you can create works with a much more realistic and organic painting effect than with standard brushes. To use the Art History Brush, follow these steps:

1. Select the History state or snapshot you want to use as the source by clicking in the left column in the History palette. A brush icon appears next to the History state or snapshot.
2. Select the layer in which you want to paint. This layer must have existed in the History state or snapshot you selected in step 1, but can have been drastically changed. Additionally, you can limit the area in the canvas to be painted by making a selection.
3. Choose the Art History Brush tool from the Toolbox.
4. Set your brush options in the Tool Options bar:
   - Choose a brush type and set the brush's master diameter from the Brushes pull-down or Brush Presets panel in the Brushes palette.
   - Choose the painting style you want to use from the Style pull-down menu. This controls the shape of the stroke being used to repaint the layer.
   - Choose a blending mode and set the opacity and flow rate for the paint being applied to the canvas.
   - Set the area to be covered by the strokes. The larger the value, the more strokes added.
   - Set the tolerance, which will limit the color of pixels that strokes are applied to by defining how different the color can be from the first pixel clicked when starting the stroke. Higher values restrict the area in which you can paint.
   - Adjust additional brush settings in the Brushes palette.
5. Place the mouse cursor in the canvas where you want to begin your stroke and click and drag to paint a stroke. Repeat this step as many times as desired.

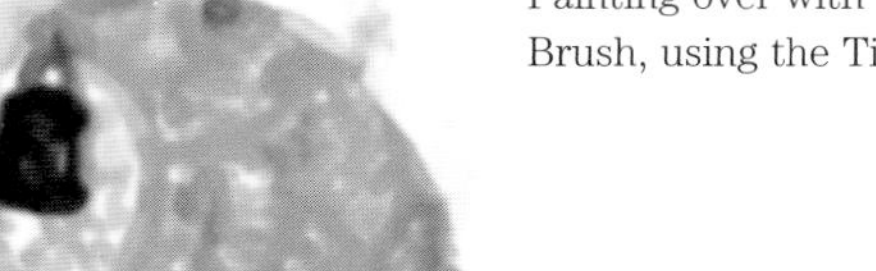

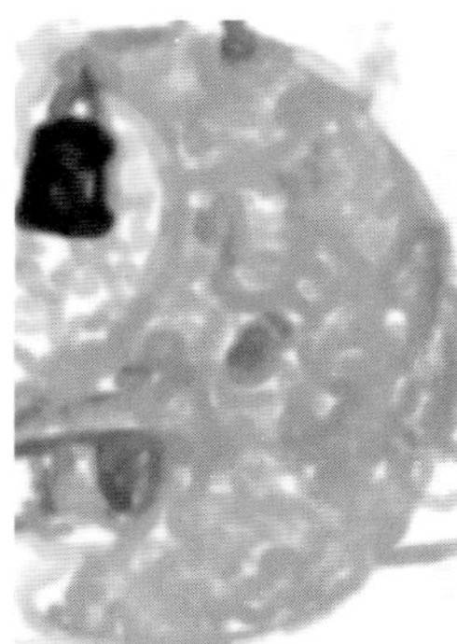

Painting over with the Art History Brush, using the Tight Long style.

15.8 Painting with Shapes

Chapter 12 describes how to draw paths and shape layers using the shape tools. You can also use these tools to create bitmap (painted) shapes rather than path (vector) shapes. The process for preparing to paint a shape into the canvas is outlined in Section 12.6.

➠ 3.20 Shape Tools

➠ 12.4 Setting Shape Tool Options

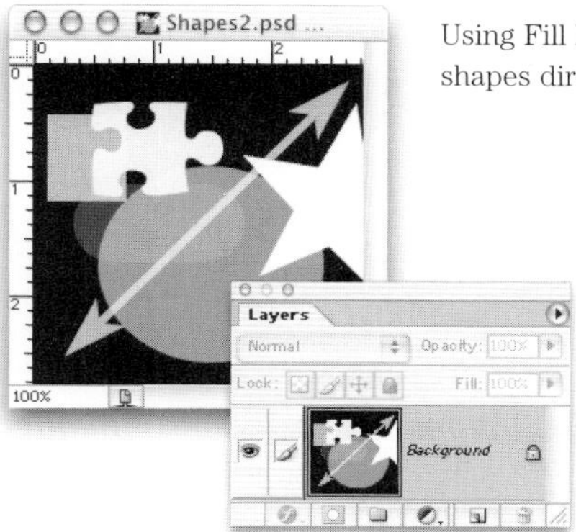

Using Fill Pixels, you can paint shapes directly into layers.

Shape tool U

Cycle shape tools
Shift U

Force proportion while drawing
Shift

Skew and distort shape while drawing
Option
Alt

Cycle blending modes in tool options bar (with shape tool)
Shift + *or* Shift −

Cycle Shape Presets (with Custom Shape tool)
[or]
Choose Opacity (example 7 = 70%)
0 *to* 9

1. Choose a shape tool and click the Fill Pixels button ☐ in the tool options bar.
2. Select a layer in the Layers palette. Additionally, you can limit the area in the canvas to be painted by making a selection.
3. In the tool options bar, set the appropriate shape tool's options, blending mode, and opacity, and check Anti-Aliased to smooth the edges of the shape.
4. Click and drag to draw the shape. Release the mouse button when the shape is the desired size.

USING PAINTING TOOL PRESETS

You can use the Tool Presets with virtually any tool in the Tool Box, but they are especially useful with painting tools. Brush Presets only save the brush options, which can then be used with any of the painting tools except for the Healing Brush and Background Eraser. The Tool Presets allow you to associate a brush with a particular painting tool and save that as a preset. See Section 4.10 for more details on Tool Presets.

15.9 Erasing

➠ 3.2 The Tool Options Bar

➠ 3.13 Eraser Tools

➠ 28.5 Extracting Parts of the Image

Eraser tool E

Cycle eraser tools Shift E

Remove content in selection Del

Switch to Eraser from Erase To History (reverts after release) Option Alt

Destruction is always a part of creation. One of the most common ways to delete content in Photoshop is to simply make a selection and press the Delete (Mac) or Backspace (Windows) key. However, you can also remove content using the brush strokes using the Eraser tool. In addition, Photoshop provides two sophisticated eraser tools that allow you to selectively erase a background or a particular color range in an image.

Using the Eraser tool in an image removes paint with the brush rather than adding it

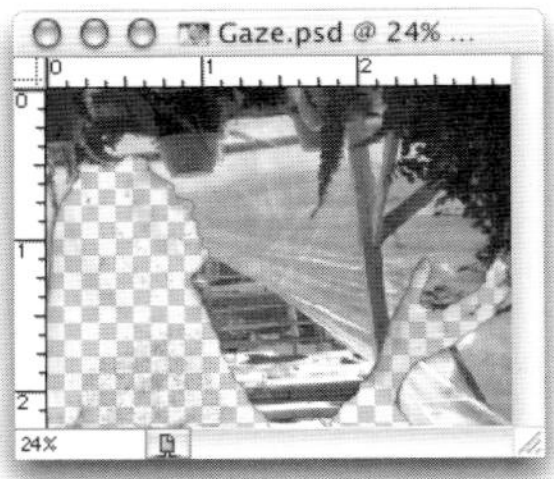

Use the Background Eraser to erase areas of similar but inconsistent color on the canvas—in this case, the foreground figure.

The light-gray plastic tarp is erased with the Magic Eraser.

Using the Eraser

The Eraser tool simply removes any pixels that get in its way. It uses a brush, pencil, or block to paint away unwanted parts of an image.

1. Select the layer from which you want to erase content. Additionally, you can limit the area in the canvas to be erased by making a selection.
2. Choose the Eraser tool from the Toolbox.
3. Set your eraser options in the Tool Options bar:
   - Choose the Eraser mode from the Mode pull-down: Brush (brush with soft edges), Pencil (brush with hard edges), or Block (rectangle with hard edges).
   - If you are using Brush or Pencil mode, choose a brush type and set the brush master diameter from the Brushes pull-down, set the opacity to specify the strength of the erasure (100% completely erases pixels).
   - If you are using Brush mode, set the flow rate. If you want to use the eraser as an Airbrush, choose that option in either the tool options bar or the Brushes palette.
   - If you want to erase the layer back to a previous History state or snapshot, select the History state or snapshot you want to use as the source by clicking in the left column in the History palette. A History Brush icon appears next to the History state or snapshot. If the selected state or snapshot has an analogous layer in the current image, you can then check the Erase To History option and continue.
   - Adjust the brush settings as desired in the Brushes palette.

15.9 Erasing *(Continued)*

4 Place the mouse cursor in the canvas where you want to begin erasing and click and drag. The content along the stroke will be removed either completely (if opacity is 100%) or partially, and the area will now be fully or partially transparent. Repeat this step as many times as desired.

Erasing the Background

You use the Background Eraser to remove part of an image while leaving other parts unaffected, by specifying a base color to be erased and then a tolerance of similar colors that can be erased. The tool samples the color at the center of the brush and uses that as the base color to determine whether other colors should be erased as the brush is moved across the canvas. One important difference between the Background Eraser and other painting tools is that it does not use the Brushes palette, instead using a simplified brush picker that allows only circular and elliptical brushes.

1 Select the layer from which you want to erase content. Additionally, you can limit the area in the canvas to be erased by making a selection.

2 Choose the Background Eraser tool from the Toolbox.

3 Set the eraser options in the tool options bar:

- Use the brush picker to specify the diameter, hardness, spacing, angle, roundness, and dynamic controls.
- Set the erasure limits: Discontiguous (anywhere on canvas), Contiguous (must be in touch with the first pixel erased), Find Edges (must be a high-contrast boundary).
- Set the tolerance, which will limit the pixels that are erased based on their difference from the sampled base color. Higher values restrict the area you can erase.
- Check Protect Foreground Color to protect the selected foreground color from being erased.
- Set the color sampling method for use to determine the base color to be erased: Once to sample the first pixel erased as the base color; Continuous to resample every pixel as the base color; Background Swatch to use the selected background color as the base color.

4 Place the mouse cursor in the canvas where you want to begin erasing and click and drag. The content along the stroke will be removed. The color at the center of the brush will be used as the sampled base color if you choose the Once or Continuous sampling method. Repeat this step as many times as desired.

The Background layer will not erase to transparent. Instead, erasing on the Background layer erases to the selected background color.

Another way to erase is to use the Brush, Pencil, or Paint Bucket tools in the Clear blending mode. Rather than applying paint, the Clear mode removes paint from the canvas, leaving behind transparent pixels. Brushes in Clear mode do not work on the Background layer.

Another way to extract complex shapes such as smoke and hair from a background is to use the Extract command (see Section 28.9).

Using the Magic Eraser in Continuous method can slow down your machine.

Don't forget that the Eraser tool in Brush mode can have all the same brush options as any brush, allowing you to do things such as erase with noise or erase with a texture.

A nondestructive way to "erase" parts of an image without actually removing the content is to use Masks (see Chapter 11).

The Background eraser overrides the transparent lock set for any layers.

Using the Background and Magic erasers can produce some gritty weathered effects.

Erasing a Color with the Magic Eraser

If you need to quickly erase a color from the image, the Magic Eraser is the tool for you. By simply clicking a pixel, you can remove all pixels of that or similar colors. To use the Magic Eraser, follow these steps:

1. Select the layer from which you want to erase content. You can limit the area in the canvas to be erased by making a selection). The Magic Eraser is one of the few tools that also allows you to work in all layers simultaneously.
2. Choose the Magic Eraser tool from the Toolbox.
3. Set the Magic Eraser options in the tool options bar:
   - Set the tolerance, which will limit the pixels that are erased based on their difference from the base color. Higher values restrict the area you can erase.
   - Check Anti-Aliasing to produce smoother edges in the erasure.
   - Check Contiguous if you want erased pixels to be in touch with the first pixel erased.
   - Check Use All Layers to sample the base color from any visible layer.
   - Set the opacity in the tool options bar to specify the strength of the erasure; 100% completely erases pixels.
4. Place the mouse cursor in the canvas over the color you want to erase and click. The color at the center of the cursor will be used as the sampled base color, and all colors within tolerance of this color will be erased. Repeat this step as many times as desired.

PAINTING TOOL CURSORS AND BRUSH TIPS

When you apply a stroke to the canvas using one of the painting tools, the cursor you see depends on the option you selected for the Display & Cursor Preferences (see Section 5.5). Your best option is to view the Brush Size3. This not only displays the brush at the size at which it will create a stroke, but also shows an outline of the exact brush tip, allowing you to preview how the stroke will appear.

CHAPTER 16

Painting with Filters

YOU USE FILTERS TO QUICKLY APPLY stylized special effects directly to an image. Unlike layer styles, which are vector-based and can thus be hidden and shown at will, filters are bitmap-based and directly affect the layer to which they are applied. Although this makes editing and making changes more difficult, pixel-based effects like these provide endless options for manipulating an image. In addition, you can use filters to manipulate the canvas as if it were a three-dimensional object or to add realistic lighting effects.

This chapter introduces you to filters, but see the "Filters" section of the color insert for a complete set of examples of all Photoshop filters. The following topics are covered here:

16.1 Filter Basics

➠ 2.8 Filter Menu

➠ 13.12 Setting Posterize and Threshold Levels

➠ 14.12 Using the Pattern Maker

➠ 27.7 Smudging and Liquifying Images

➠ Color Section: Filters

Move to next input field Tab

Because filters irrevocably change the content of a layer (although you can undo or use the History palette to go back), you might want to duplicate the layer before applying the filter and then hide the duplicated layer.

Several options in the Filter menu (Pattern Maker, Liquify, and Extract) do not work like other filters and are presented in relevant chapters throughout the book.

Most filters use similar input boxes, although they do not always use the same values. Many of these input boxes are self-explanatory and simply require you to experiment with specific settings to achieve the effects you want. If you are stuck on exactly what a particular input option is for, you can refer to the following list for a brief description of each.

Photoshop Filter Settings

SETTING	DESCRIPTION
Amount	Sets how strongly the filter should be applied.
Angle	Sets the angle at which or to which the effect is applied.
Background Level	Adjusts shadow contrast.
Balance, Direction Balance	Sets the direction of simulated strokes. Lower values set all strokes from left to right. Higher values set all strokes from right to left. Medium values mix stroke directions.
Brightness	Sets the color brightness. Larger values increase the brightens of colors in the image.
Brush Size	Sets the simulated thickness of the brush used for a stroke.
Cell Size	Sets the maximum length of a facet.
Chalk Area	Sets the amount of chalk (white) to use. Higher numbers add more white.
Charcoal Area	Sets the amount of charcoal (gray) to use. Lower numbers add more gray.
Contrast	Sets the contrast between highlights and shadows.
Dark Intensity, Darkness	Increases the amount of shading.
Definition	Increases highlight and shadow contrast.
Density	Sets the number of dots in a given area of the canvas.
Detail, Brush Detail, Stroke Detail	Sets the number of pixels used from the original image to create effect.
Distance	Sets how far to apply the filter effect from pixels in the image.
Distortion	Sets the size of distorted areas.
Edge	Select Lower to trace outlines of colors below the specified level. Select Upper to trace outlines of colors above the specified level.
Edge Brightness	Increases the brightness of edges. Higher numbers are brighter.
Edge Fidelity	Sets the detail used for object edges. Higher values produce more abstract results.
Edge Intensity	Increases contrast at object edges.
Edge Simplicity	Sets the abstraction used for object edges. Higher values produce more Cubist results.
Edge Thickness	Sets the amount of the edge to be used in the effect.
Edge Width	Sets the width of the outer edge of objects affected.
Fiber Length	Sets the size of the simulated fiber in the paper.
Foreground Level	Adjusts highlight contrast.
Glow Brightness	Adjusts the contrast between highlights and shadows.
Glow Color	Click a color square to open the Color Picker and select a color to use.
Glow Size	Sets the amount of glow. Positive values invert the image while applying the glow.
Grain, Graininess	Sets the amount of static-like noise used in a given area of the canvas for the effect.
Height	Sets the displacement of the effect to simulate height.

Continues

16.1 Filter Basics *(Continued)*

Photoshop Filter Settings *(Continued)*

SETTING	DESCRIPTION
Highlight Area, Highlight Strength	Increases the brightness of highlights.
Image Balance	Sets the cutoff level between black and white pixels.
Intensity, Black Intensity, White Intensity, Light Intensity	Increases contrast in the effect. The intensity favors the indicated level (black, white, light, or shadow).
Level	Sets the RGB color levels (0 to 255) to use in the effect.
Light/Dark Balance	Sets the cutoff level between dark and light pixels.
Magnitude	Sets the frequency of ripples.
No. Levels	Sets the number of posterization levels.
Paper Brightness	Sets the brightness of background areas that show through the effect.
Pencil Width	Sets the width of the simulated brush.
Posterization	Sets the number of posterization levels (see Section 13.12).
Radius	Enter how far the filter searches for differences among pixels.
Ridges	Sets the number of wave crests.
Ripple Size	Sets the height of a ripple crest.
Shadow Intensity	Decreases brightness of shadows.
Sharpness	Increases the contrast between edges.
Smoothness	Smooths transitions between shadows and highlights.
Softness	Softens the tone of an image.
Spray Radius	Sets the amount of spattering in the image.
Strength	Sets the contrast between strokes.
Stroke Length	Sets the length of a simulated stroke.
Stroke Pressure	Sets the simulated pressure used in a stroke. Higher values create darker strokes.
Stroke Size	Sets the simulated size of the palette knife.
Texture	Sets the roughness of object edges.
Texture Coverage	Controls the amount of texture visible at object edges.
Threshold	Sets the cutoff point for pixels to be used with the filter.

16.2 Applying Filters

➠ 8.2 Selecting a Layer or Its Contents

➠ 29.3 Using Video Filters (NTSC Only)

➠ Color Section: Filters

Reapply last filter using same settings
⌘ F
Ctrl F

Reapply last filter using dialog
⌘ Option F
Ctrl Alt F

Fade filter (after filter is applied)
⌘ Shift F
Ctrl Shift F

Move to next input field
Tab

Despite their great image-editing power, filters are relatively easy to apply. To apply a filter, follow these steps:

1 Select the layer to which you want to apply the filter (see Section 8.2). You can also make a specific selection on that layer to confine the effects of the filter.

2 Choose Filter, select one of the filter type submenus, and then the exact filter you want to apply. Selecting a filter that is followed by an ellipsis (...) opens the filter's dialog (continue to Step 3). Other filters are applied immediately and you are finished.

3 Set the options for the filter. Every filter has unique settings, but you set most options using an input box with a slider, drop-downs, or radio buttons. For more details about the various filter settings, see Section 16.1.

4 After you set the options, click OK.

The filter is applied to the selected layer, but applying some filters might take a while. If this operation will take more than a few seconds, Photoshop displays a progress bar.

Before and after applying the Filter > Stylize > Trace Contour filter

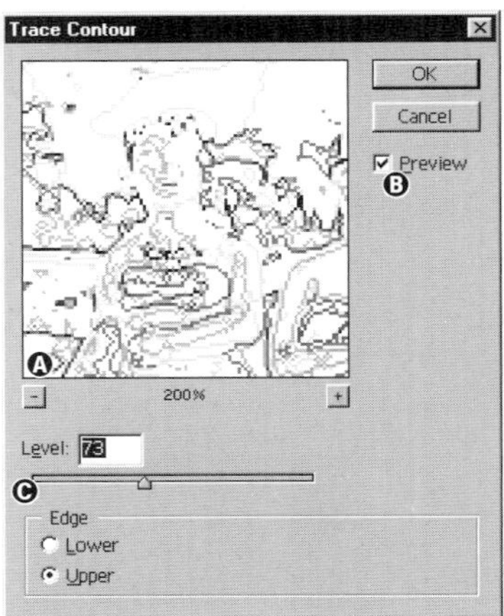

A Image preview Most filter dialogs include a preview of how the image will look like at 100% magnification after the filter is applied. You can increase the magnification by clicking the Plus + or Minus − button. You can also click and drag in the preview to move the visible area.

B Check to show the effects of the filter in the canvas. This option is not available for all filters.

C Input options You set most filter options using an input field and/or a slider. You can also set options using drop-downs, radio buttons, and check boxes.

16.2 Applying Filters *(Continued)*

Texturizing Filters

Several filters let you apply a texture while applying the effect of the filter, basically combining the Texturizer filter with the other filter. These filters include, for example, Underpainting, Conté Crayon, Displace, Glass, and Rough Pastel. This allows you to select a texture style from a list of presets or to load another texture or even another image as a texture. The texture works by simulating ripples in the image so that certain areas appear raised and lighter. If available, you will see the Texturizer controls (Filter > Texture > Texturizer) at the bottom of the filters dialog.

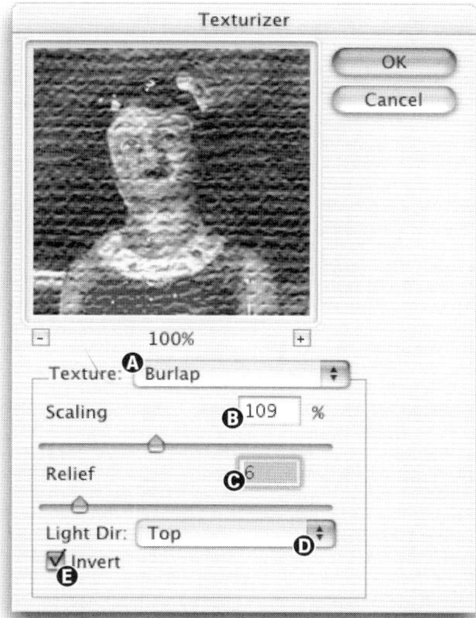

A Choose the texture type. You can also choose to load a saved texture, which can be any Photoshop native file (`.psd`).

B Use the slider or enter a percentage value (50 to 200) for the scale of the texture leaving the original image unchanged. Since textures are bitmapped, the default interpolation method is used to resize it.

C Use the slider or enter a value (0 to 50) for the contrast between raised and lowered areas of the texture. The higher the contrast, the more the original image is obscured.

D Choose a direction for the simulated lighting applied to the texture.

E Check to invert the texture. (Raised areas become lower areas.)

The most recent filter actually applied appears as the top option in the Filters menu. If you start to use a filter, but cancel before the effect is applied, that filter will not show up as the most recent filter.

You can fade the effect by choosing Edit > Fade and then setting the fade opacity and blending mode.

Sketch filters use the foreground and background colors to create their effects.

FINDING MORE FILTERS

Adobe provides dozens of filters with Photoshop, but third parties are making hundreds more. These third parties range from individual programmers hacking away to large corporations such as Procreate, which makes the popular KPT filter set (`www.procreate.com`). For more details on downloading free and low-cost filters, check out the Adobe website (`www.adobe.com/products/plugins/photoshop/`) or Plugins.com (`www.plugins.com/photoshop/`). You can also make your own plug-ins by downloading the Photoshop 7.0 Scripting plug-in (`www.adobe.com/support/downloads/`).

One important note: Filters cannot be moved between versions of Photoshop running in different operating systems. Not only can you not transfer between Windows and Macintosh, but you cannot transfer between Mac OS 9 and Mac OS X.

16.3 Sharpening and Blurring Images

➠ 27.6 Blurring and Sharpening with Tools

➠ Color Section: Filters

Move to next input field
Tab

Be sure to deselect the Preserve Transparency option in the Layers palette if you want to apply the blur filter to the edges of a layer.

Unsharp Mask has a far more prominent effect on the screen version of an image than on the printed version. It is best to print the image to check the settings.

Two of the most common uses of filters are to sharpen and blur an image. To blur or sharpen, select the layer to which you want to apply the filter, and then do one of the following:

Here's the original image.

To **blur** an image, choose Filter > Blur > Blur. To increase the blur, repeat as many times as desired. To increase the amount of blur, choose Filter > Blur > Blur More. This image is blurred 20 times.

To apply a **Gaussian blur**, choose Filter > Blur > Gaussian Blur, set the radius (the higher the value, the more pronounced the blur), and then click OK. This creates a softer looking blur, something like holding up a sheet of frosted glass. Here, the Radius used was 10.

To apply a **motion blur**, choose Filter > Blur > Motion Blur, set the simulated angle and distance for the blur, and click OK. This creates the illusion that the image was photographed in a quick linear motion. For example, the picture is of a fast-moving object, or the photographer was moving quickly. Settings for the blur shown here were Angle = 23°, Distance = 135px.

To apply a **radial blur**, Choose Filter > Blur > Radial Blur, set the blur method as either Spin or Zoom (out from all points; shown here with Amount = 45), click in the thumbnail to set the blur center point, choose the rendering quality and the amount of blur to use, and click OK. This can have the effect of either blurring the image around a center point (Spin) or stretching out from each point (Zoom).

To **sharpen** the image, choose Filter > Sharpen > Sharpen. To increase the sharpness, repeat as many times as desired; the image here was sharpened three times. To increase the amount of sharpness, choose Filter > Sharpen > Sharpen More.

16.3 Sharpening and Blurring Images *(Continued)*

To **sharpen the edges** of an image, choose Filter > Sharpen > Sharpen Edges. This affects only high-contrast edges in the image, leaving areas of solid color only. This image was sharpened four times.

Using Unsharp Mask

The Unsharp Mask filter provides you with more exacting control over how edges in the image are sharpened. It is especially useful when you need to correct blurring problems associated with photographing, scanning, resampling, and printing. Unsharp Mask works by differentiating pixels using the threshold value set and the specific amount set to increase pixel contrast. To use Unsharp Mask, select the layer or part of a layer to which you want to apply the filter, choose Filter > Sharpen > Unsharp Mask, set the options, and click OK.

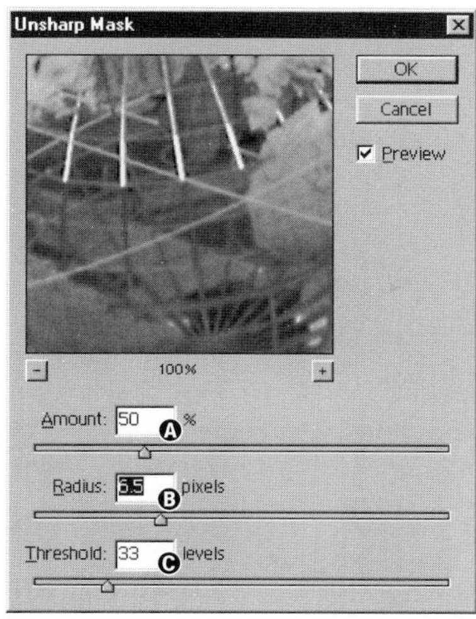

A Use the slider or enter a percentage value (1 to 500) to set how much to increase the contrast of the pixels within the threshold. For high-resolution images, an increase of 150% to 200% is generally prescribed.

B Use the slider or enter a value (0.1 to 250.0) to set the number of pixels surrounding the high-contrast edges in the image that should be sharpened. Remember, the higher the resolution of the image, the larger this number will need to be to show a noticeable effect.

C Use the slider or enter a value (0 to 255) to set the contrast the sharpened pixels need to have from surrounding pixels before they are considered edge pixels and are sharpened. You will need to experiment with your image to find the best value, but high-contrast images generally require lower values.

If you want to apply the Blur filter to the edge of a layer's content, make sure the Preserve Transparency is turned off in the Layers palette.

You can also selectively blur or sharpen areas of the image using the Blur and Sharpen tool (see Section 27.6).

Before the Drop Shadow effect was added to Photoshop, drop shadows were created by duplicating the layer, filling it with black, moving it behind the original version, and adding a Gaussian Blur.

Using Smart Blur

The Smart Blur filter provides you with more exacting control over the amount the image is blurred at one time. To use this filter, select the layer or part of a layer to which you want to apply the filter, choose Filter > Blur > Smart Blur, set the options, and click OK.

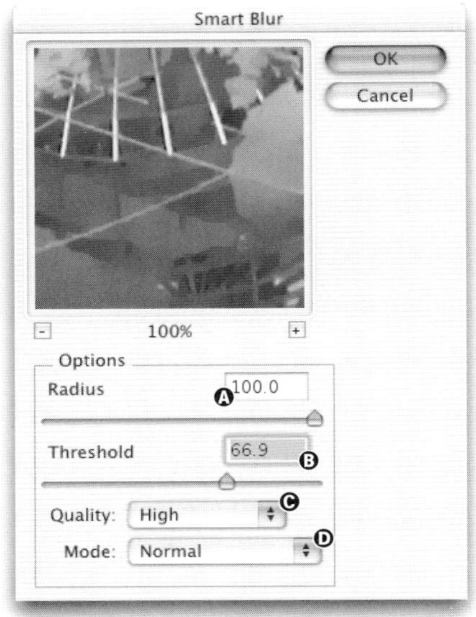

- **A** Use the slider or enter a value (0.1 to 100.0) to set how far the filter searches for dissimilar pixels.
- **B** Use the slider or enter a value (0.1 to 100.0) to set how different pixels should be to be blurred together. The higher the number, the more pronounced the blur will appear.
- **C** Choose the render quality of the blur filter. High is recommended.
- **D** Choose Normal mode (blur), Edge Only (shows edges as white and the rest of the image as black), or Overlay Edge (shows edges as white).

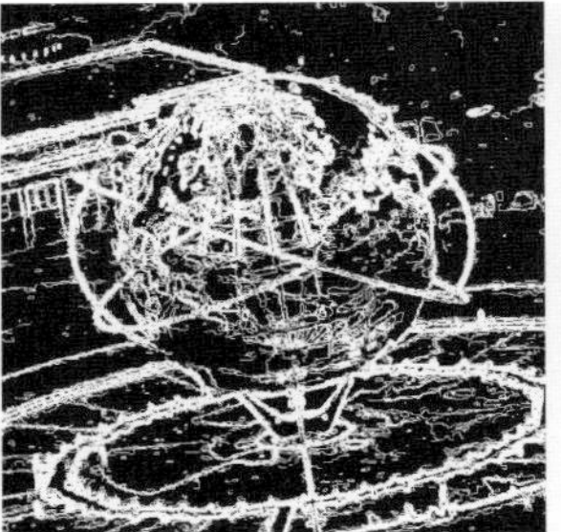
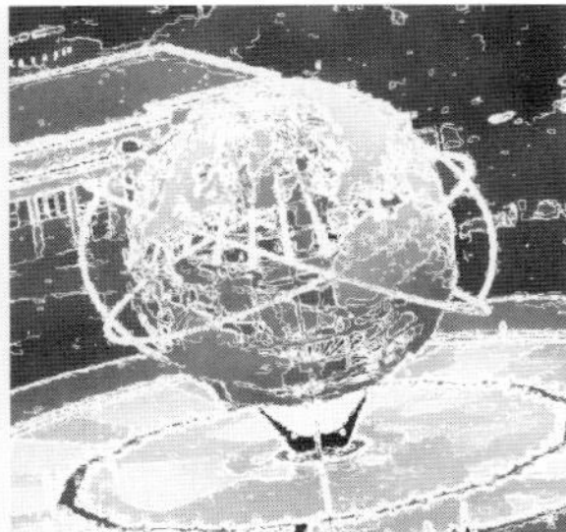

Smart Blur modes, from left to right: Normal, Edge Only, Overlay Edge

16.4 Transforming Images in 3-D

Although it will never rival the software used to create *Toy Story,* Photoshop's 3-D rendering tool lets you select an area of the image and then resize or rotate the object as if it were a three-dimensional object.

➠ 12.1 Path Basics

➠ 12.11 Reshaping Curves

➠ Color Section: Filters

Marquee Tool M

Zoom Tool Z

Hand Tool H

1. Select the layer to which you want to apply the filter. You can also make a specific selection on that layer to confine the effects of the filter.
2. Choose Filter > Render > 3-D Transform.
3. Draw shapes in the work area using the 3-D Shape tools. The 3D Transform dialog works as its own mini-interface, complete with its own toolbar on the left. Add 2-D path-based shapes to define the shapes you will then be manipulating in three dimensions.
4. After you create the desired shape, manipulate it in 3-D using the Pan and Rotate tools and the Field Of View or Dolly settings. This creates a copy of the content in the area within the path for you to manipulate.
5. When you are happy with the changes, click OK to render the 3-D shape onto the selected layer in the canvas.

The 2-D globe has been spun in 3-D.

16.4 Transforming Images in 3-D *(Continued)*

If there is not enough information to create the full shape while you are rotating, Photoshop places a simple grayscale shade on empty areas.

If the wire frame turns red as you are adjusting it, it cannot be rendered.

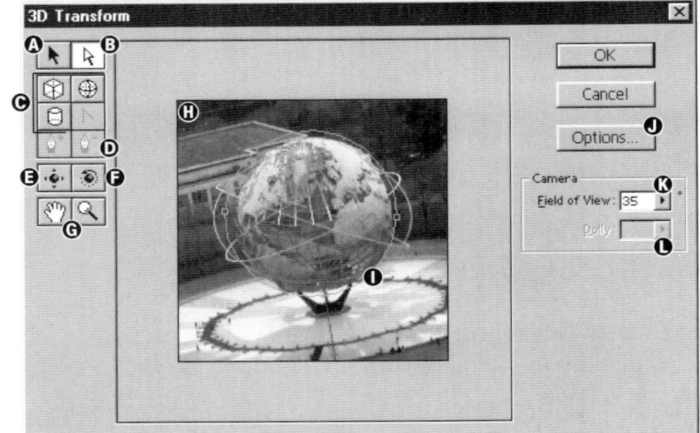

A Selection tool Choose to select and move individual wire frames. Select a wire frame and press Delete/Backspace to remove it.

B Direct Selection tool Choose to move an individual wire frame or to change its shape by clicking and adjusting anchor points.

C 3-D Shape tools Choose between a cube, a sphere, and cylinder shapes, and then draw the shapes as wire frames in the work area (see I).

D Point tools (Require Cylinder shape in the work area) Similar to Path tools, these tools allow you to convert an anchor point between curved and corner, add an anchor point, or subtract an anchor point from the sides of a cylinder wire frame.

E Pan tool Drag wire frames to move their contents.

F Rotate tool Drag around the wire frames to rotate their contents.

G Hand and Zoom tool Drag in the work area to move the viewable area of the canvas or magnify areas of the image.

H Work area Previews the image in grayscale. Draw and manipulate your 3-D wire frames here.

I Wire Frame A globe wire frame is currently selected in the work area. Drag the outer edge with the Selection tool (see A) to move it; drag the handlebars with the Direct Selection tool (see B) to resize it. Use the Pan tool (see E), Rotate tool (see F), Field Of View setting (see K), or Dolly setting (see L) to manipulate the area of the image selected by the wire frame in 3-D.

J Click to open an options dialog in which you can set the resolution of rendered objects, the level of anti-aliasing used, and whether you want the original image displayed in the work area while you are manipulating the 3-D object.

K Use the slider or enter a degree value (0 to 130) for the field of view. Larger values reduce the size of the 3-D object.

L Use the slider or enter a value (0 to 99) for the dolly (closeness) to the 3-D object. Larger values reduce the size of the object.

16.5 Adding Lighting Effects

You use the Lighting Effects filter to add simulated light sources that appear to shine on the flat surface of your image. You can place as many as 16 independent light sources, and you can control the circumference, direction, focal distance, focus, intensity, and color of each separately. To add lighting effects, follow these steps:

1. Select the layer to which you want to apply the filter. You can also make a specific selection on that layer to confine the effects of the filter.
2. Choose Filter > Render > Lighting Effects.
3. Add lights to the work area and adjust the circumference, distance, and/or direction of the light as well as the intensity, focus (for spotlights), and color of the light. In addition, adjust the properties of the simulated surface to which the light is being applied.
4. When you are satisfied, click OK to render the lighting effect onto the selected layer in the canvas.

➠ 14.3 Selecting Colors with the Color Picker

➠ 14.11 Applying Patterns

➠ Color Section: Filters

Rendering lighting effects can soak up a lot of memory. If you are using Mac OS 9, allocate at least 75 MB to Photoshop, or you might get errors.

To duplicate a light source, Option-drag (Mac) or Alt-drag (Windows) it to the new location.

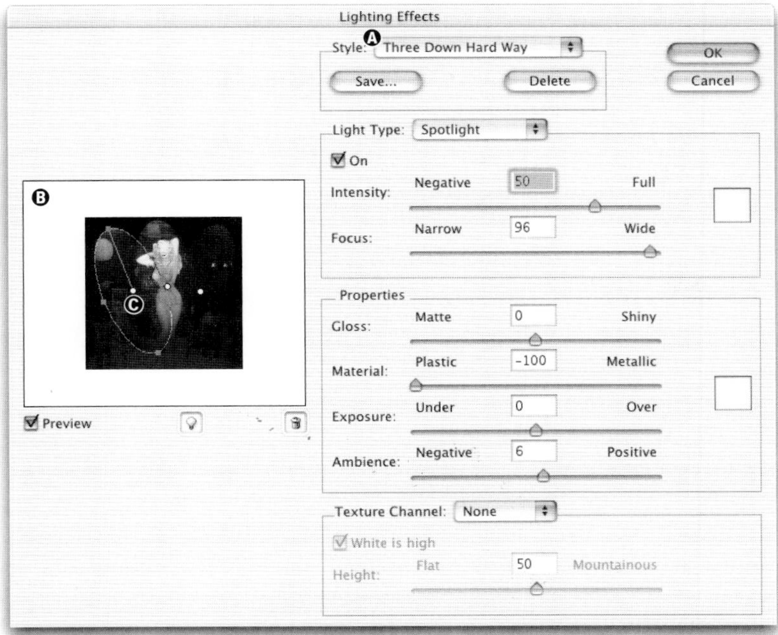

A Preset Styles Select from an extensive list of preset lighting effects. You can also save the current settings to this list or delete the current settings from the list (see G–K).

B Work Area Shows a thumbnail version of what the image will look like with the lighting effects. You will also be moving and manipulating lights in this area.

C Selected Light The round dots indicate light focal points. Click to select the light and make changes (see G–K). Click and drag to move. The currently selected light shows the circumference, direction, and/or distance of the light depending on the selected light type (see G). Click a square gray anchor point to adjust the circumference, distance, or direction of the light.

Every time you start Photoshop, it loads all the available filters. You might want to remove some filters and store them in another folder to speed up your Photoshop startup. To do this, simply drag filter files from the designated plug-in folder (most likely Photoshop/Plug-Ins/Filter) and place them in a folder not used for plug-ins. You might want to call this folder something like Plug-Ins (Disabled).

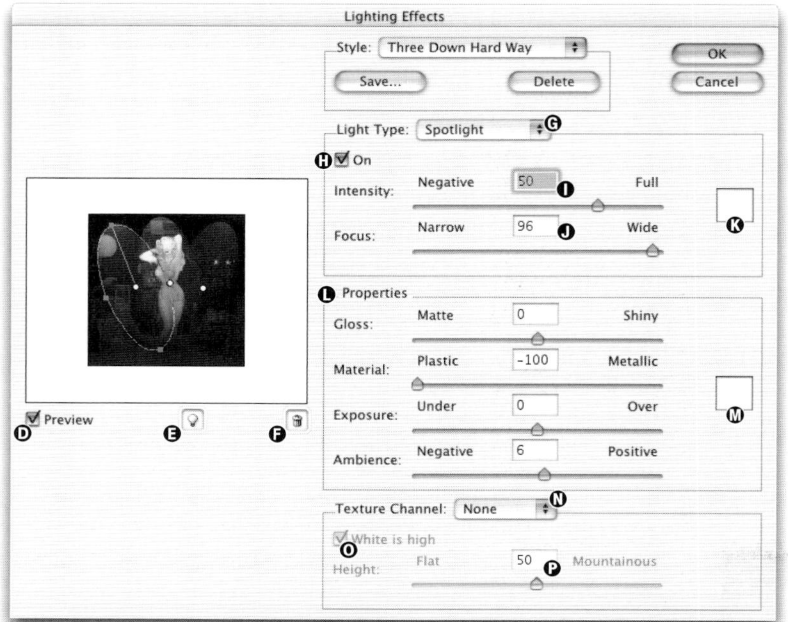

Ⓓ Check to preview the lighting effects in the work area. This will *not* preview the lighting effect in the canvas.

Ⓔ **Add Light** Click and drag into the work area to add a new light source.

Ⓕ **Delete Light** Click and drag a light from the work area to this icon to delete.

Ⓖ Choose the light type for the currently selected light in the work area (see C).

Ⓗ Check to turn the selected light on and off.

Ⓘ Use the slider or enter a value (–99 to 100) for the intensity of the selected light. Negative values use the complementary color for the light.

Ⓙ (Spotlight only) Use the slider or enter a value (–99 to 100) for the focus of the selected light if it is a spotlight. Negative values use the complementary color for the light.

Ⓚ Click and use the Color Picker to choose the color for the selected light.

Ⓛ Use the slider or enter a value (–99 to 100) for the Gloss (how reflective), Material (the simulated surface substance), or Exposure (the amount of light added) or for how much ambient light is in the image being affected by the light.

Ⓜ Click and use the Color Picker to choose the color for the ambient light in the image.

Ⓝ Choose a color channel (Red, Green, Blue) to use to create a texture in the image.

Ⓞ Check to use lighter color as the high areas in the texture.

Ⓟ Use the slider or enter a value (0 to 100) to define the texture relief. Lower numbers produce a flatter texture.

16.5 Adding Lighting Effects *(Continued)*

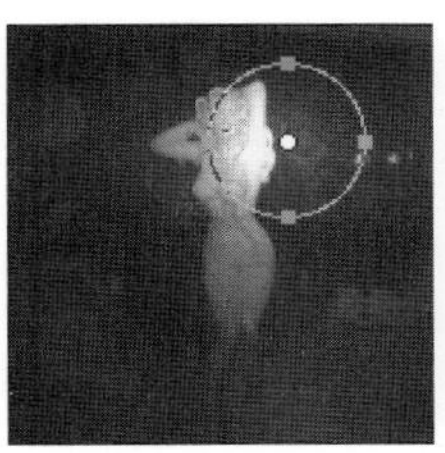
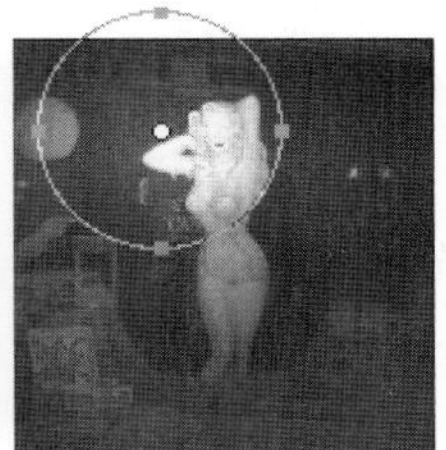

Omni lights have a circular circumference, which can be resized, but do not have direction or distance.

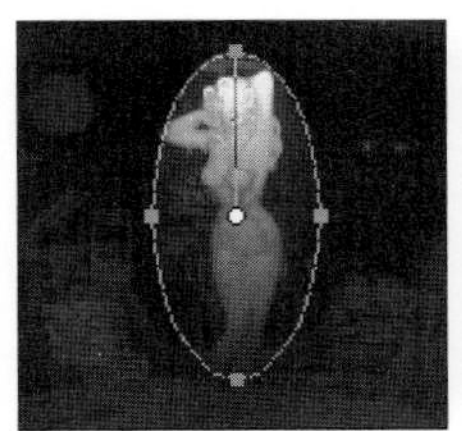
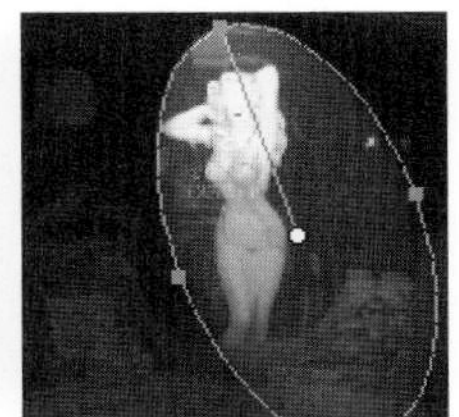

Spotlights have an elliptical circumference, distance, and direction that can be reshaped, resized, and redirected.

Directional lights have a direction and distance, which can be redirected and resized, but do not have circumference.

ADDING NEW PLUG-INS AND FILTERS TO PHOTOSHOP

Photoshop allows you to add a variety of other plug-in files to the interface by adding them to the Photoshop/Plug-Ins folder. Plug-ins can be found to allow you to add formats that images can be opened or saved as, for scanning or importing, and for saving displacement maps for textures.

Filters are a type of plug-in used by Photoshop. Installing new filters is as easy as dragging the filter file into one of your designated plug-in folders (see Section 5.9)—most likely the Photoshop/Plug-Ins/Filters folder—and then restarting Photoshop.

CHAPTER 17

Typography

WHAT YOU SAY IS NOT ALWAYS as important as how you say it. With the written word, *text* refers to the actual words (what you are saying) and *typography* refers to the way in which those words are presented (how you are saying it). There is no such thing as text without typography, and the term *type* is generally used to refer to formatted text. Even if you use the plainest, simplest fonts, you are still speaking through the presentation of the text. That said, typography is often used simply to add decoration in an image, especially in images created using Photoshop, in which the meaning of the text is obscured or even irrelevant.

In this chapter, you will learn how to add and edit text to an image and how to use the tools in Photoshop to turn plain text into formatted type.

17.1 Type Basics

➠ 3.18 Type Tools

➠ 4.16 Character Palette

➠ 4.17 Paragraph Palette

The fonts that Photoshop has at its disposal will depend on the fonts installed on your computer. If you need to add a font to Photoshop, first add it to the fonts of your operating system and then restart Photoshop.

When Photoshop starts up, it loads all currently available fonts on your system. If you have a lot of fonts, start-up can take a while. Programs such as Extensis Suitcase (`www.extensis.com/fontman/`) can help you manage your fonts more efficiently.

If you know the name of the font you want to use, you can type it directly in the Font Name field. As you type, Photoshop tries to match the font name.

Type is structured, and an individual character can be broken down and described by component parts to help better understand how letters are displayed and interact with one another. Although you can simply pour text into a Photoshop image, giving no thought to the typography, this rarely leads to pleasing results. This chapter doesn't try to provide a complete introduction to the topic of text and type, but you need to know a few terms to better format your text in Photoshop to communicate effectively.

A *font* or, in Photoshop, *font family* is a complete set of characters in a particular design, usually including uppercase and lowercase letter, numerals, punctuation, and perhaps some symbols.

Many fonts also contain several *styles*—variations that make the text **bolder**, lighter, or *italic* or in other ways change the form of characters. These styles are actually independent versions of the font that the font maker created.

In word-processing programs, you can usually boldface or italicize any font regardless of whether that style was created for the font; such on-the-fly changes are called "faux styles." The Character palette provides Faux Bold or Faux Italic styles for fonts without available styles, but these options are not recommended.

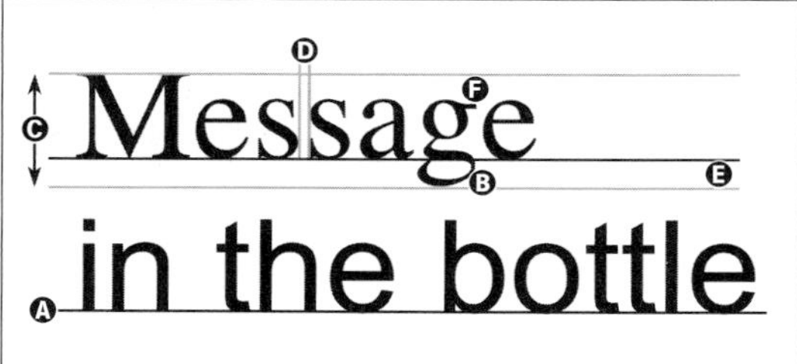

A Baseline The imaginary line connecting the lowest point of all capital letters.

B Descender The part of a letter that extends below the baseline.

C Type size The distance from the highest point of the capital letters to the lowest point of letters that have descenders.

D Tracking/kerning Adjustments to the amount of space between letters. Tracking refers to the general change in spacing on both sides of one or more letters. Kerning refers to the adjustment of space between two specific letters. For example, if you feel two letters in your text are too crowded, you would want to increase the kerning. If letters are generally too far apart, decrease the tracking.

E Leading The distance from one baseline to the next.

F Serif A small ornamentation on a character. Fonts without serifs, such as in the second line here, are called *sans serif*.

17.1 Type Basics *(Continued)*

Type size is the measure from the top of the ascenders to the bottom of the descenders. For the most part, fonts are measured in *points* (abbreviated pt), and that is the default for Photoshop. You can enter font values in several other measurement systems (enter the value and then the unit abbreviation), and Photoshop translates this measurement into point size. The alternative units are centimeters (cm), inches (in), millimeters (mm), picas (pica), and pixels (px).

Anti-Aliasing

As with other bitmap graphics, *anti-aliasing* type smoothes the edges of the letters by adding semi-transparent pixels at their edges. Using this technique increases the apparent resolution of the type on the screen and does not affect the printed appearance of the type. Resolution is especially important if you are creating graphics to be displayed on television or the Web, and anti-aliasing generally creates a much more professional and readable text especially at text sizes over 12pt. However, unlike bitmap graphics, you can choose from five anti-aliasing methods:

The original letter with no anti-aliasing

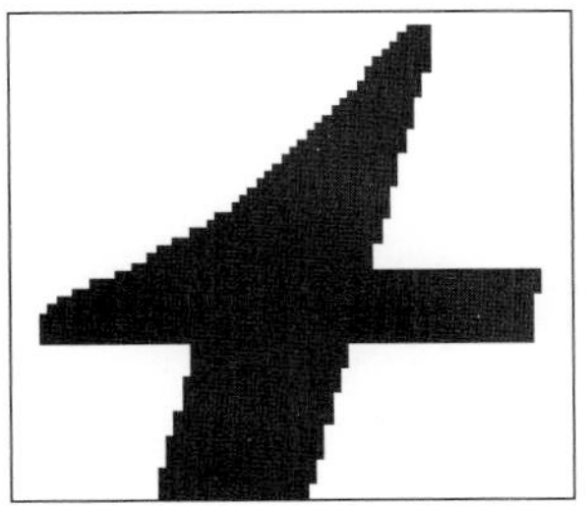

None: No anti-aliasing is used. Letterform edges appear jagged.

Sharp: Produces darker heavy type with slight anti-aliasing. Best for large sans serif fonts.

Crisp: Produces lighter type with slight anti-aliasing. Best for small sans serif fonts.

Strong: Produces heavy type with heavy anti-aliasing. Best for small serif fonts.

Smooth: Produces lighter type with heavy anti-aliasing. Best for large serif fonts.

Using Faux Italic does not truly italicize your type. Instead, it simply slants the text making it oblique. This is OK for some purposes, but tends to reduce readability.

Photoshop measures type size in points, using the PostScript value in which one point is equal to 1/72 of an inch in a 72-ppi image (ppi is an abbreviation for pixels per inch). You can switch between using the PostScript and the traditional point size definition in the Units & Rulers section of the Preferences dialog.

Which anti-aliasing method you choose depends on the font and type size you are using.

Warning: Adding type to an image using Bitmap, Indexed Color, or Multichannel mode, immediately rasterizes the text and adds it to the background layer.

Type designers use *font* to refer to the set of characters in a specific size, and *font face* or just *face* to refer to the collection of all sizes; to a designer, Helvetica is a face and Helvetica 12 is a font. We'll use the Photoshop definition: Helvetica is a font or font family.

Alignment

Alignment defines how text is positioned horizontally within a line of a paragraph if there is surplus space in the line. You can align text in four primary ways:

Left The left sides of all lines in the paragraph are flush, creating a ragged edge on the right side of the paragraph.

Center The surplus space is divided equally on either side of the line of text. Each line in the paragraph is centered.

Right The right sides of all lines in the paragraph are flush, creating a ragged edge on the left side of the paragraph.

Justified (Left, Right, Centered, Full) Extra spaces are placed in the lines so that both the left and right sides of the paragraph are flush ("justified"). However, justification can create some unattractive large spaces within lines. The Left, Right, Centered, and Full option determines how the final line of text in the justified paragraph is treated.

CREATING A TYPE MASK

You can also type to create quick masks (see Section 8.4) using the Horizontal Type Mask and Vertical Type Mask tools. Select one of the tools and follow the directions for creating a text layer. However, rather than creating a Type layer, the text you type is used to create a selection in the active layer.

17.2 Adding a Type Layer

By and large, you add text to a Photoshop image using the Type tool—of course you could draw or paint text into the image—which creates vector-based text on an independent layer called a Type layer. You can add text as a Type layer using two modes:

Paragraph mode Adjusts the flow of letters over the entire text layer. If a Type layer is in Paragraph mode, you can resize the text box. See Section 17.5 for a diagram of the text box.

Point mode Adjusts the flow of each line independent of other lines in the text layer by placing a carriage return at the end of each line. If a Type layer is in Point mode, you cannot resize the text box.

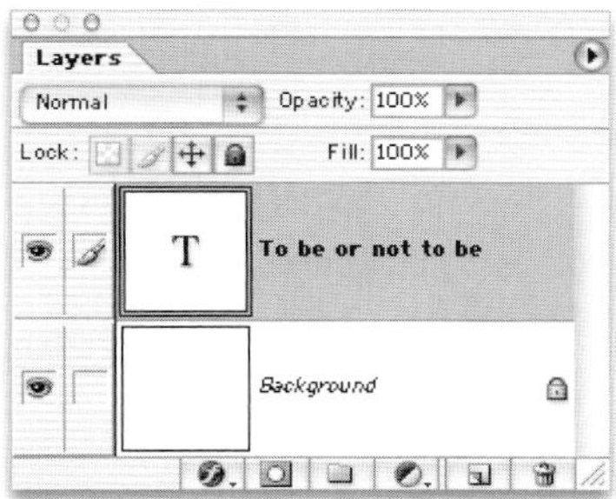

The Type layer is added to the Layers palette automatically. It uses a *T* for the thumbnail and uses the first few words in the text as the layer title.

To add type that you can edit to an image, follow these steps.

1 Choose the Type tool [T] or the Vertical Type tool [IT] from the Toolbox, and then in the Layers palette select the layer above which you want the new text to appear.

2 Set the options for the tool in the tool options bar. You can set additional options for the type in the Character and Paragraph palettes.

- Click the Orientation button [IT] in the tool options bar to switch between horizontal and vertical, which is the same as switching between the Type and Vertical Type tools. Clicking this button changes the text orientation for the entire Type layer.
- Choose a font from the font list.
- If available, choose a style for the font.
- Enter a point value (0.08 to 1085.69) for the font size. You can also directly select from a list of font sizes ranging from 6pt to 72pt.
- Choose an anti-aliasing level for the text (see Section 17.1). You can also choose the anti-aliasing level from the Layers > Type secondary menu.

➠ 3.18 Type Tools
➠ 4.15 Character Palette
➠ 4.16 Paragraph Palette
➠ 8.8 Transforming a Layer or Selected Content
➠ 8.10 Copying and Pasting Selected Content
➠ 14.3 Selecting Colors with the Color Picker
➠ 17.6 Warping Type

Type tool [T]

Cycle type tools [Shift][T]

While you are typing text in a Type layer, you can change any option in the tool options bar or the Character or Paragraph palettes. Changes affect only text typed after the changes are made or selected text (see Section 17.5).

After you click in the canvas with the Type tool, you cannot start or edit another Type layer until you either commit or cancel the current Type layer.

With vertical type, individual letters still maintain a horizontal orientation, but the letters are stacked on top of each other. To actually turn the text horizontally, you use the Rotate Text option in the Characters palette or the Transform pseudo-tool (see Section 8.8).

You can change the name of the selected layer by choosing Layer Properties in the Layers palette menu and entering a new name. This name remains with the Type layer regardless of changes made to the layer.

Warning: You cannot use the keyboard shortcuts to access tools while you are typing in a Type layer.

- Choose justification: left, center, or right. Additional justifications are available in the Paragraph palette.
- Click the color square to set the color of the text.
- If you want to warp the text, click the Create Warped Text button and use the Warped Text dialog.

3 To begin typing, place the mouse cursor over the canvas in the top-left corner of where you want to begin, and do one of the following. Regardless of which method you choose, a new Type layer is inserted immediately above the selected layer.

- Click and begin typing (Point mode). You can type across the entire width of the canvas and beyond, but text that runs off the canvas will not be visible unless you resize the canvas.
- Click and drag to insert a text box, which defines the maximum width and height that the text can occupy in the canvas, and then begin typing (Paragraph mode). A line break will be inserted between words that exceed the width of the text box, and text that exceeds the height of the box will not be visible until you resize the text box. To resize the text box, click one of the four sides or corners and drag.

4 If you want, you can also copy and paste text from other sources (either inside or outside Photoshop). Copy the text from the original source, and then choose Edit > Paste.

5 When you are finished typing, do one of the following;

- To **commit** the text changes, click the Commit button ✓. You can also commit the changes by choosing another tool, layer, channel, or path in the Toolbox or a palette.
- To **cancel** the text changes, press Esc or click the Cancel button ⦸. If this Type layer is new, the layer is also deleted.

Converting Between Text Editing Mode

To convert between Paragraph and Point modes, select the Type layer to convert, and then choose Layer > Type > Convert To Paragraph Text or Convert To Point Text depending on the current mode. This gives you the freedom to switch modes if you decide you need the advantages of one over the other.

17.3 Formatting Characters

The Characters palette provides additional options for formatting individual characters in the text. In addition to setting the font, font style, type size, and anti-aliasing (see Section 17.1), you can set the following options (and others that are self-evident from their names):

➠ 4.16 Character Palette

➠ 14.3 Selecting Color with the Color Picker

If the font you are using does not have a bold or italic style, you can use Faux Bold or Faux Italic. However, keep in mind that these are not typographically correct and will not look nearly as good as a true bold or italic version of the font.

Ⓐ Leading Leading controls the vertical spacing between two lines of text in a paragraph. If you set this value to Auto, Photoshop calculates leading based on the current type size. If you override this setting, using a leading value larger than the current font size adds space between lines; using a smaller leading value squeezes lines together. Leading is applied only to selected lines of text in a paragraph.

Ⓑ Tracking and Kerning Both tracking and kerning control the space between letters in text. You can use tracking when one or more letters of text are selected, and you can apply kerning only when the insertion point is between two characters (no selection) to change the space between those two individual letters.

Ⓒ Vertical and Horizontal Scaling You can stretch characters either horizontally or vertically from their natural state. Values below 100% compress the horizontal or vertical scale of the characters. Values above 100% stretch the horizontal or vertical scale of the characters.

Ⓓ Baseline Shift Allows you to adjust the position of the text up or down from the baseline without changing the type size.

Ⓔ Color Click the color square to select the color for the text using the Color Picker.

Typography is not only a technology but is in itself a natural resource or staple, like cotton or timber or radio; and, like any staple, it shapes not only private sense ratios but also patterns of communal interdependence. *Marshall McLuhan*	Typography is not only a technology but is in itself a natural resource or staple, like cotton or timber or radio; and, like any staple, it shapes not only private sense ratios but also patterns of communal interdependence. *Marshall McLuhan*

Leading: left Auto, right 20pt. (Font size is set to 10pt.)

17.3 Formatting Characters *(Continued)*

To be or not to be

To be or not to be

To be or not to be

Tracking: top 0, middle -75, bottom 75

T T T

Horizontal Scale: left 100%, center 50%, right 150%

T T T

Vertical Scale: left 100%, center 50%, right 150%

Typography

Base Line Shift: The T is using 8pt. The final Y is using –8pt.

Faux Bold	SuperScript^{2}
Faux Italic	Subscript$_{2}$
ALL CAPS	Underline
Small Caps	~~Strikthrough~~

Other character styles

In addition to many of the character options also accessible in the main palette, the Characters palette menu gives you access to the following options:

Rotate Character With the Type layer using the Horizontal orientation, choose this option to turn the letters so that the text is sideways rather than stacked (or vice versa).

Change Text Orientation Choose to change the text orientation for the Type layer between horizontal and vertical. Selecting this option is the same as clicking the Orientation button in the tool options bar.

Ligatures, Discretionary Ligatures, or Old Style Choose if you need to use ligatures and old-style typographic numerals available in some font sets.

Fractional Widths Choose to allow the Type layer to use a fraction of a pixel width for type spacing. This option is generally preferable for print images. Turning it off, though, might improve readability for images used for the television or computer screens.

System Layout Choose to preview the selected text using your operating system's default text handling method, which is useful when you are designing user interfaces.

No Break Choose to prevent words from breaking at the ends of lines for the selected words in the Type layer.

Reset Characters Resets the text appearance to default character values.

17.4 Formatting Paragraphs

You use the Paragraph palette to set formatting options for paragraphs of text . Besides alignment (see Section 17.1), you can set the following options for selected paragraphs:

➠ 4.17 Paragraph Palette

Type tool T

Cycle type tools Shift T

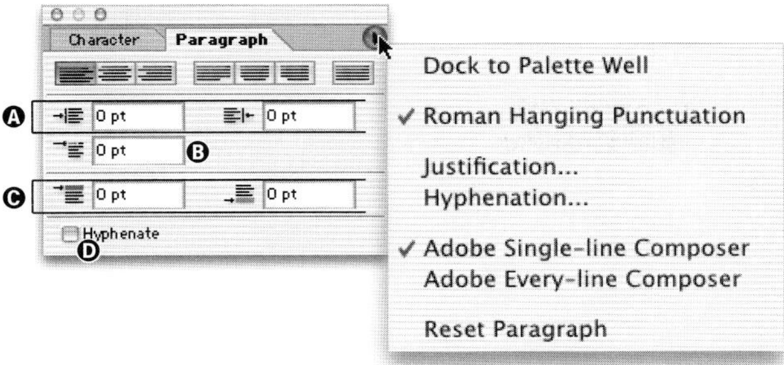

Ⓐ **Left and Right Margin Indent** Set how far in the edges of the paragraph should be from the default state.

Ⓑ **Indent First Line** This indent affects only the first line of a paragraph and is a standard way to indicate a new paragraph.

Ⓒ **Space Before and After Paragraph** Lets you add space before and after a paragraph of text. Extra space is another way to indicate paragraph breaks.

Ⓓ **Hyphenation** To make text flow more smoothly from line to line in a paragraph, you can hyphenate words at line breaks, indicating that the word continues on the next line. This works best with justified text.

Although the effect of scaling the text is similar to that of changing the horizontal and vertical scale, they are not the same, and one does not change the values of the other.

She drew her foot as far down the chimney as she could, and waited till she heard a little animal (she couldn't guess of what sort it was) scratch- Ⓔ ing and scrambling about in the chimney close above her: then, saying to herself 'This is Bill,' she gave one sharp kick, and waited to see what would happen next.

Ⓓ

Ⓐ The first thing she heard was a general chorus of 'There goes Bill!' then the Rabbit's voice along—'Catch him, you by the hedge!' then silence, and then another confusion of voices—'Hold up his head--Brandy now—Don't choke him—How was it, old fellow? What happened to you? Tell us all about it!' Ⓑ

Ⓒ Last came a little feeble, squeaking voice, ('That's Bill,' thought Alice,) 'Well, I hardly know—No more, thank ye; I'm better now—but I'm a deal too flustered to tell you—all I know is, something comes at me like a Jack-in-the-box, and up I goes like a sky-rocket!'

Ⓐ The paragraph's left margin is indented 8pt.

Ⓑ The paragraph's right margin is indented 16pt. Since this text is left justified, though, the margin sets the maximum indent.

Ⓒ The paragraph's first line is indented 16pt.

Ⓓ Four points of space is added above and below each paragraph.

Ⓔ Text is hyphenated.

In addition to the many paragraph styles, the Paragraph palette menu also gives you access to the following options:

Roman Hanging Punctuation Choose if you want punctuation marks, such as quotes, that fall at the beginning or the end of a line of text displayed outside the text box.

"We must burn the house down!" said the Rabbit's voice; and Alice called out as loud as she could, "If you do. I'll set Dinah at you!"

Roman Hanging Punctuation: The opening quotation mark is outside the text margin.

Advanced Justification and Hyphenation Choose to open dialogs in which you exactly control the justification and hyphenation used in the Type layer. Unless you are well practiced in the art of typography, leave these options at their default values.

Adobe Single-line Composer and Adobe Every-line Composer Choose to set how word breaks in a paragraph should be evaluated in order to minimize hyphenation. The Every-Line Composer is a little slower but generally produces far superior results.

Reset Paragraph Resets the paragraph appearance to default paragraph values.

MISSING FONTS

If you attempt to load an image that uses fonts that are not installed on your computer, Photoshop alerts you that one or more fonts are missing in an Alert dialog that lists all the missing fonts. If you click OK, Photoshop replaces the missing fonts, and Type layers with substituted fonts include a Warning icon ⚠ in the layer's thumbnail.

17.5 Editing Type

After you add type to an image, you can edit or add to that type in a variety of ways. Because the text is vector, rather than bitmap, you have great flexibility for formatting and editing the text and controlling the typographic appearance. In addition, text is resolution independent and can be transformed and resized without loss of image quality. However, you cannot paint on Type layers or apply filters to them until they are rasterized. After a Type layer is rasterized, however, you can no longer edit it using the Type tool, and it is subject to the same constraints as all other bitmap components in your image.

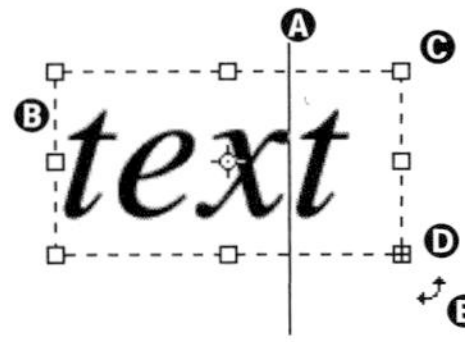

A Insertion cursor Indicates where added text is inserted.

B Text box A special bounding box that indicates the area in which text using Paragraph mode is displayed.

C Resize handles Click and drag any of these squares to resize the text box area and change the layout of the text.

D Additional text A plus sign in the bottom-right corner resize handle indicates that additional text in the text box is not being displayed. Resize the text box to display the hidden text.

E Limited transform The text box has a limited number of transform functions: resize and rotate. Press Shift to rotate in 45° increments.

➟ 3.18 Type Tools
➟ 8.8 Transforming a Layer or Selected Content
➟ 8.10 Copying and Pasting Selected Content
➟ 9 Image Layering
➟ 10 Adding Layer Styles
➟ 11 Masking Layers
➟ 14.3 Selecting Colors with the Color Picker

Selecting and Changing Type

You can directly edit text—a single character, word, or paragraph—by selecting the text to edit in the canvas and then using the tool options bar, the Character palette, or the Paragraph palette. To select and change type in an existing Type layer, follow these steps:

1 Choose the Type tool [T] or Vertical Type tool [IT] from the Toolbox and then select the Type layer you want to edit in the Layers palette. Which tool you choose does not actually matter since the Type layer's orientation determines the orientation you are editing.

2 To select text to change, do one of the following:

- To place the insertion point at a particular place in the text, click in the canvas where you want to add new text and begin typing or paste text that is in memory.
- To select specific text in the Type layer, click in the text and drag across and down.
- To select a single word, double-click the word.
- To select an entire line of text, triple-click in the line.
- To select an entire paragraph, quadruple-click in the paragraph.
- To select all the text in the Type layer, quintuple-click in the Type layer or double-click the Type layer's thumbnail in the Layers palette.

Type tool [T]

Cycle type tools
[Shift] [T]

Cut selection in layer
[⌘] [X]
[Ctrl] [X]

Copy selection in layer
[⌘] [C]
[Ctrl] [C]

Paste contents of Clipboard into selected layer
[⌘] [V]
[Ctrl] [V]

To resize the text box while editing text, click one of the four sides or corners and drag. Even though they look very much alike, this technique is different from transforming the layer box, which stretches and distorts the text rather than simply increasing the display area for the text in the canvas.

Many menu commands are not available as you add or edit a Type layer. For example, you need to either cancel or commit the text changes you are making before you can save the document.

Changing the orientation affects the entire Type layer, although other changes, such as paragraph alignment, affect only the paragraph that contains the insertion point.

When you edit a Type layer, its name changes to reflect the new text it contains unless you renamed the Type layer using the Layer Properties dialog.

3 To change the selected text, do one of the following:

- Set the options for the selected text or paragraph independent of other text in the layer by using the tool options bar.
- Set options in the Character palette for the selected characters.
- Set options in the Paragraph palette for the paragraph that contains the cursor or the selection.
- You can also press Delete or simply start typing to remove selected text.

4 When you finish editing the type, you can commit the text changes by clicking the Check button ✓ or by choosing another tool, layer, channel, or path. Cancel changes by pressing Esc or clicking the Cancel button ⊘.

Changing the Type Layer

You can also change all the text in a Type layer by simply selecting that layer in the Layers palette. With any tool selected, choose the Type layer you want to edit in the Layers palette. You can also choose the Type tool if you want to change options using the tool options bar. Then, to make changes to the text, do one of the following:

- If the Type tool is selected, you can set the options for the selected Type layer's characters or paragraph using the tool options bar.
- Set options in the Characters palette for all the text in the Type layer.
- Set options in the Paragraph palette for all the paragraphs in the Type layer.

Text as a Layer

Although they are created differently from other types of layers, Type layers are still layers, and you can edit and manipulate them in most of the usual ways:

Moving and transforming You can move Type layers using the Move tool, and you can transform (rotate, scale, or skew) them using the transform pseudo tools. Although scaling the text has an effect similar to the effect that results from changing the horizontal and vertical scale, they are not the same, and one does not change the values of the other.

Opacity and blending modes You can change the opacity and blending mode of Type layers freely at any time (see Section 9.11).

Effects and styles You can apply all effects and preset styles to Type layers (see Chapter 10).

Clipping groups You can use text layers as a part of a clipping group (see Section 9.12).

17.5 Editing Type *(Continued)*

Masks You can apply layer and vector masks to Type layers (see Chapter 11).

Painting and filters You cannot use any brush-based tools in a Type layer without first rasterizing the layer. If you attempt to use a brush or a filter with a Type layer, you will be asked whether you want to rasterize the layer first. Remember: if you do this, you can no longer edit the text with the text tool. However, you can still use brushes in the layer mask of the Type layer. You may want to duplicate the type layer and hide it, so you have a backup copy to edit if changes to the text are required.

REAL WORLD: NEIL EVANS

Neil Evans lists a wide variety of inspirations for his work, including underground comic book artists such as Winsor McKay, Jamie Hewlett, and Paul Pope as well as the "classic" artists such as Blake, Vermeer, and Samuel Palmer. "If I stopped to think about it, I'd probably conclude that I'm trying to stake out a middle ground between these two groups and have a laugh while I'm at it."

Neil's colorful images start life as black-and-white line drawings in pen and ink, usually drawn straight from his head. He then scans the drawings in through an Agfa scanner and works exclusively in Photoshop. "First I clean up the black-and-white image by adjusting the levels, so as to get a uniform black and a uniform white. I then separate the black line into its own layer by way of the Channels palette and place it at the top of the pile ready to start coloring underneath. Layer effects are good fun to play with, especially for someone like me who loves glowing things; they're also useful for giving lettering an aesthetic boost, but otherwise I try to use them sparingly."

You can find more of Neil's work at `www.nelson-evergreen.com/`.

17.6 Warping Type

➠ 3.18 Type Tools

You can click and drag to move the Type layer while working in the Warp Text dialog.

As you are making changes to warped text in the dialog, it will be previewed in the canvas. However, this can be slow depending on the image size.

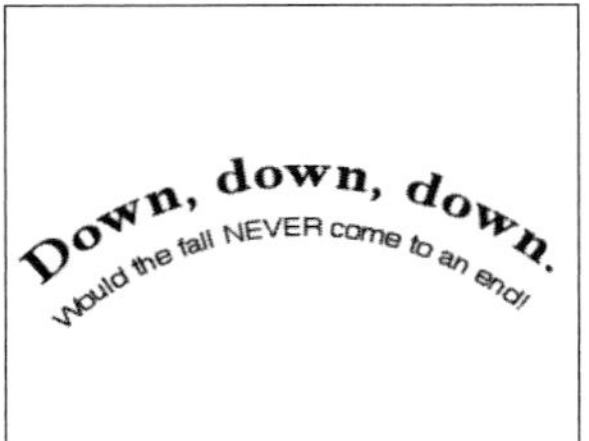

Text warped with the Arc style (horizontal)

Text warped with the Arc style (vertical)

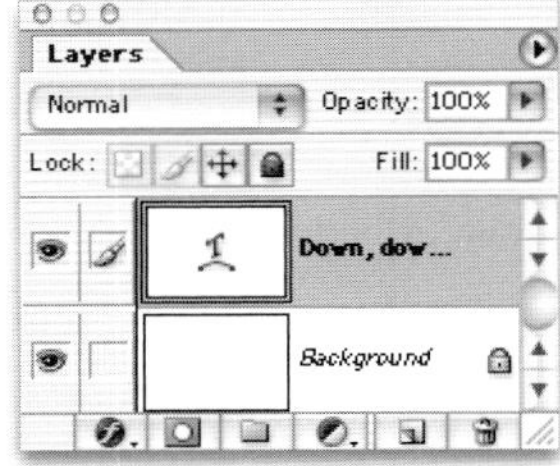

The Type layer thumbnail in the Layers palette changes to the warped text thumbnail

When you first add text to a Type layer, the text base line follows a straight horizontal line. You can use the Warp Text dialog to set a shape for the text to follow, distorting the shapes of the text in interesting ways. To distort the shape of your text, follow these steps:

1 Choose the Type layer you want to warp in the Layers palette.

2 Choose Layer > Type > Warp Text, or, with one of the text tools selected, click the Warp Text button .

3 Set the warp style, warp orientation, amount of bend, and horizontal and vertical distortion in the Warp Text dialog.

4 After you distort the text, click OK. You will notice that the thumbnail for the Type layer changes to the warped text thumbnail.

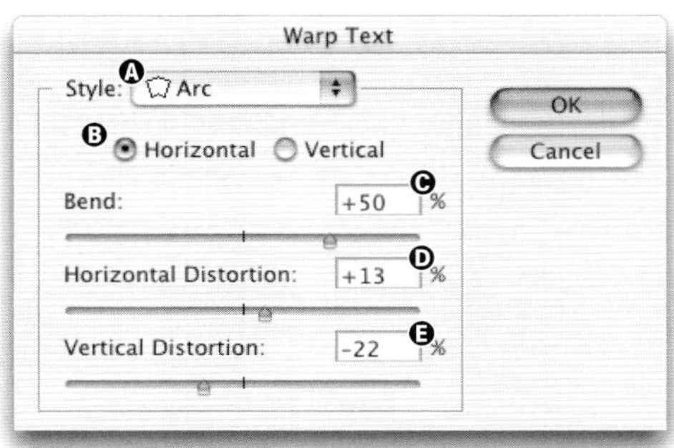

Ⓐ Choose a warp style from the drop-down. Each style has a small thumbnail next to it that indicates its general shape.

Ⓑ **Warp Orientation** Choose whether you want to apply the style (see A) to warp the text horizontally or vertically.

Ⓒ Use the slider or enter a percentage value (–100 to 100) for the maximum bend in the warped text.

Ⓓ Use the slider or enter a percentage value (–100 to 100) for the maximum horizontal distortion for the warped text. This affects the perspective, with positive numbers causing the left side of the text to appear farther away.

Ⓔ Use the sliders or enter percentage values (–100 to 100) for the maximum horizontal and vertical distortion for the warped text. This affects the perspective, with positive numbers causing the top of the text to appear farther away.

17.7 Converting Type

Because type is in vector format in Photoshop, you can convert it to other formats, including a path and a vector mask, or you can rasterize the text. To convert the Type layer, first select the layer you want to convert in the Layers palette, and then do one of the following:

- To **turn the text into a work path** based on the Type layer, choose Layer > Type > Create Workpath. This technique uses the letterforms to create a working path in the Paths palette, but does not delete the original Type layer.

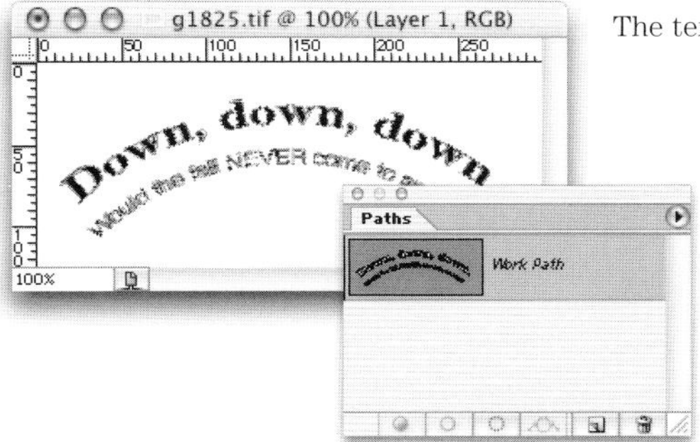

The text is now also a workpath.

- To **convert the text to a vector mask,** choose Layer > Type > Convert To Shape. This technique uses the letterforms to create a vector mask with a fill layer using the color or style of the original text. The original Type layer is deleted.
- To **rasterize the text,** choose Layer > Rasterize > Type *or* Layer. This converts the layer into a bitmap layer, which you can then edit using brushes (see Chapter 15), filters (see Chapters 16), or importing into video applications (see Chapter 29). Remember, though, that once you rasterize the text, you cannot edit it with the Type tool, and the original Type layer is deleted.

➠ 12.8 Selecting Paths and Path Components

➠ 12.9 Editing Paths and Path Components

➠ 12.10 Editing Path Segments

➠ 12.11 Reshaping Curves

➠ 12.12 Managing Paths

When Type layers are converted, they preserve the layer name based on the last text they contained.

Warning: When you convert from Paragraph to Point mode, all text that is not visible within the text box is deleted. Make sure that all text is visible before converting.

17.8 Spell-Checking and Searching Text

➠ 2.4 Edit Menu

The spellchecker always starts checking from the beginning of the text in a layer.

Photoshop 7 introduces two new, highly requested text features that greatly increase productivity: spell-checking and find and replace.

Although the new spell-checker is extremely basic, it saves time over having to copy and paste your text into a word processor. To spell-check a single Type layer or all Type layers in your document, follow these steps:

1. Select the Type layer you want to check in the Layers palette. If you want to check the spelling of all layers in the document, you do not have to select any particular layer.
2. Choose Edit > Check Spelling....
3. Use the Check Spelling dialog to scan your document for misspelled words. Click Done when you are finished checking the spelling.

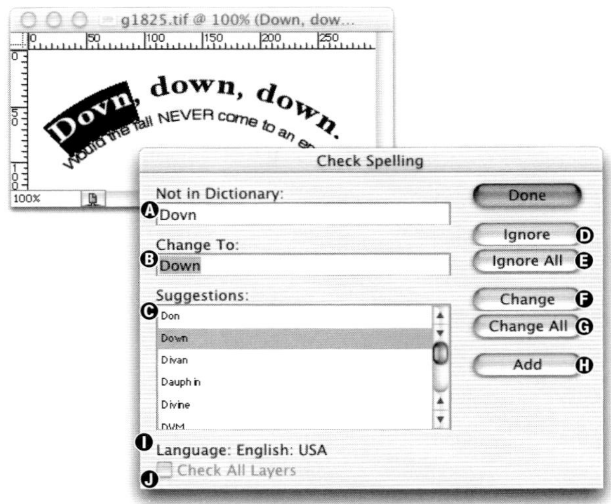

- **A** Displays suspect words that were not found in the dictionary.
- **B** Displays the most likely correct spelling for the suspect word. Click and type an alternate word.
- **C** Displays a list of other possible correct spellings. Click to select one of these suggestion.
- **D** Click to ignore this instance of the word.
- **E** Click to ignore this particular word throughout the document during this spell-checking session.
- **F** Click to use the Change To word (see B) in place of the suspect word (see A) for this one instance.
- **G** Click to use the Change To word (see B) in place of the suspect word (see A) for this and all instances throughout this document.
- **H** Add the suspect word (see A) to the Photoshop dictionary.
- **I** Displays the current dictionary being used to spell-check the document.
- **J** Check to spell-check all Type layers in the document.

17.8 Spell-Checking and Searching Text *(Continued)*

Also, Photoshop now allows you to search the text in your document and replace words. To do so, follow these steps:

1. Select the Type layer you want to search in the Layers palette. If you want to search all layers in the document, you do not have to select any particular layer.
2. Choose Edit > Find And Replace Text....
3. Use the Find And Replace Text dialog to scan your document looking for words and replacing as necessary. As you search, the words found are highlighted in the canvas. Click Done when you are finished searching.

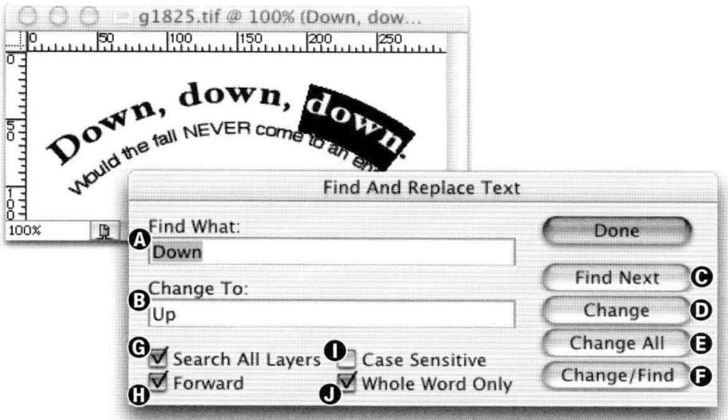

- **A** Enter the text you want to find.
- **B** Enter the replacement text.
- **C** Click to begin the search or to continue to the next instance of the find text without replacing.
- **D** Click to replace the found text with the revised text.
- **E** Click to replace all occurrences of the found text in the Type layer or document with the revised text.
- **F** Click to replace the found text with the revised text and then continue to the next occurrence of the find text.
- **G** Check to Search all layers.
- **H** Check to search forward (left to right/up to down) in the text.
- **I** Check to find only text that is the same case as the find text.
- **J** Check to find only the entire text, disregarding matches that are embedded in other words.

CHAPTER 18

Automation and Workgroups

THERE IS NO ESCAPING IT: many tasks in image editing involve repetitive operations. The automation of these tasks increases productivity and decreases errors. The latter is especially true of large projects in which the same effect or effects is applied to all images.

Photoshop 7 includes three general categories of automation tools: actions, batch actions, and droplets. You can use these tools for tasks as simple as changing a group of files from one format to the other or as complex as processing multiple images.

When more than one person is working on a document or when a project involves multiple parts with many people working on it, setting up a workgroup becomes necessary. To this end, Photoshop supports WebDAV (Web-based Distributed Authoring and Versioning), a set of extensions to the HTTP protocol that allows users to collaboratively edit and manage files on remote web servers.

18.1 Applying Actions

➠ 4.9 Actions Palette

Actions are collections of commands and tool operations that you can apply to an image (or a batch of images) in a sequential manner. For example, if you have a series of photographs that you want to desaturate and sepia-tone and then add a particular frame to, you can record an action to do this automatically rather than repeating each step yourself. You can record most commands and actions as part of an action and then apply them as desired.

Choose multiple discontiguous actions
Shift *Click action*

Choose multiple contiguous actions
⌘ *Click action*
Ctrl *Click action*

You record and apply actions using the Actions palette (see Section 4.9), which you can view and use in two modes: Button and Edit. You can toggle between these two palette modes by selecting the Button Mode option in the Actions palette menu.

To play back an action, select the layer you want to apply the action to using the Layers palette, make any additional selection, and then do one of the following:

In **Button mode**, click the button for the action, or press the associated keyboard shortcut, which, if there is one, is listed on the right side of the button.

In **Edit mode**, click the action or a step in the action, and then choose Play in the palette menu or click the Play button ▶. If you choose a step in the action, the playback begins from there and continues through the subsequent steps to the end of the action.

You can play actions only if the conditions are right for the commands being executed. For example, you cannot use the Cut command if there is no selection. If an action attempts to perform a command that is not available, you will be alerted.

Photoshop applies all the commands in the action in sequence to the selected layer. Some actions can take a long time to complete, depending on the size of the image, how complex the action is, the power of the computer, and the available system resources.

Actions created in Photoshop 7 might not run on previous versions of Photoshop if they use features available only in Photoshop 7.

The Internet contains hundreds of actions covering a wide variety of tasks. Although many of these actions are free, be sure they will work in Photoshop 7.

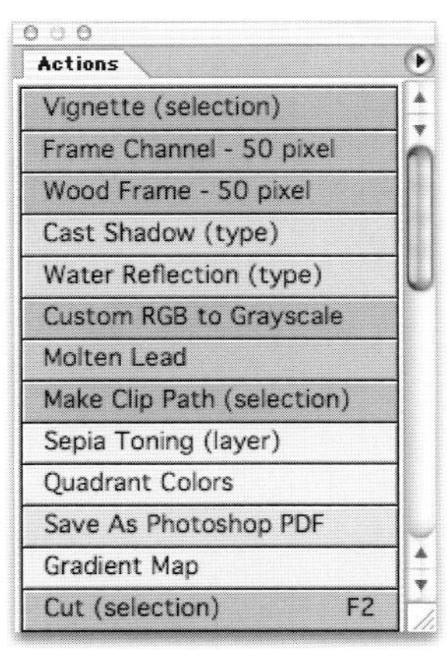

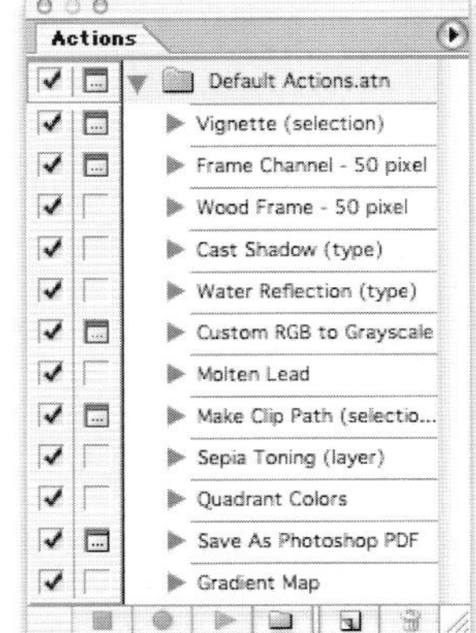

Left: the Actions palette in Button mode. Click any of the buttons to execute that action. Function key shortcuts are displayed to the right of the action name (for example, Cut is F2). Right: the palette in Edit mode (Button mode turned off). Click any action to select it, and then click the Play button or choose Play to execute that action.

18.2 Recording Actions

Although Photoshop comes equipped with dozens of actions, you can record, edit, save, and load your own actions and sets of actions. To record a new action, follow these steps:

1 In the Actions palette, turn off Button Mode in the Actions palette menu, and then click the New Action button or select New Action… in the palette menu.

2 Enter details about the action in the New Action dialog and click Record. The Record button turns red as long as the action is being recorded.

3 Do one or more of the following:

- Perform the actions you want to record. Most operations you perform while recording (tools, menu commands, dialogs, palette settings, etc.) are added to the action in the Actions palette as you perform them. However, several operations and commands cannot be recorded; these include setting preferences and applying paint strokes. Likewise zoom tools, windows, and view commands cannot be recorded.
- Choose Insert Command… from the Actions palette menu, choose a menu command, and click OK. The command is performed as a part of the action.
- Choose Insert Stop… from the Actions palette menu, enter a message, specify whether you want to include a Continue button with the stop message, and click OK. The action stops at this point and waits for the user, who can either click Stop or, if you checked the Continue option, continue.
- Select a path in the Paths palette, and then choose Insert Path from the Actions palette menu. The selected path is added to the image as part of the action.

4 To stop recording, do any of the following:

- Click the Stop button.
- Choose Stop Recording from the palette menu.
- Press the Escape key.

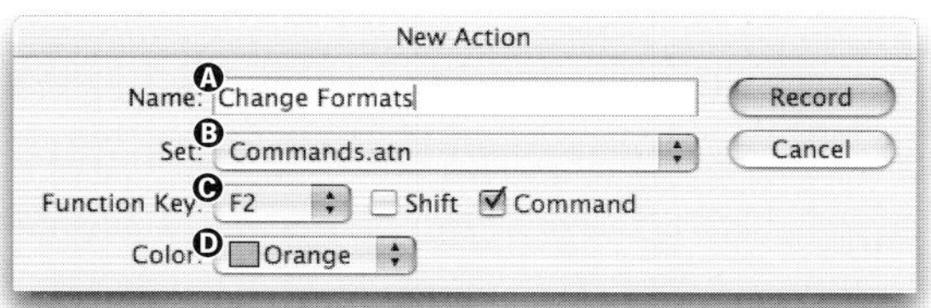

A Enter a name for the action.

B Choose the action set to which the action should be added. This action is not saved with the action set until the action set is resaved.

C Choose a function key and modifier keys to activate the action. You can choose only keyboard shortcuts not currently being used by other actions.

D Choose a color code for the action's background in the Button mode of the Actions palette.

➠ 4.9 Actions Palette

Cut selection (with `Commands.atn` **loaded)**
F2

Copy selection (with `Commands.atn` **loaded)**
F3

Paste (with `Commands.atn` **loaded)**
F4

Show Color palette (with `Commands.atn` **loaded)**
F6

Show Layers palette (with `Commands.atn` **loaded)**
F7

Show Info palette (with `Commands.atn` **loaded)**
F8

Show Actions palette (with `Commands.atn` **loaded)**
F9

Show Navigator palette (with `Commands.atn` **loaded)**
F10

Open Image Size dialog (with `Commands.atn` **loaded)**
F11

Revert to saved version (with `Commands.atn` **loaded)**
F12

The preset actions provided with Photoshop are in the Presets/Photoshop Actions folder in the Photoshop application folder on your hard drive.

One extremely useful action preset is the Commands list (Commands .atn). It includes actions for the most common menu commands, adding function key shortcuts.

It is best to plan the actions you are going to record before actually recording them. This saves a lot of editing and re-recording time.

You can cause one action to play another by recording the Play command for another action.

If the action being recorded will be applied to files of different sizes, change the ruler units to percent so that commands will be proportional to the file sizes.

Editing Actions and Action Sets

The commands used to record, edit, load, and save actions are located in the Actions palette menu.

After you record an action, you can edit it in several ways. First, turn Button mode off using the command in the palette menu; then do one or more of the following:

- To **re-record** an action, in the Actions palette, select the action and then choose Record Again…. If the action uses a tool, use the tool differently and then press Return/Enter to record the changes. If the action is a dialog, set the options and click OK to record the changes.
- To **add** to an existing action, in the Actions palette, select the action and then click the Record button. Perform the actions to be added, and then click the Stop button.
- To **create a new action set**, in the Actions palette, click the New Set button or choose New Set… from the palette menu. Enter a name for the new action set, and click OK. The new action set appears in the Actions palette menu. You can then group actions into a single folder, making it easier to save them as a set.
- To **duplicate** an action or an action set, in the Actions palette, select the action or action set and then choose Duplicate. You can also Option/Alt drag the action to another location on the Actions palette or drag the action to the New Actions button
- To set **playback options** for an action, in the Actions palette, select the action or action set and then choose Playback Options…. In the Playback Options dialog, choose the speed at which you want the actions played: choose Accelerated for best performance, choose Step By Step for slower playback, or choose Pause and enter the number of

seconds to delay. You can also pause the action after any audio annotations in the action to ensure that it plays all the way through. Generally, you want to use the Accelerated option, but if you are debugging an action, you will want to slow it down to help you detect errors.

- To change the **action options** or to **set options**, in the Actions palette, select the action or action set and then choose Action Options… in the palette menu. Change the options in the Action Options or Set Options dialog and click OK.

You can create an "undo" for actions. When recording a new action, first record Create A New Snapshot. With this as the first step, you can revert to the previous image state by clicking the most recent snapshot when you run the action.

If the action includes the Save As command, do not change the filename; if you enter a new filename, Photoshop uses that exact filename every time the action is played. As a workaround, copy the files to a new folder, and "save" the reconfigured files as the same name. This way you don't lose your source medium.

Loading and Saving Action Presets

You can save actions as independent files and then load them into Photoshop as needed. This is especially helpful if you set up specific actions for a project that you want to save for later use or to send to another Photoshop user.

- To **load** a list of preset actions, choose Load Actions… from the Actions palette menu, choose a file that has the `.atn` extension, and click OK. The actions are added to the bottom of the list in the Actions palette.
- To **quickly load** a list of preset actions, choose one of the action filenames from the bottom of the Actions palette menu. You can add a list of actions to the quick load list by saving the actions file in the Presets/Photoshop Actions folder in the Photoshop application folder. If Photoshop is running, you will need to restart before the file appears in the Actions palette menu.
- To **replace** the current list of actions, choose Replace Actions from the Actions palette menu. Choose a file that has the `.atn` extension, and click OK. The current list of actions is cleared and replaced with the selected list.
- To **reset** actions to the default list of preset actions, choose Reset from the Actions palette menu. Specify whether you want the action set to be added to the bottom of the current list (Append) or to completely replace the current list (OK).
- To **save** the current action set, with Button mode turned off, choose one of the action filenames from the bottom of the Actions palette menu. Enter a name for the new action file, making sure to preserve the `.atn` extension, choose a folder on your hard drive to save in, and click Save.
- To **clear** all actions and action sets in the Actions palette, choose Clear All Actions from the Actions palette menu, and click OK in the dialog to confirm that you want to delete all the actions. The Actions palette will now be empty.
- To **delete** actions or action sets from the Actions palette, choose the action or action set in the Actions palette and click the trashcan icon, or choose Delete from the palette menu and click OK in the dialog to confirm deletion. In addition, you can drag the action or action set directly to the trashcan icon to delete instantly. The action or action set is removed from the palette but can be reloaded if it was saved.

18.3 Performing Batch Actions

➠ 4.9 Actions Palette

It is recommended that Suppress Color Profile Warnings be turned off to turn off display of color policy messages, which can stop batch processing.

You can speed up batch procedures by reducing the number of saved history states and turning off the Automatically Create First Snapshot option in the History palette.

An action can be applied to a single image. However, you can use the Batch command to apply an action to an entire folder of files and subfolders with a single action.

In addition to applying actions to Photoshop files and other compatible files, you can apply several options files after they are processed. You can leave the files open, close them with the changes saved to the original files, or save modified versions of the files to a new location (leaving the originals unchanged).

To apply an action to a batch of files, choose File > Automate > Batch. Set the options in the Batch dialog and click OK to begin the batch action. You will see the files quickly open, actions applied, and then the file close again, until all files are processed

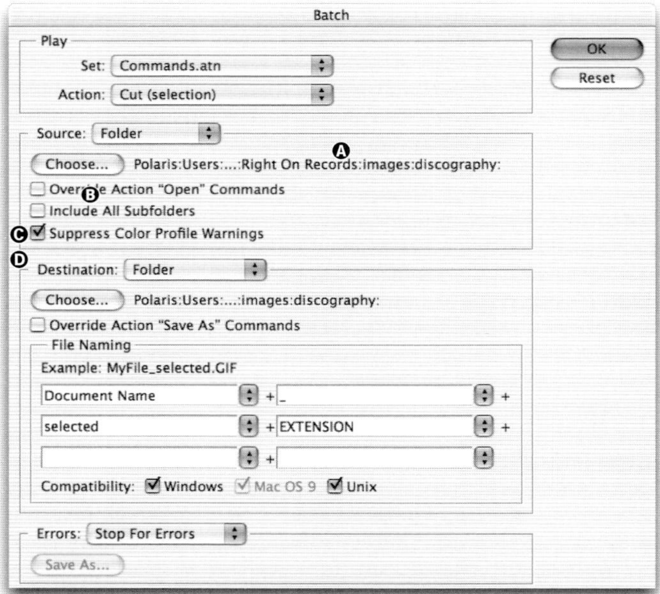

- **A** Choose a currently loaded set of actions, and then choose the action to be performed. Only sets loaded in the Action palette appear in these lists.
- **B** Choose the source for the images to be batch processed: from a selected folder, imported from a selected source, using the currently open files, or using the current folder selected in the File Browser.
- **C** If you are using a folder as the source (see B), choose the folder. The selected folder's path is displayed to the right.
- **D** If you are using a folder or the File Browser for the source (see B), check to prevent the Open command from being performed in an action. This is generally recommended as it will help prevent errors when the needed file is already open.

18.3 Performing Batch Actions *(Continued)*

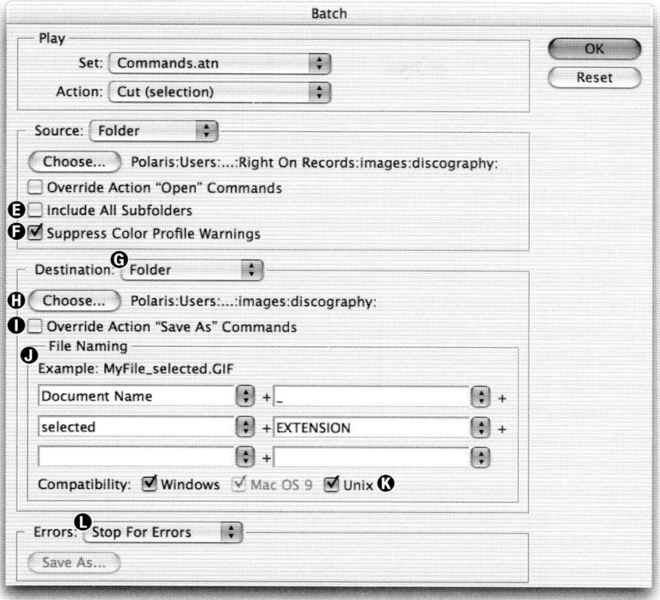

E If you are using a folder or the File Browser for the source (see B), check to include all folders within the selected folder.

F If you are using a folder or the File Browser for the source (see B), check to prevent color profile warnings. Otherwise, the batch actions will stop every time there is a color profile warning (see Section 7.3).

G Choose what is to be done with the processed files: None leaves the files open without saving changes, Save And Close saves the files in their current location overwriting the original files, and Folder saves the processed files in another location.

H If you are using a folder as the destination (see G), choose the folder in which to save the processed files. The selected folder's path is displayed to the right. Although you can save the files back into the original folder and even replace the original files, it is recommended that you save the processed files in a new folder so you can keep the originals.

I If you are using a folder as the destination (see G), check to prevent the Save As command from being executed. This prevents the process from being interrupted by the Save As dialog.

J If you are using a folder as the source (see G), choose how the files should be named by selecting options from the drop-down. An example of how the new filename will be structured appears at the top.

K If you are using a folder as the source (see G), specify the operating systems with which you want to force the filename to be compatible.

L Choose how errors should be processed: you can either stop to deal with them or log them to a text file. You can set the location for the text field by clicking the Save As... button.

Creating a new action and recording a batch command provides a way to perform multiple actions from a single action.

If you have a digital camera or a scanner with a document feeder, you can also import and process multiple images with a single action.

18.4 Creating Droplets

4.9 Actions Palette

25.3 Optimizing Images

ImageReady can also create droplets for optimizing web images (see Section 25.3).

You can drag multiple images or entire folders of images over the droplet to open the images one by one and perform the action.

You can specify that droplets save images automatically in a specific folder on your hard drive, which preserves the original version of the image.

A close relative of batch processing is the droplet. A *droplet* is a mini-application that can apply an action to an image or a folder of images when you simply drag the image or the folder over the droplet's icon. You don't even have to open Photoshop to use a droplet.

The procedure and options for creating a droplet in Photoshop are almost identical to those previously discussed for batch processing. To create a droplet, choose File > Automate > Create Droplet and enter the options for the droplet.

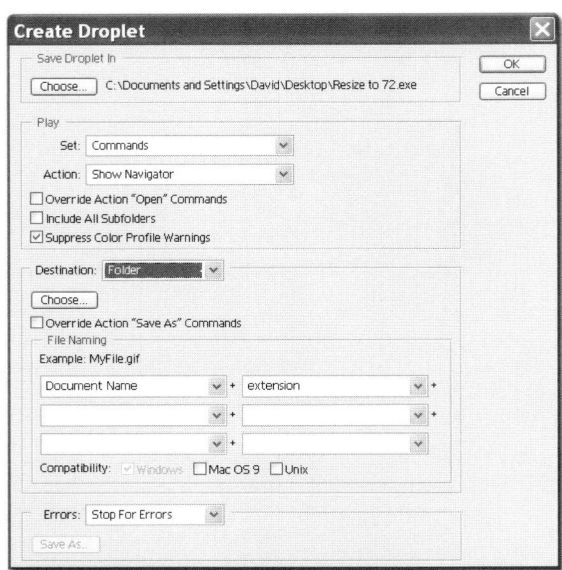

Choose a location in which to save the droplet. The current location is displayed to the right. When selecting the location, place it where you can easily drag the image file(s) or folder to it, probably the Desktop. Other options in this dialog are identical to those in the Batch dialog (see Section 18.5).

After you create the droplet, simply drag and drop a compatible image file, multiple selected image files, or an entire folder of image files onto the droplet icon to process them.

LEARNING MORE ABOUT WEBDAV

Although Adobe supports the WebDAV technology in many of its products, WebDAV is not owned by Adobe. Instead, it is an open standard being developed by the IETF WebDAV Working Group and can be included with any software that wants to support it. To find out more about the WebDAV standard, check out the WebDAV Resources website (`www.webdav.org`).

18.5 Setting Up Workgroups

If you are working in a collaborative environment and others in your organization regularly view or edit your Photoshop files, you will need to manage your files to avoid confusion. Photoshop's Workgroup commands, based on the WebDAV server technology, let you share files with other users while ensuring that files are not edited by two people at the same time and that changes made by one person are not overwritten by another person. You can use the Workgroup commands to place files on a special central computer (called a server) that allows you and others in our group to download files, lock them from being changed while you are working, and then upload the file for others to view or change. Think of this as a library from which you can check documents in and out.

➠ 5.4 File Handling Preferences

Adobe GoLive also uses workgroups to manage files.

If you are having trouble connecting to your WebDAV server, your computer or the WebDAV server might be behind a firewall that is interfering with communication. Check with your system administrator or take a look at the documentation that came with your firewall software to set options that permit communication.

When using workgroups, there are two versions of the image file:

Local This is the version that resides on your hard drive and is the version you actually edit. When you open a file from the Workgroup server, you actually download the most recent version from the server to your computer.

Server This version is available to all users in the workgroup on the WebDAV server. When you save the file, you upload your local version to the server.

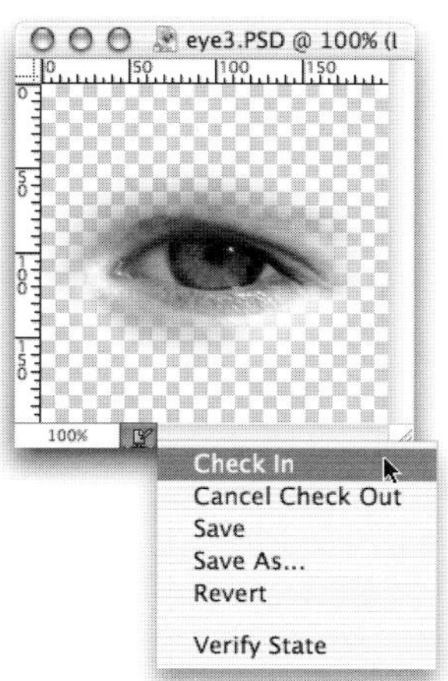

Before you begin using workgroups, you need to make sure that the functionality is enabled in the File Handling Preferences panel (see Section 5.4). Check the Enable Workgroup Functionality option and set the other Workgroup options. This opens the File > Workgroup submenu and the Workgroup drop-down (located in the document window in Mac OS or in the application window in Windows).

Before using the Workgroup commands in Photoshop, you need to connect to a WebDAV server. The WebDAV server software comes with Photoshop 7. Follow the instruction provided to install it on the computer being used as the server, which must be connected to the Internet. However, if you are not technically inclined, ask your system administrator to install the software for you.

18.5 Setting Up Workgroups *(Continued)*

Some servers require you to log on only once, the first time you use a Workgroup command. However, some servers require you to log on for every Workgroup command you issue.

When the WebDAV server software is installed, you need to connect your computer, which also has to be connected to the Internet, to the server. To do this you will need to know the URL for the WebDAV server.

- To **set the server or servers** you want to use, choose File > Workgroup > Workgroup Servers. In the Workgroup Servers dialog, specify the folder on your computer where you want to store shared files, and then choose the WebDAV server or servers you want to use. (This is where the global version of the files is stored.) Click Done when you are finished.

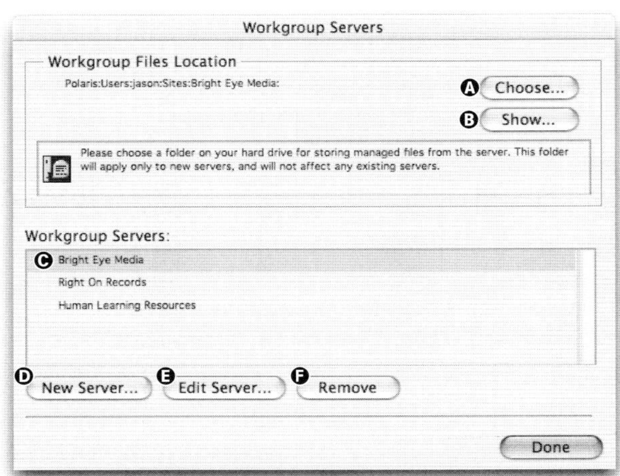

A Click to choose the folder on your hard drive in which you want workgroup files from newly added WebDAV servers saved. This is where your local version of the files will be saved; the currently selected folder is displayed to the left. You can also select a Workgroup server (see C) and then change its folder location.

B Open the local Workgroup folder using Explorer (Windows) or the Finder (Mac).

C Displays a list of connected WebDAV servers. Click to select.

D Click to set up a new WebDAV server. Enter a nickname and a URL or IP address for the server in the dialog and click OK. You must be connected to the Internet to add a WebDAV server; Photoshop will verify that you can access the server.

E Select a Workgroup server (see C), and then click to edit the nickname and the URL for the server.

F Select a Workgroup server (see C), and then click to remove the server from the list.

- To **log on to a server**, select any of the commands from the File > Workgroup submenu or the Workgroup drop-down in the document window (Mac) or application window (Windows), and choose the server from the dialog. Depending on how the server is configured, you will be asked to enter a username/ID and password, which you should get from your system administrator.
- To **log off all servers**, choose File > Workgroup > Logoff All Servers. This disconnects you from all servers you have logged on to.

18.6 Checking Documents In and Out

After you set up a Workgroup server to be used with Photoshop, you can open (download) files from the server or save (upload) files to the server. In addition, while opening a file, you can check it out to prevent other users in your group from editing the image while you are working on it. Then, when saving the file, you can check it back in, freeing the file to be edited by other members of your group.

- To **add** a new managed file to the server, open the file and choose Save As… from the File > Workgroup submenu or from the Workgroup drop-down. Enter options for which server and how you want the file saved and click Save. The file is now on the server and available to the workgroup.
- To **open** a managed file, choose File > Workgroup > Open…. Choose the server, folder, and file you want to open, and click Open to open the file *without* checking it out from the server or click Check Out to open and check out the file.

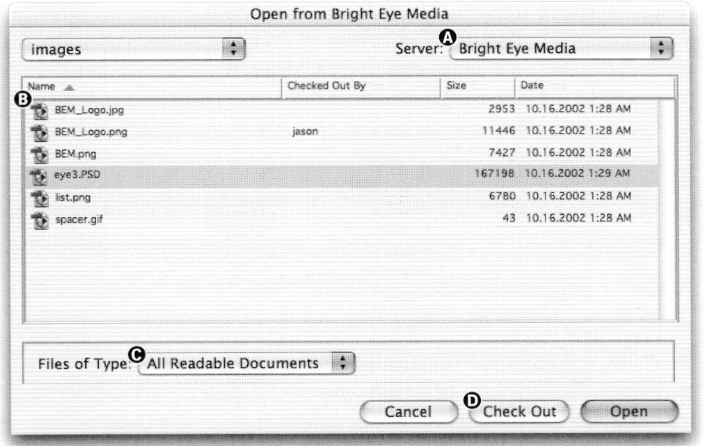

A Choose a server from the list. You can then locate the exact folder in which you want to save the file on the server.

B Choose a file to download. You can click the column heads to sort files based on that criteria.

C Choose a file format.

D Choose to immediately check out the file after saving.

- To **save** the changes to the server version, choose Save from the File > Workgroup submenu or from the Workgroup drop-down. The server version of the file is updated based on your local version.

➠ 5.4 File Handling Preferences

➠ 6.2 Opening an Existing Image

➠ 6.13 Saving and Closing an Image

If you open a managed file without checking it out, other workgroup users can still check the file out and make changes, potentially leading to confusion.

When adding a file to a WebDAV server, make sure that you include a file extension if the file will be downloaded to a Windows computer.

18.6 Checking Documents In and Out *(Continued)*

- To **check out the open file**, choose Check Out from the File > Workgroup submenu or from the Workgroup drop-down. The file must have been saved on a WebDAV server. You might want to verify the file before checking it out.
- To **verify** that a local file can be checked out, open the file and choose Verify State from the File > Workgroup submenu or from the Workgroup drop-down.
- To **check in the file while saving changes**, choose Check In from the File > Workgroup submenu or from the Workgroup drop-down. The server version of the file is updated based on your local version and unlocked.
- To **check in the file without saving changes**, choose Cancel Check Out from the File > Workgroup submenu or from the Workgroup drop-down. The file is unlocked on the server but not updated.
- To **revert** the checked-out local version of a file to the version on the server, choose Revert from the File > Workgroup submenu or from the Workgroup drop-down. All unsaved changes made to the local version will be lost.
- To **update** the local version of a file (if it has not been checked out) from the version on the Workgroup server, open the file and choose Update from the File > Workgroup submenu or from the Workgroup drop-down. All unsaved changes made to the local version will be lost.

DOWNLOADING ACTIONS AND OTHER RESOURCES FROM ADOBE STUDIO EXCHANGE

Although there are dozens of websites that allow you to download Photoshop Actions, Brushes, Custom shapes, and other Photoshop plug-ins, one of the best collections is provided by Adobe itself at the Adobe Studio Exchange website, part of the larger Adobe Studio website (`share.studio.adobe.com`). This site is stuffed with the best (mostly free!) resources you will find for Photoshop, including thousands of actions for creating frames and borders, patterns, text effects, and textures.

What really sets this site apart from other Photoshop resource sites, though, is that you can "shop" for downloads, add them to your basket, and then download everything at once. You will need an Adobe ID to use it, but this is free of charge.

PRINT TASKS

CHAPTER 19

Designing for Print

THE STEPS NECESSARY TO ENSURE that the final output will have correct color for images destined to be viewed on a computer monitor are different (and somewhat simpler) than those necessary to produce an image on either an offset press or an inkjet printer. For one thing, a computer display and a hard-copy output device use different color space. Ensuring that the printed output matches in appearance and size what appears on the computer display requires a little knowledge of resolution and how to use the Photoshop tools to control resolution. Photoshop also has tools to ensure that all the colors in an image are within the capability of the output device to faithfully print them.

This chapter explains these topics:

- 19.1 **Print basics**
- 19.2 **Resolution and printing**
- 19.3 **Previewing color for print**
- 19.4 **Checking the gamut**
- 19.5 **Working with color channels**

19.1 Print Basics

➠ 6.10 Printing Basics

➠ 21.1 Preparing to Print

All work done to prepare a project for a commercial printer is called prepress.

Whether you are using Photoshop to create a file that is to be printed on a $100 inkjet printer or a six-station Heidelberg offset press that is larger than your house, some foundational concepts apply to all printed material. This chapter introduces several terms, and understanding them will help you when printing at home or, in some cases, when getting your creative efforts printed by a printer.

Monitor versus Print Output

The first and most important concept is that the printed output can never look exactly like what is on the computer monitor. This has nothing to do with color calibration (although that is important) or color space. The image on the monitor is made out of transmitted light created by the glowing phosphors in the display, and the printed image is made up of dyes or pigments applied to paper or some other medium, and what is being viewed is reflected light from the paper. Hence, the colors on the display appear more vivid. If Photoshop is set up for color-managed workflow, it can create a "soft proof" on the monitor so that you can see an accurate representation of what the printed image will look like. This is covered in detail in Section 19.3.

Pigment versus Dye-Based Inks

The output of inkjet printers and offset printers is different. The major difference is based on how color is achieved. There are two general categories of ink: dye-based inks and pigment-based inks.

- All but the most expensive inkjet printers use an ink that is based on dyes. Ink dyes can display a wider range (also called a gamut) of colors than pigments display.
- Pigment is used to make the color inks used in some archival inkjet printers and all offset printers. Although the colors are not as vivid, they have a much greater resistance to fading. This is why, as a rule, you cannot use the output of a consumer inkjet printer to judge what the final printed version of the Photoshop file will look like when output on an offset printer.

Proofing

To ensure that both parties can agree on what the color of the finished product should look like, a special printer or proofer is used to reproduce the final output. These proof prints are correctly called contact prints, but in the trade they have come to be know as Match Prints, which is the trademarked name of the dominant proofing system used for contact proofs. Photoshop provides the tools to create both soft and hard proofs of images, which is covered in detail in Section 19.3.

Print Technologies

When deciding what type of print output to use for a Photoshop image, several considerations determine what type of printing is best. The most important consideration is the quantity to be printed. Although the actual numbers vary, for a large number of copies (more than 1000 copies), offset printing is the output of choice. There are several types of offset printing:

One-color offset This is not limited to printing with black ink on white paper. It can include colored inks on complementary colored media.

Two- and three-color offset Duotones and Tritones are used to increase the tonal range of a printed image. The use of duotones and tritons offer unique effects with the reduced costs that result from using fewer inks (and labor).

Four-color offset The most expensive and the best for reproduction of full color images, especially color photographs.

For quantities that are too small to use offset, you can select from several options.

B&W or grayscale laser printers Excellent for producing medium to large numbers of copies at relatively high speed (up to 25 pages per minute), high resolution (1200 dpi), and comparatively low cost.

Color inkjet printers The most common printers in use today, these are capable of producing excellent color for print jobs in small quantities. As a rule, inkjet printers are too slow and the cost per copy is too high for production work. There are two general classifications of color inkjet printers: color and photo. The standard color inkjet printer uses four inks, and the photo printer uses either six or seven inks. The difference between their output is in subtle color enhancement. Although some inkjets are capable of high-resolution output, avoid using this output. It slows the printing speed considerably with little to no improvement in the output.

Color laser printers Depending on the type and size of printer being used, a color laser is capable of producing short production that requires color but are not large enough to be printed offset. Color laser printers are almost always PostScript printers that can produce accurate color in small to medium production runs. The only restriction is that a color laser printer has a higher cost per page and takes longer to print than an offset printer.

Dye-sublimation printers Known as dye-sub printers in the trade. These printers produce vivid and accurate color, but they are expensive and the cost per page is high.

Once you understand the differences among print technologies, you need to ensure that you have a good grasp of the concept of resolution, which may be the most misused and misunderstood concept in the graphics industry. The next section defines in detail what resolution is and—almost as important—what it isn't.

19.2 Resolution and Printing

➠ 6.6 Setting the Image Size

All raster images are made of building blocks called *pixels*, a term used to describe the smallest part of a raster picture. Pixels have two characteristics: they are square, and they can be only one color. In that regard, a digital picture, like a mosaic, is made of colored squares.

Professional and amateurs frequently use the terms *ppi* (pixels per inch) and *dpi* (dots per inch) interchangeably. Although this is incorrect, it isn't a problem since they usually know what they are talking about. To be absolutely accurate, be aware that scanners, digital cameras, and computer monitors are measured in ppi, and printers are measured in dpi.

The dimensions of a digital picture are expressed in pixels. For example, a digital camera that uses a 5-megapixel sensor produces a photograph that is 2560 pixels wide by 1920 pixels high. (The Photoshop File Browser lists these dimensions below the selected preview image.) So, if a 2560×1920 image is printed, how big is it? Without knowing the resolution, you have no way to know the physical size of the printed output.

A digital image has no absolute resolution. It is made up of a fixed number of pixels in each dimension. As the resolution changes, the physical size of the output changes because the number of pixels that make up the image are being spread over a larger or smaller area. The only difference between these three copies of the same photo is their resolution setting. (Their filenames indicate the resolution: 75, 150, and 300 pixels per inch.) Because each photo has the same number of pixels, they appear as the same size in an image-editing program such as Photoshop.

Here, the three photos were output to a printer with each photo at the size determined by its resolution setting. The result is three different-sized images.

How big is a pixel? A pixel is as large or as small as the device needs to make it to accommodate the resolution of the image being printed. As the resolution of a photograph sent to the printer decreases, there are fewer pixels for every inch, and therefore the printer must make each pixel larger. If the resolution increases, the output device has to fit more pixels into every inch, and therefore the printer makes the pixels smaller.

19.2 Resolution and Printing *(Continued)*

Resolution is commonly (and erroneously) stated in dots per inch (dpi) even when what's being measured has nothing to do with dots. Each output device should have its resolution expressed in units of measure that is appropriate for the device. For example, displays should be expressed in pixels per inch (ppi), and scanners in samples per inch. The following table shows the relationship between the resolution of an image and the size of the printed output when the file size is the same.

RESOLUTION	FILE SIZE	OUTPUT PIXEL SIZE	OUTPUT SIZE OF IMAGE
Increases	Unchanged	Smaller	Decreases
Decreases	Unchanged	Larger	Increases

Changing the output size of an image by changing its resolution is called *scaling* or *resizing;* this is covered in detail in Section 6.6. Since scaling does not add or remove pixels from the image, it doesn't degrade the picture. So, what determines the resolution of a picture? The photo-editing program used to open the picture usually determines the resolution setting of an image. For example, many images opened in Photoshop display at a resolution of 72 dpi.

When setting the resolution for prepress, it is best to talk with the service bureau or printer that will be doing the work. They will advise you as to what resolution they are expecting. If you do not have input from the printer, setting the image to 300 dpi at a 100% output size is a safe choice for most any offset printing.

The best resolution to use with both black-and-white and color laser printers is between 200 and 300 dpi.

The best resolution for photo printers is lower due to the increase in range of colors. It is possible to get excellent output on a photo printer (inkjet or dye-sub) using a Photoshop image at a resolution of 120–150 dpi, and several manufacturers of photo printers recommend not to use an image resolution greater than 200 dpi.

Many rules determine the best resolution for offset printing. The most common is to double the line screen (which is generally 150 lines per inch), resulting in a resolution of 300 dpi. To determine the best resolution for offset printing, ask your printer. In most cases, they will provide you with a preprinted sheet of settings and file formats.

Unless specifically instructed to do so by your service bureau or printer, do not increase the resolution of a photographic image to more than 300 dpi.

When changing the size of an image, always try to do so without resampling.

If you need to resample an image, avoid increasing the size because adding pixels tends to make the image appear soft and ever so slightly out of focus.

19.3 Previewing Color for Print

➠ 2.9 View Menu

➠ 7.4 Setting a Document's Color Profile

➠ 20.2 Creating Color Proofs

The accuracy of the soft proof and hard proof produced by Photoshop is limited by many factors, including the accuracy of the color profile for the equipment being used, room lighting, and the calibration status of the equipment.

Even though the colors represented on an RGB monitor cannot accurately reproduce the color produced by an offset press, Photoshop provides the ability to view "soft proofs" of images—that is, a view on the monitor that creates a reasonably accurate depiction of the colors that will result in print. You can also create hard-copy proof sheets in Photoshop.

To display soft proofs of an image, follow these steps:

1 Choose View > Proof Setup, and from the submenu, choose one of the proof profile spaces that you want to simulate for proofing.

2 Choose View > Proof Colors to toggle the display of the soft-proof.

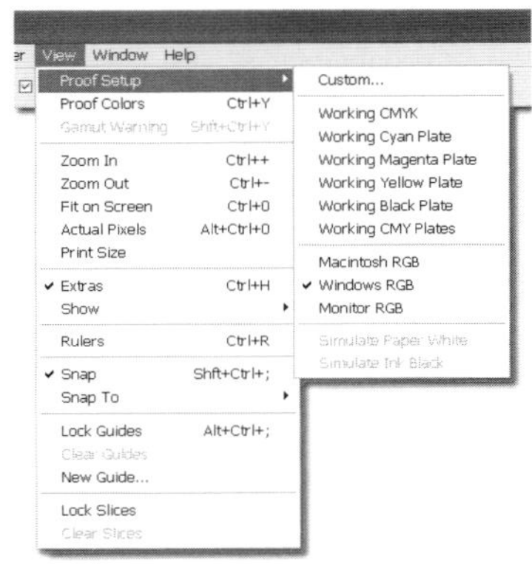

Custom Requires the availability of a specific color profile for the output device.

Working CMYK Uses the current CMYK working space as defined in the Color Settings dialog.

Working Cyan, Magenta, Yellow, or Black Plate These options provide a pre-separated preview of each of the working CMYK plates.

Macintosh RGB or Windows RGB Displays colors in the image using a standard Mac or Windows monitor as the proof profile space to simulate the output.

Monitor RGB Calculates colors in an RGB document using the current monitor color space as the proof profile space.

Simulate Paper White Previews colors against the specific shade of white exhibited by the print medium, which must first be defined using the document's profile. If the shade of white is not defined, this option is grayed out.

Simulate Ink Black Previews the actual dynamic range of the ink to be used. If the ink range is not defined in the document's profile, this option is grayed out.

In addition to displaying a soft proof, printing a hard proof helps you verify the accuracy of a custom CMYK working space profile.

19.4 Checking the Gamut

An accepted limitation of any output device is that the human eye can see a much broader spectrum of colors than any mechanical or electronic device can produce. The range of colors that a color system (device) can display or reproduce is called its *gamut*. Each device and color model has a gamut. Some color models have a greater gamut than others. Colors that cannot be accurately reproduced are referred to as being *out of gamut*.

Of the color modes available in Photoshop, only a few are of concern for purposes of establishing gamut used for printing.

Lab mode This is the only mode whose gamut is so large that, when an image is converted from any other color mode to Lab, there is minimal loss of color information. Most printers will not print files in Lab mode.

RGB mode Computer RGB monitors can display a greater range of colors than CMYK printers can reproduce, because the RGB gamut is larger than the CMYK gamut.

CMYK mode Of these modes, CMYK has the smallest gamut; it is limited to colors that can be printed using process-color inks. If an image will be printed on offset press, you can convert the file to CMYK before giving it to the printer. Or you can have the printer do the conversion. If you choose to convert it yourself, you will discover several Working Space settings for CMYK. Consult with your printer to select the proper setting for your job.

To ensure that the colors in the image can be reproduced on a printer, Adobe includes a gamut warning, which visually indicates which colors are out of gamut by displaying an icon next to the color.

When Photoshop converts an image from any color mode to CMYK, it automatically brings all colors into gamut for the selected output device. To ensure that the colors in an image are within the gamut of a selected output device, Photoshop identifies out-of-gamut colors.

If the original is in RGB color space, you can identify out-of-gamut colors in several ways:

An exclamation point appears in the Info palette to the right of CMYK values that are out of gamut any time the pointer is moved over them.

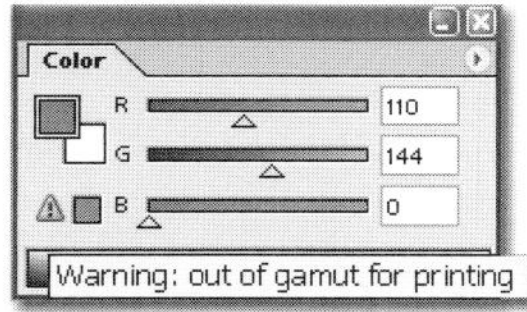

An alert triangle indicates out-of-gamut colors in both the Color Picker and the Color palette (shown here with the pop-up warning activated), and the closest CMYK equivalent is displayed whenever an out-of-gamut color is selected. Clicking either the triangle or the color patch selects the CMYK equivalent that is calculated by Photoshop.

You can also quickly identify all out-of-gamut colors in an RGB image by choosing View > Gamut Warning. All the pixels in the image that are out-of-gamut color will turn to the default viewing color (50% gray).

4.4 Info Palette
4.5 Color Palette
5.6 Transparency & Gamut Preferences
7.6 Converting between Image Modes

When selecting a new gamut warning color, choose a color that does not naturally occur in the image currently being viewed.

To change the default color of the gamut warning, locate the gamut warning in the Transparency & Gamut tab of the Preferences, click the Color box, and select a new warning color (see Section 5.6).

Even though an image contains colors that are out of gamut, the printed output may still look close, if not nearly identical, to the one displayed by an RGB monitor. It is possible for a color to be out of gamut mathematically, but the human eye cannot detect the differences between the displayed and printed versions.

19.5 Working with Color Channels

→ 4.12 Channels Palette
→ 7.5 Using Color in Channels
→ 13.10 Mixing Channels
→ 20.1 Creating Color Traps
→ 21.4 Preparing for Black-and-White, Spot, or Duotone Printing

All images in Photoshop are made up of one or more *channels*. The purpose of the channels is to store and maintain data about each of the color elements in the image. The color mode of the image determines the number of *color information channels* it contains. For example, a CMYK image must have five channels at minimum—one each for cyan, magenta, yellow, and black and a composite color information channel. Each cyan, magenta, yellow, and black channel corresponds to one of the four plates used in four-color process printing. The composite color information channel is the primary channel commonly used in most image-editing situations.

An image can contain as many as 24 channels, including the composite and separate color information channels that define the image's color mode as well as separate "alpha" channels (see Section 7.5).

In addition to standard alpha channels, Photoshop offers the ability to create *spot color channels* from selections or existing alpha channels. These sources are used for the spot application of special premixed ink or varnish that are independent of any other colors being printed using dedicated CMYK plates used in four-color offset printing.

You can create spot color channels in most color modes, although you can save them as Grayscale, CMYK, and Multichannel mode formats. While EPS DCS 2.0 is the traditional format, PDF formats can be used for exporting the spot colors to other applications for separated output.

Spot color channels are independent of the color information channels and layers and will thus be stacked over any existing layer order in the document. By default, spot color channel data overprints the existing color information channels in the order found in the Channels palette.

Creating a Spot Color Channel from a Selection

To create a spot color channel from a selection, follow these steps:

1. Create or load a selection to define the tonal values, which will be used for the spot color channel. A solid black spot color channel will separate as 100% of the spot ink, and a grayscale percentage value will separate as a tint of the spot color.
2. Choose New Spot Channel from the Channels palette menu.

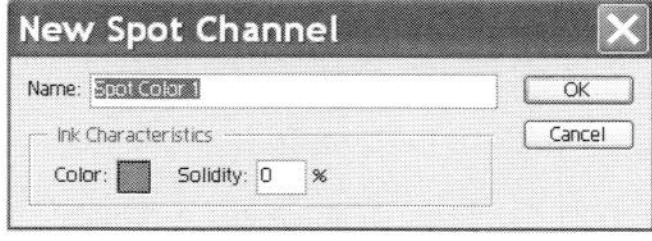

19.5 Working with Color Channels *(Continued)*

3 Click the Color box to select a color, which will most commonly be a Pantone Solid Coated Custom Color Book. The name of the selected ink will appear in the Name section and should exactly match the name used in other software if it is to separate on the same final ink plate. (Always verify that the spot color name used in Photoshop and in illustration and page-layout software is exactly the same.)

4 The Solidity option is for visual display only and will not affect the density of the final separation. As with the Duotone mode Overprint Colors option, this is intended to manually simulate the visual interaction of the combined spot inks when viewed or printed as a composite.

The alpha channel was originally defined by Apple without any specific purpose in mind. Photoshop was one of the first applications to use the alpha channels and has been instrumental in establishing the alpha channel as a space for saving selections in the form of masks as well as spot color channels.

Creating a Spot Color Channel from an Alpha Channel

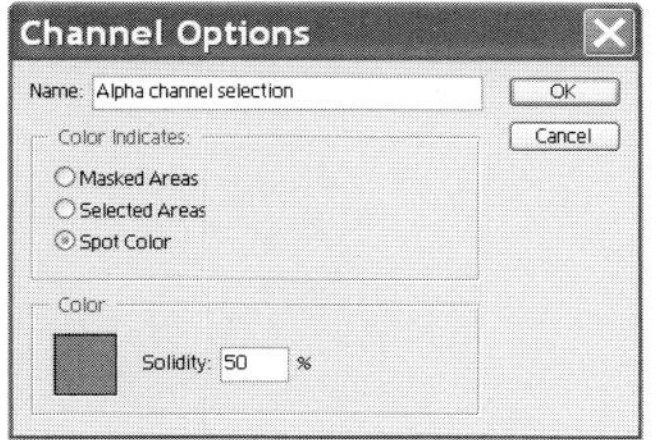

To convert a spot color channel from an existing alpha channel, double-click the alpha channel thumbnail in the Channels palette, or select the alpha channel and choose Channel Options from the Channels palette menu. Click the Spot Color radio button and appropriate Color and Solidity options as described in the preceding section.

Remember that this method will eliminate the alpha channel, which you might otherwise want to preserve. Unlike a standard alpha channel—which is often a "negative" image of white on black—a spot color channel is often a "positive" image of black on white. Simply invert the spot color channel if the results are opposite than expected after converting an existing alpha channel to a spot color channel.

SPOT COLORS VERSUS DUOTONES

Spot color channels are commonly confused with Duotone mode, which also provides users with the option to output separations in spot color ink mixes. In Duotone mode, the separate Duotone ink plates are all generated from the same original Grayscale mode source data and are varied via special Duotone transfer curves. As their name suggests, spot color channels do not have the same limitations as Duotone mode and were a later addition to the Photoshop toolset by Adobe to address a different prepress need. (Photoshop 4 or earlier requires a third-party plug-in to designate spot color and save EPS DCS 2.0 files.) A Duotone mode file that is converted to Multichannel mode allows for the separate editing of the Duotone color plates—although it is not possible to return the file to Duotone mode once any editing has taken place.

CHAPTER 20

Preparing Images for Print

ALTHOUGH USING A PRINTER connected directly to you computer is a straightforward affair (see Section 6.10), before you can print image files to printing presses, you must prepare them for output, and in some cases you must save them in a specific format to be printed. Creating accurate proofs of the final printed output is an import part of the printing process, which allows you to better preview the affects that printing will have on your image. Images that will be printed on an offset press sometimes need corrections called traps that are not necessary for inkjet printing or for the Web. Using Photoshop, you can create contact sheets as well as picture packages that automatically create an assortment of picture sizes on a single sheet of paper.

This chapter covers these tasks:

20.1 Creating Color Traps

➠ 7.2 Understanding Image Modes

Traditionally, *traps* are also known as "spreads" or "chokes;" this was originally a graphic reproduction phrase originating with the photographic preparation of film separations.

Since trapping isn't always necessary, apply it only if your printer says that it is necessary. Many service bureaus add the trap themselves, and a trap added by Photoshop will interfere with this.

Always check with your printer or service bureau as to how much misregistration can be expected. Your service bureau will provide the values to enter in the Trap dialog.

Trapping is designed to compensate for the misalignment of solid colors in Grayscale, CMYK, Multichannel, and Spot Color channels images using large areas of flat color. As a general rule, don't create traps for color photographs.

Always keep an original untrapped version of your image file, in the event you want to edit the image later.

CMYK images are printed with four separate plates, one for each ink color, and aligning these plates is critical for producing high-quality printed results. Any misalignment in the plates produces a tiny gap that contains little or no color. To compensate for any possible misalignment, you add a color trap (also known simply as trap) in areas where this is likely to happen.

The color trap is the overlap needed to ensure that any misalignment of the plates (misregistration) while printing does not visually affect the final appearance of the output. This is critical in any area of the print in which distinctly different colors touch. Overprinting them by even a small amount prevents these tiny gaps from appearing when the image is printed.

Check with your service bureau before creating traps, because many printers prefer to add traps themselves.

To create a color trap, the image must be in Grayscale, CMYK, or Multichannel mode. It is rare to use the Trap command on a CMYK-only file, but it is common to trap when using spot colors in these modes. The Trap command does not require an image to already be flat, but a flat file will result. The command is applied to the current active channel(s).

To create a trap, choose Image > Trap and, in the Trap dialog, enter the trapping value provided by the printer or service bureau.

Choose the units you will be using (pixels, points, mm) and enter a value (1 to 0) for the width of the trap. Trapping values determine how far overlapping colors are spread outward to compensate for misalignment of the printing press—hence the name of the field, Width.

Applying Knockouts

Once a spot color channel has been constructed and the composite color and solidity simulation has been defined, it is critical to consider overprints or knockouts.

By default, a spot color channel will overprint, and if a knockout is required, it must be manually constructed. Using Photoshop blending modes as an example, Normal mode is the same as creating a knockout, while Multiply mode is the same as creating an overprint. Knockouts are generally more common than overprints, so it is critical to master this simple step. Because creating a knockout will remove pixel data from the color information channels and other spot channel data, it is recommended that this operation be performed in a duplicate document so that the original data is intact.

To create a knockout, do the following:

1. Drag the spot color channel to the Load Channel As Selection icon in the Channels palette.
2. Select the appropriate color information channel or another spot channel, and fill the selection with pure white to remove any data in the area underlying the spot color channel.

Using a low Solidity value for the spot color will help with the evaluation of the interaction of the various channels when creating knockouts.

20.2 Creating Color Proofs

Colors displayed on an RGB computer monitor do not accurately reflect the colors of images that are in another color space—CMYK, for example. This is because your monitor can display many colors that CMYK offset printing can't reproduce. With Photoshop's color management, you can create *soft proofs,* which cause the monitor to better mimic what an image will look like when printed. The alternative is to print it on a printer specifically set up to re-create accurate representations of how the project would appear when printed on an offset press; this is called a *hard proof*. Using soft proofs, you can make the job look as good as possible within the limitations of your selected printing process.

To display a soft proof, open the image, choose View **>** Proof Setup, and select a proof profile that meets your requirement from the submenu. The choices on the submenu are as follows:

Custom This opens the dialog box used to define what color display device is being used as well as other information necessary to get an accurate soft proof.

Working CMYK and individual plates Selecting any of the working settings causes the active image to display a soft proof of the selected CMYK working space or individual working plate without the need to convert the color mode of the image. The title bar of the image displays the color mode of the image and the currently selected working space. For example, an RGB image with Working CMYK selected will display (RGB/CMYK).

RGB working spaces These three choices (only available when viewing an RGB image) allow the user to see what the image would look like when viewed in any of the three RGB color spaces.

Simulate (only available when viewing CMYK images) Simulate Paper White previews the shade of white of the print medium defined in the document's profile; Simulate Ink Black previews the actual dynamic range defined by a document's profile. These options are only available for viewing images that contain paper white and black ink information and can only be used for soft-proofing, not for printing.

➠ 7.2 Understanding Image Modes

➠ 7.3 Specifying Color Settings

➠ 7.4 Setting a Document's Color Profile

➠ 19.3 Previewing Color for Print

Toggle Proof Colors on and off

⌘ Y

Ctrl Y

The color accuracy of the soft color proof depends on the calibration and profiling of the monitor and the profile chosen for the Proof Setup.

Color proofs are a convenient way to see how an image will appear on different RGB monitors. For example, when working on an image in Windows, choosing Macintosh RGB will make the image on the screen appear as it would on a Mac, which is typically brighter because the Mac and Windows OSs use different gamma settings.

To convert the custom proof setup into the default proof setup for documents, close all document windows and then choose View > Proof Setup > Custom.

Using the Proof Setup Dialog Box

By default when Proof Colors is selected the default settings cause Photoshop to simulate the conversion from the documents current work space to Working CMYK. To change this setting requires changing settings in the Proof Setup dialog box, accessed through View > Proof Setup > Custom:

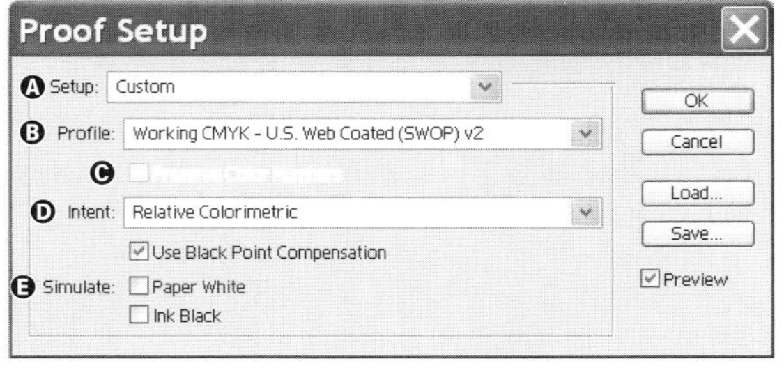

A Used to recall previously saved proof setups. If no setups have been saved, the only choice is Custom.

B Used to specify the proofing space that is to be simulated. You can choose any profile on the list, but if you choose an input device (scanner or digital camera) most of the other options will be grayed out.

C When enabled, causes the image to appear as it will look if it is sent to the selected output device without actually converting the image color space. This feature is only available when image is in the same color mode as the selected profile. When selected, the Intent menu becomes grayed out as no conversion is required.

D Select the rendering intent to be used in the conversion from the image color space to the soft proof color space.

E Both check boxes (Paper White and Ink Black) control the rendering of the image proofing color space to the monitor being used. When both are turned off, the rendering maps paper white to monitor white and ink black to monitor black. When Ink Black is enabled, the black seen on the monitor is the actual black that will appear on the output (within limitations of the monitor settings). Enabling the White Paper check box causes Absolute Colorimetric rendering to be used when rendering the proof color space to the monitor. Black Ink becomes checked and grayed out. In most cases, enabling Paper White produces the most accurate soft-proofs.

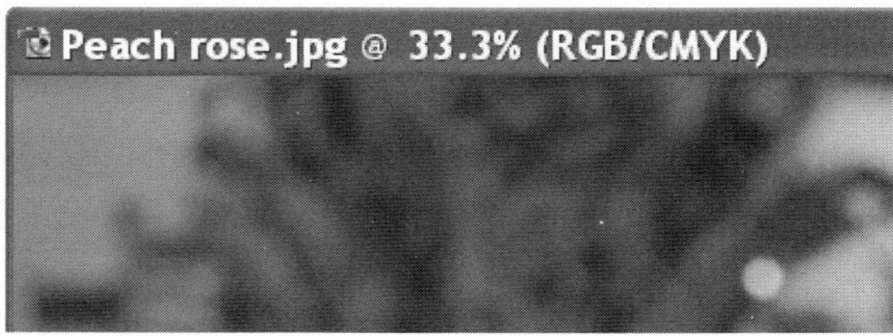

To quickly turn color proofing on and off, choose View > Proof Colors to turn the soft-proof display on and off. When soft proofing is being displayed, the name of the selected proof profile appears next to the color mode in the document's title bar and a check mark appears next to the Proof Colors command in the View menu.

20.3 Saving Files for Print or PDF

Many times you'll print on an output device that is not physically attached to the computer or you may need to save an image to be imported into another program for layout, and you must save the image as a file that can be either sent over the Internet or saved on other storage media such as a CD or DVD. Although there are many different graphic file formats, only three are predominately used between platforms and applications: Tagged Image File Format (TIFF), Encapsulated PostScript (EPS), and Portable Document Format (PDF). This section shows how to save an image in any of these formats and what options are available.

➠ 21.3 Preparing to Print to PostScript Printers

Save
⌘ S
Ctrl S

Save As
⌘ Shift S
Ctrl Shift S

To use the JPEG preview option with EPS files in Mac OS requires that QuickTime be installed.

Saving as TIFF

The workhorse file format of the graphics industry, the TIFF format is the perfect choice for any non-PostScript file. It has the advantage of being able to store alpha channels and other Photoshop-specific information that would otherwise be lost if saved using a different file format.

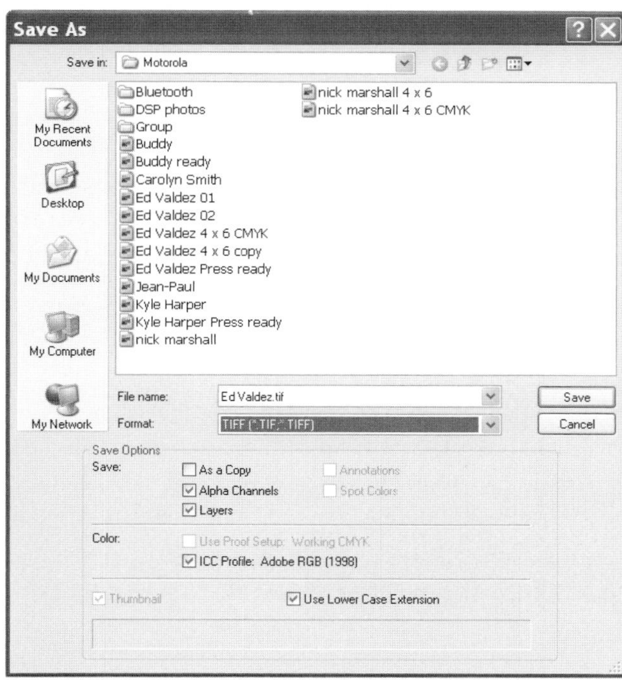

To save a file in the TIFF format, choose File > Save or File > Save As, and then choose TIFF from the Format drop-down. In the Save section of the dialog, click the Alpha Channels and the Layers check boxes, and in the Color section, click the ICC Profile check box. In almost all cases, select these check boxes when they are available. When the TIFF Options dialog opens, select the appropriate options (options will be grayed out if not available) and click OK.

When saving images as TIFF files for applications other than Photoshop, make sure that you not include selections stored in alpha channels since that will prevent most applications from opening the files.

When saving images as TIFF images, be aware that some older applications do not support TIFF files with either ZIP or JPEG compression. To ensure compatibility with these older applications, save using either LZW or no compression.

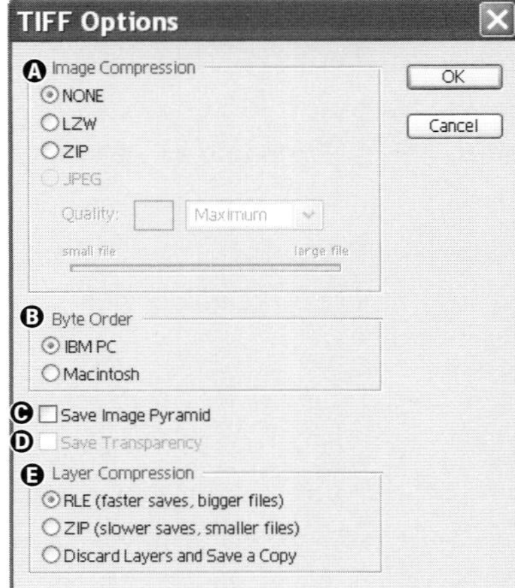

- **A** Several compression options are available. LZW is a lossless standard that reduces file size by an average of 50%. Zip provides a higher compression, but some older applications might not be able to read the TIFF file. JPEG is a lossy compression that provides the maximum file size compression but, like Zip, might be incompatible with older applications.
- **B** Since most applications today can read files saved in either byte order, change this option only if you know the file will be opened on the opposite platform from the one you are using.
- **C** Preserves multiresolution information; useful only when saving an image for an application that supports it.
- **D** Reserves an additional alpha channel to preserve transparency information. If the file being saved doesn't have transparency, the option is not available.
- **E** Selects the method for compressing data in the layers. Choose Discard Layers to save the image as a flattened copy.

Saving as EPS

Encapsulated PostScript (EPS) is the graphics format of choice for files that are to be used with PostScript-aware applications or PostScript printers. EPS files are complex and can become quite large. To save a Photoshop file in Photoshop EPS format, choose File > Save or File > Save As, and then choose Photoshop EPS from the Format drop-down. You must select several options in the dialog if the information is to be saved with the EPS file. In the EPS Options dialog, select the appropriate options (options will be grayed out if not available) and click OK.

20.3 Saving Files for Print or PDF *(Continued)*

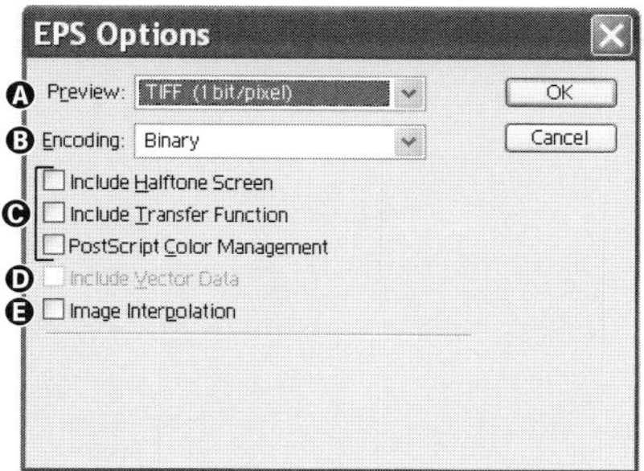

Ⓐ Select the color depth of the preview to be used by other applications to view and place the file.

Ⓑ Select how information is stored and sent to the PostScript printer. ASCII takes the most space but can be used by any PostScript device. Binary is more compact and is the default setting. If Binary doesn't work, switch to ASCII. If JPEG is selected, it produces the smallest files but can only be used to print to either a Level 2 or Level 3 PostScript printer.

Ⓒ Halftone Screen, Include Transfer, and PostScript Color Management (PCM) should only be selected if advised by your printer or service bureau. PCM converts file data to the printer's color space; don't select this option if the image will be opened in a color-managed document. PCM is not for the average user and is usually avoided, although for some very specific workflows there may be a small advantage.

Transparent Whites (not shown) If selected, the EPS displays white areas as transparent. If the image is not a bitmap (1-bit black-and-white), this option does not appear.

Ⓓ Saves any vector graphics (such as shapes and type) in the file. Even though the vector data in EPS files is available to other applications; it is rasterized if you reopen the file in Photoshop. To preserve vector data as vector data when the image is opened, it must be saved in PSD format.

Ⓔ Applies anti-aliasing to improve the appearance of a low-resolution image when it is printed. If the image is high-resolution raster, using this option will soften it.

Saving as PDF

There are several good reasons to save a Photoshop file in Portable Document Format (PDF). If the image contains large amounts of text, saving as a PDF file will retain the crisp, resolution-independent edge to the text that would not occur when the text is rasterized as a TIFF. There is even an option to embed the font into the PDF, ensuring that it will display and print correctly. The only disadvantage to Photoshop PDF files is they comply to the newest PDF specification (version 1.4), and some older applications, such as QuarkXPress 4, cannot import these files. PDF is also an excellent format for sending proofs or samples for review, since anyone can download the Acrobat Reader for free and use it to view the image.

You can create a PDF file in two ways:

- Create a PostScript file, as described in Section 21.3, and then use Adobe Acrobat Distiller to distill the file into a PDF.
- Save the image as a Photoshop PDF file.

Even though EPS files can contain vector only, raster only, or a mixture of both raster/vector, the Photoshop EPS file format is treated as a raster file by Photoshop. (Other applications will still input any embedded vector information and treat it as vectors.)

When you open an EPS file containing vector graphics, Photoshop rasterizes the image, converting any vector graphics in the file to pixels.

When saving an EPS file for placement in another application, make sure the application supports the level of preview bitmap. For example, Adobe FrameMaker can print a file with a color bitmap preview, but when this file is displayed, it appears as a gray box.

When saving an EPS file, support of PostScript Color Management (PCM) for CMYK images is available only on PostScript Level 3 printers. If you are using a Level 2 printer, you must convert the image to Lab mode before saving in EPS format. (Only use PCM if your service provider requires it.)

You can use the Save As command to save RGB, Indexed Color, CMYK, Grayscale, Bitmap, Lab Color, and Duotone images in Photoshop PDF format. To save a file in PDF format, follow these steps:

1. Choose File > Save As, and select Photoshop PDF from the Format drop-down.
2. In the PDF Options dialog, select the options you want, and click OK. The available options depend on the type of image you are creating. The most commonly used options when saving an image as a PDF are the following:

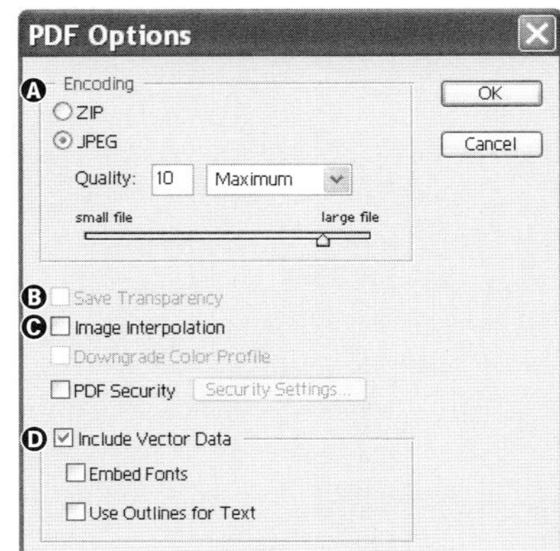

A Select the type of compression applied.

B Preserves transparency when the file is opened in another application.

C Applies anti-aliasing to improve the printed appearance of a low-resolution image.

D Only available if the image includes vector data (shapes and type). If selected, Include Vector Data preserves any vector graphics as resolution-independent objects, which results in smoother output when the PDF is printed. If vector data is included, two additional options can be selected:

Embed Fonts In short, the fonts are saved as fonts. Selecting Embed Fonts increases the size of the saved file.

Use Outlines For Text Saves text as paths rather than fonts. Selecting this option results in a smaller PDF file, but the quality of the displayed fonts can suffer, especially if the image contains display fonts. Text saved as outlines cannot be searched or selected in a PDF viewer. You can still edit the text if you reopen it in Photoshop.

A scaling option in the Page Setup dialog box is available when printing to PostScript printers such as AdobePS and LaserWriter. This scaling affects the size of all page marks, such as crop marks and captions. When you scale in Photoshop using the Print With Preview command, only the size of the printed image (and not the size of page marks) is affected.

20.4 Creating Picture Packages and Contact Sheets

In Photoshop, you can print many different-sized copies of a single image or multiple images with a single click of a button through the Picture Package command. To make multiple copies from a single image, the file need not be open. Simply choose File > Automate > Picture Package, and set the options in the dialog.

➠ 6.10 Printing Basics

➠ 6.11 Adding File Information and Watermarks

➠ 19.1 Print Basics

When applying labels, be aware that Photoshop has a tendency to write the text over the photo regardless of the position selected.

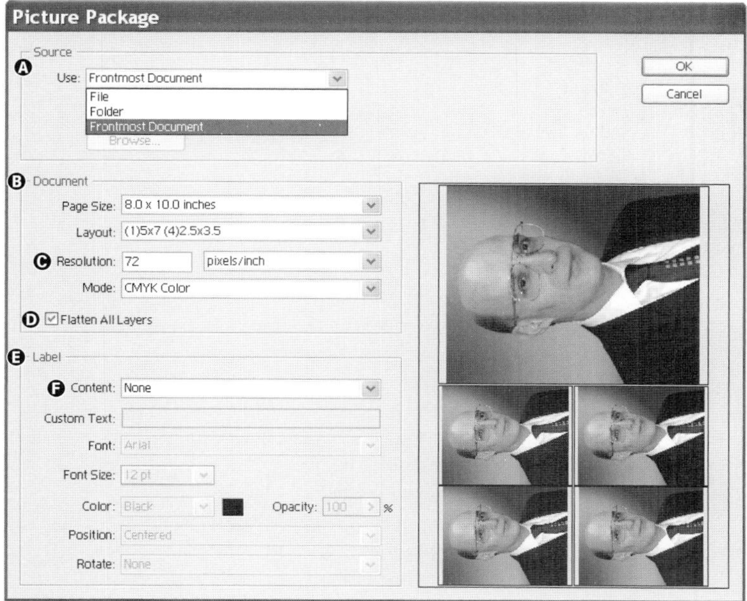

A Choose a source:

Frontmost Document This is automatically selected if an image is open.

File Click the Browse button to select an image.

Folder Click the Browse button to select a folder containing multiple image files. When you select the folder, the first image in the folder is selected.

B In this panel, set the page size of the layout, the resolution, and the color mode for the final picture package.

C **Resolution** This item sometimes causes confusion. It is in pixels per inch, which is not how this setting is usually displayed. Leave it at 72; if you want to increase it, print a test photo at 72 and a second at a higher resolution, and then compare to determine whether you can see any difference.

D Select to create a picture package with all images and text on a single layer; if not selected, each picture and caption on the resulting image will be on a separate layer, which can produce a very large file.

E In this section, you can specify font, font attributes, and position for the labels.

F **Content** The drop-down contains several choices. Selecting Custom Text allows you to add text to each photo. The other choices, such as Copyright, Caption, and so on, are printed from information that was added to the file using the File > File Info command. (If the File Info is blank, nothing will print even if it is selected here.)

20.4 Creating Picture Packages and Contact Sheets *(Continued)*

Click OK when you're done, and Photoshop creates a Photoshop file containing all the photos and whatever captions/text were selected. Copies of the original images are resized to fit into the layout. To print the photos, choose File > Print.

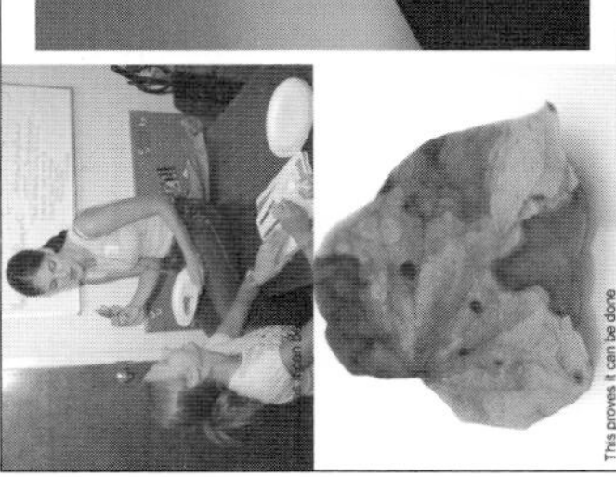

Picture Package is not limited to creating a layout from a single image. You can replace the images shown in the preview. Select the first image, preview the layout, and then click a preview to open a dialog from which you can select another image. After all pictures are in place, click OK.

Printing Contact Sheets

A *contact sheet* is a page containing thumbnail representations of image files. It provides a visual index of images. Creating a contact sheet is similar to creating a Picture Package. By displaying a series of thumbnail previews on a single page, you can easily preview contact sheets and catalog groups of images. You can automatically create and place thumbnails on a page by choosing File > Automate > Contact Sheet II, setting your options, and clicking OK when you're satisfied.

20.4 Creating Picture Packages and Contact Sheets *(Continued)*

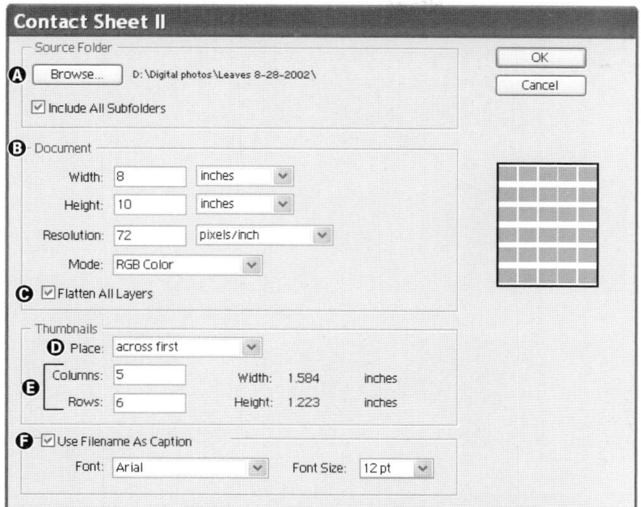

Ⓐ Click the Choose (Mac OS) or Browse (Windows) button to select the folder containing the images to be included in the contact sheet.

Ⓑ Set the dimensions, resolution, and color mode for the contact sheet.

Ⓒ Select to create a contact sheet with all images and text on a single layer; if this option is not selected, each picture and caption on the resulting image will be on a separate layer, which can produce a very large file.

Ⓓ Choose how the thumbnails are arranged: Across First (from left to right, then top to bottom) or Down First (from top to bottom, then left to right).

Ⓔ Enter the number of columns and rows that are to appear on the contact sheet. Based on the numbers selected, the maximum dimensions for each thumbnail are continuously calculated and displayed.

Ⓕ Select to produce a label under each thumbnail made up of the source image's filename.

When selecting a folder to use for Contact Sheet II, be careful of folders containing lots of images. The program will continue to generate the contact sheets until all the files in the folder have been positioned.

Because there is the potential for Contact Sheet II to create a large number of contact sheets, ensure that all open files and other applications that could consume system resources are closed.

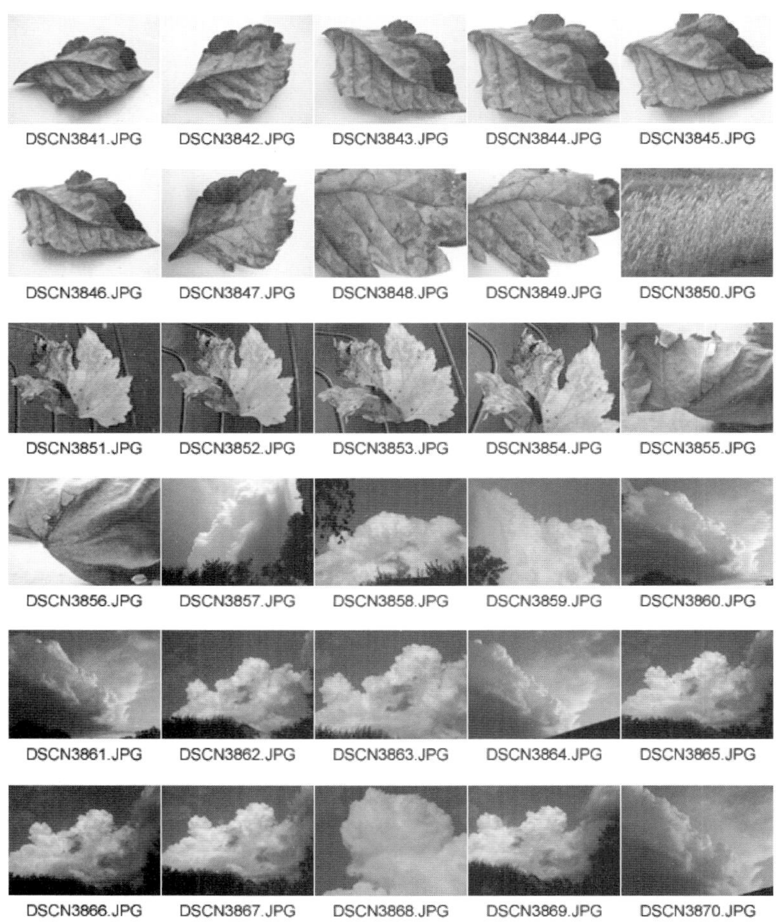

Photoshop will begin to place all the thumbnails into however many document pages it will take to fit in all that were selected. If a folder contains a lot of images, creating all the contact sheets could take a long time. Contact sheets can be saved, printed, or both.

CHAPTER 21

Printing and Prepping for Prepress

AFTER YOU COLOR CORRECT an image, it is time to print the file. You can output directly onto paper, you can convert the file to a positive or negative image on film, which is used to create a master plate for offset printing, or you can output directly from computer to plate.

This chapter covers these tasks:

21.1 Preparing to Print

➠ 6.10 Printing Basics

➠ 7.2 Understanding Image Modes

➠ 7.3 Specifying Color Settings

➠ 7.4 Setting a Document's Color Profile

Color Settings
Shift ⌘ K
Shift Ctrl K

Page Setup
Shift ⌘ P
Shift Ctrl P

Print
Option ⌘ P
Alt Ctrl P

Print With Preview
⌘ P
Ctrl P

When possible, work at the image size and resolution in which the final image will be printed.

Many printers and service bureaus accept full-color images as JPEG files with low compression (high quality) because the degradation caused by the file format is not visually noticeable.

Before you can prepare an image to print, you must decide which output device to use. Chapter 20 gives a more detailed discussion of the criteria for selecting an output device.

If an image will be printed in large quantities, offset printing is probably the best choice. Preparing an image for offset printing is not complicated, but it does involve more preparation than would be necessary for printing to an inkjet printer.

It is important to make sure that the image is in the correct color space (set in the Color Profile) for the type of printing. In addition to setting the image color space, you must select several print settings before sending an image to its output device. You'll find these options in the color settings.

Regardless of the type of printing, to ensure accurate reproduction you need to set up Photoshop for the specific printer. To do this, you use the Color Settings dialog (choose Edit > Color Settings in Windows and Mac OS 9, Photoshop > Color Settings in Mac OS X).

Working with Your Printer/Service Bureau

When selecting a printer or a service bureau, the first step is to shop around. Find a provider that has experience with the platform (Macintosh or Windows), formats, applications, and workflow that you use, and you'll save yourself time and effort. The lowest bidder or the service bureau that "everyone else" uses may not be a good fit with your requirements and methods and might end up costing you more than you thought you could save! Once you are satisfied with a printer or service bureau, stay with them and establish a working relationship. Doing so will pay great dividends in the long run—especially when you find yourself in a jam under a deadline.

Before submitting a job to a service bureau or a printer, you need to ask the following questions:

What file formats are acceptable? Although most printers can read and use Photoshop files, many times they want the files in either TIFF or even EPS format. Also check to see which platform (Windows or Mac) they prefer. Most shops can use either one, but some are platform-specific, and if they are not comfortable with the one you use, it can hamper the job. If your printer or service bureau gives you a choice of image formats, it is generally better to save them in either BMP (Windows), TIFF, or EPS format. Most shops agree that these image formats preserve both the color and the sharpness of your pictures the best. Avoid using file formats such as GIF or low-resolution (72 dpi) JPEG because the compression they use can introduce color shifts and blurring.

In what medium are jobs accepted? Many shops accept files online through an FTP site. Photoshop files can be quite large. If a shop accepts files on media, ask about any restrictions. For example, if you bring your job on a Jaz disk, you might discover that they cannot read the files. The most popular media for transporting images are CD-R and CD-RW discs.

21.1 Preparing to Print *(Continued)*

Can pictures from digital cameras be used? Although JPEG images found on the Web are too low a resolution to be used by most printers and service bureaus, the JPEG images from digital cameras can be used to provide excellent results.

What resolutions should be used? Your printer knows exactly the resolutions to use for the type of printing, so be sure to ask about the resolution requirements. Most printers and service bureaus will give you a handout that contains detailed instructions about the type of image and resolution they expect. Without direction from the printer, either scan or resize your images using a resolution of 300 dpi at the final dimensions you intend to use them. Doing this results in the best color and edge definition. If your image isn't the correct size or resolution, open it in Photoshop and resize it. This can result in loss of detail unless Resample Image is unchecked, as described in Section 6.6.

Do you need to send the fonts with the job? If you use any fonts from sources other than those found in a PostScript printer, you need to gather copies of them, archive them using a program such as WinZip, and send them with your layout file. If you don't know how to do this, go through your document carefully and make a list of any fonts used. Send that list to the printer or service bureau.

By default, all visible layers and channels are printed. To print an individual layer, make it the only visible layer before choosing the Print command.

When sending images to a printer as a TIFF file, make sure you have flattened the image before saving. This reduces the size of the resulting file and prints faster.

To print only part of an image, select that part with the Rectangular Marquee. From the Print With Preview dialog, select Print Selected Area.

USING THE CMYK WORKING SPACE

A working space is a predefined setting meant to represent a color profile that produces the most accurate color for several specific output conditions. One of the most commonly used profiles is the U.S. Prepress Defaults setting, which uses a CMYK working space designed to create accurate colors under the standard Specifications for Web Offset Publications (SWOP) press conditions. CMYK working spaces are limited to the seven profiles installed in Photoshop, which support standard perceptual settings and rendering as well as colorimetric rendering. When working with a service bureau or printer, you may be asked to use one of these preset working spaces, but the accuracy of the color that will be output still depends on the accuracy of your system's ICC profiles. If your work requires creating accurate color for prepress work, consider investing in a system that will create color profiles. Several excellent systems cost less than $50.00 and will calibrate all the parts of your system and produce an accurate ICC profile that can be used by the service bureau or printer to ensure that the color you see on your screen matches what the four-color press produces.

21.2 Preparing to Print to Inkjet Printers

➠ 6.10 Printing Basics

➠ 7.2 Understanding Image Modes

➠ 7.3 Specifying Color Settings

Page Setup
Shift ⌘ P
Shift Ctrl P

Print
Option ⌘ P
Alt Ctrl P

Print With Preview
⌘ P
Ctrl P

Using higher resolutions available with inkjet printers (that is, 2880 dpi) doesn't usually noticeably improve the output, but it takes longer and can use twice as much ink.

Pigment-based inks cannot produce colors as vivid as dye-based inks, but they have greater archival properties. If you are printing for your personal use, dye-based inks will give you more vivid colors, and, even after several years, you can print another copy.

When setting the resolution of the file to print on an inkjet printer, be careful not to set the resolution too high, which is tempting with a printer that is advertised to produce extremely high resolutions. For an inkjet printer running at a setting of 720×720 dpi, the maximum resolution of a photographic image should be 240 dpi. Anything higher is automatically resampled down by the printer's software. The newer photo printers often offer imaging at 1440/2880 dpi, even though manufacturers recommend that the files be a maximum of 360 dpi for optimum quality output. In practice, the visual difference between printed output of images at the two resolutions is almost indistinguishable. For continuous-tone digital imaging (dye-sub printers), the necessary resolution is relative to the printer's resolution; follow the manufacturer's recommendation.

Because most inkjet printers from major manufacturers (such as Hewlett Packard, Epson, Canon, and Lexmark) require that the image be in RGB mode and not CMYK mode even though the printers use CMYK or CcMmYK (photo printers) inks. The print drivers supplied with these printers cannot interpret CMYK image data and will produce unpredictable and generally unacceptable results.

Even if you plan to output your image using a service bureau, it is likely that you will be printing your image to preview on a lesser-quality printer, possibly an inkjet printer.

The kinds of built-in color management that some printers provide can interfere with the color management of Photoshop. The two color-management systems are trying to correct for each other, which sometimes produces unacceptable results. One way to get the best possible color is to use the following procedure:

1 Before opening the image, change two settings in the Color Settings dialog (choose Edit > Color Settings in Windows and Mac OS 9; Photoshop > Color Settings in Mac OS X):
   - In the Working Spaces section, choose RGB: Adobe RGB (1998).
   - In the Color Management Policies section, choose RGB: Convert To Working RGB.

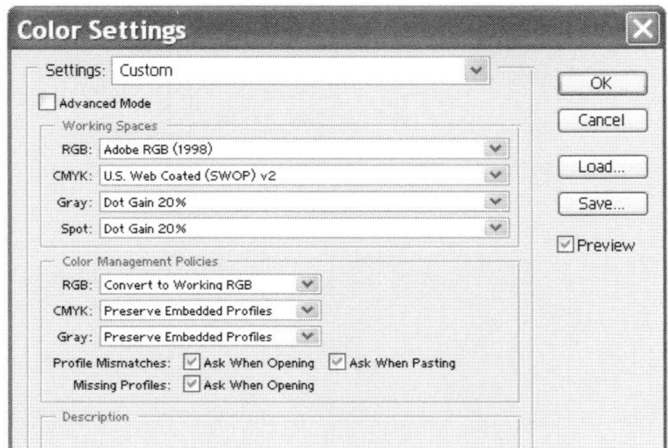

21.2 Preparing to Print to Inkjet Printers *(Continued)*

2 Open the image. If an Embedded Profile Mismatch warning appears, select Convert Document's Colors To The Working Space and click OK.

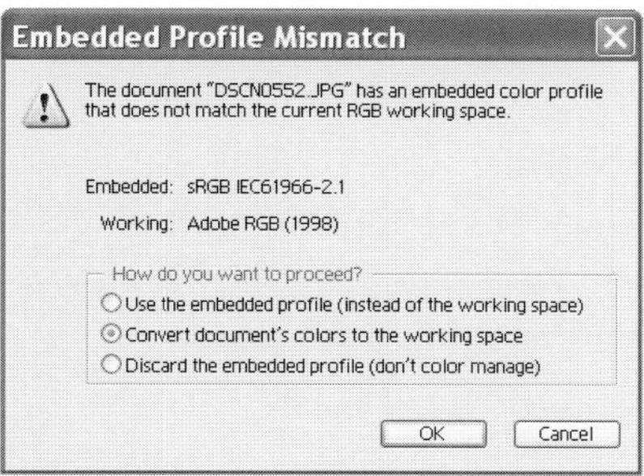

3 With the image selected, choose File > Print With Preview and, in the Print dialog, do the following:

- Check Show More Options and select Color Management from the drop-down.
- Under Source Space, select Document; in the Print Space section, select Printer Color Management from the Profile drop-down.

Show More Options
Color Management
Source Space:
Document: Document: Adobe RGB (1998)
Proof: Proof Setup: U.S. Web Coated (SWOP) v2
Print Space:
Profile: Printer Color Management
Intent: Relative Colorimetric
Use Black Point Compensation

4 Click the Page Setup button to open the printer's Properties dialog, and change the color adjustment properties to ICC Profile (this is usually accessed by clicking an Advanced button). After you set up the printer, return to the Print dialog and print the image.

If you use normal paper, print at a low resolution, such as 360 dpi. If you use special coated paper, such as inkjet paper or glossy film, print at a high resolution.

Always check the printer's Properties dialog before printing to make sure that the correct medium is selected.

Avoid using ink refill kits with your inkjet printer cartridges. The colors may not be as vivid, and, in most cases, doing so voids the printer warranty.

21.3 Preparing to Print to PostScript Printers

➠ 6.10 Printing Basics

➠ 7.2 Understanding Image Modes

➠ 7.3 Specifying Color Settings

➠ 20.3 Saving Files for Print or PDF

Save As
Shift ⌘ S
Shift Ctrl S

Page Setup
Shift ⌘ S
Shift Ctrl S

Print
Option ⌘ P
Alt Ctrl P

Print With Preview
⌘ P
Ctrl P

Most desktop color inkjet printers are non-PostScript printers, including Hewlett-Packard LaserJet, Canon Bubble Jet, and Epson Stylus.

When printing to file for a RIP at a service bureau or printer, check to see which version of the RIP software driver they want you to use.

The only way to determine which is the best print-space setting for a particular PostScript printer is to run multiple test prints. Try the various color-space settings and decide which space gives you the best results.

Many laser printers (black-and-white and color) now support PostScript. If the printer is local, all you need do to print the documents is adjust the settings that are unique to PostScript. If the target printer is a raster-image processor (RIP) at a service bureau, you need to create a PostScript file that can be sent to the output device. To do so, select the printer and then select the print to file. If the printer or RIP that is used by the service bureau or printer is not installed on your system, download it from the Internet and install it.

Before printing, ensure that the image is at the correct resolution. For grayscale halftones, the traditional rule of thumb is that the dpi (equivalent to ppi, or pixels per inch) should be twice the lpi (lines per inch). For a typical 300 dpi laser writer, which prints only up to 53 lpi, 100 dpi grayscale scans are adequate.

To print to a PostScript-capable printer, follow these steps:

1 To print to a color printer that is PostScript Level 2 or higher, it may be necessary to first convert the image to the appropriate color mode for your output device. For example, the setting that is most often used with color laser printers is CMYK.

2 Choose File > Page Setup and, in the Page Setup dialog, do the following:

- Click the Printer button; in the Printer dialog, choose the correct color printer from the drop-down. The driver for the printer must be installed on your system for its name to appear in this menu. Click OK.
- Select either Landscape or Portrait in the Orientation section. Click OK.

3 Choose File > Print With Preview; in the Print dialog, do the following:

- Choose Document as your Source Space in most cases.
- In the Print Space section, choose Printer Color Management. This option sends all the file's color information along with the Source Space profile to the printer. In this way the printer, rather than Photoshop, controls the color-conversion process.
- From the Intent drop-down, choose Relative Colorimetric.

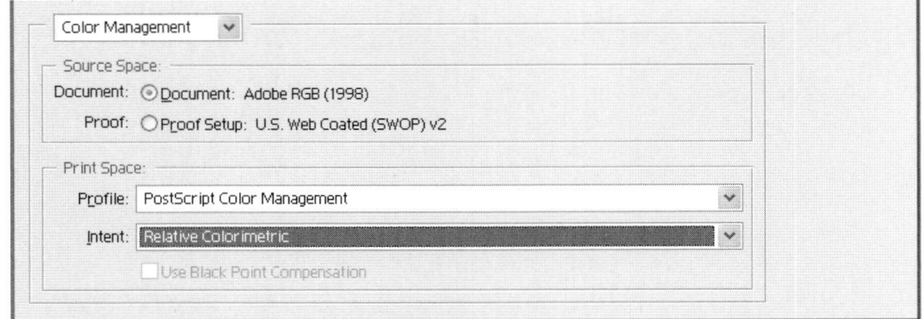

21.4 Preparing for Black-and-White, Spot, or Duotone for Printing

➠ 6.10 Printing Basics

➠ 7.8 Converting to Duotone Mode

The most important part of preparing line art (which Photoshop calls bitmapped 1-bit) images for printing involves ensuring that the quality of the original is good enough to prevent jaggy edges, disappearing fine lines, and clogged-up portions of patterns in the printed output.

When scanning in line art to be printed in Photoshop, it is always preferable to scan the image in as grayscale rather than use the line art setting of the scanner. If the original image is scanned in as line art, Photoshop's tools are not available to clean up or otherwise improve it. If the original image is scanned in as grayscale, you can control the contrast between the dark parts and the white background by using the black/white threshold and by applying sharpening to define faint or fine lines. After you correct the image, convert it to a bitmap by choosing Image > Mode > Bitmap. To produce printed images that reproduce the fine, sharp lines of the original, try the following:

- When converting grayscale images to bitmap, select the resolution and conversion method recommended by your printer or service bureau.
- Printing bitmap images to an imagesetter requires very high resolution to prevent aliasing on diagonal lines.
- Save the image at the highest resolution that the output device can produce. For example, if you are printing to a 1200 dpi laser printer, save the image at 1200 dpi. Conversely, saving an image at a resolution that is higher than that of the output device will result in larger files and longer processing time with no visible improvement in the output.

Spot color is used when printing a small number of colors (three or fewer). You can prepare spot colors in Photoshop in three ways:

- By simulating spot colors in CMYK mode
- By using Duotone mode
- By using the spot color channels, converting the image to Multichannel mode (choose Image > Mode > Multichannel), and saving in DCS 2.0 format (the preferred method)

Because spot colors occupy their own unique channel, you cannot use the layer feature with spot channels. In other words, if your image has layers, you cannot use them. If type is placed on the spot color channel, it is automatically rendered and placed in the spot channel.

You can convert a spot color channel into either the RGB or the CMYK color equivalents by selecting Merge Spot Channel from the Channel palette drop-down, which is a quick way to create comps for preview or approval. It isn't necessary to merge spot colors before printing them to a color printer.

Photoshop's recommended screen angles and frequencies for Quadtones are based on the assumption that channel 1 is the darkest ink and channel 4 is the lightest ink. If the color order in a Quadtone is different, reassign the inks for optimum results.

When printing spot color from an application other than Photoshop, ensure that the spot color appears on the correct plate and ensure that the name of the spot color matches the name of the same ink in the application.

21.4 Preparing for Black-and-White, Spot, or Duotone for Printing *(Continued)*

Use PANTONE colors for spot color jobs unless directed otherwise by your printer or service bureau.

Avoid selecting process colors or custom colors in Duotones and spot color jobs whenever possible.

Whenever possible, allow Photoshop to name the spot colors you select so that they're recognized by the application driving the output device. If you don't allow Photoshop to name the colors, the image may not print correctly or even at all.

- To prevent the mottled appearance that can result from applying a solid spot color ink on top of a CMYK image, it is generally recommended that you knock out the parts of the image that lie underneath the spot colors manually if the printing application does not do so automatically. When knocking out portions of images, ask your printer if trapping is required to compensate for possible misalignment.
- For solid spot colors (100%), halftone screens are not required. But when printing tinted spot colors that overlap, ensure that each halftone screen has a different angle to prevent moiré patterns.

When preparing Duotone mode for printing, both the order in which the inks are printed and the screen angles visually affect the final output. The screen angles are controlled in the Halftone screens dialog box. The following procedure shows how this feature is used:

1. Choose File > Print With Preview > Output > Screen to open the Halftone Screens dialog. Click the Auto button in the Halftone Screens dialog box causes Photoshop to apply the optimal screen angles and frequencies for the type of image being printed. The Halftone Screens option is found under File > Print With Preview > Output > Screen.
2. When printing to a PostScript Level 2 (or higher) printer or to an imagesetter equipped with an Emerald controller, select the Use Accurate Screens option in the Auto Screens dialog.
3. Unlike process colors, you need not convert Duotone mode images to CMYK in order to print separations. To make the separations, choose Separations from the Profile pop-up menu in the Color Management section of the Print dialog. Converting to CMYK mode converts any custom colors to their CMYK equivalents.
4. Because of the unique composition of a Duotone image when it is being prepared for exporting to a service bureau or for use in a page-layout application, save the Duotone as either an EPS or a PDF format. You cannot save the image as a PSD or TIFF file; the printer or service bureau will not be able to create the Duotone. There is an exception to this rule: if the image contains spot channels, convert it to Multichannel mode (choose Image > Mode > Multichannel) and save it in DCS 2.0 format.

21.5 Preparing for Four-Color Printing

When printing using color ink on paper, the CMYK (cyan, magenta, yellow, and black) process colors for four-color offset printing are used, and generally the PMS (Pantone Matching System) is used for spot ink color designation. The following sections present some guidelines for using CMYK effectively.

➡ 6.10 Printing Basics

➡ 7.2 Understanding Image Modes

➡ 7.3 Specifying Color Settings

➡ 7.5 Using Color in Channels

Convert to CMYK

Always use CMYK for process color work rather than RGB. Even if your printer or service bureau says they accept RGB images, they will need to convert your files to CMYK mode to create a *color separation*. In most cases, you will be charged for this additional service, although some users prefer to let professionals handle this side of things, despite the additional charge. If your image is in RGB color space, do any and all image editing in RGB mode before converting the image to CMYK. Although CMYK is a standard color model for prepress work, the exact range of colors that can be reproduced by the output device can vary. Photoshop's CMYK mode depends on the settings in the working space setting that is specified in the Color Settings dialog.

The Adobe Color Picker supports various color models. Ensure that you select the same color model that is used by the service bureau or printer.

When an image is converted between various color modes, some small image color information is always lost. Converting from RGB or CMYK to Lab or from Lab back to RGB or CMYK does not cause an identifiable loss of color information.

Ensure that your Photoshop file is the exact dimensions you want printed. If the file used a default size but your document is larger or smaller, resize your page accordingly before sending it to the printer.

Verify Bleed Settings

Bleed is the term for any printing that extends to the edge of the paper. It is impossible for most offset printers to print to the very edge of the paper so, by using a bleed, they can print the job on oversized paper and then trim the paper to the correct size, resulting in the print going to the very edge of the paper. Your printer will tell you what they prefer, but in most cases ensure that the edge of your document is about 0.25" too big in both dimensions. For example, if the final size is 8.5" × 11", make your document edge 9" × 11.5". Make sure that any photographs or backgrounds that you want to bleed extend to the perimeter of the document, past the guidelines. After the printer has printed your piece, they will trim that extra 0.125" around the perimeter, and the resulting color will extend to the edges of the printed piece.

If you intend for your image to bleed, you will need to allow for this when you originally create the file by setting the dimensions of the file to the bleed size, not the trim size. If you discover that you need to make a bleed from a slightly smaller original, you can use the Resize command in the Edit menu to increase the size of the image, which will result in loss of image detail. Another workaround is to increase the size of the canvas (choose Image > Canvas Size), and then use the Clone tool to insert the small edge around the image.

The stock (paper or other media used for printing) also has a dramatic effect on the accuracy of color reproduction, and you specify the stock in the ICC profile used to convert to CMYK. Choose Color Settings > Advanced > Custom CMYK, the legacy CMYK conversion method, to display the built-in ink and stock options. Some papers exhibit unacceptable dot gain, and the results are different on an inkjet printer and an offset printer.

When choosing a paper stock for a print job, consult with your printer. Many decorative papers cannot be used for offset printing for a variety of reasons.

Although the traditional rule of thumb is that the dpi should be twice the lpi, most printers agree that 265 dpi is more than adequate and that anything more results in larger file sizes and longer RIP time with little to no improvement in the final output.

Logos and line art will produce superior results when originally generated as vector files, especially if trapping is involved

If the line art was scanned at a resolution lower than 1200 dpi, save it as a grayscale image so that it will not exhibit aliasing.

Check for Imposition and Backup

If you are printing two-sided documents that will be folded, you have some additional considerations. The term *imposition* describes how pages and objects on pages are arranged so that, when the sheets are printed and folded, the pages will be in the correct order. The term *backup* refers to printing on the back side of the sheet that has already been printed on one side. For example, if you create a brochure, it is normally turned over from right to left (as turning the page of a book); you need to ensure that the back side reads correctly—not upside down when it is folded.

When reviewing your proof online, it is good practice to post the front and the back in the orientation that they will print. Be sure to print a copy of your online proof and attach the two sides to create a "mockup" or "dummy." This is especially important for tri-folds and multifold documents. More than one large job has had to be thrown away after printing because one part of the document appeared in the wrong orientation. By giving the printer a dummy to work with, the person doing the press work can see how it is folded and can use the first printed page to verify that everything is correct—before printing the rest of the job.

Include Fonts and Vectors

If you include unique or stylish display fonts, make it a habit to provide both screen and printer fonts with your files. In fact, make it a rule: always supply every font used in the job, no matter what. Missing fonts are the most common holdup at service bureaus.

Another common problem for PostScript Type 1 fonts occurs when users don't submit both the printer and screen font (Mac) or PFB and PFM files (PC). If text in placed graphics has been converted to paths, the printer will not require these fonts. For some service bureaus, TrueType fonts are more likely to create production problems.

Always Ask

No matter how much you know about printing, make sure you understand your specific situation—files, devices, providers. For example, a color copier with a PostScript RIP is commonly used in many service bureaus. But even though these are often 400–600 dpi devices, they only need files at 180 dpi for best results. For output to film recorders, 600 dpi is a recommended minimum, and some service bureaus recommend 1016 dpi for LVT output. LVT stands for Light Valve Technology, which is a drum-style, high-resolution film recorder that has become an industry standard. The key is to ask the printer or service bureau what they want for their images—for example, what resolution values they expect, whether they have color profiles for their output devices, and so forth.

WEB TASKS

CHAPTER **22**

Working With ImageReady

IMAGEREADY IS A SEPARATE, stand-alone program used to create and output images destined for the Web. ImageReady works much like Photoshop, and once you learn one of these programs, mastering the other will not take long. ImageReady and Photoshop include the same menus and most of the same menu options, the toolbox, and palettes that can be docked to each other.

However, there are differences. Unlike Photoshop, which is designed to create images for a variety of mediums, ImageReady is designed to create, optimize, and output graphics for the Web. To that end, ImageReady has a more limited tool set (in the Toolbox) but adds a new menu (Slices) and palettes to facilitate these operations. Some of the differences are the natural consequences of ImageReady being devoted to creating web graphics. Other interface differences, however, are less explicable and may take some getting used to.

This chapter outlines the differences between Photoshop and ImageReady and discusses how to use these two programs with Adobe's other flagship web product, GoLive.

22.1 ImageReady Document Windows

➠ 25.3 Optimizing Images

Minimize window

Ctrl ⌘ M

Alt Ctrl M

Close window

⌘ W

Alt W

Close all open windows

Option ⌘ W

Alt Ctrl W

Show/hide everything but the document windows

Tab

Show/hide all palettes

Shift Tab

Cycle through open document windows

Ctrl Tab

Alt Tab

You can have multiple document windows open and juggle them by using the Window > Documents submenu.

ImageReady maintains the same basic concept for the document window used in Photoshop: it's the place you edit the image. However, ImageReady adds and changes several features of the Photoshop window to make it more conducive to web design.

- You can preview a document using a variety of optimization settings. You access the views through the four tabs along the top of the document window.
- The information displayed at the bottom of the document window includes more options for optimizing the image for the Web.
- Rulers display only in pixels.
- The document window contextual menu also includes the layer unification commands (see Section 24.6), preview options (see Section 23.5), and Jump To options (see Section 22.6).

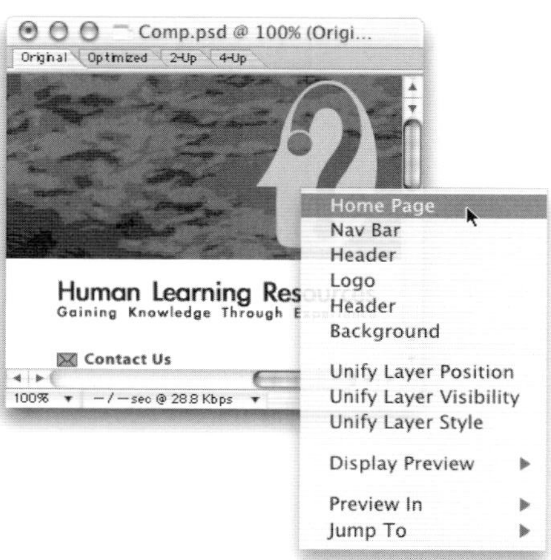

The ImageReady document window contextual menu includes options to select layers, unify layers in animations and rollovers, preview options, and send the image to other applications for editing.

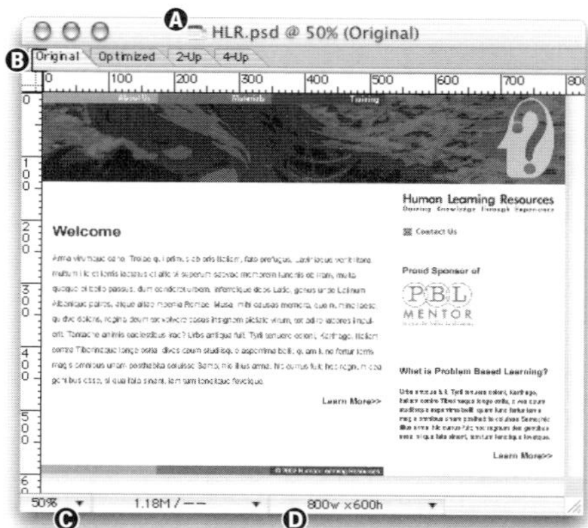

Ⓐ Title bar Not only displays the name of the file being viewed, but also the magnification and the optimization view.

Ⓑ Optimization views The preview tabs allow you to switch between the four optimization view types.

Ⓒ Magnification Displays the current image magnification, but unlike Photoshop, this is a drop-down that allows you to choose the magnification.

Ⓓ Optimization information Both drop-downs allow you to select from a list of optimization information to display, including original/optimized file sizes, information about the optimization options set, the image dimensions, watermark strength, number of undos/redos, file-size savings due to optimization, and estimated download time based on Internet connection speed.

22.2 ImageReady Menus

Although the ImageReady menu bar looks almost identical to its Photoshop counterpart—except for the Slices menu—there are some significant differences under the hood. For the most part, these differences are limited to either options not available in ImageReady or options that were not available in Photoshop. However, in several cases options in Photoshop have been moved, renamed, or replaced by similar options. The differences between the ImageReady menu bar and its Photoshop counterpart include the following:

ImageReady (Mac OS X only) Does not include the Color Settings option, and the preferences submenu contains different options (see Section 22.5).

File Adds Export Original, Save Optimized related commands (see Section 25.6), and the Preview In command (see Section 23.5).

Edit Adds Copy HTML Code and Copy Foreground Color As HTML options.

Image Adds Duplicate Optimized (see Section 25.6), Variables (see Section 23.4), Preview Document (see Section 23.4), and Master Palette.

Layer Adds New Layer Based Image Map Area (see Section 24.1), Match (see Section 24.6), Propagate Changes (see Section 24.6), Set Layer Position dialog, Lock All Layers In Set dialog, Delete Layer command (replaces Delete submenu), Layer Options dialog (replaces the Layer Properties dialog), Remove Layer Mask, and Disable Layer Mask (previous two commands replace Enable Layer Mask submenu).

Slices Menu only available in ImageReady (see Section 25.1).

Select Adds Create Selections From Slices, Create Slice From Selection (see Section 25.1), Create Image Map From Selection dialog (see Section 24.1), Delete Channel submenu, Load Selection submenu (replaces Load Selection dialog).

Filter Adds command to open the last filter dialog rather than simply reapplying the filter using the previous settings.

View Adds Preview submenu (see Section 23.5), Show 2-Up (see Section 23.5), Hide Optimization Info (see Section 23.5), Actual Pixels (replaces Actual Size option), Resize To Fit Window (replaces Print Size option), New Guides dialog (replaces Create Guides dialog).

Window Adds Optimize (see Section 25.3), Rollovers (see Section 24.4), Color Table (see Section 25.4), Layer Options/Style (see Section 23.3), Animation (see Section 24.2), Image Map (see Section 24.1), and Slice (see Section 25.1).

Help Adds the ImageReady Help option to replace the Photoshop Help option, but this is in fact the exact same help file.

➠ 25.1 Slicing Your Interface
➠ 25.2 Working with Slices

You can adjust the keyboard shortcuts for undo/redo in the ImageReady preferences (see Section 22.5).

The Slices Menu

ImageReady also includes the Slices menu that collects commands used to create and edit slices in the canvas (see Section 25.1).

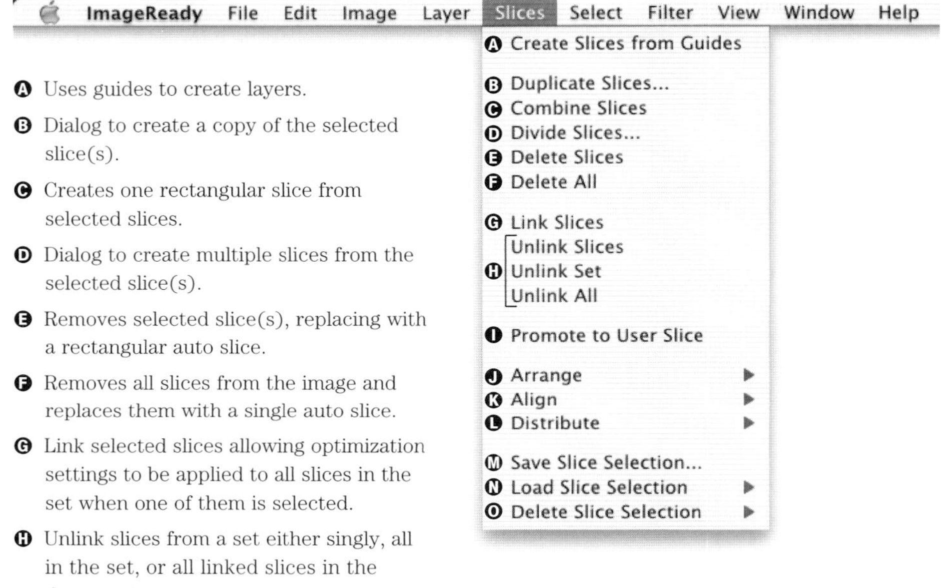

- **A** Uses guides to create layers.
- **B** Dialog to create a copy of the selected slice(s).
- **C** Creates one rectangular slice from selected slices.
- **D** Dialog to create multiple slices from the selected slice(s).
- **E** Removes selected slice(s), replacing with a rectangular auto slice.
- **F** Removes all slices from the image and replaces them with a single auto slice.
- **G** Link selected slices allowing optimization settings to be applied to all slices in the set when one of them is selected.
- **H** Unlink slices from a set either singly, all in the set, or all linked slices in the document.
- **I** Turn the selected auto slice(s) into user slice(s).
- **J** Submenu with options allowing you to set the stacking order of the selected slice(s).
- **K** Submenu with options allowing you to align two or more selected slices to their top, left, right, bottom, or centers.
- **L** Submenu with options allowing you to distribute three or more selected slices to their top, left, right, bottom, or centers.
- **M** Dialog allowing you to save one or more slices in a selection set that you can then quickly load.
- **N** Submenu listing saved slice selection sets. Choosing one set selects those slices in the canvas.
- **O** Submenu listing saved slice selection sets. Choosing one deletes that set from the list, although the original slices will remain in the canvas.

22.3 ImageReady Tools

ImageReady includes a more limited tool set than Photoshop, but the tools you will need for most web tasks are here with the same single letter keyboard shortcuts. However, there are a few important differences in how Photoshop deals with tools in ImageReady. ImageReady does not include tool preset options (or any of the preset options found in Photoshop), so you cannot save the options you set for a particular tool. Also, ImageReady's brush tools use preset brush tips and shapes rather than the robust brush engine in Photoshop 7. This is more like the brushes used in Photoshop 6 than in Photoshop 7.

Many of the tools in ImageReady are identical to their Photoshop counterparts: Move, Magic Wand, Crop, Hand, Zoom, Foreground/Background Color, and Screen Modes.

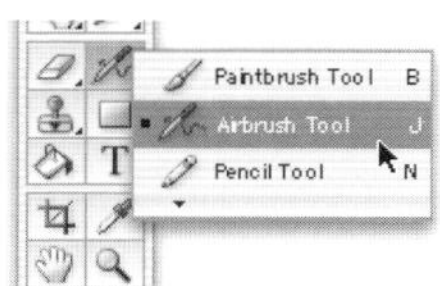

ImageReady includes a stand-alone Airbrush tool rather than the Airbrush mode that exists in Photoshop 7. The Airbrush tool behaves like the Photoshop Brush tool in Airbrush mode.

ImageReady allows you to "tear off" a tool set from the Toolbox, creating a floating palette of that tool set. Click a tool set, and then click the arrow pointing down at the bottom of the tool set.

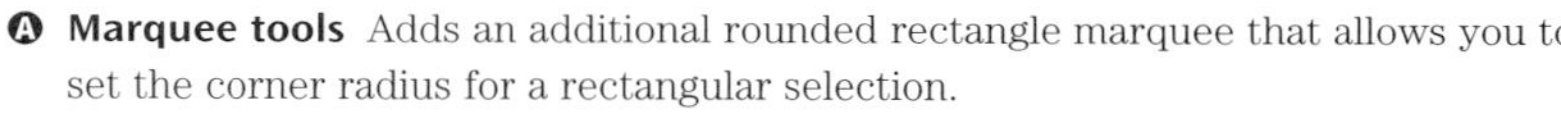

Ⓐ **Marquee tools** Adds an additional rounded rectangle marquee that allows you to set the corner radius for a rectangular selection.

Ⓑ **Lasso tools** Does not include Magnetic Lasso.

Ⓒ **Image Map tools** Tool set specific to ImageReady. See Section 24.1 for more information on creating image maps.

Ⓓ **Slice tools** Identical to Photoshop. See Section 25.2 for more details on adding slices.

Ⓔ **Eraser tools** Does not include Background Eraser.

Ⓕ **Paint tools** Includes Airbrush tool. ImageReady's painting tools resemble those available in Photoshop 6, allowing you to choose preset brush tips and sizes, but does not allow you to directly edit these.

Ⓖ **Stamp/Exposure/Distortion tools** Combines all three tool sets found in Photoshop as one tool set. Does not include the Pattern Stamp.

Ⓗ **Shape tools** Allows you to draw shape layers and filled regions as in Photoshop. Does not include the Polygon or Custom Shape tools.

Ⓘ **Fill tool** Does not include Gradient Fill.

Ⓙ **Type tool** Only includes Horizontal Type tool, but type orientation can still be changed in the tool options bar.

Ⓚ **Eyedropper tool** Measurement tool is not available.

Continues

➠ 24.1 Creating Image Maps

Switch foreground and background colors
X

Use default foreground and background colors
D

Preview In default browser (ImageReady)
⌘ Option P
Ctrl Alt P

Jump to Photoshop
Shift ⌘ M
Shift Ctrl M

Open the toolbox using the Window > Tools command.

The default browser for the Preview In Keyboard shortcut will be the last browser chosen in the Preview In submenu or toolbox drop-down.

- **L** **Toggle Image Map** Click to show or hide image map hot spot boundaries in the canvas.
- **M** **Toggle Slices** Click to show or hide the slice lines in the canvas.
- **N** **Preview Mode** Click to turn on preview mode in the canvas, allowing you to test rollovers and optimization settings.
- **O** **Preview In Browser** Click to preview the document with current slices, image maps, rollovers, animations, optimization, and other output settings in the indicated browser. Click menu to choose an alternate browser in which to preview.
- **P** **Jump To Photoshop** Send document to Photoshop for editing.

Image Map Tools

ImageReady includes the Image Map tool set, not available in Photoshop. You use these tools to draw rectangular, circular, or free-form polygon shapes to use as hot spots in the canvas. In addition, the Image Map selection tool allows you to choose and edit the shapes of hot spots created with the other tools. For more details on using the Image Map tools, see Section 24.1.

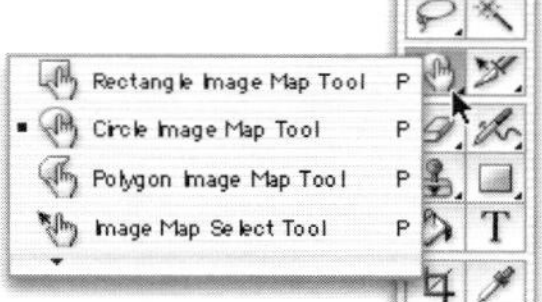

The Image Map tools include a rectangular, circular, and free-form polygon tool in addition to a selection tool for editing image map shapes.

ADDING "PREVIEW IN" BROWSERS

You can preview your Web design in a Web browser using either Photoshop's Save For Web dialog or directly in ImageReady. Both programs will use the same list of browsers for you to choose from when wishing to preview, and you can edit that list. However, to edit the list, you will need to work directly with files in your own operating system.

To add a preview browser, create a shortcut (Windows) or an alias (Mac) for the browser you want to add, and place the shortcut/alias in the Helpers > Preview In folder in the Photoshop folder. Similarly, delete any shortcuts/aliases from the Preview In folder to remove them from the Preview In list. Then you will need to either launch or re-launch Photoshop or ImageReady for the changes to take effect.

22.4 ImageReady Palettes

Palettes in ImageReady work almost exactly like palettes in Photoshop. You access them through the Window menu, you can dock them together either as a group or as palette windows, and you can save and restore their positions using the Window > Workspace menu. However there are a few important differences, notably that ImageReady does not have the Palette Well.

➠ 4 Palettes

➠ 7.10 Changing the Indexed Color Table

➠ 10.2 Applying Effects and Styles

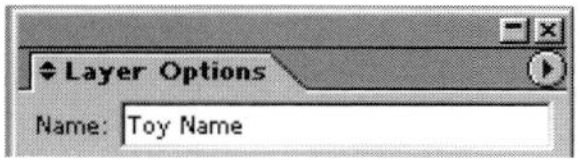

Some ImageReady palettes include a diamond-shaped icon in the tab to the left of the palette name. Clicking this tab cycles through several views of the palette displaying different information and options.

Some numeric input fields include up/down arrows to the left of the field that you can click to increase or decrease the value in the field by 1.

Show/hide everything but the document windows

Show/hide all palettes

Shift T

The ImageReady Info and Color palettes display a reduced set of modes—modes appropriate to web graphic work. The Layers and History palettes omit a few Photoshop features (such as the Adjustment/Fill layers drop-down and snapshots, respectively). The ImageReady Layers palette adds animation controls (see Section 24.3) and the Unify buttons (see Section 24.6). The Styles palette records the styles of multiple rollover states (see Section 24.5). Otherwise, you will find palettes substantially the same as their Photoshop equivalents.

In addition to the palettes that are similar to those in Photoshop, ImageReady includes seven additional palettes. Some of these palettes (such as the Image Map tool) are used with ImageReady specific tools, while others (such as Layer Styles) present options found in Photoshop but in a different format.

Optimize Used to set optimization options for an image or a slice (see Section 25.3).

Rollovers Used to add and edit rollover states to a slice or image map hot spot (see Sections 24.4 and 24.5).

Color Table Used to adjust the colors in an indexed color table used with GIF or PNG-8 optimization settings (see Section 25.3). Similar to the Photoshop Indexed Color Table dialog.

Layer Options/Style Used to set additional options for individual layers or styles associated with a layer (see Section 23.4). When in Layer Styles mode, this palette contains similar options to the Photoshop Layer Style dialog.

Animation Used to add and edit animation frames to the selected layer (see Sections 24.2 and 24.3).

Image Map Used to add information to image map hot spots (see Section 24.1)

Slice Used to add information to a slice (see Section 25.2).

22.5 ImageReady Preferences

➠ 5 Presets and Preferences

➠ 14.3 Selecting Colors with the Color Picker

Although there is some overlap with the Photoshop preferences, ImageReady includes a different set of preferences. ImageReady includes preferences for slices, image maps, and optimization. You access the ImageReady Preferences submenu through either the ImageReady menu (Mac OS X) or the Edit Menu (Mac OS 9 or Windows).

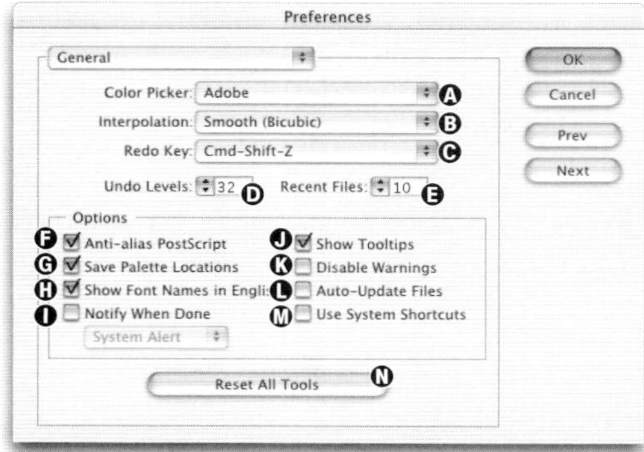

A Choose whether you want to use the Photoshop Color Picker or your operating system color picker.

B Choose a default interpolation method. ImageReady allows you to choose between Nearest Neighbor and Bicubic (recommended).

C Choose the keyboard shortcut for Edit > Undo/Redo.

D Enter the number of undo levels available. More undo levels require more memory and may slow down your system.

E Enter the number of options to include in the Recent Files submenu in the File menu.

F Check to automatically anti-alias PostScript graphics pasted into an ImageReady file.

G Check to preserve palette locations after quitting ImageReady. Otherwise, palettes will reset to default locations.

H Check if you want fonts that do not display in standard characters to use standard characters in font lists.

I Check if you want to play an alert after ImageReady finishes a command. Choose the alert from the drop-down below.

J Check if you want Tool Tips to appear when the mouse cursor is over an object in the interface.

K Check to disable warning messages when deleting most items. This can speed up your workflow, but might lead to mistakes.

L Check if you want to open documents in ImageReady but edit them in another application (such as Photoshop) and then automatically update them when reentering ImageReady.

M (Mac OS X only) Check to use system keyboard shortcuts if they conflict with ImageReady shortcuts. For example, Command-H will hide ImageReady rather than hiding slices, guides, and other extras in the canvas.

N Click to reset all tools to their default values.

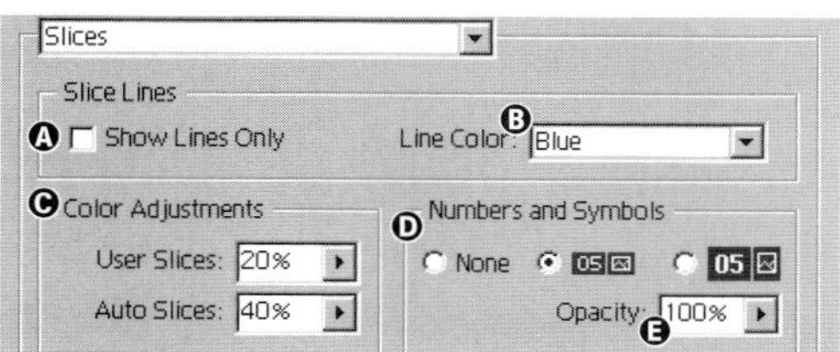

A Check to show slice lines without the icons in the top-left corner.

B Choose the color of slice lines.

C Use the slider or enter a percentage value (1 to 100) for how much the color should dim when a user or auto slice is not selected.

D Choose the size in which symbols should appear.

E Use the slider or enter a percentage value (1 to 100) for the opacity of symbols.

22.5 ImageReady Preferences *(Continued)*

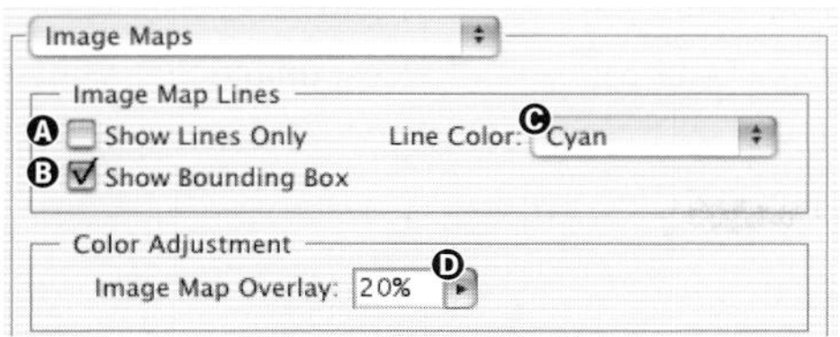

A Check to show only a borderline around an image map hot spot. If unchecked, the interior of the hot spot will be dimmed.

B Check to show a bounding box around the image map.

C Choose the color to use for hot spot borders.

D Use the slider or enter a percentage value (1 to 100) for the amount of interior dimming (see A).

In the top panel, choose the default optimization settings for new images or slices. You can use the previous settings, allow ImageReady to choose GIF or JPEG, or use an optimization preset that you choose from the drop-down. In the bottom panels, choose the default optimization settings to be used in the preview panes of the 2-Up and 4-Up previews. You can choose original (uncompressed), current (settings in the Optimize palette), Auto (allows ImageReady to determine best method), or one of the preset optimization settings.

Choose how to display painting cursors—Standard (tool's icon), Precise (crosshair), or Brush Size (circle indicating the diameter of the brush)—and choose how to display other cursors—Standard (tool's icon) or Precise (crosshair).

Choose the grid size and grid colors to use for transparent areas in the canvas. In addition, you can click either of the color squares to use the Color Picker to choose customized colors for the transparency grid.

Check if you have a secondary folder of plug-ins (separate from the folder in the Adobe Photoshop 7 folder). Checking this option automatically launches a dialog to choose the secondary folder. Click the Choose… button to change the folder. You can also select a scratch disk used by ImageReady. All available disks are displayed in the select menus. Changes will not take effect until ImageReady is restarted.

General Preferences dialog
⌘ K
Ctrl K

To delete preferences, hold down while starting ImageReady
Option Shift ⌘
Alt Shift Ctrl

22.6 ImageReady with Photoshop, GoLive, and Other Applications

Jump To Photoshop
Shift ⌘ M
Shift Ctrl M

When you move a document to another application, Adobe products refer to this action as a jump to the new application.

When jumping to Photoshop, all slices, layers, and guides will be preserved. In addition, rollovers, animations, and image maps will still be saved in the file, but will not be editable in Photoshop.

If you make changes in to an image in ImageReady that will affect the HTML use the Edit > Update HTML… command to update your files.

ImageReady allows you to create and output images graphics for viewing on the Web, including the creation of the HTML code needed to display the web page. You can create, build, and deploy an entire website using only ImageReady. However, ImageReady has limitations both as an image-editing program and as a web-development tool. This is why Adobe created ImageReady to work closely with Photoshop to add more advanced image-editing capabilities and with GoLive to add more advanced web-development tools. But even if you are not using Photoshop or GoLive, you can select alternate image-editing and web-development software to work with ImageReady.

- To jump the document to Photoshop, click the Jump To button at the bottom of the Toolbox (see Section 22.3) or choose File > Jump To > Adobe Photoshop 7.0. If not already running, Photoshop will open. The image will still be open in ImageReady, but grayed out to indicate that you are working on it in another program. You can jump back from Photoshop to ImageReady using the Jump To ImageReady button at the bottom of the Photoshop Toolbox or the File > Jump To > Adobe ImageReady 7.0 command, or you can simply return to ImageReady using your operating system. Regardless of how you jump, changes made in other applications are applied to the image.
- To jump the document to GoLive, choose File > Jump To > Adobe GoLive 6.0. Follow the steps in Section 25.6 for saving the optimized website. After you click Save, the new website will open in GoLive. To edit any of the images while in GoLive, simply double-click the image in the GoLive document window to open it.
- To jump the document to an alternate image-editing program (such as Macromedia Fireworks), choose File > Jump To > Other Graphics Editor…. Browse to find the program you want to use on your hard drive, and click Open. If you have not saved all changes to the image, you will be prompted to do so. The image will then open in the alternate image-editing software. Changes made in this program will be automatically reflected in the ImageReady version if you checked the Auto-Update Files option in the General Preferences (see Section 22.5).
- To jump the document to an alternate web-development program (such as Macromedia Dreamweaver), choose File > Jump To > Other HTML Editor…. Follow the steps in Section 25.6 for saving the optimized website. After you click Save, the new website opens in the selected web-development software.

Designing for the Web

WEB DESIGNS OFTEN START LIFE as screen comps, static versions of the web pages that include all the elements that will be used to create the final interface. You can create these designs using both ImageReady and Photoshop, using the Jump feature to move the design back and forth between the two programs. However, ImageReady was developed with web design's unique needs in mind.

In this chapter, you will learn how to start a web page in either Photoshop or ImageReady, how to consider color while designing, and how to take advantage of several ImageReady features to create web pages. You'll find the following topics in this chapter:

23.1 Designing for the Screen

➠ 2.9 View Menu

➠ 6.1 Starting a New Image

➠ 6.8 Using Rulers, Guides, Grids, and Snap

➠ 7.2 Understanding Image Modes

New File dialog
⌘ N
Ctrl N

Save As dialog
Shift ⌘ S
Shift Ctrl S

Designing a website using either Photoshop or ImageReady begins by starting a new document (in either program) with dimensions that match the screen size you want for your web page. You will then establish the structure of the page using a layout grid to define areas for specific uses as columns and rows. This is especially useful when designing using HTML tables; the grid helps align design elements and leads to a cleaner design that's easier to output to tables.

Starting a New Web Page Design

You can create a new web page in Photoshop or in ImageReady by choosing File > New.... Enter a name for the new file, select a preset size or enter the dimensions directly, and then select a background (White, Background Color, or Transparent). If you are using Photoshop, be sure that the resolution is set to 72 dpi and that the Mode is set to RGB.

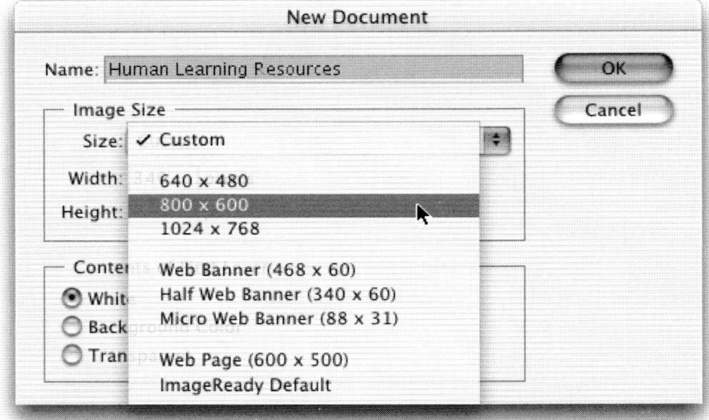

The ImageReady New Document dialog is slightly different from the Photoshop version. Since ImageReady is web only, it automatically works at 72 dpi for the resolution and RGB for the color mode. In addition, it includes several preset page sizes for Half-Web Banner, Micro Web Banner, and Web Page, which is the default web page size on monitors set to 800×600 when system chrome is taken into account.

The canvas size should reflect the screen size that people viewing your web page are likely to use. Most web surfers today use monitors set to a resolution of 800×600. However, if your audience is likely to be using older systems, set the canvas to 640×480.

23.1 Designing for the Screen *(Continued)*

Creating a Layout Grid

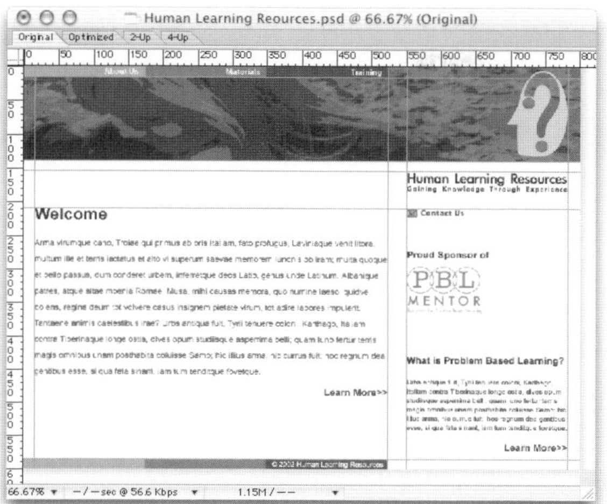

A layout grid defines the areas of the web page. The line on the far left defines the width of a web page displayed in a monitor set to a resolution of 800×600 when interface chrome is taken into account.

Most of today's monitors display at 96 dpi, although some older Mac monitors use 72 dpi. However, both web and TV designs are created at 72 dpi.

To set guides in ImageReady or Photoshop, simply drag from the ruler (see Section 6.8). ImageReady, however, adds an option that you can use to add guides in a regular grid pattern. To create a grid of guidelines in ImageReady, choose View > Create Guides… and set the options in the Create Guides dialog.

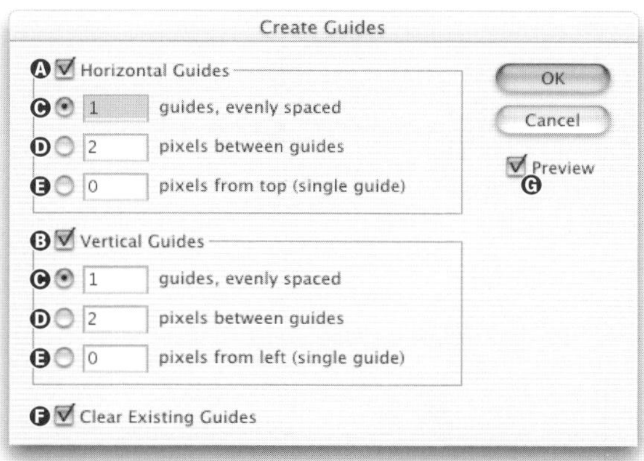

- **A** Check to add horizontal guidelines.
- **B** Check to add vertical guidelines.
- **C** Enter a value for the number of evenly spaced guidelines. The value must be between 0 and half the image width or height minus 1. (For example, an image that is 640 pixels wide can have a maximum value of 319 for horizontal guides.)
- **D** Enter a value for the number of pixels between each guide. The value must be between 2 and the image's width or height minus 1. (For example, an image that is 480 pixels tall can have a maximum value of 479 for the vertical guides.)
- **E** Enter a value for the position of the guide from the top or left side of the image.
- **F** Check to clear all guides currently in the image.
- **G** Check to preview the new guides in the canvas.

23.2 Web Color Basics

➠ 4.5 Color Palette

➠ 4.6 Swatches Palette

➠ 14 Working with Colors, Gradients, and Patterns

Although the terms seem interchangeable, *CLUT* refers to the operating system's color table and *color table* refers to an image.

The number of colors that a computer screen can display depends on many factors, and obviously the more colors your monitor can display, the better your image will look. However, with web design, how the image looks on your computer is not necessarily how it will look on the computer being used by your website's visitor. Several factors affect the final colors:

Monitor The exact size and resolution of the monitor affects the final appearance of a graphic. Generally, monitors display in 8-bit (256 colors), 16-bit (approximately 65,000 colors), or 24-bit (approximately 17 million colors).

Operating system Different operating systems use different color look-up tables (CLUTs) that define the basic colors available. This consideration is especially important for older computers that can display only at 8-bit. In addition, different operating systems have different gamma values that define how dark the midtones of colors in a graphic are displayed.

Graphic format The graphic format you choose can limit the number of colors that can be recorded for an image. For example, you can use only 256 colors with the GIF format.

Photoshop can help you overcome many of these limitations to ensure that what you see is what they get.

Color Table

A color table is an indexed list of colors in an image used with the GIF and PNG-8 formats. These lists can have a maximum of 256 color values and a minimum of 2 color values. While you are working on your design, you need not worry about the exact color table; however, when you optimize your image, the color table plays a crucial role if you are using GIF or PNG-8 formats. See Section 25.4 for more details on using the color table to optimize GIF and PNG-8 images.

Dithering

Dithering uses two or more colors placed closely together in an attempt to fool the eye into seeing a single color. The dithered image has noticeable dots rather than smooth tones.

A graphic can be dithered in two ways:

By the Browser If the operating system does not have a particular color in its CLUT that is used in a graphic, the browser attempts to simulate the color through dithering. Allowing the browser to dither graphics rarely produces seamless colors, tends to make the image look grainy, and can greatly degrade the quality of the image, especially anti-aliased text. However, this generally happens only on 8-bit computers.

In Photoshop or ImageReady You can manually dither graphics in Photoshop if you are using GIF, PNG-8, or WBMP file formats to optimize your image. When you dither manually, you can control the amount of dithering if the image is likely to be displayed on an 8-bit monitor or if there are too many colors in the image to be properly displayed using the available 256 colors in GIF and PNG-8 or the two colors in WBMP.

It is obviously preferable to set the amount of dithering in Photoshop or ImageReady rather than leaving it up to the operating system, and you do so while optimizing your image (see Section 25.3).

Using Web-Safe Colors

Web-safe colors are the set of 216 colors that older Mac and Windows computers share in their CLUTs and that display, more or less, the same across these two platforms. Should you limit yourself to these colors? Sticking to Web-safe colors slightly reduces your file size, and the colors were especially important when most web surfers were using older computer systems. However, an increasing number of web surfers now have computers that can display thousands or even millions of colors without the need to dither them. To ensure the best results without dithering, use only the Web-safe colors when you are working with graphics that contain a lot of flat areas of a single color.

You can set colors to be Web-safe in two ways:

While designing Generally if you want to use Web-safe colors, use them from the beginning of your design. To make sure that you are using the right colors, load one of the Web-Safe Color Swatch preset lists into the Swatches palette, which you can select from the bottom of the palette menu.

While optimizing Once you are ready to optimize your website for output, several settings on the Optimize and Color Table palettes let you force colors to be Web-safe (see Section 25.4).

Forcing colors to be Web-safe while optimizing takes some skill and practice to do so without degrading the quality of your image. Any anti-aliasing, gradients, opacity changes, effects filters, or adjustments will likely introduce non–Web-safe colors into your image. Start a design using browser-safe colors, and then adjust your colors during optimization. The idea is not to get *every* color in the color table to be Web-safe, but to get the large areas of color to be Web-safe.

The Visibone2 Color Swatch preset is generally the best for web design work. For more details on Web-safe colors, visit the Visibone website (`www.visibone.com`).

Adjusting the gamma changes the actual pixel values of your web design to compensate. The View > Preview option adjusts only the appearance on your monitor but does not change the image itself.

The Mac uses a gamma value of 1.8; Windows uses a darker value of 2.2.

23.2 Web Color Basics *(Continued)*

Adjusting Gamma with ImageReady

If you are designing for the Web, you must consider the gamma settings of the monitors being used by the website viewer. Most web surfers run the Windows operating system. If you are designing web pages using the Mac, your images will appear slightly lighter on your monitor than on a Windows machine. However, use this feature with caution since it will permanently alter the appearance of your image. Generally, if you are worried about Gamma, you will want to work in the Gamma Preview mode rather than altering the image.

The same image shown in Windows gamma (left) and Mac gamma (right).

To adjust for gamma settings, ImageReady lets you perform a special color correction to adjust the image for gamma values. To adjust gamma values, choose Image > Adjustments > Gamma, set your options in the Gamma dialog, and click OK.

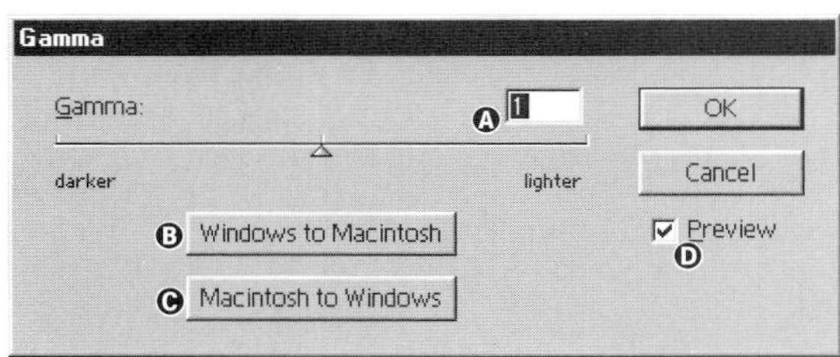

- **A** Use the slider or enter a value (0.1 to 9.99) to change the gamma value for the image from its current value. This does not set the absolute gamma value for the image, it only adjusts the current gamma level.
- **B** Click to automatically adjust the image if it is currently using a Windows gamma and you want to switch it to a Mac gamma.
- **C** Click to automatically adjust the image if it is currently using a Mac gamma and you want to switch it to a Windows gamma.
- **D** Check to preview gamma changes in the canvas.

23.3 Adding Effects with ImageReady

You can apply most of the same effects to graphics in Photoshop and ImageReady. However, in Photoshop you control these effects from a common dialog. In ImageReady, you control effects using the Layer Options/Style palette (not to be confused with the Layers palette). You generally use the Layer Options to control the advanced blending options for a layer. However, when you select an effect in the Layers palette, the Layer Options/Style palette displays the name of the effect in the Palette tab and displays the controls for the effect in the palette.

➠ 10 Adding Layer Styles

➠ 10.6 Applying Advanced Blending Options

➠ Color Section: Effects

Setting Layer Options

The Layer Options/Style palette displays the advanced blending options for the selected layer or layer set, which includes many of the same options found in Photoshop's blending options. To change the blending options for a layer, select the layer in the Layers palette, and then set the options in the Layer Options/Style palette.

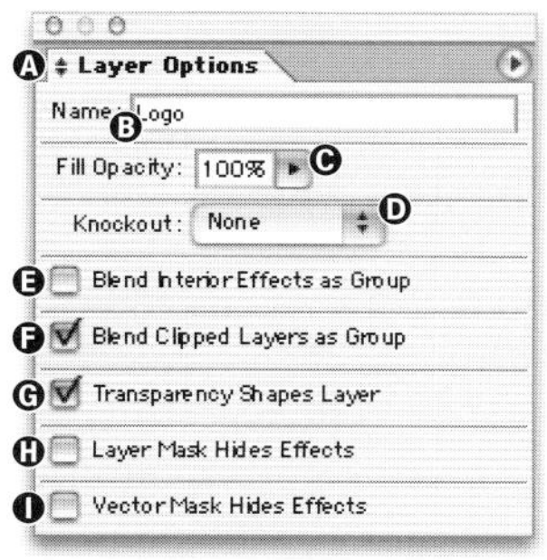

A **Collapse Palette** Click to cycle through three view modes for the palette: collapsed (tab only), show only basic options, and show advanced options.

B Displays the name of the layer. Click and enter a new name.

C Use the drop-down slider or enter a value (0 to 100) for the fill opacity of image pixels. Unlike Photoshop, you *cannot* change the fill opacity in the Layers palette.

D Choose a Knockout style. Selecting this option makes the layer transparent, showing the content of layers beneath: None, Shallow (shows the content of the layer beneath), or Deep (punches through to the background layer or transparency).

E Check if you want glow, satin, and interior effects blended with their associated layer before blending with the rest of the document.

F Check to blend the clipping groups before blending with the rest of the document.

G Check if you want the transparency of the layer to set the edges of the shape and the effects.

H Check if you want the layer mask to hide the effects rather than reshaping them.

I Check if you want the vector mask to hide effects rather than reshaping them.

If you do not see all the options you expect for a particular effect in the Layer Options/Style palette, choose Show Options in the palette's menu.

You access global lighting for effects (see Section 10.1) through the Global Light… option in the Layer Options/Style palette menu or in the Layer > Layer Styles submenu.

Setting Effects

In ImageReady, effects are applied to a layer and appear in the Layers palette exactly the same way as in Photoshop. However, the controls for the effects are in a modified Layer Options/Style palette, rather than in the Layer Style dialog. Although all of the same options are represented for the styles as in Photoshop, this palette compresses the space needed to display them.

23.3 Adding Effects with ImageReady *(Continued)*

The only option available in the Layer Options/Style palette when a layer set is selected is the name.

You cannot apply effects to a layer set.

To add an effect to the selected layer, choose the effect from the Style menu at the bottom of the Layers palette or in the Layer > Layer Styles submenu. After the effect is added to a layer, click the effect underneath the layer in the Layer's palette and then make changes using the Layer Options/Style palette, which displays the name of the effect in its tab and all the options available for the selected effect in the palette.

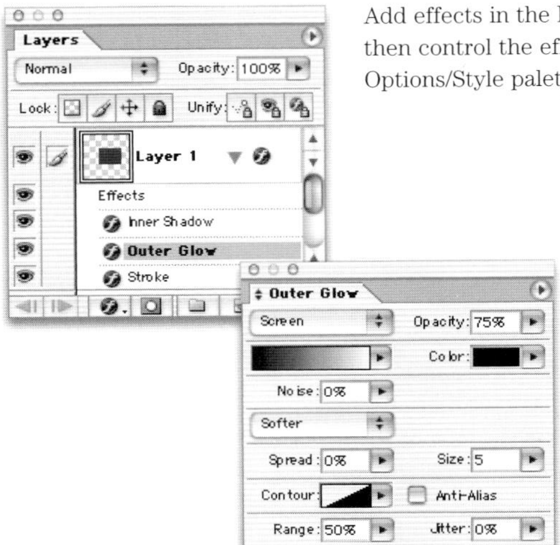

Add effects in the Layers palette and then control the effect in the Layer Options/Style palette.

COLOR SETTINGS FOR THE WEB

Remember, you can set a color profile for the image to help overcome color differences between your computer and the end user's computer. Browsers that understand color profiles will use these settings. ImageReady does not allow you to set the color profile, but you can jump the image to Photoshop and add the color profile (see Section 7.4) and then jump back to ImageReady. To preview the color settings in ImageReady, choose View > Preview > Use Embedded Color Profile.

23.4 Creating Data-Driven Graphics with ImageReady

Websites often require dozens, hundreds, or even thousands of similar, but slightly different graphics to be created based on the same template. For example, if you are creating an online toy catalog, you might have photographs of hundreds of toys that need names, prices, or other details about the toy applied to them. Further, the toy might go on sale. This would not only change the price, but might require a special sale item graphic. Rather than creating a separate graphic for each instance, you can easily set up your Photoshop graphics to interact with a database. Don't worry if you are not a database pro. ImageReady allows you to set up images as data-driven templates that you can then use with an existing database to customize the graphics or to set variables manually to create the image iterations.

If you are not setting up the database yourself, make sure you consult with your database administrator and agree to the variable names to be used.

Variables cannot be set for the Background layer.

Think of each data set as an iteration of the image.

You can preview how the different Data sets will affect the image (see Section 23.5).

Defining Variables

Variables are used to define how particular layers in the image can be changed. You can set three variables to control the visibility or content for any layer in a Photoshop document (.psd), depending on whether it is a paint layer or a text layer (other layer types cannot use variables):

A Visibility Lets you show or hide a layer between iterations.

B Pixel Replacement (Bitmap layers only) Lets you replace the image in the layer with another image in a separate file.

C Text Replacement (Text layers only) Lets you replace a string of text.

These variables require a specific name that should reflect the name of the variables defined in the database being used. After you set the variables for a layer or layers, you can use Adobe GoLive and Adobe AlterCast to bind a database to this file. Save the file as a template using the PSD format, and then follow instructions in GoLive to place the image and bind the variables using dynamic links.

You set variables for a layer in the Define panel of the Variables dialog. To set variables for a layer, follow these steps:

1. Select the layer for which you want to set variables in the Layers palette.
2. Choose Image > Variables > Define, or choose Variables from the Layers palette menu.
3. In the Variables dialog, set the variable types being used—Visibility or Pixel Replacement—and enter a variable name for each.
4. If you are working with bitmap layers using pixel replacement, you can also set Pixel Replacement options, which allows you to specify how an image should be treated if it is not the same size as the area defined by the original image (called the bounding box).

23.4 Creating Data-Driven Graphics with ImageReady *(Continued)*

5 After you set the options, select another layer to set variables for it, click Next to set options for the data sets being used, or click OK to return to the image.

After you have set up variables for one or more layers, you are ready to proceed to setting up data sets that define how the variables are defined for different image iterations.

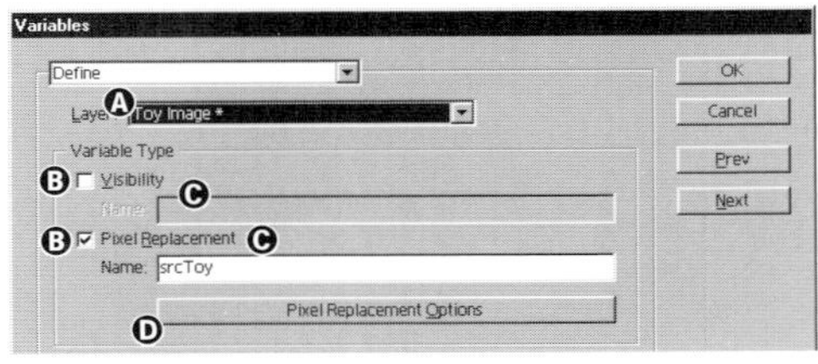

Ⓐ Choose from a list of layers in the image to define variables for that layer. An asterisk next to the name indicates that variables are set in that layer.

Ⓑ Check to use a Visibility or Replacement variable with this layer (this will read Text Replacement if a Text layer is being used).

Ⓒ If this variable type is checked (see B), enter the name of the variable being used by the database. More than likely, you will want to give a unique name to the variables used by each layer; you cannot independently control values for variables in different layers if they are using the same variable name.

Ⓓ If this is a bit-map layer, click this button to open the Pixel Replacement options which allow you to set how an image will be treated if it is not the same dimensions as the original image it is replacing.

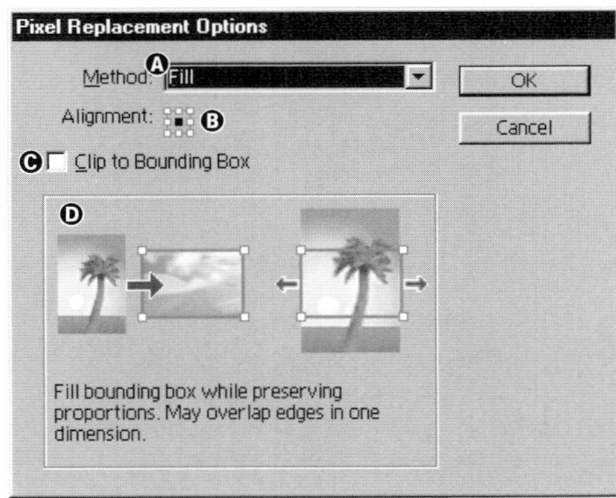

Ⓐ Choose a method for how the new image should be placed into the area of the bounding box: Fit (resizes to fit height), Fill (resizes to fit width), As Is (crops to center of image), Conform (stretches image to fit width and height).

Ⓑ Click one of the white squares to set how the replacement image should be aligned in the bounding-box.

Ⓒ Check to use the bounding box to crop the replacement image.

Ⓓ Displays a preview for how the selected method will affect a replacement image.

Working with Data Sets

You can manually create data sets to control iterations of the image using the variables you have set. This allows you to create different versions of the image, assigning different values to the variables and saving that version as a data set. This option can be time-consuming, though, and is mainly intended for use if there will only be a few iterations of an image.

23.4 Creating Data-Driven Graphics with ImageReady *(Continued)*

To set up data sets for an image, follow these steps:

1 Choose Image > Variables > Data Sets or choose Variables from the Layers palette menu. You will see the variables defined for this image listed at the bottom of the window. If the Variables dialog is open, simply click the Next button. You must have at least one variable defined to create a data set.

2 Click the New Data Set button to start your first data set, and enter a name for the data set. The name should be something that helps you remember what content is loaded for this iteration of the image.

3 Choose a variable name from the Name menu or in the variable list, and then set its value.

- If this is a Visibility variable, choose either Visible or Invisible.
- If this is a Pixel Replacement variable, click the Choose… (Mac) or Browse… (Windows) button and select the graphic file to use with this iteration.
- If this is a Text Replacement variable, enter the text to be used with this iteration.

4 Repeat step 3 for each variable, and then repeat steps 2 and 3 to create a data set for each iteration. Click OK when you are finished.

You can now use this image in GoLive with the data sets you added.

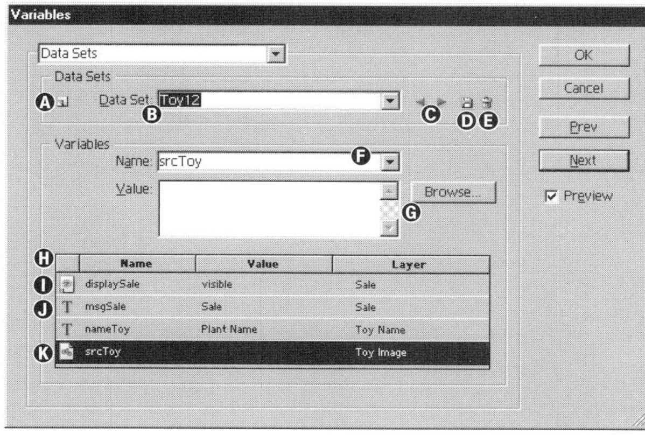

Ⓐ **New Data Set** Click to create a new data set for this image.

Ⓑ Displays the current data set. Click to choose a different data set from the drop-down.

Ⓒ Click to move forward or backward between data sets.

Ⓓ Click to save the current data set.

Ⓔ Click to delete the current data set.

Ⓕ Choose a variable name from the drop-down.

Ⓖ Set the value for the selected variable (see F and H).

Ⓗ Displays the currently selected variable. Click to select a different variable. Click a header to sort variables by that column.

Ⓘ Indicates a Visibility variable.

Ⓙ Indicates a Text Replacement variable.

Ⓚ Indicates Pixel Replacement variable.

23.5 Previewing Your Design with ImageReady

➠ 7.3 Specifying Color Settings

➠ 22.1 ImageReady Document Windows

➠ 25.3 Optimizing the Image

➠ 25.4 Setting the Optimization Options

➠ 25.5 Specifying Output Options

Often while you are working on an image, you will want to know how it will look when it hits the Web. Of course, many variables separate the original image you are working on and the way it might finally look to a website visitor. ImageReady provides several tools that allow you to preview the image and simulate a variety of conditions to help you make the best choices while designing.

Previewing in the Canvas

ImageReady allows you to preview your work directly in the ImageReady canvas as if it where a limited web browser.

- To preview the image in the ImageReady document window, choose Image > Preview Document or click the Preview Document button in the toolbox. The image in the canvas will now act like a live web page, allowing you to view animations, rollovers, and image maps, although links will be inactive.
- To preview different iterations of this image using different data sets while in Preview mode, choose a data set from the drop-down menu in the tool options bar or use the forward and back arrows to cycle through the list. As you cycle through the data set list, the image in the canvas will change to reflect the variable values set for that data set.

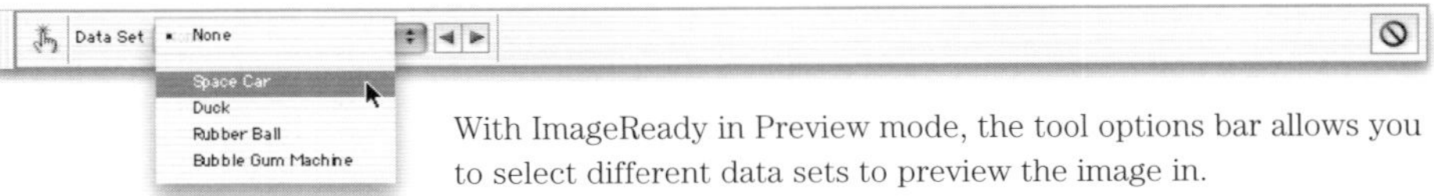

With ImageReady in Preview mode, the tool options bar allows you to select different data sets to preview the image in.

- To end the preview, choose Image > Preview Document, click the Preview Document button in the toolbox, or click the Cancel button. In addition, if you attempt to edit the image, ImageReady will alert you that you cannot edit the image in Preview mode and ask if you want to stop previewing.

Previewing Optimization Settings

You can view the image either uncompressed (original) or preview the optimization settings in one of three optimized views (optimized, 2-Up, or 4-Up) by clicking one of the tabs in the top-left corner of the document window:

Original Shows the original uncompressed image.

Optimized Shows the image with compression settings.

2-Up and 4-Up View Shows two or four views of the image side-by-side in separate panes. You can choose to show the original version in one view and/or various optimized versions in the other pains allowing you to compare how the optimizations settings affect the image.

23.5 Previewing Your Design with ImageReady

(Continued)

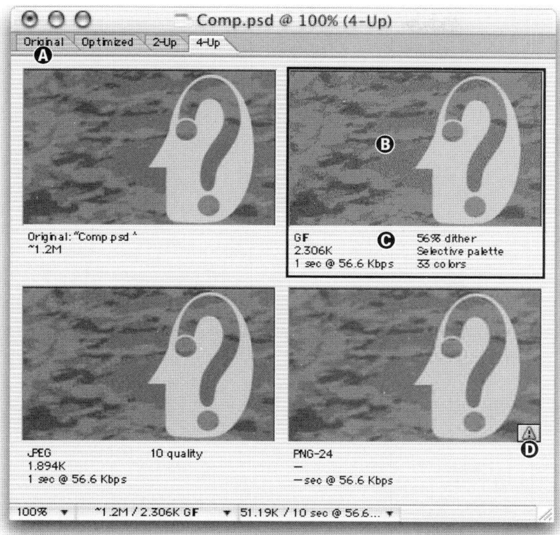

A Choose one of the tabs to select an optimization view.

B **View panes** Click anywhere in the pane to select it, The selected pane will have a black box around it. You can set the optimization settings for the images in the selected pane or select slices in that pane to optimize.

C **Optimization information** Displays the settings used to optimize the image and the estimated download time.

D **Regeneration warning** Indicates that the view has not been regenerated based on current optimization settings. Click to regenerate the view.

Show original version
⌘ Y
Ctrl Y

Cycle to next optimization view mode
Shift ⌘ Y
Shift Ctrl Y

Preview in browser
⌘ Option P
Ctrl Alt P

When optimization settings are changed, the image will need to be *regenerated* to reflect the changes.

- To regenerate the image automatically after every optimization, choose Auto Regenerate in the Optimize palette menu. However, this can slow you down if you are applying a lot of optimization settings at once. To turn auto regeneration off, choose the option again.
- To manually regenerate an optimized image, choose Regenerate from the Optimize palette menu or click the Regeneration Warning button ⚠.

You can also set the optimized views to preview as if they were using browser dithering or a particular operating system's CLUT:

- To simulate how browser dithering may affect your image, with the canvas open in one of the optimization views, choose View > Preview > Browser Dither. The image will appear dithered regardless of your monitor settings and the dithering options set for the file format.
- To simulate how the image will look using either the Macintosh, Windows, or embedded color profile, choose View > Preview and then one of the settings: Uncompressed Color, Standard Macintosh Color, Standard Windows Color, or Use Embedded Color Profile.

23.5 Previewing Your Design with ImageReady

(Continued)

You cannot edit the image while it is in Preview mode.

Slices set to No Image will not appear in the ImageReady Preview mode. Instead, the background color is used.

The Optimization setting preview tabs are also available in Photoshop's Save For Web dialog.

Previewing in a Browser

You can open the image in a web browser to preview how it will look when output. ImageReady will use the current output options to generate an HTML page and place the image slices into this framework.

- To quickly preview the image in a browser, click the browser preview button in the Toolbox. To set this button to choose a different browser, click and hold the button and choose a browser from the drop-down menu.
- To preview the image in a browser, choose File **>** Preview In **>** and choose a browser or choose Other… and then browse to an application. This browser will not be added to this list or to the list in the Toolbox, but will be used as the browser for the preview button until another browser is selected.

CHAPTER 24

Designing Web Elements

THERE ARE SEVERAL COMMON WEBSITE elements that will require more than the simple graphic design in Photoshop to create them. In ImageReady, you can create multiple states for a button to use with JavaScript rollovers, create animations to add movement to your web page, create image maps to use large graphics for navigation, and create seamless backgrounds to add texture to your web page.

24.1 Creating Image Maps

➠ 9.11 Aligning and Distributing Layers

➠ 23.5 Previewing Your Design with ImageReady

➠ 25.5 Specifying Output Options

Image Map tool P

Cycle image map tools Shift P

Toggle image maps visibility A

Using image maps is a common way to add large navigation graphics to a web page. For example, when creating a web page that shows the dates of a nationwide concert tour, you might want to allow visitors to click an area on a map of the United States to see concerts in that area. Using an image map, you can set hotspots (clickable areas of the image map) that link to pages displaying dates for that region of the country. ImageReady not only allows you to prepare the graphic for use as an image map, but also define the hotspots. If you output the image with HTML code, ImageReady uses the defined hotspots to automatically create the code for the image map in the web page.

ImageReady allows you to create image map hotspots in two ways:

- **Tool-based** You can use the image map tool to draw hotspots on the image either as circles, rectangles, or as freeform polygon shapes.
- **Layer-based** You can specify that the content of a layer is used to define the area of the hotspot. The hotspot will always readjust based on the content of the layer.

Adding Tool-Based Hotspots

You create hotspots as rectangles, circles, or polygons. Polygons allow you to draw a freeform shape with as many sides as you want. To add a hotspot to the image for use in the image map, follow these steps in ImageReady, repeating them to create as many hotspots as you need:

1. Choose the Rectangle Image Map tool, Circular Image Map tool, or Polygon Image Map tool.
2. Set your preference for the tool in the tool options bar: First specify whether you want to create a fixed-size shape, and then enter the dimensions of the rectangle or the radius of the circle. The Polygon Image Map tool does not have any options.
3. Place your mouse cursor in the top-left corner of where you want the image map hotspot to begin.
   - For the Rectangular and Circular Image Map tools, click and drag to draw the desired shape.
   - For the Polygon Image Map tool, click to set the first anchor point, and then click the next point in the polygon. Repeat around the area for which you want to create a hotspot. When you are finished, either click the first anchor point, or, to close the hotspot with a straight line from the current anchor point, double-click or Command/Ctrl-click.
4. In the Image Map palette (Window > Image Map), enter optional information about this hotspot to help Photoshop generate the image map's HTML code. Show and hide the hotspot areas in the image by clicking the Toggle Image Map Visibility button in the Toolbox.

● You can now save this image map as part of your optimized website (see Chapter 25).

24.1 Creating Image Maps *(Continued)*

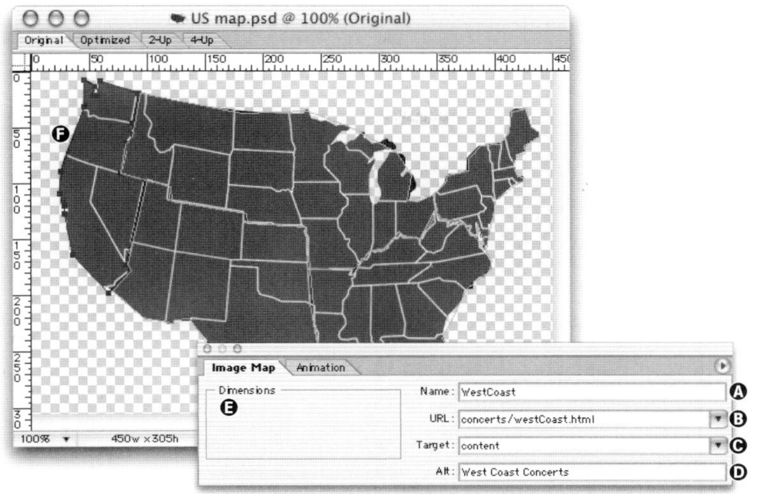

A Enter a name to be used to identify the hotspot.

B Enter the URL (either global or local) for the hotspot.

C Enter the name of the frame or window in which you want this link to appear. There are four default options that allow you to target the link to a new (blank) window, the same window or frame (self), the frames frameset (parent), or to replace the entire frameset with the new page (top) If the link should appear in the same frame or window, you can also leave this blank.

D Enter alternate text that is displayed if the image cannot be viewed. Some browsers will also use this text for tooltips that pop up when the user places their mouse over the image. Adding this text is important to ensure that your website is accessible to all visitors.

E If the hotspot is a rectangle or a circle, this area will be used to display and change the position and dimensions of the shape. If the hotspot is layer-based, this area allows you to choose the shape used for the hotspot.

F Selected hotspot in the image map.

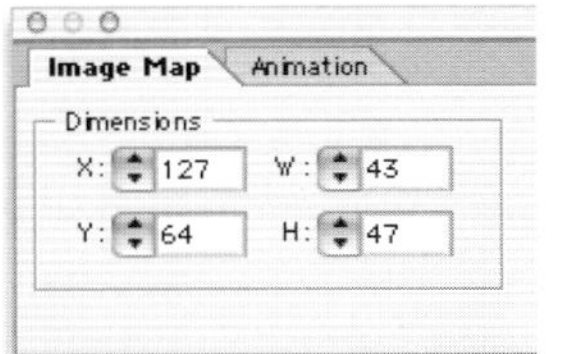

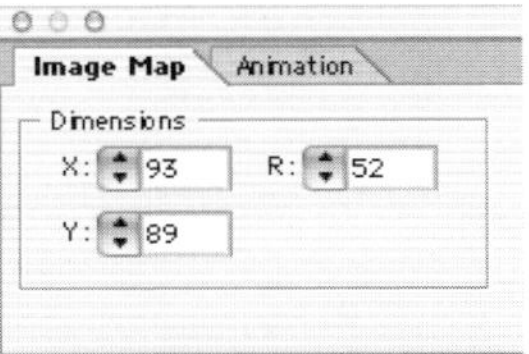

If the hotspot is a rectangle, you can enter the position and dimensions directly in the Image Map palette. If the hotspot is a circle, you can enter the position and the radius.

Layer-based hotspots are edited when their content is changed. To change the layer-based hotspot's options, click the layer in the Layers palette and then make changes in the Image Map palette.

To change a layer-based hotspot into a tool-based hotspot, choose the layer in the Layers palette and then choose Promote Layer Based Image Map Area in the Image Map palette.

You can adjust how image maps are displayed in ImageReady's Image Maps preferences (see Section 22.5).

Editing Tool-Based Hotspots

Hotspots that you create using the Image Map tools (not layer-based hotspots) behave a lot like layers in that they can be stacked, aligned, and distributed. When stacked, one hotspot will be over or under another hotspot. You can use the Image Map Select tool to not only move and reshape the hotspot, but also to restack, align, and distribute hotspots.

To begin editing an image map, choose the Image Map Select tool. In the canvas, click the hotspot you want to edit to select it and do the following:

- To **show or hide the image map**, click the Toggle Image Map Visibility button in the Toolbox or choose View > Show > Image Maps.
- To **change or add information** about the hotspot, open the Image Map palette (Window > Image Map) and enter the information.
- To **change the stacking order** of this hotspot in relation to other hotspots in the image map, click an icon in the tool options bar or choose these options from the Image Map palette's menu:

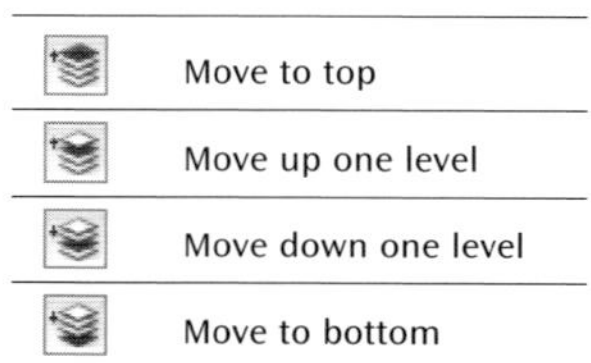

	Move to top
	Move up one level
	Move down one level
	Move to bottom

- To **move** the hotspot, with the Image Map Select tool click and drag it within the canvas.
- To **adjust the shape** of a hotspot, click and drag an anchor point. The Map Select Tool cursor pointer will turn from black to white when it is over an anchor point.
- To **align** hotspots, Shift-click two or more hotspots and then click one of the alignment buttons in the tool options bar, or choose these options from the Image Map palette's menu.
- To **distribute** hotspots, Shift-click three or more hotspots and then click one of the distribution buttons in the tool options bar, or choose these options from the Image Map palette's menu.
- To **delete** the hotspot, press Delete/Backspace, or choose Delete Image Map Area from the Image Map palette's menu.
- To **duplicate** the hotspot shape, Option/Alt-click and drag or choose Duplicate Image Map Area from the Image Map palette's menu.

24.1 Creating Image Maps *(Continued)*

Adding Layer-Based Hotspots

One of the easiest ways to create hotspots for an image map is to use existing layers to define them. This allows you to use the existing layer structure of the image, which may already be split along the needed lines, to quickly generate your image map. To use a slice to define a hotspot in the image map, follow these steps:

1 Choose the layer you want to use as an image map hotspot (see Section 8.2). If the layer does not have transparent pixels, the hotspot will fill the entire canvas.

2 Choose Layer > New Layer Based Image Map Area. This option is also available in the layer's contextual menu (Control/right-click the layer name in the Layers palette). The layer will now have an image map tool icon next to the title.

Enter information about the hotspot in the Image Map palette (Window > Image Map). You will also want to choose the shape used to define the hotspot: Rectangular, Circular, or Polygon.

You can now save this image map as part of your optimized website (see Chapter 25).

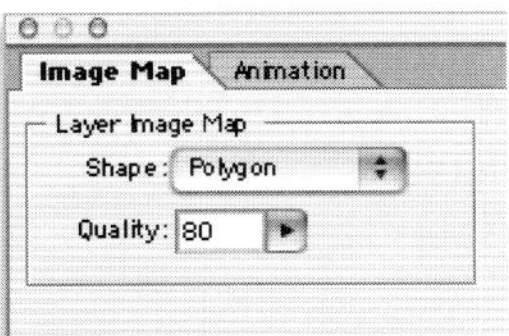

Choose the shape being used to define the hotspot for the layer. If you choose Polygon, you also need to enter the quality used to define the polygon shape around the edges.

If the layer you are using for a layer-based slice is irregularly shaped, you will probably want to use Polygon and then set the quality as high or as low as necessary to get a good fit.

Using the Higher quality setting with layer-based slices in Polygon mode requires more data to create and creates slightly larger file sizes.

ANIMATION AND ROLLOVER THUMBNAILS

You can set the size of the thumbnails displayed in the Animation and Rollovers palette using the Palette Options dialog accessed through the palette menu. With frames and states, it is especially important to display the thumbnails as large as possible because they show how the image appears for that frame or state.

24.2 Creating Animations

➠ 23.5 Previewing Your Design with ImageReady

➠ 24.6 Editing Layers for Animations and Rollovers

➠ 25.5 Specifying Output Options

Traditional animations are created using individual animation frames: still images that are part of a sequence. Displaying these images in rapid succession (each cell is displayed for a fraction of a second) creates the illusion of movement. The GIF format allows web designers to create simple animations, and ImageReady provides the tools to quickly create GIF animations from scratch or use existing images and layers to put one together. With ImageReady, you can assign a delay time to each frame, use the Tween command to quickly generate new frames, and specify looping for the animation.

Although animations are used in close conjunction with the Layers palette, all the action is in the Animation palette. To open it, choose Window > Animation. This palette is always horizontal, displaying the animation frames across the screen.

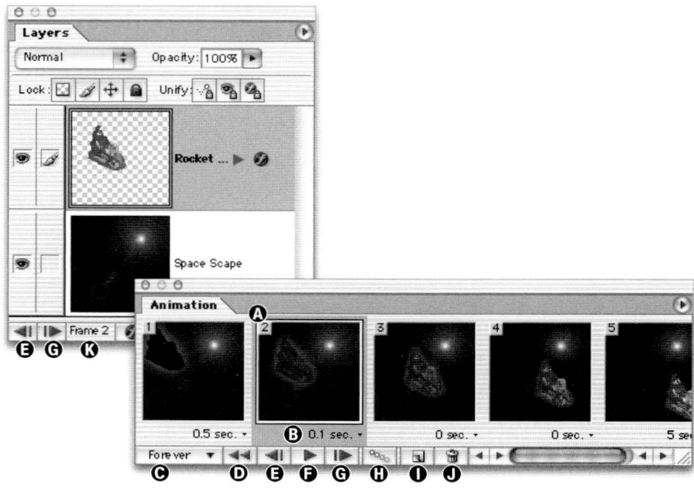

A Animation frame Each frame is numbered, and the selected frame is highlighted.

B Frame Delay Choose the amount of delay for this frame.

C Looping Options Choose a looping option for the animation.

D First Frame Click to jump to the first frame.

E Previous Frame Click to jump to the previous frame. This control also appears in the Layers palette.

F Play/Stop Click to play the animation in the canvas. Click again to stop the animation.

G Next Frame Click to jump to the next frame. This control also appears in the Layers palette.

H Tween Select two consecutive frames by shift-clicking and click to open the Tween dialog.

I Duplicate Frame Click to duplicate the selected frame.

J Delete Frame Click to delete the selected frame.

K Current Frame Displays the current frame represented in the layers.

24.2 Creating Animations *(Continued)*

Starting an Animation and Adding Frames

All images start with an initial frame that represents the starting appearance of the animation. Every time you add a new frame, ImageReady duplicates the currently selected frame, allowing you to make changes to the image for that frame. To add a frame to an animation, follow these steps:

1. Set up your image the way you want it to appear in the first frame of the animation. To add a new layer every time you create a frame, choose Create Layer For Each New Frame from the Animation palette menu. This is especially useful if you must add a new visual element to each frame.
2. In the Animation palette (Window > Animation), click the Duplicate Frame button or choose New Frame from the palette's menu. This adds the second frame to the Animation palette, which will be selected.
3. Make changes to the image as desired. This can include moving layers, adding additional effects, changing effect settings, and showing or hiding layers. You can now edit the layers for this frame (see Section 24.4).
4. Repeat steps 2 and 3 to create as many animation frames as desired.
5. Click the Play button to preview the animation in the canvas.

Always add and edit frames with the canvas in Original View mode. Although you can view frames in any of the optimization views, the editing options are limited.

You can flatten an animation into individual layers (each new layer a composite of the original layers) by selecting Flatten Frames Into Layers from the Animation palette menu. The original layers are preserved, but hidden.

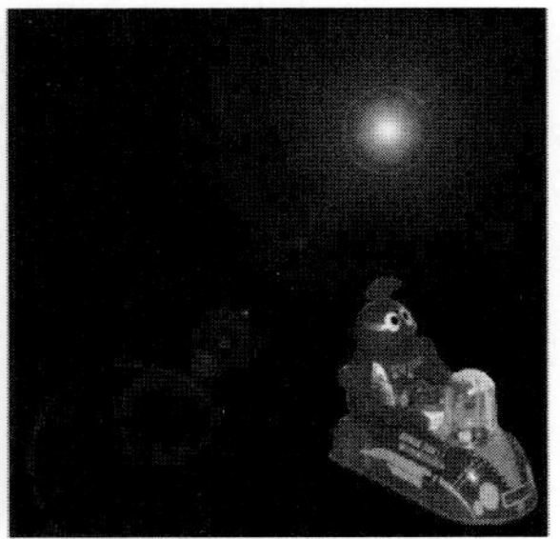

Left: The first frame. Right: In the second frame, the rocket ship has moved across the canvas.

Tweening Frames

Tweening allows you to set the beginning and ending conditions of an animation and then have ImageReady fill in the spaces, adding frames to create a seamless animation. For example, if you want to move an object across the canvas in a straight line, you can simply set the object to its initial position in the first frame, to its final position in the last frame, and then tween the two frames. ImageReady calculates the position of the object in intervening frames to make it look as if the object is moving from one spot to the next. To tween frames, follow these steps:

24.2 Creating Animations *(Continued)*

You can convert the layers in a file into frames by selecting Make Frames From Layers in the Animation palette menu.

You can have as many frames as you want in an animation—limited only by your computer's memory—but remember that every frame is a distinct image and adds to the overall download time for the image.

1. In the Animation palette (Window > Animation), select the first frame you want to use in your tween animation.
2. Click the Duplicate Frame button in the Animation palette to add the final frame for the tween animation. This creates two identical frames.
3. With the final frame selected, make changes to the image to set up how you want the animation to end. These changes can include the following:

   Position Move objects in the canvas.

   Opacity Change either the layer or the fill opacity, allowing you to fade an object in or out.

   Effects Change the settings for effects applied to the layer.
4. Select frames to be tweened in the Animation palette:
   - To animate between two adjacent frames, select the first and last frame for the tween by Shift-clicking them.
   - To animate from a frame to a copy of the previous or first frame, select the frame to use as the first frame.
5. Click the Tween button in the Animation palette.
6. Set the options in the Tween dialog, and then click OK. Frames will be added to the animation between the two frames used.

You can now save this image map as part of your optimized website (see Chapter 25).

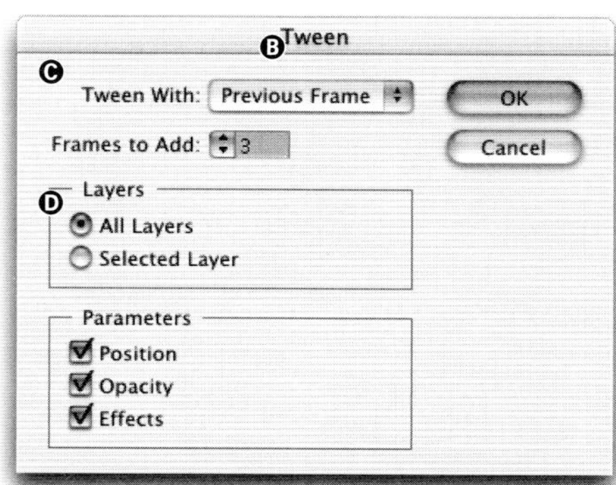

A Choose the frames to tween. If you select a single frame, specify whether you want to animate to a copy of the previous frame or to a copy of the first frame in the animation. If you select two frames, this option is set to Selection.

B Enter a value (1 to 100) for the number of frames to use to animate between this frame and the Tween With frame.

C Specify whether to animate changes in all frames in the image or only the select layer. If you are animating only a single layer, you can reduce your file size somewhat by using only the Selected Layer option.

D Check which parameters should be animated between the first and last frame.

24.3 Editing Animations

You can edit an entire animation or individual frames in a variety of ways:

- To set the **loop** for how many times the animation should play, choose an option from the Looping Options menu in the lower-left corner of the Animation palette: Once, Forever, or Other.... If you select Other, enter a value for the number of times to loop and click OK.
- To **edit** the content of a frame, click the frame to select it and then make changes in the canvas and Layers palette (see Section 24.5).
- To **re-tween** the frames between two frames, select the range of frames and click the Tween button. The frames between the first and last frame in the range will be replaced with the new tween.
- To **move** a frame, click and drag it to the desired position. To move multiple frames, Shift-click the frames to select them and then drag them to the desired position. If you drag multiple discontiguous frames, they will be placed contiguously.
- To **reverse** the order of contiguous frames, select the frames and choose Reverse Frames in the Animation palette menu.
- To **delete** one or more frames, select the frame(s) and drag them to the trashcan button or choose Delete Frame(s) from the palette menu. You can also choose frames, click the trashcan icon, and click OK.
- To **delete the animation**, choose Delete Animation from the Animation palette menu.

Setting Playback Options

The delay time determines how long a frame in an animation pauses before proceeding to the next frame; the disposal method specifies what happens to the frame image after it is played. To set the delay or disposal method for one or more frames, either select a single frame or Shift-click to select multiple frames, and then do the following:

- To set the **delay** for how long the frame paused before proceeding to the next frame, choose a delay time or choose No Delay from the Frame Delay menu under each frame in the Animations palette.
- To set the **disposal** method for a frame, Control/right-click the frame's thumbnail and select a method:

  Automatic Frames are removed after display only if the next frame contains a transparency. This method generally produces the best results.

  Do Not Dispose Frames are not removed after displaying. New frames are placed on top, but previous frames show through in transparent areas of the current frame. Places an icon next to the animation thumbnail.

  Restore To Background Always removes frames after display. Places an icon next to the animation thumbnail.

➟ 23.5 Previewing Your Design with ImageReady

➟ 24.6 Editing Layers for Animations and Rollovers

➟ 25.3 Optimizing Images

➟ 25.5 Specifying Output Options

If you are using the Redundant Pixel Removal Optimization option, you will want to choose Automatic disposal.

The actual speed at which the animation plays on the web page depends on the processor speed of the visitor's computer.

The delay time for frames will not be accurate when previewing in the canvas. You will need to preview in a browser (see Section 23.5) to get an accurate idea of how the animation will display.

You can open a GIF animation in Photoshop, but you cannot view or edit individual frames. However, the frames will stay intact.

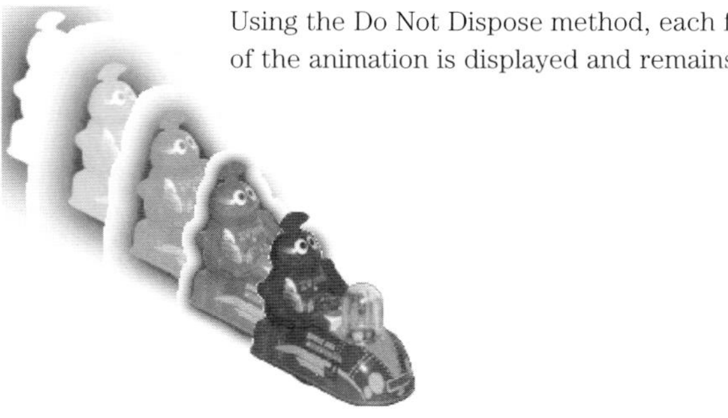

Using the Do Not Dispose method, each frame of the animation is displayed and remains.

Optimizing Animations

Optimization allows you to reduce the file size of an image, thus speeding its transmission across the Internet. Although most of the optimization in ImageReady is done in the Optimize palette, GIF animation has specific options that you can turn on or off while working. Choose Optimize Animation… from the Animation palette menu, and check the desired options:

Bounding Box Crops each frame to the area that has changed from the preceding frame. This creates smaller files and is generally recommended. However, some GIF-editing programs might not be able to open these files.

Redundant Pixel Removal Makes transparent all pixels in a frame that are unchanged from the preceding frame. This option is the default and is recommended. For this to work, the Transparency option in the Optimize palette must be selected, and the frame disposal method must be set to Automatic.

You can now save this animation as part of your optimized website (see Chapter 25).

DESIGNING BUTTONS

One common interface element that you will need to design is a button. More important, you will need to create attractive buttons that maintain a consistent look. Using style presets with the Shape tool is a quick way to create uniform buttons.

24.4 Creating Rollovers

Rollovers use JavaScript to tell a graphic to change when a certain condition is triggered through an action by the user to show a different state of the image. For example, placing the mouse pointer over an image triggers the Over state. ImageReady has six built-in states that roughly correspond to JavaScript events. In addition, you can enter your own custom states if you are using your own custom JavaScript code or development programs such as Dreamweaver.

➠ 23.5 Previewing Your Design with ImageReady

➠ 24.6 Editing Layers for Animations and Rollovers

➠ 25.5 Specifying Output Options

Toggle slices visibility

Q

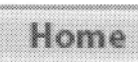

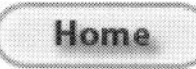

The Normal, Over, and Down states

Rollover States

STATE	DESCRIPTION
Normal	The default state used when the image initially loads. Unless otherwise indicated, all other states revert to the Normal state.
Over	Triggered when the mouse cursor is over the area without the mouse button pressed and persists until the mouse cursor moves out of the area.
Down	Triggered when the mouse cursor is over the area with the mouse button pressed and persists until the mouse button is released or the mouse cursor is moved out of the area.
Selected	Triggered after the area is clicked and persists until another area is clicked using the Selected state.
Click	Triggered after the area is clicked and persists until the mouse cursor moves out of the area.
Out	Triggered when the mouse cursor moves out of the area if you do not want to revert to Normal.
Up	Triggered when the mouse button is released if you do not want to revert to Normal.
Custom	Triggered when using your own custom JavaScript code. This is useful if you are not using the Adobe-defined states. For example, Dreamweaver includes the OverWhileDown state, which allows you to specify how the rollover should look if it is rolled over while selected.
None	Saves the state for later use, but is not output

Although rollovers are used in close conjunction with the Layers palette, you add rollover states in the Rollovers palette. To open it, choose Window > Rollovers.

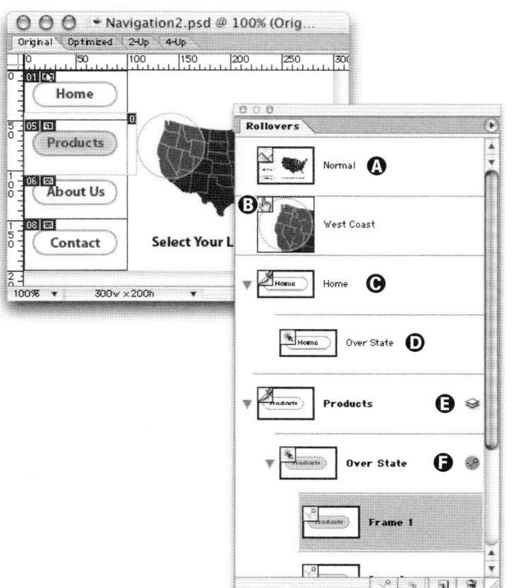

A Normal state The default appearance for the rollovers in the image.

B Image map Indicates a rollover using an image map.

C Slice-based rollover A rollover that is a collection of rollover states.

D Rollover state The Over state associated with the rollover.

E Layer-based rollover Icon indicates that this rollover is using a layer-based slice.

F Animation Icon indicates that this rollover state uses an animation.

Continues

Animations applied to rollovers in the Normal state start playing as soon as the page loads.

Although you create most of the rollover animation in the Animations palette, you can use the Rollovers palette to display, add, delete, copy, and paste frames using the palette's menu.

If you do not see all the options discussed in the Rollovers palette, open the Palette Options dialog and make sure Include Slices And Image Maps and Include Animation Frames are checked.

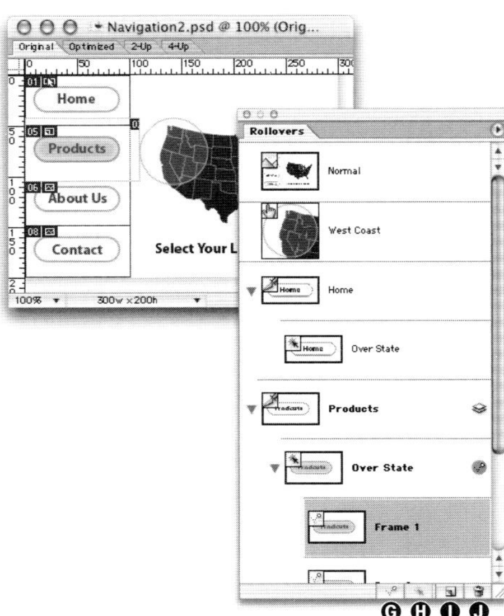

G **Add Animation Frame** Click to add an animation frame to the selected rollover state.

H **Create Layer-Based Rollover** Click to turn the selected layer into a slice with the Over rollover.

I **New Rollover State** Click to add a rollover state to the selected rollover.

J **Delete Slice** Click to delete the selected slice and its rollover.

Starting a Rollover and Adding States

Rollovers in ImageReady are added to slices of the canvas or to image map hotspots. You can then adjust the appearance of the image's layers for the various states you want in your web design. However, rather than slicing the interface yourself, ImageReady can automatically create a slice based on the shape of a particular layer that will adjust to the size of the pixels in the layer.

First, add slices or an image map to the canvas. To add slices, do one of the following:

- To manually add slices to the canvas, use the Slice tool (see Section 25.1).
- To add a rollover state associated with a layer, choose the layer (see Section 8.2) click the Create Layer-Based Rollover button at the bottom of the Rollovers palette. The new slice will appear in the Rollovers palette with the Over state default.

Once you have slices or image maps in the image, you can add rollover states. Select the slice or image map you want to add a rollover to in the Rollovers palette or in the canvas. (If you do not see the slices, click the Toggle Image Maps Visibility or Toggle Slices Visibility button in the toolbox.)

Finally, in the Rollovers palette, either click the New Rollover State Button or choose New Rollover State from the palette menu. ImageReady adds the next logical state to the slice or image map hotspot: Over, Down, Selected, Out, Up, Click, None. You can now edit the layers in the image to set the appearance for this rollover state (see Section 24.5).

You can now save your rollovers as part of your optimized website (see Chapter 25).

24.4 Creating Rollovers *(Continued)*

Adding an Animation to a Rollover

Rollover states can also use GIF animations that you create using a combination of the Rollover palette and the Animations palette. To create an animated rollover state, select the state you want to add animation to in the Rollovers palette. Click the Add Animation Frame button at the bottom of the Rollovers palette, or choose New Animation Frame from the palette's menu. If you do not see this button, open the Palette Options dialog and make sure Include Animation Frames is checked. A new frame will be added to the selected state. You can now follow the instructions in Section 24.2 for creating an animation using the Animations palette.

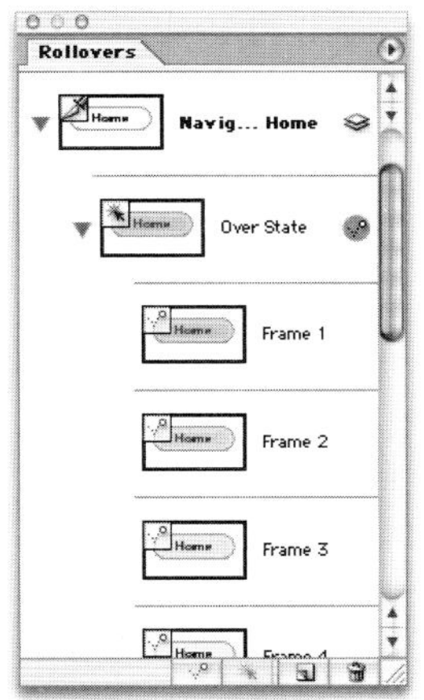

Rollovers palette displaying a state using an animation. In this example the animation causes the button to strobe slightly when the mouse cursor is over it.

Naming the rollover states becomes especially important when it's time to output the image, because you can have ImageReady automatically use the state name as part of the filename to help identify it.

BACKGROUND STATIC

You can include animations in a background image. Use this technique sparingly, but it can produce some remarkable results. A favorite is to create random static animation turning a web page into a TV tuned to a dead channel.

To do this, simply create an image in Photoshop with three to five layers, apply the Noise filter to each (Filter > Noise > Add Noise…) using uniform monochromatic noise, and apply a very slight Gaussian blur (Filter > Blur > Gaussian Blur). Then, move the whole thing over to ImageReady using the Jump command, and, in the Animation palette, use the Make Frames From Layers command in the palette's menu to create the static animation.

24.5 Editing Rollovers

➠ 23.5 Previewing Your Design with ImageReady

➠ 24.6 Editing Layers for Animations and Rollovers

➠ 25.5 Specifying Output Options

Toggle slices visibility
Q

After you add rollover states to a slice, you can edit the rollovers in a variety of ways:

- To **change a rollover's state**, Control/right-click its state and select a state from the contextual menu, double-click the rollover's state, or choose Rollover State Options… from the palette menu to select a state in a dialog. If you choose Custom, type the name of the state, or select a custom state previously used from the drop-down. If you choose Selected, specify whether you want this to be used as the default state when the web page is loaded.

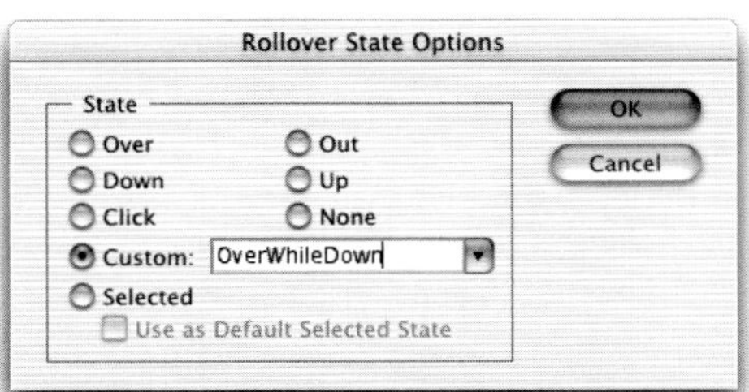

Choose a rollover state, or use Custom and enter the name of your custom rollover state.

- To **move** a rollover to a different slice or image map, click and drag the state to another rollover. This will not move the images used by the rollover state. Instead, the moved rollover state will use the images in the layers available to the rollover to which it has been moved.
- To **delete** a rollover state, select the state and click the trashcan button or choose Delete Rollover State from the palette's menu. To delete the entire rollover (including all states), choose Delete Rollover from the palette's menu
- To **copy** a rollover state, choose Copy Rollover State from the palette's menu. The state is now in a special rollover state Clipboard.
- To **paste** the layers of the copied rollover state, select a rollover state and choose Paste Rollover State from the palette's menu. This will not paste the images used by the rollover state. Instead, the pasted rollover state will use the images in the layers available to the rollover in which it has been pasted.
- To **duplicate** a rollover state, select the state and choose Duplicate Rollover State from the palette's menu, or drag the state to the New Rollover State button . The duplicated state will appear immediately beneath the original.

24.5 Editing Rollovers *(Continued)*

Applying Rollover Style Presets

As with Photoshop, preset styles can be applied in ImageReady to any layer using the styles palette (see Section 10.3). However, the ImageReady styles have one distinct advantage over their Photoshop counterpart: they also store the styles of rollover states. These special rollover styles appear side-by-side with other styles in the palette, but include a black triangle in the upper-left corner of the thumbnail. When you apply one of these styles to a layer, it automatically applies the styles for all the states that it has recorded. If the layer it is being applied to was not already a rollover, it is automatically turned into a layer-based rollover.

The ImageReady Styles palette includes styles with one or more states bundled into them, indicated by the black triangle in the thumbnail.

- To add a style to a layer, select the layer in the Layers palette and click the style in the Styles palette, or drag the thumbnail of the style directly to the layer in the canvas.
- To add a style preset based on the styles applied to an existing layer-based slice, select the rollover in the Rollovers palette, and then click the New Style button in the ImageReady Style Palette or choose New Style from the Style palette's menu. In the dialog, type the name of the style, set the style options (make sure that Include Rollover States is checked), and click OK.

The Animation and Rollovers palettes use their own separate Clipboard when copying and pasting. Copying frames or rollover states will not replace the contents of the ImageReady Clipboard and vice versa.

If you change the state of a rollover to a state that already exists for that rollover, the original state will be changed to None.

➠ 23.5 Previewing Your Design with ImageReady

Match
⌘ M
Ctrl M

You can also use warping text to create a rollover or an animation, although not all the features are available.

24.6 Editing Layers for Animations and Rollovers

Although both rollovers and animations have their own palettes, both rely on the Layers palette and the canvas to control the action of a state or a frame. Think of a rollover state or a frame as a unique version of the image that you can flip through or between using the Animation or Rollovers palette. For example, when a particular frame in an animation is selected, you are viewing the image as it will appear when that frame is showing.

Changes to specific states and frames Changes made to the layer's opacity, fill opacity, blending mode, visibility, position, and style affect only the selected rollover state or frame.

Changes to all states and frames Changes made using the painting and editing tools, adjustments, filters, type, and transformations will be applied to all states and frames in which the affected layer exists.

Unifying Layers for States and Frames

You use the unify buttons in the Layers palette to specify whether position, visibility, and/or style changes to a layer that would normally only be state- or frame-specific should be applied across all states in a rollover and all frames in an animation. To unify a layer's states or frames, select the layer in the Layers palette and click one of these buttons:

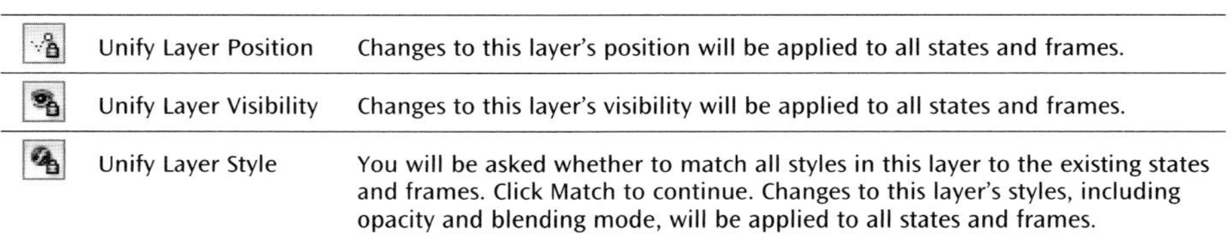

	Unify Layer Position	Changes to this layer's position will be applied to all states and frames.
	Unify Layer Visibility	Changes to this layer's visibility will be applied to all states and frames.
	Unify Layer Style	You will be asked whether to match all styles in this layer to the existing states and frames. Click Match to continue. Changes to this layer's styles, including opacity and blending mode, will be applied to all states and frames.

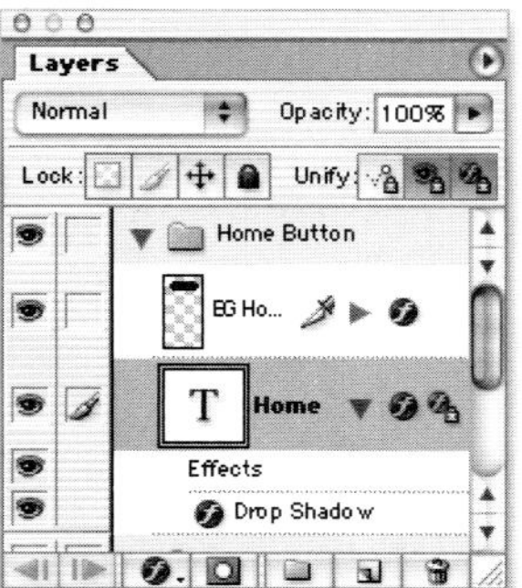

The visibility and styles of the Home Type layer are unified. The icon for the last unification button applied to a layer is displayed next to its name.

24.6 Editing Layers for Animations and Rollovers *(Continued)*

Matching Layers Across States and Frames

Matching allows you to apply the attributes of a layer in one state or frame to all the other states or frames using that same layer. For example, if you change the style of a layer in a particular animation frame and then want that layer's style change applied to all other animation frames, you can use the Match command.

To match layers, select the state (in the Rollovers palette) or frame (in the Animation palette) you want to apply to other states or frames. Then select the *layer* (in the Layers palette) that you want to match. (The layer must be a part of the rollover or animation selected.) Now, choose Match… from the Layers menu or from the Layers palette menu.

In the Match dialog, specify whether to apply attributes from the selected state or frame to all frames in the current animation, to the rollover states in the currently selected slice or image map, or to all rollover states in the image that contains the selected layer. Finally, check the attributes you want to apply from the selected layer and click OK. All the relevant states or frames will be changed to match the attributes of the selected layer.

Changes made to the Normal state or Frame 1 change all states or frames in which the affected layers exist. However, you can turn this feature off for animations by clearing the Propagate Frame 1 Changes option in the Layers palette menu.

VECTOR VS. BITMAP ANIMATION

GIF animations are a tried and true method for adding movement to your web pages, but they are severely limited in what they can do. Worse, the longer and more complex they become, the larger the file size and, thus, the longer the download time. This is because GIF animation relies on bitmap images to create the movement. Vector animation, on the other hand, allows you to create complex and interactive animations that will generally download far more quickly than GIF animations. The most common vector format for the web is Flash, but the new SVG (Scalable Vector Format) is a standard from the World Wide Web consortium that is slowly catching on.

24.7 Creating Seamless Backgrounds

➠ 14.12 Using the Pattern Maker

Reapply last filter using same settings
⌘ F
Ctrl F

Reapply last filter using dialog
⌘ Option F
Ctrl Alt F

Generally, you want to produce low-contrast backgrounds with a color that highly contrasts the foreground color you will be using for your text.

Backgrounds do not have to tile across the entire page. CSS (Cascading Style Sheets) allows you to set a background to tile once, horizontally only, or vertically only.

You can tile images into the background of a web page to add a lot of decoration and texture with a small graphic. ImageReady provides a special filter that allows you to blend the edges of an image to produce a smooth seamless background.

1 Open the image you want to use as the basis for your background and remove all slices (Slices > Delete All).

2 Choose Filter > Other > Tile Maker, choose a tiling method, and click OK:

   Blending Edges Blurs the edges of the tile together to make a seamless tile. Enter a value (1 to 20) for the width to blend (larger values blend better but might distort the image), and check whether the image should resize to fill the tile (otherwise a black border is used at the edges).

   Kaleidoscope Flips the image horizontally and vertically to create an abstract pattern.

3 To preview how the tile will look as a background, choose File > Output Settings > Background…, choose Background for the View option, and click OK. Now click the Preview In Browser button to place the tile in a temporary web page.

Original tile

Blending Edges

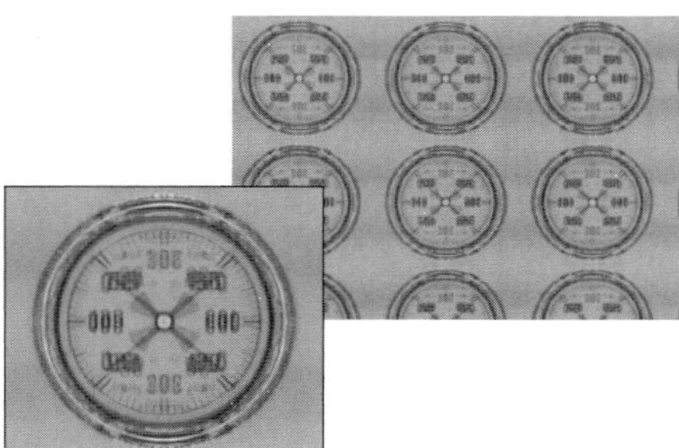

Kaleidoscope

CHAPTER 25

Outputting for the Web

BOTH PHOTOSHOP AND IMAGEREADY are set up to help you quickly optimize and save your web design to turn it into a web page. Although both programs include roughly equivalent capabilities to that end, they are implemented differently. Whereas image optimization is an integral part of the ImageReady interface, Photoshop places all optimization tools in a separate dialog, the use of which is the first step in saving the image. To begin optimizing and saving an interface, you slice it into pieces that can have separate optimization options and that can be saved as separate files.

25.1 Slicing Your Interface

Save For Web... (Photoshop only)
Shift ⌘ Option S
Shift Ctrl Option S

Draw slice from center
Option Drag
Alt Drag

Draws square slice
Shift Drag

Draw square slice from center
Shift Option Drag
Shift Alt Drag

You use slices to split your image into specific regions to which you can then apply different optimization and rollover options. More important, when you save your image for the Web, you can have Photoshop or ImageReady save each slice as an individual file, which you will then reassemble using HTML as a Web page. Every slice in the canvas is identified by small icons in the top-left corner of the slice that specify the number of the slice, identify the type of slice, and identify whether the layer is linked together with other slices to use common optimization settings. Slice icons are generally blue. If the slices are linked, however, they are automatically assigned a unique color code, a different one for each linked set. If a slice is an auto slice, the slice icons appear grayed out.

ICON	TYPE	DESCRIPTION
	User Slice	Slice defined using the Slice tool.
	Layer-based Slice	Slice defined based on the content of a specific layer.
	No Image	Slice will not be used as an image in the final output. You can add HTML text using the Slice palette.
	Rollover Slice	Slice includes rollover information that can be viewed in the Rollover palette.
	Auto Slice	Slice created to fill areas not occupied by user, rollover, layer-based, or no image slices. All auto slices are linked and grayed out.
	Linked Slice	Slice is linked to other slices. The same optimization settings are applied to slices in a linked set. Slices in the same linked set are color-coded.

Adding User Slices

You can draw slices directly into the canvas in either Photoshop or ImageReady using the Slice tool. To add slices to the canvas, choose the Slice tool from the Toolbox. As soon as the tool is active, existing slices are automatically displayed on the canvas. Next, set the style for the slice in the tool options bar:

Normal Allows you to create a free-form rectangular shape.

Fixed Aspect Ratio Allows you to constrain the height-to-width ratio. Enter values (1 to 999) for the *relative* width and height in the fields to the right.

Fixed Size Allows you to set the dimensions of the slice numerically. Enter values (1 to 999) for the width and height in the fields to the right.

Finally, click and drag from one corner of the area you want to slice, Shift-drag to constrain the slice shape to a square, or Option/Alt-drag to draw the slice from the center. You can do this as many times as you want to create slices.

25.1 Slicing Your Interface *(Continued)*

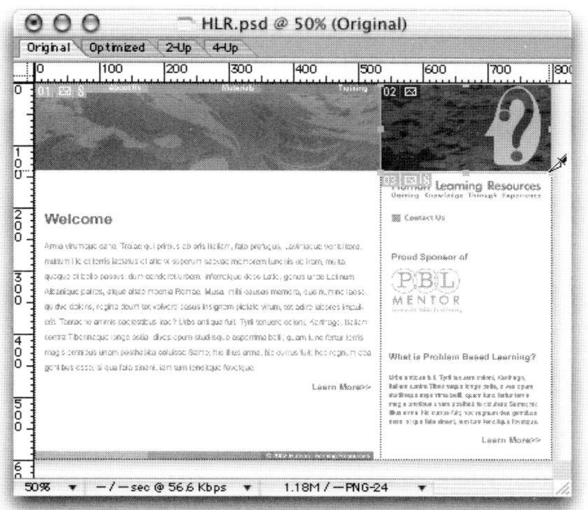

The first slice being added to the web interface around the company logo in the top-right corner. Notice that the rest of the interface is using auto slices.

Toggle slice's visibility (ImageReady)

Q

Switch between slice tools (ImageReady; reverts after release)

⌘

Ctrl

Generating Slices

In addition to drawing slices directly in the canvas, you can use other tools (guides and selections) and features (layers) to generate slices automatically. To generate slices, do one of the following:

- To generate slices based on **guides** in the canvas (see Section 6.8), first add and adjust guides as needed. In Photoshop, choose the Slice tool from the Toolbox and click the Slices From Guides button in the tool options bar. In ImageReady, choose Slices **>** Create Slices From Guides. Existing slices will be deleted.
- (ImageReady only) To generate slices based on a **selection**, make the selection in the canvas using one of the marquee tools and then choose Select **>** Create Slice From Selection. If the selection is not rectangular or if the edges are feathered, the slice will be made from the maximum width and height needed to encompass the entire selection.
- To generate a slice based on **layers** content, choose the layer in the Layers palette and then choose Layer **>** New Layer Based Slice. A layer that is used to create a slice will have the Slice icon next to its name in the Layers palette. The dimensions of the slice will adjust if the content of the layer is edited or changed.
- (ImageReady only) To generate a slice with a **rollover**, choose the layer in the Layers palette and then click the Layer-based Rollover button at the bottom of the Rollovers palette (see Section 24.4).

25.1 Slicing Your Interface *(Continued)*

Slice appearance, including line styles, colors, numbers, and symbols, is set in the Slice preferences (see Section 22.6).

Although you cannot select multiple slices in the Photoshop canvas, you can select multiple slices when using Photoshop's Save For Web feature (see Section 25.4).

Setting Slice Options

One of the most powerful features of slicing the image is that you can specify information about the image contained in the slice that will be used to generate the filenames and HTML code used to create the web page. You can also define areas in the design that will not be graphics in the final web page and even enter text and/or HTML code to use in those areas.

To access the slice options, choose the Select Slice tool, and then do one of the following:

- In Photoshop, double-click a slice in the canvas to open the Slice Options dialog. Set the options and click OK when you are finished.
- In ImageReady, with the Slice palette open (Window > Slice), select a single slice to enter information just for that slice or select multiple slices to enter information that will be used for all the selected slices.

Although their formats are slightly different, both the Slice Options dialog and palette contain most of the same options.

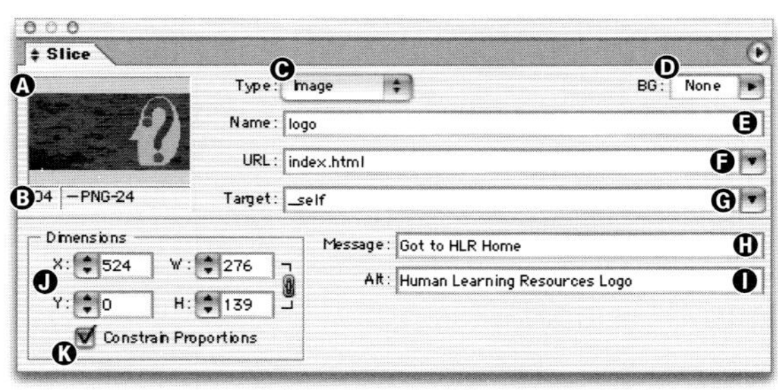

A (ImageReady only) Slice Thumbnail.

B (ImageReady only) Slice number and optimization setting.

C Choose either Image or No Image for the slice type. Image slices are output as graphics, and No Image slices are output as empty areas that can contain HTML text.

D Choose the background color for the slice. In Photoshop, select the background type (None, White, Black, Matte, or Other). If you select other, you choose the background color using the Photoshop Color Picker.

E Enter a name for the slice.

F If this slice is a hypertext link, enter the URL for the link or choose a previously entered URL from the drop-down.

G If this slice is a hypertext link, you can enter the name of a window or a frame to target or choose from a list of previously entered or standard target names.

H If this is a link, enter a message to appear in the browser's status bar when the mouse cursor is over the image.

I Enter an alternative text message to use if the image does not load or for Tool Tips. Adding the Alt message also ensures that your website is full accessible.

J Enter the position (X and Y coordinates) and dimensions (width and height) of the slice.

K (ImageReady only) Check to constrain width and height.

25.1 Slicing Your Interface *(Continued)*

If the slice is not an image, the dialog and palette will change slightly, presenting different options for the slice:

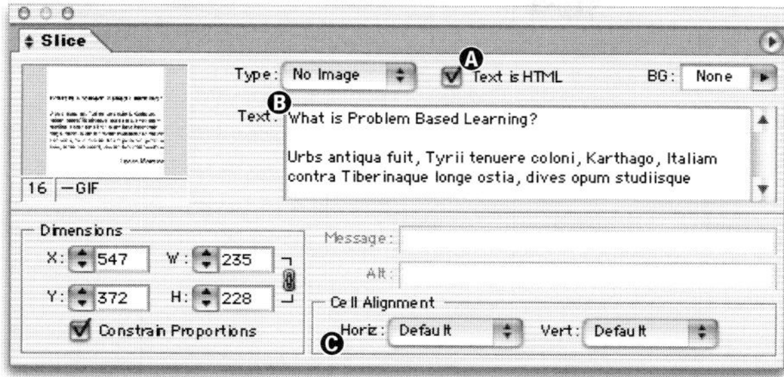

A (ImageReady only) Check if you want HTML tags in the Text field (see B) interpreted as HTML. If this option is unchecked, HTML tags will be displayed as text on the page.

B Enter HTML text and HTML tags (if A is checked) that will be displayed in this area of the design.

C (ImageReady only) Choose the horizontal and vertical alignment of the text within the area.

If snap is turned on (see Section 6.8), slices will be aligned to the edges of guides, grids, and other slices.

If you set the options for an auto slice, it is automatically changed to a user slice.

ADDING FILE INFORMATION IN IMAGEREADY

Like Photoshop, ImageReady allows you to add file information (see Section 6.11), but limits the information added to a one-line title displayed in the browser title bar and a multiline copyright notice included in a meta tag. To add file information in ImageReady, choose File > File Info..., enter a caption for the web page title, enter a copyright notice, and click OK.

25.2 Working with Slices

Toggle slices visibility (ImageReady)

Q

Switch between slice tools (ImageReady; reverts after release)

Ctrl

To specify information about, edit, or optimize a slice, you need to select it. With Photoshop, you can select and edit only one slice at a time in the canvas, although you can select multiple slices in the Save For Web dialog. With ImageReady, you can select multiple slices to edit simultaneously. In addition, slices are incredibly useful when you are optimizing your image or carving it up for output to HTML, but slice lines can be a distraction while you are editing your document.

- To **show or hide the slices**, choose View > Show > Slices or Auto Slices. In ImageReady, you can also click the Toggle Slices Visibility button in the Toolbox or click the Hide Auto Slices button in the tool options bar.
- To **select a slice**, choose the Select Slice tool and click any slice in the canvas (including auto slices). In ImageReady, you can also select slices in the Rollovers palette.
- (ImageReady only) To **select multiple slices**, choose the Select Slice tool and Shift-click as many slices in the canvas (including auto slices) as desired. You can also select multiple slices in the Rollovers palette by Shift-clicking.
- (ImageReady only) To **save a selection** of slices, select one or more slices in the canvas, choose Slices > Save Slice Selection, enter a name for the saved selection, and click OK. This saved selection will now be available in this document.
- (ImageReady only) To **load a selection** of slices, choose Slices > Load Slice Selection, and then choose one of the previously saved slice selections from the submenu.
- (ImageReady only) To **delete a selection** of slices, choose Slices > Delete Slice Selection, and then choose one of the previously saved slice selections from the submenu. The saved selection will be deleted, but the slices will not be deleted.
- To **convert** an auto slice to a user slice, select the auto slice in the canvas using the Select Slice tool from the Toolbox. In Photoshop, click the Promote To User Slice button in the tool options bar. In ImageReady, choose Slices > Promote To User-Slices.
- To **move** slices, click and drag within the boundary of one of the selected slices. Auto slices will be added or reshaped to adjust for the slices' new position. If you move the slice over other slice types, they will be stacked underneath the slice or slices being moved.
- To **resize** slices, click and drag any of the sides or corners of any of the selected slices. Auto slices will be added or reshaped to adjust for the slices' new dimensions. If you resize the slice over other layer types, they will be stacked underneath the resized slice. If you select multiple slices in ImageReady, they will adjust to each other's resizing and not overlap.
- To **divide** a slice, in Photoshop click the Divide Slice button in the tool options bar. In ImageReady, choose Divide Slice(s) from the Slices menu or Slice palette menu. Set the options for how you want the slice divided and then click OK.

25.2 Working with Slices *(Continued)*

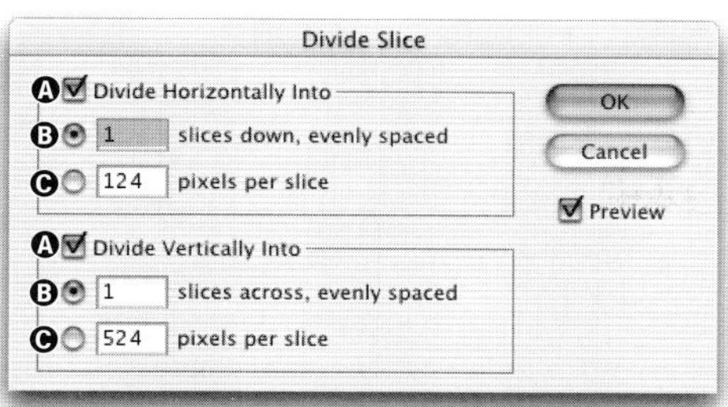

A Check to divide the slice horizontally and/or vertically.

B Choose to divide the slice evenly into the number of slices entered in the field to the right.

C Choose to divide the slice, with each new slice having a maximum width and height entered in the field to the right.

- (ImageReady only) To **copy and paste** slices, choose Copy Slice from the Slice palette menu, and then choose Paste Slice from the Slice palette menu. The copy will appear on top of the original. You can also paste the slice into anther image open in ImageReady.
- (ImageReady only) To **combine** slices, choose Slices > Combine Slices. The slices will be combined into a rectangle user slice with dimensions to encompass all selected slices even if that means overlapping other slices. You cannot combine layer-based slices.
- To **duplicate** slices, Option/Alt-drag the slice. In ImageReady, you can also choose Duplicate Slice(s) from the Slices or Slice palette menu, set your options, and click OK.

Check whether to also duplicate the Rollover states associated wit the slice, duplicate layers associated with layer-based slices, and specify where to position the duplicate slices in relation to the original slice.

- To **change the stacking order** of slices, click the Move To Top, Move Up One Level, Move Down One Level, or Move To Bottom button in the tool options bar. In ImageReady, you can also choose these options from the Slice palette's menu or the Slices > Arrange submenu. For slices, the stacking order is important for determining the order of rollovers.
- (ImageReady only) To **align** slices, Shift-click two or more hot spots and then click one of the alignment buttons in the tool options bar (see Section 9.11) or choose these options from the Slices > Align submenu.
- (ImageReady only) To **distribute** slices, Shift-click three or more slices and then click one of the distribution buttons in the tool options bar (see Section 9.11) or choose these options from the Slices > Distribute submenu.
- To **delete** slices, press Delete/Backspace or (ImageReady only) choose Delete Slice(s) from the Slices palette menu or the Slices menu. You cannot delete auto slices.
- To **delete all** slices, choose (in Photoshop) View > Clear Slices or (in ImageReady) Slices > Delete All.
- (Photoshop only) To **lock** all slices, preventing any changes from being made, choose View > Lock Slices. Choose this option again to unlock the slices.

You cannot change the stacking order of auto slices.

When you delete a user slice or a layer-based slice, auto slices are used to fill the vacated space.

Aligning and distributing slices is a good way to eliminate surplus auto slices and produce leaner files.

Saved slice groups are especially useful when you are outputting the image (see Section 25.6), allowing you to quickly choose to output only that group of slices.

25.3 Optimizing Images

➠ 18.4 Creating Droplets

Toggle Optimization Views (ImageReady only)
⌘ Y
Ctrl Y

Toggle gamma optimization views (ImageReady only)
Option ⌘ Y
Alt Ctrl Y

Toggle dither optimization views (ImageReady only)
Shift ⌘ Y
Shift Ctrl Y

The key to optimizing images for the Web is to balance the need to reduce the file size against the need to produce high-quality attractive images. This can take some practice and experimentation, but fortunately both ImageReady and Photoshop provide tools to help you preview the effects of compression and quickly make changes before you commit to any particular compression scheme. In addition, you can compress different slices in the image using different options and use masks to vary the amount of compression over an entire image.

Applying and Previewing Optimization Settings

You can apply compression to an entire image, to an individual slice, or to multiple slices to reduce the file size and thus speed transmission of graphics over the Internet. Compression settings are added to optimized images. You can optimize images in the ImageReady canvas or by using the Photoshop Save For Web dialog (see Section 25.5).

- To **apply** optimization settings to a slice, select one or more slices in the canvas, and then choose either a preset compression with preset options or a compression method. You can then set the options for the compression method as described in Section 25.4.
- To **preview** the optimized version of the image, choose one of the tabs at the top of the ImageReady canvas or in the Photoshop Save For Web dialog: Optimized, 2-up, or 4-up. Both 2-up and 4-up present multiple panel views of the image, allowing you to optimize each in each view to compare the quality and size of different possible optimization settings. Select one of the views to apply optimization settings by clicking anywhere in that panel and then clicking a slice in that panel.
- (ImageReady only) To **update** an optimized preview based on new optimization settings, choose Regenerate from the Optimize palette menu. Previews that have not been updated will display a warning icon ⚠ in the bottom-right corner of the preview. Click this icon to regenerate the preview.
- (ImageReady only) To **automatically update** optimized views when settings change, choose Auto Regenerate in the Optimize palette menu. This command can be useful if you are making a few small changes, but can be time-consuming if you are making several changes at once.

25.3 Optimizing Images *(Continued)*

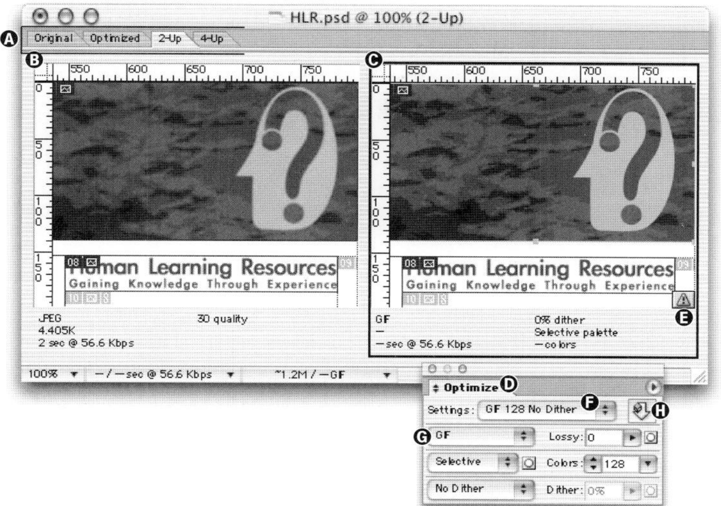

A **Preview Tabs** Click to view a single optimized version of the image, two optimized versions side by side, or four versions.

B Original Version

C Optimized Version

D Optimization options (see Section 25.4).

E An alert icon appears if the version showing in the preview has not been updated based on the current optimization settings.

F **Optimization Preset** Choose a compression method with preset options for the file format and optimization settings. You can still customize the options as desired.

G **File Format** Choose a compression method. The last settings for the method will be used.

H **Droplet** (ImageReady only) Click to save the current settings as a droplet. You can then drag and drop image files onto the icon to automatically create an optimized version of the file based on the settings.

You can also create droplets in Photoshop using the Actions. See Section 18.4 for more details.

When a slice is *not* selected during optimization, its content's color will appear dimmed. This does not affect the final appearance of the graphics.

Both Photoshop and ImageReady allow you to optimize images for the Web in real time, so that you can see the results before saving.

The advantage of using ImageReady over Photoshop for optimization is that you can set your optimization options while working to test how they will affect the final piece, which may affect your design decisions.

Remember that if you are in a 2-up or 4-up optimization view, you can use the hand tool to move the viewable area of the canvas around.

The Unlink Slice option is also available in the ImageReady Slice palette menu.

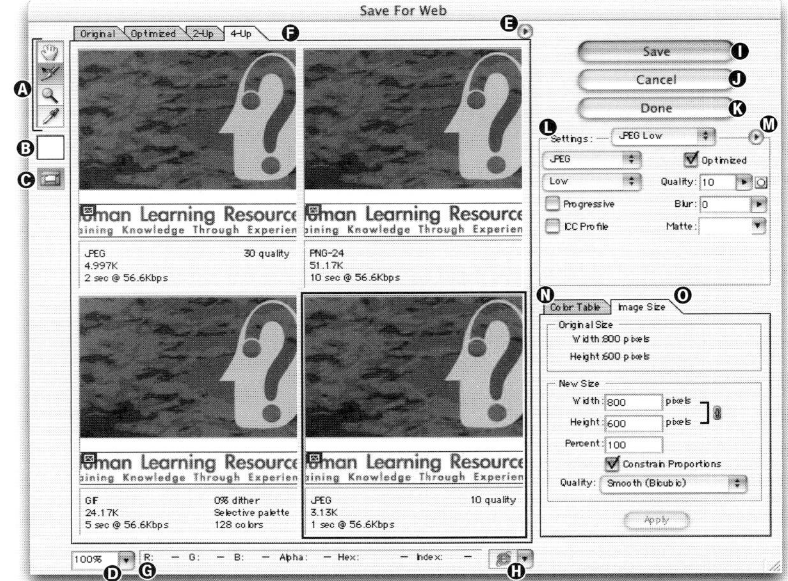

Ⓐ **Tools** This limited tool set includes the Hand, Slice Select, Zoom, and Eyedropper tools.

Ⓑ Displays the current color selected by the Eyedropper.

Ⓒ Click to show or hide slices in the display.

Ⓓ **Magnification** Enter or choose the magnification for the image(s) in the display.

Ⓔ **Preview Menu** Choose viewing options for the preview area, including Browser Dither, Hide/Show Auto Slices, preview color palette, and predicted download times based on connection speed.

Ⓕ **Preview Area** Displays the image either in its original format, optimized, or in 2-up, 4-up optimized views.

Ⓖ **Color Values** Displays various color values for the pixel the cursor is currently over in the display area.

Ⓗ Click to preview the image in a browser (indicated by the browser's icon) or choose a different browser from the drop-down.

Ⓘ Click to proceed to save the optimized image.

Ⓙ Click to return to the canvas without preserving optimization settings.

Ⓚ Click to return to the canvas and preserve the optimization settings.

Ⓛ Optimization settings (see Section 25.4).

Ⓜ **Settings menu** Contains options to save and load optimization settings, link slices, optimize to a file size, and specify output settings (see Section 25.4).

Ⓝ Click to view and edit the colors used if the image or slice is using the GIF or PNG-8 file format (see Section 25.4).

Ⓞ Click to view and change the image dimensions. Enter a new width and/or height, enter a percentage to scale the image up or down, choose the quality used to resize, and click Apply. This resizes the image for this saved version and leaves the original version unchanged.

Linking Slices to Optimize

To save time, you can link slices that will be using the same optimization settings. When one slice in the linked set is selected, changes to its optimization options affect all slices in the set. Linked images have the Link icon in the top-left corner of the slice, and slices in a linked set are color-coded.

- (ImageReady) Use the Select Slice tool to select slices in the canvas, and then choose Slices > Link Slices.
- (Photoshop) Use the Select Slice tool to select slices in the Save For Web dialog, and then choose Link Slices from the Settings menu.
- To unlink slices, choose a slice in a set using the Select Slice tool, and then choose Unlink Slice (unlinks just the selected slice) or Unlink All (removes all links in the document) from the Slices menu (ImageReady) or the Select menu (Photoshop's Save For Web dialog). In ImageReady, you can also choose Slices > Unlink Set (unlinks all slices in the same set).

Saving and Loading Optimization Settings

After you fine-tune your settings, you can save them in a variety of ways for later use:

- To **save** optimization settings, choose Save Settings in the Optimize palette menu (ImageReady) or Settings menu (Photoshop). Enter a name for the settings and save them in the Presets/Optimized Settings folder inside the Photoshop program folder. The new settings will appear in the Optimization Presets drop-down.
- To **delete** an optimization preset, choose it from the drop-down, and then choose Delete in the Optimize palette menu (ImageReady) or Settings menu (Photoshop).
- (ImageReady only) To **create a droplet** based on the optimization settings shown, click the Droplet button, enter a name for the droplet, browse to the location where you want to save the droplet, and click Save. Images or folders of images dragged onto the Droplet icon will be optimized using the saved settings.

A droplet to convert images to GIF format using a 128-color, selective palette with dithering.

Optimize to a Specific File Size

Rather than optimizing an image or a slice yourself, you can have ImageReady or Photoshop automatically optimize based on the file size you want. This method is not perfect, and there are obviously limits. You can nevertheless often achieve smaller files this way or even use this as a starting point and then modify the automatic settings to improve the image quality.

If you do not save optimization settings in the Presets/Optimized Settings folder, you can still load them, but they will not appear in the palette's pop-down menu.

Once deleted, an optimization setting is gone forever, so think carefully before clicking OK.

25.3 Optimizing Images *(Continued)*

To optimize, select one ore more slices and choose Optimize To File Size in the Optimize palette (ImageReady) or Save For Web Settings menu (Photoshop), choose your options, and then click OK. If you select Total Of All Slices, optimization might take several seconds.

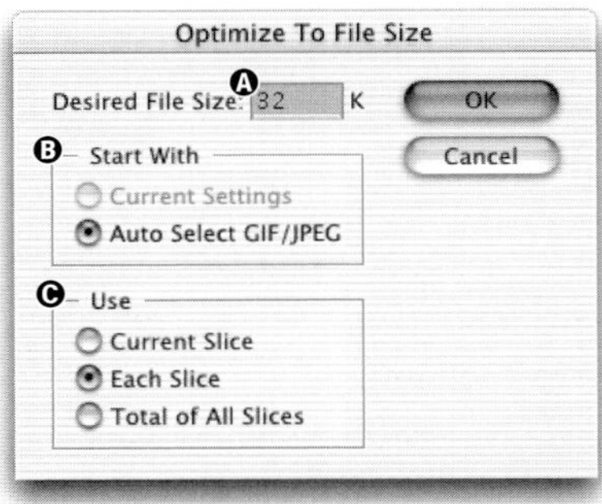

Ⓐ Enter a value for the final size of the slice or image after compression.

Ⓑ Choose whether you want to start the compression using the current settings or allow ImageReady/Photoshop to choose whether to use GIF or JPEG format.

Ⓒ Choose whether to base the optimization setting on the current slice settings, each slice individually, or the total of all slices in the image.

COPYING CODE

In addition to allowing you to save the HTML code when outputting the web page, ImageReady allows you to copy the code directly as text so that you can paste it into the HTML editing software of your choice.

- To copy the HTML code used to generate all slices or the selected slices, choose Edit > Copy HTML Code > For All Slices or For Selected Slices.
- To copy the JavaScript code used to preload the image, choose Edit > Copy HTML Code > For Preloads.
- To copy the foreground color's hexadecimal color value, choose Edit > Copy Foreground Color As HTML.

25.4 Setting Optimization Options

All images headed to the Web from Photoshop and ImageReady must be saved in one of three formats: GIF, PNG (8 or 24), or JPEG. In addition, you can save graphics that will be viewed on devices with black-and-white screens (such as mobile phones) in WBMP format (see Section 6.1). These formats take the file information and use various compression schemes to squeeze the file size down to make transmission of the files faster. All these formats are *lossy* formats in that the compression invariably leads to a little or a lot of loss in image quality.

➠ 11.1 Mask Basics

Toggle Optimization Views (ImageReady only)
⌘ Y
Ctrl Y

Toggle gamma optimization views (ImageReady only)
Option ⌘ Y
Alt Ctrl Y

Toggle dither optimization views (ImageReady only)
Shift ⌘ Y
Shift Ctrl Y

Weighted Optimization with Masks

You use masks to selectively protect areas of the image while editing (see Chapter 11). You can also use masks to selectively optimize parts of the image, allowing you to retain high quality in some regions while applying maximum compression to others. This weighted optimization allows you to control the amount of certain compression options applied:

JPEG Quality Applies higher JPEG compression to darker areas of the mask and lower quality.

GIF Lossiness Applies higher GIF compression to darker areas of the mask and lower quality.

Dithering Applies greater amounts of dithering to lighter areas of the mask.

Color Reduction Applies greater amounts of color reduction to darker areas of the mask. (Quality settings are not available.)

To use weighted optimization with an option, click the Optimize button to the right of an option in the Optimize palette. In the Modify Settings dialog, set the masks to use for the weighted optimization and then set the quality options for how the option should be treated by layers for optimization.

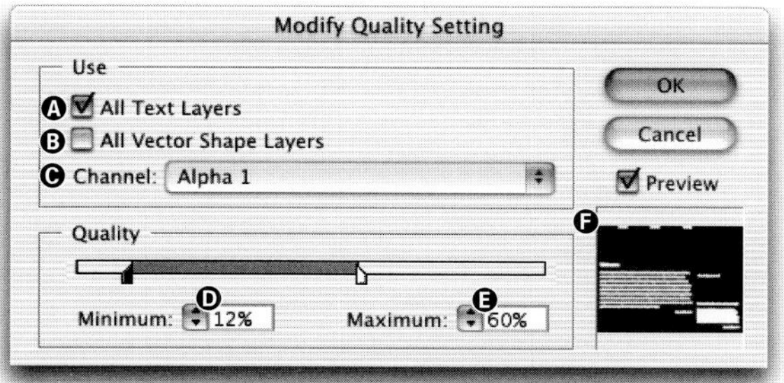

Ⓐ Check to use all text layers in the image as masks (see Section 17.2). This helps preserve text quality.

Ⓑ Check to use the vector masks in all shape layers (see Section 11.6).

Ⓒ Choose an alpha channel to use as a mask (see Section 7.5).

Ⓓ Use the slider (the black tab) or enter a value (1 to 100%) to set the minimum quality for areas that are completely unmasked.

Ⓔ Use the slider (the white tab) or enter a value (1 to 100%) to set the maximum quality for the masked area.

Ⓕ Displays a thumbnail of masked regions in an image. White represents masked areas and will be the highest quality. Black represents unmasked areas that will receive the maximum compression. Gray areas will receive compression on a linear scale.

Using the diffusion dither in adjacent slices may cause noticeable seams to appear across slice boundaries. To overcome this, link the styles and then apply the diffusion dither.

Although the PNG format is supported by most browsers, the alpha-channel feature for PNG-24 is currently only supported in Internet Explorer 5 for the Mac.

Although WBMP format is currently useful, both cell phones and PDAs are swiftly migrating to color screens that may soon render this format obsolete.

Optimizing with GIF or PNG-8 Compression

Both GIF and PNG formats work well for compressing images that have large areas of solid color. GIF format is the undisputed king of web graphic formats and is supported in every graphic-capable browser. PNG, on the other hand, is a newer format that is not as widely supported, but is supported in most of today's browsers.

Both formats work by reducing the number of colors in the image's color table (see Section 25.3) to 256 or fewer colors, effectively reducing the amount of information used to display the image, but also reducing the number of colors available to produce the image. In addition, both GIF and PNG formats allow you to specify a particular color in the image as transparent. Background colors in the web page will show through transparent images.

A (GIF only) Use the slider or enter a value (0 to 100) for the amount of compression used at the loss of image quality. The larger the value, the smaller the file, but the lower the image quality.

B **Color Reduction Method** Specify how colors in the color table should be eliminated from the color table (see next sub-section) in order to preserve the best image quality. Then enter a value (2 to 256) or choose the number of colors used for the image's color table. Fewer colors will create smaller files, but reduce image quality.

C **Dithering Method** Choose the dithering method (see Section 23.2) you want to apply to the image. Then use the slider or enter a percentage value (0 to 100) for the amount of dithering allowed.

D Check to preserve transparent regions in the flattened image as transparent pixels in the final web graphic, and then choose the color to be used behind semitransparent pixels in the image. This color should be the same color you are using for the background color in the web page. If you select transparent and do not select a matte color, semitransparent regions will be either full opaque (above 50% opacity) or fully transparent (below 50% opacity).

E **Transparency Dithering Method** If Transparency is checked, choose how partially transparent pixels should be dithered (see Section 23.2). Then use the slider or enter a percentage value (0 to 100) for the amount of dithering allowed. Setting this dithering allows you to create transparent areas that will better integrate with different colored backgrounds.

F Check to use the interlacing method with the image so that it begins displaying before the file finishes downloading. For visitors with slower Internet connections, interlaced graphics may seem to load faster, but the file size is actually slightly larger. This option is located in the top-right corner of the palette for PNG-8. This feature is not generally recommended.

G Use the slider or enter a percentage value (0 to 100) to set the tolerance level at which colors are forced to be Web-safe. The higher the value, the more colors will be forced to be Web-safe.

H (ImageReady only) Check to use the same color table for all rollover states in this slice.

25.4 Setting Optimization Options *(Continued)*

Refining the Color Table to Optimize

The color table displays all the colors currently used in the optimized version of an image or slice using the GIF or PNG-8 file format. Generally, this table is controlled by the optimization settings. However, an additional way to further refine the optimization of GIF and PNG-8 images is to edit their color table manually to change color value, turn colors transparent, force colors to be Web-safe, lock important colors, add colors that have been removed, or delete colors that are not needed.

The color table is in the Color Table palette in ImageReady (Window > Color Table) or the Color tab in the bottom right of the Save For Web dialog in Photoshop.

- To **sort** the color table, choose one of the sorting options from the palette/tab menu: Unsorted, Hue (color value), Luminance (recommended), Popularity (most used in image).
- To **select** colors, click a color square or choose one of the selection options from the palette/tab menu: All Colors, All Web Safe Colors, All Non-Web Safe Colors.
- To **save** a color table, choose Save Color Table... from the palette/tab menu, enter a filename making sure to preserve the `.act` extension, and click Save.
- To **load** a color table, choose Load Color Table... from the palette/tab menu, choose a file with the `.act` extension, and click Open. The new color table will replace the previous color table.

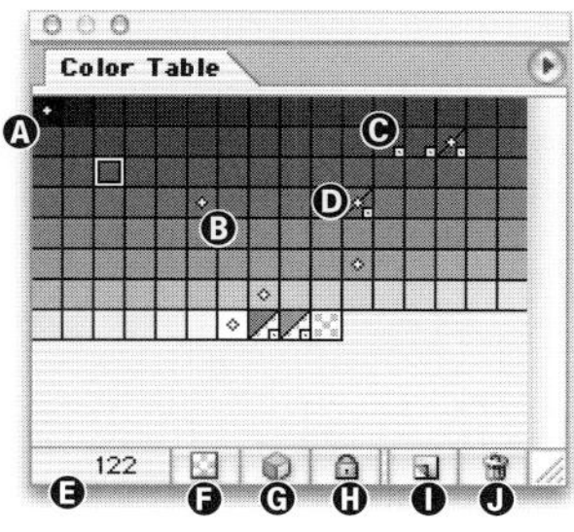

Ⓐ **Color Square** Click to select. Shift-click to select multiple colors. Double-click to use the Color Picker to change this color. Selected colors are surrounded by a white box.

Ⓑ A white diamond indicates the color is Web-safe.

Ⓒ A white square in the corner indicates the color is locked (see E).

Ⓓ A line through the color with a diamond indicates that one or more colors have been shifted to this Web-safe color.

Ⓔ Displays the number of colors in the table.

Ⓕ Click to make selected colors transparent. Click again to revert to color.

Ⓖ Click to shift color(s) to their closest Web-safe equivalents. Click again to shift colors back.

Ⓗ Click to lock color(s), preventing them from being dropped during color reduction. Click again to unlock.

Ⓘ Click to add color selected by Eyedropper to the color table. This allows you to select a color from the original version of the image to add into an optimized version.

Ⓙ Click to delete the selected color(s) from the table.

The Color Table is not accessible in ImageReady if Auto Regenerate is turned off.

You cannot use the Lossy option in the GIF format with the Interlaced or Noise or Pattern Dither options.

Using the diffusion dither with any file format may cause noticeable seams between the edges of different slices.

25.4 Setting Optimization Options *(Continued)*

Optimizing with JPEG Compression

JPEG format works best for images with a lot of colors that require smooth tone transitions, such as photographs or images with subtle gradients. Setting JPEG compression requires you to set the level of compression as a numeric value, which determines how much information is removed from the image. Lower values produce higher compression (and thus smaller file sizes) but create square artifacts in the image that decrease its sharpness and quality.

An image compressed using a JPEG value of 20. Notice the rectangular distortion artifacts.

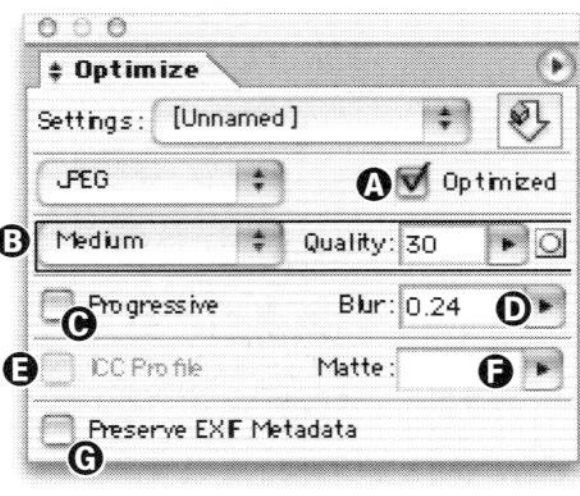

A Check to use the enhanced JPEG format to automatically produce slightly smaller file sizes.

B Select a quality setting from the drop-down, which changes the Quality value to the right. You can also use the slider or enter a numeric value (0 to 100) directly for the quality value. Low-quality values—30 or less—produce smaller file sizes but significantly reduce the image quality. You will need to experiment with quality levels to find the one that produces the smallest file size without diminishing the image quality to greatly.

C Check to use the progressive method with the image so that it begins displaying before the file finishes downloading. Progressive JPEG images require more RAM to display and are not supported in some older browsers. This feature is not generally recommended.

D Use the slider or enter a value (0 to 2) to set the amount of Gaussian Blur applied to the image to help offset the square artifacts produced by JPEG compression and producing smaller file sizes.

E Check to include the ICC profile set when specifying your color profile (see Section 7.4). This profile will be used by some browsers to ensure color consistency.

F Choose the color to be used behind semitransparent pixels in the image. This color should be the same color you are using for the background color in the web page.

G (ImageReady only) Check to include the EXIF metadata with the image (see Section 6.11).

25.4 Setting Optimization Options *(Continued)*

Optimizing with PNG-24 Compression

You can use PNG-24 to compress both images with large areas of flat color or photographs. However, using PNG-24 tends to produce larger file sizes than other compression formats. Its great advantage, though, is that unlike the JPEG, GIF, and PNG-8 formats in which all pixels are either transparent or opaque, PNG-24 allows you to include as many as 256 levels of transparency in a single image. This allows you to place the image on any background without having to worry about the matte color set when you saved the image. The down side, though, is that many common browsers (such as Internet Explorer 5 for Windows) do not support transparency with the PNG-24 format. To preserve the transparent pixels in the image, check the Transparency option.

The options for the PNG-24 format allow you to set the image to use the interlace method. You can also set the image to use transparency (transparent regions will be transparent on the web page) or to use a matte color behind transparent regions.

Optimizing with WBMP Compression

WBMP format is a black-and-white (no grayscale) format that is commonly used on mobile devices such as cell phones and PDAs. Although mobile devices with black and white screens can display images saved in color, these images are still translated into black and white, and the full color file still has to download. With WBMP you can control the quality of the image and significantly reduce its file size by eliminating color information. WBMP format has a limited number of settings that allow you to add and control dithering in the image.

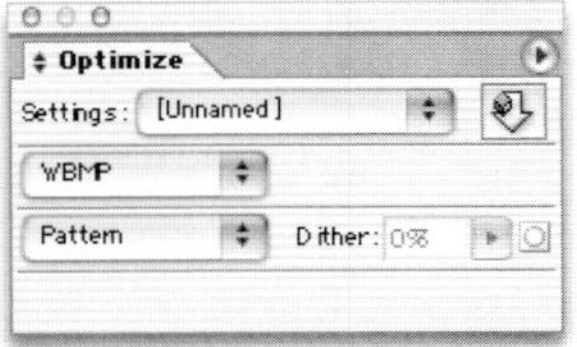

The options with the WBMP format allow you to choose the type of dithering applied to the black-and-white image (see Section 23.2) and the amount of dither applied.

25.5 Specifying Output Options

➠ 24.4 Creating Rollovers

➠ 25.1 Slicing Your Interface

HTML output settings
Option ⌘ H
Alt Ctrl H

If you are using ImageReady or Photoshop to create the HTML that you will be using to create the web page based on the image you are outputting, you will need to set the HTML, Image Map, and Slice Output settings.

Output Options are generally accessed from the same dialog associated with the Save Optimized dialog (see Section 25.6). However, you can also set the options directly in ImageReady, choosing File > Output Options and then choosing one of the sub-menu options.

HTML Output Options

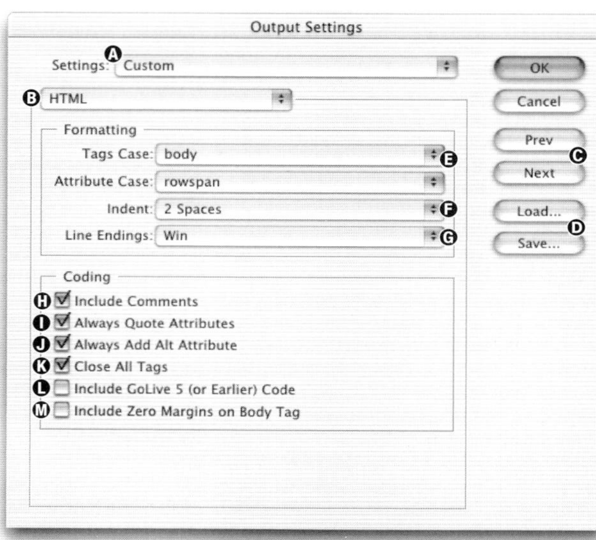

Ⓐ Choose a preset output setting.

Ⓑ Choose the output setting category.

Ⓒ Click to open the next or previous settings category.

Ⓓ Click to load or save settings using the `.iros` extension.

Ⓔ Choose the case used for HTML tags and tag attributes. Due to changes in HTML standards, all lowercase is recommended.

Ⓕ Choose how to indent the code: using tabs, none for no indenting, or using spaces (2 or 5 spaces is recommended).

Ⓖ Choose how to treat line breaks in the code: Mac, Win, or Unix. Win for Windows is recommended.

Ⓗ Check if you want Photoshop to include comments about the generated code. Recommended.

Ⓘ Check if you want attribute values in quotes. Recommended.

Ⓙ Check if you want to add the Alt attribute to all images. Recommended.

Ⓚ Check to include a closing tag for all tag sets. Recommended.

Ⓛ Check to use code compatible with GoLive 5 or earlier. This is not recommended unless you are using older version of GoLive (4 or lower) to edit your web pages.

Ⓜ (ImageReady only) Check to include attributes that will set the web page margins to 0. Otherwise, the browser will set its default margin. This is not recommended if you are using CSS for layout.

25.5 Specifying Output Options *(Continued)*

Slice Output Options

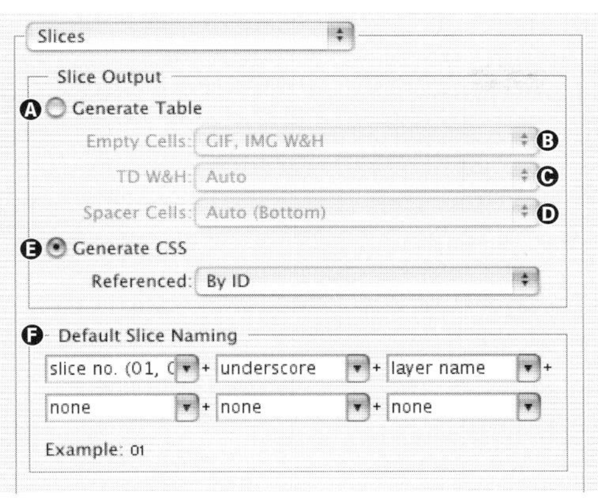

A Choose whether you want to use tables or CSS to lay out the page. Most web pages today use tables, but CSS creates faster-loading layouts.

B Choose the method for filling empty table cells: using a GIF image with width and height set in the image (recommended), using a GIF image with width and height set in the table, or using the NoWrap tag (not recommended).

C Choose how to add width and height attributes to table data tags: Auto (recommended), Always, or Never.

D Choose how to add one row and one column empty cells around the layout table to space out nonaligned slices: Auto (recommended), Never, or Always. You can also choose for Auto and Always to be placed at the bottom of the table.

E Choose how to generate CSS layers for layout: using the ID tag (recommended), placing the CSS code directly in the HTML tag, or using classes.

F Choose how to name slices automatically when added to the document. You can enter text directly in a field or choose a variable such as the document name, layer name, slice number, and date from the pull-down menus.

Image Map Output Options (ImageReady)

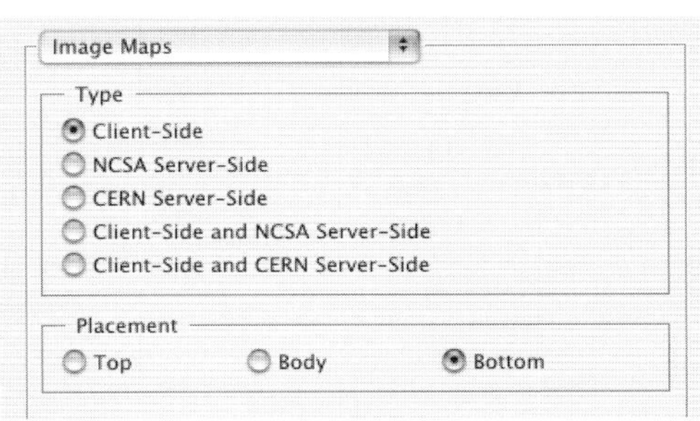

Choose how to code the image maps: as client-side (recommended) with the code embedded in the HTML, as server-side (NCSA or CERN) with the code generated as a separate file, or as a combination. If you are using client-side, specify where the image map code should be placed in the HTML. Body is recommended to keep the code with the image source tag.

Photoshop and ImageReady cannot generate server-side image maps for images that contain slices.

Almost all browsers support client-side mage maps. However, if you need to use server-side image maps for some reason, contact your Internet Service Provider (ISP) to determine whether they use NCSA or CERN specifications.

Some servers do not allow spaces in filenames, so using them is not recommended. Use underscores instead.

Background Output Options

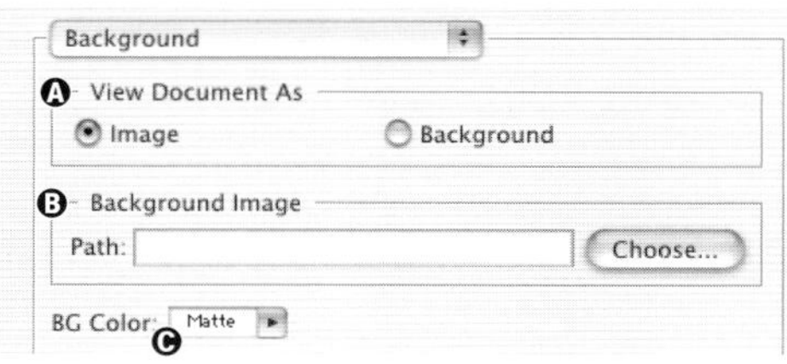

A Choose whether this is a foreground image (Image) or a background image to be tiled in the background of a web page.

B If this is a foreground image, choose a file to use as the background image on the web page. Either enter the path to the file directly, or click Choose to browse to and select the image. This image will not show up in the document but will be used when the image is previewed (see Section 22.5).

C Choose a color from the drop-down to use as the background color on the web page. This will not show up in the document window but will be used when the image is previewed (see Section 22.5).

File Saving Options

Unlike the other output options, which are primarily used to output the HTML code used to create the web pages, the File Saving options allow you to specify how image files are automatically named when output.

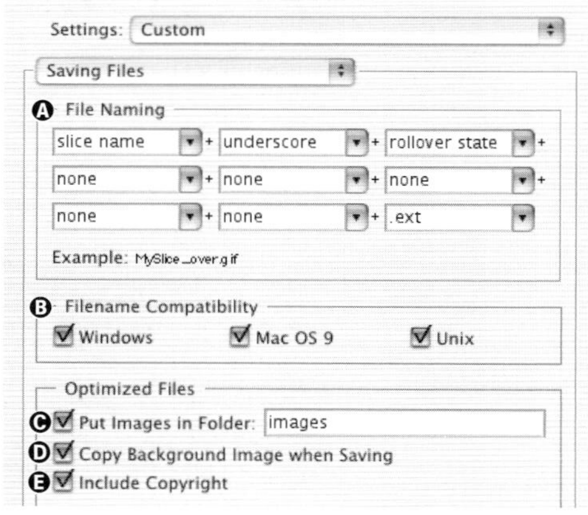

A Choose how slices should be automatically named when added to the document. You can enter text directly in a field or choose a variable from the pull-down menu such as the document name, layer name, slice name/number, trigger name/number, rollover state, and date or a symbol such as a hyphen, an underscore, or a space. Some of these will only be used if the document contains slices or rollovers.

B Check options for which operating systems the filename needs to be compatible. This will limit the length of the filename and prevent certain characters from being used to ensure that the file name will work in the operating system.

C Check to place the images into a specific folder. Enter the name of the folder to the right. If the folder does not exist, Photoshop or ImageReady will create it.

D Check to add a copy of the background image (specified in the Background options panel) to the folder when saving.

E Check if you want copyright information (see Section 6.11) included in the image files.

25.6 Saving Your Website

Regardless of whether you optimized your images using the Optimize palette in ImageReady or chose File > Save For Web in Photoshop, the rest of the process for saving the website graphics is identical in both programs. If you are using the 2-up or 4-up view, choose the version you want to use, and then do one of the following:

- In ImageReady, choose File > Save Optimized As....
- In Photoshop, click the Save button in the Save For Web dialog (File > Save For Web...).

In the Save Optimized As dialog, set your options and then click Save. Outputting the files might take a few seconds.

After you save the file the first time, in ImageReady you can quickly update the code and or images (depending on the settings from the last save) by choosing File > Save Optimized.

(ImageReady) Save Optimized As...
Shift Option ⌘ S
Shift Alt Ctrl S

(ImageReady) Save Optimized
Option ⌘ S
Alt Ctrl S

(Photoshop) Save For Web...
Shift Option ⌘ S
Shift Alt Ctrl S

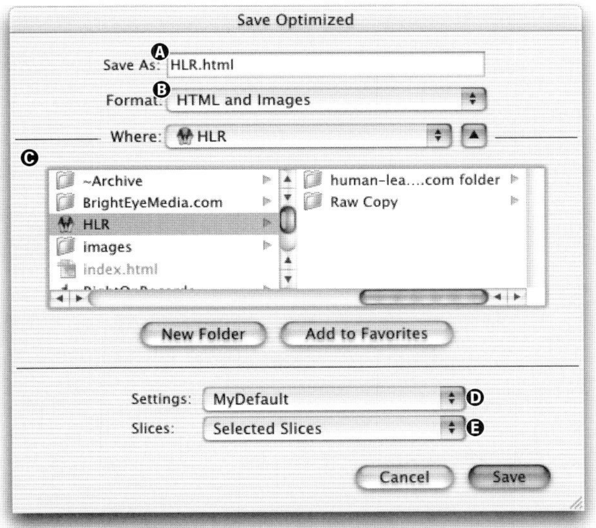

A Enter a filename. If you are saving HTML (see B), this will be used as the name of the HTML file and the `.html` extension should be preserved. If you are saving a single image only (no slices), this name will be used as the filename. If you are saving images only *with* slices, this name is ignored.

B Choose what you are saving: HTML Only generates the HTML file needed to create the web page based on the settings you have made, Images Only saves the artwork needed to create the web page, HTML and Images saves both.

C Browse to the folder in which you want to save the files. Remember, if you checked Put Images In Folder in your output options, a folder will be created with that name (unless it already exists in that location), and all sliced images will be placed there.

D Choose the output settings to use while saving (see Section 25.5). You can choose from the list of pre-saved settings or set the options by choosing Custom....

E Choose whether you want to save all slices in the image, slices selected in the canvas (ImageReady), or Save For Web dialog (Photoshop). In ImageReady, if you saved any slice groups (see Section 25.2), you can choose those to output only the slices in that saved group.

You cannot save output settings that you set while saving the optimized file. You can only save your settings in ImageReady while editing using the Output Settings command.

Often you need to output your web designs to show to clients. ImageReady allows you to quickly save a version of the file in a variety of standard formats using the File > Export Original... command. This works much like saving the file (see Section 6.13), but does not preserve slices or compression settings. It automatically flattens the image, and allows you to choose from only a limited list of file formats.

DIGITAL IMAGING TASKS

CHAPTER **26**

Acquiring Images and Color Correction

REGARDLESS OF WHAT YOU PLAN to do with or to an image, the first step is to get the picture into the computer. Although it would be nice to just stick your favorite photograph into a slot on your computer and have it appear on the computer screen, it isn't that simple. Before you can open a photograph in Photoshop, you must first convert it to a digital file, and not just any digital file. The file must be in a graphic format. Photographs taken using digital cameras are already in a usable format, but those taken with traditional film cameras must be converted to graphic files using a scanner.

Once the image is in Photoshop, you can use a variety of tools to fine-tune both color and tonal qualities. You can also correct problems with the image (such as removing shadows from the subject), enhance the photo, and produce eye-catching effects.

26.1 Scanning Basics

➠ 6.3 Importing Images

➠ 6.6 Setting the Image Size

➠ 7.1 Image Color Basics

The bottom of the scanner glass might fog sometimes; as a rule, this has little or no effect on the scanned image. Do not attempt to remove the glass unless the manufacturer has provided instructions to do so.

If the picture you are scanning will eventually need to be 256 colors for use on the Web, scan it at the highest available level (24-bit color, or RGB) anyway. This ensures the best color; also, many Photoshop filters won't work on an 8-bit image. Only after the image has been edited should you use Photoshop to convert it to 256 colors.

If you need to enlarge a picture, use your scanner rather than the Photoshop Resize command whenever possible.

Through commands in the File menu, you can access any scanner installed on the computer to scan images directly into Photoshop. The information in this section applies to most scanners. Regardless of who manufactures your scanner, the process of scanning is divided into two general stages: preparing for the scan and scanning the image.

Preparation is critical to achieving a quality scan; you can prevent many hours of work in Photoshop with only a few minutes of prep time, which includes the following tasks:

Clean the scanner glass This sounds really simple, but most users don't do it.

Clean the image being scanned Remove all dust and debris from photos using a soft brush.

Align the picture on the scanner glass Even though Photoshop has an excellent Rotate command that you can use to correct misalignment of an image on the scanner, any time a scanned image is rotated it suffers from mild deterioration that reduces the overall sharpness of the image.

Clicking the scan button on a scanner launches the scanner's software, not Photoshop. A better way is to start scanning from within Photoshop by choosing File > Import, which opens a drop-down. The choices of available input devices are determined by the equipment installed on your computer. Selecting the scanner that you want to use to scan the image launches the scanning software that came with your scanner. (Some older Macs use a plug-in to access the scanner.)

26.1 Scanning Basics *(Continued)*

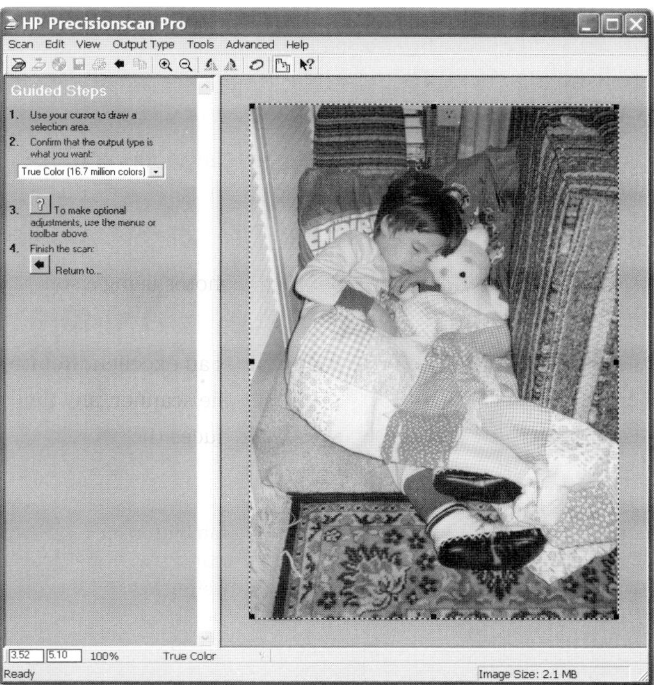

After the scanner interface opens (the HP interface is shown here), preview and define the area to be selected, ensure that the color mode is correct, and then scan.

Most scanning software performs a preview scan at startup. Select the portion of the picture that you want to scan.

You should enlarge an image during scanning for two reasons:

- You want the finished scan larger than the original.
- You plan to restore a photo.

By increasing the size to 200%, it is easier to work with the picture. When you are finished, you can resize the image to its original size. Although the picture will suffer some loss of detail when it is resized, you can more than compensate for the loss by using Unsharp Mask filter which is a sharpening filter that accessed using Filter **>** Sharpen **>** Unsharp Mask.

When you scan a printed image, such as a picture in a magazine article, it usually develops a checkered pattern or something that looks like a plaid, a *moiré pattern*, caused by the patterns of tiny dots that are used to print the picture interfering with the scanner's own patterns. To prevent these patterns, select the Descreen function on your scanner software.

When an image is scanned using Descreen, the result is a softer picture—meaning it loses some of its sharpness. This is a small price to pay for the reduction of those annoying moiré patterns.

Using Windows XP or Me, you can control the scanner using the Windows Imaging Acquisition (WIA) interface. WIA is a generic "no frills" control interface and therefore not as full-featured as the controls in the software that comes with your scanner.

The best color-quality setting that can be displayed on your computer monitor is 24-bit color. This setting goes by many names: RGB, RGB 24-bit, 16.7 Million Colors, Millions Of Colors, and True Color, to name a few.

26.2 Downloading from a Digital Camera

➡ 4.2 File Browser

Hover the cursor over a thumbnail in the File Browser to display information about the picture.

The first time you use the File Browser to view images in a folder, it must create the thumbnail previews, which will take a few moments. The next time you open File Browser, the thumbnails are displayed immediately.

When an image is modified, the thumbnail in the File Browser does not reflect the changes unless you press the F5 (refresh) key.

Use the File Browser to rotate the images to their correct orientation by Control/right-clicking the thumbnail and choosing the correct rotation.

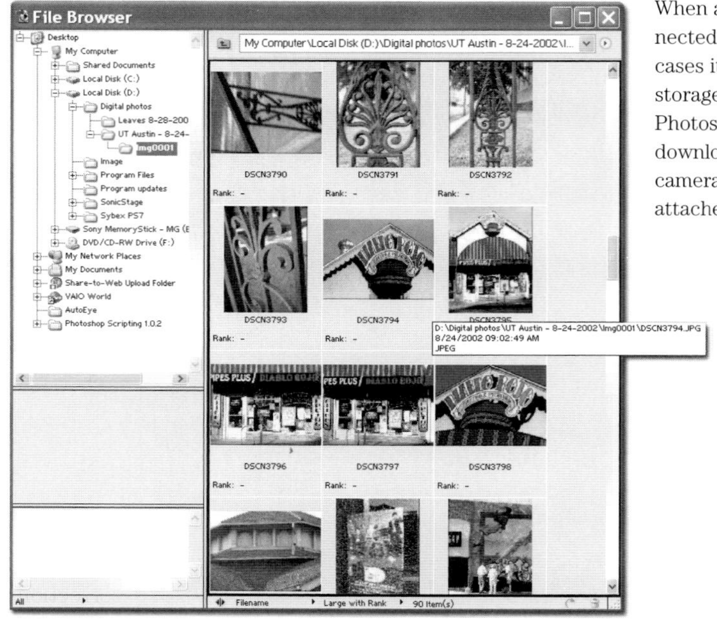

When a digital camera is connected to a computer, in most cases it appears as a mass storage device. You can use Photoshop's File Browser to download pictures from the camera as if it were any other attached hard disk.

To open files from a digital camera into Photoshop, follow these steps:

1. Choose Windows > File Browser to open the File Browser window. The first time you open File Browser, Photoshop generates preview thumbnails on the right side of the window. File Browser saves these in a special file in the same folder in which the images are kept, so that the next time you open it, the thumbnails appear instantly.
2. Select individual pictures by clicking them one at a time; select multiple individual pictures by Command/Ctrl-clicking the thumbnails; or select all the pictures in the folder by pressing Command/Ctrl+A.
3. Once the pictures are selected, you can drag them to another location by clicking one of the selected thumbnails and dragging to one of the folders on the left side of the File Browser window. You can also load the picture into Photoshop by dragging it into the Photoshop image window or by double-clicking the thumbnail.

26.3 Making Tonal Corrections

If an image is underexposed, overexposed, or low-contrast, it requires some degree of tonal correction to fix the problem. Tonal correction of an image involves adjusting the values of the extreme brightest and darkest pixels in the photograph. When pixel values in an image are predominantly at one end of the tonal range, you must redistribute the pixels throughout the image to correct the imbalance. For example, if a majority of the image pixels are in the shadow portion of the image, the image appears too dark. By using either the Levels or the Curves command, it is possible to remap the pixels in the image to make it lighter. The ultimate objective is to produce an image that has a tonal range that produces the sharpest detail possible throughout the image without causing the detail in the lighter regions to go pure white (also called a blowout) or the detail in the shadow region to go solid black. Making these tonal corrections is variously described as:

- Setting the white and black points
- Remapping or redistributing the image
- Setting the highlights and shadows

You can use several tools and methods for tonal correction. The linear tools such as Contrast and Brightness affect all pixels uniformly. For example, a traditional tonal correction adjustment involves Brightness/Contrast controls found by selecting Image > Adjustments > Brightness/Contrast. If a Brightness value of 10 is applied to an image using Brightness/Contrast, the brightness of every pixel in the image—regardless of its current value—is increased by that value. Nonlinear tonal correction tools such as Levels and Curve apply change selectively based on the value of the pixels. For example, if the highlights are remapped, pixels in the midtone and shadow regions of the tonal range are unaffected.

The original photo (left) was washed out by the bright sun. By opening Levels, moving the black point to the right, and moving the midtone (gamma) slider slightly to the left, a much more vivid image was created without loss of image detail or blowouts.

➠ 13.2 Adjusting Tonal Range Using Levels

➠ 13.3 Adjusting Color Levels Using Curves

Levels
⌘ L
Ctrl L

Auto Levels
Shift ⌘ L
Shift Ctrl L

Curves
⌘ M
Ctrl M

Both the Levels and Curves commands remap pixels in an image. The main difference between these tools is in the way that the remapping is displayed and controlled in the dialog box.

Most scanner software offers equivalent adjustment tools that act in much the same manner as the Levels and Curves tools. These can be applied to the image as it is being scanned.

While Auto Levels offers a quick and easy way to apply a level adjustment to an image, many times the values produced by the automatic setting are inadequate to resolve specific tonal correction issues.

Chapter 7 covers tonal corrections applied to the entire image. Many times, it is necessary to apply changes to parts of an image, but not the entire image. You can do so in two ways.

- Create a selection to isolate the part of the image that needs the tonal correction, and apply the desired command.
- Use one of the tonal correction brush tools to selectively apply the correction.

The principal tools for doing this are the Dodge and Burn tools and the Sponge tool, which are all located on the same spot in the Toolbox. The following sections describe these tools.

NAMING IMAGES: A REAL TIMESAVER

All digital cameras automatically assign numbers to photos when the pictures are taken. The result can be many photo files with nondescript and even identical labels such as AGF0001.JPG. To make the files more identifiable, first download the images from the camera. Although you might be able to rename the images directly on the camera, this approach is slower than renaming them on your hard disk. Also, make copies and rename those, not the originals. Then, give your pictures unique names that identify their content.

Let's say you have six pictures of Uncle Bob sitting in front of a fireplace; you can rename them something like `Uncle_Bob_fireplace01`, `Uncle_Bob_fireplace02`, and so on But since it is wise to keep the files associated with the original number assigned by the camera, it's even better to use that original number as the sequence—for example, Uncle Bob's photos would be `Uncle_Bob_fireplace_DCN0001`, `Uncle_Bob_fireplace_DCN0002`, and so on. After you apply all changes, enhancements, and corrections to the named copy of the picture, having the original number as part of the name allows you to locate the original picture file when necessary—and it is often necessary. Without the number, you have to wade through dozens of images trying to see which one is `Uncle_Bob_fireplace01`.

26.4 Dodging and Burning Images

The Dodge tool and Burn tool are called toning tools or exposure tools. You use these tools to either lighten (dodge) or darken (burn) areas of the image. The names of the tools come from a traditional darkroom technique for controlling exposure on selected areas of a photograph. To use the Dodge or Burn tool, follow these steps:

1 In the Toolbox, select either the Dodge tool or the Burn tool.

2 The tool options bar has, beyond the normal brush tool options, includes two tool-specific options that require adjustment:

   - Choose the range that the tool will affect. Selecting Shadows limits the tool action to the darker pixels in the image. Midtones affect only the middle range of grays, and choosing Highlights changes the pixels in the upper end of the tonal range.
   - Set the exposure for the tool. Typically, you set the exposure to a low value.

3 Drag the brush over part of the image you want to adjust.

When a photograph is taken with varying degrees of light falling on it (left), some areas end up in shadow, and other parts are washed out as shown. Using the Dodge tool, you can lighten the darker areas (middle). Next, you can darken the washed out areas slightly to finish the job (right).

The effects of the Dodge and Burn tools are subtle and additive. Apply the tool several times at low values (less than 10%) rather than once at a large setting.

IMPORTING FROM OLDER DIGITAL CAMERAS

Some earlier models of digital cameras did not provide USB support but instead only a serial port to connect to the computer. Using a serial connection to download images from the camera has traditionally been both slow and problematic to configure. The best solution for these older cameras is to obtain a card reader that plugs directly into the computer so that the film medium appears as a folder in a hard drive. These devices have become inexpensive in the past few years, and you can easily justify the small cost when you consider the hours necessary to download into Photoshop using a serial connection.

➠ 3.16 Exposure Tools

➠ 15.1 Brush Basics

➠ 15.2 Selecting and Adjusting Brushes

➠ 15.3 Creating Brushes

Exposure tool O

Cycle exposure tools
Shift O

When working on shadows and highlights, remember that the purpose is not to remove them but to recover detail in them. A photo with no shadows or highlights lacks detail and is uninteresting.

When applying either of the tools, select a brush large enough to cover the entire area you are working on rather than apply multiple brushstrokes with a smaller brush size, which tends to give it an uneven appearance.

The Dodge and Burn tools can only recover detail in an image; they cannot create it. If applying the Burn tool (set to Highlight) to a bright white area of an image doesn't produce any details, it is a blowout, and the Burn tool will only shade the white portions into gray. Likewise, if the detail isn't in the shadows, you can't recover it using the Dodge tool.

26.5 Using the Sponge Tool

➡ 3.16 Exposure Tools

Exposure tool O

Cycle exposure tools Shift O

When using the Sponge tool in Saturate mode, use small values such as 10% to 20% to make colors more vivid. This is especially true if you are working on an image that will be printed. Oversaturated areas tend to lose detail because all the color saturation values become too high.

An effective way to focus the viewer's attention on a particular subject in a color photograph is to partially to totally desaturate everything but the subject. This technique is quite popular with advertisers. For example, a model holds the product (in full color) while everything else in the photo is in grayscale.

The Sponge tool changes the color saturation of the pixels over which it is dragged. On color images, when it is set to Saturate mode, the saturation of the color is increased, and the colors appear more vivid. When applied to the same image in Desaturate mode, the colors appear faded. If the Sponge tool is used at 100% with Desaturate, all the color is removed, and the affected areas appear to be grayscale. If applied to a grayscale image, the Sponge tool increases or decreases contrast. To use the Sponge tool, follow these steps:

1. In the Toolbox, select the Sponge tool.
2. In the tool options bar, aside from the typical brush options such as size, choose the Mode (Saturate and Desaturate) and the Flow setting. The Flow setting of the smudge, blur, sharpen, and sponge tools control the rate the tool's effect is applied to image pixels when the tool is passed over them. At 100% the pixels are affected at the maximum rate. When set to 50% you must hold the tool over the area twice as long to achieve the same effect. Called Pressure in previous versions of Photoshop, it has a range from 1% to 100%. For weak effects use a low percentage value; for strong effects, enter a higher value.
3. Drag over the part of the image you want to modify.

SCANNING AND COPYRIGHTS

A word to the wise: just because you can scan it, doesn't mean you should. Nearly everything that is in print is copyrighted in one form or another. Most of these are obvious. For example, you wouldn't think of scanning a photograph from an issue of *National Geographic* and selling it as wallpaper for your desktop, since that would be an obvious copyright infringement; but other copyright violations are more subtle and might surprise you.

As strange as it sounds, it is not legal to make copies of any photograph that was made by a professional photographer or studio. Examples of this are school photos or wedding pictures taken by a pro. It is a fact of law that even though you may have paid this person or organization to take the picture of you or your loved ones and paid for the materials, the image still belongs to them, and it is a violation of U.S. copyright law to duplicate these pictures.

CHAPTER 27

Cleaning, Repairing, and Distorting Images

THE EFFECTS OF TIME and improper storage cause all forms of images to suffer damage in one way or another. Some photos developed creases or tears, while others fall victim to felt markers in the hands of budding young artists. There are several major tools in Photoshop that are the traditional choice for cleaning up and repairing images. While the Clone Stamp tool has been around and used for some time to replace one part of an image with another, the Healing Brush and the Patch tool are new features in Photoshop 7. In addition to correcting damage with these tools, there are other more sophisticated ways to improve the appearance of an image using the History Brush as well as the classic Blur, Sharpen, and Smudge tools. While often looked upon as a tool to distort faces, the Liquify command is a powerful tool to alter the physical appearance of a subject.

This chapter shows you how to do the following:

- 27.1 **Touch up with the Clone Stamp tool**
- 27.2 **Touch up with the Healing Brush**
- 27.3 **Patching images**
- 27.4 **Touch up with the History Brush**
- 27.5 **Blurring and sharpening with tools**
- 27.6 **Smudging and liquifying images**

27.1 Touch Up with the Clone Stamp Tool

➠ 3.11 Stamp Tools

➠ 15.2 Selecting and Adjusting Brushes

Stamp tool S

Cycle stamp tools Shift S

To use the Clone tool between two images, both must be in the same color mode.

When replacing missing areas of an image with the Clone tool, first make a rough selection around the area to prevent applying cloned pixels outside the desired area.

The Clone Stamp tool, or simply the Clone tool, is the traditional tool of choice used to remove dust and other debris from an original photograph when it was scanned, although, for cleaning up images, the Healing Brush and Patch tools are now the preferred tools. Damage to the original film negative can also be a source of photographic debris. These defects, which appear as bright specks on the photograph, become greatly enhanced and stick out when you apply any form of sharpening. You can use the Clone tool to remove tears, scratches, and stains, as well as noise on digital photographs taken under low-light conditions.

The Clone tool is a powerful tool; having all the attributes of a brush tool, it clones (copies) neighboring pixels from one area of an image and paints them to another. This can effectively remove objects from, or insert them in, your images.

The source of the pixels (sampling point) used by the Clone tool can be the same image, a different layer on the same image, or even another image. When you are retouching an image, the most common source is usually a part of the image that is similar to the part being retouched. To use the Clone tool, follow these steps:

1 Set the tool's options; the Clone tool has all the standard brush settings, plus a unique setting: the Aligned check box.

- When you select Aligned, the relationship between the sampling point and the point where the cloning begins remains fixed. For example, if the sampling point is set up being one inch above and to the left of the Clone tool brush it will always retain that positional relationship with the brush until it is reset. Regardless of where you position the Clone tool, the sampling point is one inch above and to the left of the tool. If you clear the Aligned check box, the sampled pixels are applied from the initial sampling point, and each time you release the mouse button, the sampling point snaps back to its initial starting point.
- If the source image has layers, checking Use All Layers in the tool options bar copies pixels from all visible layers in that image. When the Use All Layers check box is cleared, the Clone tool samples only from the active layer.

27.1 Touch Up with the Clone Stamp Tool *(Continued)*

2 Set the sampling point by positioning the cursor on the part of the image to be copied and hold down the Alt/Option key while clicking the point.

3 Position the cursor at the point where the copied pixels are to be painted, and click and drag the mouse.

You can restore small areas that are missing or stained in photographs restored using the Clone tool. You can also remove unwanted items using the Clone tool. To apply the Clone tool to a photo, follow these steps:

1 Select the Clone Stamp tool from the Toolbox. Place the cursor on the area of the photo that contains pixels which match the area of the photo to be replaced.

2 Choose a soft brush to prevent hard edges that make the cloned areas stick out. In the example here, the cursor was placed a short distance to the left of the sunflower stem in the middle of the photo.

3 Alt/Option-click the mouse to set the sampling point. (The cursor briefly becomes a target when the sampling point is being selected.) For the image shown, using the Aligned feature serves best as repeating patterns are not as apparent in a mixed natural background.

4 Click and apply the Clone tool. When removing an object such as the sunflower, it is tempting to click and drag the clone brush to remove the object in a single stroke. Unfortunately, this method creates a repeating pattern that is visually apparent to the viewer. The best way to apply the Clone tool is to use short strokes from several source points.. The result is that the sunflower disappears.

One of these sunflowers is facing the wrong direction, requiring the Clone Stamp tool to remove it. Eliminate the stem of the sunflower by cloning the wheat over it.

When using the Clone tool to retouch a photograph, use a lower opacity setting to blend the cloned pixels more uniformly.

When using the Clone tool to remove a defect or an object in a photograph, don't sample too close to the defect or object. If you work too close, part of the defect or object might actually find its way into the cloned pixels.

Don't use the Clone tool to clone a specific object or a person into an image. For best results, select the content and make it into a separate layer (see Chapter 28 for how to do this).

27.1 Touch Up with the Clone Stamp Tool *(Continued)*

Generally, clear the Aligned check box and apply short strokes of the Clone tool. This approach has the following advantages:

- When the area being used for source pixels is small, this method keeps the sampling point inside the area of source pixels because each time the mouse button is released, the source point snaps back to its starting point.
- When cloning large areas of natural material (clouds, trees, rocks, and so on), it prevents the appearance of visual patterns when cloning from one part of an image to another. Avoid the temptation to create a single long brush stroke, which creates a long duplicate of another part of the image.
- The human eye can quickly detect a repeating pattern; applying shorter strokes and overlapping them breaks up potential patterns.

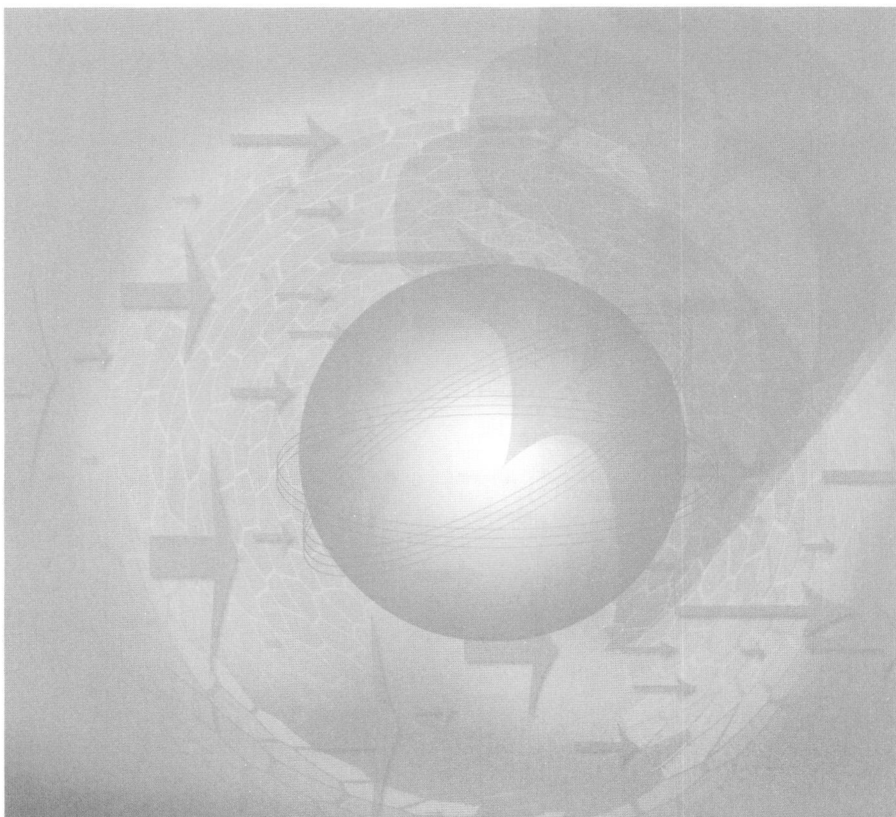

27.2 Touch Up with the Healing Brush

Introduced with Photoshop 7, the Healing Brush tool works much like the Clone tool to repair imperfections in photographs using sampled pixels from another part of an image. However, the Healing Brush tool differs in that it also matches the texture, lighting, and shading of the sampled pixels to the source pixels. As a result, the pixels painted by the Healing Brush blend much better with the surrounding image.

When the Healing Brush samples the pixels, it analyzes the texture, color, and luminosity of the source pixels. When you then paint, the Healing Brush merges the texture from the sample area into the color and luminosity of the destination area. The Healing Brush reads an area around the brush that is between 10 and 12 pixels, which is why you'll obtain the best results using a hard-edged brush

One of the most obvious differences between the Healing Brush tool and the Clone tool is the brief delay that occurs each time you apply the Healing Brush. This is because Photoshop is doing a lot of image processing to make the cloned pixels blend with their new surroundings. Because the Healing Brush must process both source and target pixels, you cannot apply it to a transparent layer.

To use the Healing Brush, follow these steps:

1 Select the Healing Brush from the Toolbox and set the options in the tool options bar:

  - Choose a source from the Toolbox options bar: Sampled to use pixels from the current image, or Pattern to use pixels from a pattern. For cleaning or repairing photographs, always select Sampled.
  - Choose brush settings. The dialog for brush types does not include preset choices. You must establish the settings for the brush (Diameter, Hardness, Spacing, Angle, and Roundness) from within the dialog. Hard brushes provide the best processing of the sample pixels.
  - If you are using a pressure-sensitive tablet, you can use the Pen Pressure option in the bottom of the Brush Settings dialog to vary the size of the healing brush by the amount of pressure applied during a pen stroke. The Stylus Wheel option varies the brush size based on the position of the pen thumbwheel (not a mouse thumbwheel).

2 To set the sampling point, Option/Alt-click the area of the photo that contains pixels that match the area of the photo to be replaced. (The cursor briefly becomes a target when you select the sampling point.)

3 Click and apply the Healing Brush tool to the area to be retouched. With the Clone Tool brush, long brushstrokes are recommended to prevent the development of telltale patterns. Because of the processing that occurs with the Healing brush, longer strokes are recommended so that the processing is accomplished in fewer strokes.

➠ 3.9 Restoration Tools

➠ 15.2 Selecting and Adjusting Brushes

Healing Brush tool [J]

Set source point
[Option] *click*
[Alt] *click*

Cycle restoration tools
[Shift] [J]

When repairing with pixels from the image, select a small area to produce the best result.

You cannot apply the Healing Brush between layers.

Avoid applying the Healing Brush tightly up against strong contrasting edges in an image. When Photoshop applies the blending algorithms, the darker pixels blur, creating a smudged appearance.

Getting the best results using the Healing Brush involves a few workarounds. When you use the Healing Brush tool to remove wrinkles on a face, at times the effect of the brush creates an unnatural appearance. Unlike the Clone tool, the Healing Brush does not have an option to control opacity because of the processing that the Healing Brush performs. One way to get the effect of opacity control is to apply the Fade command after using the Healing Brush. A second way to achieve a variable control over the Healing Brush is to duplicate the image as a layer and apply the Healing Brush to the copy. After applying the Healing Brush, adjust the opacity of the layer. With both these techniques, you can experiment with different blending modes.

USING THE BLUR TOOL WHEN CREATING COMPOSITE IMAGES

The Blur tool is a subtle tool that is often ignored by Photoshop users because the effects are not of the scale or magnitude of filters like Liquify; yet, this tool is one of the most important for creating composite images. When adding new elements to images as Layers, there are times when the edges of these layers are hard and give the appearance that they are pasted in and not part of the original image. Applying the Blur tool to the edges of these layers or even to objects that have already been flattened helps them blend into the images in a more seamless fashion.

To produce a slight blurring on the edges of new elements, it is important to use the least possible setting that will produce a visible result when applied. The larger the image, the greater the amount of the blur setting is necessary. Another consideration when using the Blur tool on large images is that large brush sizes take a lot of processor power to apply; therefore, you should be patient and apply the blurring to edges using a small brush. Applying a blur to the edge and then applying a second application with a slightly larger brush size to the same area achieves some of the best effects. As the Blur tool is applied the second time, the area nearest the edge receives additional blurring which achieves a graduated blurring toward the edge of the new object.

27.3 Patching Images

The Healing Brush and the Patch tool both repair an image by matching the lighting and shading of the sampled pixels to the source pixels. Unlike the Healing Brush, which applies sampled pixels using a brush tool, the Patch tool applies the same process to a selection. You can also use the Patch tool to clone isolated areas of an image.

Even though the Patch tool is an excellent tool for removing wrinkles and other facial imperfections, it also is the tool of choice when you need to easily and quickly remove objects such as power lines, flying birds, and other unwanted items from skies. Although you can achieve the same effect using the Clone tool, using the Patch tool is much faster. To use the Patch tool, follow these steps:

1 (Optional) Make a selection in the canvas (see Chapter 8) of the area you want to use as your source or destination patch.

2 Select the Patch tool in the Toolbox.

3 In the tool options bar, select the patching mode and choose whether to use a pattern:

Source mode The selected area will be repaired. This is the mode of choice when the selected area contains mottled but similar toned areas.

Destination mode The selected area of the image is used to repair other areas of the image. When the area being repaired needs to match a pattern or lines in the image, use this mode.

Pattern Rarely if ever used for photo retouching. Instead of bringing pixels in from part of the existing image, the source pixels are a pattern that is selected or created. You can use the Pattern feature to replace large areas with a fixed pattern.

4 If there is not an existing selection in the canvas, use the Patch tool to select the part of the image you will be using.

- If you selected Source, select the area of the image you want to repair.
- If you selected Destination, choose an image area that has the texture that you want to use to repair the damaged image area.

5 Position the pointer inside the selection and after the pointer changes shape, do one of the following:

- If you selected Source, drag the selection marquee to the area from which you want to sample to repair the area.
- If you selected Destination, drag the selection to the area you want to patch.
- Whether you picked Source or Destination, once the selection has been moved, Photoshop evaluates the lightness, hue, and saturation of the pixels in both the selection and the destination, and processes the pixels so that the pixels match and the area being replaced is almost seamless.

➡ 3.9 Restoration Tools

Healing Brush tool J

Cycle restoration tools Shift J

When using either the Healing Brush or the Patch tool, be careful not to place new source pixels too close to areas with dark or defined edges. Photoshop will include these darker pixels in the blending calculations and they will appear as a darker blur.

Here is an example of a photo cleanup using the Clone and Healing Brush as well as the Patch tool. The original image is on the left, and the cleaned-up version is on the right. The Patch tool was used to remove wrinkles, the Healing Brush was used to delete blemishes, and the Clone Stamp tool was used to remove some stray eyebrow hairs. If the Healing Brush had been used on the eyebrows, the dark hairs would blend in, making the area darker.

REAL WORLD: TEODORU BADIU

Despite their visual complexity and often intense Surrealism, Teodoru Badiu's work always starts with a simple idea. "The trigger of the idea could be religion, mythology, a quote, a book I read, or a photo I shoot."

Some of the elements in his images begin life as physical objects that he builds and photographs with a digital camera, but other times he creates 3D elements with Maya, Bryce, Poser, and Swift3D. He then imports the various elements into Photoshop to assemble the composition. "I import all the pictures and the textures and start to knock out the parts I need for my composition. For that I use different tools such as the Pen tool, alpha channels, color range, or Magnetic Lasso, depending on how the part I need to knock out looks and how complicated it is."

Despite the deep and shadowed appearance of Teo's work, he does not rely on Photoshop's built-in effects. "What I try to avoid in my work are layer effects such as drop shadows, bevels, or glows. Instead, I work with alpha channels and with blur and render filters, and, for shadows, I just use layers and selections together with blending modes and transform tools to create the shadows I desire."

You can find more of Teo's work at `www.apocryph.net/`.

27.4 Touch Up with the History Brush

The History Brush is basically a Clone tool that you can use to select previous stages of an image as the sampling point. When used for photo retouching, the History Brush allows the selective removal of effects that were applied to an image. Using the History Brush in this way provides a method for applying a filter to a portion of the image without the need to create a complex selection.

➠ 3.12 History Brushes

➠ 4.8 History Palette

➠ 15.2 Selecting and Adjusting Brushes

History Brush tool [Y]

Cycle history brushes [Shift] [Y]

Here, the original photograph (left) had a Gaussian Blur applied to the entire image (center). Then, the History Brush was used to restore the portion of the image to its state before the blur filter was applied (right), creating the effect of depth-of-field to enhance the subject.

To use the History Brush, follow these steps:

1 Select the History Brush in the Toolbox.

2 In the History palette, click the left column of the state or snapshot to use as the source for the History Brush tool. In most cases, this is the last state before the effect or tonal correction was applied.

3 Set the tool's options. Since the History Brush is a brush tool, it has all the parameters associated with brushes. Of importance when using the History Brush to restore a portion of an image is the Opacity setting. When set at less than 100%, the amount of the previous state that is restored is proportional to the Opacity setting.

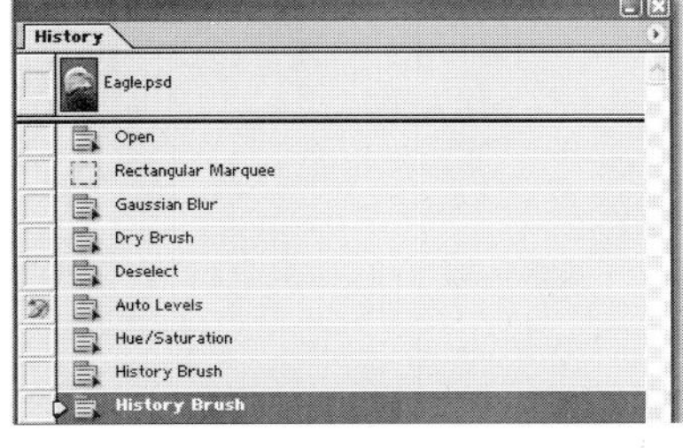

The condition of the image at the point that Auto Levels was applied will be used as the source for the History Brush.

4 Paint the areas that need to have effects removed with the History Brush tool. Like the Clone tool, the History Brush has a variable opacity, which allows the partial removal of effects or tonal corrections.

If you change either the image dimensions or the image color mode, you won't be able to use the History Brush.

Applying the History Brush with reduced opacity is a good way to partially and selectively reduce a filter effect such as sharpening.

The History palette uses a lot of memory. If your system resources are becoming low, you can clear the History states either by selecting Clear History from the History palette menu or by choosing Edit > Purge > History.

For critical work you can use a selection to restrict the application of the History brush to a specific area and prevent it from being applied to other areas.

27.5 Blurring and Sharpening with Tools

➠ 3.15 Distortion Tools

➠ 15.2 Selecting and Adjusting Brushes

➠ 16.3 Sharpening and Blurring with Filters

Distortion tool R

Cycle distortion tools Shift R

The Blur tool can make part of an image that is in focus into one that is out of focus. The Sharpen tool cannot make an out-of-focus photograph into one that is in focus.

Avoid using large brush sizes combined with long brush strokes when using the Blur tool. Because the blur action is processor intensive, the effect will lag behind the brush stroke.

It is difficult to get uniform blurring over a large area with the Blur tool. If you need to apply blurring to a large area, don't use the Blur tool. Instead, make a loose selection of the area, feather the selection, and apply the Gaussian Blur filter.

Avoid "scrubbing" a portion of an area with the Sharpen tool, because this causes repetitive applications of sharpening to be applied to the area and results in some pixels becoming white (also called blowouts).

Photoshop provides tools and filters to blur and sharpen images. You use the filters to apply the effect to the entire image; you use the Blur and Sharpen tools to apply the effect selectively without the need to create complex selections.

The operation and control of the blur filters are covered in detail in Section 16.3. The Smudge tool is covered in Section 27.6.

The Blur tool softens the apparent focus of the part of the image on which it is painted. This localized softening effect helps to de-emphasize defects or debris in a photo. You can also use the Blur tool to emphasize part of an image by making the rest of the image appear to be slightly out of focus (as shown in Section 27.4). The selective blurring of parts of an image can also produce a false depth-of-field, making some objects appear closer or farther away than they really are.

The Sharpen tool increases the contrast between adjacent pixels, making the edges in a image appear sharper and more defined. Thus, the Sharpen tool does the opposite of the Blur tool, which makes pixels in parts of an image less defined and with lower contrast, making them appear out of focus. The following procedure describes how to effectively apply either the Blur or the Sharpen tool to an image:

1 In the Toolbox, select the Blur tool or the Sharpen tool.

2 Set the options for the tool in the tool options bar. Choose a brush size and Mode, and then choose whether to blur or sharpen only the active layer or all visible layers. (With Use All Layers checked, the tool affects the pixels on all visible layers.)

3 Paint the areas that need to be blurred or sharpened. You can increase the apparent effect of blurring or sharpening by repeatedly applying.

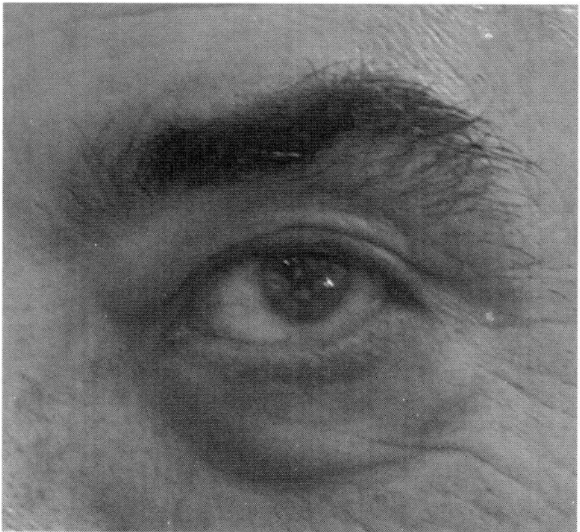

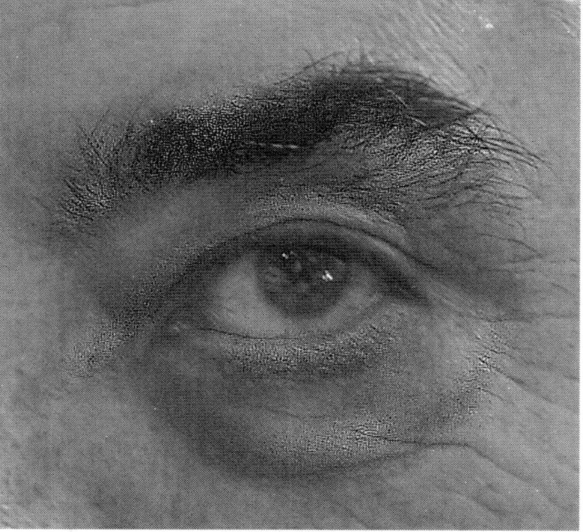

If you repeatedly apply sharpening to an area, the white pixels will lose their detail and blowout as shown on the right.

27.6 Smudging and Liquifying Images

To distort an image, you can use both the Smudge tool and the Liquify dialog . The Smudge tool smears pixels, giving the appearance of dragging a finger through wet paint. The tool picks up the color of the pixels where the brushstroke starts and pushes the pixels in the direction of the stroke. Before the Liquify command was introduced in Photoshop 6, the Smudge tool was used to perform minor distortions of images to change the shape of features and objects. Now the use of the Smudge tool is pretty much limited to creating special effects in images.

When the Liquify filter first appeared, some considered it a tool capable of creating weird distortions of images but of little other use. It has proven to be a powerful tool for retouching photographs. The Liquify filter applies one of many distortions "on the fly" as the tool is dragged across the preview of the selected image inside the dialog.

➠ 3.15 Distortion Tools

Warp Tool (in Liquify dialog) W

Turbulence Tool (in Liquify dialog) A

Twirl Clockwise Tool (in Liquify dialog) R

Twirl Counter Clockwise Tool (in Liquify dialog) L

Pucker Tool (in Liquify dialog) P

Bloat Tool (in Liquify dialog) B

Shift Pixels Tool (in Liquify dialog) S

Reflection Tool (in Liquify dialog) M

Reconstruct Tool (in Liquify dialog) E

Freeze Tool (in Liquify dialog) F

Thaw Tool (in Liquify dialog) T

Zoom Tool (in Liquify dialog) Z

Hand Tool (in Liquify dialog) H

Smudging the Image

You use the Smudge tool is used to distort the pixels over which its cursor is painted by changing their color and moving their position on the image. To use the Smudge tool, follow these steps:

1 In the Toolbox, select the Smudge tool.

2 Beyond the standard brush options, there are two further Smudge tool options: Use All Layers and Finger Painting.

- Use All Layers smears the pixels on all visible layers. If it is not selected, the Smudge tool smears only the active layer.
- Finger Painting forces the tool to use the foreground color to create each brush stroke. If this check box is cleared, the Smudge tool uses the color information under the brush pointer at the beginning of each stroke.

3 Drag the Smudge tool across the pixels to smear the color of the pixels.

Applying the Smudge tool across text makes it appear that a finger was dragged through wet ink.

Liquifying the Image

You can apply distortion effects with the Liquify filter in two ways. First, you can select one of the many tools in the Liquify dialog and apply a brush stroke across the image in the Preview window to produce the distortion selected in real time. Second, you can click the desired part of the image to produce the effect. This is especially useful with the Pucker and Bloat tools.

Distortion tool [R]

Cycle distortion tools [Shift] [R]

Liquify filter [Shift][⌘] [X] [Shift][Ctrl] [X]

You can select Finger Painting at any time by holding down the Alt/Option key as you drag the Smudge tool.

To apply the Smudge tool in a straight line, click at the starting point, and then while holding down the Shift key, click at the end point. Photoshop applies the Smudge tool in a straight line between the two points.

Ⓐ **Warp tool** Pushes the pixels along as you drag the brush across the image.

Ⓑ **Turbulence tool** Similar to Warp except that if you hold down the mouse button over a part of the image, the pixels begin to distort in all directions within the limits of the brush boundaries.

Ⓒ **Twirl tools** Placing one of these tools over part of the image and holding down the mouse button causes the area inside the brush tool boundaries to rotate either clockwise or counterclockwise.

Ⓓ **Pucker and Bloat tools** These tools can either pinch the pixels together, making them smaller, or pull them out, making the area appear bigger.

Ⓔ **Shift Pixels tool** Moves pixels at a 90-degree angle to the direction of the mouse movement. Results are similar to the results of the Warp tool.

Ⓕ **Reflect tool** Clones pixels from the area directly under the cursor and applies them to the area on the opposite end of the brushstroke. This tool is useful if you want large amounts of distortion that produce weird and unique effects but little else.

Ⓖ **Reconstruct tool** Provides the ability to selectively undo changes to portions of the image created while in Liquify without resetting or canceling the entire effect.

Ⓗ **Freeze and Thaw tools** Used to either protect (freeze) or unprotect (thaw) portions of the image from change produced by the other tools. The red overlay that appears defines the part of the images this is "frozen."

Ⓘ **Zoom and Hand tools** Zoom controls the zoom ratio of the image being viewed, and the Hand tool provides rapid movement of the image when it is zoomed in larger than the Preview window can display.

Ⓙ **Preview window** Displays the effects of the Liquify actions in real time.

Ⓚ **Tool options** Control the size and the flow (pressure) of the tools.

Ⓛ **Reconstruction options** Controls to fully or partially reverse the changes applied to an image before the OK button is clicked. The Rigid, Stiff, Smooth, and Loose options are used to extend distortions into areas of the image that are frozen or even used to repeat distortions.

Ⓜ **Freeze area options** Controls to invert the Freeze area or remove any frozen areas in the image.

Ⓝ **View options** Controls that affect the visual appearance of the freeze and mesh displays and also to turn the display on or off.

27.6 Smudging and Liquifying Images *(Continued)*

All the effects of the Liquify command are applied within its large dialog box. The operation of the filter is as follows:

1. Launch the Liquify filter by choosing Filter > Liquify....
2. Select a tool from the left side of the dialog, and apply the distortion in real time by dragging across the area that is to be modified, or click the image and hold down the mouse button until the desired effect is achieved. The brush size of the tools determines how much of the image is affected. Here are details on some of the available tools:

   Warp The brush size determines the number of pixels that actually move. If you use a large brush size (in relation to the image size), most of the image shifts in the direction of the brushstroke. If you use a smaller brush size, only a small area of the photo is displaced. This is the tool of choice for reshaping photos of people and animals.

   Turbulence The speed and amount of distortion is controlled by the settings of the Turbulence Jitter values in the Tool Options panel.

   Twirl Clockwise / Counterclockwise Because the pixels near the edge of the brush move at a faster rate than the pixels near the center of the brush, the effect is that of the pixels inside the brush boundaries being cut out and rotated as a single unit.

   Pucker and Bloat This is the best tool to change the size of parts of the human anatomy that are either naturally large or small or appear that way because of the angle from which the photographer originally took the picture.

3. Freeze and Thaw are functionally selection tools. Painting an area in the Preview window with the Freeze tool protects that area from any distortion by the other tools. The selection is not a marquee of marching ants but an overlay tint, much like that seen in the Quick Mask mode. To remove the protection from any part that was frozen, apply the Thaw tool to the area. This provides a quick and easy way to either protect existing distortions from further distortions or preserve the original image from distortions altogether.
4. View your changes in the Preview window. You can use the options in the Freeze section to control areas that are frozen, and you can use the options in the View section to control the appearance and display of indicators. The Reconstruction section provides controls that you can use in many ways to undo changes. When you're satisfied with your edits, click OK.

When working on an image, use the Zoom tool to ensure that the area being worked on fills the preview box.

You can use the Reflection tool in the Liquify filter to create a water reflection effect by applying overlapping strokes to the image.

After distorting the preview image in the Liquify dialog, you can use the Reconstruct tool or other controls to fully or partially reverse the changes or to change the image in new ways.

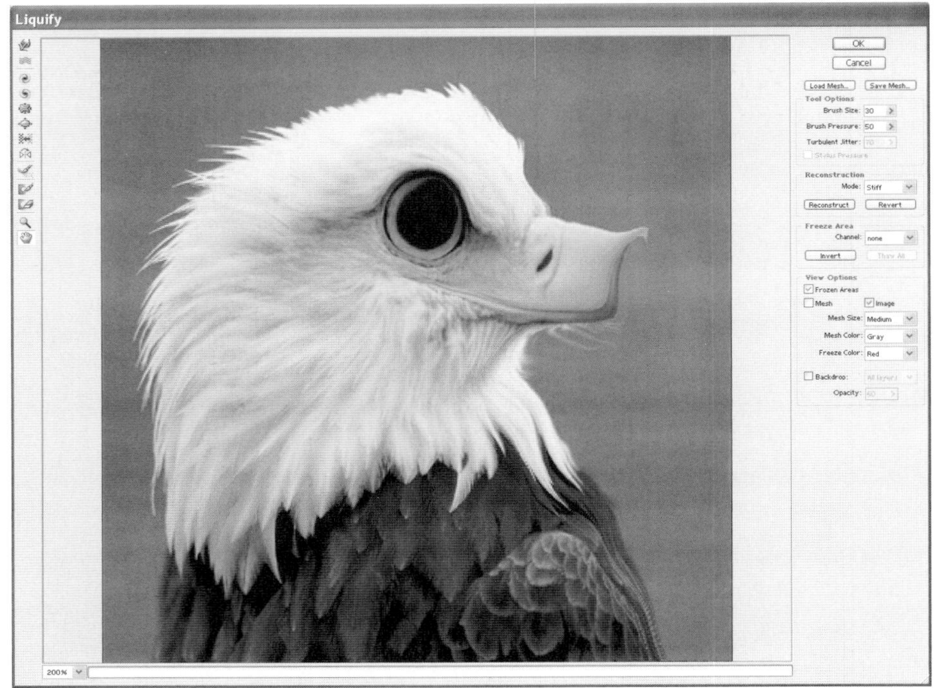

You can use the options in the Liquify dialog to alter an image in extreme ways.

CHAPTER 28

Advanced Compositing Methods

UNLESS YOU ARE SIMPLY RETOUCHING photos, you will most likely want to combine photos using Photoshop to create a collage of images. Composition is the process by which images from different sources are combined and interact with one another. The most obvious way to combine images is through copying and pasting (see Section 8.10), setting blending modes and opacity for layers (see Section 9.12), and applying effects (see Section 10.2). However, Photoshop offers several more advanced methods for compositing images. In this chapter, you will learn about:

28.1 Creating Knockouts

- ➠ 8.2 Selecting a Layer or Its Contents
- ➠ 9.6 Creating Layer Sets
- ➠ 9.12 Blending Modes and Opacity
- ➠ 9.13 Clipping Groups
- ➠ 10.2 Applying Effects and Styles
- ➠ 10.6 Applying Advanced Blending Options
- ➠ Color Section: Blending Modes

Knockouts allow you to use the content of a layer as a mask to "punch through" to the layers directly beneath the set (shallow) or to the Background or Transparency layer (deep). This works much like using layers as part of a clipping group but gives you much greater flexibility.

To use a layer's content as a knockout, follow these steps:

1. Select the layer to be used as the Knockout layer. Follow these guidelines when deciding which layer to select:
   - To use a layer to punch through all other layers beneath it to the Background or Transparency layer, you can select any layer as the Knockout layer.
   - To punch through one or more layers to another layer or layers in the image, create a layer set with the layer being used as the knockout at the top of the set and the layers to be knocked through beneath it in the same set. Make sure this layer set's blending option is set to Pass Through in the Layers palette (see Section 9.12). Place the layer or layers you want knocked through directly underneath the set.
2. Open the Blending Options panel in the Layer Style dialog (choose Layer **>** Layer Style **>** Blending Options…).
3. Set a blending mode or lower the fill opacity for the layer. This allows you to control the strength of the knockout.
4. Choose an option from the Knockout drop-down: None, Shallow, or Deep.
5. You can preview the effect of the knockout and try different blending modes and opacities before clicking OK to commit the changes.

Knockouts can also be applied to the layers of a clipping group within a layer set (see Section 9.13) with slightly different consequences. Shallow punches through to the bottommost layer in the clipping group, and Deep punches through to the layer immediately below the selected layer's layer set.

If the Knockout layer is not part of a layer set or a clipping group, both Shallow and Deep punch through to the Background layer or transparency.

None No knockout used. In this example, the Text layer and the Starburst layer are in a common set, with the photograph below the set.

Shallow Punches through all layers in the layer set to layers directly beneath the layer set. Here, the Text layer uses a shallow knockout to punch through the Starburst layer so the photograph shows through. Notice that the drop-shadow effect is still apparent.

Deep Punches through all layers directly beneath the Knockout layer to reveal the Background layer (if being used) or transparency. In this example, the Text layer uses a deep knockout to show through to the black Background layer.

28.2 Conditional Blending

You use the blending mode to specify how the pixels in one layer interact with the layers beneath it. However, this setting is applied indiscriminately over the entire layer. You can also blend pixels over certain color value ranges in the different color channels using the Blend If options in the Advanced Blending options in the Blending Options panel. These controls allow you to set the color values at which pixels are blended together or to set a smoother partially blend between layers.

To conditionally blend pixels over a particular layer, follow these steps:

1 Select the layer to which you want to apply selective blending (see Section 8.2).

2 Open the Blending Options panel in the Layer Style dialog (choose Layer > Layer Style > Blending Options...).

3 Set the Blend If options by choosing a color channel (or choose gray to affect all channels), and then use the sliders to change the black and white blending values for the channel in the selected layer (This Layer) or layers below the selected layer (Underlying Layers).

- 8.2 Selecting a Layer or Its Contents
- 9.12 Blending Modes and Opacity
- 10.2 Applying Effects and Styles
- 10.6 Applying Advanced Blending Options
- Color Section: Blending Modes

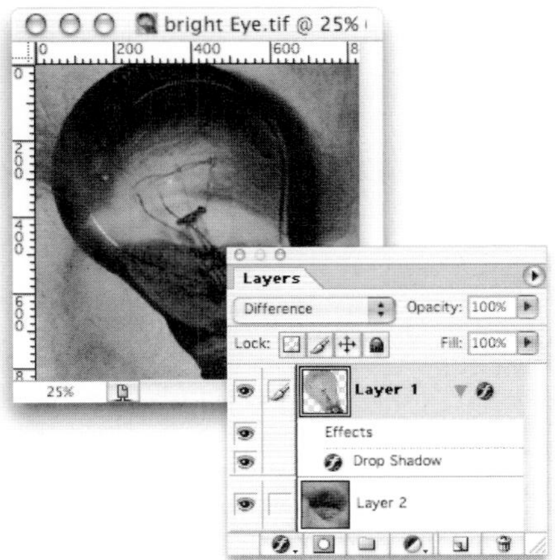

The original image with the image of a light bulb using the Difference blending mode.

This Layer (The selected layer) Pixels within the range will be blended with pixels in layers underneath. Fill pixels with values outside this range in the selected layer will be made 100% transparent. However, pixels that are created as a part of an effect (such as a drop shadow) will be unaffected by this change. Here, the blending range in the gray channel has been narrowed in the Light Bulb layer, causing pixels out of the range to be turned 100% transparent. The drop-shadow effect remains unchanged, and, because no partial blend range has been set, there are sharp colorcasts at transitions.

Conditional blending can often lead to sharp colorcast, in which parts of the image suddenly change color with no transition. Partially blended pixels, though, do not suffer from this problem and will transition smoothly.

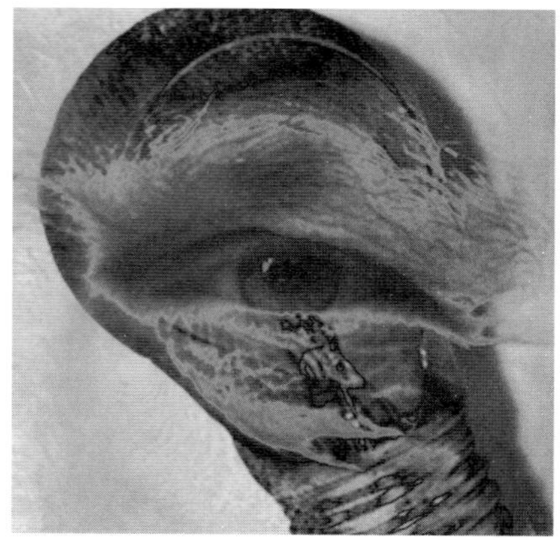

Underlying Layers (All layers below the selected layer) Pixels within the range will be blended with pixels in the selected layer. Pixels outside this range in the layers below the selected layer will be 100% opaque in place of pixels in the selected layer, including pixels created as a part of an effect. Here, the blending range in the gray channel has been narrowed for underlying layers causing pixels out of the range, in layers below the selected layer, to be turned 100% opaque. The drop-shadow effect is included in the affected pixels, and, because a range of partially blended pixels has been set, the transitions are smooth.

4 You can also split the White and/or Black blending values to create areas of partially blended pixels. To define a range of partially blended pixels, Option/Alt-click one side of a blending value slider, and move it left or right (depending on the side clicked). The range of pixels between the two halves of the slider will blend smoothly to help eliminate colorcasts in the transitions.

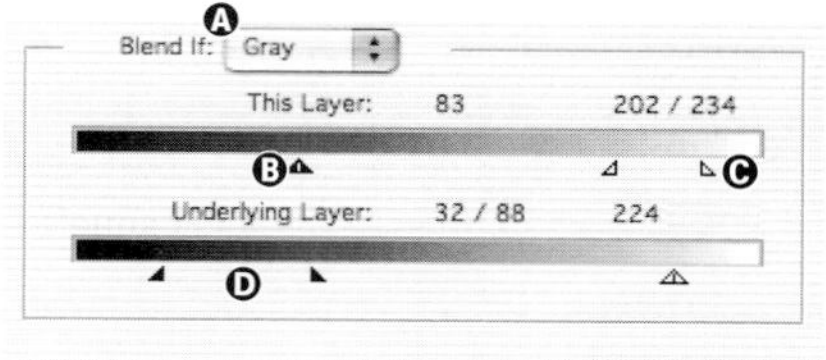

Ⓐ Choose the color channel to which you want to apply the blending options. Choose Gray to apply the blending options to all channels.

Ⓑ **Black blending value** Use the slider to choose the lower values (0 to 255) for the brightness range at which pixels should be blended. Option/Alt-click the slider to set a partial blending range to smooth transitions.

Ⓒ **White blending value** Use the slider to choose the upper values (0 to 255) for the brightness range at which pixels should be blended. Option/Alt-click the slider to set a partial blending range to smooth transitions.

Ⓓ **Partial blending range** The slider has been split, and the colors in the range between the two halves will gradually blend to create a smooth transition.

28.3 Applying One Image to Another

You can blend a layer or a color channel of any two open images using the Apply Image dialog. This allows you to select a specific layer (or merged layers) and a specific color channel (or the composite channel) using a particular blending mode. To apply one open image to another open image, follow these steps:

1 Open two images: one to be used as the target image to be changed and the other as the source image to apply to the target. Both images must have the same dimensions in pixels but can be different color modes.

2 With the target image active, select the layer you want to apply changes to.

3 Choose Image > Apply Image....

4 Set your options in the dialog and click OK. The source image will be applied to the selected layer in the target image.

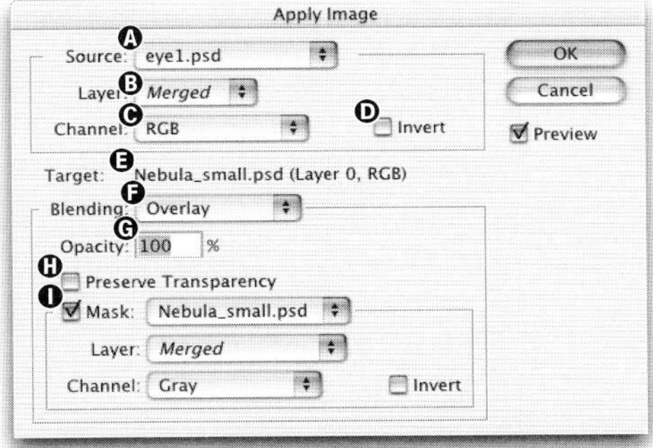

A Choose the source image. All images that are currently open and have the same dimensions in pixels as the target image will be displayed in this list.

B Choose the layer from the source image to apply to the layer you selected in step 2. Choose Merged to use the entire image.

C Choose the channel from the source image to apply to the channels for the target image. Choose Composite (RGB, CMYK, etc...) to apply the image to all channels.

D Check to invert the source image when applying.

E Displays the filename and information for the target image.

F Choose a blending mode to use when applying the source image.

G Enter a percentage value for the opacity, which sets the strength of the composite effect.

H Check if you want the composite image applied only to opaque pixels.

I Check to use an open image with the same dimensions in pixels as a mask in the composite. You then choose the image to use, the layer in that image, and the channel in that image and specify whether the mask should be inverted.

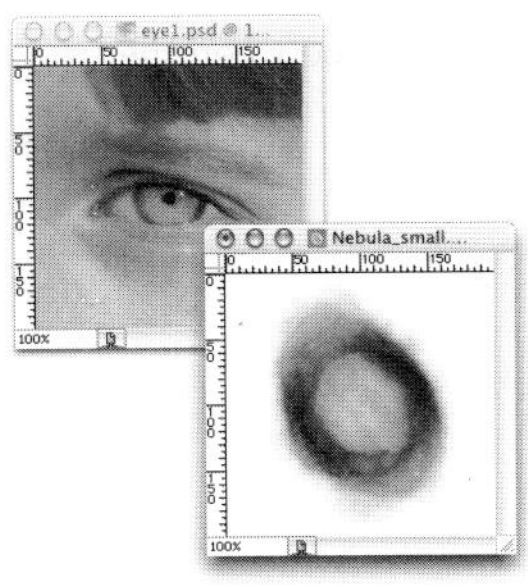

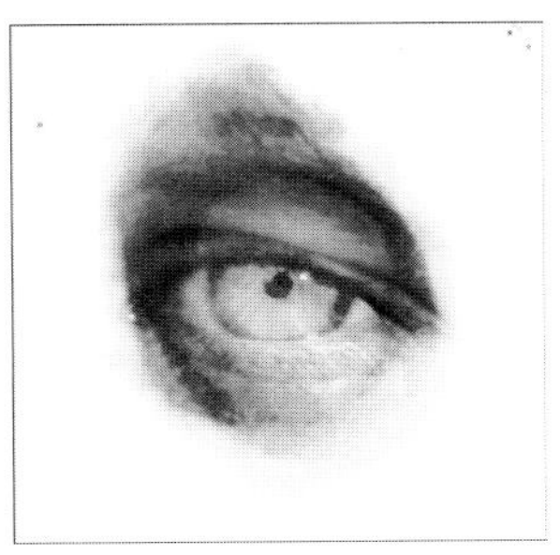

Left: The `eye1.psd` image will be used as the source, and `Nebula_small.psd` will be the destination. Right: The results of using the Apply Image dialog.

→ 6.6 Setting the Image Size

→ 7.5 Using Color in Channels

→ 8.2 Selecting a Layer or Its Contents

→ 9.12 Blending Modes and Opacity

→ 11.2 Adding Layer Masks

→ 13.14 Other Adjustments: Brightness, Desaturation, and Inversion

If the two images being applied to each other use different color modes (see Section 7.2)—for example, one is RGB and the other CMYK—you can only apply a single channel between the images and not the composite channel.

Although you can achieve a similar effect by simply copying a layer from one image to another and then setting the blending mode, the Apply Image dialog allows you greater versatility and subtlety by providing channel controls and masking.

28.4 Combining Images through Calculations

➡ 6.6 Setting the Image Size

➡ 7.5 Using Color in Channels

➡ 9.12 Blending Modes and Opacity

➡ 11.2 Adding Layer Masks

➡ 13.14 Other Adjustments: Brightness, Desaturation, and Inversion

Calculations cannot be made using the composited channel.

Calculations can help you make complex selections based on the content of the color channel. This is also useful if you want to create random-looking selections to edit, adding a more natural look to your image.

Use the Calculations dialog to select just the bright sparkler in the image.

In the Calculations dialog, you can blend two different channels in a single image or from two separate images to create an alpha channel, a selection, or a grayscale version of the composited image layers. To combine two images using Calculations, follow these steps:

1 Open two images. Both must be the same dimensions in pixels.

2 Choose Image > Calculations....

3 Set your options in the dialog and click OK.

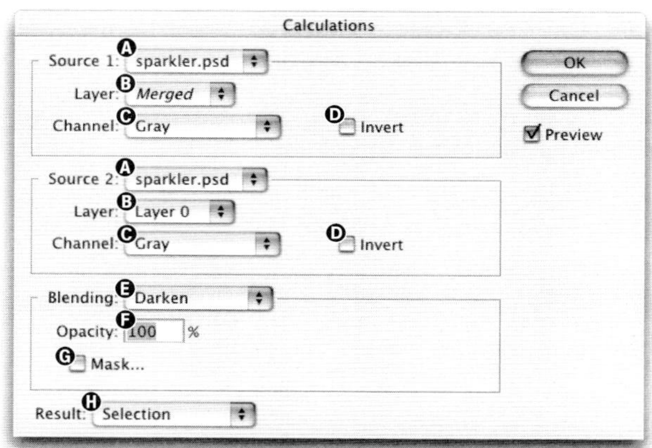

Ⓐ Choose the two source images. All images that are currently open and have the same dimensions in pixels will be displayed in this list. You can choose the same image for both, allowing you to use the image itself to make complex selections or alpha masks.

Ⓑ Choose the layer to use for the calculation in the source images. These layers will be evaluated based on the color channel and blending mode. Choose Merged to use the entire image.

Ⓒ Choose the channel from the source image to use for the calculations. Choose Gray to get the same effect as converting the image to a grayscale image.

Ⓓ Check to invert the channel performing the calculation.

Ⓔ Choose a blending mode to use when calculating the source images.

Ⓕ Enter a percentage value for the opacity, which sets the strength of the calculation effect.

Ⓖ Check to use an open image with the same dimensions in pixels as a mask in the composite. You then choose the image to use, the layer in that image, and the channel in that image and specify whether the mask should be inverted.

Ⓗ Choose how the calculations should be output: to a new document with a grayscale version of the composited layers, to a new alpha channel (see Section 7.5) that will appear in the Channels palette, or to a selection (see Chapter 8).

28.5 Extracting Parts of the Image

You can separate parts of an image from other parts of an image in many ways. You can make a selection to delete unwanted parts of the image, you can use the Eraser tool, you can erase the background, or you can erase selected colors.

However, none of these methods is particularly good for erasing an object that has fine details at its edges. For example, if you are trying to separate a cat from a complex background, you will find that the fine details of the cat's fur will be lost. If this is the case, you will want to resort to the Extract dialog, which gives you greater control over how the edges of objects form their backgrounds. To use the Extract dialog, open your image and follow these steps:

1 Choose the layer in the image from which you want to extract an object.

2 Choose Filter > Extract….

3 Choose the Edge Highlight tool, and set the tool options and extraction options. Then trace the outline of the object you want to extract, making sure to surround the entire object. If the object has fuzzy edges (such as fur or hair), make sure that the entire transition between the solid object and its edges is within the highlight. You can also use the Eraser tool to remove parts of the highlight.

4 Choose the Fill tool, and click within the area bound by the highlight area. This will protect the area from being erased. However, if the highlight was not closed, the entire image will be filled. Areas outside the highlights will be erased.

5 Click the Preview button. If you are not satisfied with the results, do one of the following:

- In the Preview controls, choose Extracted from the pull down, check Show Highlight and Show Fill, and then edit the highlighted area by repeating steps 3 and 4.
- Use the Clean Up and Edge Touchup tools to erase parts of the image directly.

6 When you are satisfied with the extraction, click OK.

Left: the original image; right: the extracted cat. Notice that the fine fur details at the edge have been preserved.

8.2 Selecting a Layer or Its Contents

8.4 Creating a Free-form Selection

15.9 Erasing

Extract dialog
Option ⌘ X
Alt Ctrl X

Edge Highlighter tool (in Extract dialog) B

Fill tool (in Extract dialog) G

Eraser tool (in Extract dialog) E

Eyedropper tool (in Extract dialog) I

Cleanup tool (in Extract dialog) C

Edge Touchup tool (in Extract dialog) T

Zoom tool (in Extract dialog) Z

Hand tool (in Extract dialog) H

It is usually a good idea to duplicate the layer you are working in with the extract dialog, so that you have a back up in case you change your mind later.

The extract dialog is also a great way to create torn/eroded edge effects around objects. Use the highlight tool, but keep the smoothness low. When extracted, you will get nicely eroded objects.

Using the Smart Highlighting option works much like the magnetic selection (see Section 8.4), allowing you to easily create highlights around well-defined edges in an image.

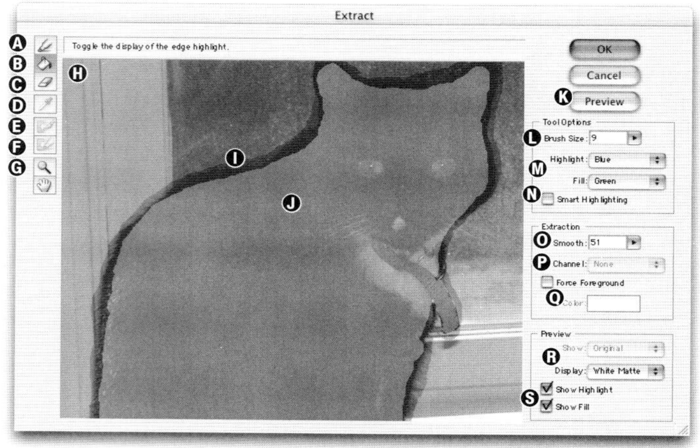

A Edge Highlighter tool Use to select the edge of the object you want to extract. Use the Tool options to set the brush size or use Smart Highlighting (see M, O, and P).

B Fill tool Use to fill an area of the image to protect it from extraction.

C Eraser tool Use to erase areas created by the Edge Highlighter tool (see A).

D Eyedropper tool Use to select a force foreground color in the preview area (see R).

E Cleanup tool Use in preview mode to erase areas or hold down Option to un-erase extracted areas. You can choose the brush size (see M) or press 0 to 9 to set the erase opacity.

F Edge Touchup tool Use in preview mode to erase stray pixels at the edge of the extraction or hold down Command/Ctrl to move the highlight edge. You can choose the brush size (see M) or press 0 to 9 to set the erase opacity.

G Zoom and Hand tools Used to zoom in the preview area and to move the image in the preview area.

H Preview area Displays the image either in its original state or after the extraction has been applied (see S).

I Highlight Selection The edge of the selection. Pixels in this area will be deleted only if they differ from the pixels in the fill selection (see K) area or forced foreground color (see R).

J Fill Selection Area of the image that will be preserved. The rest of the image will be erased.

K Click to preview the extraction in the preview area (see I). You can control the preview using the Preview options (see O).

L Use the slider or enter a value (1 to 999) for the brush size to use for selecting edge.

M Choose colors to use for the highlight selection (see J) and fill selection (see K).

N Check whether you want to use smart highlighting for the edges.

O Use the slider or enter a value (0 to 100) for the smoothness used when eliminating artifacts produced in the extraction. Higher values produce smoother results, but may not retain the fine details of edges.

P Choose an alpha channel to use for the selection. Black areas are used as the highlight selection, and white areas are treated as a fill selection.

Q Check to set a foreground color that will be extracted in the highlight area. You can then use the Eyedropper or click the color square beneath to select the forced foreground color to be used.

R Choose whether you want to view the original or extracted version of the image in the preview area (see I) and what kind of matte to use for transparent areas created by the extraction.

S Check to show highlight and/or fill areas in the preview area (see I, J, and K).

CHAPTER 29

Photoshop for Digital Video

PHOTOSHOP IS AN EXCELLENT graphic companion for video-based projects. If you're looking to go beyond the basic image and text tools available in Avid products, Final Cut Pro, and other nonlinear editors, start with Photoshop. Photoshop is also an essential design tool for motion composites with Adobe After Effects, as well as DVD-authoring tools such as DVD Studio Pro. But you must follow specific design parameters before bringing your graphic work to the blue screen.

This chapter describes these video topics:

- 29.1 **Calibrating color for TV resolution**
- 29.2 **Designing for NTSC/PAL**
- 29.3 **Using video filters (NTSC only)**

29.1 Calibrating Color for TV Resolution

➠ 2.9 View Menu

➠ 7.2 Understanding Image Modes

➠ 7.3 Specifying Color Settings

➠ 14.3 Selecting Colors with the Color Picker

NTSC is the 29.97 frames per second video format used predominantly in North America and Japan. PAL runs at 25 frames per second and is used in most of the rest of the world. If you are working on a SECAM project—a format used in Russia and France—follow the instructions for PAL.

Remember that video operates at 72 dpi on the RGB color palette. However, if you are doing "pan and scan" techniques with still images, your images' resolution should be 300 dpi.

You will probably want to save the color setting in the default Settings folder in the Photoshop folder.

Just like CMYK for print jobs and RGB for web jobs, video employs a specific color palette with a limited gamut range.

Setting Your Color Workspace

Like web projects, video projects employ the RGB color mode to define how colors are recorded and presented. Before starting with any graphic work in Photoshop that will end up in video, you must first set your Color Settings to match the color gamut used by video on NTSC (National Television Standards Committee; North America) and PAL (Phase Alternating Line; used in most of the rest of the world). To customize your color workspace for video, follow these steps:

1. Choose Color Settings from either the Photoshop (OS X) or Edit (Windows and Mac OS 9) menu.
2. In the Color Settings dialog (see Section 7.3), click the Advanced Mode check box.
3. In the Working Spaces RGB drop-down, select SMPTE-C if you are working with NTSC video projects. Choose PAL/SECAM if you are working with PAL/SECAM projects. Click OK.

Saving Your Color Profile

You can save changes to the color settings as your own customized profiles, and this is especially useful when you have customized the color workspace for special needs such as video. To save your color profile, follow these steps:

1. After you make all the changes in the Color Settings dialog, click Save….
2. In the Save dialog, type a name for the color setting (such as SMPTE-C Color Setting or PAL/SECAM Color Setting)—leaving the `.csf` extension in tact. Navigate to the place on your hard drive where you want to save this setting file and click Save.
3. In the Color Setting Comment dialog, type a comment such as NTSC Safe or PAL/SECAM Safe. This note appears in the Description box at the bottom of the Color Settings dialog the next time you load this color setting preference.
4. Click OK to save the new color setting as a profile.

To use this or other saved profiles, simply click Load…, find the color setting that has the `.csf` extension on your hard drive, and click OK.

Using Gamut Warning

Because video has a limited color gamut, be sure to turn on your gamut warning. After you load the Photoshop canvas (but before you start designing), choose View > Gamut Warning to turn on this function. (It is on if there is a check mark beside it.) If video cannot display a particular color used in the image , this function grays out the colors in the canvas and flags the colors in the Color Picker.

29.2 Designing for NTSC and PAL

Graphic design for video delivery is not as straightforward as you might think. A variety of image aspect ratios are associated with different video stocks and hardware/software applications that you must consider before proceeding. Before you begin designing graphics for your video project, be sure to talk with the editor about the video format that will be used. Find out specifically what the image aspect ratio is in terms of pixel dimensions.

For example, most NTSC projects originating in Digital Video (DV) and captured over FireWire cables (without video capture cards) have the DV NTSC 4:3 video format, which is 720×480 pixels. PAL DV projects, on the other hand, have the 601/DV PAL video format, which is 720×576.

Almost all video applications (including those with hardware dependencies) read pixels as rectangles, whereas Photoshop reads pixels as squares. Therefore, you must design your projects with this pixel difference in mind; otherwise your design will end up looking stretched on a television monitor.

➠ 6.1 Starting a New Image

➠ 6.6 Setting the Image Size

➠ 6.8 Using Rulers, Guides, Grid, and Snap

➠ 9.10 Rasterizing Vector Layers

If you're designing for DVD productions with software such as DVD Studio Pro, base your canvas size for DV NTSC 4:3 format (720×534) or the 601 / DV PAL format (768×576).

Even though you have title-safe and action-safe zones on the graphic image, you can leave design elements in the clipped out areas. Some television monitors clip out very little on the edges, so it's a good idea to have some graphical filler for those monitors.

When you create a new image (see Section 6.1), there are several video presets in the Preset Sizes drop-down to save you time.

Setting the Canvas Size for Working

You will need to start a new Photoshop document, based on the video format you are using, with the dimensions of the canvas size listed in the Photoshop (Square Pixels) column of the following table. This table applies to projects designed for all nonlinear editors, including all versions of the Avid, Final Cut Pro, and Premiere programs, as well as motion-compositing programs such as Adobe After Effects and DVD production programs such as DVD Studio Pro.

In Photoshop, start with the image aspect ratio in the Photoshop (Square Pixels) column. Remember that this is just the first step in the design process for video graphics, and that for most video applications you will need to later scale your Photoshop file to the video aspect ratio of your video format. (See the following section "Scaling Your Image" when you have completed your design.)

Canvas Sizes by Format

VIDEO FORMAT	PHOTOSHOP (SQUARE PIXELS)	VIDEO APPLICATIONS (RECTANGULAR PIXELS)
601 NTSC 4:3 (capture card)	720×540	720×486
601 NTSC 16:9 anamorphic (capture card)	864×486	720×486
DV NTSC 4:3 (FireWire)	720×534	720×480
DV NTSC 16:9 (FireWire)	864×480	720×480
601 / DV PAL (FireWire/capture card)	768×576	720×576
601 / DV PAL anamorphic (FireWire/capture card)	1024×576	720×576
720 i/p high definition	1280×720	1280×720
1080 i/p high definition	1920×1080	1920×1080

If you're unsure whether your video application requires you to manually rescale, experiment to see what happens. If your image ends up looking stretched on a television monitor, you probably need to scale the image yourself in Photoshop.

If your video application requires that you scale your graphic files to match the native video format, rasterize your image only *after* you've scaled it down to its proper aspect ratio.

When starting a video project in Photoshop, you can select from a number of preset canvas sizes.

Creating Title- and Action-Safe Images

Most television monitors clip out the edge areas of the video content. If you are inserting text in your video project, be sure that it is not clipped out. This applies to both NTSC and PAL projects in all formats. Place your essential graphic elements within the action-safe zone and your text elements within the title-safe zone. Use the Guide tool to create basic guides for title-safe and action-safe areas:

- To create **action-safe** areas of the image, pull each line approximately 35 pixels in from all sides.
- To create **title-safe** areas, set guides 70 pixels in from all sides.

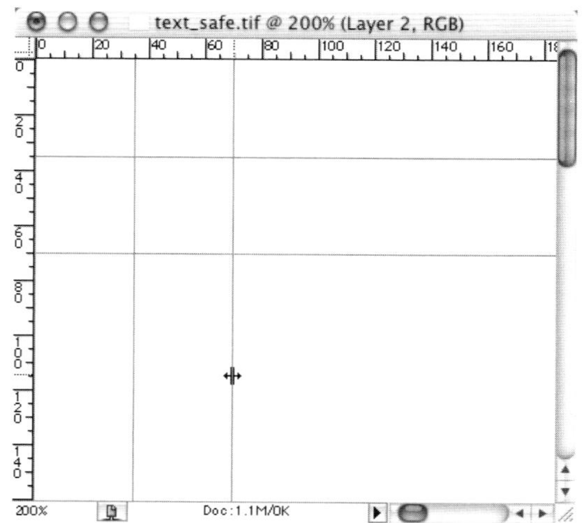

The guidelines at 35 pixels in are action-safe; those that are 70 pixels in are title-safe.

29.2 Designing for NTSC and PAL *(Continued)*

Scaling Your Image

After you finish designing your graphic masterpiece, you might need to scale the image to its proper aspect ratio for import into your video application. This technique creates faux-rectangular pixels out of Photoshop's native square pixel resolution and ends up looking best for video-based projects.

Some programs require that you scale the image, but others do not. For Final Cut Pro and DVD Studio Pro, it's essential to manually scale your image to conform to the video aspect ratio. But some versions of Avid automatically remap the pixels from square to rectangular, meaning that you won't have to scale the image in Photoshop (though you should still design with the square pixel resolutions). To scale your image, follow these steps:

1 With the image on the canvas, choose Image > Image Size.

2 In the Image Size dialog, clear the Constrain Proportions check box. This allows you to produce the faux rectangular pixels necessary for video resolutions.

3 Change the width or height displayed in the Video Applications column based on the aspect ratio for which you are designing. For example, if you are working with NTSC DV over FireWire, resize to 720×480.

4 Click OK to save your file with the `.psd` extension.

Your image will now appear to be smushed in Photoshop. But after you import it into your video application, it should look correct to the naked eye. Definitely withhold all aesthetic judgments until you see the graphic design on a television monitor. If you are working with PAL format graphic files, import them into your video application. If you are working with NTSC graphic files, continue with the next section.

RASTERIZING FOR VIDEO

If you are using Type layers, layer effects, or other vector-based content in your image, you will need to rasterize the image before you can import it into some video applications. This is especially the case with Final Cut Pro and DVD Studio Pro.

After you rasterize a layer, you cannot edit it except with the painting tools. It's recommended that you save a copy of your document *before* you rasterize it, in case you need to re-edit the file later (see Section 6.13).

For more details on how to rasterize your image, see Section 9.10.

29.3 Using Video Filters (NTSC Only)

Not all NTSC video stills have artifacts. This is the case when the two fields' video content are exactly the same. Nonetheless, it's still a good idea to use the De-Interlace filter to make sure that you have only one video field in your image.

Remember that you should always calibrate your colors for the medium in which your design work is going to be finished. For example, if you are taking video stills that will end up on a web-based project, don't use the color settings specific to video projects, but those specific to your web project.

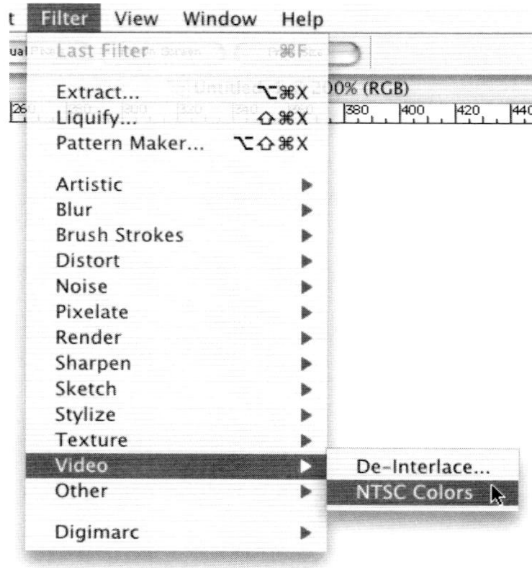

The video filters employed by Photoshop should only be used for NTSC-based video projects and do not apply to PAL projects. Nonetheless, they are indispensable for producing finer-quality images as graphical exports or imports.

Using the NTSC Colors Filter

The NTSC Colors filter is a last step to take before saving your NTSC Photoshop file to be imported into your video application. Its function is to safeguard the color gamut and prevent colors from bleeding across the television screen. If you followed the steps outlined in Section 29.1, employing the NTSC Colors filter will have minimal effect on your image, since you should not have any out-of-gamut colors. Nonetheless, you can never be too safe when working with colors that are going to be broadcast.

When your design work is complete, click Filter > Video > NTSC Colors before you save your project. You are then ready to bring your Photoshop file into your video application. You must be in RGB mode for this to work.

De-interlacing Video Stills

NTSC video works by producing two fields in one image frame at every given moment. This function is called *interlacing* and was invented as a way to squeeze the television signal down to be read quickly enough by the television monitor. The speed of video technology has since come of age in this regard, but interlaced video is still the standard for the NTSC video format.

This technology, however, does pose a slight problem for designers who are working with graphic assets taken from NTSC video. If you are working in Photoshop with video stills exported from a nonlinear editor, you will sometimes notice a motion artifact in the still image, which often looks like broken lines on areas of motion. (This is because video applications read pixels in a different way than Photoshop reads them.) The only way to cut out one of the two motion fields in Photoshop is by using the De-Interlace function.

29.3 Using Video Filters (NTSC Only) *(Continued)*

To de-interlace a video still, open or import a video still image, choose Filter > Video > De-Interlace…, and set the options in the De-Interlace dialog. When you are finished, click OK. You will notice that the motion artifacts have disappeared, leaving you with a more resolute image.

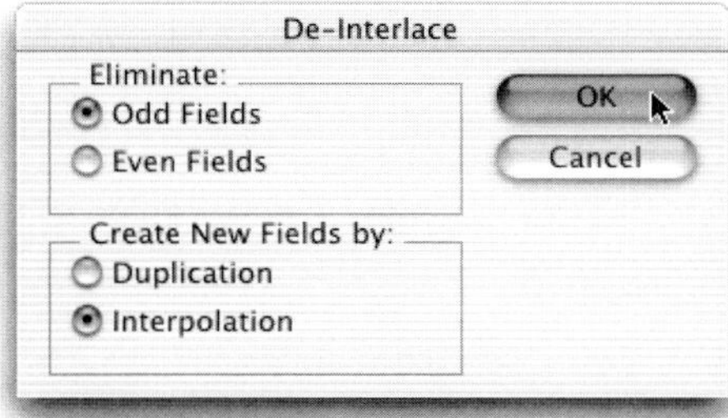

Choose which field you want to eliminate. In terms of how the action plays out linearly, the even field is the "first" field, and the odd field is the "second." Then choose to replace the field you intend to eliminate either by duplicating the chosen field or by interpolating from the chosen field. Technically, choosing Duplication maintains your colors more efficiently because it simply copies the pixels of the selected scan. Choosing Interpolation fills in the colors based on the selected image. However, in practice, you will rarely notice a difference between the two methods.

The video image (left) before being de-interlaced and (right) after.

PHOTOSHOP LAYERS IN VIDEO APPLICATIONS

Most video applications read Photoshop layers. Unless you only need a still image for your video project, you should not have to flatten your layers. In practice, however, some video applications have trouble with Photoshop files that contain 15 or more layers, especially when you are doing heavy keyframing for motion effects. Proceed with care, always keep backups of your video project files, and back up your Photoshop file before working with your graphics in your video application.

Appendix: What's New in Photoshop 7 and ImageReady 7

WHEN DECIDING WHETHER to upgrade from one version of a program to another, the first step is to consider whether the new features are worth the cost of upgrading. Photoshop 7 offers several new features that make it an excellent upgrade for illustrators (customized brushes), web designers (the Rollovers palette), and photographers (the Healing Brush and Patch tools). Of course, a new tool, a new feature, or an improvement is only valuable if you are going to use it. Following are some lists of the most important and noticeable changes between Photoshop 6 and Photoshop 7, with a brief description and a note about where in this book you can find more information.

New Tools

TOOL	DESCRIPTION	WHERE TO LEARN MORE
Airbrush mode	Turn a variety of brush types into airbrushes with the click of a button.	15.2 Selecting and Adjusting Brushes
Art Studio brushes	Use the preset brushes to simulate painting in traditional art styles.	15.5 Painting with the Brush or Pencil
Customized brushes	Set the options for a brush—size, shape, tilt, spacing, jitter, and scatter—and then save these options as a new customized brush that you can then access through the tool options bar or the Brushes palette.	15.7 Painting with the Art History Brush
Healing Brush and Patch tools	Remove scratches and other image defects cleanly.	27.3 Patching Images
Tool presets	Set the options for a tool and then save them as a new customized tool that you can then access from the tool options bar or the Tool Presets palette.	4.10 Tool Presets Palette

New Commands and Features

COMMAND/FEATURE	DESCRIPTION	WHERE TO LEARN MORE
Auto Color	Correct the color of an image with a single menu command.	13.4 Setting the Auto Color Correction Options
Customized workspace	Place your palettes where you want them on the screen and then save the layout.	4.1 Organizing Palettes
File Browser	Browse, sort, and open files on your computer from a single window.	4.2 File Browser
Pattern Maker	Create new seamless patterns from selections.	14.12 Using the Pattern Maker
Rollovers palette	In ImageReady, quickly create rollover states for websites and preview them in a web browser.	24.4 Creating Rollovers
Spelling checker	Check the spelling of text layers in the document.	17.8 Spell-Checking and Searching Text
WBMP support	Preview and save images for the Web in WBMP format (short for "wireless bitmap"), which is commonly used for PDAs and cell phones.	6.13 Saving and Closing an Image
XMP support	Read and embed XMP (Extensible Metadata Platform) image information.	6.11 Adding File Information and Watermarks

Enhancements

ENHANCEMENT	DESCRIPTION	WHERE TO LEARN MORE
Blending modes	Linear Light and Pin Light blending modes allow you to create complex blends between layers.	Color Section: Blending Modes
Liquify	Warp, zoom, and pan image with the improved Liquify plug-in.	27.7 Smudging and Liquifying Images
PDF	Increase the security of your PDF documents using Adobe Acrobat 5 security settings.	21.3 Saving Files for Print or PDF
Picture Package	Print multiple copies of an image on a single page without reformatting the document.	20.4 Creating Picture Packages and Contact Sheets
Web output	Use the improved transparency abilities to create images that cleanly blend into almost any background.	25 Outputting for the Web
Web Photo Gallery	Quickly create galleries of your images from templates for display on the Web.	25 Outputting for the Web

Glossary

action A script that, when executed, performs a single operation or a sequence of operations in Photoshop. Photoshop comes with several prerecorded actions, or you can record your own actions and save them. You access actions from the Actions palette. See *4.9 Actions Palette*.

adaptive palette An indexed color table calculated to favor the most common colors in a particular image. Using an adaptive palette for creating GIF or PNG images maintains higher quality while reducing the overall file size of the image. See *7.9 Converting to Indexed Color Mode*.

Adjustment A command or special layer type used to adjust the appearance of a single layer (command) or of all layers underneath (layer). Adjustment commands are applied directly to a layer's content. Adjustment layers can be re-edited at any time to change the appearance. See *13.1 Adjustment Basics*.

alpha channel A type of layer created in the Channels palette that records the opacity of areas of the image using grayscale values to create an invisible "onion skin" mask over the image. See *7.5 Using Color in Channels*.

anti-alias A method used by computers to "smooth" the jagged edges of graphics and text objects on the computer screen by adding semitransparent pixels along the object's edge. Anti-aliasing gives the illusion of increasing the object's resolution for screen display. See *17.1 Type Basics*.

artifact An imperfection in an image often caused by over compression, over manipulation, or a loss of color information. One of the most common examples of artifacts is the squarelike splotches in an overly compressed JPEG image. See *25.4 Setting Optimization Options*.

background color One of two selected colors, which is used for the color of background elements. For example, the background color is used to fill areas deleted from the *background layer*. The default background color is white. See *14.2 Selecting Colors*.

Background layer A special layer type, which appears behind all other layers in an image. This layer cannot be moved and deleting from it will fill the deleted area with the *background color*, but it can be hidden or completely removed, in which case *transparency* is used. See *9.2 The Background Layer*.

banding A noticeable color change in graduated tonal images. An unattractive artifact, banding occurs when too few colors are included in the image's color table. See *14.6 Creating and Editing Gradients*.

Bezier curves A system used to control the curvature of lines created mathematically for *vector* rather than *bitmap* graphics. The curves are controlled using a system of anchor points, direction handles, and handlebars. See *12.1 Path Basics*.

bit A binary digit. Computers use bits to store information. Each bit can have a value of either 1 or 0. A series of bits make up a byte, and a byte stores specific information such as a letter or a color. For example, images contain pixels, and each pixel has a specific color. The computer stores each pixel's color information as a series (byte) of bits that define the color value. See *7.1 Image Color Basics*.

bit depth The number of bits of color information devoted to a single pixel. There are two types of bit depth: image and monitor. The higher the bit depth value for an image, the more colors the image has in its color palette. For example, an 8-bit RGB image can contain as many as 256 colors. The monitor's bit depth is the number of colors that the monitor will display. This is set as an operating system preference as either 256 colors (8-bit), thousands of colors (16-bit), or millions of colors (32-bit). The number of colors a monitor can display is specific to the computer system. See *23.1 Designing for the Screen*.

bitmap image An image made out of pixels, or dots of light, arrayed in a square grid. Each pixel has an associated color and transparency value. The human eye perceives the combination of these pixels as a contiguous image. See *7.1 Image Color Basics*.

Bitmap mode A Photoshop image mode that records all pixels in the image as either black or white. See *7.7 Converting to Bitmap Mode*.

black point The *level* at which pixels in an image are black. Tones in the image are adjusted from that point so that there is a smooth transition with minimal *colorcasts*. You can adjust the black point, *gray point*, and *white point* in both the Levels and Curves dialogs. See *13.3 Adjusting Color Levels Using Curves*.

blending mode The method used to combine the information of pixels when using image-editing operations or painting. See *Color Section: Blending Modes*.

brightness The measurement of the relative lightness or darkness of a pixel using a scale from 0 (black) to 255 (white) or sometimes as a percentage from 0 (black) to 100 (white). See *13.6 Adjusting Brightness and Contrast*.

brush A brush defines the shape, size (diameter), angle, roundness, hardness, and spacing. These options define the general nature of how the brush's stroke will appear. See *15.2 Selecting and Adjusting*.

burning A technique used in the darkroom to darken areas of an image by increasing the exposure in that area. Photoshop simulates this technique, using the Burn tool, by lowering the *brightness* of pixels. The opposite of burning is *dodging*. See *26.4 Dodging and Burning Images*.

canvas The editable region of the image displayed in the document window. See *1.4 The Document Window*.

channel Channels determine the combinations of colors used to create an image. The number of channels depends on the image's mode. For example, an RGB image contains three color channels—red, green, and blue—in addition to a composite channel of all three channels (which is generally the channel you work on). You can manipulate or draw on any of these channels. You can also hide a channel, eliminating that color from the image. The Channels palette can also include one or more alpha channels or spot colors used in an image. See *1.4 The Document Window*.

chroma See *saturation*.

CMYK (cyan, magenta, yellow, black) The four ink colors used in *process color* printing. See *21.5 Preparing for Four-Color Printing*.

colorcast A sharp change in color between areas in an image sometimes produced when using *adjustments* or conditional blending. See *28.2 Conditional Blending*.

color depth See *bit depth*.

color mode The method used to record color values in an image. Each color mode has a unique color *gamut* that restricts the colors that can be recorded. Also referred to as the image mode. See *7.6 Converting between Image Modes*.

color model The method used to generate colors used in an image. The *color mode* of an image does not restrict the color model used to generate a color, but some colors generated may fall outside the color mode's *gamut*. See *14.1 Color, Gradient, and Pattern Basics*.

color table A list of color values used in a particular image file. Generally, the greater the number of colors in an image's color table, the clearer the image appears. Also referred to as a color look up table (CLUT) or color palette. See *23.2 Web Color Basics*.

compression method File format and options used to reduce the size of a saved image file. Virtually all file formats use some form of compression to reduce file size. Some compression methods are lossless and do not degrade the apparent image quality; others are lossy and can more substantially reduce the file size but also degrade the image quality. Compression can be set either at the time the file is saved or when the image is being *optimized*. See *25.3 Optimizing Images*.

de-interlacing See *Interlacing (Video)*.

dither A method used in graphics to place two or more colors close together to create the illusion of a single color. See *23.2 Web Color Basics*.

dodging A technique used in the darkroom to lighten areas of an image by limiting the exposure in that area. Photoshop simulates this technique, using the Dodge tool, by increasing the *brightness* of pixels. The opposite of dodging is *burning*. See *26.4 Dodging and Burning Images*.

dots per inch (dpi)/dots per centimeter (dpc) A measure of the *resolution* of a particular image based on the number of dots in a given linear inch or centimeter of the printed image. The higher the number of dots, the higher the resolution and the sharper the image will be when printed. However, the higher the resolution, the larger the image's file size. See *6.6 Setting the Image Size*.

droplet An *action* that is saved as a file independent of Photoshop. Images can be dragged and dropped onto a droplet to have the actions automatically performed to it. See *18.4 Creating Droplets*.

effects Vector-based styles that can be applied to a layer, but, unlike *filters*, can then be changed as desired. See *10.2 Applying Effects and Styles*.

emulsion The photosensitive side of a piece of film or photographic paper. When printing to film or photographic paper, Photoshop needs to know whether this side is up or down. See *6.10 Printing Basics*.

EXIF Information generally recorded by an image captured using a digital camera. The information includes date and time the picture was taken, resolution, ISO speed rating, f/stop, compression, and exposure time. Photoshop can display this information in the File Info dialog. See *6.11 Adding File Information and Watermarks.*

feather The gradual opacity transition from the edge to the interior of an image eliminating hard edges and *colorcasts*. Feathering, however, is different from *anti-aliasing,* which applies semi-transparent pixels in order to create the appearance of smooth edges. See *8.6 Refining the Selection.*

filters Bitmap-based styles that can be applied to a layer but, unlike *effects*, cannot be changed once applied. See *Chapter 16 Painting with Filters.*

foreground color One of two selected colors, which is used for the color for foreground elements. For example, this color is used when painting with a *brush*. The default foreground color is black. See *14.2 Selecting Colors.*

gamma The measurement of the relative contrast and saturation for a computer monitor. Gamma values generally range from 1.0 to 2.8, but can range from 0.1 to 9.99. Gamma values are generally set by the operating system, with Macintosh computers using a default value of 1.8 and Windows computers using a value of 2.2. See *23.2 Web Color Basics.*

gamut The range of colors that a particular *color mode* can produce. Colors that cannot be produced by a particular color mode are said to be "out of gamut." See *5.6 Transparency & Gamut Preferences.*

gray point The *level* at which pixels in an image are 50% gray. Tones in the image are adjusted from that point so that there is a smooth transition with minimal *colorcasts*. You can adjust the *black point*, gray point, and *white point* in both the Levels and Curves dialogs. See *13.3 Adjusting Color Levels Using Curves.*

grayscale An image that records the *brightness* of pixels using only 8 bits in which any pixel can be one of 256 shades of gray. See *7.6 Converting between Image Modes.*

halftone image The output of an image using printing screens that break down the image into a series of dots of various sizes. Resolution for a halftone image is measured in *lines per inch* (lpi) and depends on the printer's capabilities. When an image is sent to the printer, Photoshop communicates with the printer to automatically convert the pixel-based image to halftone dots. See *21.5 Preparing for Four-Color Printing.*

highlights An option that isolates the lightest parts of an image for editing separately from *midtones* or *shadows*. See *13.13 Using Color Variations.*

histogram A graph displaying the number of pixels in an image for a given input *level*. The histogram is useful for ensuring that the image maintains a uniform tonal range to produce the highest quality image and can be viewed separately in the Histogram dialog or as a part of the Levels dialog. See *7.1 Image Color Basics.*

History state Each action performed on an image in the canvas is recorded in the History palette as a History state. You can move back and forth between History states in the History palette. History state is often simply referred to as *state*, which should not be confused with *rollover state*. See *6.9 Changing Your Mind.*

hot spot The area of a hypertext link within an image map. See *24.1 Creating Image Maps*.

image cache Memory used to store fully rendered versions of the image at different magnifications. Higher values for the image cache accelerates image redrawing, but requires additional memory. See *5.10 Memory & Image Cache Preferences*.

Indexed Color An image mode used to reduce the color palette for a specific image to 256 or fewer colors. Although this can lead to some image quality loss, it generally significantly reduces the file size. There are several indexed color palette types (exact, system, web, uniform, perceptual, adaptive, and custom), each with its own benefits. See *7.9 Converting to Indexed Color Mode*.

Interlacing (Video) A method used in NTSC video to compress the image signal by creating two fields for every image. When importing NTSC video images as stills into Photoshop, you will need to de-interlace the image using the de-interlace filter. See *29.3 Using Video Filters (NTSC Only)*.

Interlacing (Web) A technique set during image *optimization* used by the GIF and PNG-8 formats to progressively display the image. See *25.4 Setting Optimization Options*.

interpolation Techniques used by Photoshop when *resizing* or *resampling* an image. See *6.6 Setting the Image Size*.

jitter Variations in the *brush* stroke that simulate the random oscillations that might occur while painting with a physical brush. See *15.1 Brush Basics*.

kerning The adjustment of space between two specific letters, as opposed to *tracking,* which sets the spacing on both sides of one or more letters. See *17.1 Type Basics*.

layer An isolated collection of image content that can be edited separately from other content in the image. Layers are controlled using the Layers palette. See *Chapter 9 Image Layering*.

layer mask A bitmap *mask* created by an *alpha channel* applied to a specific layer. See *11.2 Adding Layer Masks*.

leading The spacing between two lines of text in a paragraph. See *17.1 Type Basics*.

levels A measurement of the color or brightness values (0 to 255) in an image generally displayed in a *histogram*. The levels in an image can be adjusted in the Levels dialog. See *13.2 Adjusting Tonal Range Using Levels*.

lines per inch (lpi)/lines per centimeter (lpc) A measurement of the *resolution* when printing using *halftones*. See *21.5 Preparing for Four-Color Printing*.

lossless compression Techniques used to reduce the size of an image file while saving without loss of image quality. These techniques are not as effective at reducing file size as *lossy compression* techniques, which reduce the file size but also degrade the image quality. See *20.3 Saving Files for Print or PDF*.

lossy compression Techniques used to reduce the size of an image file while saving that result in the loss of image quality. These techniques are more effective at reducing file sizes than *lossless compression* techniques, which reduce the file size but do not degrade the image quality. See *25.3 Optimizing Images*.

luminosity See *brightness*.

mask An element used to isolate parts of a layer preventing it from being edited. *Quick masks* and *type masks* are used to create selections, while *layer masks* and *vector masks* can be used to hide parts of a layer. See *Chapter 11 Masking Layers*.

matte color The color used to turn the semi-transparent pixels at the edges of an image fully opaque. This is needed when saving an image that cannot preserve semitransparent colors, such as GIF and PNG-8, so that the edges will integrate with the background color. See *25.4 Setting Optimization Options*.

midtone An option that isolates the midtonal range of an image for editing separately from *highlights* or *shadows*. See *13.13 Using Color Variations*.

NTSC (North American Television Standards Committee) system A video standard used in North America and South America and a few Asian countries. See *29.1 Calibrating Color for TV Resolution*.

optimization Options used to set the *compression method* used to reduce an image's file size for display on the Web. Web compression methods are all *lossy compression*. See *25.3 Optimizing Images*.

overprint colors Two or more unscreened inks that are printed directly over the top of each other. See *7.8 Converting to Duotone Mode*.

paint Used either as a noun meaning any color or pattern that is applied with a *brush* or as a verb referring to the action of painting. See *15.1 Brush Basics*.

painting tools Any tool in Photoshop that uses a *brush* to add *paint* to the *canvas*. See *15.1 Brush Basics*.

PAL (Phase Alternating Line) system A video standard used in Western Europe (including the U.K.), Australia, and most of the world. See *29.1 Calibrating Color for TV Resolution*.

PANTONE A popular brand of spot color inks. The PANTONE Matching System (PMS) is a catalog of inks that are referred to by specific numeric values that can be accessed in Photoshop through the Custom Color Picker. See *14.3 Selecting Colors with the Color Picker*.

path A vector object used to mathematically define a line or a shape. Paths are created using anchor points and *Bezier curves* to set their shape. See *12.1 Path Basics*.

pixel (picture element) An individual square of colored light that can be edited in a *bitmap image*. See *23.1 Designing for the Screen*.

pixels per inch (ppi)/ pixels per centimeter (ppc) A measurement of *resolution* on computer monitors or scanned images based on the number of pixels in a linear inch or centimeter of the image. See *6.6 Setting the Image Size*.

plug-in An add-on mini-application or filter that adds functionality to Photoshop. See *16.1 Filter Basics*.

process color printing The four-color printing process using *CMYK* inks. See *21.5 Preparing for Four-Color Printing*.

proof colors A control that allows you to preview the image simulating a variety of reproduction processes without having to convert the image to that color work space. See *20.2 Creating Color Proofs*.

Quick mask A type of *mask* used to create and edit selections using *painting tools*. See *8.4 Creating a Free-form Selection*.

raster image See *bitmap image*.

rasterize The process of converting a *vector image* into a *bitmap image*. See *9.10 Rasterizing Vector Layers*.

resample To *resize*, *transform*, or change an image's *resolution*. When an image is resampled down, image information is discarded and cannot be brought back. When an image is resampled up, information is added through *interpolation*. See *5.3 General Preferences*.

resize To change the image's dimensions. This may or may not change the image's resolution, depending on how resizing is performed. See *6.6 Setting the Image Size*.

resolution The measurement of the number of units that occupy a given linear area of an image. Resolution is often measured as a ratio between the number of pixels, dots, or lines per inch or centimeter in the image. See *6.6 Setting the Image Size*.

RIP (raster image processor) Software or device used by a computer, a PostScript printer, or an image setter that rasterizes vector data for output. See *Chapter 21 Printing and Prepping for Prepress*.

rollover A web-page behavior used to change a graphic's appearance when the page visitor interacts with the graphic using the mouse pointer. Each rollover has a corresponding image *state*. See *24.4 Creating Rollovers*.

rollover state A particular action in a *rollover*. Rollover state is often referred to as simply a *state*, but should not be confused with a *History state*. See *24.4 Creating Rollovers*.

saturation A color's intensity as measured by the difference in the color values used to create the color. Colors with low saturation, or chroma, have close color values rendering the color gray. See *13.7 Adjusting Hue, Saturation, and Lightness*.

screen angles The angles at which screens used to create a *halftone image* are placed when printing. See *21.4 Preparing for Black-and-White, Spot, or Duotone Printing*.

screen frequency The density of dots in a screen used to create halftone images, most often measured in *lines per inch (lpi)/lines per centimeter (lpc)*. See *21.4 Preparing for Black-and-White, Spot, or Duotone Printing*.

SECAM (Sequential Color and Memory) system A video standard used in some European and Asian countries. See *29.1 Calibrating Color for TV Resolution*.

shadow Option that isolates the darkest parts of an image for editing separately from *highlights* or *midtones*. See *13.13 Using Color Variations*.

slice Individual pieces of an image cut out of the full image to be used to create a final web page using HTML. Individual slices in an image can be *optimized* separately for output. See *25.2 Working with Slices*.

spot color Solid ink colors used in a print job. Spot colors can be used in addition to black or *process colors* to preserve a "pure" color that will appear more vibrant than if it was created using process inks. Each spot color requires its own channel in the Channels palette and plate for printing but is *color mode* independent. See *21.4 Preparing for Black-and-White, Spot, or Duotone Printing*.

state (History) See *History state*.

state (rollover) See *rollover state*.

stroke A line applied to the border of a selection, a path, or the edges of the content of a layer. See *10.12 Applying the Stroke Effect*.

tracking The adjustment in spacing on both sides of one or more letters, as opposed to *kerning* which adjusts only the spacing between two specific letters. See *17.1 Type Basics*.

transparency Areas in a layer that contain no pixels, allowing pixels from layers underneath to show through. If there is no *background layer* and there are no pixels in the image on any layers in a given area, the transparency pattern will show through. See *5.6 Transparency & Gamut Preferences*.

trap A technique used when preparing images for *process color printing* that helps reduce the number of unwanted gaps that sometimes appear when printing using *halftone* screens by adding overlapping areas of color. See *21.1 Preparing to Print*.

type mask A type of *mask* used to create and edit selections using type tools. See *Chapter 17 Typography*.

value See *brightness*.

vector mask A vector-based *mask* created using *paths* applied to a specific layer. See *11.6 Adding Vector Masks*.

Web-safe colors The 216 colors (based on an 8-bit color palette) that the Macintosh and Windows operating systems share in common in their color palette. Web browsers on older computers display only a maximum of 256 colors, and the 216 browsers-safe colors always display on these machines with little or no change from machine to machine. See *23.2 Web Color Basics*.

white point The *level* at which pixels in an image are white. Tones in the image are adjusted from that point so that there is a smooth transition with minimal *colorcasts*. You can adjust the *black point*, *gray point*, and white point in both the Levels and Curves dialogs. See *13.3 Adjusting Color Levels Using Curves*.

XMP (Extensible Metadata Platform) The format used for file information embedded in an image file by Photoshop. XMP is an open standard based on XML. See *6.11 Adding File Information and Watermarks*.

Index

Note to the Reader: Page numbers in **bold** indicate the principle discussion of a topic or the definition of a term. Page numbers in *italic* indicate illustrations.

B

C

D

G

H

I

J

K

L

M

N

O

P

Q

R

T

U

V